Hoover Institution Publications 107

Russia and Asia

THE U.S.S.R. AND
ADJACENT REGIONS

RUSSIA AND ASIA

Essays on the Influence of
Russia on the Asian Peoples

Edited by

Wayne S. Vucinich

Hoover Institution Press
Stanford University
Stanford, California

Hoover Institution Publications 107
Standard Book Number 8179–1071–8
Library of Congress Card Number 79–152430
© 1972 by the Board of Trustees of the
 Leland Stanford Junior University
Printed in the United States of America

To Anatole G. Mazour
Professor Emeritus of History at Stanford University
who has done so much to develop Russian studies
in the United States

Contents

Preface

The extensive and pervasive Soviet presence in Asia today conforms to long historical tradition. Study of that tradition is indispensable to an understanding of contemporary relations between the Soviet Union and the peoples of Asia. As the Russians expanded eastward, they absorbed, subjugated, or made contact in one form or another with many Asian peoples, and in the process transmitted to them not only much of their own culture, but strong elements of general European culture as well. Russian contacts over many centuries with several of these have left an imprint on every aspect of their lives—cultural, economic, social, and political. And, of course, Russian civilization demonstrates at many levels that this has by no means been a one-way process.

The peculiar experience of a powerful nation sharing many cultural features with its European neighbors, yet extensively involved over an enormously broad front in Asia has provoked passionate debate about the nature of Russian civilization: is it European, or Asian, or Eurasian? The related topic of "Russia and the East" is much less explored and less understood than the subject of "Russia and the West," to which the Russian intelligentsia and, naturally, Western scholars of Russia have devoted primary attention. The present volume examines the relations between Russia and the East, with particular attention focussed on Russia's impact on Asian cultures.

Russia's *mission civilisatrice* in Asia, as it would have been called in a blither epoch than our own, has never been investigated

ix

systematically. The task is an awesome one not only because of
the enormous complexity of the interrelations, but because of the
vast time-span covered and the large number of peoples involved.
Some of the Asian peoples were subjected to Russian influence
directly; others were not. Some came under Russian rule as early
as the sixteenth century (the Bashkirs, the Tatars), others not until
the late eighteenth and early nineteenth century (the Armenians,
the Georgians, the Kabardins) and the second half of the nineteenth century (the Kirghiz, the Tajiks, the Turkmens, the Uzbeks). The Russian absorption of the Kazakhs was a long process
lasting from the thirties of the eighteenth century to the sixties of
the nineteenth. It is natural that these and other peoples subjugated by Russia should have been more intensely affected by her
than those who were not.

The modernization of Soviet Asia has come about not only as a
result of the processes inevitably set in motion by a long period of
association between small and weak peoples on the one hand and a
large and powerful nation on the other, but has been the outcome
also of a deliberate policy on the part of both the Russian and the
Soviet governments. While modern institutions and practices were
introduced by the tsarist government, the regime often found it
expedient also to support the traditional social organizations and
religion, although a shift in policy in this area had become apparent
before the end of the nineteenth century. The Soviet government,
on its part, attacked the very foundations of the old institutions
and culture, thereby precipitating a more rapid social transformation in most Oriental communities and creating a cultural symbiosis of the old with the new, the traditional with the borrowed. In
public life the culture of many of these peoples has become Russian or Soviet, but in the confines of the home and the village
much remains traditional.

The depth of Russian penetration into the lives of a given Asian
people that came under Russian sway has depended in varying degree on the length of exposure to and association with Russia, on
the size of the population involved, on its ethnic awareness and its
historical consciousness, and on the level of its social development.
The Russian culture, however, was in general more readily accepted by the more modern societies (Armenia, Georgia) than by
Muslim and other peoples with a backward or closed structure

rooted deeply in cultural and religious traditions and often lacking even a written language of their own. Georgia and Armenia succumbed readily to the weight of the Russian presence. Religious affinity between them and Russia and a long period of contact with the educational and economic opportunities afforded in Russia also favored acceptance of the Russian culture.

A variety of problems and patterns emerges in our study of the Russian impact on Asian peoples who were not politically incorporated. Historically, contacts between Russia and Turkey, for example, were restricted for the most part to diplomatic, economic, and military relations. With the exception of a brief period of Russian control over the Ottoman Empire in the 1830s and a few years of political amity and cooperation during the Turkish War of Independence (1919-22), there is hardly any evidence of lasting Russian influence in Turkey and only a few instances of Turkish borrowing from Russia can be cited. Russian political and cultural influence in Turkey came largely through the émigré Tatars and Ottoman subjects such as the Armenians and the Balkan Christians. The Tatars accepted certain political and revolutionary ideas current in Russia, invested them with Muslim garb, and from the second half of the nineteenth century on transmitted them to the Turks. The Tatars could more easily influence the Turks, their ethnic and confessional kinsmen, than could the Russians, whom the Turks traditionally distrusted.

There were initially no interrelations between the Russians and the Arabs. What Russian contacts with this part of the world did exist were restricted to the Christians, both Arab and non-Arab, and were closely bound up with the Holy Land. Only a negligible degree of Russian influence may have been transmitted by the nineteenth-century Arab merchant colonies in Russia and by a few Arab men of learning who lived and worked in Russia.

Until the beginning of the nineteenth century, Russian influence on Iran was of little consequence. From then on, however, active interest in this area took on significant dimensions. Russia maintained at varying times a strong commercial and political hold over the country through control of the ruling house, providing it with a military force and conniving with various Iranian political groups. The relations between the two countries culminated in the Russian occupation of parts of Iran in each of the two world wars.

The case of Afghanistan presents a quite special set of circumstances. Ethnically divided and geographically forbidding, this country had been exposed to Russian diplomatic intrigues since the early nineteenth century. But given the existing conditions, any effective Russian activity could hardly have extended beyond the élite of the ruling circle and the king himself. In more recent times, however, a strong Soviet Russian influence is discernible in Afghanistan, as it is in the other Middle Eastern countries.

Though Russians had visited and had investigated most of the countries of Southeast Asia, they did not exert any influence in this part of the world until recent days. In fact, there was little official or scholarly Russian interest in any of the countries of this area, with the exception of India, until after the October Revolution. Of all the Southeast Asian countries it was India that fascinated the Russians most. This was because of her geographic proximity to Russia, and because of the presence of British troops on her territory over a long period, as well as because of her rich cultural heritage.

Russian contacts with China, which began in the seventeenth century, reached out through all the time-tested channels for wielding power—military, commercial, literary, political, and ideological. By way of contrast, Russian influence on Japan was negligible until late in the nineteenth century, and even then was limited to military confrontation and trade.

Since 1917 communism has been the most important instrument for the extension of Russian influence over the Asian world. The proponents of the communist doctrine in the countries of Asia were largely the Asian peoples themselves, guided and directed from Moscow at least until the emergence of the Chinese Peoples' Republic in 1949. The Soviet Union has systematically used its own peoples (Muslims, Armenians, Kurds) as missionaries of communism among coreligionists and conationalists abroad. The depth of communist influence varies from country to country, depending on local conditions and on certain other specific circumstances. In the countries that were traditionally anti-Russian or closed to Russian influence (Turkey and Japan, for example), communist influence is weak; and the same is true of those parts of the Middle East in which Islam remains strong. The strength of Islam in the Middle East and Western control of this area were sufficient deterrents to communism in the past. However, the loss of Western prestige in the Arab world following World War II, coupled with the weakening of Islam as an institution, has markedly changed the picture.

The dramatic upheaval in Asia following the Second World War has led to a tremendous increase in Soviet activity in that vast region. The relations between the Soviet Union and the countries of Asia have expanded greatly as Russian military advisers and engineers and economic, cultural, and diplomatic missions have flooded the Asian countries. The demand for trained personnel has necessitated the expansion of facilities for the study of the present and the past of the Asian peoples, for training Oriental experts and linguists, and for publication on an unprecedented scale of scholarly works, handbooks, and propaganda brochures.

The present volume contains in somewhat revised and edited form the nine papers read at a conference held at Stanford University from 30 November to 2 December 1967 on "The Russian Impact on Asia." The purpose of the conference was to examine the nature and extent of Russian influence on a selected number of Asian countries. The contributors discuss the status of Oriental studies in the Soviet Union, the problem of Russia's geographic and cultural destiny, the impact of Russia on Armenia, on Georgia, on the European Muslims, on Central Asia, on the Siberian and Far Eastern peoples of the Soviet Union, on China, and on Japan. It was not possible within the limits of a single conference—nor within a single volume—to look into all the aspects and ramifications of the Russian impact on the countries of Asia. The author of each essay was given the opportunity to present what he considered the salient points in Russia's impact on the area of his special interest. It goes almost without saying that in the preparation of a multi-author volume such as this we are likely to find conflicting points of view among eminent scholars. The editor has made no attempt to reconcile differing interpretations or disparate views of the participants. Nor is he necessarily in accord with the opinions expressed by the various contributors.

As is frequently the case, a symposium of this type presents a problem of transliteration. Because there are several systems of transliterating Russian into English, we have adopted the system of the Library of Congress for names of persons; but for well-known Russian names we have in almost all cases used the form that has become familiar to English-speaking readers. As a guide for geographic terms, we have followed the spelling given in *Webster's Geographical Dictionary* (rev. ed., 1964). In specific cases where a contributor has expressed a decided preference for a variant spelling, we have tried to comply with his wishes.

The editor is grateful to a number of persons who were helpful in organizing the conference and in the preparation of the manuscript for publication; to Professors Ivo J. Lederer and Terence Emmons of the Department of History, Stanford University, for their counsel and guidance; to Mrs. Elise Johnson for her expert assistance in organizing the conference; to Professor Vartan Gregorian, University of Texas, and Dr. George S. Rentz, Curator of the Middle East Collection, Hoover Institution, for their help in preparing the manuscript for publication; to Mrs. Edna Halperin for her highly skilled editorial guidance; to Mrs. Priscilla Reid for the work on the index; and to my students Ivo Banac, Patrick F. Flannery, Alice C. LeMaistre, Nicholas C. Pappas, and Frank Wozniak for their assistance and their sustained interest in the progress of this work. Finally, the editor wishes to express his special thanks to the Committee on International Studies for the financial assistance that made the conference possible.

Wayne S. Vucinich,
Stanford University

Russia and Asia

Abbreviations

BSE	*Bol'shaia Sovetskaia Entsiklopediia*
CPSU	Communist Party of the Soviet Union
KSINA	*Kratkie soobshcheniia Instituta narodov Azii*
KSIV	*Kratkie soobshcheniia Instituta vostokovedeniia Akademii nauk SSSR*
KUTV	Kommisticheskii universitet trudiashchikhsia Vostoka
MGIVAN	Moskovskaia gruppa Instituta vostokovedeniia Akademii nauk SSSR
NAiA	*Narody Azii i Afriki*
NARKOMNATS	Narodnyi komissariiat po delam natsional'nostei
NIA KUTV	Nauchno-issledovatel'skaia assotsiatsiia KUTV (see above)
PV	*Problem vostokovedeniia*
RANION	Assotsiatsiia nauchno-issledovatel'skikh institutov obshchestvenykh nauk
SIE	*Sovetskaia Istoricheskaia Entsiklopediia*
UZIV	*Uchenye zapiski Instituta vostokovedeniia*
VDI	*Vestnik drevnei istorii*
VNAV	Vserossiiskaia nauchnaia assotsiatsiia vostokovedeniia Vsesoiuznaia nauchnaia assotsiatsiia vostokovedov
VUNAV	Vseukrainskaia nauchnaia assotsiatsiia vostokovedeniia

—1—

Asia Through Russian Eyes

Nicholas V. Riasanovsky

> We two, alone, stand over the steppe at midnight:
> Never to return, never to look back.
> The swans cried beyond the Nepriadva,
> And again, again they are crying. . .
>
> Blok[1]

It is presumptuous to treat, especially to treat briefly and dogmatically, such a subject as the Russian view of Asia. To begin with, as it has so often been pointed out, Asia constitutes, except perhaps for certain purposes of geography, not a precise term, but an enormous conglomerate of phenomena. In what historic or cultural sense, for instance, do Lebanon and Japan belong together? And if in our concern with the Russian appreciation of Asia, we limit ourselves to considering those phenomena that left their mark on Russian life and thought, we still have to deal with an overwhelming number and variety of topics. One might investigate Russian pilgrimages to the Holy Land or Russian rule in Central Asia, the fascination of Russian writers with the majestic natural beauty and the noble savages of the Caucasus or the relevance of Turner's frontier hypothesis to the Russian colonization of Siberia, the Russian tea trade or Russian Buddhist studies.

Yet it is my argument that in spite of the variety and the richness of the subject one may still speak of the dominant and fundamental Russian view of Asia; and one may argue that this view changed following the reforms of Peter the Great, and that the

3

new version remained essentially unchallenged until the appearance of the Eurasian outlook in the twentieth century. I shall,
therefore, discuss briefly first the view of Asia prevalent in old Russia, next the view of Asia in Petrine Russia, and finally the Eurasian
concept.

It should be emphasized that the eyes of my title are the eyes of
the intellect, and that my essay is concerned with intellectual history. There is little doubt, for example, that the old Russian esti-
mate of Asiatic nomads was a narrow and biased one, or that modern Russians shared in the gigantic falsehoods of Western imperialism. Nor do I find the Eurasian beliefs at all convincing. My purpose here, however, is not to criticize mistaken views—let alone to
attempt to redress the balance—but rather to sketch the sequence
of these views and to relate them to the general course of Russian
history.

To the inhabitants of the first Russian state, that of Kiev, the all-
important Asiatics—although Kievan Russians, to be sure, did not
use the word itself—were the neighboring nomads of the southeastern steppe. In fact, whatever the prehistoric currents and influences may have been, the light of history throws into immediate
relief the fundamental opposition of the forest and the steppe, the
agricultural society of the Dnieper Valley and the restless nomads
from Asia. Moreover, the sedentary Slavs of European Russia became Christian in the second half of the tenth century, while their
roving enemies remained pagan or, much later, adopted Islam, not
to mention the Judaism of the Khazars. It is interesting, if not
profitable, to speculate on what might have happened had the
Russians, for example, opted to join the Muslim rather than the
Christian world. As it was, Russia became the eastern flank of
Christendom and Europe, the Russian struggle against the inhabitants of the steppe assuming classic proportions: religion and ideology combined with economic, social, political, ethnic, and cultural differences to inspire and maintain it. More immediately, it
was often, and perhaps in general, the matter of survival itself,
whether in terms of the need of the Russians to protect their commercial way "from the Varangians to the Greeks" and their agricultural economy, or of the even more pressing need to check indefatigable invaders bent on plunder and destruction. Few antag-
onisms in world history were as pronounced, as long-lasting, and as
central to the lives of the peoples involved.

The main opponents of the Russians changed several times, the Pechenegs replacing the Khazars, and the Polovtsy the Pechenegs; but the fighting continued. Thus it was against the Khazars that Sviatoslav waged some of his celebrated far-flung wars during the militant decade, 962 to 972, when he ruled in Kiev; against the Pechenegs that Iaroslav the Wise won the great victory of 1037; against the Polovtsy that Vladimir Monomakh undertook in the first quarter of the twelfth century most of the eighty-three major campaigns mentioned in his *Testament*. Terror worked both ways. According to tradition, Polovetsian mothers used to scare their children with the name of Vladimir Monomakh. In contrast to the wars of medieval Europe, the wars between the Russians and the peoples of the steppe were waged on a mass scale with tremendous effort and destruction. After the Polovtsy and the Kievan Russians had virtually knocked each other out, the Mongols came to deliver the *coup de grâce*.

It may well be argued that the Mongol invasion and conquest of 1237-41 was the most traumatic historical experience of the Russian people. For the first and only time in history the whole of Russia was subjugated by an invader. Devastation and massacre spread through the land. The sources, both Russian and non-Russian, tell, for instance, of a complete extermination of the population in such towns as Riazan', Torzhok, and Kozel'sk, while in others those who survived the carnage became slaves. A Mongol chronicle states that Batu and his lieutenants destroyed the towns of the Russians and killed or captured all their inhabitants. A papal legate, Archbishop Giovanni de Piano Carpini, who crossed southern Russia in 1245-46 on his way to Mongolia, wrote of "countless heads and bones of dead people" and of Kiev reduced to two hundred houses. Or to quote *The Tale of the Ravage of Riazan' by Batu*:

> The churches of God they devastated, and in the holy altars they shed much blood. And no one in the town remained alive: all died equally and drank the single cup of death. There was no one here to moan, or cry—neither father and mother over children, nor children over father and mother, neither brother over brother, nor relatives over relatives— but all lay together dead. And all this occurred to us for our sins.[2]

The Mongol conquest of Russia was followed by some two hundred and fifty years of Mongol rule. More precisely, the Mongols had effective control over most of Russia from 1240 to 1380, the year of the great Russian victory over their oppressors at Kulikovo, and a shaky, at times nominal suzerainty for another century, until 1480, when Ivan III formally renounced all allegiance to the khan. Whatever the significance of the Mongol domination might have been for the rise of Moscow and for the eventual consolidation of Russia around the new center, that domination constituted a heavy and continuous burden on the Russian people. The terror of the original invasion was reenacted frequently, if on a lesser scale, as the new rulers killed recalcitrant Russian princes and sent punitive expeditions into towns and areas that failed to pay taxes or proved otherwise refractory. The two peoples continued to live apart, their contacts minimized by the differences in religion, in culture, and in social and economic structure. In contrast to what happened in China or Persia, the Mongols never established a dynasty of their own in Russia. They merely insisted on obedience on the part of the Russian princes and on as large a tribute as they could exact.

The balance of power shifted slowly on the great Russian plain. After the Golden Horde itself collapsed in civil strife, Muscovy had to face the successor states that continued the age-old steppe practice of constant massive raids for slaves and booty: the Russians had to rally their strength to defend the open southeastern frontier in the sixteenth, the seventeenth, and even the eighteenth centuries just as in the tenth or the twelfth centuries. After Russian offensives conquered the khanates of Kazan in 1552 and of Astrakhan in 1556, the Crimean Tatars remained as the main opponents, protected before long by a new great "Asiatic" enemy of Russia, Turkey. Southern Russia was thus to be finally won by the Russians only late in the eighteenth century, long after the reforms of Peter the Great. It should be added that in the opinion of many leading historians of Russia it was precisely this late period in the struggle against the steppe, the centuries after the Mongol power had passed its peak, that taxed to the limit the endurance of the Russians and determined, or at least conditioned, such fundamental characteristics of the emerging Russian state and society as the service gentry system and serfdom itself.[3]

For perhaps a thousand years, if one is to include speculation about prehistory, the basic Russian attitude toward the peoples of the steppe, toward Asia, was that of total apartness and extreme hostility. Other feelings, to be sure, must have been present at times, as witnessed by some princely intermarriage with the Polovtsy and the Mongols or by the fact that after the collapse of the Mongol rule many Mongols joined the ranks of the Russian gentry (apparently very few Russians ever joined the steppe peoples). But the evidence of the sources cannot be gainsaid, and all evidence points to the Russian view of the Asiatic nomads as a dreadful outside enemy, sent upon the Russians, according to the Christian chroniclers, as a punishment for their sins. The note of terror is especially strong in the depiction of the Mongols. In fact, it has been suggested by no less a specialist than A. Presniakov that Russian writers deliberately abbreviated and suppressed consideration of the Mongol activities as too painful and too shameful to record.[4] Russian scholars followed, in a sense, the attitude of their sources. The two dominant schools of historiography on the subject of the impact of the steppe peoples (principally the Mongols) on the development of Russia emphasize respectively the paucity and even absence of significant influence, that is, apartness,[5] and various negative consequences, that is, hostility.

As we have seen, the Russians began to gain the upper hand in their dealings with Asiatic nomads long before the reign of Peter the Great. Yet it was only the process of Westernization promoted by the tireless reformer and bequeathed by him to his successors that made the Russians, at last, essentially secure from the peoples of the steppe. Even Turkey, the last major opponent in southern Russia, was decisively defeated in the wars undertaken by Catherine the Great, precisely because it was less "modern" than Russia. Using its new power, Russia not only consolidated its occupation of largely uninhabited Siberia, but thrust out in other Asiatic directions: into the Caucasus, Central Asia, and the Far East. Russians came into more contacts with many more Asiatic peoples than in the days of the Polovtsy and the Golden Horde. Yet Asiatic peoples now played a much less significant part in Russian lives or in the Russian outlook.

Ideology changed as sharply as political reality. Indeed the reforms of Peter the Great and of those who came after him were probably most decisive in the cultural and intellectual evolution of Russia. Modern Russian intellectual history may be understood

only as a part of general European intellectual history, and this re-
fers to views on Asia as much as to other topics. The new orientation of the educated Russians meant several things. For one, it implied a completely Western-centered or European-centered world
view. Therefore, in relation to Asiatic peoples the emphasis on a-
partness remained as strong as in the days of steppe warfare.

Hostility, however, was drastically modified. Instead of inspiring apprehension or even terror, the inhabitants of Asia came to be
associated with backwardness and inefficiency. The Russian words
khalatniki and *khalatnichat'* referring to the "robe-wearers" illustrate the point. The superiority and even the unique validity of the
European development appeared to be the common explicit and
especially implicit assumption in Russia as in other European
countries. What is more, the empire of the Romanovs, where
Europe and Asia met, seemed to educated Russians to provide
ideal support for this view. Europeans could, and perhaps were
destined to, benefit mankind by carrying their enlightenment to
backward continents. Russian intellectuals readily joined in the
general European ideology of imperialism. On occasion, to mention an important qualification, the feeling of one's general European superiority could be combined with admiration for certain aspects of Asiatic cultures, such as Buddhism or Japanese esthetics.
Again, Russians tended to share preferences and fads common to
Europe. Yet even when such admiration produced, at least within
its narrow compass, appreciation in place of hostility and snob-
bism, it hardly diminished the apartness. More often than not elements of Asiatic cultures were admired for the very reason that
they seemed new, different, strange, and exotic.

On the whole, and speaking in broad terms, it is remarkable to
what extent the view of Asia in imperial Russia was narrow, consistent, and consistently "European."[6] In a direct and simple manner most educated Russians identified themselves and their country with the West, with Europe. Many of them, from Peter the
Great to Lenin, urged change to enable Russia to catch up with
the more advanced members of the European family of nations,
to become more "European." For Asia they usually had little time
and attention, frequently considering it, as already indicated, as a
kind of a morass. This was true of the Russian intellectuals of the
Age of Reason, of Alexander I and his enlightened advisers, of the

Decembrists, of the Westernizers, of the liberals, of the radicals, of most populists, of most conservatives, and of the Marxists, as well as of the great bulk of educated Russians in general. The main outlines of their view are well known and need not detain us. More striking and perhaps insufficiently appreciated, however, is the fact that even those Russian intellectuals such as the Slavophiles, the proponents of Official Nationality or of Dostoevskii, who rose against the West, against "Europe," in the name of a distinct and different Russian identity, retained a completely and explicitly "European" attitude toward Asia.

It was Pëtr Chaadaev who shocked his contemporaries and quickened their debate on the nature and destiny of Russia with the publication in 1836 of his "Philosophical Letter," which asserted that Russia did not belong to Europe. Yet for our purposes it is more important to realize that Chaadaev also believed that Russia had never constituted a part of Asia. "We are located in the east of Europe; this is definite; but with all this we have never been of the East."[7] Moreover, Chaadaev's eventual solution of the Russian problem was that of an extreme Westernizer. Peter the Great, he finally decided, did join Russia to Europe. In the words of a justly celebrated passage: "Peter the Great found at home only a blank sheet of paper, and he wrote on it: Europe and the West; from that time on we have been of Europe and of the West."[8]

In the subsequent debate the Slavophiles ably expounded the anti-Western view. As against the alleged rationalism, egoism, materialism, and compulsion of the West, they postulated a vision of integration, peace, and harmony among men expressed in the Orthodox Christian principle of *sobornost'*, in the Russian peasant commune, and in the family. Asia, except to the extent that the Christian tradition is to be considered Asiatic, was conspicuously absent from Slavophile thought. In fact, the largest continent in the world occupied a prominent place in only one important work to come out of the Slavophile circle, Aleksei Khomiakov's so-called world history, a huge compilation of notes, arguments, hypotheses, and examples, published in three volumes long after the author's death.[9]

In this unfinished and disjointed study, a first draft at its best, Khomiakov tried to interpret the history of mankind in terms of two principles that he identified as the Iranian principle of freedom and the Kushite principle of necessity.[10] The proponents of the two principles formed two hostile camps, based on spiritual affinity rather than on blood ties or political allegiance, and were engaged in a constant and manifold struggle for the world. The Iranian principle expressed itself in the belief in creation and in spiritual religion, in the alphabet, literature, and song. The Bible belonged to it, and Christianity was its logical culmination. Typically Iranian details included the legend of the great flood and enmity against the serpent. The link that united the Iranians was their faith, but they also belonged to the same white race which alone preserved the tradition of true spirituality.[11]

The Kushites were mute men who believed in necessity and directed their efforts toward enormous constructions, such as the pyramids of Egypt or the temples of southern India. They were engaged in hewing out of stone rather than talking; they wrote little, and they wrote only in hieroglyphics. They worshipped the serpent. The Kushites were slaves of nature, whether in the form of stone or in the sensuous form of a serpent. Although Khomiakov's scheme transcended peoples and continents, with the spirit of Kushitism inspiring the development of the West centered on the Roman state and the Roman church, most of Asia apparently belonged to the Kushite realm, typified by such phenomena as China and Buddhism. An important exception was provided by the Iranian bearers of Sanskrit and Brahmanism, who, however, in Khomiakov's opinion based on the then recent postulation of an Indo-European family of languages, were members of the white race. Khomiakov regarded the Slavs as outstandingly Iranian in their characteristics.

The proponents of Official Nationality had a little more to say about Asia than the Slavophiles. These ultraconservative supporters of Nicholas I's regime, who rallied under the banner of "Orthodoxy, autocracy, and nationality," shared the Slavophile criticism of the godless and revolutionary West, but in contrast to the Slavophiles took an entirely positive view of the Russian reality. In their affirmation of the true Russian principles or in their basic thought in general, Asia played no part at all.[12] In fact, it was the peripheral position of Asia in regard to Official Nationality that enabled some government ideologists to express far-reaching and differing views concerning the vast continent and its inhabitants. The proponents of Official Nationality included even a gifted Orientalist, as well as one of the most prolific and irresponsible journalists of the age, Osip Senkovskii, who occupied the chair of Oriental studies at the University of St. Petersburg and was strongly attracted to "the bright and original colors" of the East.[13] But the two members of the group who expressed the most pronounced and revealing views on Asia were the minister of education and "father" of Official Nationality, Sergei Uvarov, and the prominent historian of Russia and publicist, Mikhail Pogodin.[14]

Count Sergei Uvarov (1786-1855) enjoyed an aristocratic background, an excellent education, and a splendid career which made him president of the Imperial Academy of Sciences in 1818 and minister of education from 1833 to 1849. Although never a professional scholar, Uvarov concentrated his interest on the classical world and wrote a series of short studies in Greek mythology, religion, and literature. He found Asiatic influences in the material that he investigated; moreover, from his youth he was fascinated with Asia itself. In brief, the Russian minister of education belonged to that group of European intellectuals who, early in the nineteenth century, at the bright dawn of Orientalism, saw answers to the riddles of human history, life, and thought in the temples of India, the writings of Palestine, or the pyramids of Egypt. Together with his intellectual mentors, such as Friedrich Schlegel, Herder, and even Goethe, Uvarov fell naturally under the spell of the newly-discovered, fashionable, exotic, mysterious, and lavishly if vaguely promising cultures of the East.

Uvarov's most famous piece dealing with Asia was his "Project of an Asiatic Academy," which the young enthusiast presented in 1810 to Count A. Razumovskii, then the Russian minister of education. It began as follows:

> There occurred during the last years of the eighteenth century a great revolution in all our ideas concerning the history of human civilization. The Orient, recently still abandoned to the lying tales of a few adventurers and the dusty works of a small number of scholars, has been unanimously recognized as the cradle of all civilization of the universe. The accidental causes of this *rehabilitation* have been the progress of the English in India, the conquest of the sacred language of the Brahmins, of the language of Zoroaster's writings, the works of German

scholars dealing with the Bible, and the establishment of the Asiatic Society of Calcutta.

Now we have reached the stage which makes it impossible for us to deny that Asia is the central point from which all the rays of light scattered over the globe emanate. This magnificent hypothesis, which links itself admirably with all the sacred traditions, is the only one that can henceforth be considered as indisputable.

And, indeed, it would be impossible to study attentively the vast history of the human spirit in terms of this marvelous system without seeing how parts which appeared at first glance most diverse fall into a successive pattern and represent nothing but an immense development of one and the same principle. And when one joins modern discoveries to ancient notions, when one goes back to the origin of the first philosophic and religious views, one is persuaded to the point of obviousness that it is to Asia that we owe the foundations of the great edifice of human civilization.[15]

The sages of Greece, Uvarov continued, went to study in India, whence they borrowed their learning, their ethics, and their philosophical systems. Greek religion with its many gods also came from the Orient, through Phoenicia and Egypt. Later Asia exercised profound political impact on Europe through such developments as the Muslim conquest of Constantinople and Spain, and the European discovery of the maritime route to India.

It was the duty of Russia to play a special role in the renaissance of Oriental studies. The empire of the tsars included all northern Asia, possessed an enormously long Asiatic land frontier that "brought it into contact with almost all the peoples of the Orient,"[16] and maintained very close relations with such states as Turkey, Persia, and China. Special political, as well as general intellectual and cultural, interests demanded that Russia learn more about Asia. In fact, "never before has the reason of state been so much in accord with the general moral interests of civilization."[17] Uvarov concluded:

It is time that the powerful protection bestowed by His Majesty Emperor Alexander upon enlightenment be extended finally to Asia, and that Russia, having placed herself at a level with other countries, surpass them by the means which she has at her disposal and by the results which can be expected from them. For this purpose it would be necessary to establish an academy mediating between the civilization of Europe and the enlightenment of Asia, in which everything related to the study of the Orient would be brought together. An institution given over to the teaching of Oriental languages, where one would see a European critic beside an Asiatic lama, would immortalize the benefactions of the monarch and assist his liberal and generous intentions.[18]

Amplifying his project, the future minister of education dwelt with enthusiasm on the rewards of Biblical exegesis and of investigations in Oriental languages, philosophies, and literatures. The new Academy was to include Hebrew, Indian, Chinese, Manchu, Arabic, Persian, Turkish, Tatar, Armenian, Georgian, and Tibetan studies. Yet, characteristically, Uvarov's fascination with Asia went beyond specific fields of knowledge and really beyond academic learning. Surveying the remarkable continent, Uvarov wrote:

Once the knowledge of this vast and marvelous land is extended further, perhaps there will be found a thread in the labyrinth of the human spirit; perhaps there will be discovered sources, ancient, forgotten, buried in the debris, but which can give to the spirit of man new strength and freshness, those certain harbingers of the great ages which are immortalized by the presence and the works of genius.[19]

In contrast to Uvarov, Mikhail Pogodin, eventually a prominent Moscow University professor and a well-known public figure, sprang from a plebeian background and forced his own way upward. Born in 1800, and assisted originally by a friendly typographer and a helpful priest, he had the good fortune to enter in 1814 the First Moscow High School and in 1818 the university in the same city. Through ability and extremely hard work Pogodin went on to pursue a successful academic career, being elected, in 1841, to the Imperial Academy of Sciences presided over by Uvarov. While Pogodin's research represented a significant contribution to the relatively new field of Russian history, it was as an indefatigable publicist and intellectual leader of the Right that the Moscow professor attracted most attention. He became a leading exponent of Uvarov's doctrine of Official Nationality, interpreting it in the more romantic and radically nationalist sense. Devoted, sincere, and blunt as usual, he expanded this Russian nationalism into Pan-Slavism and demanded the reshaping of the world in accordance with his creed. Pogodin died in 1875. His concern with Asia had been secondary, even incidental, but nevertheless clear-cut and quite revealing.

The most important point to note is that, on the world stage, Pogodin identified himself with the so-called white race in the same wholehearted and aggressive manner in which, in Europe, he pledged allegiance to Russia and Slavdom. Pogodin's devotion to "the tribe of Japheth," like most of his other loyalties, developed early and remained unshaken throughout a long life. As a young man he had already come to the conclusion that "it is impossible to educate Africa and Asia, except by fitting out an army from all of Europe and sending it on a crusade against them. Let Europeans occupy the thrones of the Ashanti, the Burmese, the Chinese, the Japanese, and let them establish there a European order of things. Then the fate of those countries will be decided. And why should this not be done? . . .The happiness of mankind depends on it."[20]

Pogodin retained this conviction steadfastly in later years, reacting to various political developments in terms of his basic belief. Highly characteristic was his response to the news of the Sepoy Mutiny. Pogodin explained that the first reports of the rebellion evoked joy in Russia, a fact easily understandable in the light of all the damage and injury done to Russia by England in recent years. A certain countess even promised to make a pilgrimage to the Holy Trinity Monastery on foot, just so the English would be made to suffer more. But, once detailed information from India reached Russia,

> We forgot immediately that the English were our enemies, and saw in them only Europeans, Christians, sufferers; we saw in them an educated people threatened by barbarians—and a general compassion, a general sympathy expressed itself everywhere.[21]

> From the point of view of humanity, as Europeans, as Christians, as an educated people, we wish success to the English, we wish that they would establish firmly their rule in India, and that they would extend it, as far as they can, in Asia, in Africa, and in America. We wish that the other European nations would succeed in exactly the same manner and would gain footholds more and more powerfully in the other continents which must take to their bosoms, in the form of numerous well-organized colonies, the overflow of European population, and thus rescue old Europe from the troubles, worries, and dangers which are caused by crowding, by pauperism, and by the proletariat. Shem and Ham, according to the word of the Scripture, must bow to Japheth.[22]

Asia, as well as Africa and in part even America, thus represented logical areas for European expansion which would both introduce modern civilization into these huge backward regions and solve some of the most difficult problems in Europe itself. As Pogodin observed concerning the dark continent: "To establish European influence in Africa—this is a success for enlightenment; and I shall be glad to see Spain acquire Fez and Morocco, France Tunisia and Tripoli, and England the Sahara for that matter, where she will likely find ways to create plantations."[23] But for this enlightenment to be fully effective, the Europeans had to recognize the duties and the responsibilities of the white man's burden: government in colonial areas was to be guided by the true interests of the natives, not by motives of economic exploitation, as had too often been the case.

While Pogodin followed with sympathy the European penetration of Africa, he had a much more direct and immediate interest in Asia. For it was in Asia that Russia was destined to advance. In the black days of isolation and defeat in the Crimean War, the historian admonished his countrymen: "Leaving Europe alone, in expectation of more favorable circumstances, we must turn our entire attention to Asia, which we have almost entirely left out of our considerations although it is precisely Asia that is predestined primarily for us. And it is also into Asia that our enemies, following some blind instinct, although not with good intentions, want to hurl us! What would the English have done with our territorial and other connections with Asia! "[24] As the legendary Russian hero Dobrynia remarked long ago, one should go after tribute to peoples that wear bast shoes, not boots. The Europeans, Pogodin continued, wore not only boots, but lacquered boots! Russian rulers of the past, notably the greatest of them, Peter the First, maintained relations with the East and took an interest in it. "And Peter? Peter thought about India, and about China, and about Persia, and about the island of Madagascar. Just recently an order of his was found to draft boys to study Japanese."[25]

The reorientation of Russian policy in the direction of Asia could no longer be delayed. Political and cultural interests, natural links with Asiatic neighbors as well as immense trade advantages for Russia and the world, all pointed eastward. Pogodin's tone rose to a high pitch as he asserted in his customary dogmatic, blunt, and direct manner: "Let the European peoples live as they best know how, and manage in their lands as they please; whereas to us belongs, in addition, half of Asia, China, Japan, Tibet, Bukhara,

Khiva, Kokand, Persia, if we want to, and perhaps must, extend our possessions to spread the European element in Asia, so that Japheth may rise above his brothers."[26]

In sum, the proponents of Official Nationality remained as "European" in their attitudes toward Asia as Chaadaev and the Slavophiles. Although fascinated by the mysterious learning of the ancient Orient, Uvarov assumed that in contemporary Asia this learning had been "forgotten, buried in the debris," and that an academy in Russia was needed to revive it. In fact, it was the *mission civilisatrice* of Russia, so to speak, to perform that task: "Russia, ruling over a considerable part of Asia and preserving under its scepter numerous and different Asiatic languages, is selected by destiny, in preference to all other enlightened peoples, to study the East, its dialects, its literatures, and the monuments of its history and its creeds."[27] The Orient was so attractive to the Russian minister of education precisely because it was arcane and exotic.

But it was Pogodin who followed this European-centered attitude toward Asia, buoyed by the increasing material superiority of the West over the East, to reach the characteristic assumptions of modern colonialism and imperialism. Pogodin's views on Asia lacked all originality, but they were typical of his age. Whereas Chaadaev paid tribute to the Orient as "the homeland of science and of sweeping thought,"[28] Khomiakov included it in the eternal conflict of freedom against necessity, and Uvarov turned to it for mysterious wisdom, Pogodin wanted, quite simply, for Russia to expand physically in Asia. In a sense, Uvarov and Pogodin, only fourteen years apart in age and both championing the doctrine of Official Nationality, represented two different worlds, or rather two different stages of the same world in transition. Uvarov reflected an aristocratic society with its highly developed esthetic tastes, its broad but vague intellectual interests, and its social and cultural exclusiveness. Pogodin, himself of lowly origin, exemplified the rise of the common man and the coming of a new era of simple and brutal principles, mass demagoguery, wholesale imperialism, and total war.

In their view of Asia, subsequent Russian intellectuals of the anti-Western tradition followed Pogodin more often than Uvarov, although some of them, for example the writer and ideologist Konstantin Leont'ev (1831-91), continued to be fascinated by "the bright and original colors" of the East. But whether in Pogodin's terms or in those of Uvarov, this entire "anti-Western tradition" remained thoroughly Western in its attitude toward Asia. The conflict with the West, which its proponents loudly proclaimed, was essentially a fraternal conflict, perhaps all the more bitter for that reason, but nevertheless fraternal. Self-identification in terms of Orthodoxy, the Byzantine heritage, the Russian people, or Slavdom almost inevitably implied a close relationship to other Christians, other heirs of the classical world, and other European peoples or groups of peoples. Given these conditions, it is not surprising that the same Russians who vehemently denounced Europe and postulated a fundamental contrast and opposition between Russia and Western principles, nevertheless, as soon as they turned to consider Asia, identified themselves with Europe, with the West. More precisely, two aspects of their views of Asia are important in this connection: the explicit self-identification of the holders of the views with the West, and the Western nature and structure of the views themselves. Further examples need not detain us, except for the case of Dostoevskii, who has been erroneously presented on occasion not only as a staunch opponent of Europe, but also as a champion of an Asiatic nature and destiny of Russia.

To be sure, the great novelist may be easily misread, because he made a number of far-reaching statements on Russia and Asia, of which the following is perhaps the most striking: "This [the conquest of Asia] is necessary because Russia is not only in Europe, but also in Asia; because a Russian is not only a European, but also an Asiatic. Not only that: in our coming destiny, perhaps it is precisely Asia that represents our main way out."[29] Yet this very passage contains a typically imperialistic emphasis on conquest. And indeed throughout the article in question and its sequel Dostoevskii stressed the great territories and riches of Asia to be exploited by Russia, likening the perspective to the European discovery of America and expansion into it. The celebrated writer propounded enthusiastically also another imperialistic argument: acquisition and colonization of Asiatic lands would stimulate the Russians to display their talents in far-ranging, creative activity, eliminating passivity and stagnation characteristic of his countrymen and country. Checked and humiliated in Europe, Russia would do well to concentrate for a time on her *mission civilisatrice* in the East. As in so many other cases, Dostoevskii's imperialistic ideology was joined to an explicit self-identification with the West. The novelist insisted on the identity of the Russians as Slavs, as Europeans, even as "Aryans." Asia, to repeat, represented an ideal field for Russian expansion and activity. Europe was something entirely different: "Europe is also our mother, like Russia, our second mother; we took much from her, and we shall be taking again, and we shall not want to be ungrateful to her."[30]

Imperialistic attitudes and ideas spread widely in Russia—as elsewhere in Europe—in particular in the period between the Crimean War and the revolutions of 1917. Stimulated by such developments as the Russian occupation of Central Asia, the building of the Trans-Siberian Railroad, and Russian activities in the Far East and Persia, imperialistic ideology could readily combine with reactionary, conservative, or liberal beliefs, with pro-Western or anti-Western views. Frequently Russian writers asserted that their country possessed a unique nature that made it peculiarly suited to the imperialistic role, thus restating similar special claims of their English or French or Portuguese contemporaries. Even such a level-headed and practical man as Sergei Witte (1849-1915), minister of finance, industrializer of Russia, and the builder of the Trans-Siberian Railroad, wrote once to Alexander III, after affirming the true principles of Orthodoxy, autocracy, and nationality:

> It is on these bases that the whole edifice of Russian power has been built up, and it is therefore impossible for Russia to be fused with the West. At the same time she has long since appeared among Asiatic peoples as the bearer of the Christian ideal, striving to spread among them the principles of Christian enlightenment, not under the standard of Europeanization, but under her own special standard. In a word, in the Asiatic East Russia has long since taken upon herself the mission of cultural enlightenment in the spirit of those principles which have given a special character to her own development.[31]

As Witte's emphasis on Christian enlightenment indicates, Russian imperialist ideologists, like their Western brethren, enjoyed dwelling on the benefits, or alleged benefits, of colonial penetration and rule. At times they also urged protection of the natives against improper treatment by their new masters.[32] But they saw both the interests of the colonized and the policies of the colonizers only as elements within their blinding imperialist vision.

A real change in the opinion of educated Russians concerning Asia occurred only in the twentieth century among the so-called Eurasians. To be sure, for most purposes deviant views of a handful of Russian intellectuals in exile cannot be put on a par with fundamental assumptions of old Russia or with the dominant, indeed unquestioned, ideology of the entire Petrine period. Yet, in terms of intellectual history, they represented a new departure and therefore deserve attention.

Eurasianism emerged quite formally and officially in the year 1921 when four young Russian intellectuals, Prince Nikolai Trubetskoi, Pëtr Savitskii, Pëtr Suvchinskii, and Georgii Florovskii, published in Sofia a collective volume, *Iskhod k Vostoku*, that is, *Exodus to the East*.[33] The volume consisted of an introduction and ten essays. The introduction spoke of a world cataclysm—the year, it must be borne in mind, was 1921—of a catastrophic change of scenes, of a new age, of the dying of the West and of the imminent rise of the East. It concluded: "Russians and those who belong to the peoples of 'the Russian world' are neither Europeans nor Asiatics. Merging with the native element of culture and life which surrounds us, we are not ashamed to declare ourselves Eurasians."[34]

The essays that followed the introduction emphasized several themes. All four authors believed that they, their country, and the world were living through years of decisive, supreme importance. As Savitskii put it in an article entitled "A Turn to the East":

> In immeasurable sufferings and deprivations, in the midst of hunger, in blood and sweat Russia took upon herself the burden of searching for truth, on behalf of all and for the benefit of all. Russia in sin and godlessness, Russia in loathsomeness and filth. But Russia in search and struggle, in a bid for a city not of this world. . . . The ardor of history comes not to those who are calm in the knowledge of truth, who are self-satisfied and satiated. The flaming tongues of inspiration descend not on the *beati possidentes*, but on those troubled in spirit: the wings of the Angel of God have moved the waters of the pool.[35]

Or in the equally striking words of Suvchinskii hailing the coming of "The Age of Faith": "There are frightening times, terrifying epochs, like apocalyptic visions, times of great realizations of the Mystery, times frightening and blessed. . ."[36]

For Russians in particular the new revelation was Eurasia.

Savitskii made use of his essays on "The Migration of Culture" and on "Continent-Ocean (Russia and the World Market)" to help define and promote the new concept in essentially geopolitical terms. He found that cultural centers moved throughout history to colder and colder climates, from an annual average temperature of 20° C (68° F) in the second millenium B.C. in Mesopotamia and Egypt to 5° C (41° F) in contemporary northern Europe. In the case of another shift to a colder climate, two areas stood out as the likely centers of culture: on the one hand, central Canada with the adjacent northern section of the United States, "northern Minnesota," and on the other, parts of northern and central Russia together with all of eastern Russia, both in eastern Europe and in Siberia. As to the "continent-ocean," Savitskii argued that "that economic-geographic sphere which we designate by the name of Russia-Eurasia is the most 'deprived' of all the countries of the world as far as possibilities for participation in the oceanic exchange are concerned."[37] Characteristically, such exceedingly "continental" areas either remained in a primitive condition outside the world economy or became exploited servants of their more fortunate maritime counterparts. The way out of this predicament lay in the development of a continental market, essentially independent of the world oceanic economy. Instead of paying the crushing cost of long-distance transportation, continental producers and consumers should sell and purchase near by, thus creating a diversified and at the same time integrated continental economy. The larger the area and the greater its economic diversification, the stronger a continental economy was likely to be. "The economic future of Russia lies not in the aping of the 'oceanic' policy of others, a policy that is in many ways inapplicable to Russia, but in the comprehension of its 'continental nature' and in an adaptation to this nature."[38]

In a fascinating contribution, "The Upper and the Lower Layers of Russian Culture (The Ethnic Base of Russian Culture)," Trubetskoi undertook the delineation of the ethnic and cultural nature of Eurasia. Proto-Slavic dialects, from which the Russian language descended, occupied a middle geographic position and were, therefore, similar in certain respects to proto-Indo-Iranian dialects and in other respects to proto-Western-Indo-European ones. In pronunciation, for example, proto-Slavic dialects were linked to proto-

Indo-Iranian ones by consonantal changes, while their connection with the Western-Indo-European evolution was possibly limited only to certain shades of pronunciation of some vowels. As regards vocabulary, that is, words and concepts, the ties to the Indo-Iranian East consisted in particular of fundamental terms denoting religious and spiritual values and functions, as well as of prepositions, pronouns, and the negative particle and forms. Words connected with the West were mainly those concerned with material culture. Peter the Great's violent reform, Trubetskoi went on, proved fundamentally sterile, because Russians were constitutionally incapable of participating in Western culture. After the reform they remained permanently split into the superficially Westernized upper layers, and the lower layers, the masses. The lower layers, Trubetskoi insisted, included not merely, or even primarily, Slavic elements, but rather an entire many-faceted and independent cultural zone.

> In general, this culture is a separate "zone" by itself, which includes in addition to the Russians also certain Ugrofinnic "aliens" together with the Turkic peoples of the Volga basin. In the east and the southeast this culture fuses in an imperceptibly gradual manner with the "steppe" culture (Turko-Mongolian) and through it with other cultures of Asia. In the west there is a transition, again gradual (through the White Russians and the Ukrainians), towards the culture of the West Slavs which is connected to the Romano-Germanic culture, and towards the "Balkan" culture.[39]

The eastern links were especially important. For example, many Great Russian folk songs utilized the so-called pentatonic or "Indo-Chinese" scale, characteristic of the music of the Finnic and Turkic tribes of the Volga basin, of all Mongol music, and of the music of Siam, Burma, and Indo-China, but not of the music of the Western neighbors of the Great Russians. The rhythm of the Great Russian songs tended to link Russia to Asia and to separate it from the other Slavs and from the West. The same held true for the dance. In contrast to the West, the Great Russian folk dance was not based on the dancing couple, a man and a woman holding each other and dancing together, but represented a variety of elements and a freedom of improvisation also found among the East Finns, the Mongols, and Turkic and Caucasian peoples. The Great

Russian ornament exhibited originality as well as certain connections with the Balkans through the Ukrainians and with the East through Finno-Ugrian peoples. Great Russian folk literature displayed a striking originality, although again some links could be established, for instance, with Turkish and Caucasian fairy tales and with the epic of steppe hordes. The material culture of the Great Russian people differed fundamentally, to be sure, from that of the nomads of the steppe; but it indicated the closest possible association between the Russians and the Finno-Ugrian peoples, both partners apparently making major contributions to their common benefit.

Russians were thus by no means simply Slavs. Rather, they belonged to a separate cultural world, and they had strong links with the "Turanian" East as well as with Slavdom. These "Turanian" links extended not only to ethnography, but also to anthropology, "for it is certain that in Russian veins there flows, in addition to Slavic and Ugrofinnic, also Turkic blood."[40] Russians easily established rapport with "Turanians." The Russian national character differed sharply from that of other Slavs. While it also differed from the Finno-Ugrian and the Turkic characters, it at least contained certain important elements linking it to the East, such as the penchant for contemplation, the devotion to ritual, and the quality of *udal'*, extravagant daring or audacity, "a purely steppe virtue, which the Turkic peoples understand, but neither the Romano-Germans nor the Slavs can."[41] Trubetskoi concluded that in the future reconstruction of Russia the ethnic base of Russian culture would have to be taken into account. In particular, it would be entirely inappropriate to try to erect again "a Romano-Germanic roof" on this Russian foundation.

Because my essay treats only the period up to the emergence of Eurasianism, I shall not attempt to trace the course of this movement. In general, however, in the nineteen twenties and thirties Eurasianism did acquire some prominence and attracted much attention among Russian exiles in Europe. The intellectual evolution of the new teaching followed a number of distinct lines, often closely related to specific scholarly disciplines. Still, most Eurasians, whether writing as economists, geographers, geopoliticians, linguists, anthropologists, religious thinkers, political theorists, or historians, concentrated on defining and developing the new and

crucial concept of Eurasia proclaimed in *Exodus to the East.*
Savitskii followed his essays in the original volume with a constant
stream of articles and monographs on Eurasian geopolitics. Trubetskoi contributed such brilliant, if highly questionable, studies as
his "Concerning the Turanian Element in Russian Culture."[42] Following some of Trubetskoi's suggestions, another outstanding linguist, Professor Roman Jakobson, discovered the Eurasian association of languages: in Eurasia, languages, including those of quite
different genetic origins, were linked by two jointly present traits,
monotony and the distinct division of consonants into hard and
soft, which affected meaning.[43] Other members of the movement
dealt with the concept and problems of Eurasia in terms of religious doctrine, political theory, or even crude medical and anthro-
pological research.[44] Rich and many-sided Eurasian history also
appeared to receive its full development in Professor George Vernadsky's voluminous writings. Vernadsky has stressed the decisive
significance of the relation between the steppe and the forest societies on the enormous Eurasian plain, the ethnic and cultural complexity of Russia, and the major and organic contribution of Eastern peoples, especially the Mongols, to Russian history.[45]

Eurasianism represented a new Russian approach to Asia. To be
sure, there was no justification for the frequent assertions of the
opponents of the movement that the Eurasians considered Russians to be Asiatics and Russia to be a part of Asia. These assertions paid tribute, in a sense, to the originality of Eurasianism,
which many educated Russians, especially of the older generations, failed even to understand, let alone accept. What the Eurasians did in fact believe was that Russia-Eurasia constituted an
independent, self-contained, organic entity, separate from both
Europe and Asia. In other words, China or Japan were as foreign
to Russia as, for example, France or England. By contrast, the
Asiatic peoples of Russia, that is, of Eurasia, were not external influences in the historical evolution of the Russians but rather integral parts of that evolution. The Russians, to repeat Trubetskoi,
were not simply Slavs. The central dogma of the new teaching was
the dogma of an organic Eurasia with its numerous Asiatic, as well
as non-Asiatic, components. The revolutionary novelty of Eurasianism thus resided in its intrinsic incorporation of many Asiatic
peoples into the history, life, and self-definition of the Russians,

who were to be henceforth Eurasians, as well as in its unprecedented, decisive break with the West.

How can we explain the Eurasian departure in Russian thought? For one thing, Eurasianism obviously reflected great contemporary historical events, and in the first place the Russian Revolution. Indeed that revolution occupied the central position in the entire Eurasian ideology and movement, determining in large part everything in it, from the initial religious and moral fervor to the later political plans and squabbles. The Eurasians distinguished two main aspects of the Russian Revolution: the utterly destructive rebellion against God, the negative side of the cataclysm so to speak, exemplified by the Bolsheviks and marking the culmination of the entire Westernizing evolution of the Russian intelligentsia, and the activation of the masses, an essentially positive development that would lead to the overthrow of the Bolsheviks and the triumph in Russia of organic religious ideology such as Eurasianism. The members of the movement regarded their "constructive" attitude toward the Russian Revolution as a crucial distinction between them and other groups of Russian exiles and as a main reason why they, rather than these others, would lead to new Russia.

More broadly, Eurasianism expressed a general European reaction to four years and three months of unprecedented slaughter of human beings, and it may be considered as one of the post-World War I European ideologies distinguished by their bitter rejection of the past and their vague messianic hopes for the future. The fact of exile, it should be added, exacerbated the mood and the thought of the Russian prophets of defiance, despair, and resurrection. Captives in effect, rather than simply visitors, in the West, they reacted with more violence against their cold host than any preceding group of Russian intellectuals. The Eurasians were members of a generation nurtured and educated in Russia to assume their rightful place in the cultural evolution of their fatherland. Now that that place and their Russia itself had vanished, Eurasianism constituted, in a sense, a desperate bid to bring both back into existence. The scope of the dream corresponded to that of the loss.

The Eurasians reacted in a fundamental way to yet another major contemporary historical development that has been designated by such phrases as the rise of colonial peoples, the decline of imperialism, or the gradual loss by the so-called white race of its dominant global position. In effect, they tried to link their own violent turning against the West to the world-wide rebellion against control by European powers. The timing of the Eurasian interest in the colonial peoples and problem deserves attention. While *Exodus to the East* marked the inauguration of Eurasianism, it had one clear, if not comprehensive, predecessor, namely, Trubetskoi's sweeping treatment of *Europe and Mankind*, published in book form the preceding year, 1920.[46] Moreover, Trubetskoi asserted in the preface that the ideas expressed in the book "had been formed in my consciousness already more than ten years ago."[47] Earlier publication, however, had seemed undesirable because these ideas were too advanced then and simply would not have been understood.

Europe and Mankind constituted an out-and-out indictment of Western imperialism. Trubetskoi argued that the alleged universal civilization, progress, and higher values that the colonizers claimed to bestow upon the colonized were merely the chauvinism of Europe made all the more dangerous by its larger claims, which misled and seduced non-European intellectuals. If one condemned the narrow-minded and aggressive patriots of a given locality, of Prussia, or of Germany, why should one defer to the much more dangerous and far-ranging patriots of Europe? Contrary to the prevailing opinion, other cultures were bound to be hurt by their borrowings from Europe. Having disparate psychologies and cultures uniquely their own, native peoples could never enter the civilization of Europe as equal partners and develop fully and creatively within its framework. In terms of European culture they would always be second-rate. Their own cultures, on the other hand, were in no sense inferior to European culture. They were simply different. The plotting of all cultures on a continuum with that of Europe at the summit represented one of the most pernicious intellectual errors of the age. Indeed, it was precisely this insidious ability of Europeans to make the exploited peoples, that is, the educated classes of those peoples, see things the European way that accounted in large part for the European domination of mankind. Therefore, in order to throw off the European yoke, the intellectuals of other societies, blinded by Europe, had first to recover their sight and to see the falsity as well as the evil of Euro-

pean claims and pretensions. Then they could lead their peoples in
an irresistible bid for independence. The ideas proclaimed so loudly in *Europe and Mankind* became part of Eurasian thought and
literature.[48]

Whereas Eurasianism did reflect in its own manner certain mo-
mentous contemporary historical developments, its fundamental
ideological affiliations are less certain. To be sure, Savitskii's geopolitical Eurasia can be readily derived from general European,
especially German, geopolitical theories as applied to Russia.[49]
Trubetskoi's ethnic-cultural Eurasia, however, had no obvious antecedents, and indeed represented, as our brief survey has indicated, a decisive break with the entire course of Russian thought
on Asia and Europe. Still, while the Russian intellectual tradition
provided no foundation for Eurasia, two recent developments in
Russian culture contributed to the emergence of that concept.
These were the growth of scholarship in relevant fields and a new
trend in Russian literature.

The growth of Oriental scholarship—Uvarov's dream and the
subject of one of the other contributions to this volume—extended, of course, well beyond Russia. For instance, it was only
toward the end of the nineteenth century and the beginning of the
twentieth that Turkic and especially Finno-Ugrian studies, developed by many specialists in a number of countries, had progressed
sufficiently for Trubetskoi and Jakobson to engage in their fascinating theorizing concerning the Eurasian association of languages.
Even more immediately relevant for Eurasianism was research de-
tailing the rich cultural background of ancient Russia and linking
elements of Russian and non-Russian cultures. In field after field
and topic after topic Russian scholars were discovering a new and
largely "non-Western" richness in the Russian and "pre-Russian"
past, and its connections with other civilizations. Archeology, history of art with its discovery of the "Scythian style," music, literature with its new links between Kievan epos and those of Persia
and the Turkic peoples, investigations of folklore, history, and
much else, all contributed to a fuller appreciation of Russia as a
cultural and historical entity and suggested to some the need of a
new scholarly synthesis. This expansion of knowledge and awareness concerning the Russian past may be seen in a striking, even
exaggerated, manner by comparing Vernadsky's writings on ancient Russia with standard nineteenth-century accounts. In partic-

ular, it is worth noting that long before the promulgation of Eurasianism some Russian scholars, such as the leading historian V. O. Kliuchevskii, began to assign an integral and "organic" role in the development of the Russian nation to some non-Russian ethnic groups, particularly to the Finnic-speaking tribes.[50]

Yet Kliuchevskii and his colleagues did not at all consider themselves to be Eurasians. The new self-identification, the *idée maîtresse* of Eurasianism, had to come from elsewhere; and in fact it appears to be linked to an elusive, yet striking, new trend, or trends, in Russian literature. The remarkable literary and artistic renaissance that came to Russia in the first decades of the twentieth century brought with it many novel themes and visions. One of these was something like the concept of Russia-Eurasia. It emerged among several writers or groups of writers at about the same time. For example, Velimir Khlebnikov, a prominent futurist poet, declared in 1912: "I know about the mind of a continent, not at all similar to the mind of islanders. A son of proud Asia does not come to terms with the peninsular intellect of the Europeans."[51]

Fascination with Asia and identification with Asiatic or quasi-Asiatic peoples developed especially among the so-called symbolists. In 1910-11, Andrei Belyi, one of the most important and most prominent writers of the period, published *St. Petersburg,* a remarkable tale of the capital city in 1905, of a gathering revolution, violence, and nightmare. "Asiatic" elements abounded in Belyi's novel, especially in its striking nightmare sequences. A mysterious Persian, a figure of delirium, materialized, or seemed to materialize, at one point, a Mongol face glared from a wall, the horsemen of Genghis Khan again rode in the steppe. *St. Petersburg* may well be interpreted as a depiction of a fatal conflict between the city of Peter, symbol of order, organization, rationality and Westernization in Russia, and the seething, revolutionary, "Asiatic" masses.[52] "Asia," then, was inside Russia, not merely outside. But Belyi's identification with "Asia" went beyond this vague and abstract general scheme, for the main protagonists of his tale, the Ableukhovs, father and son, the important bureaucrat and the undecided revolutionary, were explicitly of Mongol origin, and it was his own ancestors that came to the younger Ableukhov in his frenzied visions.

Even more memorable than Belyi's was the somewhat similar

vision of the supreme poet of the age, Aleksandr Blok (1880-
1921), which found its best expression in a poem entitled "The
Scythians" and written on the thirtieth of January, 1918:

> You are millions. We are hordes and hordes and hordes.
>   Just try, fight us!
> Yes, we are Scythians! Yes, we are Asiatics,
>   With slanting and greedy eyes!

and several stanzas later, always addressing the West:

> Russia is a Sphinx. Rejoicing and grieving,
>   And bathed in black blood,
> It looks, looks, looks at you
>   With both hatred and love![53]

Blok's vision, like Belyi's, combined hatred and love, massacre and
the coming of a new world, all-pervasive terror and a kind of exul-
tation. As the epigraph for his poem, Blok selected the words of
Vladimir Solov'ev (1853-1900), the man who exercised in so many
ways a dominant influence on Blok's age: "Panmongolism, although the name is savage, still it caresses my ear." Again, as in the
case of Belyi who dealt quite explicitly with the revolutionary
year of 1905, Blok wrote his poem in the wake of the October
Revolution of 1917 and at the same time that he was writing his
celebrated revolutionary poem, "The Twelve." In terms of Eurasian ideology, Blok's formulation was more precise than Belyi's,
for he presented his Russians-Scythians not simply as Asiatics, but
rather as an independent third element between Europe and Asia,
which had for centuries protected the West, had "held the shield
between two hostile races, the Mongols and Europe!"[54] Blok and
Belyi were not alone. In 1916-18 there developed a movement
known as "The Scythians," linked to the symbolist school and led
by the critic R. Ivanov-Razumnik, which combined the new self-
identification in opposition to Europe with a revolutionary and
apocalyptic tone and messianic hopes. In fact many critics ascribe
Blok's poem to Ivanov-Razumnik's influence.

Neither Khlebnikov, nor Belyi, nor Blok, nor any other poet
created Eurasianism. The significant fact, rather, is that at the
same time that scholars advanced their studies of non-Russian
peoples of the Russian empire and of the relationship of these

peoples to the Russians, artistic imagination, in more cases than one, also seized upon these "Asiatics," "Mongols," or "Scythians" to the point of identification with them. The stage was set for the flowering of a full-fledged new ideology, strikingly different in its self-definition and orientation from the Russian intellectual tradition. Trubetskoi could well write on the twenty-eighth of July, 1921, the year of the formal inauguration of Eurasianism: "The new direction is being carried in the air," and cite in the first instance Blok and two other poets as evidence for his assertion.[55]

To recapitulate the history of the Russian view of Asia, we might return briefly to our scheme of the two major ideological periods and the Eurasian deviation. For ancient Russia, Asia meant the foreign intruders from the steppe who evoked hostility and, frequently, fear. The educated classes of Petrine Russia shared fully the general European ideology in regard to Asia of superiority and even imperial domination, although this ideology could at times be combined with a romantic interest in various aspects of Oriental cultures. The Eurasians, finally, called for an organic, harmonious integration, if not with Asia as such, at least with that huge part of Asia that was of direct concern to the Russians. The first outlook corresponded to the age-old wars between the agricultural Russian Slavs and the nomadic tribesmen, between the forest and the steppe. The second reflected the position of Russia as a great European power ruling numerous weaker Asiatic peoples. The third echoed cataclysmic upheavals in Europe and the developing crisis of imperialism. The Eurasian appeal for integration and brotherhood struck a genuinely new note in the attitude of the Russians toward their Asiatic neighbors. And yet, without questioning in the least the sincerity of the Eurasians, Eurasianism may be considered also as a determined defense of the Russian empire in an age when empires began to crumble. The Eurasians tried to preserve the Russian empire by denying its existence. Indeed, if there were no Russian empire at all but only one organic Eurasia, the issue of separatism lost its meaning. Moreover, behind the love and harmony of the Eurasian utopia loomed the frenzied terror of Belyi and Blok, and Vladimir Solov'ev's dread of the yellow peril. In artistic imagination at least nomadic horsemen of the first and longest period of Russian acquaintance with Asia again rode the steppe.

−2−

Oriental Studies in Russia

Richard N. Frye

If one were to divide the story of Oriental studies in Russia into parts or chapters, with an attempt at periodization, as Soviet scholars would call it, the following divisions might be proposed: 1) the pre-eighteenth century development of Russia; 2) the eighteenth century expansion into the Orient; 3) the period of Oriental institutes and Western superiority, 1804-ca. 1880; 4) missionary activity and *Kraevedenie* (or *Heimatkunde*), ca. 1880-1945; and finally 5) Orientals in expanded Oriental studies since 1945. These divisions may seem arbitrary, since they do not correspond to the traditional political divisions of Russian history; but they have a rationale and are, of course, not the only divisions one could make. We are discussing here, however, Oriental studies, not politics and economics; and the development of such studies in Russia need not correspond with other schemes of periodization.[2]

The first period of Oriental studies in Russia might be called the prehistory of development, before the time of Peter the Great. It is essential to bear in mind the outlines of early Russian history as a background for our subject under discussion. By the outlines of history, I do not mean the succession of princes and tsars, but the story of the peoples who composed the Russian state. It is generally agreed by historians that at the time of the Varangian expansion into Russia in the eighth and ninth centuries there were few Slavs to the north and east of present-day Moscow. Finno-Ugrian peoples, or Turkified natives such as the Bulgars, Bashkirs, Chu-

30

vash, and others along the Volga, occupied this vast area.[3] The steppes of the lower Volga, the Don, and the Dnieper rivers contained not only various Turkic-speaking tribes, but also settled Iranians, the leftovers from the Scythians and Sarmatians.[4] With the expansion of the Slavs to the east, not only was there a continuous contact with Oriental peoples and cultures, but there was a continuous absorption of them into the Russian people. Throughout Russian history many famous Russians have been non-Slavic in origin, some proud of this, others concealing it. The study of the Orient in Russia, therefore, has developed against this unique background, unparalled elsewhere in the world.

One may well believe that from the establishment of the first Rurikid state at Kiev, the Russian principalities had need of translators and persons acquainted with the Volga Bulgars, the Polovtsy or Cumans, and other peoples occupying the vast area east of the Ural Mountains and north of the Black Sea and the Caucasus. Although some Russians may have served in such capacities, it is more probable that Oriental merchants living in Kiev, Vladimir, or elsewhere supplied interpreters. The Mongol conquest, however, was a forerunner of change.

Many historians have attributed to the Mongols the responsibility for the backwardness of Russia vis-à-vis Western Europe, just as the Mongols have been charged with the decline of Persia and of the Islamic world in the eyes of many Persians and Arabs. Whether the Mongols really changed the course of Russian history, forcing the Russian princes to turn their attention to the East rather than to the West, is debatable, since from both the geographical and ethnic sides Russia was already bound to the Orient. Indeed, in pre-Christian times much of the religion and mythology of the eastern Slavs was borrowed from Iranians. Since the strong Iranian influence on the early eastern Slavs is well known, it need not be elaborated here.[5] The significance of all this background in the formation of Russian attitudes toward the Orient and the Orientals is difficult to assess. It is also difficult to believe that before the Mongol conquest the Russians had any conception or sentiments about their position between East and West. A *Busurman* (Muslim) from Khwarizm or a *Nemets* from Germany was probably regarded with equal disdain in the Russian domain, one an eastern, the other a western, barbarian, in the Greek sense of barbarian. The spread of Christianity among the eastern Slavs, however, would seem to have laid a basis for future beliefs that Russia was different from, superior to, and opposed to the Orient.[6]

In spite of close contacts of the Russians with the Mongols and even with Mongolia, we have no Russian literature such as the travel accounts of Marco Polo, Giovanni de Piano Carpini, Hethum, King of Cilician Armenia, and others about the Mongols. Even the Golden Horde, which for long ruled over Russia, left only faint echoes in Russian literature. The reason, I believe, is twofold. First, the Russian literary output was miniscule compared with that of Western Europe, and infinitesimal compared with that of the Islamic world.[7] Second, the trade activity and contacts in the pre-Mongol period came from the East to the West, not vice versa. Merchants from distant Khwarizm and Bukhara could be found in Russian cities, whereas the only Russians in the Orient were probably prisoners-of-war or slaves. Nonetheless, as stated above, the Mongol conquest changed Russia and the passive relationship of Russia to the East to a more active phase.

It is commonly believed that the rule of the Golden Horde over Russia, ca. 1240-1480, isolated Russia from the West. Actually, in my opinion, it was during this period that Western Europe really discovered Muscovy, for this is the time of the movement of Western centers of commerce and industry from south to north. The Italian city-states had dominated trade with the Orient, and only in the Mediterranean world had centers of trade and crafts developed to any degree. But the Low Countries, England, and Germany began to expand their trade in the thirteenth and fourteenth centuries. We must not forget that the Russian cities of Pskov and Novgorod joined the Hanseatic League; hence Western European merchants and envoys came to Russia in greater numbers than previously. The expansion of the Ottoman Turks and their conquest of Constantinople in 1453 made the Russian route to the Orient more attractive than it had been. There were many Western Europeans, artisans, and others at the court of Ivan III of Moscow (1453-1505), and the number continued to grow. Therefore, although the Mongol yoke may be held responsible for many facets of life in Russia, such as Oriental protocol at the court of the tsars, the Russians were hardly cut off from the West by the Mongols.

With the political growth of Moscow there came also a cultural development and an interest in peoples to the east. The khanate of Kazan was absorbed by Moscow in 1552 and Astrakhan in 1556, which brought not only a large Oriental population inside the borders of Muscovy, but also another culture and civilization. Before this time, however, the tide of merchants and ambassadors from the Orient to Russia had already begun to shift, for Russians had been forced to go to Sarai, the capital of the Golden Horde, to pay tribute; and some had even traveled to Karakorum in Mongolia. One of the most famous of the early Russian travelers was Afanasii N. Nikitin, who went as far as India on a trip lasting six years, from 1466 to 1472. Nikitin and later voyagers reacted much as did their Western European counterparts traveling to the Orient. For both, the peoples they met were infidels; and the church, which dominated learning in both Russia and Western Europe, fostered a hostile attitude toward Islam and Muslims. Other heathens, such as Buddhists, were too far away from Europe to be of much concern.

The post-Mongol period, to the time of Peter I, could be characterized as the period in which many Orthodox Russians had begun to develop an antagonism toward the heathens, mostly Muslims, but this had not reached the stage of a feeling of superiority against a backward foe. Any academic knowledge of Islam came more from translations from Western European languages than from first-hand contact with Muslims, even though the Tatars of the Volga were close at hand. The conquest of Astrakhan in 1556 brought Russia into contact with Persia, across the Caspian Sea, and with the khanates of Central Asia. In this area the Cossacks of the Yaik River, who caused great trouble for their neighbors, served as the military arm of Muscovy. Gradually, primarily because of the trips of Russian ambassadors to Persia and Central Asia, more became known about these parts. The Arab world and Turkey were distant and separated from Russia by the khanate of the Crimea.

The Russians conquered Siberia at a rapid pace. From 1581, when the Cossack Ataman Yermak started his operation, until the founding of Yakutsk in 1632, followed a short time later by the advance to the coast of the Pacific, there is a period of just two generations. Most of the area crossed by the hardy adventurers was empty, and only the Tatars of the khanate of Sibir, the Buriat Mongols, and the Tungus tribes offered any resistance to this movement. The first ambassadors of Tsar Alexis arrived in Peking in 1656, which marked the beginning of contacts with China; but until the time of Peter I the contacts were usually hostile and there was no permanent representation of Russia at Peking.

Thus, before the time of Peter I the Russian advance into the relatively empty regions of Siberia, as the advance into the vacuum of the Golden Horde area, the heritage of the conquest of the Kazan Tatars, failed to bring Russia into direct contact with one of the great Oriental powers or civilizations. But under Peter I contacts with China on the one hand and the Ottoman Empire and Persia on the other did bring Russia into direct relations with strong foreign powers. This changed Russian attitudes toward the Orient as it increased her knowledge of this part of the world.

The reign of Peter I marks a new era in the history of Russia, symbolized by the founding of a new capital, St. Petersburg. In regard to Russia's relations with the Orient, however, the reign of Peter might be considered not so much as the culmination of the process of previous expansion, but as a high point in the self-realization of the Russians, or at least of some ruling Russians, that Russia was part of Europe, different from the Orient. For it is significant, I believe, that Peter was a tsar who, in his dealings with the Orient, behaved wholly as a Western European monarch. Before Peter I some Persian sources had called the Russians *Uzbek-i ferengi* (European Uzbeks), but Peter I altered the character of Russia so much that after him such a designation had become impossible.[8]

Although, on the whole, the Volga Tatars were serving as translators and middlemen for the Russians with Central Asia, the Caucasus, and even farther afield, Peter resolved to enlarge contacts with the Orient by establishing a more permanent means of obtaining information. In an *ukase* of 18 June 1700, Peter provided for two or three monks to go to China to study the Chinese and Mongolian languages. After they had learned the languages they were to continue to study the native religions and to propagate the Orthodox faith and to contribute to the political and commercial interests of Russia in the field.[9] The monks did not reach Peking until 1716, but this was the beginning of the permanent Russian religious mission in the Chinese capital. An embassy was not opened until 1729, after the treaty of Kyakhta was concluded between the two powers on 14 June 1727. The Russian religious mission in Peking was active in scholarly work with such monks as Ioakinf Bichurin and others. Japanese studies were slower in formation. Several Japanese came to St. Petersburg in the time of Peter; but the teaching of Japanese on a regular basis was not established until 1736, when the Academy of Sciences was given the task of setting the program in motion.[10] Unfortunately, little was done in this domain until much later.

The activities in Oriental studies under Peter, as I have mentioned, were an essential part of his attempts to Westernize his country. Not only were Western Europeans invited to come to Russia, but Peter tried to understand the Orient in terms of Western Europe. The creation in 1725 of the Russian Academy of Sciences brought into being an institution that could serve as a center for developing Oriental studies. Before that time, however, Peter had founded his *Kabinet Redkostei* (Cabinet of Oddities), which was not only the first establishment in Russia for the investigation and study of the Orient, but also the basis on which the later *Aziatskii Muzei* was built. This institution was opened in 1818, a century later. In the Cabinet, Oriental manuscripts, coins, and art objects were collected for study. (Before the founding of the Academy of Sciences, Oriental studies had for the most part been pursued in the Ministry of Foreign Affairs.[11])

Activities in other directions during the time of Peter have a direct bearing on our discussion, since they indicate the extent of scholarly pursuits. In 1716, by order of Peter, the Koran was translated into Russian, not from the Arabic but from a mediocre French translation.[12] In the same year the Tsar sent five scholars to Persia with the Russian ambassador to study the Arabic, Turkish, and Persian languages. Furthermore, the conquests of Peter in the Caucasus gave impetus to the study of Near Eastern languages and cultures. The capture of Derbent on the Caspian in 1721 brought valuable Oriental manuscripts to St. Petersburg.[13] All these activities were carried on despite the fact that at the time there was hardly anyone in Russia qualified to work on the sources. Yet by his foresight Peter did provide rich materials for future research on the Orient.

Without seeking to detract from the immense significance of the reign of Peter for Russia, his ideas of scholarly work in the domain of Oriental studies seem to have been far ahead of those of his fellow countrymen. It is true that the founding of the Cabinet of Oddities and of the Academy of Sciences and the collection of manuscripts were very important for the future; but their influence in his day was negligible, at least as far as the development of Oriental studies is concerned. In 1722, when Peter returned from his Persian campaign, he visited the ruins of the city of Bulgar on the Volga and gave orders to restore certain remains and to copy the inscriptions on the site, primarily in the Tatar language.[14] In spite of the brilliant foundations laid by Peter, no further contributions were made by his immediate successors. It was not until the closing years of the eighteenth century that progress resumed. In 1742, in reply to a request for aid in the Tatar language, the Academy of Sciences declared that "not one person competent in Asiatic languages remained [in the Academy]," and the Academy was therefore unable to offer any help.[15] It is because of this lapse, after the time of Peter, that the next period of Oriental studies may be assigned to the Napoleonic age, which changed the face of the world in many ways.

This does not mean that all activity in Oriental studies in Russia during the remainder of the century came to a complete halt with the death of Peter. On the contrary, the war with the Ottoman Empire of 1735-39 and more particularly the wars of 1768-72 and 1787-92 did excite great interest in the Near East among the Russians. Not only did military and diplomatic contacts increase, but trade flourished, too.

In a survey of Oriental studies, the contributions of Mikhail Lomonosov (1711-65) and the founding of Moscow University in 1755 stand out. Already in 1733 a German Arabist, G. J. Kehr, who had been invited to St. Petersburg to teach in the School for the Foreign Ministry, had proposed the establishment in Russia of an academy or institute of Oriental languages. Kehr linked the creation of the academy with a plan for the Russian conquest of Turkey and Central Asia.[16] Whether Kehr had any influence on the Russian expedition in 1734-35 into the steppes east of the Urals is not known. One concrete result of that expedition, however, was the founding of the town of Orenburg, which became the center of administration of the eastern steppes. Orenburg quickly took over from Astrakhan the role of making contacts, both diplomatic and commercial, with Central Asia. The movement of Russia toward the conquest of all the Central Asian khanates had begun.

Lomonosov had the same idea as Kehr, to create an Oriental academy, but again nothing came of his plan.[17] Even the great interest in Turkey aroused by the wars of Catherine the Great failed to persuade the authorities to establish a scholarly institute or a section of the Academy for the study of the Orient. Practical concerns, however, furnished a certain impetus not provided by academicians or scholars of St. Petersburg and Moscow. In 1744 a school of interpreters was created at Orenburg, and in 1759 a middle school or gymnasium was opened in Kazan wherein a plan was formulated to teach Oriental languages. It was not until a decade later, however, that the teaching of the Tatar language began there.[18]

The acquisition of the Crimea by Russia in 1783 and the incorporation of many new Muslim subjects into the empire of the tsars became a source of concern for St. Petersburg. The edict of religious toleration for Muslims and others promulgated in 1785 seems to have led to an expansion of Tatar influence and even of Islam in the following manner. The Russian government sought to introduce schools into the steppes, with the teachers, for the most part, coming from Kazan. In 1782 the government decreed that Arabic should be taught in schools where Muslims lived, and the Chinese language in Irkutsk and farther east.[19] While these measures did not in themselves lead to the advancement of Oriental studies in Russia, nevertheless they did create a milieu in which such studies could generate wide popular interest and involvement. The Tatars, of course, took advantage of the expansion of education to spread their influence to the south and east.

In 1790 the Koran was again translated into Russian from the French, and a third time in 1792 from the English. Attached to the translation of 1790 was a life of the "false prophet" Muhammad.[20] Other works of a polemical nature about Islam appeared also. These gave an indication of the anti-Muslim feeling among some Orthodox Russians—a feeling that was to grow considerably during the course of the nineteenth century. A detailed discussion of the policies of the Russian government or of the Orthodox church toward the non-Christian religions in the empire, and especially toward Islam, would take us too far afield. On the other hand, there can be little doubt that such general attitudes on Islam as those exemplified by the views of the Orthodox church did exert an influence on the development of Oriental studies. Because of limitations of space, we can make only passing mention of some of the forces at work during this period. The expansion of Russia, the development of education among the Muslims, which was mainly in the hands of *mullahs* and others from the Kazan area, and the growth of the intelligentsia in both numbers and influence in St. Petersburg and Moscow, all helped to create a milieu in which Oriental studies were to flourish in the Russia of the nineteenth century.

All these activities are merely a prelude to the nineteenth century, when the scholarly and academic study of the Orient was put on a solid and permanent basis. Although attitudes of the earlier period did persist into the nineteenth century, we may speak of a new age even in Russia after the French Revolution and Napoleon. The nineteenth century in Russia was not only a period of development and growth, but it also saw the creation of new institutions and new attitudes toward Oriental studies. In Western Europe, especially in Germany, comparative philology of mostly Indo-European languages opened new vistas to the study of the Orient. Before this period, as we have seen, there was much activity in Russia in the practical study of Oriental languages for administrative and diplomatic purposes; but scientific or scholarly investigations were few and led to meager results since they usually came to an end with the passing of the individual who had undertaken them. Thus there were isolated sporadic bursts of activity, especially under Peter, but no solid basis on which to build for the future. Although detailed information is unavailable, it may very well be that the efforts to promote Oriental studies during Catherine's reign were aimed either at training translators and teachers in the Muslim areas or at preparing missionaries for the propagation of the Orthodox faith among the heathen.

We may take as a purely arbitrary date the fifth of November 1804 as a turning point in the development of Oriental studies in Russia, for the university constitution issued at that time provided for instruction in this area. Shortly afterward chairs for Oriental studies were established at the universities of Moscow, Kazan, and Kharkov. Although there were no quick or startling results, this decree did provide for permanent organizations or professional chairs (*kafedra*) to train scholars in the disciplines necessary to the scholarly investigation of the Orient. Such activity could be carried out only in the universities, since the Academy of Sciences existed for research and not for teaching or preparation of successors.[21] Action was slow for many reasons, mainly the lack of qualified teachers; but at least the groundwork had been laid for the preparation of Orientalists who in the future could not only staff the universities, but also the Academy of Sciences, museums, and libraries, the primary organizations for the investigation of the Orient.

Kazan University with its surrounding Muslim population was the first to implement the decree. In 1807 a chair of Oriental languages was established primarily to teach Arabic and Persian. (Such a chair in Europe means much more than the equivalent in an American university, for in Europe it implies a library, assistants, and the like.) Although the Tatar language had been taught earlier, a chair of the Turco-Tatar language was not established in Kazan until 1828. There followed Mongolian in 1833, Chinese in 1837, Armenian in 1839, Sanskrit in 1842, and Manchurian in 1844, all of which combined to make Kazan the foremost university in Russia for the study of the Orient.[22] For many years there were very few students in these classes until the government undertook to train some of its officials there. For many reasons, however, Oriental studies other than those connected with the Muslim peoples did not flourish in Kazan; and in the 1850s the chairs of the Oriental section of the university were abolished.[23] Perhaps the main reason for the decline of Kazan as an academic center for the study of the Orient was the founding of a teacher's college and other schools for the local native inhabitants. These institutions seem to have been considered more important than the classical instruction in Oriental languages usually performed by German professors.

The place of Kazan was taken by St. Petersburg, where, at the beginning of the nineteenth century, there existed the Academy of Sciences with the attached Asiatic Museum, but no university. The

Asiatic Museum had been brought into existence by a decree of S. S. Uvarov, president of the Academy of Sciences, on 11 November 1818. This decree provided for an Asiatic "Cabinet" to be installed on the first floor of Peter the Great's *Kunstkammer* on the Neva River. Oriental manuscripts, books, coins, archeological remains, and objects of ethnography were gathered there under the direction of the Academician and Orientalist C. M. Frähn (1781-1851).[24] All this material was fine for research but not for teaching. The actual teaching of Oriental languages in St. Petersburg was introduced in 1816 in a pedagogical institute, which in 1819 was transformed into the University. Two chairs were created, one for Arabic, the other for Persian; and in 1822 Turkish was added.[25] St. Petersburg University grew, as did its role in Oriental studies, until in October 1854 a special faculty of Oriental languages was established. This faculty, which became the center of Oriental studies in the empire of the tsars, soon outstripped all other centers in the land.

We come now to a discussion of the development of Oriental studies in Moscow. The situation here was unique. A beginning had been made according to the decree of 1804, and from 1811 until 1837 Arabic and Persian were taught in the university. An attempt was made to revive activity in the 1850s, but after a few years this was abandoned. The failure of the Oriental studies program in Moscow University has been attributed to the development of a competing institution—the Lazarev Institute.[26] This institution grew out of a private school, primarily for Armenians, called the Moscow Armenian Educational Institution of the Lazarevs. The first Oriental language taught there was, of course, Armenian, with Persian added a few years later. Although the name of the institution was changed at the end of 1827 to the Lazarev Institute of Oriental Languages, the program of the school was not altered; it remained a general high school where Oriental languages were taught.

In 1835 the aims of the school were set forth after it had acquired from the government a certain status as an educational institution of the second category.[27] The first of these aims was to prepare translators; and the second, to prepare teachers for all the other educational institutions of the Armenians, and to educate priests or other ecclesiastics for the Christian Gregorian faith.[28]

The interest of the government in the Institute is evidenced by its sending five south Caucasian students there in 1843 to prepare for service in the customs department. Later the Minister of Internal Affairs, Prince Aleksei Orlov, basing his argument "on the opinion of the Caucasus Committee [which dealt with problems of the union of the Transcaucasian lands with Russia], pointed out to the trustee(s) that the institute needed a basic reform to achieve the aims proposed by the government, to prepare, on the one side, officials for the Transcaucasus area, who knew the native languages well, and on the other side translators well acquainted with all languages current in Transcaucasia."[29] The Lazarev Institute thus became the instrument of the government training of officials for the Transcaucasian service.

Nor was trade with the Orient neglected. New regulations in 1848 gave the Lazarev Institute a higher government rating, that of first-class school, with the expanded aim of helping commercial enterprises. An eight-year course of study was created, the last two years of which were reserved for the study of Oriental languages. Thus the Institute, according to an announcement of the new program, sought to prepare students for entry into a university or directly into government service or into commerce. And not forgotten, above all, was the preparation of youths for service in the Armenian Gregorian faith.[30]

The Lazarev Institute, more than any other organization, embraced the full range of Russia's activities in the promotion of Oriental studies. Whereas Kazan, in the midst of a Tatar population, was obviously a special case, and St. Petersburg was a center of research, museums, libraries, and all the other facilities needed for the study of the past, conditions in Moscow seemed to be most favorable for the extension into the academic world of government aims and needs in the field of Oriental studies. In promoting training for officials the government may have been more able to secure cooperation from a private institution than from a public school or university. It is interesting to read between the lines about the controversy in 1852 between the Caucasian Committee and the Lazarev Institute. The committee wished to have its students freed from the necessity of studying Arabic, whereas the faculty of the Institute insisted on the scholarly goals of its institution. As is usual in such cases, the compromises that had to be

made satisfied few of the disputants. The Ministry of Foreign
Affairs did not become involved in the controversy, since a school
for training diplomats in practical foreign languages continued to
exist throughout the nineteenth century; and the Ministry did not
look to any of the academic centers of Oriental studies for aid.
The Ministry of the Interior, and especially the Caucasian Committee, on the other hand, needed trained administrators, especially natives. It was only natural, therefore, that they should turn
to a school in Moscow founded to teach Armenians. This accounts
for the special role in the history of Oriental studies filled by the
Lazarev Institute.

Because of the special circumstances of its creation, still another
organization deserves mention, the Kyakhta school for the Chinese
language. In 1832 Russian merchants joined together to create a
school to teach the spoken Chinese language for practical usage.
This institution flourished for a time, until the teaching of Chinese
and Manchu under Russian government auspices was shifted to
Peking. Although the Kyakhta school was closed in 1867, it did
serve as an interesting experiment in private enterprise.[31]

Finally, we must examine another important facet of Russian
interest in the Orient, the religious activity. In the academies and
seminaries of the Orthodox church Hebrew and other Semitic languages were taught and studied. The preparation of missionaries,
however, was undertaken considerably later. In 1855 a missionary
section was created in the religious academy of Kazan for activities
among the Tatars, the Mongol tribes, the Chuvash, and the
Cheremiss. Not only languages but also the Islamic and Buddhist
religions were studied. Kazan seems to have become the center for
missionary work, for in 1873 a special commission of the Academy
of Sciences in Kazan issued the *Missionerskii protivomusul'manskii
sbornik* (the missionary anti-Muslim collection), a series that lasted
to the Revolution. V. Rosen, the head of the Oriental faculty in
St. Petersburg, attacked the missionary publication as antischolar-
ly; and we find traces of the quarrel between the academics and
the missionaries in writings on Islam during the second half of the
nineteenth century.[32]

Nor did the Russian army and military academies neglect the
practical teaching of Oriental languages for selected officers who
might be needed. In Omsk a military school taught the Mongolian

and Tatar languages, while in Orenburg Arabic and Persian were taught, as well as Tatar.[33] The conquest of Central Asia, beginning with the occupation of Tashkent by the Russians in 1865, gave fresh impetus to Oriental studies because new administrators and officials were called for. Furthermore, an immense area of untold archeological and historical riches had been added to the empire that spurred investigations by Russian scholars. New manuscripts and art objects were added to the already world-famous collections of St. Petersburg. Russian Oriental studies were to blossom at the end of the nineteenth century; and in all aspects of this field Russia was to become the equal of any western European country in quality and far ahead in quantity.

The expansion of Russia into Turkestan was followed by an increasing number of Orientalists, primarily from Kazan. The Kazan ecclesiastical academy provided many teachers for schools opened in the territories newly acquired by Russia. Consequently the study of Islam as a religion was promoted there more than purely philological or historical studies. The leader of the Islamicists in Central Asia was N. P. Ostroumov (1846-1930), a graduate of the Kazan Academy, who lived in Tashkent from 1877 until the end of his life.[34] Others from Kazan followed his lead or were even more polemical against Islam, a heritage of their training in Kazan.

Until the end of the nineteenth century, as we have seen, Oriental studies in Russia followed different routes with little contact between the various organizations, schools, or even individuals. With the expansion of Russia into Central Asia and the pacification of the Caucasus, railroads provided easier communication; and there was a consequent centralization of government activities. Oriental studies matured along with other scholarly and cultural disciplines.

In the nineteenth century the establishment of the various institutes, chairs, and academies for Oriental studies laid the basis in Russia for Oriental studies in the Western European sense of the term. The word "European" may be taken as a key to this period, which was one of Russian military supremacy over Persia in two wars, leading to the loss by Persia of all of Transcaucasia to Russia, the acquisition by Russia of the delta of the Danube River after a war with Turkey ending in 1829, as well as the Russian conquest of Central Asia. Kars and Batum were secured from Turkey after a

war ending in 1878. By the nineteenth century the military, as
well as the cultural and social, superiority of the Russians over
Orientals seemed unquestioned in the eyes of most Russians. Even
the Slavophiles, who opposed the pro-Westerners in tsarist Russia,
maintained the superiority of Russia over the Orient. Hence the
third period of Oriental studies in Russia I have called the age
of Oriental institutes if one is thinking in terms of the many
academies established; or the age of Western superiority, from the
standpoint of the general sentiment then prevailing in Russia regarding the Orient. There were, however, romanticists in this period of the early nineteenth century who showed the way for the
growth of what I have called *Heimatkunde* in the fourth period.

This is not the place to discuss in detail the rise of Romanticism
in Russian literature and its intellectual ramifications in the nineteenth-century empire of the tsars. Ideas of such people as Rousseau, and later of Schelling, Hegel, and others, did of course exert
some influence among the Russian intelligentsia; but whether the
Western European Romanticist discovery of the Orient, as exemplified in Goethe's *West-Östlicher Diwan*, had any influence
on Pushkin or on other Russian writers is questionable. Probably
Pushkin's visits to the Crimea and the Caucasus were enough to
stir the imagination of the great poet to write such works as
Ruslan i Ludmilla, the *Bakhchisaraiskii, Fontan*, and *Podrazhaniia
Koranu* (Imitation of the Koran). It seems we may distinguish two
movements among the Russian intellectuals concerned with the
Orient, one group maintaining that the Oriental peoples were incapable of progress and thus inferior to Russians or Western Europeans, while the other followed a line of thought with echoes of
the "noble savage" of Rousseau. One may conjecture that the influx into Russia of Christian Armenians and Georgians may have
provided a leavening for the ideas of the latter group, since the
Caucasian peoples were middlemen between Russians and Muslims.
Furthermore, the ancestry of Pushkin was a decisive answer to any
Russian who preached any racial or ethnic superiority of Russians
over others.

We have mentioned in passing a number of German Orientalists
who came to Russia in the eighteenth and early nineteenth centuries, but this would not give an adequate indication of the overwhelming influence of German scholarship on Russia. It is im-

possible here to discuss this influence which shaped the Russian learned academies, but more especially the universities and the teaching in them. For Oriental languages one of the most important figures in the introduction of ideas of teaching languages, as well as methods of research, was Friedrich Adelung (1768-1843), who was the director of the section on the teaching of Oriental languages at the Ministry of Foreign Affairs in St. Petersburg and an honorary member of the Academy of Sciences. His writings had a great influence throughout Russia on the literary and intellectual circles concerned with the Orient. The views of A. W. Schlegel, especially on India, also were very popular in Russia at the beginning of the nineteenth century; and his ideas were followed by many literary figures.

The real founder of scholarship in Near Eastern studies in Russia, however, was Christian M. Frähn, whom I have already mentioned, but the list of Orientalists who wrote important works or who had students is long indeed. The German influence on scholarship in Oriental studies was paralleled by the expansion of the tsarist empire into Central Asia and the Caucasus, where, like the British in India, Russian officers and civil servants acquired rich field experience that enabled them to contribute to Oriental studies. For instance, the works of A. N. Khanykov on the khanate of Bukhara (1843), and of the monk Ioakinf Bichurin on Chinese sources regarding the peoples of Central Asia (1851), are excellent examples of scholarly works by Russian authors who were "from the field" rather than trained in the libraries or classrooms of St. Petersburg. In the area of Oriental studies Russia enjoyed an advantage over other countries in the two-way direction of efforts, those from the field and those from the libraries. As a result of this combination, Oriental studies in Russia rose to world preeminence, a status she still enjoys to our day. While many of the foreigners in Russia were attacked in writing by Slavic chauvinists, advocates of Pan-Slavism, and the like, the Russian students of Frähn on the whole depended on him for his contributions to the development of Oriental studies in Russia. Not only did he help many students of the Orient, but also he developed a school of numismatics in Russia. His many writings in this field laid the basis for a Russian school of Oriental studies. He found a willing colleague in O. I. Senkovskii (1800-58), also known as Baron Brambeus from Vilna, who became the head of the section on Arabic and Islam in the University of St. Petersburg from 1822 to 1847.

The fourth period of Oriental studies in Russia may seem to correspond to the Marxist designation as the capitalist and imperialist periods of Russian history; but this, if true, is purely fortuitous. It would seem, rather, as one Soviet author remarks, "unfortunately, a concrete, detailed periodization of the history of Russian Oriental studies during the time of the strengthening and development of capitalism in Russia (including its imperialist stage) has not been worked out."[35] One might rather regard the period from the last decades of the nineteenth century down to the Revolution as the separation of two tendencies in Oriental studies, neither of which was revolutionary, or materialist, or Marxist. One group was the "academic" Orientalists, who were sympathetic to, if not followers of, the earlier Romanticists. The pure academics found allies among those liberal thinkers who promoted ideas of *Heimatkunde,* or the need to promote as well as study the languages and cultures of the non-Russian peoples of the empire. The great specialist on Central Asia, V. V. Bartol'd, was a prime representative of this group. The more extreme supporters of the opposite camp fell in very well with those at the court of Tsar Alexander III (1881-94), who advocated a government policy of Russification and discrimination against minorities in the empire. Most of the students in the Lazarev Institute in Moscow and in St. Petersburg followed their professors in the first category, as we may gather from a letter by a professor in the Kazan Theological Academy, N. I. Il'minskii (1822-91), in the name of the famous conservative K. P. Pobedonostsev (1827-1907), written in 1884. "In my opinion, the students of the [faculty] of Oriental languages of Petersburg University and of Lazarev Institute are unsuited for our Asiatic areas, since they study the literature, history, and ethnography of the Asiatic peoples objectively, and carry to them their own sympathies. . .and they are unacquainted with alien [*inorodicheskii*] and missionary affairs."[36] The use of the term *inorodicheskii,* which is pejorative here, indicates the group to which Il'minskii belonged. The name of Pobedonostsev has become synonymous with reaction and ultraconservatism, not only for Soviet writers but even in prerevolutionary Russia and elsewhere in the world. There is no doubt that some intellectuals, including Orientalists, followed Pobedonostsev. Needless to say, only the academic group continued to exist after the Revolution.

In a sense again Bartol'd is a symbol of the continuity of the prerevolutionary feeling of sympathy for the cultures of Oriental peoples with the new conditions of Soviet Russia. The academic prerevolutionary Orientalists such as Bartol'd, S. F. Ol'denburg (in Far Eastern studies), I. Iu. Krachkovskii (Arabistics), and F. I. Shcherbatskoi (Indology) continued in their positions after the Revolution. Although they are characterized by Soviet authors as apolitical, non-Marxist, hence reprehensible, still their achievements cannot be, and are not, denied by Soviet intellectuals. There were, of course, revolutionaries among the students of the Oriental institutes in pre-1917 Russia, as elsewhere; and much has been made of these early Bolsheviks and their contributions to Oriental studies. After the Revolution the two main centers of Oriental studies, Leningrad and Moscow, continued to exist, whereas the provincial centers, as well as the various tsarist military and religious schools and academies, either vanished or declined radically. The religious activities of tsarism were transformed into antireligious activities of the communists. Instead of missionary publications there now appeared atheist journals and books such as *Ateist* and *Bezbozhnik* (atheist). Likewise, the tsarist schools for the foreign service were revised but continued under the Soviets. Dialectical materialism and other communist subjects were, of course, introduced into the curricula everywhere, but it is interesting to observe the marked continuity of traditions in Oriental studies from the prerevolutionary period. Whatever the climate, scholarship was maintained under the most trying economic and physical conditions.

Perhaps the dominant characteristic of Oriental studies in the Soviet Union before the Second World War was the groping for Marxist guidelines, first for assessing, within the communist framework, the roles of tsarism and native revolts against tsarism; and second, for establishing the periodization of the past. Orientals were regarded with great sympathy, especially if they had been won over to communism; but they had neither the education nor the political sophistication requisite for managing themselves or for studying their own complicated history. Questions of Russification and the nationality problem were naturally much discussed during the pre-World War II period.

A great deal has been written about the Russification policy of

the Soviet government as it affected the various minority peoples
of the U.S.S.R. Individual feelings about Russification may have
contributed to the generally held picture of the Soviet government
as forcing minorities to become Russianized. This position I would
regard as completely untenable. A sinister policy of *divide et
impera* has been attributed to Moscow every time an alphabet has
been created or changed for the Uzbeks, the Tajiks, or others,
as if Moscow really needed to divide in order to rule.[37] If little
was done in the various republics to promote Oriental studies, it
was simply because money was scarce and conditions were difficult for everyone during the period between the two wars. Russians were prominent in higher educational and research institutes
of the various republics and areas only because they made up the
majority of the trained and qualified personnel. All this was to
change after World War II.

World War II, I believe, may be regarded as a more significant
dividing line in Oriental studies than even World War I and the
Revolution. After World War II two tendencies became clear. First
the younger scholars were better trained than their predecessors
and their number had greatly increased. Furthermore, the *Sturm
und Drang* of the early Soviet and the Stalinist periods (the Stalinist influence was felt, of course, until his death but the writing on
the wall had appeared earlier) had welded the survivors into a
cohesive, cooperative body of scholars who enforced high standards of scholarship for their group above either membership in the
party or other considerations. Communism was now taken for
granted and performance was valued above words. In the second
place, the republics of the U.S.S.R. had come of age, and new
native scholars were competing with graduates of Leningrad and
Moscow. Some native Russians might complain of special privileges shown Uzbeks, Tajiks, Buriat Mongols, or others in the greatly expanding Oriental studies in Moscow and in Leningrad, not to
mention Tashkent, Baku, Tbilisi (Tiflis), and other areas; but such
privileges were personal favors and were hardly based on the preeminence of any ethnic or linguistic group or on any overall policy.

The practical study of Oriental languages for radio, foreign service, or other governmental service continues in the U.S.S.R. but
so does the study of classical or dead Oriental languages. Archeology flourishes as do modern history and economics. The polemics

directed against deviationists, such as those aimed at the "anti-Marxist" school of history of the Soviet historian Mikhail N. Pokrovskii (1868-1932), or at bourgeois Orientalists such as Krachkovskii and others, have now subsided, just as the antireligious propaganda is now stale. All this may be accounted for mainly because it is now difficult to find anti-Marxists in the U. S. S. R.[38] Whether the Soviet state foresaw or wished the growth in national feeling among Georgians, Armenians, Tajiks, Uzbeks, and others is debatable; but it does exist and flourishes on a cultural level. As far as politics, economics, or social feelings are concerned, the Soviet man or citizen is now, I believe, a reality. Knowledge of Russian is essential for any of the local peoples to advance in their professions or in their work. But it is also becoming important for Russians to learn Georgian, for example, if they expect to go far in the Georgian S.S.R. This is true, at least, for Oriental studies in the U.S.S.R.

At present Leningrad still maintains its lead as the center of the study of the classical Orient, whereas Moscow has become the Soviet center for the investigation of the contemporary Orient and Africa. Leningrad's Branch of the Institute of the Peoples of Asia and Africa (formerly the Oriental Institute) of the Academy of Sciences is located in the old building that housed the Lazarev Institute. The Tashkent Institute of Oriental Studies of the Uzbek Academy of Sciences is probably the third largest and most significant center in the U.S.S.R., while Tbilisi, with its Oriental Institute of the Georgian Academy of Sciences, comes next. The Armenian, Azerbaijan, Turkmen, Tajik, Kazakh and other republics and autonomous areas of the R.S.F.S.R. have Oriental institutes that produce many publications in local languages as well as in Russian. The flow of books has become a flood. Indeed, many Soviet savants instead of writing an article when they have a new idea prefer to survey the field and all past work on the subject before making their point. Since payment is usually made on the basis of the number of words or pages produced, obviously it is more profitable to write a book than an article. Needless to say, the great development of Oriental studies in the U.S.S.R. is thoroughly familiar to scholars everywhere in the world from Tokyo to Cambridge.

The greatest problem of the Soviet Orientalist is travel and access to foreign literature in his field, especially to unpublished manuscript collections in the West such as those in the British Museum. A few have managed to go abroad: the Russians have participated in archeological excavations in Mongolia and in China, and have thereby continued an old tradition.[39] But in general, research and study abroad are possible only with great difficulty. If the Japanese scholar would like to go to Japan or the Arabist to Egypt to study for a year, he would almost have to join an aid mission or a road-building group or become an interpreter in the Soviet Embassy in the foreign country. Such subterfuges are rarely resorted to, however, because the scholar usually has to weigh the advantages to be gained against the time lost in performing daily chores not relevant to his primary concern. Offers of such special jobs with rewards, either in the form of money or in the opportunity they afford to live abroad, though few in number, obviously hold a certain attraction. With a bureaucratic incompetence typical the world over, a specialist in modern colloquial Egyptian Arabic may be sent to Baghdad for a year, or a Pashto specialist to Karachi rather than to Peshawar or to Afghanistan. Furthermore, a scholar known all over the world may, for numerous imagined or whimsical reasons justified on political or on security grounds, be refused permission to attend an international congress in London. But such is the nature of the ponderous bureaucracy that weighs on the backs of all in the U.S.S.R.

As everywhere else in the world, so in the U.S.S.R. the personalities of the various individual leaders of Oriental studies have contributed to shaping the development of these studies. I. A. Orbeli, director of the Hermitage Museum for more than two decades that spanned World War II, dean of the Oriental faculty of the University, and head of the Oriental Institute of the Academy of Sciences for several years, was the leading figure among Leningrad Orientalists. His classical training shaped his goal to keep the old Leningrad traditions alive and flourishing. In Moscow, the former secretary of the Communist Party of Tajikstan and friend of top Soviet officials, Babodzhan Gafurov, was able to expand the size and number of personnel in the former Lazarev Institute to unheard-of proportions. Modern and classical Oriental studies, as well as African, could flourish under Gafurov's regime since he could and did get things done. The bimonthly journal *Narody Azii i Afriki*, published in Moscow, is concerned primarily with contemporary problems, whereas the *Kratkie Soobshcheniia Instituta Narodov Azii* is devoted largely to philology and history. Journals such as *Epigrafika Vostoka* and the *Palestinskii Sbornik* are devoted to more specialized studies. During recent years the number of Orientalist articles in the publications of the academies of sciences of the various republics has increased. All over the country there has been great activity.

It appears likely that in the foreseeable future both classical and contemporary Oriental studies will flourish in the U.S.S.R., for here, just as in the U.S.A., where moneys and grants are much more available for the study of the contemporary Orient, the power of appointment in the universities and in the research positions is still in the hands of the classical scholars or academics. Indeed it must remain there, for the future of scholarship in any country, under any system, must remain with the scholars. Otherwise, there will be no scholarship.

The Structure of Soviet Orientology:
Fifty Years of Change and Accomplishment

Wayne S. Vucinich

The First World War and the Revolution that followed seriously disrupted the work in Oriental research in Russia. Some Orientalists perished, while others left the country as refugees. Of those who survived and remained in Russia, many could not at once adjust to the rigid Marxist-Leninist interpretation of history. There were those who preferred not to publish for fear they might express views inconsistent with official ideology. In the years immediately following 1917 the death of several of the older distinguished Orientalists set the program back even further and left academic institutions and research centers with depleted staffs.

The Soviet government was not at first able to give much attention to building a Marxist school of Oriental studies.[1] Yet there was no lack of official interest in the Orient. The communist leadership, which saw great revolutionary potential in the Orient, addressed itself to the Oriental peoples and attempted to spread the communist revolution to several Eastern countries. Orientalists were urged to concentrate on the study of political struggles and on socioeconomic relations in the Orient. During 1918-21 Soviet historians "rediscovered" the works on Asia by Karl Marx and Friedrich Engels, whose writings, together with those by V. I. Lenin, "provided the basis for the new methodology in the study of the contemporary East." Many of the articles by Marx and Engels were published in Russian for the first time in the 1920s. Soviet historians derived direction from Lenin's work on imperialism, capitalism, colonialism, the noncapitalistic path of development, and agrarian problems. At the Second Congress of the Communist International (1920), the First Congress of the Eastern Peoples at Baku (1920) and the Congress of the Peoples of the Far East in Moscow (1922), Lenin supplied the line for the interpretation of the national and colonial question.[2]

The greatest need of the Soviet government during this era was to gain the support of the Oriental peoples and to train experts for the party, for government, and for military work. Thus, on 16 March 1918 the Turkestan People's University was founded in Tashkent, and at the end of the same year the Turkestan Eastern Institute was established. In 1924 the Eastern Institute became the Oriental Faculty of the Central Asian (Turkestan) State University.[3] Institutes of Oriental languages were founded in 1918 in Kiev[4] and in Rostov-on-Don, while the existing Kazan center of Oriental studies was secularized.

In 1919 and the years immediately following, many new centers for Oriental studies were established or existing ones transformed.[5] Of the new organizations two were particularly significant: the Moscow Institute of Oriental Studies[6] and the Leningrad Institute of Living Languages. In September 1920 in Moscow the Central Institute of Living Languages[7] was created for the purpose of teaching languages and history and preparing students for government and party work. On 2 May 1922 all the Moscow institutions engaged in Oriental studies were incorporated into the Moscow Institute of Oriental Studies (*Moskovskii Institut Vostokovedeniia*).[8]

The Moscow Institute was at first under the People's Commissariat for Nationality Affairs (NARKOMNATS), and after 1924 under the Presidium of the Central Executive Committee. The Institute concentrated on languages and contemporary affairs of Eastern countries. It served the needs of the government by providing it with data and reports on materials. Although the Institute's faculty consisted largely of young scholars, by 1936 it had become so sophisticated that it was in a position to train research scholars, instructors for higher institutions of learning, and top-level government and party experts. The Institute survived until 1954, when a new system for the training of Orientalists was adopted.

The situation in St. Petersburg was comparable to that in Moscow. First, in 1919 the Eastern Faculty of St. Petersburg University and the faculties of History, Philology and Law were merged into a single Faculty of Social Sciences, and the Orientalists in the faculty were grouped into the College of Orientalists (*Kollegiia vostokovedov*), organized on 26 June 1920 and on 14 May 1921 attached to the Asiatic Museum of the Academy of Sciences.[9] As in Moscow, all teaching, research, and other institutions in Leningrad (St. Petersburg) concerned with the Orient were organized into the Leningrad Institute of Living Oriental Languages. And like the Institute in Moscow, the Leningrad Institute was first under the jurisdiction of NARKOMNATS and later under the Presidium of the Central Executive Committee of the U.S.S.R.[10]

Despite the rapid growth of these new institutes, the bulk of the more serious research on the Orient was still being done in the Asiatic Museum and in certain other specialized bodies of the Academy of Sciences. And long after the Bolshevik Revolution the best Orientalists in the Soviet Union were those trained before 1917.

Before the Revolution there existed in Russia no single research center which concentrated exclusively on the Oriental studies. The most serious research was done under the auspices of the Eastern Section of the Archeological Society, the Geographical Society, and the Academy of Sciences.[11] After the dissolution of the Russian Archeological Society in 1924 its Eastern Section was absorbed by the College of the Orientalists,[12] which took over the journal published by the Eastern Section and issued it under a new name (*Zapiski Kollegii vostokovedov*).[13] Gradually nearly all major professional societies were in one way or another brought into affiliation with the Academy of Sciences.

Under the Soviet rule the Asiatic Museum which since its founding in 1818 had become one of the world's largest repositories of Oriental manuscripts and published works, became the main research center on the Orient in the Academy of Sciences. It continued to collect manuscripts and it trained specialists, organized professional meetings, and prepared exhibits of Oriental artistic, ethnographic, historical, and other materials.

Besides the Asiatic Museum and the College of Orientalists, a number of other departments and units of the Academy of Sciences participated in the study of the Orient. The Department of Historical Sciences and Philology, for instance, had chairs of literature and antiquities of the Eastern peoples. Two of the most active institutes in the Academy of Sciences were the Institute of Japhetic Languages and the Institute of Buddhist Culture.[14] The Institute of Japhetic Languages was founded in 1921 on the initiative of N. Ia. Marr, who became its first director. From 1923 on there was also in Moscow a North Caucasian Committee of the Japhetic Institute. In time the Institute of Japhetic Languages, or the Institute of Language and Thought, as it was known from 1932 on, became a center of controversy when N. Ia. Marr advanced the so-called Japhetic theory that all languages evolved through a number of identical stages. This theory, which was the subject of debate for many years,[15] and its ultimate rejection led to the closing of the Institute in 1950 and to the establishment in its stead of the Institute of Linguistics (*Institut iazykoznaniia*), divided into eight sections.[16]

The Academy of Sciences had the Turcological Cabinet, founded in 1928, which sponsored translations of Turkish classics and historical records, published monographs on the history and culture of the Turkic peoples, and had a commission that devised Latin alphabets for Turkic languages.

In 1928, I. Iu. Krachkovskii attempted to revive Arabistics by organizing the Arabic Cabinet (*Arabskii kabinet*) in the Academy of Sciences. Originally limited in the size of its staff, the Arabic Cabinet was eventually expanded by the inclusion of Arabists from other parts of the Soviet Union and became the Association of Leningrad Arabists (*Assotsiatsiia Leningradskikh arabistov*).

In the twenties there were within the Academy of Sciences many other specialized groups engaged in Oriental studies. Among these were the Caucasian Historical-Archeological Institute (later merged into the Historical-Research Institute of Transcaucasia), the Byzantine Commission with a cabinet in Byzantine studies, and the Institute for the Study of the Peoples of the U.S.S.R.[17] The Academy had a Permanent Commission for the Study of the Composition of the Population of Russia, with at least three of its groups (Caucasian, Siberian, Turkestanian) being involved with the Orient.

In 1929 a Group for Oriental Studies was created in the Academy of Sciences with the purpose of improving and coordinating the activities and research projects of various parts of the Academy. At the same time, steps were taken to strengthen the Academy of

Sciences both financially and organizationally. A special government commission, formed in 1929, investigated the Academy, its
organization, and its personnel. Official critics accused the All-
Union Scientific Association of Orientalists (*Vsesoiuznaia nauchnaia assotsiatsiia vostokovedov* [VNAV]) and *Novyi vostok* of
pseudo-Marxism and of close collaboration with apolitical academic Orientalists. They charged that *Novyi vostok* published inferior
papers and book reviews in which authors were unjustly criticized.
As a result, the Academy of Sciences in 1929 received a new constitution, which was ultimately replaced by still another in 1935.
Under the new constitution all scientific work in the Academy was
organized to serve the interests of the Soviet state. The Asiatic Museum and the College of Orientalists, together with the Institute of
the Buddhist Culture and Turkological Cabinet, were merged in
October 1930 into the single Institute of Oriental Studies.

Despite all the changes, however, the Soviet regime still lacked
confidence in its Orientalists. Official spokesmen continued to believe that the Academy was isolated from people, that it was
tradition-bound and apolitical. It was the aim of the Soviet leaders
to transform the Academy into an instrument of the party and the
state. Thus, until 1934 the work of the Academy was under the close
surveillance of the Central Committee of the Soviet Communist
Party. The Society of Marxist Historians (*Obshchestvo istorikov
marksistov*) actually had a "cell" in the Institute of Oriental Studies of the Academy of Sciences of the Soviet Union[18] to make certain that the study of Oriental societies conformed to officially
accepted theories.

From the very beginning the Soviet government undertook to
establish completely controlled communist centers of Oriental research and training. It wanted Orientalists to be militantly missionary, to dedicate themselves to the cause of communism and to interpret, popularize, and implement the policies of the government
and the party.

The General Staff of the Red Army of Workers and Peasants acquired an Oriental Section in 1919, which later became the Oriental Faculty of the General Staff's Military Academy.[19] The same
instructors taught in both the Oriental Faculty of the Military
Academy and in the Moscow Institute of Oriental Studies. Because
of the great need for agents and agitators proficient in the tongues

of the various Oriental peoples and familiar with their history, the Military-Revolutionary Council of the Turkestan Front established in October 1920 a special program of Oriental studies. This served as the nucleus of the Higher Military School of Oriental Studies founded in 1922.[20]

The Institute for the Training of Red Professors (*Institut po podgotovki krasnoi professury*), established in Moscow and Leningrad in 1921, heavily stressed the Marxist interpretation of contemporary developments in Eastern countries.[21] Within its department of history there was a special Oriental section. On 21 April 1921 the Communist University of the Workers of the East (*Kommunisticheskii universitet trudiashchikhsia Vostoka* [KUTV]) was opened in Moscow. This institution had a Scientific-Research Group for the study of the history and the socioeconomic problems of Soviet and non-Soviet Asia (after 1928 called the Scientific-Research Association of the Communist University of the Workers of the East (*Nauchno-issledovatel'skaia assotsiatsiia* or NIA KUTV).[22]

The NIA KUTV had a linguistic commission that formulated the party's linguistic and literary policies, composed grammars, furthered literacy, and worked on the Romanization of the alphabets of the Asian peoples.[23] After 1932 the NIA KUTV became exclusively a research center, comprising several cabinets (Japan-Korea, India, the Near East, Central Asia, and the Soviet East), a linguistics commission, an editorial staff, and a library. It published a journal called "Revolutionary East" (*Revoliutsionnyi vostok*), a "Bulletin" (*Biulleten*), and other materials. It served as "the avant-garde of the struggle for Soviet Oriental studies." During the thirties the spokesmen of the Association frequently criticized the Marxist deviationism in Orientology. They were particularly vocal in this regard at the Kharkov Congress of Orientalists.

During the 1920s there were special institutes and organizations within the Communist Academy[24] that gave much of their attention to problems concerning the East. These were the Institute of World Economy and World Politics (*Institut mirovogo khoziaistva i mirovoi politiki*), the International Agrarian Institute (*Mezhdunarodnyi agrarnyi institut*), and a commission on the literatures of the Oriental peoples. In March 1928 the section called History of the Orient was founded within the Society of Marxist Historians.[25] This unit had "cells" in the major centers for Oriental studies.

Throughout the period the communist centers of Oriental studies were active professionally. In January-April 1928 the Communist Academy helped organize a special discussion on Afghanistan. From December 1928 to January 1929 it sponsored the First All-Union Conference of Marxist Historians. At this conference most of the discussion concerned the research done in the Scientific Research Institute on China in the Communist University of the Workers of China (*Nauchno-issledovatel'skii Institut po Kitaiu pri Kommunisticheskom universitete trudiashchikhsia Kitaia*)[26] and in the Scientific-Research Institute of the University of Workers of the Far East Region in Vladivostok (*Nauchno-issledovatel'skii Institut pri Universitete Trudiashchikhsia Dal'nevostochnogo kraia*). During 1929-30 the Society of Marxist Historians and the First All-Union Conference of Marxist Agrarians[27] debated the so-called "Asiatic mode of production" and several other questions.

By the later twenties, the Society of Marxist Orientalists of the Communist Academy had developed into a center of considerable importance. It sponsored research on agrarian, colonial, and nationality questions, and rapidly expanded the scope and variety of its work. Marxist historians fought against deviationism in their own ranks and criticized bourgeois interpretations of history.[28] Most of the work published by the communist Orientalists consisted, however, of brief and highly doctrinaire studies[29] that were a source of constant embarrassment to scholarly Orientalists.

After the reorganization of the Communist Academy in 1928-30 its sections were raised to institutes and were greatly strengthened through fusion with the corresponding institutes of the Russian Association of Scientific-Research Institutes of Social Sciences (*Rossiiskaia assotsiatsiia nauchno-issledovatel'skikh institutov obshchestvennykh nauk* [RANION]).[30] But while the Communist Party research affiliates lagged in their work and were beset with difficulties, both ideological and professional, the Academy of Sciences had steadily expanded its activities and research in Oriental studies. The result was a growing conviction that parallel "communist" and "academic" systems of Oriental research and study were no longer needed. Yet it was not until February 1936 that the government and the party decided to abolish the Communist Academy and to transfer its facilities and staff to the Academy of Sciences.

THE VNAV

During the twenties a number of special societies, commissions, institutes, and museums contributed to the development of Oriental studies in the Soviet Union. Several of these bodies, many of which specialized in a particular geographical region or on a specific aspect of Oriental studies, published their own periodicals and/or occasional papers.[31] The proliferation of organizations engaged in some kind of Oriental study required a centralizing agency that could coordinate, plan, and direct research in Oriental history and culture in the Soviet Union. Accordingly, on 13 December 1921 the Soviet government established in Moscow the so-called All-Russian Scientific Association of Oriental Studies (*Vserossiiskaia nauchnaia assotsiatsiia vostokovedeniia* [VNAV]).[32] This agency, which began operation on 14 January 1922, was attached to NARKOMNATS, then headed by Stalin.[33] It was hoped that VNAV would bring the old and the new Orientalists closer together,[34] and that it would centralize and coordinate research, mobilize all those working in Oriental studies, and organize and expand the documentary materials on Asia.[35] VNAV was to encourage the investigation of contemporary life in the East, the training of specialists for the central and regional governments, the production of guidebooks, surveys, and monographic studies, and the collection of documentary materials.[36] In 1924 the name "All-Russian Scientific Association of Oriental Studies" was changed to "All-Union Scientific Association of Orientalists."

VNAV was divided into two sections, political-economic and historical-ethnological. The political-economic section had two units (the Near East and Middle East and the Far East), which investigated contemporary developments in Eastern countries; and two cabinets (the cabinet for economics and the cabinet for revolutionary movements of Eastern countries). The historical-ethnological section concentrated on research in ancient and modern history, archeology, ethnology, literature, and Oriental languages. VNAV organized the First All-Russian Congress of Egyptology (1922), the First All-Union Congress of Turcology at Baku (1926), and a number of other meetings.[37] It watched over and helped organize instruction in the languages and the history of Oriental peoples in the higher educational institutions. In this connection

VNAV sponsored in 1923 a conference of the heads of such institutions. The VNAV constituted a special commission for the study of natural productive forces of the Soviet and foreign East, and organized field expeditions for the collection of documentary materials. It assisted the government and the party in the implementation of official policy and with propaganda work in the Asian regions of the Soviet Union. It had "cells" in Moscow and in several other places both at home and abroad whose members forwarded information to VNAV.[38]

One of the major tasks of VNAV was to promote Oriental studies in Asian regions of the Soviet Union. It had branches in Chita, in Irkutsk, in the Crimea, in Kiev, in Kharkov, and in Tashkent, as well as a Transcaucasian Branch. The All-Ukrainian Scientific Association of Oriental Studies (*Vseukrainskaia nauchnaia assotsiatsiia vostokovedeniia* [VUNAV]), whose purpose was to promote scholarly study of the East, to popularize Oriental studies and the struggle of the Oriental peoples for freedom and independence, was founded in Kharkov with branches in Kiev and Odessa.[39]

The principal periodical organ of VNAV was *Novyi vostok* (New Orient).[40] Over the ten-year period 1921-30 many important works—monographs, symposiums, documents—were published under VNAV's auspices. *Novyi vostok* printed articles on all aspects of the history and society of the Oriental peoples, and on the major theoretical questions concerning the history of Oriental peoples. Most of the space in the journal—articles and correspondence—was allocated to China (VNAV had branches in Peking and Harbin).[41] Under the auspices of VNAV several books were published on the structure of Oriental societies and on national revolutionary movements, as well as a series on the "proletarian struggle" in the Eastern world.[42]

The head of VNAV was Mikhail Pavlovich (Vel'tman),[43] one of the principal founders of Soviet Orientology. His Marxist interpretations of history provided the model for others to follow. Pavlovich wrote several works on colonialism, on imperialism, and on the national liberation movements in Eastern countries. He endeavored to bring together the old ("academic") and the young (Marxist) Orientalists. The two groups had little respect for one another's work. The academics looked upon their Marxist colleagues as upstarts committed to communist propaganda rather than to genuine scholarship. The young Marxists considered themselves scientific historians, and looked on their non-Marxist colleagues as falsifiers of history. With great difficulty Pavlovich did succeed in attracting to VNAV a few of the older men, including V. V. Bartol'd (1869-1930) and S. F. Ol'denburg (1863-1934), who submitted occasional articles to *Novyi vostok*. This was an uneasy collaboration, to be sure, and it took years before the old and the young Orientalists would work together harmoniously.[44]

While prewar Oriental studies were concentrated at Leningrad and Moscow, thanks to VNAV a number of peripheral centers emerged, especially in the Soviet Eastern republics—in Central Asia and the Caucasus. A chair in Oriental languages and one in history were founded in the universities of Leningrad and Moscow, and a chair of Semitic languages in the Georgian University in Tbilisi.

Although VNAV contributed substantially toward the promotion of Oriental studies, the institution became an object of official criticism, especially after the death of Pavlovich in 1927. [45] Some attributed its limited success to general political conditions in the Soviet Union and to the stifling influences of the "cult of personality." The Central Committee of the Communist Party noted that VNAV did not produce a sufficient number of solid scholarly works containing meaningful analyses of social relations.[46] It was further pointed out that the members of VNAV were not well enough trained, that they did not know Oriental languages, that they spent too much of their energy on mere "sociologizing," that they were victimized by Pokrovskii's ideas concerning commercial capitalism, and that they erred in their interpretations of capitalism, feudalism, and imperialism. Finally, VNAV was criticized for having neglected the collecting of documentary materials. The critics conceded, however, that VNAV did produce a number of important studies of national liberation movements, of socioeconomic problems, and of imperialism. The sum of these accomplishments, however, did not carry enough weight to save the institution.

The Institute of Oriental Studies

The year 1930 witnessed the liquidation of VNAV and the founding of the Institute of Oriental Studies in the reorganized Academy of Sciences. The four principal existing Oriental centers (the Asiatic Museum, the College of Orientalists, the Turcological Cabinet, and the Institute of Buddhist Culture) were merged into a single Institute of Oriental Studies,[47] which inherited a library of some half-million volumes and an archive that held about forty thousand Oriental manuscripts. The new set-up eliminated much of the duplication in the Academy of Sciences and established guidelines for research efforts. The assigned tasks of the Institute were to serve as the main center for Oriental studies in the Soviet Union, to maintain contacts with other Soviet research centers, and to assist them professionally, to stimulate contacts with Orientalists[48] in both Soviet and non-Soviet Asia, and to serve the state and the party.

The historical-economic sector was assigned the job of investigating socialist change in Soviet Asia, and the national liberation movements, imperialism, and various other problems in non-Soviet Asia. The Literary Sector was instructed to investigate Eastern literatures and languages, to compile dictionaries, and to collect and interpret early writings. The compilation of dictionaries was subsequently turned over to the Institute of Japhetic Languages (Institute of Language and Thought), which also devised alphabets for some of the Oriental peoples. The theories espoused by the Institute of Japhetic Languages, however, led to heated linguistic controversies, with the result that the bulk of linguistic research was transferred in 1938 to the Institute of Oriental Studies.[49]

In 1936 the Presidium of the Academy of Sciences directed the Institute of Oriental Studies to investigate several basic problems concerning the history and languages of the peoples of Asia, and to produce histories of India and Japan.[50] In addition, the Institute was directed to give greater attention to the training of specialists in Marxist-Leninist methodology. Aspirants of the Institute were henceforth obliged to attend special seminars in the Communist Academy, to consult with established Orientalists, and to engage in field work.[51] As interest in Oriental studies increased, the field expanded and the decision was made to train more specialists by narrow disciplines and to give young Orientalists a better linguistic training.[52] In furtherance of this policy the Institute was instructed in 1938-39 to catalogue the Oriental manuscripts located in Soviet repositories and to publish a textbook on the modern history of colonial and dependent countries, an historical survey of

China, a symposium on colonialism, and a number of other special studies and dictionaries.[53]

Despite frequent complaints from official quarters during the thirties about the shortage of Orientalists and about the fact that many important subjects were not being adequately researched,[54] the Academy of Sciences grew steadily in importance and in prestige throughout this period. In 1936 it established bases and branches in various parts of the Soviet Union, and in 1937 absorbed institutions formerly under the Communist Academy. Soon afterward the Academy of Sciences took over the History of Material Culture, the Central Scientific-Research Institute of Language and Writings of the Peoples of the U.S.S.R., the Geographical Society, and the Institute of World Literature. Yet the Institute of Oriental Studies was still at this stage a modest establishment. In 1937 its staff comprised only seventy-five "scientific workers."[55] Critics complained that research was ineffectively planned, that it was not coordinated with the work in the republics and other institutions, and that few prominent Soviet Orientalists were seriously investigating contemporary developments in the Orient.[56]

Besides much undistinguished work, however, largely of propagandistic and agitational character, some scholarly contributions did appear during the interwar period. Included among these were works on the history and languages of Eastern peoples by I. Iu. Krachkovskii, V.V. Bartol'd, B. Ia. Vladimirtsov, A.A. Semenov, and V. L. Viatkin. Soviet writers contend that the Stalin cult of personality, the Stalinist arrests and purges of Orientalists in the thirties, and the repressive policy of the government had greatly impeded scholarly efforts. Many scientists tended to shy away from controversial contemporary problems and to work on less sensitive topics.

In the thirties the Institute of Oriental Studies concentrated for the most part on the general history and culture of the Soviet Asian peoples and on such specific topics as the history of the October Revolution and Civil War in the Soviet Asian republics and the socialist reconstruction of Soviet Asia. Much effort was directed toward such areas as colonialism and imperialism, Eastern feudalism, the nationalities problem in the Orient, and the history of political currents and social thought. Important source materials were collected, some of which were published,[57] as were also many books on contemporary literature and languages of Oriental peoples.[58] A comprehensive bibliography on the Orient was compiled.[59]

Always a popular subject, the history of the Mongols continued to attract Soviet Orientalists. In 1934 Vladimirtsov published a fine study of the Mongol social order. Many works appeared on the classical and contemporary literatures of Oriental peoples, including studies of the lives and works of Firdausi, Nizami, Alisher Navai, and Shota Rustaveli. The influence of Gor'kii on Eastern literature and the poetry of the modern Chinese poet Lu Hsun were subjects of special studies.

The Institute of Oriental Studies was involved at the same time in the popularization of Oriental studies and in propagandizing among the Oriental peoples the cause of the Soviet Union and world communism. The Institute organized popular lectures, special programs, and exhibits of Oriental books and art. It sponsored a number of conferences, meetings, and commemorative sessions. It organized or participated in a number of expeditions that investigated archeological and historical monuments as well as the contemporary life and culture of Soviet Asian peoples. Very useful work was done in ethnography and folklore by the Institute of Anthropology and Ethnography and by the Institute for the Investigation of the Peoples of the U.S.S.R.[60]

In furtherance of the Institute's aim to expand the Oriental studies program, the Cabinet for the History of the Ancient East was established in the late thirties under the leadership of V. V. Struve.[61] Associations of specialists were organized within the Institute, the first of which was the Association of Japanese Studies (*Assotsiatsiia Iaponovedenii*), founded in December 1932.[62] This body, which was headed by N. I. Konrad, had two sections, one of them concerned with scholarly research and the other with the training of specialists and with carrying on propaganda work. The main stress in research was on the contemporary period. The Association for Mongolian Studies (*Assotsiatsiia Mongolevedeniia*) was founded in 1933, bringing together specialists from a number of Leningrad institutions.[63] Besides these there were the Association for Study of Turkey (*Assotsiatsiia po izucheniiu Turtsii*) and the Association of Arabists (*Assotsiatsiia arabistov*), founded in January 1934 and headed by Krachkovskii.[64] Each of these groups engaged in research and promoted Oriental studies by sponsoring lectures and exhibits and by holding professional meetings. The Association of Arabists united Arabists of various Leningrad institutions. It organized a first meeting of the Arabists on 14-17 June 1935, at which research problems were discussed.[65] At the Second All-Union Meeting of the Arabists, held on 19-23 October 1937, Krachkovskii reviewed twenty years of Soviet Arabic studies.[66]

As for work in Iranistics, the Soviet Iranists published several works on Iranian history and culture and did a great deal toward popularizing Iranian studies by means of public lectures and exhibits. Several meetings and congresses were held, among them the Third International Congress of Iranian Art and Archeology held in Moscow in 1935.[67]

A number of special sessions honoring prominent Russian and Soviet Orientalists were organized throughout the Soviet Union. There were commemorative gatherings honoring great historical figures and events of the various Soviet Asian peoples. In the thirties Soviet Orientalists attended several international congresses. The scope and the character of Soviet research in Oriental history and culture are vividly reflected in *Zapiski Instituta vostokovedeniia* ("Notes of the Institute of Oriental Studies"), a journal published in seven volumes (1932-39). The journal's name was changed in 1940 to *Sovetskoe vostokovedenie* ("Soviet Oriental Studies"). Two volumes were published before the war broke out (1940-41), after which publication was suspended until 1945, when the third volume appeared. Much Orientological material was published also in the series *Trudy Instituta vostokovedeniia* ("Works of the Institute of Oriental Studies"), of which forty-six volumes appeared between 1935 and 1946.

During the thirties, in addition to the Institute of Oriental Studies several other institutes were founded in the Academy of Sciences in which important work on the history, languages, and literatures of the Asian peoples was carried on. Among the more active institutes were the Pacific Ocean Institute (*Tikhomorskii institut*), the Institute of the History of Art (*Institut istorii iskusstva*), and the Academy of the History of Material Culture (*Akademiia istorii material'noi kul'tury*). The Pacific Ocean Institute[68] existed from 1934 to 1950, when it was absorbed by the Institute of Oriental Studies. Thus, by 1940 the Soviet Union had gone a long way toward the establishment of a solid and many-sided program in Oriental studies.

Oriental Studies During the Second World War

The Second World War found most of the Orientalists either at the front or, with pen in hand, taking to the defense of the country and the promotion of the communist cause. Although reduced significantly, the basic research on Asia was not arrested. In October 1941 the Orientalists met to discuss fascism, imperialism, colonialism, and war.[69] Special measures were introduced to protect library and archival collections. The most important of these measures was the formation of the Leningrad committee to protect manuscripts and books and to collect private libraries and entrust them to the Institute of Oriental Studies.

The conditions of war forced the authorities to move the Institute in 1942 from Leningrad to Tashkent, where the Uzbek government extended whatever assistance it was able. The organization of the Institute remained much what it had been. It was natural that the emphasis in research during the war should be placed on contemporary developments, and on the relations between the Russians and the Eastern peoples. Soviet Orientalists investigated the fascist threat to Iran, the Chinese national liberation struggle, German economic imperialism in the Far East, the war in the Pacific, and the activities of Japan. Yet, even during the war the Orientalists were criticized for spending too much time on the early history of Asia and not enough on the contemporary developments in that continent. The imbalance in research was attributed to the surviving strength of the "academic tradition" and to the shortage of experts trained to work on contemporary problems.[70]

During the war the Institute of Oriental Studies worked closely with the party and the military organization. It published propaganda materials and organized public lectures. The Institute maintained contact with other Orientological centers in the Soviet Union, even to the point of organizing professional conferences.[71] Thus, in January 1944 it held in Tashkent a conference on the culture, history, and language of the Uighurs. Two months later a conference on Central Asian folklore took place, also in Tashkent.[72] The Institute participated in a special session that celebrated twenty years of the Uzbek Soviet Socialist Republic. It sent expeditions to investigate the Pamir languages, the Tajik dialects, and the culture of Central and Inner Asia. The Institute also sponsored a symposium on India.

One particularly valuable contribution of the Institute during its Tashkent period was that it succeeded in training a number of young native Orientalists. After the founding of the Uzbek Academy of Sciences a few members of the Institute of Oriental Studies were made members of the Academy. Their presence gave strength to Uzbek Orientology. Some members of the Institute also joined the faculty of the Central Asian State University. With the war over, the Institute of Oriental Studies moved back to Leningrad, where its staff was strengthened by the inclusion of new members.

At this point we may backtrack to give an account of the activities of the Moscow Orientalists during this period. Before the war they had been grouped into the Sector of Colonial and Dependent Countries within the Institute of History of the Academy of Sciences of the U.S.S.R., and their chief function was to investigate recent history and socioeconomic developments. A number of those who were affiliated with this group of Orientalists left Moscow after the war broke out. The Moscow Institute of Oriental Studies, which was primarily a pedagogical center, was evacuated from the city. The few Orientalists who remained behind in Moscow were joined by a number of their colleagues from the Institute of Oriental Studies and the Pacific Ocean Institute who arrived from the beleaguered Leningrad.

In 1944, as the war neared its end, there was established within the History Faculty of Moscow State University a department of the East.[73] This department, consisting of Near East, Middle East, and Far East chairs, could not encompass all Orientalists in Moscow. Krachkovskii, therefore, organized in Moscow an informal group called the Moscow Group of the Institute of Oriental Studies of the Academy of Sciences (MGIVAN).[74] On 9 February 1944 this group was formalized and became a part of the Department of Literature and Language of the Academy of Sciences, with Krachkovskii as president.

In 1944 a few Orientalists who had spent the war in Moscow, among them Krachkovskii, returned to Leningrad. What Moscow lost was offset, if not in quality at least in numbers, by the new arrivals of Orientalists to Moscow from Tashkent.[75] Actually, more than half the members of the Institute of Oriental Studies were now in Moscow.

The Moscow group studied national liberation and democratic movements in Asia and recent developments in India, Iran, and Turkey. Its staff investigated the formations of nations and states and sought to refute bourgeois ideas concerning the nonparticipation of Eastern peoples in the development of "world culture."[76] The group pioneered in writing textbooks on Asia that covered the ancient and medieval periods. It investigated the literatures and literary heritage of the Soviet Asian peoples. It organized several professional meetings at which such problems as the relations between Russia and Asian peoples and Russian literary influence on Oriental literatures were discussed. Several monographs and surveys of histories of Oriental peoples were initiated during the war and published later.

A number of symposiums and many books were published during the war, but much of the material was of propagandistic nature. Several monographs and surveys of the history of Oriental peoples were initiated but not published until after the war. A number of Orientalists were decorated for their work during the war, but a good many had perished in the war years. After the war commemorative volumes were published for some of those who had died. The third volume of *Vostokovedenie*, published in 1945, was dedicated to fallen Orientalists.

Oriental Studies After the War

It was not until after the Second World War that Soviet Orientalists produced a significant amount of worthwhile scholarship on the Eastern World. After the war they were confronted with many ideological and political problems. Riding on the wave of a great military victory and of an officially cultivated Great Russian nationalism, they found themselves troubled as to how to reconcile Marxist-Leninist theory with these facts of life and how to interpret the past and present of the Oriental peoples. The problem of

Russia's relations with Asian peoples received a high priority in Soviet research.

The end of the Second World War opened for the Soviet Union an unprecedented opportunity for hegemony over Asia. The Soviets suddenly found themselves deeply involved in every part of Asia without a sufficient number of trained Orientalists. It became urgent to expand research facilities, to train linguists and specialists, and to provide handbooks on individual countries. The amount of propaganda and agitation had to be sharply stepped up, and Asia was soon flooded with Soviet agents, brochures, and leaflets.[77]

The primary objective of Soviet Orientalists was to present universal history in accordance with the teachings of Marx and Lenin. Thus, the historian was expected to write history in terms of class struggle and the development of productive forces, and to fit it into a Marxist periodization scheme. Because Marxist-Leninist guidelines did not provide answers to all aspects of social development, there was room for disagreement. This accounted for never-ending debates on how to interpret this or that historical problem. Often the interpretation of history was complicated in that it required reconciliation of Marxist-Leninist ideas with the interests and objectives of the Soviet state and party.

Soviet Orientalists were directed to wage a "militant" war against colonialism, to refute scientifically "imperialism" and "racism," and to espouse "genuine internationalism." They were expected to discredit many bourgeois ideas concerning the historical past of the Oriental peoples and to rewrite the history of Asian peoples in accordance with the principles of Marxism-Leninism. Critics pointed out that neither the Institute of Oriental Studies nor the Pacific Ocean Institute had published a major work on Asia explaining contemporary developments in the "crisis of the colonial system of imperialism." Soviet Orientalists were repeatedly told that they must with pen in hand participate more actively in the ideological war, and that they must interpret the consequences of colonial rule, must explain the national liberation and communist movements in the colonial and dependent countries, assess the general political and economic developments in the Asian "people's democracies," and refute the bourgeois historians.

In view of the dramatic developments in Asia and the enormous new opportunities for the Soviet government and the Communist

Party, the program and the organization of Oriental studies in the Soviet Union had to be brought up to date. For several years after the war there was lively discussion on how to organize this activity. Until after the Second World War Oriental studies were carried on in separate institutions and branches of the Soviet Academy of Sciences, the republican academies of sciences, the few higher educational institutions, the Moscow Institute of Oriental Studies, and in the Military Institute of Foreign Languages. The Institute of Oriental Studies in the Academy of Sciences had failed to become the main directing and coordinating center of Oriental research in the Soviet Union.

Official wartime laxity regarding nationalism and religion permitted a resurgence of national feelings and religious practices. This trend, which was reflected in the historiography of different Soviet Asian peoples, led in turn to the introduction of repressive measures. State authorities took vigorous action to eradicate national, cosmopolitan, and anti-Russian sentiments from historical and literary works on the Soviet Asian peoples. From 1949 until 1951 leading Soviet newspapers and journals often published warnings to historians and literati, as well as to the institutes sponsoring them, and offered acceptable interpretations of controversial issues in the history of the Soviet Muslim and certain other Asian peoples. At various professional conferences Pan-Islamism and other forms of "cosmopolitanism" and "bourgeois nationalism" were condemned. A number of Orientalists were reprimanded or purged and their works condemned. New studies with ideologically acceptable interpretations were produced. In their writings Asian authors were obliged to refrain from expressing any ideas or interpretations that were anti-Russian, and were told to honor and extol the many virtues of the "Great Russian people," under whose leadership the Soviet peoples would attain a common supranational culture for the entire "Soviet family" of nations.[78]

In July 1950 a decision was finally reached to transfer the Institute of Oriental Studies from Leningrad to Moscow and to merge with it the Pacific Ocean Institute and other centers of Oriental studies. Moreover, the Institute of Oriental Studies was transferred from the Department of Literature and Language to the Department of History and Philosophy of the Academy of Sciences.[79]

After its transfer to Moscow, the Institute of Oriental Studies was enlarged and given a new directorship and a set of guidelines.

S. P. Tolstov was named director. As now constituted, the Institute had sectors for China, Mongolia and Korea, Japan, Southeast Asia, India and Afghanistan, Iran, Turkey and the Arabic countries, the Soviet East, and Eastern manuscripts (the last-named remained in Leningrad). The sectors were further subdivided into units specializing on specific disciplines or periods of history or historical problems. As needed, new units were created for particular research assignments, on completion of which they were dissolved. The number of units in the Institute therefore varied from time to time. The Academic Council of the Institute had three sections—historical, economic, and philological.

The purpose of the Institute of Oriental Studies was to coordinate Oriental research in all disciplines and to solve the most important historical and current problems. By the decision of the Presidium of the Academy of Sciences of the U.S.S.R., announced on 1 July 1950, the Institute was instructed to engage in research and publication, to train young scholars in the fields of Oriental studies (history, economics, literature, language), and was to hold professional conferences for discussion of important problems and for interpretation of controversial questions. Director Tolstov was asked to complete the staff of the Institute and to draft a plan of work for 1951.[80] The Institute's task was to implement the direction of research and to provide authoritative interpretations of historical events and personalities. It would offer programs of graduate study (*aspirantura*) and doctoral research (*doktorantura*), would avail other centers of research of its professional counsel and help, and would organize and coordinate research in the Soviet Union.

A Branch of the Institute in Leningrad (*Otdelenie Instituta vostokovedeniia*) consisted of several sections (*otdels*). These were sections for the Near East and the Middle East, the Arabic countries, Japan, China, Korea, Mongolia, Viet Nam, and for Turco-Mongolian studies as well as a few others. With some exceptions, the work done in Leningrad was predominantly on ancient, medieval, and modern history, while that done in Moscow was largely on contemporary and recent times. In 1959 a Section of Ancient History was organized within the Leningrad branch whose principal function was to coordinate the work done in the Soviet Union in the field of ancient history (Sumerology, Assyrology, Hittitology, Iranistics, Indology, etc.). It is of some interest in this connection that other institutes, councils, and commissions of the Academy of Sciences, such as the Institute of Linguistics (which includes a chair in Chinese Philosophy), the Institute of Ethnography, and the Institute of Archeology, continued to publish important studies on the history and culture of the Asian peoples.

Under Tolstov the Institute was instructed to investigate early as well as contemporary history, but to concentrate on the "real" problems and to analyze them from the standpoint of "Marxist-Leninist methodology." Members were obliged to refute the theories of "reactionary bourgeois Oriental studies" and to spell out the major theoretical questions, such as the crisis of the colonial system, the national liberation movements, the socioeconomic and cultural transformation of Eastern peoples' democracies, and the policy of the Anglo-American imperialists in Asia.[81] All this was embodied in the research and publication plan for 1951, which provided also for the issuance of collective works on and histories of a number of Asian countries. In regard to ancient and medieval history, Soviet Orientalists were to continue investigating the problems of class struggle, agrarian relations, crafts, culture, and medieval towns. Whereas earlier plans had placed the accent on philological research and on ancient and medieval history, after the reorganization the emphasis was put on the study of contemporary history, economics, politics, literature, and language. The 1951 plan called for "capital" works in these areas.[82]

One very real problem was the lack of Oriental experts in several disciplines.[83] In 1950-51 only four scholars in the Soviet Union covered the history, literature, economics, and languages of Southeast Asia, exclusive of India. The shortage of economists was particularly acute. This situation resulted in the lumping together in single sectors of Turkey and the Arab countries, Korea and Mongolia, and India and Afghanistan.[84]

As heretofore, the Institute continued to sponsor meetings and discussions on major historical problems. Especially important and sensitive were discussions held in 1950 and 1951 on Shamil and Muridism,[85] and on the Mongol epic poem "Geseriade." Conferences were held on China, Korea, Mongolia and Viet Nam, the people's democracies in Asia, the historical significance of the Russian annexations, and Oriental languages. At a conference held on 12-23 November 1951 Soviet Orientalists examined the "social structure of people's democracies" (government without proletarian leadership). Under official promptings they undertook to assess the "revolutionary potential" of the Asian countries,[86] and in late 1955 organized a conference on the "Impact of the Russian Revolution of 1905-1907 on Asian Countries" at which several leading Orientalists spoke.[87]

The Institute of Oriental Studies produced a large number of monographs, symposiums, collections of documents, and brochures. It participated in several collective ventures and itself initiated large projects. The Institute was professionally active and had sponsored and organized a number of conferences and meetings whose proceedings it had published.

Yet, despite rather impressive accomplishments, Soviet leaders complained that the Institute had not become the real center of Oriental studies and that it had not achieved the research objectives assigned to it. Many of the works it published were inferior, and the Institute, according to its critics, had failed to meet the planned output of scholarly works. It was further pointed out that the Institute did not enroll and train a sufficient number of young Orientalists, especially in the field of economics, and that many of those who were enrolled did not complete their work on time. Despite urgent need for economic experts on Eastern countries, only fifteen "aspirants" were enrolled in the Institute to specialize in economics and politics, while 117 were allowed to select humanities as their field of specialization.[88]

The Institute was criticized further for not giving sufficient professional assistance to republican academies and research centers, for ignoring the idea of criticism and self-criticism, and for failing to coordinate its work with other institutions engaged in Oriental research.[89] To facilitate such coordination, which was required by the constitution of the Soviet Academy of Sciences, a special Council for the Coordination of Scholarly Work of the Academies of the Federal Republic had been set up.[90] For the coordination of Oriental research specifically there was established the Central Coordinating Council for Oriental Studies (*Tsentral'nyi koordinatsionnyi sovet po vostokovedeniiu*). Under its auspices there are currently commissions for special fields, such as the Coordinating Commission for Eastern Literature (*Koordinatsionnaia komissiia po vostochnom literaturovedeniiu*).

The heaviest charges leveled against the Institute of Oriental Studies were that it had not complied with the decisions of the Nineteenth Conference of the Central Committee of the All-Union Communist Party held in October 1952, that it had published works that contained "grave ideological errors" and "mistaken political ideas," and that it had allowed the "anti-Marxist teachings" of N. Ia. Marr to permeate linguistics, archeology, and ethnography. It was noted also that the Institute had been slow in cooperating with other Soviet Oriental centers and with its counterparts in the people's democracies, and that it had not done enough toward refuting the bourgeois interpretations of history.[91] The Institute was instructed to do better work in a number of disciplines and on a whole list of specific subjects, especially in the investigation of national liberation movements in Asia.[92] It was expected, moreover, to produce scholarly works on Oriental languages and literatures, to expose bourgeois "falsifications" of history, and to write about the successful struggle for liberation by different Oriental peoples. The Institute was ordered to give more help to the academies of sciences of the federal republics and to its own branches in solving major historical and ideological issues and to training young specialists.[93]

Above all else, the Institute was expected to examine in conferences and meetings the workers' struggle for hegemony in the national liberation movements in Asia, the position of the peasantry as the principal ally of the workers in the national colonial revolution, the role of the national bourgeoisie in the Eastern colonial and dependent countries, the character of Eastern feudal land ownership, and the path of noncapitalistic development in the Eastern people's democracies.

The Institute of History fared no better than had the Institute of Oriental Studies, for it was criticized just as severely. As early as 1948 critics charged that the Institute of History tolerated the dissemination of certain "ideological fallacies" in historical writings. At the Central Committee meeting of the All-Union Communist Party in October 1952, the Institute of History was held responsible for the existing confusion in historiography on the grounds that it had failed to provide an accurate interpretation for a number of controversial points in Asian history,[94] and had thereby allowed "bourgeois conceptions" to creep into Soviet historical works. It was pointed out that the Institute's organ, *Voprosy istorii* (Problems of History), had published materials including bourgeois ideas and that it had failed to carry out a single basic study of Soviet society (i.e., on collectivization or industrialization or culture or socialist construction). The critics further contended that the editors of the journal gave too little attention to resolving fundamental historical questions.[95]

The Institute of History was criticized further for failing to provide an adequate number of trained persons for work on the history of Central Asia and Kazakhstan,[96] and for allowing two especially damaging errors to circulate. These were the erroneous ideas concerning the role of the Muslim heroes Shamil (c. 1798-1871) and Kenesary Kasymov (1802-47) and the nationality question. Both the Institute and the editors of *Voprosy istorii* were accused in addition of tolerating and protecting historians who had fallen into bourgeois ideological waters.[97] A number of historians were purged, many completed works were put aside or subjected to revision, and studies still in manuscript were recast to conform to official interpretations of controversial historical questions.

Like the Institute of History, the Institute of Oriental Studies was reminded that it must carry out the decisions of the Nineteenth Congress of the Communist Party (December 1952).

On 13 February 1953 on orders of the Presidium of the Academy of Sciences, the Institute of Oriental Studies was reorganized and given a new structure. This consisted of three sections, one on the Far East, one on India and Southeast Asia, and one on the Near East and the Middle East. Each section was divided into two sectors, one concerned with history and economics, the other with language and literature. There were in addition three independent sectors (History and Culture of Soviet Asia, the Ancient East, and Leningrad Oriental Manuscripts), a sector for information, and a group in charge of publishing.[98] During the next two years further organizational changes were made.

After 1954 the Central Committee (CC) of the Communist Party of the Soviet Union (CPSU) demanded a carefully planned research program in all disciplines and on all Eastern countries.[99] The new research plans and the theoretical questions to which the Orientalists were to address themselves were embodied in the Institute's Plan for 1953-55.[100] But the Soviet leaders were still dissatisfied with both the Institute's organizations and with its work, and the Presidium of the Academy ordered a further reorganization of the Institute of Oriental Studies on 12 August 1955. This time it was divided into twelve sectors.[101] Groups of experts working on a specific problem were organized.[102] To facilitate research, "scientific cabinets," whose purpose was to collect basic literature, were organized within the sectors.[103]

The Presidium spelled out the objectives of the Institute's journal *Sovetskoe vostokovedenie* (Soviet Oriental Studies), which after several years of suspension resumed publication in 1955. The journal would carry in its pages the discussion of "real" problems of history, economics, culture, and literature and languages of Asian countries, particularly those concerning the people's democracies. It would explain the nationality question in Soviet Asia, would conduct discussions regarding major problems and implement officially acceptable interpretations, would report on the accomplishments of Soviet Orientology, would review books and other publications on Oriental countries, and would continue the struggle against bourgeois theories on Oriental history.[104] Besides *Sovetskoe vostokovedenie*, the Institute also published *Uchenye zapiski Instituta vostokovedeniia* (Scientific Papers of the Institute of Oriental Studies)[105] and *Kratkie soobshcheniia Instituta vostokovedeniia* (Brief Reports of the Institute of Oriental Studies).

In 1955 the Institute of Oriental Studies had 220 "scientific collaborators," of whom 105 were historians, 37 economists, 50 linguists, and 25 specialists on literature. Interestingly, 45 of the specialists worked on China, 44 on India, and 66 on the Near East and the Middle East.[106] The topics investigated remained much the same as under earlier arrangements: ancient and medieval social and economic relations, the agrarian question, colonialism, the working class and its struggle for hegemony in the national liberation movements, American aggression in China, the People's Republic of China, Japan in the Second World War, postwar Japan, and the people's struggle in Viet Nam.[107] Short accounts of the history of China, India, Korea, Japan, and Mongolia, and guidebooks on contemporary Iran, Turkey, and Syria were initiated.

The Institute was assigned formidable work in linguistics and literature. The All-Union Philological meeting, held in 1955, decided to intensify the study of numerous modern and ancient Oriental languages, to produce grammars and dictionaries, and to train specialists. Thus, the study of Eastern languages and literatures and the publication of historical, literary, and linguistic monuments remained an important part of Soviet Oriental studies. A whole list of linguistic and literary works were published.[108] The Institute continued to organize and sponsor various kinds of professional meetings.[109] Also, it sent representatives to a number of meetings abroad.

Despite feverish activity in Oriental studies, critics continued to complain that the scholarship was not of high caliber, that the Orientalists were ignoring some basic issues, that many works lacked originality, that some studies were too dogmatic and betrayed the influence of the cult of personality, that Orientalists often erred in the way they explained such subjects as the national-democratic regimes, colonialism, and the struggle for national liberation. Some writers were charged with exaggerating the role of the working class in the national liberation movements and others with underestimating it and exaggerating the role of the middle classes. There were mistakes in interpretations of the roles of leaders of national bourgeoisie (Atatürk, Gandhi, Nehru). The subject of state capitalism in the Orient was given insufficient attention.[110] Once again the Institute of Oriental Studies was charged with failure to become the real center of Oriental studies in the Soviet Union and with giving insufficient attention to the contemporary problems of Asia and to the criticism of bourgeois theories.

At the Twentieth Congress of the CPSU (1956) the Institute of Oriental Studies became the object of sharp criticism. In consequence, the Presidium of the Academy of Sciences on 7 September 1956[111] issued a directive for the reorganization of the Institute. The Institute was ordered to strengthen its staff in a number of disciplines, to make improvements in the training of the "aspirants" for teaching careers, to initiate the rapid publication of Oriental works and manuscripts. For this purpose, in 1957 a Publishing House for Eastern Literature (*Izdatel'stvo vostochnoi literatury*) was founded.[112] This board remained under the administrative control of the Institute of Oriental Studies and its successor (Institute of the Peoples of Asia) until 1964, when it was transferred to the Academy's publishing house Nauka (Science) and its Principal Editorial Board for Eastern Literature (*Glavnaia redaktsiia vostochnoi literatury*).[113] Under the Presidium's direction a popular journal, *Sovremennyi vostok* (Contemporary East), was launched. In addition the Institute was instructed to begin joint research and publication projects with other institutes and to invite specialists from various Eastern countries for consultation. After the founding of the Principal Editorial Board for Eastern Literature, *Uchenye zapiski* and *Kratkie soobshcheniia* ceased publication, and in their place symposiums of shorter studies were published at irregular intervals.[114]

The Presidium charged that the Institute had not produced major works on the breaking down of the "colonial system of imperialism," on the growth of the national struggle for freedom and independence of the Oriental peoples, and on basic studies of the history and economy of China and India. It noted that the literatures and languages of Eastern peoples had been neglected, and that the role of the masses and the national bourgeoisie struggle against imperialism had been slighted. The Institute was told that the works issued under its imprimatur were not scholarly enough and that they suffered from dogmatism and uncritical presentation of material (*nachetnichestvo*). The Presidium demanded more criticism of "reactionary" scholarship.[115]

The Presidium noted further that the Orientalists often worked in isolation and failed to consult with colleagues either within the Institute of Oriental Studies or outside. Nor did they consult sufficiently with Orientalists in the "progressive" Eastern countries. The Presidium charged that the Institute did not provide needed opportunity for discussion of major issues. In addition, according to the Presidium, many Orientalists lacked linguistic training and the Institute had failed to build up a qualified staff.

In compliance with the Presidium's new directive[116] the Institute of Oriental Studies was obliged to adopt a Five-Year Plan (1956-60), to fill vacancies in its staff with qualified personnel, to provide for a more effective organization, to improve the training of specialists, to give more attention to the study of Southeast Asia, the Arab World, and Southern Africa, to invite foreign specialists for consultation, to improve publication and to expand publishing facilities, to enlarge opportunities for linguistic study, and to coordinate its research with the Institute of World Economy and International Relations, founded in the Academy of Sciences in 1956.[117] The Institute was told that it must not only fill the vacancies on its own staff and send young trainees to Asia for study, but must also invite experts from Asia and Africa for consultations and must publish literary monuments.

After the 1956 reorganization, the Institute of Oriental Studies consisted of six sections subdivided into sectors established on a regional basis.[118] There were, in addition, four independent sectors.[119] B. G. Gafurov, a capable administrator sufficiently pliable to adjust to the ideological and political zigzags of the Soviet government and party, was made the new director, a position he retains to this day.[120]

The Leningrad Branch of the Institute, of which I. A. Orbeli was made head, was divided into sectors on history, philology, and Eastern manuscripts. Further organizational changes involved the creation of a special Sector for Philosophy and Religion, and the Section on Languages of Eastern Peoples, with three sectors.[121]

On 4-11 June 1957 the First All-Union Conference of Orientalists was held in Tashkent. On this occasion Director Gafurov spoke on the status of Oriental studies and their purpose, noting *inter alia* that Soviet Orientalists still continued to neglect the study of the contemporary East.[122] Much of the discussion concerned the Institute's Five-Year Plan (1956-60), whose main emphasis was laid on the investigation of contemporary problems.[123] Forty-three out of 224 research topics concerned some aspect of the "Colonial System in Decay and Break-Up." Special studies were projected on several aspects of the contemporary history of Oriental countries. There were to be studies on class struggle, colonialism, imperialism, national liberation movements, workers' movements, national democratic revolutions, the Communist Party, economic developments, land reforms, and relations between the Soviet Union and individual Oriental states.

Prominence on the list of research projects was given also to the origin and development of slave-holding relations in Oriental countries, to the genesis and the growth of feudalism, to the genesis of capitalism, to the history of Oriental studies, to the development of social thought, to the role of religion in the lives of Oriental peoples, to the analysis of Oriental languages and dialects at different stages in social history, to the publication of dictionaries and grammars for Eastern languages, to the investigation of Oriental literatures, and to the assessment of the role of literature in the people's struggle for socialism, peace, and freedom. This Five-Year Plan provided for the publication of monographs, symposiums, and brochures, historical and literary monuments and manuscripts. Historical surveys and guidebooks (*spravochniks*) were planned for nearly all Oriental countries. Much of this Five-Year Plan was accomplished and the late fifties and sixties witnessed a great expansion in Soviet Oriental studies,[124] although the output on China declined appreciably as a result of the strained relations between the Soviet Union and the Chinese People's Republic.

Besides historical sketches and guidebooks, grammars, documentary collections, and literary works, many special studies were published. The output included books on agrarian relations in India, literary studies, Firdausi's life and writings, studies on workers' movements, on Russian and Soviet relations with Asian countries, on American imperialism, on the agrarian transformation in the people's democracies, on the national uprising in India (1858-59), on the national liberation movement in India, on the economy of Southeast Asia, as well as on several other topics. Soviet Orientalists were particularly proud of two symposiums, one on the "Great October and the Peoples of the West," the other on "Lenin and the Orient."

Collections of writings by I. Iu. Krachkovskii and V. A. Gordlevskii were issued. The Institute organized and participated in various collective efforts such as the ten-volume "Universal History" (*Vsemirnaia istoriia*).[125] It participated in the project "Peoples of the World" (*Narody mira*), initiated by the Institute of Ethnography, and in the collective work, "Modern History of the Countries of the non-Soviet East" (*Novaia istoriia stran zarubezhnogo Vostoka*), and "History of the Countries of the East in the Medieval Period" (*Istoriia stran Vostoka v srednie veka*). The Institute made significant contributions to the "Great Soviet Encyclopedia." It sponsored several professional meetings, sent delegates to meetings of Orientalists abroad, and cooperated with socialist countries on various projects. The Institute participated in Warsaw (1957) and Prague (1958) meetings at which Oriental sources on Eastern and Central Europe were discussed.

A new Five-Year Plan (1960-65)[126] brought important changes in Soviet Oriental studies, many of which were reflected in the Institute's journals. In 1959 *Sovetskoe vostokovedenie* and *Sovets-*

koe Kitaevedenie (Soviet Chinese Studies) were suspended and their place taken by a new periodical, *Problemy vostokovedeniia* (the Problems of Oriental Studies). Two years later *Sovremennyi vostok* (the Contemporary East) was replaced by another popular journal called *Aziia i Afrika segodnia* (Asia and Africa Today) and in 1961 *Narody Azii i Afriki* (Peoples of Asia and Africa) succeeded *Problemy vostokovedeniia.*

Although the Institute of Oriental Studies published some excellent scholarly tracts, it still could not escape official criticism. The same familiar charges were repeated: not enough publication, inferior quality of published works, mistaken interpretations, too much on early and not enough on contemporary history, no consultations or cooperation with other institutes, insufficient criticism of bourgeois historians, etc. The strained relations with China and the Middle Eastern crisis forced the Institute to drop or modify some research projects and to adopt others.

On 22 July 1960 the Presidium of the Academy of Sciences ordered a merger of the Institute of Oriental Studies and the Institute of Chinese Studies into a single Institute of the Peoples of Asia (*Institut narodov Azii*) with a branch of the Institute in Leningrad.[127] B. G. Gafurov was retained as director of the new Institute and I. A. Orbeli of the Leningrad Branch. A directive of the Presidium issued on 16 December 1960 defined the functions of the Institute of the Peoples of Asia,[128] and another directive issued on 10 February 1961 gave the Institute its organization. The new Institute had seven regional and country sections, each with two or more sectors,[129] and three problem sections. The Leningrad Branch had three sectors—the Near and the Middle East, the Far East and Southeast Asia, and Manuscripts; also a number of cabinets[130] and problem groups.[131] From time to time special additional problem groups were organized, one of the first of which investigated the workers' movements in Asia.

The executive apparatus of the Institute of the Peoples of Asia was much like that of its predecessors, and consisted of an Academic Council (*Uchenyi sovet*) presided over by a director. As before, the Academic Council had three sections (history, economy, and philology), with a chairman for each. The Academic Council passed on the doctoral and candidate dissertations, the research plans, and the completed manuscripts.

As then constituted, the Institute of the Peoples of Asia had a staff of more than fifty persons with the degree of doctor of philosophy—a degree hard to come by in the Soviet Union—and four hundred candidates in sciences. Aspiring Orientalists from all parts of the Soviet Union enrolled in the Institute for an eight-year program of study toward the degree of *aspirantura* in one of several disciplines.[132] The Five-Year Plan (1959-65) provided for further research in the topics already under investigation[133] and for some new ones. The director announced that the Institute's aim was to work closely with "the practical needs of the building of communism" and to assist the Central Committee of the Communist Party and the Soviet Government in their efforts to secure general peace and security for the people.[134]

In October 1964 the Presidium of the Academy of Sciences directed the Leningrad Branch to concentrate on the study of the culture of the Oriental peoples from the earliest times to the most recent period, to publish and interpret ancient Oriental writings, to investigate the beginnings of class society and the evolution of precapitalistic formations in the East, to produce a history of written language in the East, to assess the development of literature and art, and to present the history of ideological currents in the East. One of the most important assignments of the Leningrad Branch was the publication of Eastern manuscripts. Thanks to the presence in Leningrad of such able scholars as V. V. Struve, A. N. Kononov, N. V. Pigulevskaia, I. M. D'iakonov, V. A. Livshits, A. G. Perikhanian, L. N. Men'shykov, and F. I. Kychanov, important work was done on the social and economic history of the ancient and medieval Near East and Middle East, and on Iranian, Turkish, and certain other languages.

The Five-Year Plan for 1966-70 provided for the continuation of many major research projects, as well as for investigation in such areas as the theory and practice of socialism in the Asian people's democracies, Asian international relations, monopoly capital in Japan, the proletariat and its part in the growth of the international workers' movement, the role of the Soviet Union in the social and economic development of the countries of Asia and North Africa, the economy of the developing countries, agrarian and nationality questions, ideological conceptions of national revolutions and liberation movements, development of Oriental socioeconomic formations, culture, language, literature, and social thought.[135]

By 1970 the Institute of the Peoples of Asia had published an impressive quantity of books, symposiums, brochures, and source collections. It sponsored conferences on many different topics and published their proceedings. The Institute sponsored also thousands of lectures and maintained close ties with the countries of the people's democracies; and the members of the Institute participated in foreign conferences. During 1970 the earlier name of the Institute, *Institut vostokovedeniia* (Institute of Oriental Studies), was restored.

The journal of the Institute, *Narody Azii i Afriki*, mirrored the vitality and character of Soviet Oriental studies. It carried articles on a wide range of topics, discussed research problems, and supplied the latest interpretations of Oriental history and culture. It published reviews, book announcements, professional notes and reports on Orientological activities in the Institute and elsewhere in the Soviet Union and on professional meetings, conferences, and international congresses. This publication reported also on the examinations for academic degrees, supplying the names of examiners and the titles of subjects examined.

Other Centers of Oriental Research

Although it is true that the great bulk of the work in Oriental studies is carried on in the Institute of the Peoples of Asia and its Leningrad Branch, a very considerable amount of research on Asia is done in other institutes and branches of the Academy of Sciences of the U.S.S.R., particularly the Institute of Ethnography,[136] the Institute of the History of Material Culture,[137] and the Institute of Ancient History.[138] The same is more or less true of the institutes that fall under the Department of Philosophy and Law,[139] Economics,[140] Literature and Linguistics,[141] and the institutes and branches of the Siberian Department.[142] Much research is done also in the many republican research centers.

In most instances the republican centers, though they originated before the October Revolution or before the Second World War, have attained real importance only since the end of the war. Armenia, for example, did not acquire a full-fledged Academy of Sciences until 1943, although until that time there was a branch of the Soviet Academy of Sciences in Erevan. The Armenians, however, can trace the beginnings of Oriental studies in their country to the Lazarev Institute founded in Moscow in the early nineteenth century.[143]

The Armenian Academy of Sciences is organized into five departments (*otdelenie*), one of which is the Department for Social Sciences. This department has five institutes: History, Archeology and Ethnography; Economics; the P. Acharian Institute of Linguistics; the M. H. Abegian Institute of Literature; and the Institute of Arts. There are also within the Department of Social Sciences sections for Oriental languages, philosophy and law, and a Commission for International Scientific Contacts. The activities of all these institutes, sections, and commissions deal almost entirely with the Orient: the study of the past and present of Armenia, its precursors, and its Soviet and foreign neighbors. The Historical Museum and certain other specialized institutions are also under the jurisdiction of the Armenian Academy of Sciences.

In 1954 the Institute of History of the Armenian Academy of Sciences organized a group for the study of modern and recent history of the countries of the Near East and the Middle East. This group, whose head is O. G. Indzhikian, was transformed in 1958 into a sector for Oriental studies[144] in which research is concentrated on the history and economics of the Near Eastern and the Middle Eastern peoples (Turks, Kurds, Arabs, Iranians).[145] In 1969 the group celebrated its tenth anniversary.[146]

Armenian Orientalists have investigated the history of the Near East and the Middle East since the fifth century and have published several studies on workers' and national liberation movements, on the foreign and domestic policies of Near Eastern and Middle Eastern countries, on Soviet foreign policy, on the Ottoman expansionist policy in the First World War, on the imperialistic countries in the Near East and the Middle East, and on oil and agrarian problems. The Armenians have published some Arabic and Turkish sources and works on middle-class ideology, on political parties, on the anti-imperialist struggle, and on minorities in the Near East and the Middle East. Much effort has been devoted to publishing Armenian sources, literary works, studies of Armenian colonies abroad, and general developments in the Near East and the Middle East. Armenians have a strong program in Kurdish history, literature, and language.

In 1945 the branch of the Academy of Sciences of the U.S.S.R. in Baku was transformed into the Academy of Sciences of the Azerbaijan S.S.R. This institution is divided into five departments, one of which is the Department of Social Sciences, which in turn is made up of the Institute of History, the Nizami Institute of Literature and Language, the institutes, of Economics and of Oriental Studies, and the section on philosophy. The Republican Archives of Manuscripts and the Commission on International Scientific Contacts as well fall under the Department of Social Sciences. The Institute of Oriental Studies, established in 1958, was renamed in 1967 the Institute of the Peoples of the Near East and the Middle East. The Institute was made up of the following sections: History, Economics, Literature, Languages, Social and Philosophical Thought, Textology and Publication of Sources, and a Group for Kurdish Studies.

The main interest of Azerbaijan's Orientalists is in the history of Azerbaijan itself and of its Caucasian and Near Eastern and Middle Eastern neighbors. In recent years the Institute has been working on the national liberation and workers' movements in Iran, Turkey, and the Arabic countries, on the Kurdish question, on contemporary developments in Turkey and Iran, and on the publication of historical and literary documents.[147] The Institute sponsored jointly with the Institute of the Peoples of Asia the All-Union Meeting on History and Economics of Afghanistan, Iran, and Turkey, held in Baku, in May 1962.[148] Much valuable research on the Caucasus and the Middle East has been done also in the institutes of History and Literature and Language (*Institut literatury i iazyka im. Nizami*).

During the interwar period a modest amount of research and publication was sponsored by the appropriate departments and chairs of the university and the branch of the Academy of Sciences of the Soviet Union in Tbilisi.[149] Research on national and regional history, languages, and literatures expanded greatly after 1941, when the branch of the Academy became the Academy of Sciences of the Georgian S.S.R. The Academy has six departments, one of which is for social sciences. Within the Department of Social Sciences are institutes of Oriental Studies, Linguistics, History of Georgian Arts, Economy and Law, Philosophy, the Shota Rustaveli Institute of History of Georgian Literature, the K. S. Kalidze

Institute of Manuscripts, and the I. A. Dzhavakhishvili Institute of History, Archeology, and Ethnography. Under the jurisdiction of the Department of Social Sciences are also the Southern Ossetian Research Institute, the Batumi Research Institute, the Abkhaz Research Institute, the Committee for International Scientific Contacts, the Commission for Publication of Oriental Manuscripts on the History of Georgia, as well as a number of libraries, museums, and other cultural centers.

In 1960 the Institute of Oriental Studies was incorporated into the Georgian Academy of Sciences.[150] The Institute consists of sections for the investigation of modern and recent history of Eastern countries, feudal history of Eastern countries, Semitology, languages of the Ancient East, Indo-Iranian languages, Persian philology, Turcology, and Byzantine studies. Georgian Orientalists are investigating Babylonian, Persian, and Byzantine literatures and their impact on Georgian literature. They are working on the ancient tongues of the Near East peoples (Hittites, Urartu, Sumerians, and others), on feudalism, on medieval towns in the Near East and the Middle East, on national liberation movements, on the genesis of capitalism, and on the histories and languages of the peoples of the Near East and the Middle East. A special commission in the Academy of Sciences of the Georgian S.S.R. is working on the publication of annotated documents. In 1968, when the Institute of Oriental Studies of the Georgian Academy of Sciences was reorganized, G. V. Tsereteli, a prominent Orientalist, became its director.

In Kazakhstan the program of Oriental studies is a very modest one. The Kazakh Academy of Sciences has five departments, one of them devoted to the social sciences, and its own publishing facilities. The Department of Social Sciences has institutes of linguistics, philosophy and law, economics, the M. O. Auezov Institute of Literature and Arts, and the Ch. Ch. Valikhanov Institute of History, Archeology and Ethnography.

The Academy of Sciences of the Kirghiz S. S. Republic has four departments. The Department for Social Sciences has institutes of history, language and literature, economics and philosophy. The Department of Geography operates the Tien-Shan Physical Geography Station in the village of Pokrovka. The Department for General Turkish and Dungan History is staffed with experts in history, economics, linguistics, and literature. Perhaps the best work done in Kirghizstan is on the origin, history, and culture of the Dungan, the Dungan language, and on Chinese sources and language. In the sector for Turcology important work is done on the ancient and medieval Turkic languages, and on the study of languages of small Turkic peoples in South Siberia and Central Asia.

Oriental studies in Tajikstan began to develop after the October Revolution. In 1941 the Tajik branch of the Academy of Sciences of the U.S.S.R. was established. Ten years later the branch became the Academy of Sciences of the Tajik S.S.R., with three departments. The Department of Social Sciences has the Ahmad Donish Institute of History, the Rudaki Institute of Language and Literature, the Institute of Economics, the Section of Philosophy, and the Section for Archival Studies. A special Department of Oriental Studies and Written Heritage (*Otdel vostokovedeniia i pis'mennogo naslediia*) was established in 1958 and is made up of a number of sectors: Contemporary East, History of Literature, Oriental manuscripts, Textology and Publications.[151] The Orientalists of Tajikstan are specializing in the ancient and medieval history of the peoples of Central Asia, Iran, Afghanistan, and India.

The Turkmen branch of the Academy of Sciences of the U.S.S.R., which was founded in 1932, two years later acquired the Oriental Institute with several sections: North Indian philology, Eastern Turkestan philology, Iran-Afghan philology, and history of the countries of the Near East and the Middle East. At the end of the Second World War, in 1946, the branch became the Academy of Sciences of the Turkmen S.S.R., with four departments. The Department of Social Sciences consisted of the Makhtumkuli Institute of Linguistics and Literature, the Sh. B. Batyrov Institute of History, and the Institute of Economics. The Institute of Linguistics and Literature has five sections: art, philosophy, economics, architecture, and Uighuro-Dungan studies. Of these, one of the most successful is the section on Uighuro-Dungan studies (*otdel Uigurovedeniia*), which specializes on folklore, literature, and the Uighur language.[152] In 1957 chairs of Arabic and Chinese philologies were added to the Institute.[153] Three years later, in 1960, a sector for Oriental studies was established in the Institute of History, Archeology, and Ethnography.[154] The Museum of Literature and the Southern Turkmenistan Complex Archeological Expedition also came under the jurisdiction of the Academy.

In recent years one of the major projects in which Turkmen Orientalists have been engaged is the study of the impact of the Great October Revolution on the national liberation movements in Iran, Afghanistan, Turkey, and Arabic countries, and on the relations between Turkmens and these countries. Turkmen Orientalists have also published many historical documents.

Uzbekistan has the best-developed Oriental studies program in Central Asia thanks to a number of local institutions. Since 1933 the State Public Library in Tashkent had housed a section for Eastern manuscripts, with several prominent Orientalists on its staff, including A. E. Schmidt and A. A. Semenov. In 1943 the section for Eastern manuscripts of the State Public Library became the Institute for the Study of Eastern Manuscripts, which during the Second World War worked closely with the Institute of Oriental Studies, which had moved from Leningrad to Tashkent after the war broke out.

By this time the Oriental studies program in Uzbekistan had been enhanced by other important developments. The Uzbek Academy of Sciences was created in 1943 out of the existing branch of the Academy of Sciences of the U.S.S.R. The Academy's Department of Social Sciences was made up of the institutes of philosophy and law, the A. S. Pushkin Institute of Literature and Linguistics, the Institute of Economics, the Karakalpak Branch of the Uzbek Academy of Sciences (in Nukus), and the Institute of History, Linguistics, and Literature of the Karakalpak Branch. In 1950 the Institute for the Study of Eastern Manuscripts became the Institute of Oriental Studies of the Uzbek Academy of Sciences.[155]

Under the auspices of the Uzbek Institute of Oriental Studies a number of studies of varying length have appeared. These include many works of prominent medieval Muslim thinkers, such as al Biruni and Ibn Sina.[156] The Institute concentrates on regional history; that is, Soviet Central Asia, the Soviet Middle Eastern neighbors (Afghanistan and Iran), and Southeast Asia (India and Pakistan). It publishes early historical and literary sources as well.

Important collections of sources are published also by the Uzbek Institute of History and Archeology. The study of Western imperialism in Iran, the Middle East, and Central Asia and the relations between peoples of Soviet Central Asia and their neighbors abroad are major research interests of Uzbek Orientalists, and books and short studies have been published on both of these topics. Among other major preoccupations of Uzbek historians[157] are the national liberation movements, the study of workers' movements, and the refutation of bourgeois historians who in their works allegedly minimize or ignore the role of the people of the East in the development of "world civilization."

Works published by Uzbek Orientalists in recent years have related to such topics as the history of the workers' movement in India, pre-Hindu principalities of northern India, ethnographic studies of Indian peoples, studies of the national liberation movement at different places and at different stages, the Soviet annexations of Central Asia and their historical meaning, history of Badakhshan, the Afghan agrarian problem, Russian and Soviet relations with Afghanistan and Persia,[158] and the struggle of Afghanistan for independence.

Once a fairly important center of Oriental studies, the Ukrainian Academy of Sciences, as well as other institutions in the Ukraine, have been eclipsed by Oriental centers of other republics, although some work in Orientology is being done at the universities of Lvov and Kharkov and in the Section for the Foreign East in the Institute of History of the Ukrainian Academy of Sciences. Because the history of the Ukraine is closely associated with the history of the Tatars and Ottoman Turks, the study of these peoples and the Near East in general is of primary interest to Ukrainian historians. But since the end of the Second World War Oriental studies in the Ukraine, both in the Academy of Sciences and in educational institutions, have been drastically curtailed.

Modest work in Oriental studies is being carried on in many other places in the Soviet Union. Each of the smaller research centers on the republican and lower levels in Soviet Asia investigates the history of its own region and regions bordering on it. This applies, for instance, to Kazan, the traditional center of Oriental studies; to the Institute of History, Language and Literature of the Bashkir Branch of the Soviet Academy of Sciences; and to the Buriat Complex Scientific Research Institute of the Siberian Branch of the Academy of Sciences of the U.S.S.R.,[159] the Scientific Research Institute of Language, Literature, and History attached to the Council of Ministers of the Kalmyk Autonomous Soviet Socialistic Republic,[160] the Daghestan Branch of the Soviet Academy of

Sciences (at Makhachkala), the S. M. Kirov Kole Branch of the Academy of Sciences of the U.S.S.R. (at Akademgorodsk), the Komi Branch of the Academy of Sciences of the U.S.S.R. (at Syktyrkar), and the Institute of Social Sciences of the Siberian Section of the Academy of Sciences of the U.S.S.R. (at Novosibirsk).

Numerous research centers publish their findings in regular journals, symposiums, occasional papers, or in the form of monographs. However, not all have their own printing facilities. Many centers published "Brief Announcements," collections of short papers. Most important for students of Oriental studies are the publications of the Academy of Sciences. Besides the publications of the Institute of the Peoples of Asia, already discussed above, of great importance are the journals *Voprosy istorii* (Problems of history), *Istoriia S.S.S.R.* (History of the U.S.S.R.), *Novaia i noveishaia istoriia* (Modern and recent history), *Sovetskaia etnografiia* (Soviet ethnography), *Sovetskaia arkheologiia* (Soviet archeology), *Vestnik drevnei istorii* (Journal of ancient history), and the symposiums *Epigrafika vostoka* (Oriental epigraphy), published by the Leningrad Branch (Central Asian Sector) of the Institute of the History of Material Culture, and *Palestinskii sbornik* (Palestinian symposium), published by the Russian Palestinian Society of the Soviet Academy of Sciences.

Universities and Pedagogical Institutes

From the very beginning of Soviet rule, several universities have offered work in Oriental history and languages, and newly founded universities and pedagogical institutes have included in their offering work in Oriental studies. Oriental research has been carried on in Turkestan University, founded in 1918 as the first center of higher learning in Central Asia.[161] Although the primary function of the higher institutions of learning is to teach and to train public servants, they engage also in research work. The Oriental Institute (*Vostochnyi institut*), which was established in Tashkent in 1918, offered instruction in languages and in the history of Central Asia and the bordering countries. It was replaced in 1924 by the Eastern Faculty of the Central Asian State University (now V. I. Lenin Tashkent State University). [162] On the staff were several prominent

Orientalists who wrote a great deal and trained young historians and philologists.

The Department of the Historical and Philological Faculty at Baku State University, founded in 1919, became an independent Oriental Faculty in 1922.[163] In the autumn of 1919 the Eastern Department of the Faculty of the Humanities of what later became the Irkutsk State University offered a program of Oriental studies.[164] When the Armenian People's University was founded in 1921 it included an Eastern Faculty headed by the prominent Orientalist Ia. A. Manadian. In 1925 this Faculty was reduced to the status of Eastern Department within the Faculty of Pedagogy.[165]

In 1920 the Far Eastern State University at Vladivostok had an Eastern Faculty that had grown out of the Eastern Institute, founded in 1899, and the Polytechnic Institute. This faculty derived strength from the facilities and the personnel of the Society for the Study of the Manchurian Region and the Harbin Society of Russian Orientalists. Its main function was to train specialists on China, Japan, and Korea, although it engaged in research, too. For a short time in 1929 the Society of Oriental Studies in the Far Eastern University published a periodical called *Biulleten'*.

In 1936 the Department of Oriental Languages was established in the Institute of Languages, History, and Material Culture of the University of Tbilisi. Some years later, in 1942, the Department became the Department of Near Eastern Languages. In 1945 the University of Tbilisi acquired the Faculty of Oriental Studies with sections for History and Philology. An Eastern Faculty had existed in Azerbaijan University since its founding in 1920. In 1944 this Faculty was reorganized and expanded to include departments of Turkish and Iranian philology. The Faculty emphasizes teaching and research in the Turkish, Iranian, and Arabic languages. Other faculties, such as the Historical Faculty, also engage in both teaching and research. In Azerbaijan's Historical Faculty the study of Soviet and Russian relations with Caucasian, Near Eastern and Middle Eastern peoples has been one of the major subjects of investigation.

The Crimean State University at Simferopol acquired an Oriental Department within the Faculty of Social Sciences in 1921. In 1922 this department became the Eastern Faculty.[166] Oriental languages and history were taught also at Kazan, which acquired

an Eastern Pedagogical Institute in 1922. Some work is done in the
Cabinet of Oriental Studies in Tartu (Estonia) State University,
which celebrated its tenth anniversary in 1965, and in nearly every
Soviet university and pedagogical institute.[167]

It is not surprising that Oriental studies did not progress at an
equal pace in all republics and regions. In the Ukraine, for example, an effort was made during the first years after the Second
World War to revive interest in the Orient. But at the beginning of
1950 it was decided for various reasons to curtail Oriental studies.
Individual efforts to preserve some work in Oriental studies under
the auspices of the Institute of History of the Ukrainian Academy
of Sciences were not too successful. Even Lvov University, which
has a good library holding, was obliged to reduce its offering in
Oriental history and languages. In recent years, however, there has
been a campaign in the Ukraine in favor of the resurrection of Oriental studies to at least the prewar level.[168]

On the university level the most important work in Oriental
studies is done at Moscow and Leningrad State universities. Moscow State University is the largest and the most significant center
of Oriental studies in the Soviet university system.[169] The program
in Oriental studies, which developed rapidly after 1925, received a
further boost when in 1943 the Eastern Department was created
in the Faculty of Philology. This department had chairs in Turkish
and Iranian philology. In 1944 a chair in Arabic philology and in
1953 one in Chinese philology were added. Also in 1953 the Faculty of History acquired the Oriental Department with three chairs:
history of the Near East, history of the Middle East, and history of
the Far East. Four years later a chair of Eastern languages was added, with specialization on the history and literature of China and
India. One of the major functions of Moscow State University is
to train specialists for the government and for the teaching pro-
fession. The university likewise trains teachers of the Russian language for non-Russian schools (Tajik, Uzbek, Turkmen, etc.). Many
of the present Soviet Orientalists are Moscow-trained.

A new period in the history of Oriental studies in Moscow State
University began in 1956 with the founding of the Institute of Oriental Languages (*Institut vostochnykh iazykov*) consisting of two
faculties: historical-philological and faculty for training of language
specialists.[170] In 1967 the Institute had chairs in Arabic, Turkish,

Iranian, and Chinese philologies; in Far Eastern and Southeast Asian Languages and Literatures; in the Near East and the Middle East, Indian, Chinese, Far Eastern, and Southeast Asian histories; African studies; economics and economic geography of the countries of Asia and Africa; and Western European languages.[171]

Moscow State University is strong in the field of ancient history, with some of the country's leading authorities on ancient Egypt, the Near East, Rome, and Central Asia on its teaching staff. Included among these are S. P. Tolstov, A. V. Mishulin, V. I. Avdiev, N. A. Mashkin, A. B. Ranovich, K. Zel'in, A. G. Bokshchanin, D. G. Reder, and O. I. Savost'ianova. Many prominent regional experts and ethnographers are also on the staff, among them N. A. Smirnov, a specialist on Russo-Turkish relations in the sixteenth and seventeenth centuries; A. A. Guber, the country's leading authority on Southeast Asia; A. L. Gal'perin and B. V. Rodov, leading authorities on Japan; M. N. Pak on Korea; L V. Simonovskaia and G. B. Erenburg on China; I. M. Reisner, A. M. D'iakov, B. N. Zakholder, M. M. D'iakonov, N. Gol'dberg, A. M. Osipov, and K.A. Bol'dyrev on India, Iran, and Afghanistan; A. F. Miller, N. A. Smirnov, Kh. Z. Gabidullin, and E. F. Ludshuveit on Turkey; and V. B. Lutskii on the Arab world. Also on the staff are several prominent ethnographers-Orientalists, among them S. A. Tokarev[172] (seventeenth- and eighteenth-century Yakutia), K. S. Kozlov[173] (Volga Region), A. V. Fadeev (the Caucasus), and S. V. Kiselev (South Siberia).

Next in importance to Moscow State University as a center of Oriental studies is Leningrad State University, whose Eastern faculty (*Vostochnyi fakul'tet*) is dedicated exclusively to Orientology. The university has chairs for Mongolian, Iranian, Turkic, Arabic, Indian, Japanese, and Chinese philologies; chairs of the Far East, the Near East, and Ancient East history; and a number of seminars (e.g., the seminar for Caucasian studies). Since the end of the Second World War the program of Oriental studies has undergone rapid expansion.[174]

Several prominent Orientalists have been affiliated with Leningrad State University. For five years after the war the chair of Arabistics was occupied by the distinguished Arabic scholar I. Iu. Krachkovskii. In this department the principal stress remained on teaching and research in the field of Arabic language and literature.

The chair of the history of the Far East was occupied by G. V. Eftimov and emphasized the modern and recent history of China, international relations in the Far East, imperialistic expansion into China, and China's foreign relations and resistance to colonialism. The chair of Near East history was occupied by I. M. Petrushevskii, also a prominent Orientalist who is best known for his work on feudal agriculture in medieval Iran and Azerbaijan.[175]

The broadening of relations between the Soviet Union and various Oriental countries and peoples has made it urgent to produce grammars, dictionaries, and translations of works by Oriental authors. As had their colleagues in Moscow, the Orientalists of the University of Leningrad produced a number of textbooks on languages and literatures of Oriental peoples. One of the best of these is the grammar of the Chinese language written by A. A. Dragunov. Under the auspices of the newly found chair of Korean philology (1952), a Korean-Russian dictionary and a Korean grammar were published; also a grammar on contemporary Turkish by A. N. Kononov,[176] a talented Turcologist, and a book on modern Mongol literature by L. K. Gerasimov.

Leningrad University has the strongest program in the Soviet Union in the field of history and languages of the ancient Near East and China. In recent years specialists at the university have published studies of ancient Egyptian, Chinese, and Near Eastern languages. Several prominent Orientalists (E. Ia. Liusternik, I. N. Vinnikov, A. D. Novichev, A. N. Bol'dyrev, K. N. Bogoliubov, A. T. Tagudzhanov, and V. V. Struve) are on the staff of the Eastern Faculty—and, until her recent death, N. V. Pigulevskaia.

In the fifties and the sixties the members of the university community published several works on China and Japan. Much effort was devoted also to the study of Oriental historiography and to the publication of source materials. For a long time Leningrad was an important center for the translation of Oriental works, and before the Second World War the Institute of Oriental Studies even held a translation seminar. But since 1956, a group of Orientalist translators has been created, representing primarily the Eastern Faculty in Leningrad University and the Leningrad Branch of the Institute of the Peoples of Asia.[177]

For the benefit of the instructor and the researcher on the faculties of universities and other higher educational establishments periodic conferences are held at which the problems of historiography and source materials are discussed. These conferences have been sponsored by the U.S.S.R. and Russian S.F.S.R. ministries of higher and secondary special education. A number of such conferences have been dedicated to the problems of history and historiography of Oriental countries. [178] At the Converence of Higher Educational Institutions (*Mezhvuzovskaia nauchnaia konferentsiia*) held in Leningrad on 25-27 January 1963 a large number of problems were discussed, such as bourgeois historiography on the modern and contemporary Far East, American historiography on China, problems of interpretation of ancient Chinese history, Tibetology and sources on the north Arabian tribes in the fourth to sixth centuries. There were papers on the Tanguts, Saffavids, Ismailis, Afshars, and certain other Oriental peoples.

At the Conference held in Moscow on 20-26 December 1966 short papers were read on the role of the All-Union Scientific Association of Oriental Studies [VNAV] in the development of Soviet Orientology, on the problem of the "Asiatic mode of production" in Soviet historiography, on the status of research on Southeast Asia and the Middle East in the Institute of Oriental Studies of Uzbekistan, on the status of Soviet Islamic studies, and on a number of other topics involving the modern history of China, Japan, India, Indonesia, Afghanistan, the Arab World, and Korea. The papers are important in that they summarize what has been done, tell how the various problems were interpreted, and assess the availability of sources. The Moscow Conference, which was dedicated to the fiftieth anniversary of the October Revolution, adopted a resolution calling for intensified historical investigation of the Oriental world and improved quality of scholarship and class instruction. It was decided to hold conferences every two years in Moscow and Leningrad alternately.[179]

One result of the much expanded offering in Oriental studies in universities and pedagogical institutes was the creation of a textbook crisis. There was a severe shortage of good textbooks and other reading material on Oriental history, languages, and literatures. The few existing textbooks and sourcebooks were antiquated. To add to the problem, the uncertainties of Soviet politics made it difficult for anyone to produce acceptable texts. In 1947 A. A. Zhdanov spoke of the ideological tasks of Soviet social scientists and suggested that an acceptable textbook should expose "alienism" and "cosmopolitanism" in Soviet historiography and extol the achievements of the Soviet and Russian peoples.

By 1948 faithful historians had produced a number of textbooks, several of them dealing with ancient history and embodying the latest Soviet findings and interpretations based on new archeological and documentary materials. Soon there was an abundance of textbooks for universities and institutes (*vuzovskie uchebniki*) on early history, but none of them escaped criticism. V. I. Avdiev's inferior textbook on the history of the Ancient East,[180] though criticized, was officially considered the best of the lot and was cited as a model of how the history of the ancient world should be presented by a Marxist-Leninist historian. Avdiev won the Stalin Prize for his book, which besides treating the ancient history of the Near East and the Middle East covered also the ancient history of India and China.[181] The branch of the Institute of Oriental Studies in Leningrad is currently preparing for publication a large three-volume study of the ancient East. In this study Soviet historians are expected to assess the economic and social position of various categories of producers in ancient civilizations, to discuss the class struggle, and to provide an adequate treatment of the role played by slaves and peasants in ancient society.[182] Moreover, they will attempt to destroy bourgeois theories about ancient history.[183]

The need for ideologically acceptable textbooks in the more sensitive period of modern and contemporary history of the Eastern peoples was even greater. Discussions on the "ideological" content of textbooks and their general improvement went on both before and after the death of Stalin. The revision of existing textbooks was imperative also because they were being translated into the languages of the "people's democracies," and unless corrected they would disseminate ideas not officially approved.[184]

The question of what a textbook should contain and of how and what to teach was a never-ending problem in Soviet pedagogical and political circles.[185] There were constant complaints about the lack of textbooks and reading materials.[186] The critics complained that the textbooks were not up to date, that histories of the peoples of Asia and Africa were being slighted, that the textbooks did not include sufficient illustrative and audiovisual material.[187] Ideological errors continued to appear.[188] In more recent years the textbook situation has become less serious, since many new texts on the history of the peoples of Asia and Africa have appeared and the new sourcebooks on modern history (by A. A. Guber, A. V. Efimov, B. G. Gafurov, I. M. Maiskii, A. I. Molok, etc.) include a representative amount of reading material on Asian and African peoples.

The problem of how to achieve a balanced teaching program on Asia and Africa at all school levels is still being debated.[189] One author has suggested that on the university and pedagogical institute level more special courses and seminars be offered in which the students could work with source materials and familiarize themselves with historiography.[190]

Various promotional devices are used to encourage students to specialize on the Orient. One issue of *Narody Azii i Afriki* carried articles by three generations of Orientalists on "Why I became an Orientalist,"[191] no doubt with the intention of inspiring others to follow in their footsteps. In addition, much effort is directed toward giving students practical research experience, training in the use of archival materials and even affording them opportunities to publish their work. Conferences are held at which candidates for higher degrees read papers on a wide range of subjects.[192]

Archival and Library Resources

Several Soviet repositories and libraries have excellent collections of both published and unpublished materials on the Orient. A great many documentary collections have been issued and a number are currently being prepared for publication. Important sources on ancient and medieval history have been published, including very valuable Sogdian documents and Seleucid and Parthian inscriptions found on Mount Mug.[193] There are collections of documents on such subjects as policies of European powers in Southeast Asia in the eighteenth and nineteenth centuries, on social laws of Daghestan from the seventeenth to the nineteenth century, on Russo-Indian relations in the seventeenth and eighteenth centuries, on Russo-Chinese relations since 1689, on Russo-Mongol relations, 1607-36 and 1921-66, and on the Taipei Rebellion.

The most extensive collections of documentary materials have been those concerning the workers' movement, the first and second Russian revolutions, the civil war, and the establishment of Soviet rule in various parts of Soviet Asia. There are a number of documentary volumes also on the relations between Russia and the Soviet Union and individual Asian peoples. Two multivolume collections of Russian foreign ministry documents, covering the years 1801-15 and 1878-1917 contain valuable materials on the relations between the Russians and Asian peoples. Documentary materials on the work and activities of Russian generals and admirals in the eighteenth and nineteenth centuries likewise contain important data on Russian policies toward Oriental peoples and Asia.

Under official direction Soviet libraries and archives have expanded existing collections of documentary materials and have classified and published many of them. Increased contact with Asian countries has made it possible for the Soviet Union to add large quantities of documents to existing collections and to enlarge the library holdings. The most important repositories in the Soviet Union are located in Leningrad, Moscow, Kazan, Tbilisi, Erevan, Tashkent, Dushanbe, and Baku.[194] In addition to archives, several major libraries house collections of rare manuscripts and xylographs.[195] As a result of systematic collecting from the time the Asiatic Museum was founded in 1818 until today, the Archive of the Institute of Oriental Studies of the Soviet Academy of Sciences now contains the most important collection of manuscript materials in the Soviet Union.[196] These materials are stored in the archive and library of the Leningrad Branch of the Institute of Oriental Studies.

The finest manuscript collections of the Institute of Oriental Studies are in Arabic,[197] Turkish,[198] Persian/Tajik,[199] Syrian,[200] Ethiopian, Mongol,[201] Chinese,[202] Tangut,[203] Manchurian,[204] Tibetan,[205] Hindi and Punjabi,[206] Uighur,[207] Kurdish,[208] Korean,[209] Japanese,[210] Armenian,[211] Georgian,[212] Buriat,[213] and Oirat.[214] The Institute has in addition a small collection of Indian, Ceylonese, Burmese, Siamese, and Indonesian manuscripts.[215] Of all these, the largest and most important is the Arabic collection, which sheds light on the history of Muslim and non-Muslim peoples of the Soviet Union and neighboring countries, although the collection of manuscripts in Turkic languages (Uighur, Uzbek, Turkish, Tatar, Kazakh) is of special importance as well.[216]

Among noteworthy collections found outside of Leningrad and Moscow, the manuscript section of the Institute of Oriental Studies of the Uzbek Academy of Sciences houses about a hundred thousand Oriental manuscripts, of which some 48 percent are in Arabic, 40 percent in Persian, and 10 percent in Uzbek. Publication of these documents, which began several years ago, is still in progress. The Institute has been issuing a catalogue of its collections, of which eight volumes have already been published.[217] It has published volumes of documentary materials on specific questions and translations of medieval classics and works of prominent thinkers.[218]

The Academy of Sciences of the Tajik S.S.R. has a collection of some six thousand Oriental manuscripts.[219] Its Department of Oriental Studies and Written Heritage, which has published several volumes of documents and works of famous medieval Muslim thinkers, has conducted successful expeditions to the Gorno-Badakhshan Autonomous Region in quest of manuscripts and other documentary materials. In 1963 the fifth such expedition was organized.[220]

The study of the manuscripts in Tajikstan, which have considerable historical and geographical import, was begun only a few years ago. Of special value are creations of poets and medieval thinkers, and manuscripts on medicine, astronomy, and theology, as well as a number of other subjects. Additional documents are located in the Firdausi Public Library and in the pedagogical institutes of Dushanbe, Kuliab, and Leninabad.

An excellent collection of books and manuscripts is to be found in the Armenian State Archive of ancient manuscripts, Matenadaran,[221] which is attached to the Council of Ministers of the Armenian Soviet Socialist Republic. The unpublished materials are in Armenian, Arabic, Turkish, and Persian.[222] The Persian collection is superb.[223] The study and classification of the Matenadaran manuscripts, which are based on the holdings of Armenian monasteries including Echmiadzin, have been entrusted to the scientific research institute of ancient manuscripts. Matenadaran has more than ten thousand book manuscripts and about four thousand manuscript fragments in Armenian dating from the fifth to the eighteenth centuries. The collections contain the works of Nizami, Hafiz, Firdausi, Ibn Sina, and others. Of great value are about fifteen hundred documents in Persian, Turkish, and Arabic on the history of the Caucasus and neighboring regions.[224]

The Academy of Sciences of the Georgian S.S.R. contains a fine collection of Georgian, Turkish, and Persian documents.[225] The State Museum and Central State Archive in Georgia hold about two thousand documents, both originals and copies, in Persian, Georgian, and other languages.[226] The Academy of Sciences of the Azerbaijan S.S.R. has a good collection of Turkish and Persian materials, both unpublished and published, and the Buriat Complex Scientific Research Institute holds valuable materials on the Mongols.[227]

A number of Soviet libraries have, in addition to a good collection of published works, some manuscript holdings. Among such institutions are the Library of the Eastern Faculty of Leningrad State University, the Library of the Academy of Sciences, and the Public Library Saltykov-Shchedrin.[228] In the Saltykov-Shchedrin Public Library in Leningrad is to be found a fine collection of books and periodicals on China. The Library of the Leningrad Branch of the Institute of Oriental Studies has good collections of printed works on Arabs, Persians, Turks, Indians, Mongols, Chinese, and Jews. The Institute's library in Moscow, too, has a strong collection on Oriental peoples. Important holdings exist in the Lenin State Library in Moscow,[229] in the All-Union State Library of Foreign Literature,[230] in the State Public Historical Library of the Russian Socialist Federal Soviet Republic,[231] and in the A. M. Gor'kii Scientific Library of Moscow State University.[232] On China alone the V. P. Volgin Basic Library of Social Sciences in Moscow has fifty thousand volumes and well over a thousand periodicals,[233] the Lenin State Library has two hundred thousand books, and the Library of the Institute of Oriental Studies in Leningrad about a hundred thousand.[234] The libraries at Tashkent, Tbilisi, Erevan, Baku, Kiev, Kazan, Ulan-Ude, and Alma-Ata have good collections of printed works, as do several other Soviet libraries.

Progress in Soviet Oriental studies is greatly facilitated by a number of professional societies and museums. The All-Union Geographical Society promotes the study of Asian geography, holds meetings, and sponsors publications.[235] The State Museum of Art of the Peoples of the Orient in Moscow has rich holdings divided into three sections: Soviet Asia, the Far East, and the Near East and the Middle East.[236] The Museum of Eastern Cultures in Moscow contains Oriental manuscripts, miniatures, textiles, paintings, and other objects.[237] After the Second World War, Korea, China, and India made valuable contributions to this museum, which had been founded on the basis of the confiscation of the P. I. Shchukin private collection.

Several organizations attached to the government or to the party engage in Oriental research and publication. Among these are the Sector on the Non-Soviet East of the Institute of Art (*Sektor zarubezhnogo vostoka Instituta istorii iskusstv*) attached to the Soviet Ministry of Art,[238] the Moscow Institute of National Economy (*Moskovskii institut narodnogo khoziaistva im. G. V. Plekhanova*), and the Academy of Rural Economic Sciences (*Akademiia sel'skokhoziaistvennykh nauk*), founded in 1929. The principal party agencies concerned with the Orient are the Institute of Marxism-Leninism of the Central Committee of the Communist Party (*Institut Marksizma-Leninizma pri TsK KPSS*), which has a chair in Oriental history and publishes its own journal;[239] the Higher Party School attached to the Central Committee of the Communist Party of the Soviet Union (*Vysshaia Partiinaia shkola pri TsK KPSS*); and the Academy of Social Sciences attached to the Central Committee of the Soviet Communist Party (*Akademiia obshchestvennykh nauk pri TsK VKP* (b)), founded in Moscow in 1946.[240] The Academy has an Institute of the Far East, in which work is done primarily on China.

Bibliographical Output

Both in variety and in volume the bibliographical material on the Orient published by the Soviet Union is impressive. Books and periodical and newspaper articles are listed in a number of bibliographies. In addition to many general bibliographies, there are bibliographies classified by country, by region, by institution,[241] or by subject.[242] Many short bibliographies of works by prominent Orientalists are available. Of great value is a ten-volume "Bibliography" on Eastern countries published in Russia.[243] The All-Union Book House currently publishes a "Yearbook of the Books of the U.S.S.R."[244] and the "Bibliography of Soviet Bibliography."[245] On the history of foreign countries there is a "Bibliography of Russian Bibliography Published from 1857 to 1965."

Before and after the Second World War various centers of learning published bibliographies under their own auspices. Nearly all Soviet republics, autonomous republics, and small administrative regions are now publishing bibliographies of works printed on their own territory or under the imprimatur of their institutions. Most republics and regions also issue "Annals" in which they list books and newspaper and periodical articles.[246]

Since 1959 the Institute of the Peoples of Asia has published bibliographies on a number of non-Soviet Asian countries. There are, for example, bibliographies on Afghanistan,[247] India,[248] Iran,[249] Japan,[250] the Mongol People's Republic,[251] Turkey,[252] and Southeast Asia.[253] A complete bibliography of Soviet and Russian materials on China, first published in 1932, was expanded, corrected, and republished in 1966.[254] This work, which was translated into English in 1948, was initiated by the Scientific-Research Institute on China in the Communist Academy and lists works published in Russian between 1730 and 1930. It was revised and brought up to 1957 by the staff of the Institute of Chinese Studies of the Soviet Academy of Sciences and published in 1966. The bulk of material listed in the "Bibliography of China" deals with Soviet-Chinese relations, with Chinese Communist activities, and with the founding of the Chinese People's Republic. Soviet scholars tend to identify with Sinology any materials that deal with China, even the latest items on ideological and political bickering.

Among the works on separate regions of Soviet Asia[255] are an "Annotated Index of Literature on the History, Archeology and Ethnography of Kirghizia,"[256] and a four-volume "Bibliography of Kirghizia."[257] A bibliography of the published works in Russian on Turkestan before the Revolution is being issued, the first volume of which has appeared.[258] At least one volume of a comparable bibliography on Kazakhstan has also come out,[259] as well as a short bibliography of Uzbekistan.[260] There are bibliographies on the Tuva Autonomous Region (covering works published between 1774 and 1958),[261] on the Iakut Autonomous Soviet Socialist Republic, covering works published between 1931 and 1955,[262] on the history and literature of Kamchatka,[263] and on Kurdish[264] and Mongolian[265] studies in Russia. In short, there is available a bibliography of one sort or another for nearly every one of the Soviet Asian peoples and regions. The multivolume historical surveys of individual peoples contain lengthy bibliographies; and a number of journals, particularly *Voprosy istorii*, publish bibliographies regularly.

Collective Works and Series

Soviet Orientalists appear to place great value on collective scholarly efforts, as is evidenced by the numerous symposiums, historical surveys, and reference works, such as *Sovetskaia istoricheskaia entsiklopediia* [266] (Soviet Historical Encyclopedia) and the fifty-one volume *Bol'shaia Sovetskaia Entsiklopediia* (Great Soviet Encyclopedia). One of the collective efforts of which Soviet Orientalists are most proud is the ten-volume *Vsemirnaia istoriia* [267] (Universal history). This work and the two encyclopedias contain the most up-to-date information on Soviet historical research and interpretation.

Probably no Western encyclopedia, with the exception of the Encyclopedia of Islam, has so many entries on Oriental history and civilization as the "Great Soviet Encyclopedia." The vast amount of material included in it, especially on Soviet Asia, is in itself impressive. For the 1969-74 period the Soviet Union has embarked on the third revision of this work in order to bring it up to date, to expunge undesirable evidence, and to modify some earlier Soviet interpretations.

The ten-volume "Universal History," the first volume of which appeared in 1955 and the last in 1965, is intended to serve as the Soviet answer to the Western presentation of world history. Relying on the Marxist-Leninist philosophy of history, Soviet scholars undertake to discredit bourgeois interpretations of the history of the Asian peoples. [268] They criticize the so-called "Eurocentrism" and the "Kulturträgerism" of Western historians, charging that Western scholars continue to apologize for colonialism [269] and to deny the Asian peoples their due place in universal history. Western historians are accused further of ignoring the internal development of individual countries, their national specifics, and their contributions to "the common culture of humanity." The long period of colonial hegemony of European imperialism over other peoples has conditioned the bourgeois scholar to see in the history

of Europe "the basic content of historical process."[270] The editors
of "Universal History" explain that the "scientific" interpretation
of history destroys legends and "religious fantasies," and enables
the reader to understand how the world reached "the contemporary stage of development" and where it is headed.[271] The "Universal History" as written by Soviet historians is intended to show
that the historical epoch which brings the greatest change in world
history is that which ushers in "the communist society." The Soviet version of "Universal History" consequently serves as a guide for
the working class and the "progressive peoples of the world." It
helps them comprehend the laws of social development and teaches
them how to utilize those laws in the "revolutionary struggle."

During the past few years a number of collective projects have
been initiated. The Institute of History has published a twelve-
volume "History of the U.S.S.R. from the Earliest Times to Our
Own Day" (*Istoriia S.S.S.R. s drevneishikh vremen do nashikh
dnei*), a work consisting of two series of six volumes each. The
first six volumes cover the period up to the October Revolution,
and the second six from the Revolution on. The purpose of the
work is to provide a unified and integrated history of all the Soviet
peoples.

For several years the Institute of Ethnography has been publishing its series of "Peoples of the World" (*Narody mira*). Among the
more important symposiums in the series are "Peoples of Asia,"
"Peoples of the Caucasus," "Peoples of Siberia," "Peoples of Central Asia," and "Peoples of Southeast Asia."

A collective five-volume History of Soviet Literature (*Istoriia
sovetskoi literatury*) is being published, as well as a four-volume
"Languages of Asia and Africa" (*Iazyki Azii i Afriki*). Also projected by the Institute of Philosophy is a four-volume work on the
"Culture of Pre-Class and Early Class Societies."[272] The A. M.
Gor'kii Institute of World Literature is publishing a multivolume
history of world literature (*Istoriia vsemirnoi literatury*), which
shows the origin and development of "the new socialistic literature" and the reflections in it of the national liberation struggle.[273]
The study of world literature is considered especially important
for the Soviet Union because the literatures of the peoples of the
Soviet Union are closely associated with foreign literature.[274]

Besides numerous collective projects, the Soviet Union is publishing many series of works which in varying degrees involve the history and culture of Oriental peoples. In a series called "Ethnogenesis and the Formation of Nations" monographs entitled "Ethnic History of Northeastern Siberia," "Paleoanthropology of Central Asia," and "Russian Old Settlers in Siberia" have already appeared. The series will include as well studies of Eveny culture and Hunnic monuments in Buriat Mongolia.

A series of "Travels in Eastern Countries" (*Puteshestviia po stranam Vostoka*) consists largely of translations of well-known Western works; and the series called "Russian Travels in Eastern Countries" (*Russkie puteshestvenniki v stranakh Vostoka*), as the title indicates, is a collection of earlier and contemporary Russian travels to Asian countries.[275] A series entitled "In the Wake of the Extinct Cultures of the East" (*Po sledam ishcheznuvshikh kul'tur Vostoka*) consists of Russian works and translations of foreign books. Several important works have appeared in this series, including books on the discovery of Khazariia, the travels of Przheval'skii and Kozlov and the findings at Karakhoto, investigations of the territory between the Caspian and the Amu Darya ("the cradle of ancient civilizations"), the results of the archeological findings in the Pamirs and the Tien Shan, and several others.

A particularly worthwhile series is the "Monuments of the Literatures of the Peoples of the East" (*Pamiatniki literatury narodov Vostoka*), which consists of translations of many early written monuments. This series is divided into a "Large Series" and a "Small Series." In the first appeared nine volumes of Firdausi, Sa'di's "Gulistan," Nakhichevani's "Dustur al-kitab," and a number of other works. The second series included 'Umar Khayyam's "Ruba'iyat" and "Tracts," Khorezmi's "Mukhabbat-name," and the works of certain other authors. The series known as "Translations" (*Perevody*) includes Muhammad Kazim's "Nadir Shah's Campaign to India," 'Abd al-Rahman al-Jabarti's works on Napoleon in Egypt, and others.

In the series "Policy of Imperialistic States in the Countries of Asia and Africa" (*Politika imperialisticheskikh derzhav v stranakh Azii i Afriki*) appear books on the activities of American, English, French, and other "imperialistic" countries in various parts of Asia and Africa. There are books, for example, on U.S. policy in the countries of the Far East, Southeast Asia, and the Near East and the Middle East. Somewhat different is the series "Countries and Peoples of the East" (*Strany i narody Vostoka*), which was initiated in 1959 by the Eastern Commission of the Geographic Society of the Soviet Union. Several volumes of this work, edited by V. V. Struve and A. V. Korolev, have already been published. They contain essays on the geography, history, language, literature, and economics of different Asia peoples. The series "Countries of the Near East and the Middle East" (*Strany Blizhnego i Srednego Vostoka*) includes books on such subjects as the economics and politics of the Near Eastern countries, on the Kurdish question, on the French expedition to Syria in 1860-61, on the contemporary economy of the countries of the Near East and the Middle East, on ethnic problems in the Near East, and on CENTO. There are also series on the "History and Economy of the Countries of Africa, the Near East and the Middle East" (*Istoriia i ekonomika stran Afriki, Blizhnego i Srednego Vostoka*) and on the "History and Economy of the Countries of South and Southeastern Asia" (*Istoriia i ekonomika stran Iuzhnoi i Iugo-Vostochnoi Azii*).

Soviet Orientalists, especially those in the Leningrad Branch of the Institute of Oriental Studies, are currently making intensive studies of the culture of Oriental peoples, with the result that much work is being published in this area. The series "Monuments of Oriental Writing" (*Pamiatniki pis'mennosti Vostoka*) has issued a number of studies, including Arabic, Turkish, and Persian epigraphic materials from the Northern Caucasus, Chinese classics in Tangut, ancient Indian ethical and philosophical works, materials on the seventeenth- and the eighteenth-century Japanese village, and many more. The series "Monuments of the History of the Peoples of Central and Eastern Europe" (*Pamiatniki istorii narodov Tsentral'noi i vostochnoi Evropy*) consists of specific kinds of source materials, such as the Byzantine Book of Eparch, Alexiad, and Ecloga.

The series "Universal Literature" (*Vsemirnaia literatura*), "Monuments of Literatures of the Peoples of the East" (*Pamitaniki literatur narodov Vostoka*), and "Literatures of the Orient" (*Literatura Vostoka*) publish a variety of works on early and contemporary Oriental literature. More than a hundred books have been published since 1957 in the series called "Literature and Folklore of the Peoples of Asia, Africa, Australia, and Oceania" (*Literatura i Fol'klor Narodov Azii, Afriki, Avstralii i Okeanii*). These titles cover a wide range of subjects taken from the literature and folklore of many Asian peoples.[276] Finally, there is a series entitled the "Contemporary Eastern Novel" (*Sovremennaia vostochnaia novella*) and one called "Tales and Myths of the Peoples of Asia" (*Skazki i mify narodov Vostoka*). In both of these series many translations of Oriental works have appeared.

In addition to all of these, many symposiums have been published on the literature of both Soviet and non-Soviet peoples. At least four issues of "Brief Reports" of the Institute of Oriental Studies (*Kratkie soobshcheniia*) have been devoted to literature and literary problems.[277] A determined effort has been made to provide surveys of the history of literature for each of the Soviet Asian peoples. The study of the ancient literatures of Eastern peoples, for example, has received serious attention.[278] Epic poetry and folklore are being investigated extensively, too. Though space does not permit the listing here of studies of specific literary problems, Soviet authors have shown special interest in the impact of Russian and Soviet literature (Chekhov, Pushkin, Chernyshevskii, Tolstoi, Gor'kii) and events (the First Russian Revolution, the October Revolution) on Eastern literature. Oriental poetry and writings dedicated to the Soviet Union and communism are being collected. In the past several years Soviet authors have investigated the relations between the various Oriental literatures and between them and Western literature.[279] Among the topics that have rereived greatest attention are socialist realism[280] in and the periodization of Eastern literatures.[281] A variety of literary problems concerning Eastern literatures has been discussed in professional meetings and in print. These include the question of humanism and the theory of literature and esthetics in Asian countries.[282] In March 1962 in Moscow and in June 1963 in Tashkent, conferences were held on Oriental textology, and a standing committee on Oriental textology was chosen. At the All-Union Coordinating Meeting, held in December 1962 under the sponsorship of the Institute of the Peoples of Asia, unified plans for research in Oriental literature were agreed upon. The Coordinating Council for Literary Studies met in Baku in June 1965 to assess the work done in Oriental literature.

In the field of Oriental art and culture many books have been
published. The same is true of philosophy and social thought and
of Oriental science from ancient to modern times. The degree of
interest in Oriental science and the variety of topics investigated
are reflected in the three-volume symposium, "The History of Science and Technology of the Eastern Countries."[283] Another symposium under the same editorship[284] but a different title appeared
in 1966.

A large quantity of material has been published also on Oriental
languages. These include many serious studies in philology, dialectology, phonetics, morphology, lexicography and lexicology, and
other aspects of language. Soviet Orientalists have made detailed
investigations of the history and character of many major and
minor Oriental languages. They have written a variety of grammars
and compiled numerous dictionaries. The best work is that on the
Turkic, Iranian, and Chinese languages; the least impressive, that
on the languages of the peoples of Southeast Asia. About eighty
books have been published in the one series alone on "Languages
of the Peoples of Asia and Africa" (*Iazyki narodov Azii i Afriki*).
These are short discussions of various groups of languages. A number of issues of *Kratkie soobshcheniia* (Brief Reports of the Institute of Oriental Studies) that have been devoted to Oriental
languages reflect the character and the quality of the Soviet
linguistics. [285]

An Appraisal of Oriental Studies by Regions and Peoples

When we speak of Soviet Oriental studies we must distinguish between two categories: works on Soviet Asia and works on non-
Soviet Asia (*zarubezhnaia Aziia*). It is not unnatural that the best
and most extensive efforts of Soviet scholarship should have been
directed toward the study of Soviet Asia. In the quantity and quality of published work on non-Soviet Asia, there is wide variation
from region to region and from people to people. For different
reasons the Russians have traditionally given more attention to
Turkish and Iranian studies than to other branches of Orientology;
but Sinology, Indology, and Arabistics also have a strong tradition

in the Soviet Union. Only modest results have been achieved in the Japanese and Korean studies, and the investigation of Southeast Asia has barely begun.

Many historiographies, both general and special, have been published. A good account of the history of Russian and Soviet Oriental studies is available in the four-volume "Sketches of the History of Historical Science in the U.S.S.R." [286] Another important work is the five-volume "Sketches of the History of Russian Oriental Studies" before the October Revolution. [287] This work consists of a series of separate essays on several branches of Oriental studies by a number of contributors.

Many short general accounts of Soviet Oriental studies have been published. [288] In 1967 the Institute of the Peoples of Asia issued more than two dozen brochures, in English, on different fields of Soviet Orientology. Though hastily compiled, these brochures are useful. Occasionally individual research centers publish accounts of Oriental studies carried on under their own auspices. Such accounts are available on the work done by centers in Leningrad, [289] Tashkent, [290] and Kazan. [291] There are many reports also on Oriental studies in particular regions, among them Central Asia, [292] Uzbekistan, [293] Tajikstan, [294] Turkmenistan, [295] Kirghizia, [296] Kazakhstan, [297] Iakutia, [298] Armenia, [299] Azerbaijan, [300] Georgia, [301] and Siberia. [302] Short statements are available also on the work done on individual peoples: Mongols, [303] Manchurians, [304] ancient Turks, [305] Kurds, [306] Arabs, [307] Semites, [308] and even on the tiny nations of Daghestan, [309] Abkhazia, [310] and Pamir. There are good works on Russian and Soviet investigations of Islam and Islamic institutions, [311] on the ancient East, [312] and the "History of the Discovery and Investigation of Soviet Asia. [313] Periodic reports are published in *Narody Azii i Afriki* and *Voprosy istorii*, as well as in other journals, on Orientological activities in both the leading and the provincial centers of the Soviet Union. [314]

As already indicated, Soviet Orientalists have done their best work on Soviet Asia, the vast region which for the most part is inaccessible to foreign scholarship. [315] Monographic studies, documentary collections, and detailed historical syntheses exist on nearly every Soviet Asian nation. The history of Soviet Asian peoples is presented within an established system of periodization, and the main stages in the social evolution of each people are interpreted in nearly identical fashion, in accordance with Marxist-Leninist teachings and the objectives of the Soviet state. In the process every aspect of the history of the Soviet Asian peoples is being painstakingly investigated.

Extensive archeological projects have been carried out in many parts of Soviet Asia, with the result that a great quantity of new evidence on ancient peoples has been uncovered.[316] This evidence has enabled Soviet scholars to work out a system of periodization for the stone, the bronze, and the iron ages of the Soviet Asian peoples. As a result of archeological excavations, Soviet scholars have broadened their knowledge of early peoples and of the primeval-communal and slave-holding orders in Soviet Asia. Ethnographic investigations[317] and manuscript-hunting expeditions[318] have in recent years greatly expanded the material and written evidence on medieval and modern history and the culture of the Soviet Asian peoples.

A large quantity of material has been published on the prehistory and the ancient history of the Oriental world as a whole. Included among the works on ancient history are studies of specific problems and historical surveys of one or more ancient civilizations. Soviet historians are particularly interested in the origin of early civilizations and in the character of their social organizations, and seek to establish continuity between them and some of the Soviet peoples of today. The peoples of Soviet Central Asia, for example, are looked upon as the cultural and ethnic heirs of Bactrians, Khwarizmians, and Sogdians, and the Armenians as the heirs of Urartu. Long debates have been held on how to periodize the ancient history of individual civilizations, on the applicability of Marxian ideas regarding the "Asiatic mode of production," on what is common and what specific in ancient Oriental societies.

Monographic studies, collections of documents, symposiums, and periodical articles have been published on nearly every aspect of the history of the Soviet Asian peoples. Historical surveys have been produced for nearly every Soviet Asian people.[319] Georgians and Armenians are the only major ethnic groups who lack up-to-date general modern histories, though in both cases there are adequate surveys of their early history.[320] Broad surveys of the history of these two peoples, however, are in progress. In 1970 the Volume

VIII of the *Istoriia armianskogo naroda* (1941-1965) was published by the Institute of History of the Armenian Academy of Sciences.

Heated debates have raged over the ethnogenesis of various peoples, the breaking down of tribal order, and the rise of class society, as well as on the whole problem of the genesis and growth of feudalism. Much attention has been given to socioeconomic problems and to the culture of the peoples of Asia. The history and culture of Oriental peoples in medieval times has been investigated intensively, with many historical and literary monuments being published.

The problem of the periodization of the history and literature of Asian peoples has been discussed extensively. The history of social thought and religions from the earliest times is an important topic of inquiry in the Soviet Union. The negative influence of religion and religious institutions is shown and the materialistic trends in philosophy played up. The works of several early and modern Oriental philosophers have been translated and analyzed.

The attempt to write histories of Soviet Muslim peoples while disregarding or minimizing their ethnic and cultural ties with peoples across the border and to claim for the Soviet Muslims the famous medieval Muslim thinkers and Muslim cultural greatness has created difficulties for Soviet historians. Soviet historians have continued to investigate the history of the economic, cultural, and other contacts between the Russians and the Soviet Asian peoples.[321] In the years immediately following the Second World War no historical topic attracted more attention than the problem of the Russian union with or annexation of Asian peoples. It was not in the interest of the Soviet state, for instance, to treat the annexations as Russian aggrandizement tantamount to imperialistic acquisitions of other great powers.[322]

Since the late 1940s a major task of the Soviet historian has been to promote the Communist Party's nationality policy. This has required the creation of the myth that friendly relations among the peoples making up the Soviet Union existed from the beginning of their association and the historian has been obliged to stress the role of the Russian people "as cultural leader, military defender, and political genius." The myth has been at variance with earlier Soviet interpretations. The non-Russian leaders and resistance movements which opposed Russian colonialism and which were previously labeled "progressive" are now declared "retrogressive" or part progressive and part retrogressive. Russian annexations of non-Russian peoples that were once seen as "absolute evil" (outright conquests) or as the "lesser evil" (a view widely accepted in the thirties) are now interpreted as results of the "voluntary" union of non-Russian peoples with Russia, and former Russian military actions against the non-Russian nationalities looked upon as defensive actions to aid local populations against their foreign enemies (Iran, Turkey, England).

This debate over historical interpretation has been accompanied by bitter polemics, purges of professional historians, and the repudiation of their earlier works. For a fleeting moment in 1956 the "new scholarly climate" allowed a more objective assessment of the tsarist aggression against the Oriental peoples but this was not tolerated long. In the meantime, the implementation of the official nationality line has resulted in an outpouring of an unprecedented quantity of published material.

The Russian occupation and administration of the annexed territories and the Russian cultural and revolutionary impact on the subject peoples have led to lengthy discussions and heated debates on how to interpret various resistance movements directed against Russian rule. The controversary came into the open with the publication of *History of the Kazakh S.S.R.*,[323] whose authors argued that the struggle of every people for national independence was "a progressive factor."

Other topics requiring an acceptable interpretation were the epic poems[324] of several of the Asian peoples. Regardless of their literary quality and of their value as a source of historical data, many of the poems spew forth hatred of the Russians or other members of the Soviet community. Soviet leaders, disturbed by the uncritical dissemination of epic poems, demanded that they be subjected to ideological assessment.

The native leaders, who were likely to be anti-Russian, were condemned as reactionaries, along with such middle-class movements and ideologies as Pan-Islamism, Pan-Turkism, Pan-Iranism, Pan-Afghanism, and the Jadid[325] and Basmachi movements. Some movements, such as the 1916 revolt in Jizzakh, for example, were at first interpreted as progressive developments and later as reactionary and anti-Russian.[326] One of the main difficulties for Soviet historians was to reconcile facts with preconceived schemes, to find a class struggle where none was in evidence.

Since Stalin's death in 1953, the tendency has been to praise the Russian state rather than the Great Russian nationalism. One author writes that "The accommodation that has been reached between the party ideologist and the historian permits a range of interpretation considerably more flexible than that of Stalin's day, when a numbing uniformity was the rule."[327] Some of the Muslim heroes, such as Shamil, and the epic poems, such as *Manas*, are no longer rejected as being entirely reactionary. This zigzag in historical interpretation is illustrative of the highly politicized nature of Soviet historiography. History continues to be used as an instrument for the furtherance of communist objectives both at home and abroad.

The formation of Soviet Asian peoples into nations has been a subject of many written works. Many studies have been published on the impact of the Russian Revolution of 1905-07 on the Soviet and non-Soviet Oriental peoples. Soviet historians emphasize the importance of the Revolution and of the role played in it by the proletariat; and they lay great stress on Lenin's words to the effect that the Revolution marked the beginning of the "Asian awakening." Their purpose is to show that nearly all revolutionary undertakings in Asia were inspired and precipitated by the Revolution of 1905 and 1907, particularly the October Revolution.

The part played by Soviet Asian peoples in the Bolshevik Revolution and the Civil War that followed is a subject that has yielded many monographic and documentary works. So has the subject of socialization and the development resulting from various five-year plans, as well as the role of individual Soviet Asian peoples in the "Great Fatherland War." Especially significant for Soviet historians has been the topic of the social transformation of individual Asian peoples.

The development of socialism by by-passing capitalism and the noncapitalist path of development have furnished almost unlimited material for investigation. These studies, whether long or short, are for the most part theoretical and general, and many are based on specific countries and regions. They are likely to discuss, for example, the development of individual Soviet republics from "feudalism to socialism," or from "nomadism to socialism," or simply their development "on the way to communism."

Some of the best work on the Soviet Asian peoples has been done in the field of ethnography and the study of culture. Teams of specialists have investigated the way of life, the customs, and the traditions of each of the Asian peoples, as well as their transformation under Soviet rule, that is, the impact of socialism and modernity on their traditional culture. Thus, there are studies of the "transformation of life and culture" of a particular people "in the epoch of the building of socialism"; of the changes in the lifestyle of this or that people; of the building of communism and the overcoming of "religious survivals."[328] The cultural revolution in Soviet Asian regions and the formation and development in these areas of a "technical intelligentsia" are also the subject of investigation.

Voluminous literature is available on the history of collectivization in various Soviet regions and republics. The authors discuss the beginning of collectivization, the initial difficulties and setbacks, and the successes and achievements of collective farming and livestock breeding. There is an equally impressive body of literature on the formation and history of the working class in various republics and parts of the Soviet Union. The discussion of nationality, nationhood, consolidation of small nations, state-building, and national and Soviet culture has furnished the subject matter for many studies of varying length.[329]

The Second World War and its aftermath in non-Soviet Asia have inspired a prodigious literature on contemporary history. A number of studies have been written on national liberation movements, on the noncapitalistic path of development, on revolutionary democratic dictatorship, on class struggle, on socialism and capitalism in the developing countries, and on the Marxist-Leninist position on nationality and colonial questions. The emergence of the developing nations is investigated systematically, with emphasis on the position of the working class, the peasantry, and the middle class, agrarian reform, the economies and governments of the developing countries, and relations among the Asian peoples.

Much effort has gone into the study of relations between the Asian peoples and the Soviet Union. Stress is laid on the progressive character of the Soviet Union, on its dedication to peace and the destruction of colonialism and imperialism, and on its many-sided benevolence toward the developing peoples. Many studies have been made, too, of Soviet economic and cultural relations with contemporary Asian states and peoples.

A mass of literature exists on colonialism and imperialism. Some of the studies are theoretical; others concern imperialistic domination and colonial oppression of particular Asian countries by European powers and the United States, which serves as a special target. The various activities of the United States are discussed at length, with the country being dubbed an apologist for colonialism and the creator of neocolonialism.

As indicated elsewhere, not all branches of Soviet Oriental studies are equally well developed. One of the oldest, however, is Arabistics.[330] Russian scholars have long been interested in the Arabs, in their civilization, their language, and their religion. The eighteenth century brought forth unprecedented interest in the Orient, and since then many Russians have traveled to that part of the world on official assignments or out of curiosity or interest in learning. V. R. Rozen (1849-1908) actually was the founder of the Russian school of Arabic studies. Three of his students, I. Iu. Krachkovskii, A. E. Schmidt, and A. E. Krymskii, were the mainstay of Soviet Arabistics.

Before the October Revolution the bulk of research centered on medieval Arab history and on Arab literature and language. Since the Revolution more and more attention has been given to modern and contemporary Arab history. Also, before the Revolution Russian Arabists limited their studies almost exclusively to the Arabs of the Arabian Peninsula, the Fertile Crescent, and Egypt. Since then, especially in more recent years, they have extended their research and scholarship to the southern part of the peninsula, the Persian Gulf, and North Africa.

After the Second World War Soviet scholars for the first time had a real opportunity to study in Arabic countries. Various cultural agreements were concluded with the United Arab Republic providing for exchange of scholars and students. Soviet and Egyptian archeologists participated in joint excavations, and a variety of Soviet scientists visited and worked in Egypt, Lebanon, Syria, Algeria, and Tunis.[331]

Apart from a few works of some merit on the ancient history of the Near East and the Middle East,[332] Soviet scholarship has not produced worthwhile studies of pre-Islamic Arabs and Arabia. The Soviet output has consisted for the most part of official interpretations of social conditions in Arabia before the advent of Islam and on the nature of Islam. Nor have Soviet scholars produced any significant contribution on medieval Arabs and Islam. Petrushevskii's much-praised "Islam in Iran" adds little to what is known about the subject.[333]

In the large volume of published material in the Soviet Union on the Arabs, there is hardly a work that will survive with time. With a few exceptions the Arabists have done no more than compile known information and squeeze it into a Marxist mold. Short accounts of modern history and contemporary developments have been written for each Arab state. In the series "Arabic Countries," published by the Soviet Academy of Science, about sixty books have appeared. Some treat the Arab world in general and others concern individual Arab countries.

The topics that most interest contemporary Soviet Arabists are the national liberation movements, the Arab struggle against Ottoman rule and Western imperialistic powers, the winning of independence and the building of a state, current politics and economics in Arab countries, the Israeli threat, neocolonialism and new efforts by Western powers to penetrate the Arab world, society and social classes, the role of the national bourgeoisie in the struggle for independence, the history of workers' movements and the present status of workers in Arabic countries, the role of government in noncapitalist development, the peasantry and land reform. The largest amount of published material is in the nature of propaganda diatribes directed against the United States, Israel, and the West. These efforts do not include a single comprehensive history of the Arabs. Beliaev's book on the "Arabs, Islam and the Arab Caliphate in the Medieval Period" covers only a part of Arab history.[334] The much-praised book by V. B. Lutskii entitled "Modern History of the Arab Countries"[335] concentrates on the nineteenth and twentieth centuries. The most comprehensive work on Arab history is a collectively written "Modern History of the Arab Countries," published in 1968.[336] Since the death of I. Iu. Krachkovskii (1883-1951) no comparable figure in Soviet Arabic studies has emerged.[337]

Recent Soviet writings on the Arab world furnish a good case study of adjustments to political expediency. In compliance with the decisions of the Twentieth Congress of the Communist Party of the Soviet Union (February 1956) and with new Soviet political objectives in the Middle East, the attitude toward the Arabs and Islam has changed in word and action. Soviet writers have abandoned their earlier rather dogmatic interpretation of the national liberation struggle, and the role of different social classes in the national liberation movement is currently being reassessed. It is now recognized that the bourgeoisie in the Arab countries and the bourgeois leaders can successfully lead the national liberation movement.

After 1956 the Arab bourgeoisie was no longer outrightly dismissed as a reactionary force, but was divided into the "upper bourgeoisie," which was allegedly betraying national interests, and the "national bourgeoisie," which played a progressive role. The Egyptian revolution and Nasser were seen as progressive forces in the development of contemporary Egypt. The movement toward Arab unity (the Arab League) was no longer rejected as a reactionary force but was seen as a positive development, since all the requisite conditions (political, economic, cultural, ethnic) exist for Arab national unity.

Comparable changes may be seen also in the Soviet treatment of Arab and Yemen. Until the assassination in 1958 of King Faisal II and Prime Minister Nuri as-Sa'id, Iraq merited little attention and little sympathy in Soviet literature on the Middle East. Since then, however, Soviet authors have often given Iraq greater respect, praising the Iraqi movement for national independence and heaping criticism on Ottoman, British, and American policies toward Iraq. Between 1928, when Yemen and the Soviet Union concluded a treaty of friendship, and the end of the Second World War, Soviet writers were for the most part soft on Yemen, but subsequently did not hesitate to speak out against its antiquated social and political institutions. In contrast, since 1957 one again notes in Soviet literature a friendly attitude toward Yemen, which grew even friendlier after the establishment of the republic in 1962.

During the twenties Saudi Arabia was treated with relative kindness. The Soviet Union established diplomatic relations with the Hijaz in 1924 and in 1926 with King Ibn Saud, whose son Amir Faisal visited the Soviet Union in 1932. But the thirties and the years following the Second World War witnessed strong criticism of Saudi Arabia because of its close relations with Britain and the

United States. After 1955 the Soviet attitude toward Saudi Arabia changed abruptly. This is apparent from a comparison of the Soviet interpretation of Wahhabism before and after that year. While Soviet authors in their earlier writings condemned Wahhabism as a totally negative movement, they now view it not only as a religious but also as a political movement, which they treat with greater tolerance and understanding.

After the Sudan won its independence in 1956, Soviet writers changed their line in regard to that country, too; they no longer advocated Egyptian-Sudanese union. The interpretation of the Mahdi movement has been modified as well. At present Soviet writers see in Mahdism both a political and a religious element; they describe the movement as a people's war against British rule.

The Soviet position with regard to Zionism has not been consistent. The Soviet Union condemned Hitler's persecution of Jews and was one of the first to recognize the state of Israel. Within a few years the Soviet Union reversed its position from one of sympathy to one of enmity for Israel; and since 1951 it has depicted Zionism as a capitalist ideology and Israel as a capitalist creation.

Islamic studies likewise have a long tradition in the Soviet Union. Initiated in formal fashion in the eighteenth century, they expanded greatly during the following century.[338] With the advent of communism, however, Islamic studies suffered badly. The investigation of religion and religious institutions was forced to follow the officially accepted line. Yet much has been published, though often under the sponsorship of antireligious organizations.

For Soviet scholars Islam is no different from any other religion. Islam is seen as the ideology of the ruling classes, which justifies human exploitation and social injustice. Though Soviet historians are not in agreement in all details regarding the character of social conditions that led to the emergence of Islam, they have provided a Marxist-Leninist explanation of the origin of Islam and of its role in history. They have written critiques of Pan-Islamism and various other movements within the Islamic community, such as Muslim modernism. Several authors have produced critical assessments of Western interpretations of Islam and its institutions.

Among the few acceptable studies of Islam are V. V. Bartol'd's "Islam," "The Muslim World," and "Muslim Culture." In more recent years several interesting works on Islam have appeared with a strong political and ideological flavor. These works treat Islam in general,[339] Shamil and Muridism,[340] the ideology of contemporary Islam,[341] Islam and the contemporary world,[342] the class content of Islam,[343] Islamic sectarianism,[344] the origins of Islam,[345] Islam and its reactionary essence,[346] Muslim survivals,[347] Ismailism,[348] and Wahhabis.[349] Krachkovskii published a new translation of the Koran in Russian, with a lengthy introduction.[350]

The Russians have been acquainted with various Turkic peoples from the beginning of their history, though serious scholarly investigations of the Turks did not start until the middle of the nineteenth century. The greatest Russian Turcologist was V. Radlov, who died in 1918. During the interwar period the leading Turcologists were A. N. Samoilovich, S. S. Malov, N. Ashmarin, E. Polivanov, V. V. Bartol'd, and N. N. Poppe. The quantity of Soviet research and publication on the Turkic peoples is enormous, and much of it is first-rate. Soviet scholarship on the Ottoman Turks is less good. After the Twentieth Congress, research and publication on Ottoman history and on modern Turkey expanded, particularly following the Turkish *coup d'état* of 1960 and the conclusion of various Soviet-Turkish agreements in 1963. Relations between the two countries have steadily improved and Soviet writers in general have become more tolerant of Turks. They contend that while the *coup* of 1960 did not bring basic changes in the country, it did spur the growth of democratic forces.

The Soviet interpretation of the origins of the Ottoman state, the character of Ottoman feudalism, the Ottoman conquest of Constantinople,[351] and the nature of Ottoman society are based partly on Marxist-Leninist ideas and are dictated partly by Soviet political interests. The social, ethnic, and religious movements in the Ottoman Empire against the Sultanic government are popular topics in Soviet historical circles.

The best Soviet survey of Ottoman history is A. D. Novichev's two-volume "History of Turkey,"[352] covering the period from the eleventh century on. The work is intended for the use of university students and lacks documentation. The first volume covers the period of feudalism from the eleventh to the eighteenth century. Part 1 of the second volume treats Ottoman history from 1792 to 1839; and Part 2, which has not yet been published, will cover the period since 1839. The short accounts of modern Turkish history by A. Miller and A. D. Novichev are too sketchy to be of much value.

Soviet historians are keenly interested in the Eastern question, in the Tanzimat reform movement, in the Ottoman constitutional struggle, and in the Young Turk Revolution. Russian relations with the Turks in the eighteenth and the nineteenth centuries, a very significant portion of Russia's history, have been treated in numerous studies. On this subject a great deal of documentary material has been published, treating in detail the Russo-Turkish wars and the careers of Russian military leaders. No work of real scholarly merit has appeared in the Soviet Union on Turkey in the First and Second World Wars, nor on Turkish international relations and internal developments since 1918. Two series of Russian foreign ministry documents dating from the beginning of the nineteenth century are currently appearing; they contain extensive material on Russo-Turkish relations.[353]

The greatest volume of Soviet publication on Turkey concerns the Kemalist period, the national liberation movement of the Turks (1918-23), social and economic questions, classes and the class struggle, the peasants and agriculture, the Turkish economy, foreign capital in Turkey, Turkey in the Second World War, Turkish relations with the United States, the working class, and recent trends in the Turkish political and economic scene. Much of this material has been hastily compiled and is superficial and clumsily slanted.

The shifts in Soviet policy toward Turkey since 1960 are reflected in historiography. For a brief period after the First World War, when the relations between the U.S.S.R. and Turkey were cordial, the Soviet historian was assigned the task of rendering sympathetic accounts of Kemalist Turkey. In the late thirties, when Soviet-Turkish relations had become strained, Soviet writers were less kind to the Turks. During the Second World War and for some years after, Soviet historians were severe critics of the Turkish government and of Turkish history. Since 1960 the Soviet historian is more reasonable in his presentation of modern Turkish history. Cultural relations with Turkey expanded after the conclusion in 1964 of an agreement on cultural and scientific exchange. This has enabled Soviet scholars to consult Turkish linguists, archeologists, and historians. One Soviet author observes that full cultural cooperation has been impeded somewhat because the Turks lack a single institution for coordinating scientific work.[354]

Russian contacts with Iran and India were established as early as the fifteenth century.[355] A. Nikitin visited Persia, India, and Turkey between 1466 and 1472 and recorded his observations of the Oriental world he saw. His work represents not only an important literary monument but also a valuable historical document on the countries he visited as well as on the Russia of his time. Several prominent men studied in Iran at the end of the eighteenth century and from then on. V. A. Zhukovskii (1858-1918) and K. G. Zaleman (1849-1916) were Russia's greatest Iranists. Zhukovskii specialized in the Iranian language, folklore, and ethnography, while Zaleman's specialties were Iranian languages, especially Ossetian, and lexicography. V. V. Bartol'd (1869-1930), the well-known Russian Orientalist, was equally at home in Turkic, Iranian, and Mongolian studies. He was the editor of the journal "Iran" and of several other publications issued during the interwar period. Two others who made valuable contributions are A. A. Freiman, expert on the Ossetian language and probably the greatest Iranist, and F. A. Rozenberg.

Excellent work has been done on the ancient period of Iran.[356] The work on Urartu, Media, Parthia, and other early civilizations has helped explain many obscure points concerning the territories of present-day Iran and adjacent regions of the Caucasus and Central Asia. Particularly distinguished historians of ancient Persia are V. V. Struve, I. M. D'iakonov, and a promising young historian M. A. Dandamaev.

Among several good studies on the medieval period are works treating Iran's international position,[357] agrarian and feudal relations,[358] medieval towns,[359] and Islam and Islamic institutions.[360] I. P. Petrushevskii is probably the best Soviet medieval historian of Iran. Most of the work written on the nineteenth century deals with Russo-Iranian relations, with British encroachments on Iran, with Babis and Bahais, and with social and reformist movements. Yet not one of these studies may be considered first-rate.

Developments in Iran at the beginning of the twentieth century are of great interest to Soviet historians. These involve Russo-Iranian relations, British and American penetration of Iran, and particularly the Iranian revolution of 1905-11, which has been the subject of several studies. Every aspect of the revolution has been investigated: leadership, class composition, ideology, and the impact of the Russian Revolution (1905-07) on the Iranian Revolution. Iran's position in the First World War has not received the attention it deserves, while the influence of the Bolshevik Revolution on Iran and Soviet-Iranian relations at the time have been the subject of several short works.

Before the Revolution Russian Iranists were primarily interested in the early history of Iran and in its language and literature. Since the Revolution Soviet scholars have branched out into the study of contemporary Iran. Iranian history since the First World War has received special attention. Soviet Iranists have written on the coming to power of Reza Shah, on the Iranian national liberation movement in the twenties, on the nationality problem, and on political, economic, and cultural developments.

The Second World War and its aftermath have been intensively investigated also. The topics that most interest Soviet writers are the democratic and anti-imperialistic movement, the socioeconomic transformation, the peasantry and agrarian reform, the working class and communism, the development of a national bourgeoisie, the problem of oil, and the policies of imperialistic states toward Iran. A few short studies have also been published on various peoples who inhabit Iran, such as the Armenians, the Kurds, the Bakhtiaris, and the Baluchis. Soviet-Iranian relations still remain one of the most studied subjects.

Of a number of short surveys and guidebooks published on recent political and economic developments, none appear to have real merit. The two best, however, are a collective history of Iran from the earliest period to 1800,[361] edited by the late N. V. Pigulevskaia and some of her colleagues; and a short survey of Iran up to the end of the Second World War.

Soviet pressure on Iran in the years immediately following the Second World War hampered the normal development of cultural relations between the two countries, and the animosity toward the Iranian government was reflected in Soviet historiography. Cultural relations have steadily improved, however, since 1954, when Soviet delegates participated in the one thousandth anniversary celebration in honor of Ibn Sina. Since that time Soviet scholars have been able to visit the country freely and to engage in research.[362]

We come now to Kurdistan, a land that has probably received more attention in recent times from Soviet writers and historians than from those of any other nation. This interest on the part of the Soviets is dictated by politics, by tradition, and by the fact that a portion of the Kurdish nation lives on Soviet soil. Although some good work has been done on the ethnogenesis of the Kurds and their early history, the bulk of the published materials is on the so-called Kurdish question, on the national liberation movement of the Kurds, and on present social and economic questions involving the Kurds, Soviet writers find themselves in an anomalous position regarding their attitude toward Kurdish history. While sympathetic to the Kurdish national liberation movement, they criticize Westerners who talk of a united Kurdistan, because Soviet historians see in this a move designed to detach territory from the Soviet Union.

Although contacts between Russia and Afghanistan have existed since the seventeenth century, it was not until after the Second World War that relations between the two countries became cordial. This opened up many-sided cultural cooperation and enabled Soviet scholars to visit the country and to study there.

Whereas Russian scholars for the most part neglected Afghanistan before the October Revolution, since then, and especially since the Second World War, all aspects of the country's history and society have been researched. The friendly relations between the two countries in recent years have made it possible for Soviet historians and other scholars to investigate Afghanistan more extensively than at any previous time, and for Soviet archeologists and geographers to do field work there.[363] The principal topics covered in Soviet works are development of feudalism and the founding of the Afghan state,[364] tribal relations, socioeconomic problems, formation of the national government, the struggle for independence in the nineteenth and twentieth centures, the Afghan struggle for independence in 1838-42, and relations between Afghanistan and the Central Asian khanates.

Published materials relating specifically to Afghanistan's history after the Second World War cover the country's foreign relations, especially its relations with the Soviet Union, postwar political, socioeconomic and cultural development, the growth of capitalism and commercial capital, economic planning and foreign aid, agriculture, and the working class. Many works have appeared on the country's postwar economic development. Among the more ambitious studies are R. T. Akhramovich, "Afghanistan after the Second World War,"[365] E. S. Nukhovich, "The Foreign Policy of Afghanistan,"[366] and L. B. Teplinsky, "Soviet-Afghan Relations, 1919-1960."[367] In addition, one or two short accounts of Afghanistan's general history have appeared, as well as a two-volume historical synthesis of Afghanistan from earliest times to 1965.[368] Soviet scholars have not produced a comparable survey for any other Near East or Middle East country.

We turn now to India, a country in whose history and culture the Russians have long been interested.[369] It is largely to the credit of I. B. Minaev (1840-90), who founded Russian Indian studies, that this branch of Soviet Orientology has become one of the more advanced. After the Bolshevik Revolution two of Minaev's students, S. F. Ol'denburg (1863-1934) and F. I. Shcherbatskoi (1866-1942), continued his work. Ol'denburg investigated Western Buddhism and Buddhist iconography on the basis of materials found at Karakhoto, while Shcherbatskoi specialized in Indian logic, on which he published a two-volume study. These men in their turn went on to train a number of excellent students, among them A. Barannikov, whose field is Indian linguistics; V. Kal'ianov, who is specializing in Indian philosophy; and N. Vinnikov and A. Freiman, experts on Indian literature and languages.

Russians trace their relations with India to A. Nikitin's visit to that country in 1466-72. Contacts with India expanded in the seventeenth and eighteenth centuries. After the founding of the Russian Academy of Sciences by Peter the Great more and more interest was shown in India. Russians began the study of Sanskrit in the middle of the eighteenth century; and before the close of the century G. Lebedev made three trips, while both Ol'denburg and Shcherbatskoi visited the country and studied there.

For a time after the October Revolution Indian studies were neglected, but since the Second World War the Soviet government has systematically encouraged research in this area. Soviet historians and other scholars are trying to provide a Marxian interpretation of and periodization for Indian history. In this connection they have been for some time discussing the so-called "Asiatic mode of production" and the nature of Indian feudalism.[370] Debate on these subjects continues, with the experts expressing a wide array of views.

After the Second World War the Soviet Union concluded cultural agreements with independent India that provide for the exchange of scholars. In addition various Soviet scientific teams and expeditions have been sent there. Soviet historians have shown particular interest in ancient and medieval socioeconomic formations, in agrarian relations, in ethnic and confessional problems, and in the history of different regions of India. They have produced studies on southern India from the fourteenth to the eighteenth century and on the agricultural structure of India between the thirteenth and the eighteenth centuries.

Several Indian classics have been translated and some good original work has been done on national and social movements and on literary, philosophical, and political developments since the seventeenth century. There are studies on the Mughal miniature paintings, on the economic situation in eighteenth-century Bengal, on the French colonies in India, and on the English conquest of India in the eighteenth century. Indian political activities and social unrest in the nineteenth century, relations with England, the 1857-59 uprising, Russo-Indian relations, and the Indian National Congress have been extensively treated. Among other subjects investigated have been the philosophy and work of Indian revolutionary leaders: Rama, Gandhi, and Nehru. Special interest has been shown by Soviet scholars in the impact on India of the October Revolution.

In the case of India, as with several other Eastern countries studied by Soviet researchers, the largest volume of published material covers the period since the end of the Second World War. There is a fine study on India during and after the Second World War.[371] A number of studies have appeared on the country's political and economic problems, on the working class and communism, on the national bourgeoisie, on industrial development, on agrarian reforms, on the peasant and nomad question, on the growth of capitalism, on the threat to India of Western neocolonialism and imperialism, on the expansion of American influence over India (1947-61), on the problem of food, on India's transportation system, on national liberation movements in India, on economic thought in modern India, on the history of the workers' movement, on the Indian princes, on the national question, on labor legislation, on the caste system, on economic problems, on relations with the Soviet Union, on the specifics of development of Indian capitalism and foreign monopoly capital, on American credits, on demography, on industry, on the Sikhs, and on the tea plantations. Soviet literary historians and critics follow closely the trends and activities in modern Indian literature. Several short surveys and guidebooks on India have been published, as well as a four-volume survey of Indian history from the earliest period to contemporary times.[372] This work, which is in general sketchy, is valuable primarily as a Soviet attempt at a Marxist interpretation of Indian history.

Modern Pakistan has received far less attention from Soviet scholars than has India. Nonetheless, cultural exchanges have broadened since 1945 and Soviet scholars have had the opportunity to visit and study in Pakistan. It is only since the fifties that some worthwhile research on Pakistan has been done, but there are probably no more than a half dozen persons in the whole of the U.S.S.R. working on this area. Some Soviet scholars have shown interest in the history of the relations between Pakistan and the peoples of Soviet Central Asia. Apart from many short studies of specific problems, several brief geographical and economic surveys have been published. The leading Soviet authority on Pakistan, Iu. V. Ganovskii, has published works on the "Peoples of Pakistan,"[373] and on "The Nationality Question and the Nationality Movement in Pakistan,"[374] and has participated in the writing of the "History of Pakistan.[375]

The most neglected segment of Russian and Soviet Oriental studies has been Southeast Asia. Most of the work on this subject is inferior in quality, highly political in tenor, and concerned primarily with current events. Probably the first serious contacts between Russians and the peoples of Southeast Asia were made by N. N. Miklukho-Maklai (1846-88) during his travels in the Pacific, when he visited New Guinea, Indonesia, Australia, Malaya, and the Philippines. Serious interest in Southeast Asia did not develop, however, until after the Second World War.[376] It was then that close cultural relations were established with Ceylon and that several Soviet scholars visited that country. Soon after the establishment of Soviet-Indonesian diplomatic relations in 1954, cultural relations were established with that country too. This afforded the opportunity for Soviet scholars to study the Indonesian language, history, and literature. Cultural relations established with Burma in 1955 led to a series of exchange visits between Soviet scientists and Burmese, and cultural relations were initiated with Thailand in 1957 and with Nepal in 1963.

Despite many short works on modern and contemporary Southeast Asia, Soviet accomplishments in this field are not impressive because of the lack of specialists. Most of what has been written concerns Indonesia. The main topics investigated are colonialism and imperialism, national liberation movements, economic developments, the Second World War, the formation of a bourgeoisie and a nation, the workers' movement, agrarian reforms, state capitalism, postwar development, American imperialism, and contemporary politics.

Collections of documents on Southeast Asia and a number of guidebooks on individual countries have been published.[377] In recent years short contemporary histories have been written on Burma, Ceylon, Thailand, North Viet Nam, and one or two other countries. The leading Soviet expert on Southeast Asia is A. A. Guber, the author of short studies on modern Indonesia and the Philippines and an organizer and promoter of Southeast studies in the Soviet Union. A. E. Belen'kii[378] and Guber have written books on the national awakening and national movement in Indonesia, and N. A. Simoniia on the Indonesian bourgeoisie and the formation of the Indonesian nation. There is also a brief account of Soviet-Indonesian relations between 1945 and 1962.[379] The collapse of the Sukarno regime in 1966-67 led Soviet historians to abandon some and to resume other research on Indonesia. The best studies on Indonesia and the rest of Southeast Asia are scattered through a number of symposiums. Several superficial works have been published on Viet Nam since the fifties, including studies of politics and war, agrarian reform, the working class, and the national liberation movement.

The Russians have manifested an interest in China since very early times, especially after the visit of I. Petlin[380] to that country in 1618. The foundations of Russian Sinology were laid by the Russian Religious Mission in Peking, sent there in 1714 by Peter the Great. From this Mission emerged the first Russian Sinologists.

Although there had been several distinguished Sinologists before
him, V. M. Alekseev (1881-1951) was probably the greatest Russian and Soviet Sinologist. His interests were many-sided. He wrote
on the history of Chinese literature, on culture and writing in
China, and conducted ethnographic investigations. Besides his own
original studies, he translated several Chinese works.

Sinology suffered a setback as a result of the Bolshevik Revolution from which it did not stage a recovery until after the Second
World War. This is not to imply, however, that the interwar period
was barren. On the contrary, several good works appeared in the
twenties and the thirties, and the prewar journals[381] carried among
many propagandistic articles a number of scholarly studies that
raised and attempted to solve many major historical questions
drawn from China's long, rich history.

The successful communist resistance and victory in China after
the Second World War generated feverish activity in Soviet Sinological circles.[382] A voluminous amount of material has been published in the past two decades dealing with all major phases of Chinese history and culture. In the promotion of this study of China
the government has invested generously. For a brief period of
time, 1956-60, there existed a separate Institute of Sinology in the
Soviet Academy of Sciences, but this was later merged with the
Institute of the Peoples of Asia. A determined effort was made to
produce as quickly as possible a large number of Chinese-speaking
experts, and scholars were encouraged to draw up ambitious research and publication plans. The result was that many persons
learned Chinese, and a large number of books and shorter works
on China were published.

A number of professional meetings were held on Chinese history, on Soviet studies of China, and on Chinese literature and language. Debates took place on the interpretations of the socioeconomic order in ancient China,[383] on the question of periodization
of history of ancient China, on the meaning of Marx's ideas concerning the "Asiatic mode of production," [383a] on the interpretation of the peasant uprisings in the medieval and later periods, and on
the genesis of Chinese civilization.[384] Although rich archeological
findings in China in recent years have thrown new light on many
aspects of ancient China, historians are still unable to agree on the
genesis of Chinese civilization.

Other topics currently being debated concern the interpretation of the ideology and class composition of the antifeudal uprisings in China in the medieval period.[385] Soviet scholars have published a number of monographs on the peasant rebellions and antifeudal uprisings from the tenth to the nineteenth century. Closely related problems studied by Soviet historians are the role played by non-Chinese peoples in the various uprisings and the character of medieval Chinese despotic rule and the guild system.

Soviet scholars have published prolifically on ancient and medieval Chinese authors, on art,[386] on culture, on philosophy, on learning, and on military science. Most active in these fields have been N. I. Konrad, A. A. Petrov, M. V. Shtein, and S. L. Tikhvinskii. The nineteenth-century topics investigated are social and national disturbances, economic conditions, Western encroachments, and Russo-Chinese relations. Among other works there is an interesting study on the "First Russo-Chinese Agreement, 1689."[387] The Taipei Rebellion is another much-discussed topic.[388] Soviet historians appear to be highly interested in the Revolution of 1911 and Sun Yat-sen. Besides two books on the 1911 Revolution (by E. A. Belov in 1958 and V. I. Danilov in 1959), several articles have been published on the revolution itself and on the political views of Sun Yat-sen.[389]

On the interwar developments in China the topics of most lively interest to Soviet scholars are the emergence and growth of the Chinese Communist movement, the Chinese national liberation movement, Soviet relations with Chinese communists, and Soviet volunteers in China. Some of the most impressive work has been that on Chinese literature, both classical and modern. Among the scholars particularly active in this area are V. I. Semanov, B. L. Riftin, V. Sorokin, L. Eidlen, L. Cherkasskii, N. T. Fedorenko, O. L. Fishman, and N. I. Konrad. At least two histories on Chinese literature were published after the war, as well as a great many studies on individual authors and specific literary topics.

The largest volume of work has been that concerned with the period since the founding of the People's Republic of China. The topics investigated in this connection are Sino-Soviet relations, China and Western imperialism, political and economic developments in the Chinese People's Republic, Chinese foreign relations, and the United States and China. On this last topic alone at least a half dozen books have appeared since 1960. The most controversial problems in recent history have been the definition and the periodization of the Chinese Revolution. Some Soviet historians have contended, for instance, that the Chinese Revolution had a peasant character. This controversy was resolved by the acceptance of Mao's doctrine that the 1949 Chinese Revolution was socialistic.

Another much-discussed question was whether the military form of Chinese revolutionary struggle should be the model for revolutionary movements in colonial and semicolonial countries. Soviet historians were of the opinion that armed struggle was not requisite for successful revolutions in other countries.[390] They explain that until 1959 historians accepted many "dogmas" from Chinese writings, but that since 1960 they have returned to independent investigation, trying to revise what they previously accepted. Soviet historians reject the Chinese identification of the Chinese revolutionary movement with the leading international (communist) workers' movement.

Even though the amount of published material on China is large, much of it is mediocre. The short account of the recent history of China by G. V. Eftimov[391] and a multiauthor work published later[392] are sketchy and superficial. The same is true of a short survey of Chinese history from the earliest period to the mid-seventeenth century.[393] Soviet scholars have not yet produced a comprehensive history of China.

As for Tibet, long before the Revolution Russian Orientalists were interested in this country and had acquired a fine collection of Tibetan manuscripts. G. Ts. Tsybikov (1873-1930), linguist and ethnographer of Buriat origin, was first to visit Tibet (1899-1902). He wrote several works on Tibetan and Mongol philology. Well-known Sinologist V. P. Vasil'ev (1818-1900), who produced many studies on Buddhism and Oriental religions, was the only one of his contemporaries in Russia who knew both Tibetan and Chinese. N. Kiuner (b. 1877), geographer and historian, had to his credit more than three hundred works on different Oriental questions, including one on Tibet. Like other branches of Orientology, Tibetology was set back by the Revolution and did not recover until the return to the Soviet Union of Iu. N. Rerikh (1902-60), who had spent many years in India (1923-57). Rerikh, an expert on Oriental languages, religions, and history, produced several works on Tibetan history and language. In recent years a number of studies on Tibet and some chronicles have been published. Of the latest studies the best are "A Sketch of the History of the Tibetan Peoples" by V. A. Bogoslovskii[394] and a book on Tibetan historical literature by A. I. Vostrikov.[395]

So far as investigations on Manchuria, the Soviet Far East, and the regions bordering China are concerned, these have been uneven in quality. Most of the work of consequence in this broad area has been on archeology and ethnography rather than on history.[396] Whatever investigation of Manchuria has taken place has been primarily in the context of Chinese-Manchurain relations; the internal history of Manchuria has been neglected. A few historians of note have written on Manchuria, among them L. I. Duman, G. S. Kara-Murza, E. V. Shavkunov, E. I. Kychanov, V. E. Larichev, and M. V. Vorob'ev. Much interesting material appeared in the *Vestnik Man'chzhurii* (Manchurian Herald), which was for years published in Harbin. Manchurian studies are not as well developed as are Altain and Mongol studies.

The study of archeology, ethnography, language, and literature of the Mongols and Altais has been impressive. Mongol studies began in earnest in Russia in the second quarter of the nineteenth century. By the time of the October Revolution there were several good Mongolists, but most of them left the country after the Revolution. The best Soviet experts on the Mongols were B. Ia. Vladimirtsov (1884-1931) and N. N. Poppe. The Soviet Union had probably the largest collections of Mongol and Tibetan books and manuscripts existing anywhere. This fact, combined with the accident of geography, as well as the relations between the Russians and the Mongols, helped to create a climate that favored the development of Mongolian studies. Vladimirtsov was equally at home in ethnography, in linguistics, in literature, and in history. He wrote on Mongol literature and language, on epic poetry, and on religion. Probably his three best books are "Buddhism in Tibet and Mongolia" (1919), "Genghiz Khan" (1922), and "The Social Order of the Mongols" (1934).

A variety of investigations have been in progress in connection with the early history of the Mongols, with their social organization, with their expansion and relations with neighbors, especially

China, and with their language and literature.[397] The most compre-
hensive work on this people is Grekov and Iakubovskii's study of
the Golden Horde.[398] There have also been investigations of the
Mongol chronicles and other types of historical literature.[399] One
Soviet author published a collection of Chinese documents on the
Mongols,[400] and another a study of Mongol social organization
based on the work of a seventeenth-century Mongol historian.
A great deal has been published on the contemporary Mongol
People's Republic, but the main focus has been on the building of
socialism in the country[401] and on the country's relations with the
Soviet Union. The topics most thoroughly investigated in regard to
modern Mongolia are the people's democracy and socialist construction, rural transformation, cultural development, formation
of the Mongol nation, and Soviet-Mongol relations. The few available surveys on modern and contemporary Mongolia have little
merit.[402]

Russian historians and Orientalists seriously neglected Japanese
history and culture until the end of the nineteenth century. The
Russians had tried to establish contact with Japan in 1738 and
again in 1791 and 1793. But it was not until a hundred years later,
when a chair of Japanese language and literature was established in
the University of St. Petersburg in 1898, that the first really serious effort was made to investigate the history and culture of the
Japanese people. The leading experts on Japan were O. Rozenberg
(1888-1919), a specialist on Buddhism, which he studied on the
basis of Chinese and Japanese sources, and D. M. Pozdneev (1865-
1942), a philologist, historian, and economist, who, among other
accomplishments, compiled the first Russo-Japanese hieroglyphic
dictionary. To these names one should add N. I. Konrad (b. 1891),
who is considered the founder of the Soviet school of Japanese
studies and has published many works on the literature, language,
and history of Japan, China, and Korea.

After the Second World War Soviet historians began to devote
even more attention to Japan. The changed political situation and
the capture of Japanese military archives by the Red Army may
have contributed in some ways to the increased interest in Japan.
But it was more than this. The strategic location of Japan and its
remarkable economic recovery[403] were also contributing factors.
Various aspects of Japanese history, economy, culture,[404] and literature have been investigated. There is a book on the social and

economic history of Japan in the period of late feudalism by A. L.
Gal'perin (1896-1960),[405] and four works on Russo-Japanese relations, including one on the period from 1697 to 1895,[406] one on
the period from 1905 to 1945,[407] and one on the period from 1895
to 1907.[408] Soviet scholars are interested in the Japanese workers'[409] and peasants' movements[410] and have produced several studies of Japanese literature and language. Besides a number of general
guidebooks, they have written also on Japanese monopoly capitalism, on the position and the activity of the working class and the
peasantry, on the major political parties, on the development of
capitalism, on the nature of feudalism, on the essence of the Meiji
revolution, and on philosophical trends and Marxist thought. The
best short survey to appear on modern Japanese history, a collective effort,[411] is more important for the way it reflects the Soviet
historian's interpretation of Japanese history than as a scholarly
contribution.

Studies on Korea represent the newest branch of Soviet Orientology.[412] The first serious investigations in this area began in the
fifties. Some work has been published on the ancient[413] and medieval period of Korea, on tribes, feudalism,[414] on culture and cultural monuments, and on peasant uprisings.[415] But most of the
published material relates to the modern and recent period of
North Korea. There is a short history of Korea since the nineteenth
century.[416] The most popular topics on Korea have been the national liberation movement,[417] the formation of the working class and
the national bourgeoisie[418] and their part in the liberation movement, agriculture and the peasantry[419] and the building of socialism,[420] and economic development.[421] There is a good study of
Korea in the second half of the nineteenth century,[422] as well as a
few short guidebooks on Korea in general.

In this brief survey of Soviet Oriental studies it has not been
possible to discuss every major work on the Orient published in
the Soviet Union. The aim has been rather to present an overall
picture of Soviet Oriental studies and to focus on the main trends
and tendencies in it. Planned research on the Orient in the Soviet
Union has yielded an enormous quantity of published material.
Yet there are glaring gaps. The most obvious is the lack of acceptable surveys of the histories of the non-Soviet Asian peoples. Soviet Orientalists apparently shy away from historical syntheses because these involve too many controversial problems. They also

shy away from topics that are peripheral to or incompatible with official ideology.

The Soviet Orientalist works under difficult conditions. Not only is he obliged to write in accordance with the ideological and political requirements of the state, but he is frequently directed to produce propaganda brochures. It is all too obvious that this has stifled creative efforts and has demanded compromises. The task of the Orientalist is further complicated by the fact that Soviet leaders have arrogated unto themselves the sole right to interpret history for the communist world, and to proclaim historical dogma. This monopoly, challenged by China and by one or two other communist countries, must be defended by the Soviet Orientalist.

Full development of Soviet Oriental studies has been further impeded by the lack of trained specialists on some of the Oriental countries, by excessive official interference, by frequent reorganizations of research centers, and by a shortage of printing facilities and Oriental typeset. Progress is hampered, too, by changes in the Soviet government's internal and foreign policy which periodically requires revisions of interpretations of men and events in history. These arbitrary shifts in policy account for the repudiation of many fine studies on Soviet Asian peoples written before 1950, as well as for the discrediting of much work on China produced before 1960. The Soviet Communist Party has succeeded in standardizing the interpretations of basic historical questions and in coordinating research efforts. The firmer party control no longer permits historiographic controversies reminiscent of the early postwar years, with the result that opposing views on basic historical problems are neither presented nor tolerated. Yet Oriental studies continue to grow and to enjoy high priority in Soviet scholarly work. In light of the existing situation, the new contributions of Soviet Orientologists are bound to arouse considerable attention.

—4—

The Muslims of European Russia
and the Caucasus

Alexandre Bennigsen

In this essay we are interested in four Muslim regions of Russia: the Mid-Volga region, the Crimea, the Northern Caucasus, and Muslim Transcaucasia. These regions lack territorial, ethnic, or even cultural unity. Territorially the Muslims of European Russia are separated one from the other by vast areas that are populated exclusively by Russians or by other Christian peoples such as Georgians and Armenians. Ethnically the Muslims of European Russia are predominantly people of Turkish race: Tatars and Bashkirs on the Mid-Volga; Nogais, Kumyks, Balkars, and Karachais in the foothills and in the mountains of the Northern Caucasus; the Azeris in Transcaucasia; and Tatars in the Crimea. In the mountains of the Caucasus live peoples belonging to the Ibero-Caucasian ethnic group: Adygeis, Cherkess, Kabardians, Abazin, Abkhaz, Chechen, Ingush, and the smaller ethnic elements of Daghestan. There are also Muslims who belong to the Iranian group: Ossetians in the Central Caucasus, Tates in Daghestan, Talysh and Kurds in Transcaucasia.

The religious unity of the Muslims considered in this study is more real. The great majority of the Muslims of European Russia and the Caucasus are Sunni of the Hanafite rite (the Daghestanis adhere to the Shafiite rite). Only in Transcaucasia do we find a majority of Shiites.

Historical and cultural traditions, too, vary from region to region. The Volga Tatars, the heirs of the Kama Bulgars, were Islamicized very early and preserved vivid memories of the traditions of the Golden Horde and the Kazan khanate. The historical traditions of the Bashkirs, a peasant and seminomadic people, resemble more the nomads of the Kazakh steppes. In the Crimea, an Ottoman vassal state until the end of the eighteenth century, the predominating cultural and ethnic influence was Turkish, while in Shiite Transcaucasia the paramount ethnic and linguistic influence was Iranian. During the nineteenth century the culture of the mountaineers of the Central Caucasus and Daghestan was given the indelible imprint of Shamil's *Imamate*.[1] which in the name of Arab culture and language unified them for more than half a century.

Finally, the Muslim peoples whom we are discussing varied in their stages of social evolution from those who lived as clans or as tribes to those who were already formed into nations. In general, the peoples whose land had previously been conquered by the Russians had already been drawn into the current of capitalistic development. Their social structure, however, differed from region to region and according to the different types of administration that the Russians imposed upon them. In the Crimea, for instance, the landed nobility preserved its privileges, while that of the Volga region had been displaced by the bourgeoisie. In the lands that the Russians conquered during the nineteenth century, on the other hand, the Muslim peoples remained in a stage of feudal or prefeudal development. On the eve of the Revolution, the mountaineers of the Caucasus still lived in a perfectly preserved clan organization.

THE RUSSIANS AND THE MUSLIMS BEFORE 1917

The first contacts between Russians and the Volga Muslims go back to the Middle Ages, to the time of the conversion of the Golden Horde to Islam.[2] At the outset these contacts were noteworthy for their spirit of religious liberalism—a policy that was to be abandoned in the sixteenth century. The sovereigns of the Golden Horde, faithful to the Genghis Khan tradition of religious tolerance, prohibited all manifestations of religious fanaticism. If the "Tatar Yoke" weighed heavily on the back of Russia, the Orthodox Church got along with it well. Alongside the Muslims and Jews, the Christians of all confessions (Orthodox, Nestorian, and Roman Catholics) had churches in Sarai, the capital of the Horde. Proselytism was prohibited by the Mongol-Tatars. Moreover, the sovereigns of the Golden Horde, being quite indifferent to religious matters, were not seriously interested in converting their Russian vassals. Those who were converted became quickly "Tatarized." Numerous Tatars of the feudal nobility abandoned the Horde and entered the service of the Russian princes. These "Vykhodtsy" were considered equals by the Russian nobility; they and the troops they brought with them were in general converted to Orthodox Christianity. In taking this course and by adopting the language and the outlook of their new fellow-countrymen, these Tatars soon became Russified. This sort of fusion explains the presence among the old Russian nobility of families with such Turkish names as Mansurov, Urusov, Bakhtiiarov, Uvrov, Davydov, Iusupov.

For a long time the Tatars and the Russians tolerated one another's religion. This was true even when, in the fourteenth century, the young Muscovite state, under Dimitrii Donskoi (1350-89), tried to shake off the Tatar yoke. In this period the Tatars refused to give their wars against the Russians the character of a "Holy War." During the sixteenth century, when the Muscovite state launched an offensive against its former Tatar suzerains and initiated its conquest of eastern and southern Muslim territories, this situation changed. This conquest of the Muslim lands, which was neither a preconceived plan nor an established policy, lasted until the end of the nineteenth century, when the Russian armies reached the frontiers of India and China.

The Muscovite state, a unified Great Russian state, launched an offensive against the khanate of Kazan in 1552. At that time the terms "Russian" and "Orthodox" were indistinguishable, and the war against the Volga Muslims was looked upon as a "crusade" led in the name of the Christian faith against the "impure" (the *Busurmans*). The Tatars themselves justified the defense of their country as the *gazavat* (Holy War against the Infidel). The brutal character of the struggle and the merciless Russian repression of the Tatars greatly affected the relations between the Russians and the Volga Muslims. This explains why of all the Muslims of Russia the Tatars knew best how to oppose the Russian influence and became the main opposing force to Russia and the Russians.

The Crimea was annexed by Russia in 1783, under Catherine II, at a time that was from many standpoints the most liberal of all Russian history. The peninsula was annexed by an aristocratic and multinational empire, governed by a sovereign who did not conceal her sympathies for the Prophet's religion and who was aware of the importance of national problems. The take-over did not encounter any serious opposition nor was it accompanied by destruction. The Russians tried, at least in the beginning, to gain the sympathies of a fraction of the Muslim population, the feudal landed nobility and the "clergy."

By contrast, in the Muslim territories of the Caucasus conquered by arms during the second half of the nineteenth century, when the tsarist empire was entering the era of capitalistic development, the Russian administration did not try to rally the local population to itself. The Northern Caucasus became pacified only after long and bloody wars against the mountaineers. The country was too poor and too populous to support rural colonization, and until the Revolution of 1917 remained a typical military colony, an unviolated territory where the Russians were content simply to maintain order.

In eastern Transcaucasia, which the Russians had wrested from the Iranian Empire, they did not encounter nation-wide resistance on the part of the local population, for the arrival of the Russians put an end to a long and bloody period of unrest and was not followed by any appropriation of the land. There was no Russian rural colonization; and only the army and some administrative officials represented the power of St. Petersburg, which, although interfering occasionally, was a long way off. The landed nobility retained its economic power, and the local bourgeoisie profited by the exploitation of the country, gaining great additional power after the discovery of oil at Baku.

The various policies pursued by the tsarist government in each of these four regions followed logically from the modes of conquest themselves.

The Muslim Mid-Volga

In the Volga region, the Russian military conquest was followed by systematic occupation. The Muslims were expelled from the city of Kazan and the best lands were confiscated and distributed among the Russian landed gentry, the Kazan Archbishopric, and the numerous monasteries that began to appear on the Mid-Volga immediately after the conquest. This first occupation was followed during the second half of the sixteenth century by the flow of Russian peasants escaping from serfdom who came to settle on the most fertile lands. Finally, in order to maintain order and to protect the territory against the incursions of nomads, the country was covered with a net of fortresses populated exclusively by Russians. Russian colonization, interrupted for a while during the Time of Troubles, was resumed in the beginning of the seventeenth century and continued until the reign of Catherine II.[3]

At the end of the eighteenth century, the population of the Volga territory was already predominantly Russian. The Muslim Tatars constituted less than forty percent and the Russians fifty percent, the remainder being represented by various eastern Finnish peoples (Maris, Udmurts, Mordovians, etc.) or by non-Muslim Turks (Chuvash).[4] The ratio of the Tatars to Russians has remained unchanged until today.

This phenomenon has had a great influence—an influence that still persists—on relations between the Russians and the Volga Muslims. Tatars were overwhelmed by Russian colonization. The two communities were tightly bound one to the other, with compact Russian villages next to purely Tatar settlements, or living together in mixed localities. Under these conditions, any active resistance to the Russian presence was impossible. On the other hand, from the seventeenth century on, the most dynamic elements among the Tatars developed the habit of expatriating themselves. At certain times this movement resembled a mass exodus. Today, among the five million Tatars found in the Soviet Union, only 1,345,000 inhabit the national territory of the Volga.[5] As a consequence, there developed a Tatar diaspora with merchant colonies scattered throughout Siberia, the Caucasus, Central Asia, and even European Russia. This phenomenon, which put the Volga Tatars in contact with their coreligionists from Turkestan and from the Caucasus and, beyond its borders, even with those from the Ottoman Empire, was to have profound influence on their *Weltanschauung*, by reinforcing their attachment to Islam.

In addition, it gave rise to still another obstacle to their assimilation by the Russians. Over more than two centuries, from 1552 to 1764, the Russians practiced a rigid policy aiming at the absorption of the Volga Muslim community. The Tatars and the other Volga peoples, whatever their religion, were considered subjects of the Russian state, bound to all obligations, but at the same time second-class subjects to whom all the rights recognized for Christians were denied.

Since the Tatar feudal nobility and the Muslim clergy, who in the sixteenth century had inspired all the revolts against their domination, were the most dangerous adversaries of the Russians, the Russians first conducted their attack against these two classes. The Muslim clergy lost all material power through the requisition of property in mortmain (*waqfs*), religious officials were pursued and jailed, the mosques and the koranic schools (*mektebs* and *medreses*) were destroyed. Between 1738 and 1755 alone one particularly zealous archbishop of Kazan ordered the destruction of 418 of the 536 mosques of the Kazan region.[6] The offensive against the landed nobility, who were decimated by the conquest, was begun under the first Romanovs by a series of measures that prohibited the possession of Christian slaves by Muslim landowners.[7] The long decline of the Tatar nobility commenced at the beginning of the seventeenth century and was accelerated even more under the reign of Peter the Great, when a decree gave the Muslim landowners of the Volga six months to be converted to Christianity or see their lands and serfs confiscated by the State.[8] This measure was a mortal blow to the old indigenous nobility, who from that time played only a minor role in Muslim society. Its most dynamic elements became merchants or small manufacturers; the others, ruined, rejoined the mass of free peasants.

The destruction of the ruling classes represented the negative aspect of assimilation pursued with tenacity by the Russian state. The positive aspect consisted of converting the Muslim Tatars and the animist peoples of the Volga to Orthodox Christianity. Inaugurated as early as 1555 by the first archbishop of Kazan and pursued during the whole second half of the sixteenth century, this policy of forced conversion was crowned, at least in the beginning, by apparent success, since it led to the appearance about the end of the sixteenth century of an important community of Christian Tatars, the *Kriashens* (or rather *Staro-Kriashens*, Old Converts, to distinguish them from the *Novo-Kriashens*, Neo-Converts, baptized in the eighteenth and nineteenth centuries).[9]

Although the policy of conversion to Christianity was somewhat deëmphasized during the Time of Troubles and under the first

Romanovs, it was resumed under Peter the First and was pursued with increasing vigor until the reign of Catherine II. Various means were attempted either progressively or simultaneously, such as the use of propaganda, creation of special schools attached to the monasteries and to the archbishopric of Kazan for the children of baptized Tatars, administrative measures designed both to prompt conversions and to penalize those who persisted in their attachment to the religion of the Prophet. The neophytes were exempted from all duty, taxes, corvees, obligations, and conscription, whereas the Tatars who remained Muslim were forced to assume the burden of taxes and conscription for their converted brothers. Moreover, to prevent any contact between Christian and Muslim Tatars and to protect the Christian faith of the neophytes, the Muslims were expelled from the villages in which there were converts and deported into the farthest regions of the country. Finally, all Muslim proselytism was prohibited under pain of death.

To coordinate these measures there was founded in Kazan in 1731 a semicivil, semiecclesiastic organization called the "Office of the Neophytes" (*Novokreshchenskaia Kontora*), which had broad administrative powers and possessed its own military force. The activities of the "Office," in particular the forced conversion of children, the systematic destruction of mosques, and the deportation of Muslims, were to leave a bitter and indelible imprint on the memory of the Tatars; and the balance sheet of almost two centuries of direct offensive against Islam appears very meager. Of course, this offensive contributed to creating an important community of converts, the *Novokriashens*, apparently numbering some 400,000 souls at the end of the eighteenth century. But only in appearance were these neophytes Christians; and for the most part they were former animists, not Muslims. In spite of the support of the civil authorities, the "Office" was not able to put an end to Muslim proselytism among the Finnish animists, but provoked the massive flight of Muslims toward the Urals, the land of the Bashkirs, and Siberia. Finally, the hatred caused by the "Office's" policy was not unrelated to the participation of the Muslim Tatars and especially of the *Kriashens* in the great popular uprisings of the second half of the eighteenth century, in particular the Pugachev Rebellion.[10]

The policy of forced assimilation completely stopped under

Catherine II, and for almost a century afterward the relations between the Russian authorities and the Muslim Tatars were marked by tolerance. This spectacular sudden change may be variously explained: the lesson of Pugachev's revolt; the empress's personal sympathies for Islam; but above all the desire to use the dynamism of the Tatars in order to facilitate the penetration of the young Russian state into Asia.

In 1764 the "Neophytes' Office" was suppressed and Christian proselytism was discouraged. In 1767 the Muslims received authorization to build mosques in the city of Kazan, and then in other cities of the Volga. In 1773 a decree conferred religious freedom over the whole expanse of the Empire,[11] and in 1782 Catherine II granted Russian Islam a supreme spiritual authority, the Orenburg *Muftiat*,[12] the immediate consequence of which was the widespread apostasy of the Neo-Converts. At the end of the century the number of Christian Tatars who were ready to revert to Islam was estimated at 250,000.[13] At the same time that it abandoned the policy of assimilation, the government of Catherine II granted the Tatar merchant class exceptional favors that made it the intermediary between Russian industries and markets of Central Asia still closed to Unbelievers. Tatar merchant colonies were thus able to branch out toward the east and the southeast of the Empire, in the track of the Russian armies or even preceding them into the Kazakh steppes and the mountains of the Urals, into Turkestan, the Caucasian foothills, and Siberia.[14] Everywhere the Tatar merchants brought Muslim culture and religion with them, reinforcing their economic ascendancy with cultural and political influence. As a consequence, by an apparently paradoxical phenomenon the extension of the Russian administration into Asia was accompanied not by the Russification but by the Islamization and the Tatarization of the animist, or superficially Muslim, natives.[15]

The era of liberalism in Russian-Muslim relations ended around 1860, when a new period of pressure on Islam began. At that time the conception of the Empire was beginning to be modified under the influence of Slavophile ideas. From then on, for the ruling class and for the Russian church, the Russian-Orthodox identification was continuously strengthened. In this context, the abjuration of the Orthodox faith by the indigenous masses became apostasy and a veritable national treason. But all the measures applied in the preceding centuries had shown their ineffectiveness. The Tatars and the Bashkirs of the Volga-Urals were citizens of the Empire but still formed a heterodox bloc, loyal and submissive to the authorities, but resolutely attached to its own faith and culture. The decade of the 1860s also corresponded to the beginnings of the awakening of Islam. Almost everywhere, in Muslim India, as well as in the Arab countries, in Persia, and of course in the Ottoman Empire, modernistic thinkers who were determined to shake off the long torpor that had characterized the inaction of the *Dar ul-Islam* sought to reconcile Islam and progress in order to regain power and to free themselves from the ascendancy of the Occident. The ideas of the Turkish reformers of the epoch of the *Tanzimat* began to penetrate, though still almost imperceptibly, into the Muslim world of Russia, bringing the hope of a possible renaissance.

But, at the same time, with Central Asia being annexed to the Empire,[16] the Russian merchant class could henceforth avoid the Tatar intermediary. Former associates, the Russian and Tatar bourgeoisies now became rivals; and the Russian authorities then sought to limit the economic and cultural influence of the Tatars over their coreligionists, the Bashkirs, the Kazakhs, and the Turkestanis. A new crisis between Russians and Tatars was inevitable.

The offensive begun in 1860 reassumed the old policy of Christianization that had been abandoned a century earlier, but the methods were more supple and more efficient; they tried to attract the Tatars and the other indigenous peoples of the Volga to Christianity through education and propaganda.[17] Conjointly pursued by the Orthodox Church and the civil authorities, this original policy of indirect assimilation sought to turn the indigenous peoples to Christianity, without directly Russifying them; the new converts were to preserve their own tongue and culture. The creation of a net of indigenous schools, the development of literary languages (in Cyrillic characters), and intense proselytism—an effort comparable to that which the Soviet government was to undertake among the same peoples in the thirties and forties in order to denationalize them—all these bear witness to the prodigious effort to succeed where the record of preceding centuries had been marked by failure.

By the end of the nineteenth century about 200,000 Tatars, as well as all of the Finnish animists, had been converted to Orthodoxy.[18] This policy deeply marked relations between Russians and Muslims. More than the economic rivalry, the mortal menace of

Christianization aroused all the Tatar elite against Russia and provoked a deep and abiding aversion to everything Russian.

By the outbreak of the Revolution of 1917, the pressure exerted by Russians over the Muslim Tatars led, as noted above, to the total transformation of the social structures of the Tatar community. The landed nobility completely disappeared; the Muslim "clergy" became indigent and was dispersed. This phenomenon is worth noting because it gives to Tatar Islam its unique character in the *Dar ul-Islam*. On the eve of the Revolution it was a popular religion, strongly rooted in the *peasant milieu* (not, as everywhere else, a religion of city dwellers), and was represented by a thick stratum of clerks (*mullahs*) of peasant extraction, very poor, pugnacious, and often ready to accept the most revolutionary ideas (it is enough to recall that there were many *mullahs* or sons of *mullahs* among the first Tatar socialist leaders).[19] The peasant mass—more than ninety percent of the Tatar population at the beginning of the twentieth century—although poorer than the neighboring Russian peasantry, had a surprisingly high cultural level. In 1897, twenty percent of the Tatars of the Kazan government knew how to read and write, a percentage superior to that of the Russians in the same region (eighteen percent). It was the unshakable faith of the Muslim rural masses in Islam that caused all attempts at assimilation to fail. Finally, above the other classes there was the commercial or industrial bourgeoisie, rich, powerful, dynamic, and convinced that without profound modification of the mental structures of the whole Muslim society, the Tatar community would not long be able to resist Russian pressure. The reformist movement in Russian Islam was the result of the action led by the Tatar bourgeoisie supported by the "clergy" and sustained by all other strata of the indigenous society.[20] At the beginning of the twentieth century, the Tatars were the only Muslims in the world to possess such a "modern" social structure, and they seemed better equipped than anyone else to withstand the pressures of a foreign civilization.[21]

On the level of material borrowings, the Russian influence on the Tatar rural masses was minimal. Up to the twentieth century, the Tatar wooden house, although resembling the Russian *izba*, retained its special character; the furnishings remained traditional—rugs and pillows instead of furniture. As for men's and women's clothing, this was perfectly suited to Tatar living conditions and bore not the slightest resemblance to Russian garb. Finally, the Tatar traditional cuisine did not undergo any changes; it was rather the Russians who adopted Tatar dishes.

As for activity in the indigenous arts and crafts, the Tatars had well-developed handicrafts before 1917 that were of purely Oriental inspiration and owed nothing to Russian influence. Eighty percent of the population were craftsmen in woodworking, fabrics (wood and linen), leather, and precious metals. Only in the domain of agriculture did the Volga Tatars adopt, from the eighteenth century on, the methods of cultivation and the ploughing instruments of the Russians.

Russian intellectual and spiritual influence is more difficult to evaluate. It is known that the long policy of Christianization had attained undeniable results, since some 200,000 Tatars were Orthodox Christians. But the majority of this number was actually composed of crypto-Muslims ready to return to Islam—which they in fact did after the Revolution. On the religious level, therefore, the Russian effort appears to have met with almost total failure. But Russian influence on the Tatar language was more substantial. After more than 350 years of the two peoples living side by side, it was inevitable that many Russian words and expressions should enter the Tatar language. As an example we may cite the stenographic reports of the two congresses of the Muslims of Russia of 1905 (held in Nizhnii Novgorod) and of May 1917 (held in Moscow).[22] It may easily be seen that the borrowings from Russian were particularly numerous in the domain of administration and in the political vocabulary, where Russian expressions succeeded in displacing the Arabic terms formerly used, as, for example, *zakon* (law), *sobranie* (assembly), *prighovor* (decision), *siktsiia* (section), *program, istatiia* (article).

But in other political areas the borrowings from Russian remained limited. The brilliant pleiad of writers who illuminated Tatar literature at the end of the nineteenth century and the beginning of the twentieth succeeded in guarding the Tatar language from contamination. On the eve of the Revolution of 1917, the Kazan Tatar was certainly less "Russified" than the Osmanli Turk was "Frenchified."

On the spiritual level the secular menace had given Volga Islam its fiercely conservative character. For centuries the whole Muslim community retired within itself, and refusing all contacts with the Russians lived in a climate of intellectual conservatism and of intransigent religious formalism. This made any cultural symbiosis with the Russians doubtful. Lacking indigenous spiritual leaders, it was to Bukhara and to Daghestan, the two great centers of rigorous Islamic traditionalism, that the Tatars turned for spiritual direction.

After 1880, when the reformist movement began, the modernist Tatar theologians, such as Musa-Yarulla Bigi or Rizaeddin Fahreddinoglu, sought their inspiration in Turkey and in the Arab countries, but never in philosophical Russian trends. In the spiritual domain, Russians and Tatars lived on two very different levels up to 1917.

As for Russian influence on the intellectual level, this is even more difficult to evaluate. Practically nonexistent up to 1880, it was becoming stronger and stronger until 1905, when some other influences, especially Turkish ones, began to make themselves felt. Beginning with the closing years of the century, when a small number of the Tatar intelligentsia were completing their studies in Russian universities, the Russian influence became ever more pronounced. On the eve of the Revolution of 1917 the Tatar intellectuals spoke Russian and their *Weltanschauung* was very deeply penetrated by Russian ideas. This penetration was noticeable in all domains: the new Tatar bourgeois literature was directly inspired by Tolstoi, Chekhov, and later Gor'kii; and on the political level, the role of Russian ideologies was greater still. From the extreme clerical right, which found its inspiration in the Russian monarchist conservative movement, to the extreme socialist left influenced by the Socialist Revolutionaries or the Social Democrats, Bolsheviks, or Mensheviks—not to mention the liberals who copied the programs of the Russian Kadets—Tatar political movements were nothing but reflections of the currents that stirred the Russian milieux. Likewise, on the level of doctrines, Pan-Slavism, populism, or later socialism and communism found deep echoes in the Pan-Turkic and Pan-Islamic theories of the Tatars.[23]

In short, on the eve of the Revolution, if the rural masses were almost unpenetrated, the Tatar intelligentsia presented a curious mixture. Intellectually and technically they were very advanced, certainly one of the most advanced groups of the whole Muslim world at that time. Politically, too, they were very mature (it was the Kazan Tatars who were to be the propagators of modern ideologies in the Ottoman Empire).[24] Yet at the same time, having profited greatly from Russian culture, this intelligentsia remained very close to its national culture and to its religion (among Tatars of that time there were almost no freethinkers who had broken with tradition). If it drew its inspiration from, and even copied, Russian models, it was in order to defend itself better against assimilation. Nationalism, this product of modern times, formerly unknown in Islam, was born among the Volga Tatars before it spread into the Ottoman Empire, and nowhere else was this ideology so deeply and so seriously felt.

The Crimea

In its apparent liberalism the policy of the tsarist government in the Crimea contrasted sharply with that practiced in the Mid-Volga. In the Crimea the Tatar feudal nobility assumed its place, retaining its rights and prerogatives, in the hierarchy of Russian society without being obliged to adopt Christianity. Its loyalty to the Romanov dynasty, if not to Russia itself, was thereby insured. The Muslim religious leadership also retained its power and wealth, as well as its title to the *waqf* revenues. It therefore remained very conservative, and was hostile toward any reform that might affect its privileges. Moreover, since the Crimea, the "Côte d'Azur" of Russia, was a consumer and not a producer country, the Crimean merchants, unlike those of Volga and Transcaucasia, could never rise to the status of a strong commercial middle class capable of assuming leadership of the reformist movement. Only a few isolated intellectuals, such as Ismail Gasprinskii, members of the small noble class who had studied in the schools and universities of Istanbul, were able to kindle the torch of Tatar renaissance.[25]

No systematic effort of assimilation was attempted in the Crimea. A few rare representatives of the Crimean high aristocracy—the princes Shirinskii, for example—voluntarily converted to Christianity; but such cases were exceptional. The Russian authorities were in fact opposed to any Christian proselytism, and the Orthodox missions were refused the right to operate in the Crimea. On the other hand, the influx of European colonists—Serbs, Greeks,

Germans, Balts, Moldavians—and the requisition or acquisition of the best lands by the Russians, encouraged the Tatars to emigrate to Turkey. It is estimated that between 1783 and 1905 nearly a million Crimeans, mostly peasants, left their native peninsula.[26] On the eve of the Revolution, the Tatar community had been reduced to some 150,000 souls, a small minority drowned in the mass of Christians. But neither from the cultural nor from the material point of view was this minority penetrated by Russian influence. Nearby Turkey was the pole of attraction toward which the Crimeans turned. To the intellectuals especially, the Young Turks were the political model *par excellence*, and it was only on the eve of the Revolution that Russian socialist ideas (particularly those of the Socialist-Revolutionaries) were found spreading among some groups of young revolutionaries.

The Caucasus

The mountains of the North Caucasus were conquered after a century of effort—an effort that necessitated some fifty years of exhausting military campaigns. These struggles served to undermine the Russian state and contributed in no small way to hastening the process of disintegration that was to end with the collapse of the tsarist regime and the October Revolution.

Inhospitable, poor, and overpopulated, the Caucasian chain, which was pacified only after 1880, was not very favorable to Russian rural colonization. Only the low region of the foothills, the rich steppes of the Kuban and of the Terek, and the oil zone of Grozny received colonists in successive flows, Cossacks and Russians who drove the Muslims toward the mountains. The Russian presence made itself felt there merely by a few scattered officials and military posts. The highly influential native nobility retained enough of its privileges to make it loyal to the tsarist monarchy; but the clergy, which was also very influential, was implacably hostile. The Russian authorities abstained from interfering in the internal affairs of the country and contented themselves with maintaining law and order. Up to the twentieth century, the peoples of the North Caucasus had no national consciousness in the modern sense of the term, and Islam in its most conservative form was their only real bond of unity. Resistance to the Russian presence took on a character that was more religious than national; and, since it lacked the support of the feudal nobility and the merchant middle class, its principal agents were the religious leaders, the *ulama*.

There was no attempt to assimilate the native, who did not receive the status of a full-fledged citizen but remained a "foreigner" (*inorodets*). All Christian proselytism was severely prohibited. The Ossetian country was the only place in the North Caucasus where Russian authorities tried without much success to convert the native population to Orthodoxy. Their failure resulted from the fact that the Ossetians were formerly Christians who had either been converted to Islam during the seventeenth and eighteenth centuries or had fallen back into animism. The nearly total absence of Russians in the mountains explains why the Caucasian mountaineers succeeded in preserving until the beginning of the twentieth century the most archaic traditions and customs, such as their endogamous and exogamous tabus. The Russian language was unknown, and literary culture was of exclusively Arabic inspiration. Russian influence was felt only in the domain of material civilization, but even there was not a matter of imitation but rather of symbiosis. The Russians copied the clothing of the mountaineers, whereas the mountaineers drew inspiration from the Russian agricultural techniques (iron ploughshares, introduction of the workhorse), copied the habitations (the *khata* of the Kuban cossack slowly replaced the old Caucasian *saklia*), and adopted Russian food (introducing potatoes, cabbage, sugar, and bread). From the very first years of the century, however, the mountaineers began to go abroad to work in the oil refineries of Grozny and Baku or in the fisheries of Petrovsk, where they inevitably met Russian, Armenian, or Azeri workers. By these means Russian cultural, technical, and later political influence slowly began to penetrate the mountains. In particular, it was due to these contacts that the socialist ideas spread around 1914 among some small groups of Daghestanian Muslim intellectuals from whose midst came the future Caucasian communist leaders after 1917.[27]

Transcaucasia

In Transcaucasia, a country of old, settled civilization with a dense population, all rural colonization was equally impossible; and the rural Azeri masses who formed the major part of the Muslim population of the country remained virtually untouched by any Russian influence. On the other hand, the discovery, at the end of the past century, of the oil deposits of Baku, was to contribute powerfully to the introduction in Transcaucasia of Russian and European techniques and customs, and of Russian and European ideological trends.

At the beginning of the century, Baku was a great intellectual and industrial center, especially rich in industrial plants that were among the most important in the Muslim world. The total number of workers probably reached 100,000, of whom more than half were Muslims, Azeri Turks, Northern Caucasians, or Persians from the nearby Iranian provinces of Azerbaijan and Gilan. In the modern factories of Baku the Muslim workers labored side by side with Armenian, Georgian, and Russian comrades; and very early, because of the social conflicts between workers and bosses (among whom there were numerous Muslims), they were able to acquire a true class consciousness and to form an industrial proletariat in the modern and occidental sense of the term, the only proletariat of its kind in the *Dar ul-Islam* of the time. Baku was the only spot in the world where socialist ideas could penetrate a milieu of Muslim workers as well as a few select circles of leftist intellectuals.

The same revolutionary ideologies agitated intellectual circles that were products of the industrial bourgeoisie and the landed nobility, the latter being still powerful and rich. Even more than the Tatar intellectuals of the Volga or of the Crimea, the representatives of the Azeri intelligentsia were "occidentalized" people of Russian education. Most of them had completed their studies in Russian educational institutions; but contrary to their Kazan or Crimean coreligionists, the Azeris submitted only to a limited degree to Russian political influence. Torn by the political and economic rivalry between Armenians and Muslims, the country was further divided by the conflict between conservative and religious elements oriented toward Persia, and by liberal elements in whose view national and linguistic unity with Turkey outweighed the spiritual relationship with Shiite Persia. The Russian presence was less felt in Transcaucasia than in other Muslim territories. The hostility of its indigenous peoples toward the Russians was partially neutralized by the violence of the antagonism between Muslims and Armenians. In Transcaucasia Russian authorities neither directly attacked Islam nor attempted a policy of assimilation. Russian cultural and political influence made itself less felt here than did that of Turkey.[28]

In trying to draw up the balance sheet of tsarist policy in the Muslim possessions, one can only note the absence of any systematic or uniform policy. The action of St. Petersburg varied constantly according to regions and periods. It is, however, possible to isolate some main trends.

From the middle of the nineteenth century, the Russians tried almost everywhere to win over the Muslim nobility. The aristocratic families of the Crimea and of the Caucasus were admitted into the nobility of the Empire without having to be either converted to Orthodox Christianity or even Russified. The Muslim nobility was treated in the same way as the German nobility of the Baltic countries. The Russians demanded only loyalty to the monarchy, not to Russia, a policy whose success was evident. At the time of the February Revolution, it was the Muslim nobility that was the last to demonstrate its loyalty to the Romanov dynasty (for example, the general, Khan of Nakhichevan, who in 1914 commanded the entire Cavalry of the Guard). But the feudal nobility played only a minor role in the life of Muslim society and its example could not be dictated to the other strata of society.

The political line vis-à-vis the peasant masses is difficult to determine. The attempt at assimilation by conversion to Orthodoxy was carried on only in the Tatar region of the Mid-Volga and received there only doubtful results. Everywhere, even completely isolated groups of Muslims, for example in Byelorussia, in Lithuania, or near Riazan',[29] survived all pressures.

In the Northern Caucasus and in Transcaucasia, the Russian authorities were content to maintain order without trying to elevate the cultural level of the masses, or even to introduce them to the rudiments of Russian culture. With rare exceptions, the Russians never attempted there what the French did in North Africa or the Dutch in Indonesia—to spread their culture among the masses.

It was, however, vis-à-vis the Muslim intelligentsia that the contradictions and irrationality of tsarist policy were the most apparent. In the first place, the Russian rulers never tried to attract the powerful merchant and industrial bourgeoisie (with the only exception under Catherine II). This course led to profound consequences. All nationalist movements and all separatist trends that

occurred after 1905 originated in the bourgeoisie. Up to 1917 the
authorities of St. Petersburg were invariably distrustful of the modern Muslim intelligentsia. It was thus that Nikolai Ivanovich Il'minskii (1822-91), an educator, theologian, and Islamicist, proclaimed:
"A Muslim fanatically hostile to the 'Infidels' was less dangerous
for the Russian state than a Muslim educated in European style,
with a degree from a Russian or Western university." In spite of
this official mistrust, the Muslim intelligentsia was able to attend
Russian secondary schools and universities without any restrictions, thanks to the racial liberalism of the Russians. This resulted
in the creation of an elite of exceptionally high level. Thus, the
Russian "way of life" was spreading on all levels of Muslim society,
not by conscious imitation but by some kind of osmosis: Muslims
and Russians coexisted side by side, generally ignoring one another,
sometimes despising one another, but also becoming accustomed
to one another.

RUSSIANS AND MUSLIMS
UNDER THE SOVIET REGIME

The break produced in the history of Russo-Muslim relations by
the October Revolution appears either more or less significant, depending upon one's interpretation. For some, the establishment of
the socialist regime in Russia meant complete rupture with the
past, which radically modified Russo-Muslim relations. Others saw
in the Soviet regime the heir to tsarist policy. In this view, relations between Russians and Muslims, i.e., between governing and
governed peoples, with the exception of some formal changes, remained what they had been before 1917.

Although this problem is hard to resolve, we may find some
helpful clues in the case of the Volga Tatars, who had been under
Russian domination for centuries. The Soviet nationalities policy
is hard to follow because of its constant changes and contradictions. To understand it, therefore, one must consider its ambiguous
character. From the very beginning, Soviet policy had to reconcile
two contradictory tactics. On the one hand, the regime advocated
a liberal, humanitarian policy, defended by all those who sincerely
believed Marxist socialism would answer the questions that the capitalistic world could not solve. They believed, in particular, that it

would solve the problem of the relations between ruling peoples and subject minorities; and for them, indigenous nationalism, including that of the Muslims, was nothing but a reaction against the oppressive "chauvinism" of the Russians. By ending the Russian domination they anticipated, *ipso facto*, the disappearance of all obstacles to friendship between the peoples of the U.S.S.R. On the other hand, there was a realistic tactic: to stop the disintegration of the empire and to reestablish the unity of the country on new ideological bases, while still preserving the supremacy of the Russian people.

These two contradictory principles were taken into account simultaneously at the time of the elaboration of the Soviet nationalities policy as it began to appear from 1918. Indeed, after the seizure of power, the Bolshevik leaders, meaning to demonstrate their intention of breaking with the past, took a series of steps that were to give the Soviet state a character fundamentally different from that of the tsarist empire. The latter had been a unitarian state, dominated by Great Russians, with Orthodox Christianity as the state religion. The Soviet state was to be a confederation of peoples, lay and atheist, and equal in rights.

One of the first measures adopted by the Bolshevik government was aimed at ending the policy of religious assimilation practiced in the Tatar region. This was announced by the famous call to "the Muslim workers of Russia and the East" of 24 November 1917. Both Lenin and Stalin signed this proclamation of freedom of religion.[30]

A year later, in December 1918, spectacular measures favoring Islam were taken. They concerned mainly the Volga Tatars. Among these measures we may mention the return to the Muslims of especially venerated relics (Osman's Koran, the tower of Suyum-Bike in Kazan, etc.),[31] and at the same time steps were taken to stop once and for all the missionary work of the Orthodox church.

Very soon the consequence of this favorable attitude toward Volga Islam began to be felt. The majority of the Christian Tatars (the *Kriashens*) returned to Islam. In 1926, according to the census, there were a little over 100,000 of them. In 1939, at the time of the second Soviet census, they had already been completely absorbed by the mass of Muslim Tatars. Thus the unique attempt of forced assimilation of a Muslim community dominated by a governing Christian community ended in complete failure. From these measures favoring Islam, an undeniable current of sympathy toward the new regime arose among the Volga Tatars—a sympathy that survived for many years. This explains in particular why during the Civil War the Volga Muslims as a general rule supported the Reds against the Whites.

If there was religious equality (or rather equality in the lack of religion), there was also officially administrative equality. The Great Russian people lost its rank of a governing people, Russian ceased to be the only official language in the country, and the important nationalities of Russia were given the right to constitute national territorial unities. For the Muslims of European Russia and the Caucasus, in spite of many delays this policy ultimately led to the creation of new nations, each of them having a territory and an administration of its own, as well as a national language.[32]

It is not the task here to analyze how well founded these national unities may be nor to decide whether or not these new nations are viable. It will only be recalled that, with the exception of the S.S.R. of Azerbaijan, whose territory already corresponded to a historical reality, the creation of the other Muslim national unities, rather than being sought by the Muslims, was actually imposed by Moscow. For even after the October Revolution the aspirations of the Muslim intelligentsia of the Volga and the Northern Caucasus were completely dominated by the Pan-Turkic and the Pan-Islamic idea. They were oriented toward the unification of various human groups around nations that were already consolidated or were in the process of being consolidated. They did not look forward to a dispersion into small entities too weak to resist Russian pressure. They thus demanded the creation of a Tataro-Bashkir nation on the Volga, the creation of a Daghestan unified around the Kumyk tongue, the fusion of Chechen and Ingush into one single nation, etc.

It was also against the wish of the Muslim elite of the time that various literary languages were created, as, for example, Bashkir and numerous tongues of Daghestan (Tabarasan, Lak, Darghin, spoken only by very small groups); and Ingush and Abaza, too, were transformed into literary languages. The effect of this was to separate peoples who could have been united. The Muslim elite, on the contrary, tried to promote two or three languages of civilization—in particular the Tatar of Kazan and the Azeri—to the rank of Pan-Turkic "languages."

Thus, during the twenties a desperate fight took place between the Muslim communist leaders who were defenders of the unifying Pan-Turkic ideal and the Moscow administration. It was Moscow that triumphed when, around 1928, the Tatar communist leaders were condemned for "nationalistic and pan-Turkic" deviationism. [33] Then the peoples of the Volga and of the Caucasus were divided into a multitude of micronationalities, none of which was strong enough to oppose efficiently the new *policy of integration* which the Soviet government was progressively applying from that time on with the final goal of constructing on the ruins of the past a new civilization and a new "soviet" man. But this new "homo sovieticus" was nothing but a Russified Muslim, capable of sharing the ideals of the "Leningrad workman" according to Kalinin's famous phrase. And so, around 1928, there began a last stage in the history of Russo-Muslim relations—that of "sovietization." This last stage was different from the policy of assimilation practiced under the tsarist regime, but at times it could indeed be confused with "Russification."

The Policy of Integration

Thus, in the first days after their seizure of power, the Bolsheviks proclaimed administrative, juridical, and political equality between Muslims and Russians; and in the first years of the new regime they supported this proclamation of equality by various measures. But all this could not of itself secure effective equality between the Russian people and the Muslim peoples. It was only the Russian people who had an industrial proletariat and a modern intellectual and professional elite, whereas the Muslims were essentially peasants, with neither a proletariat nor a modern intelligentsia of significant numbers. The Soviet leaders strove for many years, if not to realize this unity, at least to bring Muslims and Russians together on the economic, cultural, and spiritual levels.

There was both a negative and a positive aspect to this policy of integration. On the negative side the policy was destined to destroy any possible obstacle to the rapprochement of the peoples, such as religion, or customs, or "subnational" (tribal or clan) or "supranational" (Pan-Turkic or Pan-Islamic) loyalties. The positive aspect concerned the cultural and technical elevation of the Muslim population "to the level of the Russian proletariat." Consequently, the

Moscow government harnessed itself to the Herculean labor of working a thorough metamorphosis among the Muslims. This undertaking, which formed no part of any preestablished plan, had to be implemented by a painful process of trial and error. Of the human material with which it dealt, part had already achieved the capitalistic stage (Volga Tatars, Azeri) and part was still in the feudal or tribal stage (Northern Caucasians). Any uniform treatment was therefore out of the question.

The negative aspect of the Soviet policy is the one with which we are best acquainted, for both Soviet and Western writers have often analyzed this destruction of the heritage of the past. All "subnational" traditions that blocked the transformation of Muslim human groups into modern nations were to be obliterated. This policy received its broadest and most energetic implementation—and success as well—in the mountains of the Northern Caucasus. It consisted in particular of the interdiction by legal means or by propaganda of family customs inherited from the clan-tribal system: the *kalym* (payments or presents to the parents of the bride), exogamous and endogamous tabus, the levirate, polygamy, seclusion of women, etc.

The campaign against "supranational" traditions, above all in the Tatar region, was waged over a long period and brought more serious consequences. These traditions were delaying the appearance of national consciousness, in the narrow meaning of the term, among the Muslims of Russia. Thus, the offensive was aimed at both the Islamic religion on the one hand and at the Pan-Turkic ideology on the other.

As for the problem of religion, all communists, Muslim as well as Russian, were in agreement from the outset. All saw the necessity of separating church and state, as well as church and school, as proclaimed in the Decree of the Council of People's Commissars of the R.S.F.S.R. of 23 January 1918, on "Freedom of conscience and religious societies. . ." From then on, Islam, like any other religion, became a "private matter," but this was the extent of the identity of views. For the Russians, Islam had to be completely destroyed, for the major obstacle to the "sovietization" of the Muslim peoples was the "Muslim way of life." In it there was that element which differentiated Muslim peoples from their Russian countrymen. But the Muslim communists considered that all that was necessary was to "laicize" Islam, by destroying its purely dogmatic and spiritual aspects while retaining its cultural and social ones. For them attachment to Islam meant the guarantee against assimilation by the Russians.

One of the main leaders of the Tatar Communist Party, Mir Sayid Sultan Galiev, in a now-famous article in *Zhizn' natsional' nostei* (14 and 23 December 1921) defined perfectly the attitude of the communist Muslims.[34] Sultan Galiev accepted the need to combat Islam because, like any other religion, it was "an obstacle to the building of socialism." But discretion and the right touch were indispensable in battling it, for Islam, "the youngest of the great religions," was more vigorous, and also more "democratic" than Christianity; and its teaching, being part and parcel of the social life of its believers, admitted of "progressist" attitudes which it would be folly, in his view, to attempt to scotch. The communist state should avoid giving the Muslims the impression that, in attacking the religion of the Prophet, it was merely prosecuting the campaign opened in the nineteenth century by the Christian missionaries. Such confusion was the more possible since, on the admission of the Bolshevik leaders themselves, the early anti-Muslim propagandists included a certain number of missionaries, apostate by conviction or self-interest, who succumbed to the logic of pursuing under their new employers the work which they had begun under the aegis of the Orthodox church.

Sultan Galiev advocated a policy that would pave the way for the establishment of a truly Muslim communism, not a carbon copy of the Russian model. From 1923 on, his policy was severely condemned by Stalin,[35] and from then until the war of 1941, it was almost exclusively Russians who led the antireligious campaign in Muslim territory which aimed at the total destruction of Islam. The campaign, which reached its culmination in 1938,[36] was brutal and "global." It was aimed at the closing of religious schools, the confiscation of *waqfs* properties, the prohibition of religious (*shari'at*) or customary (*adat*) jurisdiction, and, after 1928, the closing of mosques and the waging of intense antireligious propaganda warfare.

The onslaught on religion was massive, violent, all of a piece— and often clumsy. It mattered not what the circumstances or the religion, or whether the populations involved were barely Islamicized or, like the highlanders of Daghestan, closely wedded to their beliefs. Clergy and congregations alike were henceforward persecuted not only as "parasites" but as "counter-revolutionaries," even as "the most active representatives of counter-revolution," and, after 1935, as "spies in the pay of Japan and Hitler's Germany."[37] Stopped during the war, the campaign was resumed after 1945 and has been going on ever since. The methods are more elastic and more "scientific," but certainly less efficient than the frontal attack of the thirties.

In parallel with the antireligious campaign, the central authorities in Moscow proceeded to liquidate the Muslim intelligentsia that had rallied to the new regime after the Revolution but had preserved intact its attachment to Pan-Turkic and Pan-Islamic ideologies. From 1924 to 1938 a series of purges of the party apparatuses and the Soviets annihilated the indigenous cadres in all the Muslim republics. The crisis was particularly violent in the Tatar territory on the Volga.

The years between 1930 and 1937 represented the culminating point of the antinationalistic struggle in the Tatar region. The Tatar Communist Party (CP) was almost totally purged of its nationalistic elements (annihilation of "Sultangalievism"), and in Azerbaijan almost all the leaders of the Azerbaijan CP were liquidated in 1937-38.[38]

The positive aspect of Soviet policy was the raising of the cultural, economic, and political level of the Muslim peoples, allowing them to become truly equal to the Russians. In all domains, particularly in the domain of education, a gigantic effort was undertaken. Space does not permit us to describe it here, even in its main features. It is sufficient to recall that by today's standards the Tatar and the Azeri peoples are now among the most advanced Muslim peoples in the world. However, in spite of the huge amount of progress, the envisaged goal could never be fully reached. Economic equality could be achieved only by developing industries in regions which had so far lacked them. But this kind of operation, conducted in essentially agricultural areas, ran into technical troubles sufficient to slow down progress and to thrust into the distant future the creation of a native proletariat that would be comparable to the Russian. Genuine cultural equality was even more elusive. In spite of the Soviet leadership's evident goodwill, it was not possible to bridge the educational gap between the Muslims and the Russians. As for political equality, the want of a proletariat and the numerical weakness of the intelligentsia rendered that illusory, too. Nonetheless, from 1921 onward the authorities endeavored to give practical effect to it by means of what was called the policy of *korenizatsiia* (literally, the striking of roots), which meant assigning so far as possible to Muslims a percentage of administrative posts proportionate to their weight in the population of a given territory. The expectation of the time was that this policy would prove to be the best method of furthering the growth of national cadres, would satisfy nationalist aspirations, and would end the conflict on that score once and for all.

But Moscow's *korenizatsiia* was inherently delicate. The heavy administrative apparatus of the Soviet state called for more and more bureaucracy, more and more centralization; and to keep pace with these a trained army of bureaucrats and technicians was demanded which only the Russians could supply. From 1928, when the U.S.S.R. entered the era of five-year planning and accelerated industrialization, the plea of sheer efficiency was added to everything else as an argument for going slowly with *korenizatsiia*. After 1928, when the great purges of the Muslim bourgeois nationalists began, the *korenizatsiia* policy lapsed gradually into the background, until the leadership eventually shelved it on the eve of the Second World War.

To sum up Soviet policy toward the Muslim nationalities and to compare it to that of the tsarist regime, we must recall that the prime objective of the policy was the "sovietization" of Islam. If to the first Bolshevik rulers, for the most part internationalists and cosmopolitans, "sovietization" meant a break with the cultural and historical traditions of the Russian people, to Stalin and his collaborators who held absolute power from 1928 on, the words "Soviet" and "Russian" became almost interchangeable. The Russian people (or rather the Great Russian people) became once again *de facto*, and later *de jure*, the leader of the Soviet peoples ("the elder brother"). The Great Russian historical and cultural traditions were officially generalized for the whole Soviet Union. Russian was supposed to be the "second native language" of all citizens of the Union. The role of the Russians in the party was overwhelming. Nowhere was there a Russian rural "decolonization." In short, "sovietization" became the synonym for "Russification." These circumstances explain the resurgence of Tatar and Azeri nationalism after the war, a nationalism with a smattering of Russophobia. Its theses were akin to those defended by the nationalist reformers of Kazan and Baku before 1917.[39]

CONCLUSION

The first question to arise in the summing up of the Russian impact on the Muslims is a fundamental one and relates to Islam as a religion. Are the Muslims of the U.S.S.R. still Muslims? This is difficult to answer. If one may judge from formal appearances alone, they are no longer Muslims. In the first place, the knowledge of Arabic indispensable for the performance of the prayers is dying out. Neither in Kazan nor in Baku is there religious teaching. Observance of the rites is decreasing (except for circumcision, the only rite that is regarded as essential). Ignorance concerning the dogmas and ritual is very general. But at the same time, and in spite of the lack of interest in religious practices, almost all intellectuals, peasants, and even workers feel they are "Muslims." This is unchallengeably attested to by the findings of many inquiries made either by ethnologists or by Soviet antireligious propagandists. It is especially true of Central Asia.[40] Even convinced atheists declare themselves "Muslims," since for them religion is confused with the national belongingness. "I am a Muslim since I am an Uzbek or a Kirghiz." This is the typical answer. We know less about the religious situation in Tatar territory and in Azerbaijan, but indirect evidence allows us to believe that the feeling of belonging to Islam is even stronger there than it is in Central Asia. Kazan, Ufa in Bashkiria, Baku in Transcaucasia remain spiritual centers (the seats of Muslim leadership for European Russia and Transcaucasia are in Ufa and Baku), and the majority of the *mullahs* in the U.S.S.R., just as before 1917, are Tatars from Kazan.

The Tatar region and Azerbaijan apparently follow the same evolution as the other Muslim countries, particularly Turkey, and the Arabic countries of the Maghrib, where laicism evolves more rapidly than anywhere else. But the Russian pressure has not produced a radical "deislamization."

On the other hand, the Northern Caucasus and more especially the Chechen region and Daghestan are still almost untouched fortresses of the most conservative Islam. The use of Arabic is maintained, and the Muslim brotherhoods (*tariqa*) are still active there.

The importance of anti-Islamic propaganda in these three regions (Caucasus, Volga, and Transcaucasus) gives evidence of the strength of religious feeling there. It may be recalled that in the course of three years (1962-64) 210 antireligious pamphlets specifically intended to fight Islam were published in the U.S.S.R. in various Muslim languages. The North Caucasus is far ahead with 81 pamphlets (74 in Daghestan alone), and in Central Asia only 79, although 75 percent of the Muslims of Russia live there. In Azerbaijan there were 14, and 13 in the Volga (9 in Tatar and 4 in Bashkir).[41]

For the Muslims of the Volga and of the Caucasus, as for those of Central Asia, Islam remains a social bond of union that enables them to differentiate themselves from the Russians. The somewhat rapid evolution of the formerly patriarchic Muslim family toward the small monogamic family could be ascribed to Russian influence, but this same process characterizes almost all Muslim countries. Similarly, the Muslim social traditions—seclusion of women, the wearing of veils, endogamous and exogamous tabus, abduction or buying back of the betrothed, levirate, etc.—all are disappearing at varying rates of speed according to region (the rate is somewhat slower in the North Caucasus). The evolution is noticeable also in Turkey, in Iran, and in the Maghrib. Nevertheless there is nowadays a resemblance at least in appearance between the Azeri and especially the Tatar family and the Russian or Western family. Henceforth the great Russian dream of an ethnic fusion between Russians and non-Russians seems to become theoretically possible. At the moment, it is nothing of the sort; mixed marriages between Russians and Muslims are still exceedingly rare.

Before the Revolution, Muslims—and above all peasants and intellectuals—could marry Russian girls. Such marriages were permitted by the *shari'at* and did not give rise to serious opposition on the part of the bridegroom's parents, since in the majority of cases the Russian wives were converted to Islam. On the other hand, the marriage of a Muslim girl with a Christian or a Jew was forbidden by Muslim law and was practically impossible. At the present time, marriages between Muslim men and Russian women, although rare, are possible, but they often occur among individuals who are no longer closely associated with their respective communities, or they are entered into by Muslim men who have left their national territory and are living among Russians. Such marriages are likely to be more frequent among intellectuals. On the other hand, it seems that marriages between Muslim women and Russian men are exceedingly uncommon and are still considered as a veritable betrayal of family and nationality.

The material and cultural influence exercised by the Russians over the Muslim communities depends partly on the percentage of the Russian element in the total population of given Muslim territories. This percentage has varied a great deal in Central Asia since October 1917, and still more since the last war. By contrast, the percentage of Russians in the Tatar region (44 percent), as in Transcaucasia, did not vary much. These regions of venerable civilization had too dense a population to accommodate new Russian rural or industrial colonies. In the Northern Caucasus the Russians form very important minorities (49 percent in the Chechen-Ingush A.S.S.R., 29 percent in Daghestan). In places they even represent the majority of the population (70 percent in the Adygei A.R., 51 percent in the Karachai-Balkar A.R.). But as a general rule the Russians represent the urban element or else the lowland population, whereas the Muslims populate the mountains. To sum up, there was no demographic overthrow after 1950 in the regions that interest us here, as there was in Kazakhstan or in Kirghizia.

All the same, there appears to be abundant evidence of Russian influence in some areas, particularly in the matter of housing. In the Tatar region there is no longer any distinction between the indigenous peasant house and the Russian *izba*. This, however, came about through an earlier symbiosis and not by recent imitation. But on the Volga, as in the Caucasus, the furnishings of the house have everywhere remained traditional and indigenous. With regard to clothing, the Russian impact is more obvious, although Tatars and Caucasians have retained some of the typically local characteristics in their dress. The Russian influence on diet has been strong, too, but in general, Muslims still observe the pork tabu. As an example, the number of pigs per inhabitant is only 2.2 in Azerbaijan against 3.7 in the R.F.S.R.

In the techniques of production, no difference exists any longer between Russians and Muslims. There are almost no indigenous crafts left except in Daghestan, and these no longer play a role in the economic life of the country. Agricultural and industrial methods, as well as educational systems, are everywhere identical. This is a new state of things that will no doubt contribute to the establishment of material uniformity between the Russians and the Muslims.

Less felt and more difficult to assess is the Russian cultural impact on the Muslims. One precise criterion, however, does permit us to appreciate the power of the Russian cultural and spiritual attraction: the extent to which the Russian language has been a force for assimilating the Muslim people. Soviet authorities appear to hope that in time Russian will become the supranational language spoken by the most advanced elements of the population of the Soviet Union. The national literary languages, transcribed since the Second World War in Cyrillic (Russian) alphabets, are therefore subjected to a two-pronged attack delivered from both the inside and the outside. The internal attack aims at modernizing the languages by purging them of "outdated" words—that is to say, Arabic and Persian expressions. The campaign is rounded off with "enrichment" of local languages of Russian or international origin. The linguistic policy thus tends to superimpose Russian on the Muslim languages. Russian borrowings have now become so extensive that complete knowledge of the national languages is no longer possible without a mastery of Russian. But this process, which is mainly confined to the current language as used in the press, is not irreversible. In recent years it has been possible to detect attempts by Muslim intellectuals—specifically in Azerbaijan—to rid their languages of excessive Russian accretions.

"External" Russification, i.e., the actual introduction of the Russian language, is another method of bringing the Muslim and Russian peoples together. So far, however, this has had little effect on the rural masses. Living as they do in isolation, the Muslim peasants do not know Russian any better than their ancestors did before the Revolution. Very often the young villager does not encounter the Russian language at all until he starts his military service. In the towns the situation is different. Russian is taught in all the primary and secondary native schools, and is the language of instruction in most of the disciplines in higher education. For professional advancement and success in life, a thorough knowledge of Russian is indispensable.

There is not, however, any question of the local languages disappearing. "Advanced" Muslims do not lose the use of their mother tongue; they simply become bilingual, Russian being the professional and administrative language while the national languages are used only outside working hours—a situation not unlike that prevailing in India during the British period. Statistics contained in the 1959 census show that the actual replacement of the national languages by Russian is a very long way from fulfillment.

However, from 2 percent in 1926 the number of Tatars who considered Russian their native tongue increased to 7 percent in 1959. This increase is noted mainly among the diaspora of the Tatars of Siberia and those of European Russia, and far less among the Volga Tatars, who did not abandon their homeland.

Among the Caucasian peoples the percentage is much lower: 1.2 percent among the Azeris, 1.6 percent among the Karachai-Balkars, and 1.9 percent among the Ingushes. Even among the Adygeis, a small minority surrounded by Russians, the percentage of Russified Adygeis does not exceed 3 percent. The reader may be reminded that among the Uzbeks only about 0.3 percent of the population declared Russian as its native tongue.[42]

The Muslim intelligentsia of the U.S.S.R. has often been compared to that of the Middle East and of Asia, a comparison often giving the advantage to the Muslims. The Soviet Muslims are the only ones in the whole *Dar ul-Islam*, with the exception of Turkey, to possess scientific and technical cadres comparable to those of Europe. In this domain the Volga Tatars and the Azeris occupy first place, far ahead of their Central Asian brothers.[43]

The present-day Muslim intelligentsia, especially in Azerbaijan, seems to have all the necessary ideological and political qualifications, and its claims to lead its own republic cannot therefore be brushed aside by the Soviet government as easily as could those of the intelligentsia of the twenties and thirties.

To all outward appearances, the Tatar or Azeri intellectual seems almost completely Russianized. He is a man of the twentieth century, and he is probably grateful to the Russian people—"the elder brother of the Soviet peoples"—for having enabled him to make, in a single generation, the great leap forward that has brought him straight from feudalism to socialism. Russian is his "second mother-tongue," but there is no linguistic assimilation. The more Russianized Muslim intellectuals may become bilingual, but they use their mother-tongue outside working hours. On the surface, too, the modern Muslim intellectual has completely broken with Islam. He no longer observes the traditional rites; and, without being openly hostile, is simply indifferent. Here also, however, it is easy to go wrong unless the attitude of the modern intellectual toward the faith of his ancestors is seen in its proper perspective. He may be indifferent to religious dogma and practice, but he remains attached to the whole body of customs and traditions that make up the special character of the Muslim way of life. His consciousness of belonging to the "community of believers," a consciousness symbolized by the universally practiced rite of circumcision, is evidence of this. Furthermore, in spite of the considerable extent to which it has assimilated Russian culture, the Muslim intelligentsia continues to hold out against any racial intermingling, even in the upper strata of society. Mixed marriages remain rare, even among the most Russianized elements of the Volga Tatars.

To conclude this brief account, we must return here to the case of the Volga Tatars. They have been citizens first of the Russian state, then of the U.S.S.R., for four centuries. No Muslim people has been subjected for so long a period to such systematic, unrelenting pressure to become assimilated. From this ordeal the Tatar people have emerged with honor. They have preserved all their originality and uniqueness, losing only 7 percent of their numbers to assimilation by the Russians, an amazingly low proportion. However, it would be erroneous to see in the Russian impact on the Tatars only the negative results. No Muslim people has profited as much from the benefits of modern civilization as have the Tatars, whose elite has no reason nowadays to envy the Russians.

The Russian influence has not only been a denationalizing one—attempts at outright assimilation, or at Russification, sometimes yielded to a policy of integration around a supranational idea and loyalty, such as Orthodox Christianity and communist ideology, for example. This kind of policy could have allowed the Tatars to preserve in part, at least, the originality of their national culture.

The racial liberalism of the Russians facilitated and still facilitates contacts with the Tatars, but the Russian air of cultural superiority erects a barrier to improved relations. The Russian accepts the Easterner, but only on condition that the Easterner become impregnated with Russian culture. The Russian himself, on the other hand, never becomes Orientalized. In spite of these four hundred years of living side by side, there has been no cultural symbiosis between the Russians and the Tatars. The two peoples do know one another and they do not necessarily hate one another. In fact, they sometimes seem to understand and sympathize with one another; but they are not on the point of meeting in a fond embrace.[44]

—5—

The Impact of Russia
on the Armenians and Armenia

Vartan Gregorian

The study of the impact of Russia on the Armenian people and on
Armenia presents great methodological and historical problems.
Unlike many other nationalities of the Russian Empire, the Armenians, while endowed with an ancient culture and a national
church, were dispersed not only within the Russian Empire but
also throughout the world. Long before the Russian conquest of
Eastern Armenia in 1828, the Armenians had established a number
of major viable communities in Russia. Thus any study of the impact of Russia must inevitably deal with two problems: the influence of Russia on Armenians throughout the empire in general and
on the region of Armenia in particular. In addition, such a study
should logically deal with Russian political and cultural influence
on Armenians abroad.

While examining the influence of Russian culture on the Armenian culture, the historian is confronted with the additional difficulty of assessing the interaction and mutual influence of the
Eastern and Western Armenian cultural heritages, the former consisting chiefly of the contributions of the Armenians of Russia,
Persia, and India; and the latter of the Armenians of the Ottoman
Empire and Europe. This investigation poses special problems in
our attempt to assess Russia's historical role as an agent of modernization, as transmitter of socioeconomic change, and as bearer not
only of Russian culture but of that of Western Europe as well.

Finally, there are many unresolved historical, methodological,
and ideological questions relating to the function of Russia as a

continuous political and cultural influence over the non-Russian nationalities after the formation of the Soviet Union. These problems entail a study of such factors as social mobility, trends in regional economic developments, the dynamics of demography, and the interaction of various cultural heritages within the Soviet Union. Also necessary is an examination of the evolution of the Marxist theory of nationality, national culture, and the nature of the periodic manifestations of "Great Russian Chauvinism" and outbursts of nationalism within particular Soviet republics and various nationalities of the Soviet Union, as well as the attitude of the non-Russian intelligentsia of the Soviet Union toward "Russian orientation" and Russian national culture, and its present and future historical role on the road to, and position within, communist society.

DISPERSION OF THE ARMENIANS

The disintegration and extinction of Armenian statehood and political power in Eastern Armenia was accelerated by the Seljuk invasion, resulting in 1064 in the fall and sack of Ani, the capital of the Bagratid dynasty; in Western Armenia the Mameluks of Egypt delivered the *coup de grâce* in 1375 to the last independent Armenian state, the Kingdom of Cilicia. Both of these developments, concurrent with and followed by centuries of Turco-Mongol invasions, internecine strife, and protracted Ottoman-Persian wars (in which the Armenian Plateau was either a theater or an object of contention, with consequent intense suffering),[1] reached their climax when the two empires concluded a settlement that ended the partition of the Armenian Plateau and historical Armenia. The agreement, which brought peace to the ravaged territories, was additionally important in that it divided Armenia into two *separate* parts and institutionalized in them the Ottoman and Persian rules respectively.[2] The larger part was the Western, Ottoman or Turkish Armenia, which grew up around five vilayets: Van, Erzurum, Kars, Diarbekir, and Sivas (Sebastia). (Large numbers of Armenians also lived within Childer, Adana, and Trebizond provinces.) The focus of Persian Armenia lay in the khanates of Erevan (Yerevan), Nakhichevan, and Karabakh. Within the latter khanate were five small Armenian principalities: Gulistan, Djraberd, Khachen, Varanda, and Dizak. Between the fifteenth and the sixteenth centuries, under the auspices of Uzbek and later Persian rulers, these had received autonomous rule and were being governed by their respective *meliks* (princes).[3]

In the wake of these events, significant demographic changes took place in the Armenian Plateau and in historical Armenia. Large numbers of Armenians had earlier moved to Byzantium, Cilicia, and later to Western Georgia, the Northern Caucasus, the coastal regions of the Black Sea, the Ukraine, and Poland. These emigrations were accompanied by forced mass transplantations of Armenian populations under the orders of successive Persian, Ottoman, and local petty rulers.[4] The major outcome of these developments was the creation and continuous rejuvenation of the Armenian colonies in Georgia, the Crimea, the Ukraine, Rumania, Bulgaria, Holland (Amsterdam), Italy, France, India (Madras and Calcutta), Egypt, New Julfa (Isfahan), Astrakhan, and New Nakhichevan in Russia.[5]

STATUS OF ARMENIANS WITHIN THE RUSSIAN EMPIRE BEFORE 1828

Russian-Armenian relations before 1828 may be divided roughly into five periods. During the first period, which extends from the time of Kievan Russia to the thirteenth century, relations were haphazard. The second period, extending from the thirteenth to the fifteenth centuries, was marked by the establishment of Armenian colonies among various Slavic peoples and in Russia and by meaningful commercial and other contacts. The third period includes the time from the reign of Ivan IV to the second half of the seventeenth century. At this time the Armenians were carrying on commercial activities with Russia through the Ukraine, Poland, the Crimea, and the Caucasus. The occupation of Kazan and Astrakhan had widened the contacts of Russia with Transcaucasia and had opened further opportunities for Armenian commercial activities in and with Russia. The fourth period spans the years from the 1660s to the end of the seventeenth century, when the Armenians managed to receive important commercial privileges from Russia affecting their dealings with East-West transit trade and when they established systematic contacts with Russia. The last period begins with the eighteenth century and the emergence of important Armenian communities in Astrakhan, New Nakhichevan (near Rostov-on-Don), Moscow, and St. Petersburg. These developments attracted Armenian merchants and capital from Persia and the Transcaucasus. The merchants were active in internal transit trade as well as in manufacturing enterprises. Some of them obtained important economic concessions from Russia and attempted to interest Russian rulers in the liberation of Eastern Armenia.

Direct Armenian relations and contacts with Russia and with Russians, which may be traced to the role played by the merchants, date back to the ninth and tenth centuries. Armenians came into contact with Russians through both the Balkans and Byzantium, as well as via the Black Sea, the Caspian Sea, and the Caucasus.[6] The Russo-Armenian contacts were not, however, confined to trade. Historical records indicate also close Russo-Armenian religious cooperation and cultural influence. Thus in the twelfth and thirteenth centuries manuscripts on the life of Armenian saints and martyrs were translated into Russian and Russian manuscripts into Armenian.[7] Various historians also attest to the influence and contributions of Armenian and Georgian art on Rostov-Suzdal and even to the transformation of certain features of the Vladimir-Suzdal architecture of Kiev.[8]

From the thirteenth to the fifteenth centuries Armenian merchants of the Crimea, along with Venetian and Genoese traders, controlled the commercial traffic of the Black Sea region and trade with Russia. The strong position of the Armenian merchants in the region continued even after the Ottoman annexation (1475) and the formation of the Khanate of Crimea.[9]

There were also Armenian merchants and the nucleus of a colony in Kiev which according to certain sources dated back to the eleventh and thirteenth centuries. There are records that indicate, for instance, that Vladimir Sviatoslavich married Anna, an Armenian, and that among doctors attending Vladimir Monomakh there was an Armenian physician.[10] According to I. A. Linichenko, "In southern Russia and Poland it was so customary to see the Armenians in the role of traders of the eastern commerce that a whole series of oriental goods were known as 'Armenian goods'."[11] In the twelfth and thirteenth centuries there were Armenian communities in Lvov, the city of Vladimir, and in the region of Kamenets-

Podol'sk, where there were two villages named Armiane and Armi-
anki. The Armenians of Kamenets and Lvov were chiefly artisans,
merchants, and entrepreneurs. They enjoyed certain privileges and
were active in the transit trade of southern Russia, Poland, and
Eastern Europe in general, while at the same time they also dealt
with banking transactions. The Armenians of Kiev are even reported to have taken active part in the battles of Grunwald (1410)
and Varna (1440).[12]

In the sixteenth and seventeenth centuries under Polish rule, the
Armenians of Lvov (Lemberg), Kamenets-Podol'sk, Vladimir, etc.,
continued to thrive economically. They enjoyed autonomy in Lvov,
controlled its commerce, and contributed to the development of
its goldsmithing. Armenian merchants were not only allowed to
partake in the internal trade of the Polish Kingdom but were
even freed from paying duty on transit trade. They maintained
trade relations with Russia and served as bankers to Polish rulers
(Władysław II, Zygmunt III). They also took part in the Viennese
expedition of Jan Sobieski. In the seventeenth century many Armenians, on account of their devotion to the Polish cause, were
granted titles of nobility.[13] By this time they had established a cultural center at Lvov in 1616, had founded a printing press, had
built a school and churches, had codified their laws, and had even
established a regular school theater presenting plays in Polish, in
Armenian, and in Latin.[14] The Ukrainian-Polish Armenian colonies
maintained active trade and commercial representatives in Constantinople, Izmir, Isfahan, Amsterdam, and Moscow, and controlled most of the transit trade of Poland and Eastern Europe
with Russia.[15]

In Russia proper there was reportedly a small Armenian trading
colony at Moscow.[16] According to Nikolai M. Karamzin (1766-
1826), the Armenian merchants of Moscow in the fourteenth century dealt in imports of the luxury trade of the East and exported
furs and metals from Russia.[17] A major development that widened
the sphere of activities of Armenian merchants with Russia and encouraged the settlement of an additional number of them within
the empire was the Russian capture of Kazan (1552) and Astrakhan (1556). According to Vasilii O. Kliuchevskii (1841-1911), for
Russia in the East, Astrakhan occupied a similar position to that of
Archangel in the West. Both centers became the most important

focal points of Russia's foreign trade.[18] The strategic location of Astrakhan and the vast economic opportunities it afforded contributed to the establishment of an important Armenian community there in the sixteenth and seventeenth centuries that subsequently became a major link with Russia for the Armenian merchants and trading houses of Persia and India.

During the time of Olearius, Tsar Aleksei Mikhailovich, who had turned down the attempts of the Swedes, the Dutch, the French, and the English to participate directly in the Eastern trade through Russia, in 1667 granted the Armenian merchants of Isfahan the right to travel north from Astrakhan across Russia and to sell Persian merchandise (mainly silk) to European buyers. This agreement, which placed Russian merchants at a disadvantage and drew periodic protests from them, was of great importance for the future relations of Armenian merchants and capital with Russia, since the grant was not given to a particular Armenian house but rather to the Armenian merchants of Isfahan, who had achieved great prominence in Persia and India.[19] The monopolistic position of the Armenian merchants in Russia was further strengthened after 1688 when they concluded a commercial agreement with Sweden dealing with the export of Persian goods via Russia to Scandinavia.[20] The trade of the Armenian merchants thus was not confined to silk. According to Olearius, from Astrakhan they carried on "a great traffic with all sorts of goods": the volume of trade through that city was so large as to bring the tsar an annual revenue of some 12,000 rubles in customs alone.[21]

For the Russian authorities Astrakhan provided a base for economic and political participation in the Caucasus and an opportunity, aided by the activities of the Armenian merchants, to link the commerce of the Transcaucasus and Persia with Russia. This was necessitated by the fact that not until the end of the eighteenth century did the Russian merchants begin to play a significant role in trade with Asia and Europe. The tsars therefore not only encouraged the establishment of the Armenian merchants in Astrakhan, but granted them many privileges in addition to Russian citizenship: religious freedom, the building of an Armenian Church, exemption from forced military or other services, an elected ruling body for self-government, and permission to use Armenian laws for the regulation of the internal affairs of the community.[22]

At the beginning of the eighteenth century Armenians, who constituted twenty percent of the population of Astrakhan, held complete control over the import of cotton, dyes, and textiles. A substantial segment of the artisans of the city was drawn from their ranks. By the middle of the century they had founded some of the first silk- and cotton-manufacturing enterprises in Russia.[23]

Astrakhan was but one of the commercial centers where Armenian merchants and capital prospered under Russian rule. Between the sixteenth and the eighteenth centuries they established themselves in various regions of Byelorussia, where they took part in the founding of various manufacturing enterprises.[24] In Russia proper we encounter many Armenian merchants in the middle of the eighteenth century. There were in 1754 some 150 Armenians in Moscow, most of them merchants.[25] Some prominent Armenians of Moscow and St. Petersburg became interested in manufacturing, too. Ignatii Sheriman, for instance, in 1721 became one of the founders of the first silk-manufacturing enterprises of Moscow and its first director-general.[26] According to Liubomirov, in the 1760s three of the five silk-manufacturing establishments of Moscow belonged to Armenians, and they shared in the ownership of the other two.[27] Vasilii Khastatov, the director of one of the first major joint stock-trading companies of Russia, founded to carry on trade with Constantinople and the Mediterranean, was an Armenian.[28] A similar joint stock company, dealing with Persian trade, was established by the Isakhanov brothers in St. Petersburg; and at the time there were also other major Armenian commercial establishments (Manvilov, Bogdan Akhverdov (Hakhverdov), Petros Shirvanov, and the Manucharian brothers).[29] In addition, Armenians were given permission and concessions by Peter the Great and his successors to develop the cultivation of rice and cotton in the regions of Astrakhan and Terek. In the 1760s the Lazarev brothers established what was considered the best and largest silk-manufacturing enterprise in Moscow, and between 1760 and 1800 invested their capital in the mining industries of Russia as well.[30]

In 1774, after the conclusion of the Treaty of Kuchuk Kainarji (Küçük Kaynarca), Russia reacquired Azov and adjacent territory. The Crimean khanate, until then a vassal of the Ottoman Empire, was declared independent. In order to undermine the economy of the khanate and strengthen southern Russia's artisanry and trade, the government of Catherine the Great decided to transplant the Armenian population of the Crimea to Russia, a task that was entrusted to General A. V. Suvorov.[31] In 1778 some fifteen or twenty thousand Crimean Armenians were settled near Taganrog. They were given land and financial compensation and established a town, New Nakhichevan, and five villages. By 1781 the town, which had some twelve thousand inhabitants, had become a major trade center dealing with Black Sea-Caucasus-Russian trade.[32] Side by side with this new community the small Armenian colonies of Mozdok and Ghzlar grew so rapidly (to some three thousand) that in 1785 the tsarist government declared Mozdok an Armenian-inhabited town. The Armenians of both towns, in addition to their activities in agriculture and trade, established manufacturing businesses dealing with silk, wine, and alcohol.[33]

Another Russian Armenian colony was created as the result of the Russo-Turkish wars (this time the war of 1787-91), when, after the peace of Jassy (Iasy) some four thousand Armenians under the direction of General Suvorov were transferred from Moldavia and Wallachia to the valley of the Dniester where, near the city of Dubasar, they founded the town of Grigoriopolis and a few Armenian villages. The Russian government on this occasion also lent financial assistance and granted land to them.[34]

To Armenian merchants and artisans Russia of the eighteenth century provided a fertile and secure ground for institutionalizing and expanding their economic power. The Russians, who had granted the Armenians religious freedom and limited internal autonomy to run their community's affairs in Astrakhan, extended similar privileges to the Armenians of New Nakhichevan.[35] The Russian Empire gave the Armenian communities freedom not only to organize their churches, but also to establish printing presses in St. Petersburg (1781), New Nakhichevan (1790), and Astrakhan (1796). These presses printed Armenian classics, medical compendia, religious-historical works, and autodidactic Russian language manuals.[36] Armenians were allowed also to establish schools in Astrakhan, Moscow, St. Petersburg, Mozdok, Ghzlar, and Grigoriopolis. A major Armenian educational establishment was set up in New Nakhichevan.[37]

Armenians were given the privilege, too, of serving in the Russian army. A few of them, in fact, rose to the higher echelons, achieving the ranks of colonel and major general, and, as early as during the War of 1812, receiving decorations.[38] Security, economic opportunity, religious and cultural freedom, and personal advancement—all these were among the early advantages enjoyed by the Armenian communities of Russia. In such circumstances some influential Russian-Armenian leaders attempted in the eighteenth century to take advantage of the financial-commercial and geopolitical interests of Russia in the Caucasus for the purpose of securing the liberation of Eastern Armenia—a goal that Armenian leaders of Eastern Armenia and India had been pursuing unsuccessfully since the sixteenth century.

ARMENIAN POLITICAL ACTIVITY

Between the sixteenth and the eighteenth centuries Armenian attempts to liberate Armenia and to reëstablish an Armenian political entity were confined mainly to Eastern Armenia. Although these attempts were initially limited to the diplomatic arena, they later developed into ideological political programs, and ended up in a national armed insurrection against various khanates of the region. The first moves of national liberation were made by the leaders of the Armenian Apostolic Church at Echmiadzin and Sis (Cilicia), who hoped to secure the support of the papacy, and through the coalition and cooperation of some European powers to free Armenia. If needed they were even ready to accept the union of the Catholic and Armenian churches (v. projects and missions of Catholicos Stepannos Salmastetsi in 1547, that of Catholicos Michael [1562], and of Catholicos Azaria Djughayetsi [1585]).[39]

In 1675-76 a fourth initiative, undertaken and led by Catholicos Hakob Djughayetsi, attempted a similar plan: to secure the intercession of the papacy and through a possible political coalition of Austria, Poland, Venice, and perhaps Russia to embark upon the liberation of Armenia. This program envisioned the participation of the Armenian meliks of Karabakh as well as the cooperation of Georgia.[40] In connection with this mission the Catholicos also asked Tsar Aleksei Mikhailovich (1629-76) to intercede diplomatically on behalf of the Armenians to prevent their being "mistreated and tortured."[41] During this period a similar petition was addressed to the tsar by Catholicos Petros of Gandzasar, who asked his help in not abandoning "the Armenians without consolation amongst the infidels."[42] These moves coincided with the activities of Grigorii M. Lusikov in Russian government circles. He was the representative in Russia of the Armenian merchants of Isfahan and an emissary of the Persian Court working to secure a possible anti-Ottoman coalition between Russia, Poland, and Persia. If such an alliance were successful in its objectives, Lusikov, through separate private negotiations, hoped to secure some political and economic concessions for the Armenians.[43] Of definite significance in this episode was the arrival upon the scene of Israyel Ori, a rare combination of Armenian patriot, political visionary, maverick diplomat, and adventurer. Encouraged probably by the defeat of the Turks at Vienna and by Peter the Great's occupation of Azov, he revived the Armenian liberation attempts of 1687. To stimulate European (Polish, German, Russian) interests and cooperation in such an endeavor,[44] he held forth two inducements: the adherence of the Armenian Church to the papacy and the crown of the restored Armenian throne to Johann-Wilhelm of the Palatinate. The international situation and his own lack of realism, however, doomed Ori's European projects to failure. Sure that Russia, for strategic and commercial reasons, was interested in Transcaucasia, Ori tried to swing the support of the Karabakh meliks to the eventual advance of Peter the Great, and through Russian support to establish some kind of Armenian political entity in Eastern Armenia.

Throughout the eighteenth century there followed various attempts to secure active Russian participation or help in liberating Armenia. These hopes were bolstered in 1722 by the Afghan and Ottoman invasions of Persia and by Peter the Great's expedition to Transcaucasia. The Karabakh meliks, who took up arms with high expectations of Peter the Great, were disillusioned. Russia concluded peace and the Armenians were left to their fate. They fought against the Turks and Persians under the leadership of David and Mkhitar Begs (1723-30).[45]

Some thirty years later Armenian political activities were revived when Catholicos Hakob Shamakhetsi presented a petition to the Russian government asking for its help and protection for the Armenians.[46] In 1762 Hovsep Emin, son of a rich Armenian merchant from India, who had received military education in England

and who counted among his English friends Edmund Burke and the Duke of Cumberland, conceived a project for resurrecting the statehood of Armenia with Russian and Georgian assistance. The outcome was to be a modern Georgian-Armenian state having a joint European-style army and enjoying Russian protection. The plan envisaged the founding of a network of schools that would educate the youth of both countries and would instill a sense of patriotism in them, as well as promoting a cultural rebirth. Though Emin secured the support of some wealthy Armenian merchants of St. Petersburg in his attempts to promote this project, his hopes nevertheless came to nothing.[47]

Among various Armenian leaders both in Russia and abroad, the Russo-Turkish war of 1768-74 raised fresh hopes and expectations of establishing an Armenian state. These hopes are embodied in the projects of Movses Sarafov (Sarafian) of Astrakhan, the owner of a silk factory and a shipbuilding concessionaire. In consultations with various merchants of St. Petersburg in 1769, Sarafov proposed the formation of a military contingent composed of Armenians of Russia and armed at the expense of the Armenians themselves, who, through an alliance of King Erekle (Irakli) and King Soloman of Georgia and the meliks of Karabakh, were to occupy Erevan and use it as a base for the liberation of Van. The projected Armenian state was to be independent, was to enjoy Russian protection, and was to be an ally of Russia.[48]

In the following decades some leading members of the Armenian colony of Madras and, in Russia, Archbishop Hovsep Arghutian and Hovhannes Lazarian (a prominent figure in St. Petersburg) revived similar plans. The archbishop and Lazarian called for the formation of an Armenian military force to be led by an Armenian general that would occupy Gandzha and Shemakha, joining forces at this base with the Karabakh meliks, freeing the valley of Ararat, and creating an Armenia. This plan envisioned the assistance of Russian artillery and, once Armenia had achieved its independence, the temporary quartering of Russian troops, to allow the Armenians the needed time to organize their state.[49]

A far more liberal and radical program of action was prepared by the Madras group, of which Shahamir Shahamirian, Movses Baghramian, and others were members. Their line of action called for the mobilization of Armenian resources, including the resources of the church, to open a network of schools to educate the Armenian youth, to give them military training, and, through the cooperation of the military resources of the meliks and the assistance of Georgia, to establish an Armenian republic with a constitution.[50]

The sponsors of both projects hoped to exploit Catherine the Great's and later Paul I's Eastern policies to secure their aims. In this they were once again disappointed.

ARMENIA UNDER RUSSIAN RULE

At the beginning of the nineteenth century, Russian expansion into the Caucasus took on a systematic form. In 1801 Russia annexed Eastern Georgia; between 1803 and 1810, the Georgian provinces of Mingrelia, Imeretia, Guria, and Abkhazia. In 1804 Russia moved against the khanate of Gandzha and through the cooperation of the Armenian population occupied the city of Gandzha. By 1805 Russia had annexed the khanates of Karabakh, Sheki, Shirvan, and in 1806 those of Baku and Derbent. The two Russian attacks on Erevan in 1804 and 1808, though they did not result in the permanent occupation of that khanate, did create greater difficulties for the local Armenian population. The conquests of Russian imperialism were legitimized by the Russo-Turkish Treaty of Bucharest in 1812 and the Russian-Persian treaty of Gulistan in 1813. Persia forfeited its rights in Eastern Georgia, Gandzha, Karabakh, Sheki, Shirvan, Baku, Kuba, Talysh, Derbent, and Daghestan. [51]

The war between Persia and Russia was renewed in 1825. This time it resulted in the Russian conquest of the khanates of Erevan and Nakhichevan. The Treaty of Turkomanchai was concluded, which, in addition to these new territories, secured for Russia economic and political concessions in Persia.[52]

In both the Russo-Persian war of 1804-10 and that of 1826-27, the Armenians lent military and political support to the Russians in anticipation not only of liberation from the rule of Persians and of local khans, but also of achieving a base for an autonomous Armenian development.[53] In 1826, for instance, Archbishop Nerses Ashtaraketsi, in a famous "Appeal to the Armenian Nation," reminded the Armenians that the Russians were coming not in their own self-interest but for the peace, security, and well-being of the Armenians. He therefore asked the Armenians, in the name of their glorious forefathers, for the sake of God and Christianity, not to spare either their goods or their lives for the success of the Russians.[54] The archbishop himself led a detachment of Armenian volunteers against Erevan.

In his *ukase* (*ukaz*), while thanking the Armenians for their devotion to Russia and their assistance in the 1826-28 Russo-Persian war, Tsar Nicholas I made amply clear Russia's true and ultimate intentions toward Armenian political aspirations. He interpreted the Armenians' adherence to the Russian cause as a natural consequence of their realization that under Russian rule their legal status and their life were much better than under any other arrangement.[55]

Those Armenian leaders who had fulfilled their functions in the execution of the Russian conquest of Transcaucasia were now discarded or banished.[56] For the Armenian leadership only its minimal demands had been satisfied—Armenians of Transcaucasia had been freed from the rule of the shah and his vassal khans. Otherwise, however, the change had merely substituted the tsar for the shah. In such circumstances, most Eastern Armenian religious and lay leaders, both in Russia and abroad, though disillusioned, accepted the reality of Russian colonial rule, hoping to make Russian Armenia a secure ground for nation building, a beacon to immigrants, and a concentration point for Armenian populations, as well as a political base. Others, however, decried the absence of self-rule for the Armenians and the blow to the realization of their national aspirations.[57]

In 1828 Tsar Nicholas I, by an executive order, created the Armenian Province (*Armianskaia Oblast*) on the newly occupied territories of the Erevan and Nakhichevan khanates. This did not satisfy those Armenian leaders who were hoping to regroup Armenians under a single administrative unit. The oblast had left out the substantial number of Armenians of the Karabakh, Akhalkalak, Kazakh, and Lori regions. Those who had been hoping to establish at least local self-government in the Armenian Province were also soon disappointed. Of the five men who formed the administration of the province, which was headed by a military governor, three were military and two were civilians. Of the latter, only one was to be an Armenian, and he was to be drawn from the upper classes. Most of the administrators of the province were Russians.[58] By 1833 the collegial nature of administrative authority had been changed, and the power of the province was centered in the hands of the military governor. In 1840 even the "Armenian Oblast," a pleasing name and concept to some Armenian leaders of Russia, was abolished. Instead, all Transcaucasia was now divided into two provinces, Georgia-Imeretia and the Caspian Oblast. The Armenian Oblast became part of the former, and mountainous Karabakh was included within the latter.[59] This move was an effort to centralize and Russify the administration of the region, and administratively to merge it within the general framework of the empire, disregarding national, historical, and regional particularisms. It also eliminated the vestiges of local rule. Most of the government bureaucracy and the judiciary were now placed in the hands of Russian officials.

The move revealed clearly the fact that for Russia, Transcaucasia and Armenia were colonies. This had already been reflected in 1827 in the official report of E. F. Kankrin, finance minister of the tsar, and in the subsequent reports of 1836 and 1840, in which it was stated that the founding of universities, major industries, and manufacturing enterprises in Transcaucasia was either unnecessary or undesirable. The region was to provide only raw materials and commercial routes for Russia.[60] Its administrative unity and merger with Russia were further consolidated in 1844 with the formation of Kavkazskii Krai, to be headed by a viceroy. This was a far-reaching administrative reorganization. By 1849 Transcaucasia was divided into five provinces: Tbilisi (Tiflis), Kutaisi, Shemakha, Derbent, and Erevan.

In 1862, 1868, 1875, and 1880 Transcaucasia was the subject of still further administrative reorganization.[61] The tsarist government's constant administrative changes reflected more than necessary normal policy changes; they were designed to check regional and ethnic separatist movements or tendencies and at the same time to prevent any nationality from becoming a preponderant majority in any major province. The dictum seems to have been *divide et impera,* a measure that was reflected also in tsarist land and peasant policies.

Agrarian relations in Transcaucasia were diverse and complicated. In Georgia feudal relations were much more developed than in Eastern Armenia and in the future Azerbaijan. Like Russia, Georgia too had serfdom, whereas in Armenia and Azerbaijan the majority of the peasants were from a legal point of view outside the bonds of serfdom. The landlords had no right to sell or donate peasants as they could in Russia and Georgia. The tsarist government from the very outset recognized the rights of Georgian nobility. As for the legal rights of the khans, begs, aghas, and meliks, however, these were considered controversial and subject to further study and clarification. In the 1830s and 1840s the landlords were asked to provide legal proof of their rights to their lands. At first the tsarist regime, in order to increase the revenues of the state and to limit the administrative and economic privileges of the Muslim landlords, was inclined not to recognize the traditional rights and the feudal holdings of khans, begs, and aghas. Later, however, in order to avoid alienating the Muslim elite and with the intention of strengthening its rule in Transcaucasia, the tsarist government made a radical change in its policies.

Under the administration of M. S. Vorontsov, Viceroy of the Caucasus, the tsarist government ended its noncommittal policy toward the khans, begs, aghas, and meliks. By the rescript of 6 December 1846, it recognized them as the legal owners of their lands, and by this means returned various confiscated lands to their owners. The landlords were allowed to will, donate, or sell their holdings to members of the upper class. The tsarist regime went even a step farther in strengthening feudal relationships in Russian Armenia. It gave the holders of *tiule* (temporary possession of land) the right to transform *tiule* into inheritance properties.[62] Since the Armenian peasantry on the eve of Eastern Armenia's annexation to Russia occupied an unfavorable socioeconomic position in relation to the ruling Persian and Turkish feudal elements,[63] this measure, by legitimizing and institutionalizing their rule, constituted a blow to Armenian hopes of achieving not only political liberation but a degree of socioeconomic emancipation as well.

In general, both as an ethnic group and as a class, the Armenian peasants occupied an unenviable position in comparison to the Turkic and Muslim element. The number of entire feudal landowning elite of the former khanate of Erevan, for instance, was 1,778, of which the Azeri and Kurdish khans, begs, and aghas numbered 1,573, their Armenian counterparts 205. The situation was the same throughout Transcaucasia when as late as 1897 the number of Muslim feudal and other major landowners was 43,020, and only 8,511 Armenian.[64] The tsarist regime had no interest in breaking the dominant socioeconomic position of the Turco-Tatar landowners nor of alleviating the taxes levied on the peasantry. On the contrary, between 1828 and 1836 the taxes of the *Armianskaia Oblast* increased from some 47,736 to 334,869 silver rubles. The same was true in the case of the khanate of Nakhichevan and the Okrug of Ordubad, where they increased from 13,997 to 95,875 rubles.[65] Generally speaking, despite the strenuous post-1945 and post-Stalinist attempts of the Soviet Armenian historiographers to prove the contrary, the difference between the burden of the combined taxation of the Persian and local petty rulers on Eastern Armenian peasantry and that imposed under Tsar Nicholas I does not seem to be great.[66] Until 1836 in the *Armianskaia Oblast*, the Russian government retained not only the former Persian system of taxation but even the tax collectors. In 1836, under General V. Bebutov's administration, the taxation system was revised; and for the next six years the major development in the rural economy of Russian Armenia was the collection of taxes not only in kind but in money as well. Townsmen in Erevan, Nakhichevan, and Ordubad districts were obliged to pay money taxes. Even the nomads were ordered to pay such taxes.

In 1843 taxation in kind was replaced by money. On the one hand, this was a noteworthy economic development since it constituted a blow against a natural economy system and marked the development of capitalism in the rural economy; but on the other, it contributed to the process of dispossession through indebtedness and to the increase of the economic problems of the peasants.[67] A significant feature of the 1840 taxation system was the fact that it divided the Armenian and Muslim peasantry into two legal categories: peasants living on state lands and those on the estates of landlords. Theoretically the tsarist regime's move meant that it was not recognizing the full feudal rights of the Armenian and Muslim landlords as it did in Russia and Georgia. In reality, however, it did not abolish the prerogatives of Armenian and Muslim landlords or reduce the peasantry's manifold obligations to them. Thus, the peasants were forced to pay taxes in kind to the landlords in addition to the direct taxes that they paid to the government.[68] The result was constant peasant unrest, passive resistance, and petitions to the tsarist officials to alleviate the taxation burdens.

For the Armenian peasants on Muslim landholdings the socioeconomic unrest and dissatisfaction were often colored with an ethnic-
religious conflict as well. Thus, in their petition to Tsar Nicholas I,
the Armenian peasants of the Kazakh region complained of "Turkish Aghalar," who at the time of the Persian expeditions to Transcaucasia were looting them and were now governing them. Similar
petitions complained of heavy and illegal taxes and exploitation of
the Armenian peasantry by the Turkish landlords.[69]

In the 1880s the tsarist regime also took over the pasturelands
of Transcaucasia and declared them state property. In the Gandzha
and Erevan provinces this involved the take-over of some 424,269
and 353,755 *desiatins* of land.[70] Aside from establishing a tighter
economic and administrative control over the region, this move
was another in the tsarist government's attempts to colonize the
region, a policy that had been in effect in the Caucasus before the
annexation of Eastern Armenia. As early as 1818 the tsarist government was already spending vast sums of money in an attempt to
establish German immigrants in Georgia.

In Transcaucasia colonization had been in effect since the 1830s.
Initially there were far-reaching proposals to settle some 80,000
Russian Cossacks on the Russo-Persian border, as military outpost-
village types of settlements. From the 1830s on, the first waves of
colonizers in Transcaucasia, however, consisted of the members of
various Russian-persecuted and exiled religious sects (Old Believers,
Molokane, Dukhobors, etc.). In 1846 the number of such sectarians in the region was 15,751.[71] By 1857 there were in Transcaucasia some fifty Russian villages with a population of 22,392.
Of these villages seven were in the khanate of Erevan.[72] By 1864
their population had increased to 29,487 and in 1866 to 31,223.[73]

The Russian villages of Transcaucasia were divided into three
categories: veteran soldiers, sectarians, and Orthodox. The establishment of the Orthodox settlements and in general the Russian
colonization of Transcaucasia and Eastern Armenia were officially
justified as providing model villages that might help the postal and
commercial communications of Russia and introduce new crops
and artisans into the region.[74] In reality, however, the purpose was
in line with the prescriptions of General Dmitrii A. Miliutin (1816-
1912), chief of staff of the Russian army of the Caucasus, who advised the government that the best way to strengthen Russian rule
in the region was to colonize it.[75] By 1898 the number of Russian

villages in Transcaucasia had increased to 102.[76] As far as Armenian peasants and villages were concerned, some of their land was confiscated and given to Russian settlers. In other instances, the Russians were allowed six times more land per family than their Armenian counterparts and their taxes were relatively lighter. In cases of redistricting, it often happened that more land was passed to the Russian villages at the expense of Armenian peasants. The same situation occurred throughout Transcaucasia.[77]

The policy of colonization reached its peak under the rule of Prince Grigorii S. Golitsyn, Viceroy of the Caucasus (1896-1904), who attempted to establish a Land Bank in the Caucasus dedicated to the colonization of the region. He argued that because most of the landlords of the region were in debt while most of the capital funds of Transcaucasia lay in the hands of the Armenians, the establishment of such a bank was a necessary instrumentality for averting an Armenian take-over of the land and for facilitating a Russian one instead.[78] Under Golitsyn the process of dispossession of Armenian and Muslim landholders was accelerated to the benefit of the Russian colons. The agrarian relations of the region between 1898 and 1904 give ample illustrations of the well-protected status of Russian colonization.[79] Even as late as 1906, when the new Viceroy of the Caucasus, Count I. I. Vorontsov-Dashkov, in order to forestall the dangerous revolutionary trends in the Caucasus, proposed to the tsarist government the distribution among landless peasants of some of the free state lands and forests, Finance Minister Shipov postponed a decision. He proposed referring the question to the Duma, which might utilize such lands not only for the needs of the local inhabitants but also for the Russian colonization of that borderland.[80]

In general, the position of the Armenian peasantry in Transcaucasia was not strong. The peasants were scattered, they lacked regional cohesiveness, and they did not form an absolute ethnic majority in any province. The 1,293 villages in which they lived were spread throughout the six provinces of Transcaucasia: in Erevan province 464 villages, in Gandzha 365, in Kars 80, in Tbilisi 331, in Baku 46, in the region of Batum 7. In many of these villages they lived together with Georgians, Turks, and Kurds. Some 467 villages belonged to the upper classes, to monasteries, and to churches.[81] Russian colonial policies, while providing physical security, did not create conditions for the economic emancipation of the peasantry. The reform laws of 1864-65 in Georgia and those of 1870 in Armenia and present-day Azerbaijan did not provide remedies, but rather placed the majority of the Armenian peasants in a temporarily dependent position. The reforms did not eliminate the tax on produce (which took one-tenth of all crops grown by the peasants), nor a capital tax on the upper classes; nor did the reforms delimit the rights of the upper classes or of the peasants as to the disposition of water, forests, and pastureland. Without the landlord's consent the peasant could not even redeem his land.[82] The reform laws of the 1870s applied the same principles in regard to the Armenian and Muslim peasants as to those of Georgia and Russia, despite the fact that in Georgia the peasants were not obliged to render personal services. In many respects the emancipatory laws of 1870 institutionalized and legalized the privileges of the major landholders. Unlike the situation in Russia, in Armenia the peasants had to buy back the land without governmental assistance. From a legal point of view, until the repurchase of the land was accomplished, the peasants were in a dependent position with an obligatory relationship to the land.[83]

Dependent relationships in Russian Armenia were abolished only in 1912, when a legislative act provided for compulsory redemption of the land by the peasants. The government had to pay twenty-four million rubles to landlords in freeing the peasants from temporary, undetermined, and other modes of semifeudal dependence. The peasants in return were to pay that sum with interest within twenty-six to fifty-six years. While the measure was a noteworthy one, its execution was repeatedly postponed. Between 1913 and 1916 only fifteen percent of the dependent peasants were freed from their semifeudal relationship.[84] In the meantime, however, the growth of the rural population, the hunger for land, the development of capitalist relations in the rural economy, dependent relationships, heavy taxation, and resulting indebtedness of the peasants forced many of them either to rent additional land, often on a short-term basis (a process which brought on rapid exhaustion of the soil), or else, as was often the case, to move to the towns in search of work. The growth of industrial and commercial enterprises in Baku and Tbilisi was an attraction. In 1913, for instance, some thirty thousand peasants left the villages of Erevan Province for these centers; and another twenty thousand moved within the province to various smaller urban centers.[85] The Armenian peasantry was thus further weakened and dispersed—a weakness that was reflected in the fact that whereas in Georgia the aristocracy and the landed gentry took an active part in the national liberation movements, among Armenians that role was reserved for the bourgeoisie or for the intelligentsia.

THE GROWTH OF THE ARMENIAN BOURGEOISIE

During the first seventy years of the tsarist administration, urban centers of Transcaucasia grew rapidly, while in Armenia the pace was somewhat slower, as indicated in the following tabulation:

City	Year	Population	City	Year	Population
Baku	1865	14,714	Erevan	1865	14,070
	1897	112,252		1897	29,023
Tbilisi	1875	67,770	Aleksandropol'	1831	3,444
	1897	160,645		1886	24,230
				1897	32,230

The spectacular growth registered by Aleksandropol' was linked to the development of communications, trade, and the gradual introduction of industries.[86]

Statistics of the period indicate the rapid growth of trade. Whereas in 1862-66 the annual commercial transactions of Transcaucasia totaled some 11,815,891 rubles, between 1872 and 1876 the sum had increased to 14,139,270 rubles, reaching in 1886 the figure of 39,264,547 rubles.[87] With the growth of the economy and the process of urbanization in Transcaucasia came the emergence of a viable Armenian bourgeoisie, a distinct characteristic of which was the fact that it had developed mainly outside the territories of present-day Armenia, asserting itself in Tbilisi, Baku, Batum, and in the Northern Caucasus.

Both as an ethnic element and as a bourgeoisie the Armenians enjoyed a well-entrenched position in Tbilisi. In 1876, out of some 66,147 male inhabitants of the city 21,516, almost 32 percent (including the Russian garrison of 10,615), were Russians. The Armenians constituted approximately 32 percent of the population, the Georgians only 20 percent, with other nationalities making up the difference.[88] The 1876 statistics set the total number of merchants of the city at 6,851, of whom 4,249 were Armenians. Those who dealt with production numbered 13,137, of whom 5,919 were again Armenians.[89] The data of 1886 shows that almost all the cigarette factories were in the hands of the Armenians.[90] In 1890-1900 the Armenians controlled somewhere between 62.5 percent and 74.6 percent of commercial industrial enterprises of Tbilisi; 73.7 percent of workers and servants employed in these enterprises were Armenians. In Tbilisi four out of six banks were under the control of the Armenian bourgeoisie, while almost half the real estate was reportedly Armenian-controlled.[91]

A similar situation prevailed in Baku, where Armenian capitalists controlled more than half the city's oil wells. Armenian companies owned and controlled 155 oil wells, Europeans and Russians 79, others 61.[92] Some 25 percent of the trading enterprises and 10.5 percent of the real estate of the city and most of the shares of Transcaucasian banks, valued at some forty million rubles, were under the control of this bourgeoisie. The capital of the Armenians in Russian high finance was also noteworthy. According to estimates, in 1917 12 percent of the capital of the 53 joint-stock commercial banks of Russia (that is, some 81.6 million rubles) belonged to the Armenian bourgeoisie and such major capitalists as the Mantashians, the Jamharians, and the Ghuskassians.[93] The following statistics for the city of Baku serve to illustrate the numerical and financial strength of the Armenian element in Transcaucasia:

Year	Total Population	Number of Armenians	Percentage of Armenians
1873	15,105	755	5
1900	222,412	51,205	23

In 1898 Muslims of Baku owned some 6,279 properties valued at 10,898,580 rubles, and in 1905 some 6,600 properties worth 15,815,910 rubles. During the same periods the Armenians of Baku owned 778 and 842 properties with values of 11,603,070 and 17,390,070 rubles, thus surpassing the Muslim element in wealth.[94]

Similar situations prevailed in other cities of Transcaucasia, such as
Batum:

Year	Total Population	Number of Armenians	Number of Georgians
1878	1,000	-	-
1882	5,751	908	809
1898	14,674	3,091	3,526

During the period of 1898 to 1902 the Armenians were in charge
of 25 percent of the shipping transactions of Batum.[95]

The strong position of the Armenian bourgeoisie presented peculiar problems. It placed the power of the Armenian bourgeoisie
outside the area of what later became Armenia. In Tbilisi and Baku
this power provoked the wrath of the Georgians and Turks, particularly in local and municipal elections. The situation was especially
alarming to the Georgian nationalists and nobility, who in Tbilisi,
their capital, were finding themselves isolated. Georgian-Armenian
relations deteriorated further as a result of the increase in the Armenian population of the city. By 1897, according to Nikoladze,
47 percent of the population was Armenian.[96]

The following figures show the approximate breakdown by
groups of the 2,412 voters of Tbilisi in 1892:

Ethnic Group	Number of Voters	Percentage
Armenians	1,285	53
Russians	506	21
Georgians	381	16
Germans	106	4
Turks	56	2
Poles	45	2
Jews and other groups	10	0.4

As the result of municipal elections between 1875 and 1902, Armenians consistently occupied 53 to 55 seats in the 72- to 80-seat
municipal council. Their preponderance in municipal elections and

affairs was a result of those Russian laws that preserved electoral and other rights to those who owned houses in the cities. Thus by 1900 Transcaucasian cities presented the following situation: the cities of Tbilisi, Erevan, Aleksandropol', Gori, Akhaltsikhe', and Signakh had Armenian mayors and municipal councils in which they formed majorities. Baku and Gandzha had Russian mayors. In the council of Baku, Armenians occupied 21 seats, Muslims 27, Russians none. Batum was the only city under discussion whose mayor was Georgian, but even here Armenians and Russians formed the majority in the municipal council.[97]

After some seventy years of Russian rule, and the resulting economic unity and development of Transcaucasia, in 1897 the social structure of the Armenian population of Transcaucasia broke down as follows:

Class Structure	Numbers (family members incl.)	Per cent- age
Landholding nobility and clergy	9,457	0.8
Peasantry:	821,510	70.0
a) well-to-do	(106,800)	(9.1)
b) middle income	(328,604)	(28.1)
c) poor	(386,106)	(32.8)
Bourgeoisie (industrial and commercial)	85,760	7.3
Workers	190,210	16.2
Artisans, craftsmen in home industries, retail merchants	66,159	5.7
	1,173,096	

The Armenians of Transcaucasia were spread throughout the region, a fact that was not true of other ethnic groups of the area. Thus, while some 99.7 percent of all the Georgians lived in the territories that constitute present-day Soviet Georgia, and 64.6 percent of all the Turco-Tatars lived in what is today Soviet Azerbaijan, only 40.9 percent of the Armenians lived in the territories of present-day Soviet Armenia at the beginning of the century. Of the Armenians of Transcaucasia, 31.7 percent lived within the confines of what is now Soviet Azerbaijan and 20.3 percent in Georgia.[98]

The numerical strength of the Armenians in various provinces of Transcaucasia in 1886 is shown below:

Province	Total Population	Number of Armenians
Erevan	670,405	375,000
Elisavetpol	728,943	258,324
Baku	712,703	55,459
Tbilisi	808,143	193,610
Kars okrug	174,044	33,094

In 1886 Armenians in Transcaucasia numbered 939,131 out of a total population of 4,702,898.[99] Thus Armenians constituted only 20 percent of the population, Georgians 25 to 30 percent, and Tatars and other Muslims 45 percent.

While in many areas of Transcaucasia the Armenians presented little threat in terms of ethnic preponderance, the dominant position reached by their bourgeoisie—a position bolstered by the general growth of trade, industry, and communications against the largely favorable matrix of the Russian legal and administrative rule—tended to create serious friction between them, on the one hand, and the Georgians and Tatar-Turks on the other. This situation, of course, played into the hands of the tsarist government.

The Armenians needed the support of the government to retain and protect their commercial interests and their preponderant economic role. On those occasions when the tsarist government struck out against manifestations of Armenian nationalism and the power structure of the Armenian church, schools, and political parties, it found it easy to exploit the ready distrust and animosity of the Georgian aristocracy and the Turkish feudal landed gentry toward the Armenian bourgeoisie. In revolutionary situations, Transcaucasia thus had religious, ethnic, and socioeconomic conflicts that could have been, and eventually were, easily exploited by the tsarist government.

ECONOMIC DEVELOPMENT OF ARMENIA UNDER RUSSIAN RULE

The establishment of a network of modern communications in Transcaucasia played a significant role in the socioeconomic devel-

opment of the region from which Eastern Armenia benefited greatly. In 1871-72 the tsarist administration finished the construction
of the Tbilisi-Karakilisa-Erevan road and subsequently the Erevan-
Julfa, Karakilisa-Aleksandropol', Aleksandropol'-Koghb, and Na-
khichevan-Gori roads. In 1872 the first railway in Transcaucasia,
the Tiblisi-Poti line, was built. By 1883 a Batum-Baku line was operating, and by 1899 the Tbilisi-Aleksandropol'-Kars line had been
completed.[100] Thus between 1872 and 1900, a total of some 1,948
kilometers of railway lines were built in Transcaucasia, 350 of
which passed through what constitutes present Armenia.[101] In
1899 Baku was linked with Vladikavkaz, two years later Aleksandropol' with Erevan, and in 1908 Erevan with Julfa.[102] This network of railroads, together with the system of postal communication that had been established throughout the region, contributed
greatly to the economic integration of Transcaucasia, to closer
links with Russia and the opening of the region to an influx of
both Russian and foreign capital, and to the rapid growth of industries. In this connection various representatives of industrial enterprises of Moscow, Warsaw, and Tbilisi attempted to tap raw material in the present-day Armenian territories for the use of these
industries.

At the same time, the volume of production of various agricultural commodities grew, as shown below for Erevan province. Figures are given in puds (1 pud = 16,390 kg.).

Year	Commodity	Quantity (in puds)
1861	cotton	30,000
1870	cotton	270,000
1889	cotton	508,764
1893	cotton	646,885
1896	tobacco	7,231

The opening of new markets and the availability of modern means
of transportation contributed to the rapid growth of Transcaucasian trade as well. In the 1862-66 period the overall annual commercial transactions of Transcaucasia averaged 11,815,891 rubles,
but by 1872-76 this total had climbed to 14,139,270 rubles and in
1886 to 39,264,547 rubles.[103] Most of the transit trade of Persia
and the Ottoman Empire with Russia passed through Erevan province. In 1892 the exports from Erevan markets alone totaled some

1,652,000 puds with a value of 6,125,000 rubles. From Russia and other centers of Transcaucasia manufactured goods and petroleum products filled the markets of Armenia. Statistics indicate that in 1893, in three districts of Erevan province the import of such products amounted to one million puds.[104] Russian goods, notably tea, sugar, coffee, and textiles became standard articles in Armenian imports.[105] Tea, especially, became an important item in the Armenian diet.

The process of industrialization in Armenia, in contrast to that of Russia and the rest of Transcaucasia, was very slow. Before the Russian annexation of Eastern Armenia, the only industries in Armenia were small-scale copper- and silver-mining enterprises that were developed under the rule of Erekle, the Georgian king, and were completely gutted during the 1795 Persian incursions into Transcaucasia.[106] A printing press and a small paper-making mill had been established in 1775-76 at Echmiadzin, the spiritual center of the Armenian Apostolic Church. There were some small silk- and glass-manufacturing enterprises in the late eighteenth century, which were destroyed during the 1795 invasion of Transcaucasia by Agha Muhammad Khan. Just before Russia's annexation of Eastern Armenia some of these enterprises had been reactivated: small-scale copper-mining was in evidence, and there were two silk-manufacturing and rudimentary glass-making establishments in the region.[107]

After the annexation of Armenia, and particularly after the 1860s, certain industries began to develop in the country, the most important of which were copper- and salt-mining and wineries. In 1865 the copper mines of Alaverdi were producing annually between 3,000 and 6,000 puds of copper. The mining industry had been held back because of primitive methods and outmoded machinery. Beginning in 1887, when a French company took over a thirty-year concession to exploit the mines of Alaverdi, the situation improved dramatically. In 1894 the investment by this company of some two million francs brought about great technological advances and increased motivation. The extension of the Tbilisi-Aleksandropol'-Kars railway at this time contributed to the volume of production. Between 1900 and 1908 copper production increased from 19,682 puds to 123,731 puds.[108] Similarly, in the region of Ghapan (Zangezur) it rose from 51,783 puds in 1900 to 72,000 puds in 1908.[109]

Other notable economic developments in Armenia under Russian domination were the expansion of the wine industry and the large-scale exploitation of salt-mining. The first modern factories producing alcoholic beverages were those of Saradzhev and Tairov, which imported machinery from Switzerland and went into production in 1889-90. During the next four years the Soghomonov, Afrikov, Giozalov, and Melik-Babakhanov brandy factories were built. While the quality of Armenian wine was not good and its markets were very limited, major markets in brandy were found not only in Transcaucasia but in Russia at large. By 1909 the number of brandy factories had increased to thirteen, the most notable of these belonging to the Shustov, Saradzhev, Abramov, Khakhnazarov, "Arax," and "Na Vere" firms.[110] Of the twelve major brandy factories of Transcaucasia eight were in Armenia; and as early as 1906 Armenia ranked as the number one producer of brandy and alcohol and number two in the production of wine.[111]

Between 1890 and the early 1900s a number of industries were developed on a somewhat smaller scale. For instance, systematic exploitation of salt mines in Erevan and Nakhichevan provinces and Kars *okrug* was undertaken. Salt production in Erevan and Kars increased from 1,504,285 puds in 1897 to 2,599,297 puds in 1903. Until 1908 the major concessions of the salt mines of Erevan, Kars, and Nakhichevan were controlled by the Janpoladian family.

This same period saw the development of cotton-ginning enterprises. By 1913 there were some fifty small cotton-ginning factories in the province of Erevan. Also, during these years, a number of small-scale silk-manufacturing businesses were established.[113] The production of olive oil, too, was increased and modernized. By 1903 some 137 small enterprises in the province of Erevan were producing olive oil.[114]

Of far greater importance than any of these, however, was the modernization of the dairy industries, which took place between 1860 and 1900. The first modern dairy enterprises in Transcaucasia and Armenia were founded by European, mainly Swiss, businessmen. Their example was followed by Armenians, Georgians, Russians, and Azerbaijanis. In the region of Lori (in Armenia) some twenty modern dairy establishments were formed, each producing annually an average of 29,000 puds of cheese. Modern dairy farms were founded also in the regions of Kars, Erevan, and Aleksandropol'. Whereas in 1905 there were only six European-style large modern farms in Armenia with 2,413 cows producing 1,079 puds of milk and 2,730 puds of cheese, by 1912 there were 64 modern farms with 18,539 cows producing 5,656 puds of milk and 34,108 puds of cheese.[115] The market for these products, including Swiss- and Dutch-style cheeses, was chiefly in Tbilisi, Rostov, Odessa, and Moscow. Most of these enterprises were owned by Europeans and Russians, with Armenians controlling only five or ten percent.

In 1906 the total number of dairy farms and other small enter- prises (leatherworking, etc.) in the province of Erevan was 2,773, with an estimated annual production worth 1,236,000 rubles. Par- allel to the development of small-scale industries and business en- terprises in Eastern Armenia was the growth of an Armenian fac- tory labor force estimated between 10,000 and 12,000. Of these, 5,000 were employed in major industries, eighty-six percent of them in the copper industry.[116] The Armenian factory workers, like the Armenian bourgeoisie, however, were not concentrated in Russian Armenia proper; there were large numbers of Armenian workers in the various industrial centers of the Caucasus, especially in Baku, where between 1889-1913, for instance, they constituted between 25 and 32 percent of the oilfield work force.

The process of urbanization kept pace with the introduction in- to the Transcaucasus of various industries, as well as with the growth of trade and migration of the landless peasantry. In 1914, 1,300,000 inhabitants of Transcaucasia (out of a population of 7,600,000) lived in urban centers. In Russian Armenia, an esti- mated 100,000 (10.5 percent) of 1,000,000 inhabitants lived in towns and cities. The population of Erevan had meanwhile climbed to 31,000, that of Aleksandropol' to 33,000.[117]

THE GROWTH AND SECULARIZATION
OF ARMENIAN CULTURE

On the eve of the Russian conquest, the *Jarangavorats* of Echmiad- zin, founded in 1813 for the purpose of training Armenian clergy- men, was the only school of any note in Eastern Armenia. Stand- ards were low and the curriculum archaic. After the annexation of Eastern Armenia, however, the Russians in 1831 established two modern-style provincial elementary schools, one in Erevan, the other in Nakhichevan. Admission to these schools was determined both on a legal and on a class basis. Within the next few decades, however, the tsarist government had established a network of primary and secondary schools; and the fact that they were coeducational provided a major challenge to the tenets and religious character of the traditional Armenian school. By 1878 there were 24 secondary schools and 583 elementary schools in the Caucasus; in 1900 these numbers had risen to 51 and 1,693, respectively. These schools attracted an ever-increasing number of Armenian students. In 1878, for example, there were 1,257 Armenians attending the secondary schools and 2,037 in the elementary schools, while by 1900 there were 5,250 in the secondary schools and 23,218 in the elementary. In addition, the Russian administration allowed the establishment of private schools with modern curricula. In these schools the Armenian enrollment was 2,640.[118]

By 1890 the ethnic breakdown of the student body in the three secondary schools (gymnasiums) of Tbilisi was as follows:[119]

	Percent Georgians	Percent Armenians	Percent Russians
Gymnasium I	16.6	28.2	38.4
Gymnasium II	19.0	26.9	38.9
Gymnasium III	11.6	56.7	21.3

The appeal of Russian education to the Armenians was widespread, especially in the urban centers. Despite this situation, the education of the majority of the Armenian youth remained under the control of the local Armenian communities, who operated their schools through legal privileges granted to the Armenian Church by the Russian autocracy.

The *Polozhenie* of 1836, which recognized some of the traditional privileges of the Armenian Church, legitimized and institutionalized the existing unity and the economic and spiritual powers of the Armenian Church and its educational function. Under the provisions of the *Polozhenie*, the tsarist government recognized the spiritual and administrative control of the Catholicos of Echmiadzin over all the Armenian congregations of the Russian Empire, and the right of the Armenian communities of the empire to full freedom of worship. The Armenian clergy was exempt from civil burdens. The document recognized the principle that the Catholicos, the supreme spiritual head of the Armenian Church, was to be chosen by the elected representatives of the Armenian people of Russia and those of the Diaspora. The tsarist government also allowed the opening of Armenian schools provided they were under the control of the church. A few restrictions on the authority of the Armenian Church were imposed: the decisions of the Supreme Synod of the Church, for instance, had to be sanctioned by a procurator appointed by the Russian government; and the appointments and removals of bishops in various dioceses were to be sanctioned by the tsar, who also had the authority either to confirm or choose between two candidates selected for the office of the Catholicos. The names of these two candidates, however, were to be submitted to him by an Armenian National Assembly gathered in Echmiadzin to select the next Catholicos.[120] Notwithstanding these restrictions and the intentions and attempts of the tsarist autocracy to control the Armenian Church, its wealth and its educational activities, or its attempts through such control to exercise influence over the Armenians outside the Russian Empire, the *Polozhenie* was probably the most generous document granted to a non-Orthodox Church in Russia.

Contrary to the belief of the tsarist regime that the Armenian Church-administered parochial educational system was moribund, the Armenians, under the leadership of both a European- and a Russian-trained educated elite, managed to revitalize and modernize their school system, its finances, and its curriculum. (Some prominent members of the Armenian bourgeoisie of Russia, India, and Persia left legacies to the Armenian Church for the express purpose of helping to fulfill the educational needs of the Armenians.) The network of parochial schools was used to promote Armenian national culture, to resist tsarist assimilationist policies, to politicize the Armenian masses, and to contribute to the growth of their national consciousness and self-assertiveness. Taking advantage of the provisions of the *Polozhenie*, the Armenian Church assumed a dual function by fusing nationalism to religion. The process of democratization of the structure of the church and secularization of education transformed it not into a bastion of orthodoxy but into one of nationalism. By 1885, in its six dioceses of Russia (Erevan, Karabakh, Tbilisi, Shemakha, Astrakhan, and New Nakhichevan-Bessarabia) and in the region of Kars, the Armenian Church controlled some 330 schools, 247 of which were for boys and 83 for girls.[121]

The gradual secularization of the Armenian parochial schools brought about a counterreaction from the Russian government, which attempted to bring under its control a substantial part of the curriculum of the parochial schools. The government required that all teachers of the elementary schools must be Russian subjects, that instruction in Russian language, history, and geography were to be obligatory, and that government-appointed supervisors would oversee the proper instruction in these subjects. In 1884 the Russian government tried to extend such control to the finances as well. To reach its goal of curbing nationalism and eliminating the seeds of separatism, Russians tried to circumscribe the definition of religious instruction and to remove from the Armenian Church the unrestricted right to found schools. These demands the Holy Synod at Echmiadzin rejected. In 1885 the Russian government ordered Armenian parochial elementary schools closed, and two years later it demanded that throughout the Armenian secondary schools instruction in the Armenian religion must be given in the Russian language. These demands, too, were opposed by the Armenians. In addition, the government ordered that all teachers in Armenian schools must have credentials from a state teacher-training institution, and banned the teaching of Armenian history and geography (1889). The Russian government's campaign against the Armenian school system continued into 1894.

The parochial schools, reopened after some concessions and compromises, were shut down again in 1895. A decree of 1897, while sparing seminaries, deprived the Armenian Church of the right to operate the parochial schools. The government moved also to undercut the financial sources of such schools and took measures to revise the by-laws of various Armenian charitable and educational organizations. All such organizations were forbidden to establish new branches, and existing ones were ordered to decentralize, to divest themselves of libraries and educational endowments, and to confine their activities to purely charitable ends. In addition, the tsarist government banned some major Armenian publishing associations (1900).[122] In 1903 the tsarist government decided to deal the final blow to the dominant socioeconomic position of the Armenian Church. A decree ostensibly recognizing the Church's title to its properties ordered the transfer and control and administration of all Church properties, both movable and immovable, to the Ministry of Agriculture and Public Domains and to the Ministry of the Interior. This transformed into an open conflagration the protracted but smoldering struggle between tsarist autocracy and the Armenian Church. The Armenian people saw clearly that the object of the Russian autocracy was to undermine their cultural and religious autonomy. After an initial phase of more or less passive resistance, or failure to comply, the Armenians, through their political, religious, educational, and revolutionary organizations, decided to take direct action. This mass active resistance, occurring at the same time as the outbreak of the 1905 Russian Revolution, forced the tsarist regime to reconsider its policies in an effort to stabilize the situation in Transcaucasia. The government therefore made some concessions to the Armenians. The decrees confiscating Armenian Church properties were annulled and Armenians were allowed to reopen their parochial elementary schools on the basis of the tsarist guideline of 1874.[123] By 1914 the parochial schools had recuperated some of their losses and the total number of Armenian pupils in the elementary parochial schools of the Transcaucasus had reached 34,845. By then, however, the Russian state school had asserted its primacy: there were 42,594 Armenian students in Russian elementary schools. More important, whereas there were only 1,528 pupils in Armenian diocesan secondary schools, there were 8,713 attending the Russian ones.[124]

The influence of the Russian educational system predominated not only in the state schools but in the parochial elementary and secondary diocesan schools as well. Over the period between 1850 and 1879 most of the curricula of these institutions had gradually been secularized. Even the curriculum of Armenian seminaries included, among other things, logic, psychology, mathematics, pedagogy, and physics.[125] Russian secondary schools, as well as Armenian institutions patterned on them, prepared the ground for the emergence of an Armenian literati in Russian Armenia who were to become the transmitters of Russian and European cultures, advocates of social change, spokesmen for national liberation movements and national self-assertion, and apostles of revolution. Such famous Armenian secondary schools as the Nersisian school in Tbilisi (founded in 1825) played a prominent role for an entire century and produced many of the famous Armenian intellectuals, writers, and political activists. A similar institution was the Gevorgian Djemaran (Academy). This institution of higher learning, founded in Echmiadzin in 1874, attracted the elite of Armenian students from all parts of Russia as well as a few from abroad. Although its avowed aim was to serve as a seminary and as a teacher-training school, it was rather in the second category that it had greater success. In its first twenty-five years the institution produced some 284 graduates, of whom only 47 chose to become clergymen. The Academy became a hotbed of student activism, producing not only eminent writers and educators but revolutionaries as well. Many prominent Armenian members of Dashnak, Menshevik, Bolshevik, Social Revolutionary (S.R.), and the Kadet parties, among them Anastas Mikoyan, came from the ranks of the student body of this institution.[126]

Armenian secondary schools taught not only the Armenian language and history but Russian, mathematics, physics, logic, psychology, and geography as well. Armenian youth was thus exposed to Russian culture and scientific thought not only in the state-operated secondary schools but in its own private and parochial schools as well. In this respect the Lazarian Djemaran (Academy) of Moscow played an important role both in the development of a secular Armenian culture and in the propagation of Russian literature and scientific thought among the Armenians. Founded in 1814 (and opened in 1815) by the Lazarev (Lazarian, in Armenian) family for the promotion of modern higher education among Armenians, the Lazarev Djemaran was transformed in 1827 into the Lazarev Armenian Institute of Oriental Languages.[127] It thus assumed a dual function, preparing Orientalists for the Russian government and universities, and educators, publicists, and intellectuals for the Armenian community. Between 1815 and 1848 alone, out of some 726 students who attended the Lazarev Academy and Institute, 112 went on to become university graduates.[128] Concurrent with these developments, Armenian studies became institutionalized in the universities of St. Petersburg, Moscow, and Kazan. Many Armenian students, who graduated from Lazarev Djemaran, and from Russian gymnasiums and Armenian diocesan secondary schools, continued their education in such centers of higher learning as the universities of Heidelberg, Berlin, Jena, St. Petersburg, Moscow, and Dorpat. Thus by 1850-60 there had been created a west-European and Russian-trained Armenian intelligentsia, eager not only to promote European and Russian culture and scientific thought among Armenians but also eager to secularize the Armenian language, to create a popular vernacular literature, and to democratize and modernize the structure of the Armenian school system.

The movement to establish vernacular Eastern Armenian as a literary language and to remove classical Armenian as the medium of popular education, which was led by Khachatur Abovian and Stepannos Nazariants, set off a major debate between modernest proponents of the vernacular as a literary language and traditionalist champions of classical (*grabar*) Armenian. The first steps in the direction of establishing the vernacular were taken by Lazarev Djemaran and Nersisian school.

Abovian, a product of Nersisian school and a graduate of Dorpat University, upon his return to the Transcaucasus in 1837, armed with modern pedagogical theories and a high sense of patriotism, attempted to open a model secular school (endowed by private funds or sustained by the rich resources of the Armenian Church) that would revolutionize the educational system of Eastern Armenia. As a teacher in Tbilisi, he envisioned the means to modernize the educational system of the Armenian schools and to spread literacy. While he conceded his admiration for the beauty, richness, and logic of classical Armenian, nevertheless he found the gulf between this language and the masses so great that it constituted an obstacle to mass education and the subsequent enlightenment of the people. His attempts to bring about such reforms within the establishment having failed, he undertook to reach the "ordinary people through a language understood by all." In 1841-42 he wrote a patriotic historical novel, *Verk Hayastani* (The wounds of Armenia), depicting the "liberation of Eastern Armenia by Christian Russia," hailing the significance of Russian rule and the potentialities it held for the enlightenment of the Armenian nation. But the obstructionism of the tsarist bureaucracy, the opposition of the Armenian traditionalists, and the petty intrigues of his colleagues frustrated his efforts. He also became disillusioned about the probability that "cross-worshipping Russia" might ever help the Armenians to transform the structure of their society, revitalize their culture, or regain their historical identity and role through enlightenment and self-confidence. His novel, however, published in 1858 ten years after he had vanished under mysterious circumstances, became extremely popular, and showed forth as a beacon for the champion of a secularized Armenian language and secular education.[129]

Nazariants, like Abovian, was a graduate of Nersisian and Dorpat. In 1842 he became a professor of Armenian language at the University of Kazan and in 1849 a lecturer in Arabic, Persian, and Latin in the Lazarev Institute. Like Abovian, he too believed that enlightenment must be brought to the Armenians, and that this was possible only through a secular education, secular language, literature, and theater. In university circles and among educators Nazariants fought for these goals. In 1858, in order to widen his audience, he launched a monthly publication, *Hiusisapayl* (*Aurora Borealis*), patterned on and greatly influenced by the famous Russian periodical *Sovremennik*. This periodical, which continued until 1864, championed educational and economic reforms. Nazariants, like Abovian before him, saw in Russia a welcoming hand to the "exploited and enslaved Armenian people," a bridge to European civilization. While aware of the colonial policies of tsarism, he hoped that Russia, under the leadership of the reformist Tsar Alexander II, would grant internal autonomy to Armenians and thus enable them to develop their national existence. Giving due consideration to the Armenians' historical background and to the stage of their current socioeconomic development, Nazariants urged the Armenians to adhere to a Russian orientation: "politically the Armenian must be Russian." *Hiusisapayl* contributed to the development of a literary generation which institutionalized the use of vernacular Armenian and developed a new East Armenian literature.[130]

By the 1890s vernacular Eastern Armenian had become the established secular and literary language of the Armenian communities of Russia. Translation of Russian and European literary works became one of the chief preoccupations of the Armenian nationalist-modernists. The press of Lazarev Institute (founded in 1829) published Russian-Armenian dictionaries, some of the works of Pushkin and Lermontov in Armenian, and selections from Krylov, Lomonosov, Derzhavin, Dmitriev, Zhukovskii, Khemnitser, and many others. Abovian made translations from Karamzin, Krylov, and Zhukovskii. *Hiusisapayl*, too, printed some translations from Lermontov and Pushkin.[131]

It was not only through the media of schools and *Hiusisapayl* and the works of Abovian that the influence of Russian culture and the Russian language spread. The Armenians, aside from forming a strong bourgeoisie, an expanded school system, and a growing intelligentsia, developed also a press of their own and publishing houses. Starting with such short-lived periodicals as the bilingual *Vostochnaiia Izvestiia* of Astrakhan (1816), and *Kovkas* of Tbilisi (1846-47), both of which were published in classical Armenian, and *Ararat* of Tbilisi, the first journal in vernacular Eastern Armenian, by the second half of the nineteenth century the number of Armenian periodicals in Russia had reached 246. Most of these publications carried original Armenian contributions and translations from Russian journals and works of literary figures. In the Armenian press of the 1890s there appeared some 700 translations from Russian literature, as against an average of 150 in previous decades. In such periodicals as *Murdj* (Hammer) of Tbilisi, there regularly appeared translations from west European and Russian literary figures (Pushkin, Lermontov, Pisarev, Belinskii, and others). Many Armenian writers who had received their education in Russian or Armenian schools not only submitted original contributions but translated the works of eminent Russian literary figures and critics. Among these writers were H. Hovhannisian, Gh. Aghaian, Y. Shahaziz, H. Tumanian, Av. Isahakian, and Alexander Dzaturian. Dzaturian alone translated 150 poems from Pushkin, Lermontov, Nekrasov, Pleshcheev, and Kolstov. In addition, the Armenian publishing houses in Tbilisi and Baku, and the Armenian presses in New Nakhichevan, Moscow, and elsewhere published, along with original works of Armenian authors, translations from Dobroliubov, Krylov, Gogol, Belinskii, Tolstoi, Nekrasov, Saltykov-Shchedrin, and Gor'kii.[132] Most nineteenth-century Armenian authors of Russia readily acknowledged the great impact of Russian literature on their works. In addition, the Russian language left a strong imprint not only on the Eastern Armenian vernacular but on the literary language as well, especially in the technical field.[133]

The influence of Russian culture extended to the modern Armenian theater in Russia, initially developed from 1824 to 1859 in the Armenian high schools of the Crimea and in New Nakhichevan and Tbilisi. In Moscow, from 1858 on, theatrical performances, under the direction of one or two contemporary famous Russian actor-directors,[134] were presented by the Armenian students of Lazarev Djemaran and of Moscow University (in 1860 the university had some sixty Armenian students). The Armenian theater in

Moscow was influenced by the works of Griboedov, Gogol, and Ostrovskii; the theatrical group of Lazarev Djemaran presented Armenian and Russian plays, particularly works of Gogol. From 1863 on the Armenian communities of Tbilisi and New Nakhichevan as well as others organized professional theatrical groups with regular repertoires. In 1873 the Tbilisi company recruited additional Armenian members from Constantinople. Included in its repertoire were plays of Shakespeare, Schiller, and Molière, in addition to works of Ostrovskii and Griboedov.

Armenian literary critics in the 1880s demanded more presentations of the works of Gogol, Turgenev, and Ostrovskii and praised the realism of Russian literature and drama, bringing these works to the attention of Armenian dramatists to be used as examples and guides.[135] In general, Armenian dramatists of the 1850s and 1860s, such as M. Patkanian, N. Pughinian, M. Ter-Grigorian, and especially G. Sndukian, the leading dramatist of the 1880s, were influenced not only by West European dramatists but also by the esthetic views of Belinskii and other Russian literary critics. Some were influenced by *Sovremennik.* (Sndukian, while studying at the University of St. Petersburg, was a classmate of N. Chernyshevskii.) The influence of such Russian dramatists as Gogol, Ostrovskii, Turgenev, and Gor'kii is easily traced in the East Armenian rationalist-didactic, historical, as well as realist drama.[136]

As for modern East Armenian music, in this area too there appears the imprint of Russian culture. Some of the major Armenian composers of the nineteenth century, like Kara-Murza, Yekmalian, Korganov, and Tigranian, received their training from Russian composers in the conservatories of Moscow and St. Petersburg. Korganov, for example, was influenced by his teachers Anton G. Rubinstein, Tchaikovsky, Ipolitov-Ivanov, and S. Taneev. Yekmalian had a close association with Kazachenko; N. Tigranian was influenced by Rimskii-Korsakov. A. Spandarian, another famous Armenian composer, had close links with such Russian composers as Gluazunov, Liadov, and Arenskii; Kara-Murza and Spandarian composed Ukrainian songs.[137]

A similar situation prevailed with Armenian painters of Russia. Most of them had studied at the school of painting in Tbilisi (the first such school in Transcaucasia, inaugurated in 1874), and at the Academy of Fine Arts in St. Petersburg, where an entire generation of Armenian painters had received their training. Among these are such names as H. Hovnatanian, S. Nersisian, H. Shamchinian, G. Bashinjaghian, and, of course, Hovhannes Aivazovsky, the most famous of them all.[138]

ARMENIAN SOCIOPOLITICAL THOUGHT
AND THE NATIONAL LIBERATION MOVEMENT

In the second half of the nineteenth century the Armenian bourgeoisie enjoyed a well-entrenched position in Russia, Persia, India, and the Ottoman Empire. Outside of Russia, a modern Armenian culture flourished in such centers as Venice, Vienna, Constantinople, Smyrna (Izmir), and Calcutta; and an educated Armenian generation, product of Armenian and European schools, provided a fertile ground for the development of Armenian nationalist and social movements, interested in the social and economic state of the Armenian nation and in its future. Reports of the exactions, injustices, and indignities suffered by Armenians outside major urban centers of the Ottoman Empire and the possible future of the Armenians as a cohesive, organized, cultural and political entity aroused the concern not only of the Armenian bourgeoisie but also of the Armenian intelligentsia of Russia. A faction led by such nationalist-conservatives as G. Hakhverdian, P. Shanshian, M. Aghabekian, and P. Simonian was aware of the new economic and political realities created by the Russian annexation of Eastern Armenia and the scattering of both the Armenian bourgeoisie and intelligentsia throughout Russia and Transcaucasia. They knew that the importing of Russian-manufactured goods was ruining the Armenian artisan class, and that inflation and taxes were pauperizing the Armenian peasantry, driving them from their homeland to seek security in urban centers of Russia. To ameliorate the situation, they proposed to stabilize the economy of Transcaucasia by promoting local trade and local industries and by improving means of communication between the Caspian and Black seas, improving and modernizing the agriculture of Erevan province, and establishing harmonious relations with neighboring nations. Some of the adherents of this faction advocated the opening of Armenian business and vocational schools in Transcaucasia and the concentration of Armenian capital in them.

Although the nationalist-conservatives labored to preserve and improve the social and economic position of the Armenians in Russia, they generally considered Ottoman Armenia as the most desirable base for nation-building. Gabriel Patkanian, a leading representative of this school of thought, argued that the religion of the Armenians had helped them preserve their language and that the language in turn had sustained their nationality. In spite of this, however, Armenians could not call themselves a nation in the European sense of the word. For that they needed unity and common purpose. Unity could be achieved only if they banded together on their ancestral lands. Common purpose, on the other hand, depended on the degree to which Armenians became educated and modernized. Nationhood and progress for Armenians thus depended on their adoption of European culture and of modern technology. Here, Russia and Europe could provide Armenians the necessary means and stimuli, while at the same time they had the power to press the Ottoman Empire to end its discriminatory and exploitative policies toward Armenians. Thus the Armenians could establish a solid basis for achieving unity, enlightenment, common purpose, and freedom.[139]

A Russian orientation was strong among Armenian liberals too. Grigor Ardzruni, a leading liberal and editor of *Mshak,* for instance, welcomed the historical role of Russia. Without Russia and her influence, he said, the Armenians would have remained static as they had been for the past five or six centuries, silent and immobile.[140] Russia had enabled the Armenians to develop a strong bourgeoisie, which must now take advantage of existing conditions and help the Armenian people not to become just a religious sect but a true nation. For this the Armenian language, along with its secular culture, must be developed, and a fatherland must be secured as a crucial factor in the preservation and development of the nation.[141] Furthermore, Ardzruni promoted the view that the Armenian bourgeoisie should help develop with its own capital the commercial and industrial potentials of Russian Armenia; that it should help the Armenian artisans to develop and concentrate in their hands the various trades in Russian Armenia and provide work to Armenian workers, thus helping to prevent the outflow of Armenian emigrants from East Armenia to the rest of the Russian Empire. An alliance between the Armenian bourgeoisie and the Armenian intelligentsia was necessary to the maintenance of an Armenian nation within the Russian Empire.[142]

Ardzruni also held the view, shared by many other Armenian liberals in Russia, that the social, economic, and cultural position of Armenians in the Russian Empire was far superior to that in the Ottoman Empire. In Russia Armenians did not face physical extermination or social degradation, and the Armenian bourgeoisie was not threatened. In Russia, which was dynamic and in the process of industrializing, the Armenians had a strong economic position. The Ottoman Empire, on the other hand, was feudal, autocratic, and stagnant. In the event of a collapse of the Ottoman Empire, the "sick man of Europe," the Western Armenians were advised to shy away from England and to look to Russia for their political orientation. If the Russians were unable—or unwilling—to accept the union of the two Armenias, then Ottoman Armenians had to seek independence. An independent Armenia could be of mutual benefit to Armenians and Russians; Russia, Ardzruni hoped, would rather see a grateful, friendly, and faithful independent Armenia as a neighbor than a conniving England.[143] If Ottoman Armenians joined the Armenians of Russia, for the first time a majority of Armenians would come under one rule; Ottoman Armenians would enjoy physical security and would bolster the numerical strength of the Armenians of Russia. In addition to promoting the cultural, economic, and political unity and the integration of the two Armenias, the Armenians would benefit from the cultural and economic advantages that a modernizing Russia could provide them. Furthermore, Ottoman Armenia could serve as an adequate market for the Armenian capital, thus reconciling the class interests of the Armenian bourgeoisie and the national aspirations of the Armenian intelligentsia. If and when the Russian Empire also disintegrated, the Armenians would already have established a secure cultural and economic base for their continued development as a nation.

Other Russian Armenian liberals also considered the ownership of land, the conquest of a fatherland and a collective existence, and an end to the continuous dispersion and emigration of Armenians from historical Armenia as the most crucial historical problems confronting the Armenian nation. As one of them put it: "Even if the Armenians lived in slavery but lived on one land and led a collective social existence," they would still have a future as a nation.[144] Without a fatherland the Armenians as a nation were doomed. Russian orientation was thus a means and not an end for the majority of the Armenian liberals and nationalist-conservatives, and as such it figured prominently in their plans to win a fatherland and to preserve or reconstruct a modern Armenian nation.

Russian revolutionary movements left a deep imprint on the Armenian national liberation movement, on its revolutionary parties and its ideologies. The revolutionary wave of the 1850s and 1860s, for instance, gave the first major impetus to the Armenian national liberation movement. Such Armenian intellectuals as Mikael Nalbandian (1829-1866) became the transmitters of revolutionary ideology and later a source of inspiration to Armenian revolutionaries. Educated in the universities of St. Petersburg and Moscow, a teacher at Lazarev Academy and a collaborator on *Hiusisapayl*, Nalbandian was an early admirer of such utopian socialists as Owen and Fourier and of anarchists like Proudhon. He enjoyed close personal ties with Herzen, Bakunin, Ogariev, Turgenev, and Dobroliubov, and was acquainted also with Belinskii, Chernyshevskii, and Serno-Solov'evich. Under the influence of these figures he became a "revolutionary democrat," participated in the "Zemlia i volia" revolutionary movement, worked with Russian émigré revolutionary circles in London, and advocated both national and social liberation for Armenians.[145] And in turn, Armenian nationalists, liberals, and revolutionaries found their inspiration in the writings of Nalbandian.[146] He was arrested by the tsarist authorities in 1862 and confined to the Petropavlovsk prison for three years. Upon his release in 1865 he was exiled to Kamyshin, where he died of tuberculosis the following year.

Nalbandian was not the only Armenian intellectual who was influenced by the writings of such men as Belinskii, Chernyshevskii, Nekrasov, and Herzen. Others, such as Barsegh Bastamiantz, Mikael Patkanian, and Gevork Yevangulian, between 1855 and 1865 tried to develop esthetic theories based on their understanding of Belinskii, Chernyshevskii, and Herzen. *Sovremennik* had subscribers in almost all the major Armenian urban centers. Such popular writers and poets as Ghazaros Aghayan and Hagop Hagopian, among others, wrote of the influence of the works of Chernyshevskii, Dobroliubov, and Nekrasov on their own intellectual formation and artistic theories during their formative years in the 1880s. According to a censored article of Avetik Araskhanian, a leading Armenian liberal publicist of the 1880s and editor of *Murdj*, Chernyshevskii and the Russian revolutionary movement had deeply affected both the Armenian and the non-Armenian youth of the Caucasus.[147]

THE IMPACT OF RUSSIAN POPULISM (NARODNICHESTVO)

In the 1870s and during the 1880s the most important single influence on the formation of the ideologies of the Armenian national-liberation movement was Russian populism. Such was its influence that one major authority on the history of the movement maintained that "It was the Russian populist revolution that through the intermediary of the Armenian intelligentsia began the revolutionary movement among the Armenians of the Ottoman Empire."[148] Aside from Russia proper, where many Armenian students came into contact with the Russian populists, in Transcaucasia itself there was in 1875 a local populist organization which had Georgian, Azerbaijani, Russian, and Armenian members.[149] In addition there were Transcaucasian populist organizations in St. Petersburg and Moscow as well as in Zurich and Geneva.

In 1879 the conspiratorial Russian revolutionary society "Land and Freedom" (founded in 1876) split into two groups: the "Black Partition" (*Cherny peredel*) and "People's Will" (*Narodnaia volia*); the former emphasized gradualism and the use of propaganda, while the latter proposed all-out terroristic assault and a revolutionary offensive against the tsarist government. The split influenced the character of the Armenian populist groups, too.

In 1879-80 the "Black Partition" established a branch in Tbilisi that was followed by a branch of the "People's Will." According to tsarist police reports, some Armenian members of these organizations, like S. Ter-Grigorian, had established contacts between various Armenian national-liberation organizations and *Narodnaia volia's* branch in Tbilisi.[150] The executive committee of *Narodnaia volia* in Tbilisi was composed of three Georgians and three Armenians.[151] From the 1880s on many Armenian intellectuals drifted into liberal, legal populism following reformism and gradualism. The important Armenian figures of this movement were A. Kalantar, H.

Ter-Movsisian, S. Ghorghanian, Hratchia, G. Iuzbashian, A. Amirian, L. Sarkisian, G. Vartanian, and A. Adelian. Most of these "legal narodniks" were students at the universities of Moscow and St. Petersburg, and were influenced by such Russian ideologues of the legal *narodniki* movement as S. N. Krivenko, V. Vorontsov, and their major periodical *Russkoe bogatstvo*. The Armenian legal *narodniks*, who continued their activities into the 1900s, wrote in such prominent Armenian periodicals as *Mshak, Meghu Hayastani,* and *Gordz*. In general, the Armenian legal *narodniks* advocated concrete measures and reforms to ameliorate the plight of the peasantry. They stressed improvement in agriculture, opening of agricultural schools, and encouragement of intellectuals who wished to go to live in the village; and they stimulated a distaste for unnecessary hardships attributed to capitalism. They advocated also communal ownership of the land as a means of saving the people from the malevolent aspects of capitalism. Such a program, they reasoned, would stop the flight of Armenian peasants from their lands and would provide them with the necessary conditions to free themselves economically and to benefit culturally.[152]

It was the revolutionary wing of Russian populism, however, that together with Socialism and Marxism became the dominant force among Armenian radical students and intellectuals; this movement had a far-reaching impact on the formation and the ideologies of Armenian revolutionary groups and parties. Among the existing Armenian revolutionary and nationalist groups of the early 1880s (in Tbilisi, Erevan, Shushi [Karabakh], etc.) those of Moscow and St. Petersburg became the principal proponents of Russian revolutionary populism. The Armenian revolutionary organization of Moscow, known as *Hayrenaserneri miutiun* (The Union of Patriots) and founded in 1882, established the first illegal and secret Armenian press and published the paper *Azatutian Avetaber* (Herald of Freedom), which was the first Armenian revolutionary paper. Its emblem was a dagger and a gun. This publication echoed the views of the Russian populists and advocated the socioeconomic liberation of Armenians: "If the working, productive forces of Armenia [the peasant, the artisan and the worker] are going to be exploited, then for the Union of Patriots no political liberty has meaning and significance." "The cornerstone of the [Armenian] people's freedom lies in its economic independence."

As for the nationality question, the *Azatutian Avetaber* attacked both chauvinists "who imagine that by hating other nations, they love their fatherland"—and those colorless "world citizens" who hide behind cosmopolitanism and universalism. Instead it advanced a plea for cooperation between the various nationalities living in Armenia. Equal respect for each nation's language, culture, religion, and independence could in no way be detrimental to mutual progress and development. The paper also advocated social unity and social solidarity: "one for all and all for one" was its ideal, hence its plea that all private and crown-held lands should pass to the peasant communes (*mir* or *obshchina*). Only the peasant commune was entitled to ownership since it alone was the productive force. Furthermore, the communes were to serve as the social and political units basic to the formation of a large and stable political confederation.

In the matter of Armenian national liberation from Ottoman rule, the Union of Patriots derided those Armenians who sought to beg for liberty and justice. To free itself from "the barbarian yoke" the Armenian people had but one means: it could purchase its freedom only through blood and toil. The paper appealed to the Armenian youth to become the leaders, the backbone of revolutionary-liberation movements. The organization's ideals and tactics were not only reflections of *Narodnaia volia*—propaganda, agitation, organized bands, and terror—but bore the imprint of Peter Lavrov's theories. The organization adhered to Lavrov's view "That humanity's single main desire was to achieve happiness, to possess such a social and cultural state, where every man's physical, intellectual and moral development would be secured equally."[153]

The *narodniki* (as well as other Russian revolutionary ideologies) left their imprint also on the program and the ideology of the first all-Armenian revolutionary party, the Hnchakian party, which within the following three decades carried out its political activities and propaganda among Armenians of the Ottoman Empire, of Russia, and of the Diaspora. The Hnchakian party was founded in Geneva in 1887 on the initiative of six Armenian university students from Russia. The founders of the party, including its leaders, Avetis Nazarbek[ian] and his fiancée, Maro Vartanian, were in contact with Russian émigré revolutionary circles of Europe (including G. Plekhanov and Vera Zasulich, the founders of "Emancipation of Labor," the first Russian Marxist organization). The Hnchakian party took its name from the party's organ, *Hnchak* (the Armenian word for bell), which most likely was borrowed from Alexander Herzen's *Kolokol* [Bell]. The motto of the Hnchakian party, which appeared in the first issue of its paper, was "Among the people, with the people, for the people."

Although in its program the party adhered to socialist and Marxist ideologies (and later designated itself as social-democratic), the influence of Russian populism, especially that of *Narodnaia volia,* remained strong. The populist influence manifested itself both in the ideological tenets as well as in the adopted methods of the party. For instance, whereas in the case of Europe the party denounced the exploiting and dehumanizing character of capitalism, which it saw being displaced by a proletarian revolution, by the triumph of socialism, and by the reorganization and restructuring of society, in the case of Armenia the party held fast to the populist view of socialism. According to Nazarbek, the Armenian people and Armenia had not entered the industrial-capitalist phase of development, nor was it necessary for them to do so. To aid in the introduction of capitalism in Armenia and among Armenians was incompatible with socialism and therefore constituted a crime. He advocated instead the preservation among Armenians of the *mir* (the peasant commune) as the most positive foundation for a future socialist order. To enable the Armenian people to receive the "benefits of capitalism without its yoke and evils" Nazarbek proposed the formation of communal land ownership in liberated Armenia and the organization and management of industrial production on the basis of workers' associations, assisted by government credit. These associations were to serve as bridges to socialist order, sparing Armenia from the nefarious impact of capitalism.[154]

The tactics of the Hnchakian party also reflected the impact of *Narodnaia volia.* The party adopted political terror as a revolutionary means of eliminating its opponents, police spies, and informers, driving fear into the hearts of oppressors, and elevating the spirit of the Armenian people. To accomplish its objectives the party called upon the Armenian intelligentsia, "the educated and understanding class, especially the youth." Even the party's structure, a highly centralized system directed by a central committee, was patterned upon the *Narodnaia volia.* Socialism was a distant goal of the party, however. Its immediate goal was to liberate historical Armenia from the Ottoman Empire and thus to afford the Armenians the possibility of developing themselves unhindered, both socially and culturally, in a free and independent fatherland with a democratic form of government. This fatherland would then serve as a base for the liberation of the rest of the Armenians. Quoting the anarchist Kropotkin, *Hnchak* stressed the belief that freedom is not given, it is taken. Arms and armed rebellion were therefore essential in carrying out their program. On the basis of cooperation with other national-liberation movements in the Ottoman Empire, the Hnchakians expressed the hope of contributing to the formation of a general federation of independent fatherlands in the East.[155]

Like the Hnchakian party, Hai Heghapokhakan Dashnaktsutiun (the Armenian Revolutionary Federation) party was also formed by Armenians of Russia. Its three principal organizers, Kristapor Mikaelian, Stepan Zorian (or Rostom), and Simon Zavarian, were products of Russian universities. All three were influenced by the Russian populist and socialist movements. Mikaelian was especially influenced by the writings of Chernyshevskii, Dobroliubov, Lavrov, and Mikhailovskii. He became an active member of *Narodnaia volia* (with which he had come into contact while a student in a secondary school). According to Mikaelian, the ideal of the radical students at that time was international socialism. Zavarian too speaks of the influence of Chernyshevskii, Nekrasov, and Perovskaia, in his memoirs; and he too participated in the *Narodnaia volia* movement. Zorian, on the other hand, took part in radical student activities at the Petrovsk Academy in Moscow and at the Novo Aleksandrskii Agricultural Academy near Warsaw.[156]

The Armenian Revolutionary Federation was founded in 1890 with the objective of unifying all the scattered Armenian revolutionary groups and their activities around a central goal, self-assertion and the political and social emancipation of the Armenian nation. While organizing with this objective, the Armenians, according to the party's organ *Droshak* (Flag), could not and should not pin any hopes on unreliable European diplomacy as a sole source of succor. They could obtain their rights only through the shedding of blood. Similarly, to speak of the triumph of socialism in Armenia was to manifest a total disregard for the stage of historical development in which the Armenians found themselves, and showed ignorance of the cultural and historical characteristics of Armenia and the Armenians. The defense of the Armenian nation's rights and its cultural, economic, and political renaissance presupposed the disintegration of the corrupt and oppressive Ottoman power. Dashnaktsutiun was to become the voice and the will of the Armenian nation, with arms for revenge as well as for self-defense. Thus, like *Narodnaia volia* it believed that armed resistance and political terror were essential revolutionary tools for national and social liberation.

The party programs that expounded the themes of administrative, cultural, and economic freedom of Ottoman Armenia (as well as the tactics the party adopted) show its similarities to and affinities with *Narodnaia volia* and later with the Russian Socialist Revolutionary Party. The first party program of Dashnaktsutiun, for instance, saw in "the physical and moral decline of the ruling class" the approaching final victory of labor, entailing the elimination of all classes, and the transfer of the ownership of means of production and its products to the workers. It also pledged to fight against the exploiting class, to defend the interests of the working people, and especially to preserve "the communal principles, to advance communal ownership, communal labor," in preparation for and in anticipation of a social organization that was to emerge from the forthcoming proletarian revolution.

While the party's main goal and priority was to secure autonomy and political freedom for the Armenians of the Ottoman Empire (within the framework of a federative system), the party was drawn by events (including tsarist assimilation and oppressive policies) to engage in a struggle against the tsarist regime as well. This policy, at first characterized as one of self-defense, was gradually transformed into one with a revolutionary platform, thus expanding the sphere of Dashnaktsutiun's activities and making it the most powerful, the most attractive, and the most influential Armenian political party. In Russia, especially in the Caucasus, the party ordered its working-class members to participate in labor strikes ("when they were related to the general interest of the working class"). Dashnaktsutiun established close political relations with the Russian Social Revolutionaries (S.R.) throughout 1903-17 and adopted revolutionary terror and agitation as part of its program of action in Russia. The resemblance between the S.R.s and Dashnaktsutiun did not stop at method (terror) or organization (after an initial centralization following a decentralized system).[157] Its program and ideology reflected also the impact of the S.R. platform and thought. Dashnaktsutiun stressed the historical role of the intelligentsia in preparing and leading a revolutionary movement, and in promoting a consciousness for revolution.

Like the S.R.s, Dashnaktsutiun rejected a narrow definition of the labor class in favor of one that included the great bulk of the peasantry. It too stressed that struggles for political-social and national liberation were interpenetrated and formed a unity, that land was essential for freedom, that democracy too was essential for freedom, and that democracy was to be socialistic and socialism democratic. Like the S.R.s, Dashnaktsutiun advocated universal suffrage; an end to class privileges; communalization of land; the eight-hour working day; the end of indirect taxes; national insurance against unemployment, accident, and illness; pensions for old age; freedom of speech, press, conscience; organization of labor; and the right to strike. For Transcaucasia, Dashnaktsutiun advocated the formation of a federated democratic republic with its own parliament (elected on the basis of universal suffrage and direct, equal, and secret ballot), and complete equality for all the nations and nationalities within the confederation. The confederation was to enjoy complete administrative and cultural autonomy.

The closeness of the S.R. and Dashnaktsutiun extended beyond method, organization, and identity of views on the many issues. A member of the Second International, Dashnaktsutiun participated in various meetings of revolutionary parties of Russia, with the view of forming a united front against tsarist autocracy. In 1904, for instance, in the Latin Quarter of Paris, at a gathering of the leaders or representatives of the Russian S.R., the Kadets (Constitutional Democrats), the Polish National League, the Finnish "Active Resistance" Party, the Georgian Socialist-Federalist Party, the Latvian Social Democratic Labor Party, and Dashnaktsutiun,[158] Dashnaktsutiun agreed on a common platform that called for cooperation among revolutionary parties to end Russian autocracy, and to supplant it with a democratic system based on universal suffrage; and in addition to guarantee the right of national self-determination and free development.[159] On various occasions Dashnaktsutiun, in its struggle against tsarist assimilationist and colonial policies, cooperated with the Hnchakians, the Armenian socialist revolutionaries, and certain Armenian elements of the Russian Social Democratic Party. The active Armenian resistance (1903-06) against the tsarist policies toward Armenian schools, church, and publications (a policy that was regarded as threatening the role of Russian Armenia as a secure base for the liberation of Ottoman Armenia) received the support of such socialist-revolutionary leaders as Chernov and such constitutional democrats as Struve. The relations with the S.R. became even more cordial after 1907 when Dashnaktsutiun, under the influence of the Russian revolutionary movements (and with an eye toward obtaining the help of international socialism in general, and Russian socialism in particular, for the liberation of Ottoman Armenia), adopted a comprehensive socialist program.

The S.R. and Dashnaktsutiun contacts were carried on by V. V. Lunkevich, one of the leading members of the S.R. party and a member of that party's central committee. Lunkevich, who was half Polish and half Armenian, was a close friend of many Dashnak leaders, and collaborated on *Droshak* under the pseudonym of Araratski. Dashnak publications of Geneva and Tbilisi published many works of leading Russian socialists.[160]

In 1911, during the political trial of Dashnaktsutiun by the tsarist regime (Aleksandr Kerenskii was one of the chief defense lawyers), the party enjoyed the support not only of the Second International but that of the Russian S.R. and the Constitutional Democratic parties as well. The cooperation between Dashnaktsutiun, the S.R., and the Kadets continued until 1918. In the Russian Duma, the Dashnaktsutiun entered the S.R. parliamentary faction and pressed for programs similar to those of the S.R.: demands for an eight-hour working day, minimum wage, all land to the peasants, the granting of equality to all nationalities and the transformation of Russia into a decentralized democratic federative republic, cultural autonomy to nationalities, and a demand for a Russian pledge to defend the same principles in the Ottoman Empire.[161] The S.R. and the Kadets defended in general the reforms in Turkish Armenia, demanding autonomy for the area. As for Transcaucasia, Dashnaktsutiun demands for a *Zemstvo* system (that would have allowed the Armenians to form an ethnic majority in a few provinces of the region) were supported by the S.R. and the Kadet parties.

Finally, the Russian revolutionary movements also contributed to the formation of Armenian revolutionary Marxist groups. During 1901-02, Armenian students who had attended Moscow, St. Petersburg, Kiev, Kharkov, Riga, and Kazan universities (and who had been drawn into Marxist organizations) founded social democratic groups in Tbilisi, Erevan, Baku, Aleksandropol', and other centers and started the publication of Marxist newspapers and literature. They attempted gradually to organize the students of secondary schools for Transcaucasia and to recruit and revolutionize the ethnically heterogeneous labor force of the region.

Among these groups was the Hai Sotsial-Demokratakan Miutiun (The Armenian Social-Democratic Union), which was organized in Tbilisi in 1902 and which faced great difficulties. At a time when Armenian nationalism was at a high pitch, when all Armenian political parties were preoccupied with the defense and liberation of the Armenians of the Ottoman Empire and were championing the cultural economic position and rights of Armenians against tsarist Russia and were speaking of the defense of Armenian ethnic and national rights against actual or potential Georgian or Turco-Tatar encroachments, the Russian Social-Democratic Workers' Party's platform on the agrarian and nationality question was internationalist but not comprehensive enough to attract the support of the Armenian masses, politicized through nationalism and direct action. The divisions between the two wings of the Russian Social Democratic Workers' Party, the Mensheviks and the Bolsheviks, on nationality and other questions, the ethnic heterogeneity of the working class in the Transcaucasus, and especially the absence of a strong factory labor force, hindered the organizational efforts of the social-democrats outside of Tbilisi and Baku. Fully aware of this situation, a group of Armenian Marxists, following the example of the Jewish Bund, attempted to draw up a platform that would satisfy the national as well as the social aspirations of Armenians. The new party that emerged in 1903 in Baku called itself Hai Sotsial-Demokratakan Banvorakan Kazmakerputiun (Armenian Social-Democratic Workers Organization). This group opposed the Social Democratic platform on municipalization and nationalization of land and that dealing with the nationality question. The various Armenian social democratic groups, on the other hand, in 1903 fused into the Russian Social Democratic Workers' Party, becoming a Caucasian branch of it.[162] The Armenian Marxists within the Russian Social Democratic Workers' Party, while under the influence of the Bolshevik-Menshevik rift, produced a great body of Marxist thought, contributing to the growth of an Armenian Marxist literature. They also produced many eminent leaders who left their impact on the history of the Transcaucasian labor movement (Kamo, S. Shahumian, B. Knuniantz, S. Kasian, M. Melikian [Dadushka], A. Begzadian, S. Zurabian, A. Khumarian).[163]

CONCLUSION

To sum up, between 1829 and 1917 Russian rule and Russian culture left a deep imprint on both the culture and the social organization of the Armenians and Armenia. The Russians not only contributed to the secularization of Armenian culture, thus creating circumstances favorable to the formation among Armenians of a strong and viable bourgeoisie and an intelligentsia, but they played an important role as well in the formation of Armenian political parties that were often either modeled on the Russian ones or profoundly influenced by them. Scattered throughout Russia, Armenians strove hard to defend and expand their national and cultural rights in Russia and to use Russian Armenia and Armenians as a means of bringing about the emancipation of Ottoman Armenia. The Armenians in Russia, who were aware of their tenuous positions and of their weaknesses, made minimal demands and followed a Russian orientation which, while advocating an end to autocracy and envisaging national self-determination and cultural autonomy, did not look to a breakdown of the unity of Russia. They regarded such a democratization and national and social liberation as the eventual rescuers of that unity. The site of the longed-for fatherland where they might build a viable nation was historic Ottoman Armenia. World War I and the Armenian massacres torpedoed that hope.

The triumph of Bolshevism in Russia, followed by the formation and then the dissolution of the Transcaucasian Republic, placed the Armenians in a position to found a small fatherland where they had least imagined it—in Erevan Province, the most underdeveloped part of Transcaucasia. The social revolution in Russia and the national self-assertion of Georgians and Turco-Tatar elements of Transcaucasia dealt a heavy blow to the strong Armenian bourgeoisie that had flourished outside of Armenia proper. The impact of Russian culture, however, had been strong and remained strong in the region among the Armenians, who had undergone a century of Russian political and cultural influence. This influence continued in the Soviet period, which followed the creation in 1918 of the Armenian fatherland and its short-lived independence (1918-20).

—6—

A Century of Russian Impact
on Georgia

David M. Lang

Georgia, like Armenia, presents special features of interest in the context of the Russian impact on Asia over the past century. The peoples of both countries are possessors of ancient Christian cultures, and inheritors of traditions of statecraft that extend back over more than two thousand years. Both peoples are noted for their high average intelligence and literacy rating; and both have produced cadres of professional men, doctors, artists, actors, and administrators who have themselves made an impact on Russia out of proportion to their numerical strength. The case of Stalin is an extreme instance of the Georgian counterimpact upon Russia, but this could be paralleled in many examples of a more subtle and less conspicuous nature.

Visitors to Georgia are often struck by the self-confident air of the people there, and by their pride in their national and cultural past. Svetlana Alliluyeva speaks contemptuously of "the petty, narrow-minded nationalism of Georgians nowadays," and depicts them as "tactlessly speaking Georgian in front of those who don't understand" and "praising everything Georgian to the skies and running down everything else."[1] This assessment, of course, springs partly from Miss Alliluyeva's deep affection for her mother's memory, and partly from her unconscious revulsion from the Georgian background of her father and his Caucasian associates. However, it is an attitude sometimes shared by other Russians, and one which the Georgians by their exuberance and their refusal to be assimilated do foster to some extent, in very much the same way as do the Welsh, the Irish, and the Scots in the British Isles.

Less prejudiced observers, such as Boris Pasternak, find in Georgia qualities of charm, sincerity, and genuine human values that are in danger of disappearing in our present-day automated and mechanized society. The spiritual affinity for Georgia of such Russian poets as Boris Pasternak and Nikolai Zabolotskii has its roots in the Decembrist period, when a number of the conspirators were sent as common soldiers to the armies of the Caucasus. Griboedov married a Georgian princess, while Pushkin passed through Tbilisi on his famous journey to Erzurum. Lermontov's great poems "Mtsyri" and "Demon" have a Georgian setting, while his ballad "Tamara" presents a picturesque though unhistoric image of the great queen. Well could Belinskii observe: "The Caucasus seems to have been fated to become the cradle of our poetic talents, the inspiration and mentor of their muses, their poetic homeland!"[2]

In discussing the impact of Russia upon Georgia, we must not forget that Georgia, like Armenia, had a cultural and political past extending back far longer than that of Russia herself. Ancient Colchis, the present Western Georgia, was renowned for its fabulous riches in gold and for its advanced metallurgy, as symbolized by the Greek myth of Jason and the Argonauts who sailed there in quest of the Golden Fleece.[3] Converted to Christianity by Saint Nino in the time of Constantine the Great,[4] Georgia participated fully in the Christian culture of the Byzantine Empire, to which it made its own distinctive and outstanding contribution in the fields of architecture, fresco painting, and icon working, as well as in learning and in philosophical inquiry. Under King David the Builder (1089-1125), Georgia became a mighty Christian feudal state, a major power in the Near East, able to enter into alliance with the Crusaders, and to inflict mighty blows on the Turks and the Saracens. Queen Tamar (1184-1213) continued this tradition of independent Georgian statecraft. As patroness of the Georgian bard Shota Rustaveli, author of the incomparable epic, "The Man in the Panther's Skin," Tamar presided over a literary culture which could compare on a more modest scale with that of the Persia of Nizami and Saadi, and the Italy of Dante and Ariosto.

The key date in the Russian impact on Georgia is 12 September 1801, when the ancient kingdoms of Kartli and Kakheti were incorporated into the Russian Empire, three days before the coronation of Tsar Alexander I. Outwardly, at least, the incorporation bore the character of a voluntary amalgamation of the two states. The Georgian kings were surrendering their sovereignty to the more powerful Russian tsars in return for a guarantee of support for the Georgian Bagratid dynasty, which had ruled in Georgia for over a thousand years and which proudly claimed descent from two kings of ancient Israel, David and Solomon. This amalgamation had been one of the major clauses of the treaty of Georgievsk, signed in 1783 between King Erekle II of Georgia and Empress Catherine the Great.[5] Decimated by the slave trade with Turkey, by ruthless invasions by the Persian Qajar dynasty, and by the incessant raids of the Lezghians of Daghestan, the Georgians were by the end of the eighteenth century in no condition to stick out for terms; they were faced by the choice of virtual extermination or of a merger with the Russian elder brother.

The Russians were well aware of the inherent weakness of the Georgian national position. Even the liberal Alexander I, pressed by chauvinistic advisers, could not resist the temptation to exploit this position. The surviving members of the Georgian Bagratid dynasty, far from being confirmed in their royal prerogatives, were systematically removed from Georgia and placed under surveillance in honorific positions at St. Petersburg and elsewhere. In reaction against this, Prince Alexander, one of the sons of the Georgian King Erekle II, had fled to Persia, whence he was now waging a continuing campaign against the Russian dominion over Georgia. Even more dramatically, Queen Mariam, the widow of King Giorgi XII, when ordered by the Russian General Ivan Petrovich Lazarev to pack her belongings and prepare to leave Georgia, stabbed her tormentor in the breast with her dead husband's dagger, an act for which she was imprisoned for many years in a Russian monastery.

The Georgian National Church, which had enjoyed autocephaly or independence within the Orthodox communion for over a thousand years, was forcibly absorbed into the Russian Church. The last of the old Georgian Catholicos-Patriarchs, Antoni II, was stripped of his rank in 1811 and sent into enforced retirement at St. Petersburg. He was replaced by a representative of the Russian Holy Synod, the Metropolitan Varlaam, with the title of exarch of Georgia. Varlaam, himself a Georgian by birth, was soon replaced by a line of Russian exarchs who did all they could to abolish the Georgian Church liturgy and assimilate the Georgian Church entirely with the Russian.

The policy of assimilation of Georgia by Russia was reflected also in fundamental changes in the administrative and judicial systems. Under the Georgian kings, justice had been largely oral in character, each party appearing before the royal tribunal together with his witnesses, and a verdict being often delivered on the spot. Now, lawsuits had to be conducted in Russian according to the methods of the creaking Russian bureaucracy, which often referred them to St. Petersburg for a verdict that could take years to arrive. This in itself might have been tolerable had it not been for the poor quality of the officials sent to administer Georgia, many of whom were both incompetent and corrupt. An official report by Senators Kutaisov and Mechnikov, who made a tour of inspection in Georgia in 1829-30, painted a terrible picture of "abuses, malpractices and oppression of the people," and recommended a thorough shake-up. When Tsar Nicholas I visited Georgia in 1837, he dismissed dozens of high-ranking officers for profiteering and corruption. The French consul in Tbilisi, in a secret report dated 1834, asked:

> What can one expect of an administration in which the subordinate officials have no other aim but to enrich themselves, and in which besides there is never the least question of supervision? Each district or province is a satrapy destined to augment its governor's private fortune, just as each regiment is, for its colonel, a collection of men whose various skills he exploits for his own benefit.[6]

The economic situation of the population was adversely affected by the constant wars waged by the Russian armies of the Caucasus against Persia and Turkey, and against the Muslim tribesmen of Daghestan and Circassia. In a report dated 1828, the dramatist Aleksandr Griboedov, who was also a high-ranking Russian diplomat, commented that during the Persian campaign of 1826-28, Georgia had "suffered in the aggregate heavier losses in cereals, pack animals and beasts of burden, drovers, etc., than the most flourishing Russian province could have sustained, while in population and extent she equals only three *uezdy* of the Governorates of Great Russia."[7] Compulsory requisitions of produce and livestock, often taken with little or no compensation, were the order of the day.

These conditions produced widespread discontent among the population. Differences of social class were forgotten in a determination to unite against the Russian overlord, whose rule now seemed more burdensome than that of even the Persian or the Turk. At first, the uprisings had a spontaneous, popular character, as in the case of the Kakheti rebellion of 1812, and the Western Georgian insurrection of 1820, in which Archbishop Dositheus of Kutaisi was killed by Russian Cossacks. In 1832, the Georgian aristocracy planned to annihilate the Russian governor-general and his staff at a grand ball to be held in Tbilisi, and to set up a revived Georgian monarchy under one of the Bagratid princes. The plot was betrayed in advance, however, by one of the conspirators. The official inquiry that followed unearthed a seething mass of resentment against the Russian tsar and his agents on the spot.

It was under the skilled and statesmanlike rule of Prince Mikhail Vorontsov, Viceroy of the Caucasus from 1845 until 1854, that matters first took a turn for the better. Vorontsov's father, Count Semen Vorontsov, had been for many years Russian ambassador to England and a friend of the younger Pitt. Mikhail Vorontsov was himself a man of Western sympathies and excellent education, far better equipped to tackle the multiracial society of the Caucasus than the rough-and-ready army generals who preceded and also who followed him. Vorontsov was no social reformer. The iron hand of Nicholas I gave him little scope in this direction. But more than reform Georgia needed justice, prosperity, order, education. Here Vorontsov excelled. He injected some needed efficiency into the Russian bureaucratic machine and punished corruption. He built bridges and roads and improved communications. He patronized schools, had a theater built in Tbilisi, and vastly increased the output of journals, newspapers, and books, both in Russian and in Georgian. He encouraged the founding of the Tbilisi Public Library and the Caucasian branch of the Russian Geographical Society, as well as enabling the outstanding specialist in Georgian history, M.-F. Brosset, to make a thorough survey of ancient Georgian churches and antiquities.

Vorontsov devoted much attention to commerce. He persuaded the Russian Ministry of Finance to restore certain customs concessions designed to facilitate the international transit trade through Georgia, from the European capitals to India and Central Asia. He supported merchant and craft guilds in the cities of Tbilisi and Gori, while also enabling entrepreneurs to start up several modern factories. A trading depot was established at Tbilisi by a syndicate of Russian manufacturers, as well as warehouses and showrooms. The number of industrial organizations in Georgia grew between 1843 and 1850 by 94 percent, while their total output went up by 105 percent. There existed in Georgia in 1850 some 132 industrial concerns, with a total production valued at 256,000 rubles. Growth over the next few years continued at so rapid a tempo that in 1864, when serfdom was abolished in Georgia, there existed 465 factories and industrial concerns of all kinds, with a total production worth over 860,000 rubles.[8] During this period efforts were made to improve methods of farming, cotton planting, silk raising, and wine production—for which Georgia was already famous. A branch of the Russian Agricultural Society was founded in Tbilisi.

However, the countryside was already in the grip of a serious agrarian crisis. The old manorial economy and feudal relations based on serfdom were breaking down under the harsh impact of modern economic realities. The steady increase in the population resulted in acute land hunger throughout Georgia. At the beginning of the nineteenth century, the average peasant holding ranged between 10 and 20 *desiatins* (1 *desiatin* = 2.7 acres); by the time the Georgian serfs were freed in 1864, the average holding had dropped to about 5 *desiatins*. The position was aggravated by the seizure of communal lands, forests, and pastures by the state and by powerful landed proprietors. Peasant unrest broke into disorders in Imeretia in 1857, in Guria in 1862, in the Ksani valley and around Surami in Kartli in 1863, and near Tbilisi in 1864.

The cause of the Georgian peasant was championed by the new generation of Georgian intellectuals, many of whom were steeped in the ideology of such pioneer Russian radicals as Belinskii and Herzen, while some were in personal contact during their student days in Russia with Chernyshevskii and Dobroliubov. These young Georgian intellectuals were in fact known as "Tergdaleulis," signifying "those who had drunk from the River Terek," i.e., had crossed the Terek and gone for their education to Moscow and St. Petersburg universities. When the Georgian serfs had been finally emancipated, these young intellectuals continued to campaign for improved conditions of life for the rural and urban poor. They also agitated for the introduction of the *Zemstvo* system into Georgia, which was in fact excluded from the benefits of it. Nor did Georgia enjoy the benefit of the jury system, which was introduced into European Russia in 1864.

The last thirty years of the nineteenth century saw the beginnings of a major industrial revolution in Georgia. This was accelerated by improved communications. Roads were built, and the main towns of Transcaucasia were connected in 1870 by the telegraph. Two years later, a regular service was inaugurated on the Poti-Tbilisi railway, built by British engineers. (The engineers taught the Georgians to play soccer in their spare time—a sport in which they greatly excel today.) The manganese industry set up in Chiatura in 1879 soon attained international importance, and by 1892 Chiatura manganese represented 38 percent of the entire world production. Batum on the Black Sea became an international outlet for Baku oil, which in 1888 represented no less than 21 percent of the entire world supply.

With her frontiers protected by Russian bayonets, and the slave trade with Turkey stamped out, Georgia's population continued to increase. In 1866, it totaled 1,300,400; by 1897, it was 2,034,700. Between 1865 and 1897, the population of Tbilisi more than doubled—from 71,051 to 159,590. The capital of Georgia became more and more of a cosmopolitan city, complete with European amenities such as hotels, a horse tramway, new bridges, paved streets, a piped water supply, schools, an opera house, and various municipal and government institutions housed in imposing stone buildings.

Two contrasting but at the same time complementary phenomena made their appearance—nationalism and revolutionary activity. Georgian nationalism aimed at the restoration of the Georgian language as the medium of instruction in state schools, at the preservation of all that was specifically Georgian in public and private life, and at local self-determination, to culminate in the eventual political separation of Georgia from tsarist Russia. The Georgian revolutionary movement, while following outwardly the Russian patterns of populism, anarchism, and finally of Marxist social democracy, also had strong patriotic overtones.

The chief protagonist of Georgian nationalism toward the end of the nineteenth century was Prince Ilia Chavchavadze (1837-1907), renowned equally as poet, novelist, banker, and political leader. He stood for the solidarity of all classes of the Georgian population in face of Russian attempts at assimilation. However, the ideas of his movement, known as the *Pirveli Dasi* or "the First Group," did not extend farther than a form of bourgeois liberalism and home-rule aims; nor was the *Meore Dasi* or "Second Group," founded in 1869 by Giorgi Tsereteli and Niko Nikoladze, much more militant in its social objectives. It was left to the young Marxists who band-ed themselves together in the 1890s as the *Mesame Dasi* or "Third Group" to institute a truly Georgian revolutionary movement, in close community with the Social Democrats of Russia itself. Geor-gian Anarchism, represented by Varlaam Cherkesov, a disciple of Pëtr Kropotkin, and Georgian Populism, which was quite active in the 1870s, turned out to be dead ends, and left no lasting imprint on the country's political evolution.

These political activities took place against a background of in-creasing Russian chauvinism and persecution of everyone and every-thing that diverged from the officially accepted Great Russian model. This trend set in under Tsar Alexander III (1881-94) and continued under Nicholas II, the last of the Romanovs. Dissenting sects, the Uniate Church and the Lutherans in the western prov-inces, Lamaist Kalmyks, Buriat Mongols, and especially all Jews, suffered a systematic campaign of cultural and political pressure. In Georgia, even the Tbilisi Theological Seminary, where Stalin re-ceived his early training for the priesthood, became a hotbed of re-sistance against the campaign of Russification. In 1886, an expelled student named Laghiashvili assassinated the rector, Chudetsky, a bigoted Russian who described Georgian as a "language for dogs." The Tbilisi Armenians, at that time a dominant element in Georgia's capital city, formed in 1890 the Dashnak patriotic organization, which began its activities by composing patriotic songs and by drilling the people in the use of arms and in physical fitness pro-grams. Originally formed with a view to liberating the Armenian communities under Ottoman rule, the Dashnak organization was driven more and more to secret opposition work against the tsarist regime itself. The movement gained momentum particularly after 1903, when the governor-general Prince Grigorii Golitsyn confiscated the property of the Armenian National Church and closed down Armenian schools in both Georgia and Armenia itself.

The original nucleus of the Georgian Social Democratic movement of *Mesame Dasi,* which met for the first time at Zestafoni in 1892, included the proletarian writer Egnate Ninoshvili (1859-94), the future president of independent Georgia, Noe Zhordania, and several others who were later to become prominent in the tsarist Dumas and in the Georgian Republic of 1918-21. Later, in 1898, the organization was joined by the young Stalin, fresh from his early struggles in the Tbilisi Theological Seminary. Stalin soon parted company with the more moderate, "legal" Marxists like Zhordania, and with a group of associates embarked on a career of underground organization work and terrorist activity directed against the tsarist government and the local capitalists of Tbilisi, Baku, and Batum. A whole series of strikes and demonstrations, beginning with the May Day demonstration of 1899, established the Caucasus as one of the strongholds of revolutionary militancy in Russia.[9]

The Revolution of 1905 was greeted with enthusiasm by Georgian public opinion. Everywhere, clashes took place between workers and peasants, and tsarist troops and gendarmes. Landowners who sided with the Russian authorities were boycotted or even assassinated. The Georgian bishops assembled and demanded the restoration of the autocephaly of the Georgian National Church, only to be dispersed and beaten up by armed police. On 29 August 1905 a peaceful public meeting in Tbilisi Town Hall was attacked by Cossacks, with the loss of sixty lives. Parts of Western Georgia, notably the province of Guria, became virtually independent, and functioned for some months as autonomous communes free of Russian interference. From Kutaisi, capital of Western Georgia, the head of the secret police reported to the Russian Viceroy, Prince Vorontsov-Dashkov, that the Georgian revolutionary movement resembled

a huge cauldron filled with water and hermetically sealed and suspended above an enormous furnace. Beyond a doubt, when the sides of the cauldron can no longer withstand the pressure of the steam which is formed by the heating of the water, and has no other outlet, then they will burst into splinters and fly in all directions as a result of the force of the blast.[10]

The Revolution of 1905 failed in its aim to overthrow the Russian monarchy, and reprisals were terrible everywhere. The repression was especially severe in Georgia, where gangs of the Russian extremist "Black Hundreds" (the so-called League of Russian Patriots), joined with the Cossacks in wreaking vengeance on the Georgian population. In January 1906 General Alikhanov-Avarskii was appointed military governor of Western Georgia, where he restored order with fire and sword. At the same time, the Georgians soon attained considerable power and prestige in the Russian Imperial Duma, where the Georgian Social Democratic faction led by Noe Zhordania was seconded in the Upper House or Council of State by Prince Ilia Chavchavadze, the spokesman for the Georgian national cause.

During World War I, Georgia was a focal point in the struggle between the Russian and Turkish armies on the Transcaucasian front. On the Russian side, many Georgians took part in these campaigns, which imposed severe economic strain on the towns and countryside. On the Turkish side, a somewhat farcical spectacle was presented by the "Georgian Legion," recruited by the Germans from Georgian émigrés and stationed during the campaign of 1916-17 at Tirebolu, near the Black Sea coast to the west of Trebizond. The légion, which had made no substantial contribution, was disbanded early in 1917. German interest in Georgia, however, remained strong.

The collapse of the tsarist regime in March 1917 was greeted with rejoicing throughout Georgia. A special committee known as the Ozakom was set up by the Provisional Government in Petrograd to deal with Caucasian affairs. [11] After the Bolshevik Revolution in November 1917 the local authorities in Georgia, Armenia, and Azerbaijan found themselves cut off from the center of power in Russia. Public opinion and the stark realities of the situation led them to set up a separate provisional government, of a largely Menshevik character, which was known as the Transcaucasian Commissariat. The Commissariat repudiated Lenin and his party, and sought to salvage what it could from the ruins of the now crumbling Russian Caucasian front by making a separate peace with the victorious Turks.

The Treaty of Brest-Litovsk, signed on 3 March 1918 excluded from Russian territory the districts of Batum, Ardahan, and Kars, where the fate of the population was to be decided by a free plebiscite. In prevailing conditions, this meant abandoning the Armenian and Georgian Christian inhabitants to the mercy of the advancing Turks. After the Turkish army entered Batum on 15 April 1918, an ultimatum was issued to the Transcaucasian Commissariat to conclude peace on terms most advantageous to the Ottoman side.

There seemed to be every prospect that Georgia and the rest of Transcaucasia would be entirely overrun by Turkish forces intent on capturing Baku and realizing Enver Pasha's Pan-Turkish dream of a fusion of Asia Minor, Transcaucasia, and Turkestan into one great Turanian empire. At this point, however, the Germans unexpectedly stepped in. The Germans, who now dominated the Ukraine and the Crimea, were themselves in urgent need of the Baku oilfields, and had no desire to see the entire Middle East fall into the hands of their ambitious Turkish friends. A strong and alert German delegation attended the peace conference at Batum in May 1918. At railway stations and other strategic points, German helmets were soon to be seen. These the Christian Georgians thought vastly preferable to the Turkish fez. The result of this German intervention was the break-up of the Transcaucasian Federation, and the setting up on 26 May 1918 of an independent Georgian Republic under the presidency of the Social Democratic leader Noe Zhordania and the patronage of the commander of the local German expeditionary forces. Following the defeat of Imperial Germany in November 1918, the Germans were replaced by a British occupation force, which remained in Georgia until 1920.

The Georgian Mensheviks, who were returned to power in February 1919 by an overwhelming free vote of the population, pushed through agrarian reforms, nationalized basic industries, founded a Georgian state university, and in general did their utmost to revive the independent Georgian nationhood that had been submerged by more than a century of Russian rule. They had to contend with appalling difficulties. The country was flooded with refugees, both from Armenia and Anatolia to the south and from communist Russia to the north. Inflation and hunger were rampant. The Moscow regime regarded Tbilisi as a center for counterrevolutionary activity, especially as the government there now included such stalwarts of the former Kerenskii cabinet as Irakli Tsereteli and Karlo

Chkheidze. Moscow therefore agitated and intrigued for the overthrow of the Georgian Mensheviks.

Not less dangerous were the Russian Whites. In the West, the
representatives of the former tsarist regime campaigned against diplomatic recognition of the Georgian and other Transcaucasian republics by the Allied powers. This recognition was in fact accorded
to Georgia, largely through the efforts of Lord Curzon, and of Sir
Oliver Wardrop, lifelong friend of Georgia and a prominent Georgian scholar, who was for a time British High Commissioner in
Tbilisi. The main threat from the White Russian side derived from
the Volunteer Army of General Denikin, who refused to admit any
less comprehensive aim than the restoration of Russia's frontiers as
they were in 1914 under Tsar Nicholas II. In regard to Denikin and
his policies, it is worth quoting the views of Sir Harry Luke, who
succeeded Wardrop as British High Commissioner in Georgia:

> Instead, therefore, of making common cause with the other enemies of
> Bolshevism, with Rumania, Poland, the Baltic and Caucasian States,
> Makhno, Petlura and the rest, he not only rejected the help but definite-
> ly provoked the enmity of these valuable, indeed indispensable, poten-
> tial allies. Had he possessed the most rudimentary political acumen he
> would have made friends with Rumania and left the Bessarabian ques-
> tion to be settled after the Bolsheviks were beaten; he would have acted
> similarly, *mutatis mutandis*, with regard to Poland, the Baltic Repub-
> lics, the Caucasians, the Transcaucasians and other Russian "Succession
> States" instead of antagonising them and in some cases actually engag-
> ing in hostilities against them.[12]

During 1920, the war-weary British evacuated Transcaucasia; and
the Americans, in spite of President Wilson's high-minded pledges
on the American mandate for Armenia, did nothing to stop the rising tide of Kemalist nationalism in Turkey and Bolshevik advance
from the north. Both Azerbaijan and Armenia fell to the Russian
communists during the year. On 7 May 1920 the Georgian repub-
licans signed a treaty of friendship and nonaggression with Soviet
Russia. S. M. Kirov, a member of the Caucasian Bureau of the all-
Russian Communist Party, was appointed the first Soviet ambassador to Tbilisi. The British Commissioner Luke noted in his diary
on 20 June 1920:

> The Bolshevik Diplomatic Mission to Georgia, which has been dribbling
> in by installments, now almost complete, with the arrival today of Head

of Mission, Kyrov. Staff of Mission, including attendants and a group of seventeen persons ostensibly despatched to settle details regarding Peace Treaty, numbers about seventy. Georgian Government are alarmed at its size and have protested, but Bolsheviks continue to pour in. I understand they propose to make Tiflis headquarters of their eastern propaganda. Kyrov on arrival harangued the crowd which had collected outside his residence.[13]

One of the secret clauses in the Russo-Georgian treaty of 1920 provided that "Georgia pledges itself to recognize the right of free existence and activity of the Communist Party. . .and in particular its right to free meetings and publications, including organs of the press." This was one of the points on which Kirov laid the strongest emphasis during his mission to Georgia. The Georgian Menshevik government, which had formerly proscribed the local Bolshevik party, was forced to release communist party members and sympathizers from prison. Many of these promptly embarked on an overt campaign to overthrow the Mensheviks by force, with the result that Noe Ramishvili, the capable Minister of the Interior, clapped them back in jail, provoking a fiery exchange of notes between Kirov and the Georgian Foreign Ministry.

The events leading to the Soviet annexation of Georgia are rather interesting. On 27 January 1921 France and England recognized Georgia *de jure* as an independent sovereign state. However, plans had already been made in Moscow for the overthrow of Georgia. In December 1920 A. I. Gekker (Hecker), commander of the Eleventh Red Army, sent to Moscow a secret appreciation of the prospects of a military conquest of Georgia. Gekker stressed that it would first be desirable to reach an understanding with the Turkish Kemalists at Ankara, with whom the Kremlin was already friendly, to ensure that there was no interference from that side. In the meantime, reinforcements and stores were massed in Azerbaijan, now under Soviet control, all ready for a propitious moment to invade independent Georgia.

On 11 February 1921 disorders broke out in the Lori district, south of Tbilisi. Simultaneously a revolt began in the nearby town of Shulaveri, near the Armenian and Azerbaijani frontiers. The insurgents were mostly Armenians and Russians, who attacked local Georgian military posts. By 14 February, a regular battle was raging on the Armeno-Georgian border, near a place called Vorontsovka.

Gekker telegraphed the Soviet envoy in Tbilisi: "Resolved to cross the Rubicon. Take action in the light of this decision." A Communist Revolutionary Committee (Revcom) that included such prominent Georgian Bolsheviks as F. Makharadze, Mamia Orakhelashvili, and S. Eliava had by now been formed in Shulaveri. This Revcom constituted a "shadow cabinet," all ready to take over from the Zhordania government in the event that the coup was successful.

Red Army detachments poured into Georgia from the direction of Baku, as well as from the north through the Mamison and Daryal passes, and along the Black Sea Route past Sukhumi. Soviet forces under the leading Georgian Bolshevik and friend of Stalin, Sergo Ordzhonikidze, entered Tbilisi on 25 February. After a brief but determined rearguard action by the independent Georgia forces, the country was in a matter of days in Soviet hands and a Georgian Soviet Republic was proclaimed.

In spite of the versions given in Soviet official historiography, there can be no denying the initial hostility of the vast mass of the population to Soviet rule. When Stalin arrived in Tbilisi in July 1921 to supervise the establishment of the Soviet order there, he was greeted with hisses and shouts of abuse. This was one of the considerations that led Stalin to force Georgia into a new Soviet Transcaucasian Federation. It was his idea that Georgian nationalism would be counterbalanced and kept in check by the influence of the Armenians and Azerbaijanis, with their differing aspirations and communal aims. A reign of terror ensued of such proportions as to reach the ears of Lenin himself.[14] In his Testament and other documents dictated shortly before his death, Lenin wrote that he "felt strongly guilty before the workers of Russia for not having intervened vigorously and drastically enough in this notorious affair." He was disgusted at the "swamp" in which the Russian Communist Party had landed over the Georgian business. Stalin, wrote Lenin, had let his personal vindictiveness against his old rivals in Georgia run away with him, showing himself "not merely a genuine social chauvinist, but a coarse brutish bully acting on behalf of a Great Power." This Georgian affair became a notorious test case, with the local Georgian communists in Tbilisi struggling desperately to retain some measure of local autonomy, while Stalin and Ordzhonikidze intrigued against them at the center, in Moscow, and spread all manner of slanders and lies against them through the Communist Party branches generally. Lenin several times prepared to come out into the open against Stalin and Dzerzhinskii, head of the Cheka. Only Lenin's series of strokes (the first of them came in the spring of 1922) and his premature death in January 1924 saved Stalin from being exposed to Lenin's wrath, which might well have cost him the succession to the first place in the Soviet state.[15]

The Georgian people were now preparing for a last desperate effort to regain their independence. Plans were laid for a general insurrection, scheduled for 29 August 1924. The plan, however, miscarried. Through some misunderstanding the mining center of Chiatura and the surrounding district rose up in arms on 28 August instead of on the appointed day. At first the insurgents achieved considerable success. A number of Red army units were eliminated, but the Russian commander in Georgia finally overcame the forces of the patriots, who were led by Colonel Kaikhosro Cholokashvili. Conservative estimates place the number of prisoners and hostages killed by the victorious communists at between seven and ten thousand.

The suppression of the 1924 rising was followed by a period of uneasy calm. The relative prosperity brought to Russia by Lenin's New Economic Policy (NEP) had a beneficial effect on Georgia, a country of ample natural resources which had in any case never been subjected to the extremes of famine which had overcome Armenia to the south and European Russia to the north. The Communist Party of Georgia preferred for a time to use peaceful persuasion rather than armed coercion to extend its hold over the masses, and substantial progress in the industrialization of Georgia was achieved even in the NEP period. The impressive Zemo-Avchala hydroelectric scheme, which was completed during this time, was inaugurated by M. I. Kalinin in June 1927. During the purges of the 1930s the builders of this project were executed by order of L. P. Beria.

The inception of the first Five-Year Plan in 1928 and the drive toward full-scale collectivization of Soviet agriculture marked the opening of a new phase in Georgian social and economic history. The Georgian peasantry, who had won their right to individual small holdings during the Menshevik republican era of 1918-21, when the landed proprietors had been largely dislodged, now clung to these holdings with the courage of desperation. Opposition to the new measures was by no means confined to the rich peasants or *kulaks*, but was prevalent among the majority of the middling or poorer peasants also. Bloody clashes took place between NKVD detachments armed with machine guns and angry peasant women armed with sticks and stones. When the disturbances eventually died down, the net result of Georgia's first collectivization drive was the creation of some 3,400 *kolkhozes*, incorporating about 170,000 former peasant holdings.[16] A score or more of *sovkhozes* or state farms were formed, too. At this time there were not more than thirty-one tractor stations in the whole of Georgia, and it was a long time before peaceful collectivization could be resumed and agricultural production rescued from the chaotic condition into which doctrinaire haste had plunged it.

At the same time, a determined attack was launched on commercial private enterprise; restaurants, hotels, and shops were completely municipalized, though this did nothing to benefit the consumer. A number of metallurgical works, paper combines, and chemical and pharmaceutical laboratories were set up. These heralded a definite improvement in the country's industrial position, which had hitherto lagged far behind its agricultural potential. The cultivation of the vine and special subtropical plants and trees, which had a long history in Georgia, was stimulated further by the regime. Spas and rest homes were built and tourist trade was encouraged.

Education, which included the study of the native Caucasian languages, was given a definite boost during this period. By 1928 both Georgia and Armenia had higher proportions of school attendance than did the U.S.S.R. as a whole. In that year, 11 percent of the Georgian population was attending full-time school, as against 8.2 percent for the Soviet Union generally. The education of women in Georgia was already well advanced; by 1926, 45 percent of all Georgian women were literate, as opposed to only 19 percent in neighboring Muslim Azerbaijan. Higher education was represented by the great Tbilisi State University, founded in 1918, and by a number of training colleges and polytechnic institutes. By 1927, Transcaucasia, with 4 percent of the Soviet population, had 10 percent of the total students in higher education. There also existed in

Tbilisi a branch of the Soviet Academy of Sciences, elevated in 1941 to the status of a separate Academy—the present Academy of Sciences of the Georgian S.S.R. Although Russian is a compulsory second language in the higher grades of all Georgian schools, nonetheless Georgian remains the general medium of instruction. A Russian or other non-Georgian student attending Tbilisi State University would find himself severely handicapped, especially in the Arts Faculties, without a fluent knowledge of Georgian.

Because of the role played by the Georgian Church as a center for opposition to Russian communism, the antireligious campaigns of the 1920s and 1930s were marked by even greater bitterness in Georgia than in Russia itself. One of the first acts of the Georgian bishops on the news of the outbreak of the February Revolution in 1917 had been to assemble at the ancient patriarchal cathedral in Mtskheta and declare the independence of the Georgian Orthodox Church from that of Russia. In September of the same year, Bishop Kyrion was elected Catholicos-Patriarch of All Georgia; and the succession of supreme heads of the Georgian Church, all of them of Georgian birth, has continued unbroken to the present day.

A leading part in national resistance to Russian communism was played by the Georgian Catholicos-Patriarch Ambrosius Khelaia who in 1922 addressed to the Genoa Conference a memorandum denouncing the communist oppression of the national and religious life of Georgia, and demanding the establishment of an international commission to organize a plebiscite in the country. In 1924 the communists staged a show trial of the Georgian Catholicos and eight other church leaders. The proceedings took place in the city theater, in front of which a "spontaneous" demonstration of four thousand workers was stage-managed by the authorities demanding that the prisoners be condemned to death. At the end of a ten-day travesty of justice, the Catholicos and his associates were found guilty and deserving of death. However, the regime did not dare to execute Ambrosius; he died in captivity in 1927.

As a consequence of the national church's role in anti-Russian resistance, the godless campaigns of the 1930s were waged with more violence in Georgia than in many other parts of the Soviet Union. The man chiefly responsible for the suppression of opposition in Georgia, including religious opposition, was the notorious

L. P. Beria, at first head of the Georgian GPU, and from 1932 to 1938 supreme chief of the Transcaucasian Communist Party organization. He successfully built up the Georgian League of Militant Godless from 101,586 members in 1931 to 145,413 in 1938, representing over 4 percent of the total population of the republic. The Georgian atheist organization was warmly praised by Emel'ian Iaroslavskii, Chairman of the League of Militant Godless, and used to stage hostile manifestations against Catholicos-Patriarch Kallistrates at the Sioni Cathedral in Tbilisi.

During World War II, the Georgian Church displayed the same patriotic attitude as that to be found throughout Russia itself. As a reward, Stalin personally gave instructions in 1943 for the newly reestablished Moscow Patriarchate to recognize the autocephaly of the Georgian Church, which the Russian clerics had previously refused to do. However, the number of churches actually operating has remained very small. Of the 2,455 Georgian churches of the pre-1917 period, only about a hundred are still officially open, including eleven in Tbilisi itself. It is instructive to run through the list of fifteen Georgian episcopal and archepiscopal sees, as listed in the official Georgian Church calendar. In 1950, only five of the Georgian bishoprics were occupied, namely the Patriarchal see of Mtskheta and Tbilisi, the bishopric of Dsilkani, the Metropolitan archbishoprics of Manglisi, of Urbnisi, and of Gelati and Kutaisi. In 1962, we find the number of active dioceses increased to nine, though closer examination of the list shows that in four cases the diocese was being administered either by a neighboring bishop or by the Catholicos-Patriarch through a Vicar-General. At the time of writing, the picture is much the same as in 1962, except that the ancient see of Alaverdi in Kakheti, occupied for a few years around 1960 by Bishop David Burduladze, is again vacant.

The Georgian Church today, though poor, is undeniably accorded general respect as a visible symbol of Georgia's ancient national past. Gone are the days of antireligious parades and show trials of leading clerics. The present Catholicos-Patriarch, Ephrem II Sidamonidze, is a man of cultured and benign appearance, well-loved by communist and Christian alike. On his installation in 1960 Ephrem was the subject of warm panegyrics in the *Journal of the Moscow Patriarchate*. Ephrem is in regular correspondence with the Archbishop of Canterbury, His Grace Michael Ramsay, and he manages also to cultivate friendly relations with the Supreme

Catholicos of Armenia, Vazken I, in Echmiadzin. At official functions such as the state session of the Georgian Parliament on the occasion of the jubilee of Shota Rustaveli in 1966, Ephrem may be seen occupying a seat of honor near the front of the hall, with an attendant bishop. He is also a council member of the Georgian Society for Friendship and Cultural Relations with Foreign Countries and of the Society for the Preservation of Cultural Monuments. In a sense, all this is a symbol of weakness rather than of strength, for the Kremlin knows that the Georgian Church no longer represents a danger to the regime. The institution has been systematically purged of rebellious elements; and the Georgians, never very prone to religious overindulgence, have found other, more innocuous outlets for expression of their cultural individuality, such as their football teams, their drinking rites, the Georgian Popular Dance Ensemble, and the universal cult of their national bard, Shota Rustaveli.

Before concluding this survey of religion in Georgia, it seems appropriate to add a few words about the state of the Jews of modern Georgia. As a recent special survey states, "the Georgians treat 'their' Jews as an integral part of the area's population."[17] Indeed, many Jewish intellectuals and writers are prominent in Georgian literary life. For the most part they bear surnames in the Georgian form ending in "-shvili" or "son of," for instance: Danielashvili, translator of Minsky's *Dibbuk*; Kurshishvili, translator of Sholem Aleichem; and Rose Tadvidishvili, chronicler of the Jewish community in Kutaisi, capital of Western Georgia. In the 1959 Soviet census, 51,582 persons in Georgia declared that they were of Jewish nationality; and of these, 35,322, or close to 70 percent of the Jewish population of Georgia, indicated the Georgian language as their native tongue. Georgia is thus the only republic in the Soviet Union where the language of the majority—the official language of the republic—is also recognized officially as the language of declared members of the Jewish nationality. In the Russian Republic, in the Ukraine, and in all other Soviet republics of the Union, Jews cannot list the language of the majority as their "national language." There, only Yiddish and the languages of the Oriental Jews are the official recognized languages of the Jewish nationality.

According to Joshua Rothenberg, the Georgian Jewish community is "at present the best organized Jewish community, or perhaps the only organized Jewish community in the Soviet Union, and a citadel of Soviet religious Jewry." No fewer than thirteen of the sixty-two synagogues at present functioning in the U.S.S.R. are to be found in Soviet Georgia. Thus, 20 percent of all Soviet synagogues are in Georgia, while Georgian Jews number only 2.5 percent of the total Jewish population in the Union as a whole. About half the former students of the Moscow *yeshiva*, now defunct in all but name, came from Georgia. There is a flourishing Georgian Jewish literature, written mostly in Georgian, but with strong Jewish overtones. Prominent in this field was the talented novelist Herzl Boazov, executed for "nationalistic tendencies" in the purges in 1937. The Soviet Yiddish periodical *Sovetish Heimland* for November 1966 gives a comprehensive survey of current literary and theatrical activities among the Georgian Jews, in which specifically Jewish life and customs are treated with a realism unknown in other Soviet republics.

The 1930s in Georgia were dominated by the unsavory personality of L. P. Beria (1899-1953), a man who was many years later to be unmasked as an enemy of the people. Although it is wrong to blame all the excesses of Stalin's era on Beria—as Svetlana Alliluyeva tries to do—Beria nonetheless does bear a heavy responsibility for the decimation of the Georgian intellectual and professional managerial classes which took place during the Great Purges.[18] On the other hand, Beria could surely have achieved nothing had he not found willing supporters and sponsors in Stalin himself, as well as in his own ill-fated predecessors as head of the NKVD—the sadistic Yezhov and Yagoda.

Lavrenti Beria came of a poor Mingrelian peasant family, living in the Sukhumi district of Abkhazia near the Black Sea. He joined the Bolshevik Party in 1917 while studying at a technical college at Baku, and became a member of the Caucasian Cheka in 1921. By the time he was thirty-two, he had been vice-president of the Cheka in Azerbaijan and Georgia, president of the Georgian GPU, and then president of the Caucasian State Police and chief representative of the OGPU in Transcaucasia. In October 1931 Beria became second secretary of the Transcaucasian Communist Party, the first secretary of which was a decent man named Kartvelishvili, who disliked Beria's unsavory personality and methods. Within a few years, Beria had fabricated a series of false accusations against his superior Kartvelishvili, who was soon deported and put to death. Beria, naturally, took his place.

From 1932 to 1938 Beria exercised dictatorial powers in Georgia. On the credit side, he played a leading role between 1933 and 1937 in implementing the Second Five-Year Plan. This period witnessed the completion of such projects as the Zestafoni ferro-alloy plant, the Tbilisi machine-tool plant named after Kirov, the Avchala cast-iron factory, a new industrial plant in Kutaisi, and tea factories in Western Georgia. However, Beria kept up a constant barrage of denunciations to Stalin of Georgian Bolshevik leaders, officials, writers, and teachers. The 1936-37 purges were even more terrible in Georgia than elsewhere because Stalin and Beria used the opportunity to wreak vengeance on their many personal foes and rivals, as well as on many innocent persons who knew too much about their obscure beginnings and shady past. The decimation of Georgian writers and artists was particularly cruel. Among the victims were such prominent writers as the novelist Mikhail Javakhishvili and the poets Titsian Tabidze and Paolo Iashvili (both great friends of Boris Pasternak). The toll included also leading theatrical producers, a world-famous specialist in ancient history (Grigol Tsereteli), and a number of doctors and industrial managers who could ill be spared. Needless to say, the ranks of the Georgian Communist Party were ruthlessly thinned, and scarcely a single government leader of the 1920s was allowed to survive.

At a congress of Georgian writers held at Tbilisi in July 1954, the first secretary of the Georgian Communist Party, V. P. Mzhavanadze, in referring to the terrorism exercised by Beria and his henchmen, announced:

> Comrades, you all know what injury was done to our people by that gang of murderers and spies who now have been unmasked and done away with by our Party. That gang killed many leading and progressive scientists... The Central Committee of the Georgian Communist Party has found out that the outstanding masters of the Georgian language—Mikheil Javakhishvili, Titsian Tabidze and Paolo Iashvili—became victims of the intrigues of that abominable gang of murderers. I have pleasure in declaring in the name of the competent organs that these men have been rehabilitated.

While welcoming this declaration by Georgia's leading contemporary statesman—and a very fine patriot and gentleman he is—one cannot help recalling a saying by Ilia Chavchavadze, to the effect that when you have broken your neck, or merely one or two legs or arms, apologies are very nice, but do not help you to recover.

Nor can one help wondering if there is not something wrong with a system which permits a "gang of murderers and spies" to gain control of society, and to carry on their crimes for so many years without any intervention by the powers of law and order.

Beria's last master stroke was the invention and "discovery" in 1951 of a nationalist organization centered on Mingrelia, the western province of Georgia adjoining his own homeland. There is little doubt that this discovery was fabricated by Beria in order to curry favor with Stalin, whom Beria did not long survive.

As was to be expected, drastic upheavals took place in the Georgian government and in the party machinery after Stalin's death. In the upper echelons a complete shake-up occurred. The post of first secretary of the Georgian Communist Party was filled in September 1953 by a new man, V. P. Mzhavanadze, a former lieutenant-general in the Red Army. The second secretary, who is usually a Russian, was P. V. Kovanov, later succeeded by P. A. Rodionov, who is still in office. A forty-one year old engineer and geologist, Givi D. Javakhishvili, was elected Prime Minister of the Georgian Republic. Both Mzhavanadze, a candidate member of the Presidium of the Central Committee of the Soviet Communist Party, and Javakhishvili are wise and popular statesmen. Javakhishvili accompanied Kosygin on his visit to Great Britain in 1967. The Georgian communist M. P. Giorgadze was in 1958 appointed Secretary of the Supreme Soviet. Although the power of Georgians in Moscow has waned since the death of Stalin, they can at least no longer be blamed for all the failings of the central government. Attempts by Khrushchev to brand Stalin as a wicked tyrant were greatly resented in Georgia, provoking a full-scale riot at Tbilisi in 1956. Stalin's shrine and museum at Gori are still much visited, and are shown proudly to foreign visitors by the local guides.

Something has been said in these pages about the appalling loss of life in Georgia and other parts of Transcaucasia as a result of the revolution, the Civil War, the purges, and World War II. However, these losses have since been somewhat offset by remarkable improvements in the health and general standard of living of the population, which has greatly reduced the death rate and increased life expectancy. Georgia is famous, of course, for its sprightly centenarians, some of whom are reputed to marry and have families right up to the age of a hundred. While certain of these reports are surely exaggerated, after the manner of travelers' tales everywhere, there is no doubt that the Georgians and the Caucasians generally are a robust and long-lived stock. In Western Georgia, the deadly scourge of malaria, once almost universal in the low-lying Colchis basin, has now been virtually eradicated through drainage of swamps, as well as through provision of drugs and medical services.

The dramatic advance in medical standards in Georgia may be measured by the statistics. In 1913, there were only 700 doctors and 1,300 auxiliary medical staff in the whole of Transcaucasia, for a population of some six million. The ratio was thus one medical worker (including nurses and midwives) for three thousand members of the population. By 1940, there were 8,700 doctors in the Transcaucasian republics, 8,000 more than in 1913. By 1960, the number of doctors had risen to 26,400—that is to say, it had trebled in twenty years. This situation resulted at one time during the 1920s in a rapid expansion of the population. Had it continued to increase at the prevailing rate, the population of Georgia would have doubled every thirty years or so. It is noticeable that partly because of housing shortages Georgians today tend to limit their families as far as possible, particularly in Tbilisi and the large towns, with the result that families with more than two or three children are relatively uncommon.

If we compare the position of Georgia and adjoining Soviet republics with that of Turkey and Persia, the improvement in the Soviet zone looks even more striking. The crude death rate in Turkish towns in 1959 was 12.9 per thousand, and that in villages, where medical care is largely unknown, much higher. The rate for Georgia was 7.6 per thousand in 1950, lowered to 6.8 per thousand in 1963. Since infant mortality in Turkey is responsible for as high as 43 percent of the total deaths recorded, it is necessary for proportionately more children to be born per family in order to keep the population on a rising trend. Thus, the crude birth rates for Turkey in the later fifties is of the order of 37 per thousand, as against 24 per thousand in Georgia.[19] This does not mean that the population of Turkey was increasing much more rapidly, but that the wastage through infant deaths there was higher than in Georgia.

This is all part of a general trend noticed recently in the U.S.S.R., and is typical also of developments in many Western societies over the past century. As industrialization and urbanization proceed, families tend to shrink in size. Improvements in medical services make it unnecessary to maintain a high birth rate as infant mortality drops to a very low level and the elderly live longer. Birth control practice and the employment of women in qualified work—an extremely common phenomenon in Georgia—tend to reinforce this drop in the birth rate.

An amenity enjoyed by the Georgians is that of excellent health resorts. The numerous medicinal springs in the country, the mountain air, the subtropical climate, and the splendid Black Sea beaches attract holiday-makers from every part of the Soviet Union, as well as from foreign countries. There are alpine resorts and also resorts situated in the medium-mountain forest belt and in low-lying regions, including the coast. The visitors include large numbers of persons suffering from pulmonary, gastrointestinal, rheumatic, cardiovascular, nervous, and skin disorders, as well as from many other conditions. Tbilisi itself (the name comes from Georgian *tbili*, "warm") has been famous for centuries for its natural hot springs and mineral baths. Some other resorts, which had been organized before the Revolution, were not developed on a large scale until Soviet times. Borjomi, the Georgian Vichy, enjoys international renown for its mineral water, of which no less than 96 million bottles were distributed to many countries in 1962. The resort of Abastumani, lying some 4,000 feet above sea level on the Ajar-Imeretian range, has excellent facilities for treatment of tuberculosis patients, while skiing and all winter sports are available in season. Many of these amenities are used by both Georgians and visitors from outside. Even when visitors are in the majority their presence is welcome because it contributes to the wealth and economic activity of the local population.

Another branch of public service that has developed rapidly in Georgia under Russian rule is that of transport. Up to the year 1800 roads were mere unpaved tracks that could be negotiable only on horseback, on foot, or by merchant caravans. Even carriages had difficulty in crossing the Caucasus range, or in proceeding between the principal towns. The building of a railway network, which was achieved in tsarist times, linked Tbilisi with the Black Sea, with Baku, and with Erevan in Armenia. Some of the trains were so slow, however, that it was commonly said in jest that peasant women were afraid to ride in them, as they were slower than going by horse or donkey. Roads have not been greatly improved, even during Soviet times; but one great feature in contemporary Georgia is the excellent and cheap air services linking Tbilisi with Moscow, Leningrad, Tashkent, and also with the smaller towns of Georgia itself. This facility has widespread effects on the economy and on welfare generally. I have myself stood on Kutaisi airport in western Georgia and watched helicopters and light aircraft landing every half-hour or so, bringing peasants to market from outlying villages in the mountains, children to school, or even animals to the skilled care of a veterinary surgeon. (There is probably some truth in accounts appearing from time to time in Western newspapers that tell of Caucasian peasant women who can afford to fly to Moscow to sell subtropical fruit, flowers, or vegetables in "free" markets in Moscow.) And the Tbilisi Metro, the first subway in the Caucasus, opened in 1966, is still another addition to the long list of achievements.

Incomes, by Western standards, are low. There is certainly underemployment among the intellectual classes, and a number of "perpetual students" crowd the literary institutes rather than embarking on teaching in the villages. However, the industrial workers and peasants are by and large better off than in most places in European Russia, except perhaps for Moscow, Leningrad, and Kiev and the immediate vicinity. Because the climate is mild and sunny, heating is less of a problem; life can be carried on out-of-doors for much of the year. The fertility of the soil and the native energy and cheerfulness of the people make for a delightful way of life that is very pleasing to foreign visitors.

Statisticians have calculated that Soviet economic policy has by and large tended to favor growers of rare, subtropical produce, such as tea, citrus fruits, and vines, rather than producers of staple commodities such as cereals, potatoes, and hay. Compulsory deliveries at very low prices, as practiced under Stalin, did not affect Georgia to the same extent as it did Russia and, particularly, the Ukraine. The Glasgow economists Nove and Newth conclude that available evidence supports the following propositions:

(1) By and large, with the possible exception of Azerbaijan, the Caucasian and Central Asian republics have contributed a less than average amount per capita to the total revenue of the Soviet Union.

(2) These republics were permitted to retain, on the whole, a higher than average proportion of all-Union revenues raised in their territories to finance economic and social development. This was a consequence of the fact that investments in these areas and expenditures for education and health were greater, relative to local resources, than in other parts of the Soviet Union. In addition, especially before 1955, much industrial investment in these areas was financed directly out of the Union budget.

(3) One may feel, with justice, that the pattern of expenditure was decided in Moscow, and that the direction of industrial and agricultural development related to the interests of the U.S.S.R. as a whole. However, it follows from the financial evidence that the Russian connection, membership of a large and more developed polity, greatly facilitated such social and economic progress as was achieved in these areas.[20]

There is evidence, certainly, that the central government in Moscow has pumped vast sums of money into such economically wasteful but socially and politically beneficial projects as the great Rustavi steel mills. One has only to contrast the bustling atmosphere of Soviet Georgian towns with the charming but decayed sloth of many cities of independent Ireland to reach some meaningful, if disquieting, parallels and contrasts.

It is often charged, and with some justification, that Georgia is one of the most "nationalistic" of the Soviet republics. Memories of the forcible annexation of 1921 and of the terrible purges are still vivid. Behind groaning beards, and after innumerable toasts in the traditional style, one sometimes hears jovial Georgians lamenting their long-lost independence and uttering confident boasts of the wonders they could achieve if Moscow would leave them alone. Visitors are sometimes startled to hear Georgian acquaintances point contemptuously at some harmless Russian passer-by and wish that he was out of the way. Certainly Georgians keep a watchful eye on the population ratio in their republic, where they constitute some 64 percent of the total. They would not tolerate the kind of mass immigration from Russia and the Ukraine that has become universal in such areas of Central Asia as Kazakhstan.

During the 1920s the Georgian issue was a lively one in international socialist circles. Most of the members of the Zhordania cabinet were able to get away safely before the advancing communists could catch up with them. They set up their headquarters in Paris, where they had a fine country house at a place called Leuville-sur-Orge. One or two of the less fortunate were murdered or committed suicide, but most of them lived to a ripe old age, President Zhordania himself attaining the age of eighty-five. These social democratic leaders were strongly attacked in exile by other, more right-wing, nationalists, who accused them of preparing the way for socialism in Georgia and thus contributing to the communist takeover. The chief among these antisocialist groups was called Tetri Giorgi (White George, named after Georgia's patron saint, who was also conceived as a moon god). In 1937 a "Georgian Fascist Front" was formed, under the chairmanship of Sh. Maghlakelidze. Feeble attempts were made by Hitler to mobilize émigré Georgians during World War II. Since he could never decide whether or not Georgians should be exterminated as "non-Aryans," these attempts did not get very far. During the past few years, U.S. intelligence agencies have attempted to revive Georgian nationalism, largely through the able intermediary Isaac Don Levine, the well-known expert on Soviet affairs. Radio Free Europe in Munich maintains a Georgian desk, as does also the Institute for the Study of the U.S.S.R. in the same city.

It is doubtful, however, whether these activities will serve any useful purpose now that a more enlightened policy toward Georgia and other Caucasian republics is being adopted in Moscow. It is sometimes forgotten that complete cultural Russification has not been the order of the day in Georgia under the Soviets, whatever political policies may have been in effect.[21] A conscious effort is made to instill pride in national cultures, as witness the remarkable scale of the jubilee of Shota Rustaveli, celebrated on an international and all-Union basis in September 1966. In some respects, these celebrations constituted a massive vote of confidence by the Kremlin leadership in the present Georgian local regime, which has continued in office uninterruptedly for seventeen years, through all the vicissitudes of the Khrushchev era, and has proved most successful in establishing an honorable *modus vivendi* between Moscow and the local population. If there has been an undermining of traditional Georgian culture, this is in large part due to the universal cult of "pop" music, refrigerators, motor cars, and other features of the "decadent" West that are now becoming commonplace aspects of the Soviet way of life. Against this must be set the increased national solidarity that is the result of fifty years of education conducted in the Georgian tongue and the impact of the Soviet Georgian-language newspapers and radio and television programs. Regions that were once separate enclaves of backward tribesmen now feel themselves fully drawn into the orbit of a new, united Georgian Soviet nation. As a Soviet showplace and a most popular resort, there seems no reason why Georgia should not continue to reap increasing benefit from its many natural advantages without severing its connections to the larger economic and political entity of the Soviet Union as a whole.

Such increasing benefits are confidently foreshadowed by the current Five-Year Plan for Georgia (1966-70). Progress is to be concentrated in electricity, in engineering, and in the chemical industry, and also on the further growth of the food and light industries. The total volume of industrial production is to be increased by approximately 60 percent, electricity by 90 percent, good road vehicles by 100 percent, mineral fertilizers by 100-120 percent, silk textiles by 40 percent, knitwear by 60-70 percent, wine production by 50 percent, tinned goods by 160 percent. The first sections of the Inguri, Vartsikhe, and Namakhvan hydroelectric power stations are to be put into operation, and the Tbilisi power station is to be expanded up to 960,000 kw. New coal mines at Tqibuli and Tqvarcheli are to be completed and Stage 2 of the Rustavi nitrogenous fertilizer plant finished. New construction projects in hand include the Madneuli copper concentration plant, a factory for industrial control computers, two knitwear factories, and nine plants for the primary processing of tea.

Agricultural expansion involves increased production of citrus fruits, grapes, tea, and tobacco—all these principally by increases in yield, but also by the cultivation of new ground. Some 60,000 hectares of dry steppe land is to be made productive by irrigation. Drainage work projected for 90,000 acres in the Kolkhida valley will expand greatly the land area under cultivation in Western Georgia near the Black Sea. Further development of holiday resorts is envisaged, as typified by the opening in 1967 of the large new Iveria hotel in Tbilisi.

The present situation in Georgia, from both the political and the economic point of view, may not be entirely to the taste of every Georgian. Human nature being what it is, some may prefer to run their own affairs badly rather than let someone else run them better on their behalf. But the sharp contrast between the dynamic economic and industrial system and the excellent cultural facilities of Georgia, on the one hand, and, on the other, the chronic instability of some modern countries of the Middle East, or the deplorable backwardness and stagnation of others, leaves little room for denying the positive side of Russia's impact on Georgia. The Soviet formula of a federation of European and Asiatic communists is far from perfect; but at least Georgia is at present well insured against drifting back into the vicious circle of ignorance, poverty, and disease, and is able to stand on her own feet economically and industrially in this highly competitive modern age.

Russian Conquest in Central Asia:
Transformation and Acculturation

Manuel Sarkisyanz

It was Russia's claim to forming a part of Europe and to being Europe's shield against the onslaughts of Asia that constituted, in a manner of speaking, her credentials for admission into the Concert of European Powers.[1] During a long period of her history Russia's intellectual life had been directed westward. While the content of the classical Russian culture was Western in origin, its manifestations were often called Oriental in intensity; and in its extremism it was more ecstatically medieval than modern. For the most part, even anti-Western trends in Russian thinking, such as Slavophilism, viewed Russia as belonging to Europe, not to Asia. On the other hand, the Slavophile Aleksei S. Khomiakov valued Islam higher than Catholicism and "Arab character" higher than "German character."[2] The ultraconservative Konstantin Leont'ev desired Russia to prefer Hindu or Tibetan hierarchies to European egalitarianism and hoped that the "Turanian elements," shaping Russian culture more than did the Slavic, would produce something "spiritually distinct" from Europe.[3]

By way of contrast, however, Russian revolutionaries, in the spirit of the European Enlightenment, initially despised Asia. It was disappointment in both the European proletarian ("the future bourgeoisie") and the European middle classes (suspected of betraying their liberal and democratic slogans) that directed the hopes of Alexander Herzen (1812-70), Russia's most prophetic revolutionary, to the East, for the East had suffered misfortune from European civilization and would one day rise against it. Herzen blessed the Mongol Yoke for preserving such Russian peculiarities as the rural *mir* commune.[4] From this folk institution the *narodniks* (populists) expected a purer economic and political democracy to rise than would be possible in Western mass society. Folk Russia had never fully followed St. Petersburg into Westernization;[5] its peasant rebels against the early St. Petersburg state had cooperated again and again with Turkic and other Muslim nomads, as for example during the Pugachev Rising of 1773. Even as did the colonists in Siberia and on the steppes of Central Asia, the Russian Orthodox peasants may have felt a religious (or "ideological") distance from the indigenous Asians. But no racial distance separated them as in the case of those West European colonial conquerors who carried their White Man's Burden into their empire-building in Asia. The gradual and continental character of the colonization of Central Asia by the Russians tended, on the whole, to reduce the gap between them and the various native Asians, binding them together in what has been called the historical destiny of the Eurasian spaces.

KAZAKHSTAN
Russian Conquest

The unification of the Eurasian spaces by the Russian Empire began with the absorption in the sixteenth century of the Golden Horde and its Tatar succession states, and was followed in that century and the next by the conquest of Siberia. In the St. Petersburg period began the expansion of the Russian Empire from the forest zone across the steppes of what is today called Kazakhstan. The ancestors of the Kazakh rulers in the fifteenth century had moved out of the dissolving Golden Horde.[6] Like the Tatars, they were descended from Islamicized and Turkicized Mongols and derived their position from the heritage of Genghis Khan. In 1730 a Russified Tatar intermediary prompted Abu'l-Khair, the first Kazakh khan, to ask for Russian overlordship. To Abu'l-Khair's Western Kazakhs (the Younger Horde), subjection to Russia seemed at the time a desirable alternative to the devastating raids of a rival Eastern nomad power, that of the un-Turkicized and Lamaist Western Mongol Dzhungars who were overrunning the pastures of the Eastern Kazakhs. Furthermore, Abu'l-Khair expected that Russian power would enable him to bring the other two Kazakh hordes under his rule, an eventuality that he had almost effected by 1741. His successor, Nur 'Ali, collaborated with Russian Orenburg to the extent of combatting the Bashkir rebels in defiance of Orenburg. But during the great Russian peasant war under Pugachev in 1773-74, Western Kazakhs collaborated with both Russian belligerents.

The expansion of Cossack garrison lines into the Kazakh steppes provoked guerrilla resistance by the Kazakhs defending their pastures against Russian Cossack military colonization. Sultan Ablai of the Kazakh Middle Horde used his buffer position between the Russian and the Manchu Chinese Empire to attempt a Muslim Iranian oasis-type of absolutism, even going so far as to try to force his Kazakhs into a sedentary mode of life. But after conquering the Central Asian oases, the Uzbeks (who, competing with the Kazakhs, had likewise moved out of the dissolving Golden Horde) turned to sedentary life earlier and more successfully than the Kazakhs. From the Ferghana area and the Uzbek state of Khokand, Uzbek agricultural colonists were, after 1808, advancing northward into central and eastern Kazakh pastures, while the Western Kazakhs were being pressed by the Uzbek state of Khiva. All this made the alternative of Russian overlordship acceptable, certainly until the centralization of Russian administration after the Napoleonic wars.

In 1824 the Russian government abolished the office of khan in the Kazakh Younger Horde, and in 1846 the Older Horde passed from Chinese to Russian overlordship. Losses of Kazakh pastures to Russian military colonization by frontier Cossack garrisons contributed to the Kazakh independence struggle under Kenesary Kasymov (1802-47). His struggle against the Western Siberian administration was supported by some Tatars and Bashkirs and by the Uzbek rulers of Khiva and Bukhara. He was killed in 1847, however, by Kirghiz vassals of Khokand.[7]

After Russia's frustration in the Crimean War, the Russian Empire resumed its expansion into Central Asia.[8] Her victory over Khokand in 1864 permitted the Kazakhs to expel sedentary Khokand Uzbek colonists. In 1865, however, some Kazakh areas were tightly incorporated into Russian Turkestan while others were administered from Orensian state property in 1868, although the right of the inhabitants to use the land was confirmed. Russian

measures restricted nomad migrations, and those Kazakhs who resisted by force were sentenced to death or deportation in 1869.

Russian peasants had begun to settle in Kazakhstan in 1866, and
this colonization grew during Russia's famine of 1891-92. By 1895,
though Russians constituted only one-tenth of the population of
Semirechie, they owned all of its agricultural land. After 1906 the
policy of Pëtr A. Stolypin sought to relieve peasant pressure on
landlords in European Russia by channeling that pressure into Russian colonization of the steppe areas and of Siberia. This resulted
in drastic losses of pasture land and gradually pushed the Kazakh
nomads back toward desert areas. During the period 1902-13 the
Kazakh population declined by nine percent. Its flocks suffered
under heavy winters because hay feeding had not yet been learned
from the Russians. Impoverishment forced the Kazakhs to abandon
nomadism in favor of sedentary agriculture. Denomadization, particularly in the vicinity of Russian settlements, led to the rise of
private property over previously communal lands and the selling or
mortgaging of pastures. But denomadization was accompanied also
by a transition from Kazakh customary law to Muslim canonic law.
Actually the Kazakhs became more Islamicized under Russian tsarist rule than ever before. The *Pax Russica* had linked them with
the Muslim cultural center of Bukhara. On the other hand, pre-
Soviet Russian culture had far deeper impact on the Kazakhs, who
had previously participated very little in medieval Muslim civilization, than on the peoples of sedentary areas of Central Asia who
had a strong Islamic cultural tradition.[9]

Early Russian Cultural Impact

In the north more Kazakh children attended the Russian schools,
founded from 1789 on, than Muslim schools. In this connection,
Soviet research may tend to overemphasize the cultural impact of
Russian revolutionary deportees among the Kazakhs. During his deportation to Semipalatinsk, Fedor M. Dostoevskii (like the Fourier-
ist socialist Sergei F. Durov and the Populist Nikolai M. Iadrintsev)
became a friend of the first Kazakh modernist, Chokan Valikhanov
(1835-65), son of an alumnus of a Russian Siberian military school

and one of the first Kazakhs to possess a command of the Russian language. After acquiring familiarity with the medieval Chagatai Turkic literature and even the Uighur script, Chokan was enrolled in the Russian military academy at Omsk. There he became a fellow pupil of the famous Russian explorer Grigorii N. Potanin.[10] Among his Russian teachers were Nikolai G. Chernyshevskii's friend V. Lobodovskii and the Orientalist Nikolai F. Kostyletskii, an admirer of Vissarion G. Belinskii. It was in Russian translation that Chokan read Rousseau, Carlyle, Dickens, and Thackeray; and it was through Russian scholarship that he became attracted to field research on Central Asian folklore and social institutions. While in the service of the tsar's General Hasford (Gasford), Governor-General of Western Siberia, Chokan explored Kazakhstan and Semirechie. For the "sake of. . .closer fraternization" of Kazakhs and Russians Hasford recommended him for decoration. Informed through Chokan's research on "Traces of Kazakh Shamanism," Hasford came to launch the propagation of "Hasfordism," an intermediary religion to facilitate a transition from Kazakh Islam to Russian Christianity.

Of greater consequence were Chokan's associations with the Russian explorer Pëtr Petrovich Semënov-Tian-Shanskii (1827-1914),[11] who encouraged his studies at St. Petersburg University, introduced Chokan's discoveries on Kirghiz history (which refuted Humboldt, Ritter, and Klaproth) into Russian scholarship, and recommended his election into the Russian Geographic Society. In 1858-59 he was the only scholar of Central Asian origin to have a broad-based Western education. Thus Chokan was entrusted with a caravan exploration of Kashgaria (the first since Marco Polo and Jesuit Hoes of 1603) in the service of Russia, and St. Petersburg policy-makers subsequently benefited from his insight into Chinese Turkestan.

Chokan soon came under the influence of Alexander Herzen's followers, the brothers Vasilii and Nikolai Kurochkin, members of the secret society "Land and Freedom," and began to criticize such Kazakh institutions as trial by clan elders (*bays*), and feuds, demanding for Kazakhstan liberal administrative reforms in the spirit of the Russia of 1861.[12] As a result, Chokan was prevented from assuming the elective office of "senior Sultan." He even served with General Mikhail G. Cherniaev against Khokand before withdrawing, shocked by the crimes of that conquest. When this enlightened descendant of Genghis Khan died in 1865, he had probably achieved a greater impact on the Russia of Alexander II than on contemporary Kazakh society. One reason for this was that he wrote mainly in Russian, his works remaining mostly unpublished during his lifetime.

Modern Kazakh prose began with Ibrai Altynsarin (1841-89), the compiler of the Kazakh Chrestomathy of 1879, the textbook anticipating modern Kazakh literature. This literature was pioneered by Abai Kunanbaev (1845-1904), the son of a clan elder in the Semipalatinsk region. While studying at a Muslim theological institution, he briefly attended a Russian school. As the use of Arabic letters was spreading in contemporary Kazakhstan, Arabic, Persian, and Chagatai Turkic classics were stimulating Abai, as were oral Kazakh folklore and its bards of the steppes. It was from his brother, a pupil of the same Russian Orientalist Kostyletskii who had taught Chokan Valikhanov, that Abai learned about the writings of Belinskii, Turgenev, and Tolstoi. Apparently under the influence of such Russian humanists, Abai attempted, upon his election as district administrator in 1875, a policy of enlightened reforms from above. His Kazakh rivals, however, soon denounced him as an enemy of the tsar and a danger to ancestral customs. He resigned from administrative service in 1898 but remained head of his Aul settlement, continuing to direct seasonal migrations and the choice of pastures. In 1885 he participated in a clan discussion of such reforms as ensuring freedom of women to choose for themselves their marriage partners, prohibiting the relatives of a deceased man from inheriting his widow, and abolishing collective responsibility for theft.

Through the Russian revolutionary E. P. Mikhaelis of the "Land and Freedom" society, who had been deported to Semipalatinsk, Abai became acquainted with the writings of Plato, Spinoza, and Spencer, as well as with those of the Russian Nihilists Chernyshevskii and Pisarev, in addition to Dobroliubov, and also with the social satire of Mikhail E. Saltykov-Shchedrin. He was soon advocating utilitarian popular instruction for the Kazakhs. Shortly before beginning to translate Pushkin and Lermontov into the Kazakh language (in 1886), Abai began writing Kazakh poetry himself.[13] Though his poems were lyrical, they contained criticism of the social injustice and the Russian bureaucratic arbitrariness that had continued after Alexander II's reforms, but he also sang praises of the Russians as examples of enlightenment and progress.

In 1886 Abai was elected a member of the Russian Semipalatinsk District Statistical Committee. As a Kazakh Westernizer, he may be compared with such Muslim modernists as Sir Sayyed Ahmad. Abai attempted to reveal the causes of Kazakh backwardness, and kept admonishing his Kazakhs to become educated and to be useful (for example, in his poem "In the Boarding School They Learn"), a message that would appeal to American pragmatism though it was reiterated in verse.[14]

Kazakh Nationalistic Reactions
To Early Russian Impact

What Abai denounced as backwardness was remembered with nostalgia by Dulat Babataev (1802-74), for whom the traditions about the epic glories of the nomad Kazakh past made the social changes of his own time appear as degeneration and decline. Thus the transition from nomadism to agriculture was in Dulat's eyes an impending disaster for which he blamed the Kazakh renegades who had deserted their Islamic faith and had submitted to the Russian unbelievers. He called his age an Age of Sorrow that was to herald the approaching end of the world; and in the face of this he called for a "return to Islam." Similarly, the departure from the ways of the fathers prompted Shortam Bay Kanaev (1818-81) to warn of the approaching end of the world in a Koranic sense. His poem "Age of Grief" (after which an entire current of Kazakh nativist thought is called "Zar Zamanism") expresses longing for lost nomad freedom and old patriarchal ethics. It mourns the imitation of Russian ways, the passing to sedentary agriculture, and the impact of money economy, which had produced such greed that "even the calf is being sold for money," and "money is being charged even for mortar."

Shortam Bay lamented the degeneration of morals and the corruption and exploitation appearing with the money economy, which he blamed for raising the vicious and humbling the noble.[15] Like other apologists of the Muslim world during its contemporary crisis, Murad Mongke-uly (1843-1906) refused to attribute such decline to the will of Allah, but blamed instead human error, insisting—unlike the early Muslim modernists in Egypt or India—that it was money that had usurped the role of God. A Sufi's and yet a modernist's reaction to the crisis of Islamic Kazakh society confronts us in Aubakir Kerderi (1858-1903). In the transitoriness and fruitlessness of earthly life, which he regarded as illusory, he found some consolation for the Russian excesses. For him, too, the prototype of an ideal society lay in the past, and truly enlightened progress was something brought by the Prophet Muhammad. Though Aubakir was among the first to propagate Islam in the Kazakh language,[16] he was obviously influenced by the Crimean Tatar modernist Ismail Gasprinskii. He desired his Kazakhs to take their example of progress and enlightenment from Constantinople. At the same time he wanted them to learn from the colonial power ruling them, and to appreciate the progress brought by Russian administration and education.

After the turn of the century evidence appears of different types of Russian impact on Kazakh political thought. In the Russian Populist magazine *Russkoe bogatstvo* the explorer Potanin reported that Kazakhs gathering in the Semipalatinsk area wanted a narrator to tell them stories from Turgenev, Lermontov, and Tolstoi.[17] Russian ideological controversies between liberalism and populism (*narodnichestvo*) were paralleled by inter-Kazakh polemics about the relative merits of communal (nomad) or private (agricultural) holding of land. Turgay Kazakh Sultan Vakhitjan Karatayoghli (Karataev), a graduate of the Russian Imperial University who in 1907 became deputy to the Second Duma, protested against Russian peasant colonization.[18] He was disappointed in the Russian Kadet and Octobrist liberals, who had for a moment given him hope, and in 1917 joined the Communist Party. Muhammad Djan Seralin (1871-1929), a graduate of a Russian-Kazakh school and much encouraged by a Russian missionary educator, Nikolai I. Il'minskii (1822-91),[19] became the editor of the first Kazakh journal, *Ay qap* (1911-15). This periodical advocated a rationalized Islam and the Islamic canonic law as against Kazakh customary law.[20]

The position of *Ay qap* was challenged by *Qazaq* (1913-18), which carried the views of Bokey Khan-uli and certain other Kazakhs. Bokey Khan-uli, a member of the First Duma, represented the economically privileged Kazakh strata and was less committed to Islam (against which he defended Kazakh customary law) and more secularized (in the sense of the Russian Kadet liberals).[21] He, and those who shared his views, condemned the Kazakh mass rising in 1916 (precipitated by the draft of Central Asians for labor behind the Russian front lines). Bokey Khan-uli stood by the tsarist government even after 300,000 Kazakhs, in order to escape reprisals, had fled to China and the Kazakh land in Semirechie had been confiscated. Bokey Khan-uli's organization, the Alasha Orda, did not insist on territorial autonomy from Russia even in 1917-18. In the Russian Civil War it leaned first on the Russian Social Revolutionary government of Samara and then on the White Russian military dictatorship of Kolchak. But much of the Kypchak tribe of Kazakhs under Amangeldi Iman-uli (Imanov) (1873-1919), a prominent Kazakh insurgent in 1916, fought on the side of the Reds. For this reason Amangeldi Iman-uli was executed by the Alash Orda. However, the Russian chauvinism of the Whites eventually induced the Alash Orda, by 1919, to pass to the Red Side. Such Kazakh Muslim modernists as Muhammad Djan Seralin had by then already joined the Communist Party.

The early Soviet Russian impact on the previously Muslim thinking of Seifullin, Chairman of the Council of People's Commisars of Kazakhstan, was exemplified, in 1923, in his poem "Asia," in which God reproaches a wicked Europe for not having heeded the Huns, the Mongols, and the Tatars whom Allah had sent to warn Europe, nor God's "Semites under the leadership of Karl Marx. . ."[22] But Kazakh National Bolshevism never recovered from its failure to undo the Russian peasant colonization in 1927.

Kazakhstan Under Communist Hegemony

Under the Russian Communist F. I. Goloshchokin who, as Party Secretary, ruled Kazakhstan from 1927 to 1932, Kazakhstan was reopened to Russian colonization, a process that was soon facilitated by the completion of the Turkestan-Siberian Railway across its eastern part. Although in 1932, in resisting collectivization, the Kazakhs had resumed nomadism and had slaughtered up to half their livestock before withdrawing into Chinese Sinkiang,[23] the Russian hold over Kazakhstan increased during the period of the Five-Year Plan through the growth of towns. The total Kazakh population declined by twenty-two percent from 1926 to 1939, and the towns became Russian centers. Mining in central Kazakhstan attracted immigration. Karaganda—famous for its Concentration Camp—became the third largest coal producer of the entire Soviet Union. Since the Second World War Kazakhstan has produced also a large quantity of nonferrous metals—copper, molybdenum, tungsten, manganese, and nickel. The Kazakh people did not participate in due proportion in the economic development of their own republic,[24] either by way of making positive contribution or in the enjoyment of economic benefits.

Yet it would be misleading to see in the demarcation of a Kazakh federal entity and in the division of Russian Central Asia into ethnic territorial units, a mere Machiavellian device to split a "Turkestan" allegedly constituting a natural unity, in order to weaken and dominate the parts one by one.[25] If such had been the purpose, it could have been achieved more easily by preserving as Soviet republics the historical states that long before communism had cut across the nationalities of Central Asia. It can hardly be denied that the historical and sociological divisions between the four Turkic peoples of Russian Central Asia—not to mention the Iranian Tajiks—are no more artificial than those between the Latin peoples of Europe. Thus, for example, the Kirghiz, with whom nineteenth-century terminology used to confuse the Kazakhs, had more than six centuries of history before the existence of the Kazakhs.

KIRGHIZIA

Early Background and Russian Conquest

Between 840 and 925 A.D. the Kirghiz had been the strongest power in Central Asia, possessing an elaborate civilization that included the use of a Turkic "runic" script. Many, if not most of them, perished in the holocaust of the Mongol conquests in the thirteenth century. The survivors lost the cultural achievements, such as their script, and the agriculture that they had developed on the Yenisei River. Between the sixteenth and the eighteenth centuries most of them had been driven westward into their present habitat by Western Mongol pressure. Here they were found already at least superficially Islamicized,[26] and divided into numerous tribes and clans.

The first Kirghiz to come under Russian rule were not subdued
by Russian arms but had called upon Russia for assistance against
other Kirghiz. Menaced by the Sarybagysh Kirghiz, who had the
backing of Uzbek Khokand, the Bugu Kirghiz in 1854 requested
Russia's assistance. In 1855 their chief, Borombai, asked to be accepted as a Russian subject together with ten thousand families.
Upon Borombai was bestowed the rank of a Russian lieutenant
colonel, along with some subsidies; and his people were exempted
from Russian taxes. The attempts of the Russian explorer Semënov-
Tian-Shanskii to mediate in the feud between Borombai's Bugu
Kirghiz and the Sarybagysh Kirghiz, however, met with no success.
Upon the request of the Bugus, in 1863 a Russian garrison was stationed permanently on the Issyk Kul Lake. The Russian fortress
Aksu, built in the following year, was to protect them against the
Sarybagysh and against Khokandian collectors of tribute. It was to
restore the inter-Kirghiz and intertribal balance of power that the
other *northern* Kirghiz groups followed the example of the Rus-
sian-backed Bugu tribe and, by 1867, voluntarily requested, or at
least accepted, Russian rule. Only a minority of them fought on
the side of Khokand and resisted Russia.[27]

In contrast, the *southern* Kirghiz were subdued by Russia through
force of arms by 1876. But even in their case Russian domination
had not supplanted independence but had merely replaced an alternative foreign hegemony, that of the Uzbek kingdom of Khokand.[28]
Against Khokand's Khan Khudayar almost all southern Kirghiz revolted in 1870-74. They repeatedly hoped for Russian support
and many of them withdrew from Khokandian- into Russian-occu-
pied territory.[29] But as their oppressor Khudayar had meanwhile
become a vassal of the tsar, the independence struggle of the southern Kirghiz evolved into a kind of Muslim Holy War against Russia.
The leader of this war, Mullah Hasan Oghlu ("Polat Kan"), was executed upon the final Russian conquest in 1876; but his comrade-
in-arms, 'Abdul Dabek, son of a Kirghiz commander in Khokandian service, continued the Holy War in the Pamir Mountains until
1902 (in the name of claimants to the khanate of Khokand). His
mother, Kurban Jan Datkha, held out in a largely Kirghiz principal-
ity in the Alai Mountains until 1898; and her sons administered it
for Russia until 1922.[30]

Tsarist Russian Impact on Kirghiz Society

While most southern Kirghiz, after Tsar Alexander II's annexation of Khokand, shared the effects of the Russian impact on Uzbek Ferghana, northern Kirghizia became one of the most neglected and underdeveloped parts of Russian Turkestan.[31] Initially it continued to be administered by its own chieftains ("Manaps") on behalf of Russia. But in 1867-68 the Kirghiz clans were divided into territorial districts the demarcations of which cut across clan distinctions. This weakened the chieftains, since the "native administrators" were now to be elected—on the basis of property qualifications. In practice they could purchase these offices, for, as was found by the inspection under Count Pahlen undertaken on behalf of the tsar, the responsible Russian officials in the area were extremely corrupt.[32] Alexander II's liberalizing statutes of 1868 also subsequently enabled the Kirghiz chieftains to collect for themselves rents for communal clan lands. This was not unconnected with the transition from extensive nomad to intensive agricultural economy.

Among the Kirghiz, too, sedentarization was largely forced by the impact of Russian peasant colonization: the Kirghiz nomads were sometimes not allowed more land than was assigned to Russian agricultural colonists. The first Russian settlements had already appeared in 1868 on the Issyk Kul Lake (where the great Russian explorer Nikolai M. Przheval'skii [1839-88] desired to be buried). The Russian settlers were frequently incorporated into the newly organized Cossack army of Semirechie, which was assigned the most fertile lands. Its garrison settlements were established at the main crossroads. The famines that struck European Russia in 1891 and 1898 were followed by a second wave of Russian colonization that brought impoverished peasants. This tripled the number of Russian settlers around Pishpek. A third wave of colonization was meant to relieve the agrarian tensions that convulsed central Russia in 1905. To make way for this mass movement, entire Kirghiz groups were pushed into the mountains and steppes. In the Pishpek (now Frunze) area the Kirghiz lost more than 700,000 hectares of their most fertile pastures. As a result more and more Kirghiz land became "available" for Russian colonists, and more and more Kirghiz, no longer able to keep enough livestock to maintain themselves, were reduced to the status of hired farmhands. Between 1903 and 1913 the Kirghiz people was reduced by about one-tenth. In contrast, by 1914 there arose 131 Russian and Ukrainian settlements in Kirghiz areas.

The Russian colonists learned from the Kirghiz local techniques of irrigation and in turn taught the Kirghiz how to maintain their cattle through heavy winters by preparing hay for feeding. An elementary agricultural school for Kirghiz had functioned since 1883. In 1886 a Russian-Kirghiz School was established to promote the goals of assimilation by Russification. Some mixed marriages between Russians and Kirghiz took place in spite of the fact that Russians were forbidden to marry Muslims.

Kirghiz Opposition to Russian Colonization

Accordingly, Kirghiz opinion as voiced by "Akyns" (bards of the steppes, who inspired the independence struggles) was divided into a conservative or nativistic anti-Russian, and a protomodernistic or liberal, current. Among the former group, Kalygul and Arslan Bek during the early Russian period sang songs of mourning about the Evil Age ("Tar Zaman"), exposed the injustices of the powers of this world, and called for compassion for the misery of the people. They lamented the apocalyptic coming of the Final Age ("Akhir Zaman"). These "Zamanists" mourned the heroic steppe ideals of the past and considered the Russian infidels responsible for the decline of the Kirghiz. Among the Kirghiz participants of the Andijan uprising of 1898 who were deported to Siberia was the analphabetic bard Toktogul Satylganov (1864-1933), who allegedly became influenced by socialist ideas through contacts with deported Russian revolutionaries. In contrast to the "Zamanists" he expected the salvation of the Kirghiz not from a "return" to Muslim values but through modern enlightenment coming from Russia.[33] On the whole, however, the Kirghiz "Enlighteners" with their first printed books and modernistic Muslim schools were more under Tatar "Jadid" than Russian influence, though after the turn of the century the pro-Russian Kazakh modernist Kunanbaev came to have some influence on Kirghiz intellectuals like the satirist Togolk Moldo.

In northern Kirghizia, the Russian ("Kadet")-influenced liberalism of Bokey Khanuli had won some following since the 1905-07 period. By 1913 many Kirghiz refused to celebrate the third centenary of Romanov tsars. But the Kirghiz uprising of 1916 had no connection with Russian revolutionary movements. In northern Kirghizia, which felt Russian colonization pressures most, it became, particularly among the Sarybagysh tribe, an outright anti-Russian mass revolt led by the Manap Mukush Shabdanov and the Batyr Nogaev. The insurgents burned Russian villages and modern technical installations. But a number of Russian peasants fought and died alongside them. Among these were M. D. Vlasenko (who previously had earned three decorations from the tsar), S. Kovalenko, and F. P. Pavlov, as well as the headman I. V. Koshaev. The last three were eventually murdered by their fellow Russians.[34] Though the revolutionary Kirghiz proclaimed the Manap Kanaat Abukin as khan, he was unable to capture the decisive fortified points from the Chinese territory. Those among them who survived were enabled to return to their old pastures during the brief period of democracy in Russia in 1917.

But in order to punish the "rebels," Russian Turkestan's Governor General Aleksei N. Kuropatkin had ordered that the Russians whose property had been looted by Kirghiz insurgents in 1916 were to be "compensated" by Kirghiz property. This led to further dispossession of Kirghiz by Russian colonists, who continued to seize Kirghiz property even in 1917. Democratic Russia also failed to rescind Kuropatkin's project aiming at expelling the Kirghiz from some areas of Semirechie into desolate wilderness. Against this background there emerged, in March 1917, a Kirghiz Public Committee meant to represent Kirghiz national interests. But the leftist democratic Kirghiz organization "Puhara" had no mass influence. That the establishment of a communist dictatorship in Kirghizia was not possible until March 1918 was due to the Russian Social Revolutionaries under O. A. Shkapskii rather than to any effective Kirghiz political activity. It is true that in southern Kirghizia "conservative" Basmachi partisans cooperated with the Russian Peasant Army of Monstrov. But by 1920 the Russian communists had effectively broken resistance against their dictatorship in Kirghizia.

Demographic, Economic, and Political Effects
of Communist Russian Policies in Kirghizia

In the course of the struggles of the preceding five years almost one-third of the Kirghiz people had perished, the greatest losses being suffered by the northern Kirghiz. The north, which was constituted in 1926 into the Kirghiz Autonomous Republic and in 1936 into the Kirghiz Soviet Republic, had become almost cleared of its Kirghiz inhabitants. In 1926, however, about two-thirds of the inhabitants of Soviet Kirghizia were still Kirghiz. By 1939 they did not constitute more than half, and in 1959 only 40.5 percent, of the population. Even the Soviet Kirghiz capital, Frunze (the former Pishpek), received its name from a descendant of Russian colonists who won fame as a Red Army commander in the Civil War.

It is in and around this predominantly Slavicized capital of Soviet Kirghizia that most "Kirghiz" industries are concentrated. The principal industries are the mining of coal, oil, and lead, as well as nonferrous metallurgy. Kirghizia produces more mercury than any other part of the Soviet Union; after Kazakhstan, it is the main producer of coal in Soviet Central Asia. Since the second half of the past century Russians have promoted the production of cotton and tobacco. The growing of sugar beets particularly has been encouraged during the Soviet period.[35] The dairy industry and sheep breeding continue to be important components of the economy. In the precollectivization stage of Soviet Kirghizia, the cattle by 1928 had doubled the number of 1914. From then on the number declined until 1960, when it again reached the level of 1929.

The blame for the destruction of three-fourths of Kirghizia's cattle during the forced collectivization of the early Stalinist period was put on Kirghiz National Bolsheviks. Among them Abdulkerim Sidik-uulu was blamed both for opposing collectivization and for opposing the forced settlement of the remaining nomads. The deviationist creed of "Sydykovism" derives its name from this prominent member of the Kirghiz State Planning Commission. The fate of Sidik-uulu, who was liquidated by Stalin in 1937 along with other leading communists both Russian and Turkic,[36] was shared by Turar Riskul-uulu (Rykulov). Riskul-uulu was one of the most prominent of the Kirghiz National Bolsheviks and had risen to a position of Union-wide leadership. In 1922 he had become Stalin's

Deputy Commissar of Nationalities and subsequently Vice-Premier of the Russian Soviet Republic.

Cultural Developments in Soviet Kirghizia

Systematic purges in Soviet Kirghizia after the Second World War were limited to the suppression of suspect literature rather than of personalities. But in the field of literary activities the Communist Russian impact cannot be called wholly destructive if compared to the pre-Soviet state of Kirghiz literature, for the simple reason that before the 1920s hardly any literature as such existed aside from a rich oral folklore.[37] The Kirghiz epic "Manas," said to be longer than any other epic of world literature, was the subject of much discussion and reinterpretation. The hero of the tale, Manas, is allegedly identical with a Yenisei Kirghiz conqueror of the ninth century. The Manas epic, however, did not become fixed until the twentieth century. It has been called a compendium of nomad Kirghiz culture, an artistic monument of the culture's heroic age. The first to begin to record it was the Russian-acculturated Kazakh scholar Valikhanov in 1859. It was reserved to the Kirghiz Communist Party Central Committee to take the initiative for a full recording of this "Iliad of the Steppe" (a complete recitation is supposed to last weeks). Already in the Stalinist period the Manas epic of the Kirghiz people had been included among those cultural selections which are claimed to be a part of the heritage of "all the peoples of the Soviet Union." The epic served to document the distinctness of Kirghiz culture in relation to other cultures of the Muslim world.[38]

In the case of Kirghiz national identity this was not a wholly artificial or a purely propagandistic thesis of Soviet nationality policies. Under tsarist rule Islam spread among the Kirghiz more than ever before (pilgrimages to Mecca became customary in that period); yet the outward Muslim rites were still not strictly followed. The Arabic alphabet was the only pre-Soviet script known among the Kirghiz after the Middle Ages, but the knowledge of even the Arabic characters was very rare. Northern Kirghizia possessed very few Muslim institutions of learning. The few elementary schools of pre-Russian Kirghizia taught besides the Arabic language only the classical Chagatai, once the literary medium of all Turkic Central Asia. The Kirghiz language was not written before the Russian period, and the adaptation of Arabic letters to the Kirghiz language had remained inadequate. Although Kirghiz books (lyrics and genealogy) were printed from 1911 on, a modern textbook in Kirghiz allegedly did not appear until 1923.

In 1924 there appeared the first newspaper in the Kirghiz language ("Free Mountains"). Among those who contributed articles to this journal was Aaly Tokombay-uulu (Tokombaev, born in 1904), who was to become the most prominent Soviet Kirghiz writer. His family was among those who fled from Russian reprisals into Chinese Turkestan following the crushing of the Kirghiz rising of 1916. Here his parents perished from hunger. Aaly Tokombaev returned; he survived among the hordes of homeless and abandoned children, and was eventually enrolled in a Communist Party School. After joining the Communist Youth League, he was graduated, in 1927, from the Central Asian Communist University and joined the party. In the same year arose the association of Soviet Kirghiz writers, "Red Spark."

Subsequently Tokombaev contributed to ridiculous pseudopanegyrics of Stalin. This work reflected not only his Bolshevik dogmatism but also his—and his Kirghiz generation's—traumatic experience that inspired his "Blood-stained Years," which dealt with the Kirghiz tragedy of 1916.[39] The same trauma underlies the setting of Kasymaly Baialinov's (born 1902) novelette "Ajar" (published in 1928). The tragedy of its heroine is the tragedy of destitution, of self-defense, and of defeat. After Ajar's father is killed in the revolt of 1916, her mother saves herself with her child by flight into China. There she dies of starvation and the daughter is sold to a merchant. In a lonely night she escapes from him, but wolves overtake her. "Her desperate cries were short. The moon shone with indifference. Near the bush, in a gray, phantom-like throng, the animals were scrambling over that which a minute before had been Ajar. . ."[40]

Reaching that which existentially confronts all men, "Ajar" was within four years translated from the Kirghiz into Russian and thereafter into French, English, German, and Czech. The international recognition it received was hardly matched by any Kirghiz Soviet writing that occurred under Stalinist tutelage. Whatever possibilities for at least cultural self-realization Kirghiz Soviet intellectuals may have had ended with the Stalinist purges of 1937-38. Stalinist scholasticism questioned even whether the collective Kirghiz self-defense of 1916 had been "reactionary" or "progressive."

UZBEKISTAN

If in the intellectual sphere communist Russian domination weighed heavier on the Uzbeks than on the Kirghiz, in the physical sphere the impact was less severe. Because the Uzbeks had a far older and deeper Muslim culture than did the Kirghiz, communist Russian domination had both to eliminate and to impose more in Uzbekistan than it did in Kirghizia. But the Uzbeks in their territory were not overshadowed by Russian mass colonization. With more than five million people, the Uzbeks still remain the most numerous of the non-Slavic peoples of the Soviet Union. The Uzbeks had more state-building tradition and thus more ability to resist Russian conquests than any other Turkic people of what had become Russian Central Asia. Like their Kazakh rivals, the Uzbek rulers emerged from the Turkicized Mongol Empire of the Golden Horde during its dissolution in the fifteenth century,[41] but unlike the Kazakhs, they became to a considerable extent heirs of the old sedentary Iranian and Muslim oasis cultural centers between the Oxus and Jaxartes rivers. From the Uzbek conquest of the heritage of Tamerlane originated the Uzbek-ruled states of Bukhara, Khiva, and Khokand.

Uzbek-Russian Relations
Before the Conquest by Russia

Bukhara, the most important of the Uzbek states, had a history of relations with Russia reaching as far back as the sixteenth century, or since the Muscovite conquest of the Tatar Volga states Kazan and Astrakhan. Tatar merchants continued their trade with Uzbek Transoxiana as Russian subjects. Bukhara was an intermediary in the trade between Russia and China until the expansion of the Russian Empire in Siberia brought Bukhara into direct contact with it.

Uzbek Bukhara, however, was more dependent on trade with Russia than vice versa. In the seventeenth century sixteen Uzbek embassies went to Russia and nine Russian embassies to the Uzbeks. But Russia's diplomatic impact was not sufficient to obtain the release of captive Russians sold to Bukhara as slaves or to obtain Uzbek government guarantees for Russian Tatar caravans. Christian Russian merchants would not enter Bukhara until the consolidation of the Uzbek states in the late eighteenth century had increased potential turnover. Russian embassies came to Bukhara in 1780, 1794, 1820, and 1841. In the 1840s the Russian firm Pichugin opened branch offices in the main cities of the Bukhara state. Now Bukharan foreign trade came to be more dependent on Russia, as even British goods were imported through Russia. A greater Russian commercial impact on Bukhara and a more active Russian policy in Central Asia were demanded, after 1834, by Russian business interests represented by P. Golubkov.[42]

Muscovite protection for its Volga trade had been requested by Uzbek Khiva as early as 1559. By 1602 Khiva already found herself within the radius of raids by Russian Ural Cossacks, who stormed the town of Urgench and kidnapped a thousand persons. But in 1622 the Khivan prince Afghan Sultan found refuge in the Russian satellite state of Kazimov (Meshchersk). Russian caravans, supplying Bukhara with metals, had to pass through Khivan territory and were escorted by Khivan troops up to the Caspian peninsula of Mangyshlak. Tsar Peter I became actively interested in Khiva, hoping to reach India by way of the Oxus and to prospect for essential metal ore in Central Asia. In 1700 the ruler of Khiva requested a Russian protectorate against Bukhara, which had for a short time been Khiva's suzerain. As early as 1703 St. Petersburg was already in a position to confirm in office the khan of Khiva, Arab Muhammas II. But in 1717 the next khan, Shir Ghazi, had the Russian guard murdered that Peter I had sent him under Bekovich-Cherkasskii'. In retaliation a Khivan embassy was detained in Russia. Benevini, the Oriental Secretary of the Russian Foreign Office, in 1721 met a hostile reception in Khiva, against which he had attempted to enlist Bukharan support. Russia's expansion into the Kazakh steppes soon brought her closer to Khiva, now in deep decline and greatly impoverished. Before the middle of the nineteenth century Khiva had to some extent become dependent on Russia's Volga-Caspian trade, which had gained in importance for Russia as China was being opened for British trade. In the year of the British Opium War, 1840, sales agents of Russian firms had already dared to enter Khiva,[43] by then notorious in Central Asia as a bandit state where captives were sold into slavery.[44]

Russian Conquest of Uzbek Khokand

In contrast, in Khokand's largest city, Tashkent, Russian captives were in 1859 bought out of slavery and repatriated by the merchant Sa'id Azim Bay, who was actively engaged in Khokandian trade with Russia. Tashkent was an important commercial center, which on the eve of the Russian conquest had a population of 150,000. Of the three Uzbek states Khokand was economically and socially perhaps the least underdeveloped. There slavery played a lesser, and hired labor a greater, role in agriculture than in other Uzbek areas. It was perhaps against this background that, although torn by internal struggles,[45] Khokand offered stronger resistance to Russian conquest than had Bukhara—not to mention Khiva.

Advancing along and on the Syr Darya (Jaxartes) River, Russian forces penetrated into the populated part of Khokand, capturing its fortress Aq Meshit (present-day Qizil Orda) in 1853 after a siege of twenty-two days. The thwarting of Russia's scheme for southwestern expansion that resulted from her defeat in the Crimean War accelerated her drive into the alternate direction of Central Asia. The American Civil War deprived Russia's nascent textile industry of Southern cotton, which made the alternate cotton-growing areas of Ferghana more important to Russian economy. Thus the war ministry prevailed over the more cautious foreign office. Without explicit orders from St. Petersburg, the Russian general Mikhail G. Cherniaev (1828-98) in 1865 stormed Tashkent—which was heroically defended—after which his initiative was endorsed by the tsar. Khokand was forced to sign a peace treaty dictated by Russia that practically made it a Russian satellite. Khokand did not, however, lose its right to pursue independent foreign relations, and thus preserved for eight years more independence under Russia than was left to its Uzbek rival Bukhara within the same year, 1868.

Tsarist Hegemony over Uzbek Bukhara

Bukhara had maintained regular diplomatic relations with Russia since 1820; and its notoriously tyrannical amir, Nasrullah, preferred keeping up friendly relations with Russia to following the British advice that he join the other Uzbek states in solidarity against Russian expansion. In 1840, during the British invasion of Afghanistan, when Russia offered the amir assistance in case of British threats, Nasrullah requested and received Russian military instructors. When Bukharan expansion in Khokand collided with the Russian conquerors of that Uzbek khanate, British policy dropped Bukhara. Again without orders from St. Petersburg, General Cherniaev advanced into Bukharan territory in 1866. The Muslim public opinion incited an internal revolt in Bukhara, forcing her amir, Muzaffar ul-Din, even against his will, into a Holy War against the Russian infidels. Russian military superiority prevailed. But Samarkand's populace besieged a Russian garrison in 1867-68. The Bukharan forces were eventually routed completely in 1868. The amir ordered the decapitation of the Bukharan messenger who brought the Russian peace terms, but had to accept the terms nevertheless. Thus Bukhara was obliged to abolish slavery and to cede Samarkand to Russian Turkestan (against the will of its inhabitants). Russia reserved for itself the right to represent Bukhara in foreign relations. The amir thus became a vassal of the tsar.

The worlds that separated Bukhara from Russia are exemplified by the Bukharan emissary who brought his amir's signature to these terms, inquiring "by" which incantations [d'aa] the Russians had managed to win their victory." The Bukharan monarchy, however, benefited from the Russian protectorate, as Russian troops would now back the amir against internal Uzbek opposition and would even help him annex (or reannex) some territories he had long coveted, such as Hissar, Shahresabz, and Badakhshan, even against the will of their inhabitants. Russian forces enabled Amir Muzaffar ul-Din to crush a revolt of one of his sons and to force that son out of the realm. They helped him also to break tribal resistance of the Qungrat Uzbeks in 1870, and even to annex Khivan territory on the right bank of the Oxus (Amu Darya) in 1873.[46]

Nevertheless, the ruler of Bukhara—in vain—sought British Indian, Ottoman, and even Kashgarian support against his Russian suzerain. Even as vassal of the tsar he spent large amounts of money for the construction of the railroad to Arabia's holy places in the Hejaz. Though reduced to a state of satellite of an infidel empire, the ruler of Bukhara, a realm long famed for its Muslim piety and learning, still enjoyed enormous prestige in the world of Islam. Internally Bukhara was less affected by its protectorate status than were the Native States within British India. Although, since 1885, a Russian political agent was to represent in Bukhara the St. Petersburg Foreign Office as well as the Governor General of Russian Turkestan, in practice the Bukharan amir found ways to have direct relations with the central government of the Russian Empire. In St. Petersburg he distributed rich presents and, in case of disagreement, frequently was given preference over the wishes of the Governor General of Russian Turkestan, theoretically responsible for the amir's supervision. From 1892 on, Bukhara was included in the Russian customs frontier, although it preserved its own currency. Most of the state income (ninety percent in 1913) was spent on the court of the amir, who owned palaces in fashionable Russian resorts; and over seven percent of it went for his presents and for his army. The Bukharan army's equipment was not modernized during the tsarist protectorate and (except for the amir's guard) remained on the level of Napoleonic times.

Outbreaks of revolt continued to be crushed by public executions. Bukhara's penal institutions, long notorious throughout Central Asia, were hardly affected by the humanitarian liberalization trends of contemporary Russia.[47] Some of those sentenced to death were still thrown from a minaret. Humanitarian arguments were used by Russian critics of St. Petersburg's reluctance to promote internal reforms within its Bukharan satellite state. Against this background the Russian government repeatedly considered ending the "indirect rule" status of Bukhara and annexing it for the sake of more efficient and rational direct rule. But such annexation projects were repeatedly postponed because of foreign policy considerations.

Limitations of Russian Cultural Impact
on Bukhara, 1868-1920

Along the Russian-built railroad (1888) in the valley of the Zarafshan River and in the river ports, there arose Russian settlements with extraterritorial status, such as Charjuy, for example, which impressively demonstrated within traditionalist Bukhara an alternative way of life. But the railroad itself, for theological "reasons," was not permitted to touch Bukhara City. Russia did, however, exert an increasingly decisive impact on Bukhara's foreign trade. Russian imports tended to impoverish the Bukharan artisans but not to the extent of those in Russian Turkestan. While it is true that Russian cotton speculators did invest in Bukhara, too, the Marxist thesis that it was Russian capitalism's impact that decisively worsened the position of the Bukharan amir's subjects and caused the rise of an Uzbek middle class—allegedly represented by the Jadid modernists or Young Bukharans—lacks conviction. This probably exaggerates the sociological impact of the protectorate Russia exercised over Bukhara.

Alone in his admiration of Russian modernity was Ahmad Mahdum Kallah (Danish; 1827-97), who repeatedly visited St. Petersburg on the staff of the amir's embassies, hoping that Russian influence would give Bukhara an enlightened monarch to lead it toward progress.[48] As a rationalist in the spirit of the Bukhara-born medieval Aristotelian Ibn Sina (Avicenna, 980-1037), Ahmad Danish wrote a devastating secret history of the last Uzbek dynasty. But his pro-Russian liberalism and enlightenment were of very little influence during his lifetime. When Russian medicine discovered that Bukhara City was a focus of dangerous epidemics, a committee of Russian physicians brought a microscope to the decision-making Muslim theologians of Bukhara in order to obtain their consent for an improvement in their capital's water supply. The theologians answered that the glass of the microscope could well delude men to assume the existence of the nonexisting germs and that diseases continued to be both caused and stopped by the will of God alone.[49] The water supply of the city[50] was not modernized until after the Bukharan revolution of 1920.

The Bukharan revolutionary movement owed much less to Russian than to Young Turk models and to radical modernistic reinterpretations of Islam that were emanating in the late nineteenth century from Cairo, British India (Aligarh), and Volga Tataria (Kazan). Tatar modernistic Muslim thought, which is dealt with in this volume by Professor Bennigsen, provided perhaps the main initial inspiration of Young Bukharan modernism. It was under Russian

Tatar influence that Muhammad Atshil Murad Oghli Miryi (who died in 1898) evolved from the scholasticism of his Bukharan theological education to rationalistic, modernistic Islam. As their name indicates, the liberal Young Bukharans owed more to the example of the Young Turks than to Russian liberalism, even when they were reduced to operating from the relative safety of the Russian extraterritorial settlements. Abdalrauf Fitrat, the main ideologist of the Young Bukharans—who may have been the earliest Muslim modernist to advocate not evolutionary improvement but revolutionary overcoming of the established order in the spirit of a rationalized Holy War—derived his total refusal to collaborate with the imperialist powers and his subsequent collaboration with the Soviet regime not from Russian influences but from reinterpretations of Muslim thought and from secularized Pan-Turkism. Yet he expressed nevertheless the initial aspirations of such Young Bukharans as Faizullah Khoja-oghli Khodzhaev (killed in 1938) and Sadriddin Ayniy (1878-1954), both of whom became prominent under the Soviet regime.[51] And the Bukharan Communist Party, which emerged from the Young Bukharans, was founded in exile in Russian Turkestan—in the Tashkent of 1918.

Russian Turkestan:
Tsarist Colonial Administration

After the Russian conquest, the urban population of Tashkent, largely as a result of the influence of General Cherniaev, had initially become reconciled with tsarist rule. The general was popular among both Russians and Uzbeks and—quite unlike his successors—required no bodyguard. Even after he was recalled in 1866, his men, like A. K. Abramov, continued to serve in Samarkand, which had been annexed to Russian Turkestan. These men stood in honorable contrast to the proverbially corrupt Russian colonial bureaucracy of Tashkent. Among these "Tashkentian gentlemen"—satirized by the Russian social critic Saltykov-Shchedrin—was a certain Baron Nolde, who would collect in Chimkent a private tax of 2.50 rubles from each farmstead for his own pocket. When arraigned before a Russian court of law, he cynically explained: "After all, we too have to make a living."

Although conditions in Russian Turkestan were similar to those existing in Russia proper before the liberal reforms of Tsar Alexander II, no political policy was tolerated there—at least until 1907—because of the influence of Governor-General K. P. Kaufmann. Subordinated to his military administration was a sort of native "self-administration," which after 1867 was theoretically in the hands of elected representatives of the local population.

Trial by jury, however, newly introduced into Russia proper, was not extended to Russian Turkestan. On the other hand, the capital, Tashkent, remained the only city in the Russian Empire to preserve the municipal self-government granted in 1870 (on the basis of an elective system, the franchise being restricted by property qualifications). The representative character of this governing body was limited by the circumstance that only one-third of the City Council came from the indigenous majority of Tashkent. Because of the Russian majority in the council, most municipal expenses (for example, street lights) were limited to the Russian section of that colonial capital. In the Imperial Duma of 1906 only one deputy represented these 800,000 natives of Russian Turkestan who had been allowed the franchise. After the electoral restrictions of 1907, Turkestan was no longer represented in the Duma at all. But for a short time (in 1905-06) it had as Governor General D. I. Subbotich,[52] a liberal who chose his personnel without regard for their politics, advocated basic civil rights, and had the reputation of being a "Red General."

Educational Developments

General V. P. Nalivkin, Deputy Military Governor of Ferghana, who subsequently joined the Russian Social Revolutionary Party, was the foremost Russian expert on this area and wrote the standard history of Khokand. He had been active in Governor-General Kaufmann's educational policy of erecting common schools for both Russians and the indigenous population. This policy, which was quite contrary to British Indian patterns, had since 1871 aimed at overcoming native distrust.[53] But this did not suffice even as a point of departure for cultural Russification. Rather the opposite was true in the case of A. N. Vyshnegorodskii, who had qualms about having abused the confidence placed in him by Kazakh no-

mads for a publication about their customary law. He subsequently lived among sedentary Muslims as one of their own and was an
admirer of Islamic mysticism (Sufism).

Yet, on the whole, Russian life in Turkestan continued in relative isolation from the native population. It was not until 1899
that a Russian speaker addressed them in a public lecture about
modern applied science. Practical modern skills were popularized
more effectively by "reformed Muslim" schools with a utilitarian
and businesslike orientation ("Catechism instead of lyrics of Navai,
keeping accounts instead of reading poetry by Bedil, and practical
knowledge instead of Hafiz"), inspired and largely staffed by Russian Tatar Muslim modernists.[54] Such Tatar influence on the
"Jadids" (modernistic Muslim reformers) of Russian Turkestan
was even stronger than their impact on the Young Bukharans. But
it would be wrong to conclude from this that all of them met the
Russian colonial impact only with opposition. Among the modernist Muslim reformers of Russian Turkestan were such pro-Russian
writers as Zakir Furqat (1858-1909), whose topics included such
modern subjects as electric lights and Russian secondary schools;
Nihaniy, who wrote an ode to Tsar Nicholas II; or Karimbek Sharif-
bek-oghli Kamiiy (1866-1923), who effusively rhymed praises of
the enlightenment to come from Russian instruction.[55] Such pro-
Russian Uzbek poets were favored by Russian editors of newspapers that were beginning to appear in Tashkent, where printing
was introduced in 1868. Much writing that had previously been
circulating in manuscripts was subsequently to be published. Since
1870 there was published an Uzbek news-sheet, supplementing the
Russian Government-General's official gazette. From 1883 on the
Uzbek news-sheet was being edited by the Russian State Church
missionary N. P. Ostroumov, who also translated the Four Gospels
into Uzbek.[56]

Russian policymakers, both military administrators like M. G.
Cherniaev and missionary educators like Il'minskii, encouraged the
cultivation of the Uzbek vernacular into a literary language—at the
expense of Persian and Arabic literary links to the Islamic world
outside Russia. But it was through modernistic Volga Tatar rather
than Russian influence that modern Uzbek became a literary language, with a drama of its own after 1911. The first Uzbek play-
wright was Mahmud Khoja Behbudiy, who was one of the most

important Uzbek Muslim modernists. This Jadid modernism, suspect from the beginning to conservative Muslim opinion, became suspect also to the tsarist powers after the Russian revolutionary outbreaks of 1905. As a result, official Russian colonial policy toward Islam was reversed. After Governor-General Kaufmann's administration (1867-82), government sponsorship had been withdrawn from Muslim institutions. Contrary to his expectations, however, these institutions did not wither away. Muslim canonic law continued to be the basis of civil judicial transactions among native parties in Russian Turkestan. The number of traditional Muslim theological schools even multiplied as a result of the nationalistic and Pan-Turkic radicalization of Jadid modernism. From 1905 on, tsarist policy resumed the encouragement of traditional patriarchal Islam that had been advocated by General Cherniaev.

Economic Developments

It was, however, under General Cherniaev that the descendants of Muhammad, along with the other dignitaries of the annexed khanate of Khokand, had lost their privileged position. A part of their endowment land (*waqf*) and all "fief property" lost its exemption from taxation or became the property of the Russian state. In practice, these holdings were left to their cultivators in return for payment of taxes—which were initially lower than the customary rent of Khokandian times. Such effects of the Russian conquest (which were contrary to comparable practices in large parts of British India) seemed, at least initially, to reconcile the rural population with Russian colonial rule. But the introduction of American cotton after 1885 as an almost exclusive cash crop made Russian Turkestan (not unlike Egypt under British occupation) dependent on world markets for its prosperity and on food imports from Russia for its sustenance.

As a result of speculation on the one hand and indebtedness on the other, in the course of the transition to a money economy one-third of the peasants of Ferghana had by 1912 lost their land through mortgaging and foreclosures.[57] In Ferghana, economically the most developed part of Russian Turkestan, many artisans, such as smiths, weavers, and potters, were professionally ruined because they were not able to compete with imported industrial products.

As they were forced to resort to agriculture, they increased the population pressure on the land. In spite of the resulting shortage of land in relation to a growing population, little was done to open up new land by irrigation. The old Khokandian irrigation canals continued to be used—even by Russian settlers. Agricultural colonization was legalized after the Russian peasant revolts of 1905, particularly since 1910, although the colonial authorities of Russian Turkestan had opposed the coming of Russian colonists. The settling of the newcomers took place mainly at the expense of the nomads who, since the 1880s, still constituted five percent of the population of Russian Turkestan. The nomads, as well as seminomadic tribes, had become largely impoverished because they no longer had military employment in the service of the khanate of Khokand after its annexation by Russia. They—and the steppe Dervish sheiks closely associated with them—became the main opponents of Russian rule.

Uzbek Resistance
to Imperial Russian Domination

The infidel rule of the Russians was blamed for the misfortunes of the people by the Naqshabandi Dervish ascetic Muhammad 'Ali Khalfa (Sabir Sufiev). He fed the homeless and was reputed to be a miracle-working holy man. Thus, when in 1898 he openly preached a Holy War against the Russians, fifteen hundred of his disciples rose in arms and killed twenty-two Russian soldiers in Andijan. But no uprisings broke out in other towns of Turkestan. Russian troops captured Muhammad 'Ali. He was hanged. And the property of his followers was confiscated as "indemnity" for the Russian victims. The participation of elective native representatives in the local administration was abolished; and the populace was forced to kneel down along the travel route of the Russian Governor-General Sergei Mikhailovich Dukhovskoi (in office 1898-1901). In spite of all this, the revolutionary outbreaks of 1905 in the cities of Turkestan remained confined to the Russian population. In contrast, the modernist Uzbek Jadids hoped—in the spirit of the Crimean Tatar modernist Gasprinskii and not unlike contemporary Muslim modernists of British India—that, in return for their collaboration with the established colonial regime, liberal reforms would be granted by the

imperial power. Even after being repressed by the tsarist regime of
Pëtr A. Stolypin (1906-11), they still dissociated themselves from
the mass uprising of 1916. In Turkestan the Ishan Nazir Khoja of
Jizzakh proclaimed this Muslim revolt to be a Holy War against the
Infidels. This uprising was strongest in the nomad Kazakh and
Kirghiz areas (cf. p. 261). It was brought about by a decree which,
in spite of the objections of A. N. Kuropatkin, Governor-General
of Russian Turkestan in 1916-17, ordered the mobilization of the
heretofore exempted Central Asian Muslims for labor service behind the front.

The defeat of the insurgents was followed by fifty-one executions. They, as well as those responsible for these reprisals, were
amnestied by Aleksandr Kerenskii in 1917. Nor had Lenin's pro-
fessed policy of equal rights for all nationalities affected initially
the local Soviet regime that was proclaimed in Tashkent a week
before the Bolsheviks seized power in Petrograd. In this colonial
capital of Russian Turkestan the Soviet was an almost exclusively
Slavic body. Having refused to let Russian Peasants' Soviets participate, it refused also (by an overwhelming vote of 97 to 17) to admit Muslims to government positions. Even the local Russian Social
Revolutionary press opposed the distribution of land to landless
Turkestanian natives.[58] It was under these circumstances that an
Extraordinary All-Muslim Conference, which previously, at a time
when Russia was still a democracy, had demanded only autonomy
for Turkestan within a Russian federated republic, on 11 December 1917 proclaimed a Turkestanian Autonomous Government.
Though the autonomous government appealed to Lenin's government, the Tashkent Red Army crushed the autonomists assembled
at Khokand in a brutal massacre on 14 February 1918. This action
was not approved by the central government of Soviet Russia.
Turkestan, however, was soon isolated from communist Russia by
the White Guard Cossacks of Orenburg.

As a result, famine broke out in the no longer self-sufficient
cotton-growing areas of Ferghana. Among the suffering Muslim
population of Ferghana there developed spontaneous guerrilla resistance. "Basmachi" partisans began a sporadic warfare[59] that was
not completely ended until the close of the decade. The partisans
were soon strengthened by forces from Khiva and Bukhara as the

Soviet Russian Turkestan regime collided with these monarchies.

Armed revolt against Russian overlordship was considered by Muhammad Rahim II, the khan of Khiva, as early as 1885, during a Russian-British conflict. He failed to adjust to the Russian protectorate although it had consolidated his absolutism as it had in Bukhara. Remaining poorer than the Bukharan amir, he was unable to make frequent visits to St. Petersburg or to distribute lavish gifts there, and thus lacked the amir's influence at the Russian court. On the whole Russia's impact on Khiva was much less than that on Bukhara. Khiva remained the most underdeveloped and poorest part of "Russian" Central Asia. Not all the slaves there were actually freed after the state became a satellite of Russia in 1873; some were kept and even secured with chains. Khiva's court preserved many nomadic features,[60] such as the campfire. The modernistic Young Khivans, who had even less following than the Young Bukharans, suffered bloody persecutions after the reform attempts of 1917. Their liberal platform represented mainly interests of merchants from whom the khan would collect forced loans that remained unpaid. What endowed the Young Khivans with political attraction was the seizure of power by the Turkmen chieftain Junaïd Khan, whose Yomud tribesmen were no longer held in check by the forces of the deposed tsar.

After Junaïd Khan had killed Khan Isfandiyar of Khiva in 1918 and his Turkmen had instituted a reign of terror over the Uzbek majority,[61] the Young Khivans were forced into an alliance with the Red Army. Together they proclaimed, on 1 January 1920, the People's Republic of Khwarizm. This was to be the first "People's Democracy," the first satellite of Soviet Russia, and was to last until 1924. The continuing conflict between the traditionally ruling Uzbeks and the more warlike Turkmen offered lasting opportunities for interference by Soviet Russian representatives, who demanded that the previously privileged classes be disenfranchised. Although no actual communistic reforms were introduced, the first republican government under the Young Khivan Pahlivan Niyaz already had concluded in 1920 a military and political alliance with Soviet Russia. While this treaty provided a model for subsequent satellite relationships elsewhere, Soviet Russian influence brought about in the Khivan government of the Khwarizm Republic repeated purges.[62] This was a prelude to subsequent developments in Outer Mongolia and lasted until the republic's absorption into the Soviet Union in 1924.

Bukhara suffered a similar fate. There the Young Bukharans were being appeased with liberalizing concessions by the Amir Sa'id Mir 'Alim as long as he apprehended pressures from the Russian protectorate power. But when Russia was convulsed by civil war, he executed Russian representatives negotiating with him, as well as large numbers of Young Bukharans, on a wave of Muslim enthusiasm accompanying the failure of a Soviet Russian invasion in 1918. In an outbreak of medieval-oriented Muslim feeling in March 1918, the massacres of Russians living in Bukhara accompanied the massacre of Bukharan Jadid modernists and even the destruction of modern technical installations. The Uzbek monarchy of Bukhara, threatened once in the 1860s by native mobs for collaborating with infidel Russia, in its last years used these very antimodernistic masses to massacre the Young Bukharan minority. Isolated from the masses, Young Bukharans approached the Bolsheviks. It was with the decisive assistance of the Red Army that they were able to expel the amir on 2 September 1920 and to proclaim a republican Bukhara.

A People's Republic—like Khwarizm (Khiva)—was the first Popular Front-type dependent of Soviet Russia. Its governing Revolutionary Committee was presided over by Faizullah Khoja-oghli, the son of a Bukharan merchant second in wealth only to the amir and the most socialistic of the Young Bukharans. His first mentor, Abdalrauf Fitrat, became the Bukharan People's Republic's Minister of Culture and sought to cushion the Russian impact by revolutionary reinterpretation of indigenous institutions. Bukhara's medieval guilds became labor unions and professional Soviets. Yet on the whole the reforms undertaken were less comparable to communist Russian reforms than to those of early Kemalist Turkey, although the Bukharan Republic did not separate the state from Islam. In this category belonged the replacement of Persian by the Uzbek Turkic vernacular as the language of state, the proclamation of popular sovereignty, and the granting of the franchise to women as well as to men.

Of Russian democratic and not of Kemalist Turkish inspiration were the Bukharan Republic's declarations regarding the distribution to poor peasants of the lands confiscated from the deposed ruling strata, and about equality between the Uzbeks and the other (mainly Tajik) peoples of Bukhara. In order not to jeopardize its political hold over Turkey, Persia, and Afghanistan, contemporary Soviet Russia exercised a certain degree of restraint in its pressure on Bukhara. But the failure to distribute land to the peasants drove them into the Basmachi resistance movement, merging with Muslim resistance against the Turkestan Soviet Republic. As a result, the Bukharan republican government became completely dependent on Soviet Russia.

Bukhara, like Khwarizm-Khiva, was made to proclaim a communist regime in 1924. New territorial entities along ethnic lines were carved out of these previously Uzbek-ruled states and Russian Turkestan. The most important of them, Soviet Uzbekistan, was presided over by Khoja-oghli, who, under the impact of Russian revolutionary developments, had evolved from secularizing Muslim modernism in the direction of National Bolshevism. Without the Russian connection Young Bukharan modernists would have remained isolated from the traditionalistic majority of their countrymen. Through Russia's impact they rose—temporarily and against the will of the so-called obscurantist majority—to the status of a modernized minority elite dictatorship over an undeveloped country. The alternatives confronting them at the time are perhaps illustrated by the tragedy of the pro-Soviet Uzbek poet Ubaidullah Salih-oghli Zawqiy (1853-1921), who had written an anti-Basmachi poem entitled "The bandit Ergash"—and was tortured to death by that Basmachi chieftain Ergash in 1921.[63]

The Basmachi guerrillas had by then been strengthened by followers of the deposed amir of Bukhara operating from Afghan territory.[64] It was a heterogenous movement of old-time outlaws resisting traditional abuses of arbitrary power, of disappointed liberal and even socialistic nationalists (such as the partisans of Mustafa Chokay-oghlu), and also of restorative Muslim forces. Most—but by no means all—Central Asian Muslim authorities endorsed the Basmachi cause.[65] To counteract the appeals of "Basmachism," communist policymakers, attempting to appease Islamic opposition, made a number of concessions to local opinion. In order to justify social revolution in the name of Islam,[66] attempts were made to apply in early Soviet Uzbekistan the Islamic-Marxist syncretism as it had developed historically among the Tatars.[67] Thus, canonic Muslim jurisdiction (the Shari'a Courts), were permitted to operate in some localities until 1927.[68] Upon Lenin's explicit insistence, efforts were made to recruit indigenous personnel into the Uzbek Communist Party, reversing early Tashkent Russian Bolshevik ethnic exclusiveness. A specifically Muslim organization within the Communist Party, however, was abolished even before the establishment of Soviet Uzbekistan.

But there is no denying the fact that the Leninist period saw attempts to reverse the colonial policies of the deposed Russian regime—by seeking active Uzbek participation in building a local communist regime rather than immediately reorganizing the economic relations among these Turkic Muslims.[69] The agrarian revolts that had permitted the Bolshevik seizure of power in Russia proper were not followed by peasant risings in Uzbek Central Asia. Even in Ferghana, the most economically developed Uzbek area, where class differences were sharpest, there had been no landed nobility with large estates possessing an outlook sharply separating it from the people. Even there, spontaneous peasant risings remained exceptional and had not led to seizures of more than 5,500 acres or so from Muslim landlords. There was no organized Muslim peasant war against Muslim landlords (such as earlier Islamic history had known again and again), but only organized enforcement of decrees issued by the communist authorities.

In December 1925 the Uzbek Communist Party's Central Executive Committee decreed the nationalization of all lands, forests, waters, and natural resources. As a result, landlessness among the peasants of Uzbekistan almost disappeared, but few of them were thereby made economically strong enough to subsist without state aid. Nor were the subsidies given by the Soviet Union's government sufficient to protect small producers such as urban artisans.[70] But attempts in this direction were made by the early Uzbek National Bolsheviks. Similarly, private trade with the neighboring foreign countries was still allowed long after foreign trade had become a state monopoly in Russia proper. Thus, on the whole, the economic and social reforms applied in pre-Stalinist Soviet Uzbekistan did not differ greatly from programs accomplished by noncommunist revolutionary regimes in other Muslim countries. Thus it may be said that until about 1927 the impact of the Russian Revolution in Uzbekistan was not accelerating more than those general social evolutions that accompany secularization in noncommunist Muslim societies, which included emancipation of women and youth, dissolution of patriarchal family structures, and separation of public instruction from theology.

Soviet Uzbekistan's secularization of instruction and literature continued a trend carried over by pre-Marxist Jadid modernists of Russian Turkestan from their Volga Tatar mentors. Early communist Russian impact on Uzbek thinking was also transmitted largely through Tatar influence. Soviet Uzbek borrowings of Tatar political terminology were not devoid of involuntary irony. Thus, adapting literally from the Volga Tatar, without regard for differences of connotation between the two Turkic languages, an early communist newspaper carried the motto "*Vagabonds* of the world, unite!" (because no Uzbek equivalent was found for the concept of "Proletarians").[71]

The Jadid middle-class traditions had tended to make literature a vehicle for instruction and improvement of public morals and society through the virtues of thrift, diligence, education, enlightenment, and morality; and the Soviet Russian cultural values, with their didactic emphasis on the utilitarian, radicalized these traditions. Soviet Uzbekistan's most popular writer of the 1920s, however, Abdulhamid Sulayman Yunus Cholpan (1898-1938?), sensitive lyricist that he was, with romantic longings for the pre-Russian Uzbek past, did not fit into the strait jacket. He suffered attacks by communist "Proletcult" literary criticism that attempted to condemn all pre-Bolshevik culture, even that which present-day Soviet thought considers to be its predecessor. In turn, "Proletcult" criticism became a precursor of party-line literary conformity just as its political imperatives had been anticipated by the didactic insistence of Jadid belles-lettres. Thus, in the first Uzbek novel (*Days Gone By*, by Abdullah Qadiriy Jolqunbay, 1922), a story of suffering stemming from an arranged and polygamous marriage, the classical motif of tragically unfulfilled love became adapted to a message of social criticism calling for the emancipation of women.

Similarly, the first Uzbek opera (*Halima*, by Ghulam Zafariy) illustrated the lessons of both women's dependence and the class struggle from the tragic end of a girl who commits suicide for the sake of a poor lover while avoiding marriage with a rich but unloved man chosen for her by her father. But soon happy endings were demanded as a matter of principle by a Stalinist "literary

canon" that could not admit the existence of conflicts in a "class-
less society." Uzbek critics were instructed from Moscow that
criticism had to be set down not only on the basis of Marxism but
specifically on the basis of Soviet Russian models. A particular
Uzbek literary theory, even though based on Marxism, was not to
be acceptable. Thus the appearance of "proletarian" criticism of
Uzbek literature preceded the appearance of proletarian Uzbek
literature itself.

Since peoples such as the Uzbeks had no industrial proletariat
while the Russians could claim some, the dogma of the Dictatorship
of the Proletariat served to confirm (or restore) Russian hegemony.
Stalin had early endowed proletarian dictatorship with priority
over national self-determination. In order to avoid syncretisms that
would arise if imported Marxism were to be expounded in terms
of familiar traditional concepts, Stalinist orthodoxy insisted that
the new political terminology necessary for designations of communist concepts be borrowed from the Russian language. Yet it
would be wrong to assume that the entire revolutionary transformation of Uzbek culture was forced exclusively by a Russian imported communism against the solid opposition of unanimously
Islamic Uzbek opinion. Even militant Uzbek atheism was derived
from Jadid Uzbek thought, which in turn began with modernistic
reinterpretations of Islam. Thus the Uzbek Jadid writer Hamza
Hakim Zadeh Niyaziy had evolved to the extent of becoming chairman of the "Society of the Godless." In 1929, while converting a
Muslim shrine into a "Red museum," he was murdered by an Islamic mob. Since he later became a Soviet Uzbek hero, the town
Shah Mardan, previously named after 'Ali, the nephew and son-in-
law of the Prophet Muhammad, was renamed after Hamza Niyaziy,
a martyr of anti-Islamic Uzbek atheism.

The drive against Islam, which coincided with the first Five-Year
Plan, was intended to transform Uzbek society most radically.[72]
The cotton-growing area of Uzbekistan was to be vastly enlarged.
Though the country had doubled the 1913 acreage by 1933, still
in 1927 the Soviet Union was importing 41 percent of its cotton.
Yet by 1933 the Soviets had to import no more than 2.6 percent,
an achievement made possible through the increase in production
forced on Uzbekistan by the central planning of the Five-Year
Plan. Uzbek cotton now accounts for more than two-thirds of the

Soviet Union's entire cotton production. The policy of enforcing an increased cultivation of cotton, already promoted in the Uzbek areas in tsarist times at the expense of the area's previous self-suffi- ciency in cereals, was one of the main goals of the compulsory col- lectivization program which in Uzbekistan culminated in 1930-31.

Thus, for the sake of Soviet Russia's industries, Stalinism in- creased colonial Uzbek dependence on Russian bread imports. In- dustrial development (mainly steel and hydroelectric power) was planned as auxiliary to cotton growing, while in the production of fertilizers Uzbekistan occupies fifth place among the component republics of the Soviet Union. Such industries were built up in Uzbekistan by Russians rather than by Uzbeks. The new industrial towns, like the coal town Angren and the oil town Leninsk, coun- terbalance the historical Uzbek urban centers. Even the Uzbek cap- ital, after Stalin's rise, was transferred from classic Samarkand to Russian-developed Tashkent.

On the grounds that Khodzhaev had championed Uzbek eco- nomic self-sufficiency and had worked against the subordination of Uzbeks to the Soviet Union's interests in general and against Uz- bekistan's dependence on its Moscow-planned economy in particu- lar, Stalin had him executed in 1938.[73] With Khodzhaev perished the most prominent twentieth-century Uzbek statesman. About the same time, Stalin's purges exterminated the flower of the Sovi- et Uzbek intelligentsia, among them Fitrat, Cholpan, and Qadiriy. They and many other Uzbek writers perished because of denuncia- tions from the Writers' Union that had appeared under the guise of literary criticism.

> From the viewpoint of the Soviet government. . .the most important duty carried out by writers' unions is the policing of ideas among the literary men, who in turn shape the thinking of the remaining intelli- gentsia and the reading public.
>   Mobilizing this broader section of the population to serve specific pur- poses of the new regime inevitably introduced a conformity among the intelligentsia which perhaps paralleled the community of thought met among the old Muslim intellectuals before the arrival of the Jadids. . . A mark of the generation growing up under. . .Russian Communism in Central Asia became, therefore. . .ideological uniformity, with the state once again enforcing the official viewpoint. . . . Gone was the exhilarat- ing diversity of ideologies and rival intellectual currents which colored Central Asia life up to the 1930s.[74]

Instead came monotonous glorifications of Stalin, frequently
rhymed in the overloaded and bombastic style meant to imitate
late medieval odes.

Even the abolition of the Stalinist "cult of personality" under
Khrushchev since 1956 and the rehabilitation of some of Stalin's
Uzbek victims did not restore the cultural and ideological diversity
of pre-Stalinist Uzbekistan. And no original Uzbek thought, literary
or political, has shown itself since the Time of the Purges. There is
no longer an Uzbek *intelligentsia* in the classical Russian connotation of that term. But there are Uzbek *cadres*, commanding modern techniques learned from the Soviet Russians. As a matter of
fact, the Uzbek people have produced more such modern cadres
than the other people of Russian Central Asia, whose modernization they might therefore have come to dominate if the historically
Uzbek-ruled monarchies of "Turkestan" had not been split along
ethnic lines. In the course of this early Soviet development, the Uzbeks had taken first place among the Muslim peoples of the communist empire.

Last of the Central Asian peoples to fall under Russian domination were the Turkmen tribes. While there has never been a pre-
Soviet Turkmen state or unification of all Turkmen tribes,[75] some
of them did at certain times dominate the Uzbek-ruled state of
Khiva.[76] It is misleading to present *the* Turkmen as having been
subdued by force of Russian arms. As early as 1677 some Caspian
Turkmens had declared themselves Muscovite subjects; other Turkmen wished to do the same in 1745, 1802, and 1811. Yomud
Turkmen voluntarily fought Persia on the Russian side in 1826-
28. Persia's and Khiva's pressure stimulated Turkmen preference
for Russia. By 1850 about 115,000 Turkmen had voluntarily become Russian subjects. On the other hand, in 1877 the resistance
of Yomud Turkmen against Russian army requisitions prompted
General Kaufmann's order to exterminate them—which order his
Lieutenant-Colonel N. Ivanov refused to execute. In contrast, the
Tekke Turkmen about that time also asked to become Russian
subjects. They became alienated when General Lomakin was not
empowered to accept them, and thereupon opted for a resistance
against Russia that proved stronger than that of the three Uzbek
states.[77] It was not until 1881 that they were subdued, after one

of the bloodiest campaigns of Russian colonial history. The Saryk Turkmen south of Merv did not submit until 1884. Yet many of them then stood by Russia in the confrontation with Anglo-Afghan forces (in 1885).

Non-Turkmen remained in the towns in the Turkmen territory of tsarist Transcaspia, whose cotton boom of the 1890s paralleled that of Uzbek Ferghana. Private landed property, exceptional in pre-Russian times, spread. Turkmen tribal politicians received the authority of Russian officials. Of all Central Asians only Turkmen served in the Russian army. From 1909 on Stolypin encouraged the alienation of Turkmen communal (Sanashyq) land which had traditionally been distributed on genealogical principles to married tribesmen. Indebtedness and foreclosures resulted. But Turkmen guerrilla resistance remained isolated from early Russian revolutionary activity, although not from Uzbek Jadid influences.

The Turkmen Jadids did not demand a separation from Russia and its cotton booms. In contrast, the Turkmen of Khiva revolted in 1912 against Uzbek exploitation. As Russian forces in Khiva were reduced by 1916, the Young Turkmen chieftain Junaïd Khan became virtual dictator over Khiva, where the Russian protectorate had had little internal impact.[78] In contrast, in July 1918 in Russian Transcaspia the Turkmen spokesmen cooperated with the Russian Social Revolutionaries in overthrowing communist rule in Ashkhabad. The Turkmen Oraz Sardar headed the forces of the Social Revolutionary Ashkhabad government. But its Turkmen draftees tended to desert to the Tashkent Red Army, which had not drafted Turkmen. Hard-pressed by Turkmen hegemony, the liberal Uzbek Young Khivans also came to assist the Red Army which, in 1920, converted Khiva into the People's Republic of Khwarizm.

In 1924 the republic's Turkmen territories were incorporated into Soviet Turkmenistan, even though local Russian Soviets had distrusted the Turkmen. Indeed, Turkmen had initially not even been recruited for communism. It was probably under Russian populist influence that Turkmen Jadids like Yomudskii came to champion the Sanashyq collective landholding; that is, Turkmen democracy and socialism. In 1920 Soviet legislation made all private land in Turkmen areas Sanashyq property, but the very Sanashyq was eliminated by legislation after 1926. Even the abolition of the Sanashyq institution, however, and the distribution of confiscated land to individual peasants rather than to the commune failed to destroy the institution immediately. The Sanashyq had to be broken from within by introducing into it class-struggle situations. To achieve this, the policy was directed toward increasing the number of economic inequalities in the villages by the imposition of private in place of communal property in order to encourage contradictions between rich and poor. But even such newly created contradictions did not suffice; at the time of the elections to the local Soviets, the Turkmen peasants persisted in choosing their tribal elders as deputies, so that even local communists preferred to consult them before making decisions.

Thus it was not before 1927 that outside communist impacts converted the struggles between tribes into struggles for land within individual tribal units. This eventually made possible in practice the dissolution of tribal entities and the abolition of Sanashyq communal property. Even afterward the impact of collectivization was initially mitigated by the continued cohesion of tribal clans. Even Turkmen communists were accused of not fighting such "relics of tribalism and feudalism" as irreconcilably as had been expected in early Stalinist days. Their nationalism was repeatedly "exposed" even in the 1920s.

Longing for the past characterized such Turkmen writers as 'Abdul Hakim Qul Muhammad-oghli, who, in his *Flames of Hope* (published in 1927), awaited a "spring" to come after the "black winter" of communist Russian domination should be gone again. Early Soviet Turkmen literature was less exposed to communist Russian impacts and more to Jadid and even Pan-Turkic influences than was its Uzbek counterpart. Thus there were demands that the Turkish of Turkey, belonging to the same Oghuz family as Turkmen speech, should be made the language of Turkmenistan, rather than that the vernacular Turkmen should be developed as a separate language. The Turkmen were more successful than the Kazakhs or the Kirghiz in preserving their population majority in their territory. The Turkmen population in Turkmenistan even grew from 59 percent in 1939 to 61 percent in 1959. The Russian immigration into Turkmenia remained urban in spite of the very impressive irrigation facilities constructed during the Soviet period, as witness the Kara Kum Canal from the Amu Darya to Ashkhabad, completed in 1962. Thus, among the recent concrete achievements of Russian rule over Central Asia is the restoration of the irrigation agriculture that had been declining since the nomad advance in the pre-Russian millenium.

The descendants of the east Iranian oases agriculturists who were overwhelmed by the Turkic nomads are the Tajiks. After the Uzbek conquests of the early 1500s, the Tajiks for the most part had been pushed into inaccessible mountain territories in the Pamirs and had been discriminated against by Uzbek conquerors who, however, had absorbed sedentary Iranian traditions in Bukhara and Ferghana.[80] It was the impact of Soviet Russian nationality policies that restored to the Tajiks a territory of their own, established Tajikstan as a Soviet Republic in 1929, and developed their east Khorasanian Persian into a separate language.

It may be debated whether the pre-Soviet peoples of Russian Central Asia could be regarded as nations or whether they were nations artificially created through deliberate communist Russian policy. But to deny their common historical links is as impossible as it is to deny their historic individualities. The Stalinist prohibition of any association among them, either economic (Central Asiatic Economic Council) or cultural (Chagatai literary movement), serves deliberate political purposes,[81] just as do allegations of exiled nationalists that the Central Asian peoples had been separated artificially from a natural Turkestanian entity.[82] The formation of secular elites with allegiance to each of the five Central Asian nations may be regarded as a by-product of Soviet policies. The scope allowed to the self-realization of these policies within Leninist Russia was not unconnected with hopes to attract to communist Russia at the same time the foreign Muslim states. There are important Turkmen enclaves in Persia, while Tajik history involved not only northeastern Persia but also Afghanistan. After it appeared more likely that potential Pan-Iranism might attract the Tajiks and Pan-Turkism the Turkmens and Uzbeks away from the Soviet Union, however, subordination to centralized Russian communist hegemony was enforced by the destruction of the Asian national Bolshevik elites in Stalin's purges of 1937-38.

For similar reasons the internationalist Latin alphabet, substituted for the Muslim Arabic script, was replaced by the Cyrillic letters. This facilitated the spread of literacy—which in Soviet Central Asia by 1959 had reached 51-52 percent. But the abolition of the Arabic script also served another purpose. Only selected aspects of Central Asian culture are being preserved and promoted in the Soviet Union, such as the appropriation of the medieval Chagatai classic author Navai by Soviet Uzbekistan and of the Iranian classic author Firdausi by Soviet Tajikstan,[83] to serve the culture standing of the Soviet Union in the Middle East. Anniversary conventions popularize these writers in the general Soviet Russian cultural frame of reference. But even this is more than can be said about Russian cultural aloofness from Central Asia in tsarist days.

If Russian democracy is ever restored, it will have to offer the greatest possible concessions to the demands of the Central Asian peoples in order to make continued political association with Russia desirable for them. But should their popular majorities refuse to maintain federalized ties to Russia, their right to self-determination and separation must be respected if democracy is to make sense at all.

−8−

The Peoples of Siberia
and the Far East

Stephen P. Dunn and Ethel Dunn

This investigation was supported, in part, by Research Grant No. RD-1607-G from the Vocational Rehabilitation Administration, Department of Health, Education and Welfare, Washington, D.C. 20201.

It is our purpose to treat in this essay the Russian impact on the peoples of Siberia and the Far East from both the historical point of view and in the context of the current situation. This definition of our subject confronts us at the outset with two important methodological consequences—before we even begin to examine the empirical data. In the first place, in qualifying the impact as Russian rather than, for instance, Soviet, we define the subject in cultural or ethnic, rather than in political, terms. In the second place, in speaking of an impact, we serve notice that we shall be concerned at least in the first part of our discussion with what actually happened and is happening rather than with ideology or with the mechanics of planning. In view of both these qualifications, it will be necessary to characterize briefly the initial situation which the tsarist authorities found on coming to Siberia as well as the general nature and aims of tsarist policy.

The indigenous population of the Soviet North is made up of some twenty-five small peoples: Evenki, Khanty, Siberian Nentsy, Shortsy, Chukchi, Evens, Nanays, Mansi, Koryaks, Dolgans, Sel' kups, Nivkhi, Ul'chi, Udegeis, Asiatic Eskimos, Itel'mens, Kets, Orochi, Nganasans, Oroks, Yukagirs, Tofalars, Aleuts, Negidals, and Entsy. Some experts include also the Saami, called Lapps in

Western ethnography. According to the 1959 census, these peoples range in number from the Evenki, who are the largest group (about 24,600), to the Entsy (about 300).

ORIGINAL CULTURE OF THE SIBERIAN
AND FAR EASTERN PEOPLES

For all its variety, the culture of the Siberian and Far Eastern peoples before Russian contact (early fifteenth to midseventeenth century, depending on the area), as it can be reconstructed from early sources and surviving elements, fell into a few rather clearly defined types. The subsistence of all groups was based on dry-land hunting and gathering, reindeer herding, or the hunting of sea mammals, such as seal, walrus, and whale.[1] Sociopolitical structure was everywhere simple; the social unit was usually small (from thirty to fifty people, the inhabitants of one camp), and varied in size seasonally, with the availability of food supplies and the pressure of economic activity. In the realm of religion, folklore, and the like (what is referred to by Soviet specialists as "ideology"), the Siberian peoples present a distinctive complex of features having much in common with that found among the New World Eskimos and some North American Indian tribes: highly developed shamanism and animism, with a vast and confused pantheon of zoomorphic and semizoomorphic deities and spirits.

The main cultural types in which the Siberian and Far Eastern peoples are divided coincide with certain natural areas. They may be roughly listed as follows:

(1) Hunters and gatherers of the *taiga* (coniferous or mixed sub-Arctic forests). Some of these were, in the Russian term, *peshye* (unmounted, i.e., they had no riding or pack animals). Others kept small herds of reindeer, of a larger and stouter breed than the tundra reindeer, which they used for riding and for the transport of goods, and occasionally for milking. These reindeer, however, were not generally eaten.

(2) Fishermen and hunters of wild reindeer on the tundra. These were the smallest and most primitive groups in the North.

(3) Tundra reindeer herders, who moved with large herds of reindeer over more or less fixed routes and lived almost completely on the products supplied by these reindeer.

(4) Maritime fishermen and hunters of sea mammals, the character of whose occupations permitted them to adopt a sedentary way of life, at least in certain favored locations.

Each of these "natural-cultural types" represented a specific and usually highly effective adaptation to a particular environment. Features of social structure and ideology usually correlated with economic factors to produce a relatively fixed constellation of traits.

RUSSIAN CONTACT BEFORE 1917

The acquisition of Siberia by the tsarist Russian Empire was a fairly gradual process, extending over several centuries. It took a number of separate forms, with widely varying characteristics and consequences: 1) military conquest; 2) forced or voluntary colonization; 3) commercial exploitation. When we speak of military conquest, we are perhaps stretching a point: the tsarist government did not come into collision with any organized state or coalition of tribes anywhere in the area (if we exclude indirect confrontations with the Chinese in the Far East); there was very little actual fighting. The colonization, whether forced or voluntary—i.e., whether by convicts or by free settlers—was extensive and had considerable effect where it took place, but was also rather unevenly distributed. It resulted in the formation of enclaves of Russian population and culture, which in turn exerted a strong Russifying influence on the culture of some surrounding tribes (such as, for example, the Evenki [Tungus] of the northern part of Irkutsk Oblast).[2]

Finally, commercial exploitation was limited almost entirely to a few categories of goods—furs, lumber, fish, walrus ivory and other sea-mammal products, and precious metals. The resulting penetration had a number of important characteristics in common with the commercial penetration of the Canadian North during approximately the same period. First, it was not accompanied (except to some extent in the case of precious metals) by any marked influx of population. Secondly, it resulted in the dissemination of trade goods (weapons, traps, fishing gear, manufactured cloth, kerosene, sugar, tea, and flour in very limited amounts) and luxury items (vodka, tobacco, and certain types of utensils) which were superimposed upon the basic subsistence economy without fundamentally altering it. In other words, the proceeds of the fur trade were used by the native population to pay their taxes and to resupply their own fur-hunting operations rather than for actual subsistence. It follows from this that the degree and kind of culture change resulting from tsarist "colonization" was limited both quantitatively and structurally.

The question of missionary influence falls into a somewhat separate category. There are obvious difficulties involved in judging the extent and significance of this influence on the basis of Soviet sources, and to try to exploit the pre-Soviet sources would be a major undertaking in itself. On the whole, it appears that Christianization of the native population, except in areas of dense Russian settlement, was rather superficial. The people were given Christian names on the Russian model (which they retained for juridical purposes when the Soviet passport system was put into effect in the 1930s, although they did not use these names among themselves). They were enrolled in parishes and in many cases they were baptized. Whatever elementary education was available to the indigenous population was under the sponsorship of the Orthodox Church, which before the Revolution controlled the bulk of primary education throughout the Russian Empire. Soviet sources, of course, tend to denigrate the extent and effect of church-sponsored education, in line with the Soviet preference for distinguishing Russification from Sovietization. However, there is some evidence that for reasons not yet clear the degree of Christian influence varied widely from place to place and from people to people.[3] Russian missionaries of the nineteenth and early twentieth centuries reduced some of the Siberian languages to writing; but the practical effect of this is once again played down by Soviet authors, who maintain that the written languages created by missionaries were used only for religious purposes. Accordingly, the total effect is difficult to judge, except in the case of the Yakuts, who were culturally more highly developed than any other native people.

NATURE AND IDEOLOGICAL PREMISES
OF THE SOVIET CULTURE-CHANGE EFFORT

With the advent of the Soviet regime, the nature of Russian contact with the Siberian peoples underwent a sharp change, although as a result of political and military factors it took some time for the change to be felt. The Soviet program as applied to the territories formerly ruled by the tsar was above all one of modernization. This meant that the former specialized and limited forms of commercial exploitation and the limited degree of culture change they had brought about would no longer meet the needs of the program. Siberia and the Far East had to be integrated as rapidly as possible into the structure of a modern industrial state. Furthermore, the means by which this integration was to be carried out were laid down in the revolutionary ideology of communism. This ideology called for state ownership of virtually all means of production, for centralized allocation of resources, and for centralized decision-making in general. We will consider later the respects in which the demands of the ideology were and remain disfunctional for the development of the Siberian peoples. It will be sufficient to note here that a competition for resources, which were sometimes extremely scarce, was set up between Siberia and the other regions of the country. In the nature of things, this competition was seldom resolved to Siberia's advantage. Until fairly recently (from the end of World War II until 1956, depending on which specific region is under consideration) the priority given to Siberia in terms of investment was generally low, although precise figures are only rarely available. The Soviet cultural achievement in Siberia must always be judged against the background of overall investment and development policy, with account taken of international factors.

SOVIET-SPONSORED CULTURE CHANGE

The empirical data to be considered in this section fall under three broad headings—Economic, Social and Political, and Educational Change.

Economic Change

Under economic change we shall deal first with the general policy of collectivization, then with the traditional occupations, and finally with newly established branches of the economy.

Collectivization—Over most of the area with which we are dealing, the formation of kolkhozy (usually "collective farms," but in Siberia and the Far East more accurately translated as "producing cooperatives") was not completed until after World War II.[4] Exceptions must be made for the Amur Region and for certain other areas where there was considerable Russian settlement. Even on the Amur, however, if we may judge from data on the Nivkhi,[5] the progress of collectivization was delayed by ethnic factors: separate collectives were formed for Russians and natives.

The essence of Soviet collectivization in its present form lies in a combination of public and private property. In return for his labor, the member of the collective (kolkhoznik) enjoys the right to occupy part of the land entrusted to the collective, on which he may build a dwelling and grow food for his family; to hold private property (livestock and minor farming equipment) within specified limits; and to use the resources of the collective (major equipment, draft animals, fuel supply, lumber, and the like) for his personal economy, also within certain limits. Natural conditions and the organization of the economy in the North demand certain changes in this general model. The household plot that in other areas is used for growing food loses much of its importance where agriculture is almost or entirely impossible. A man's or a family's material well-being must be measured in the amount of basic resources (in the North these are reindeer, sled dogs, and hunting and fishing equipment) to which the man or the family has access.[6]

The overall impact of collectivization in northern Siberia and the Far East at this point in time remains questionable, because of a number of extremely stubborn facts. As long as, and in places where, the economy continues to be based on reindeer, large sections of the population must continue to wander over the tundra tending the herds. The central settlements at which the reindeer kolkhozy are supposedly based remain vacant for most of the year or are occupied only by children, old people, and officials. Furthermore, the provision of the most elementary comforts and services to a population constantly on the move over such inhospitable terrain and under severe natural conditions would in itself be a major undertaking and a very expensive one. In areas where the major resource is not reindeer but fish or sea mammals, the conditions are in some cases rather better. Permanent settlement, with all its advantages in terms of cultural services, utilities, and consumer goods, is possible in these cases provided that the site has been properly chosen. However, this is often not the case.[7]

On the other hand, collectivization did make possible some improvements in living standards and a considerable rise in educational level for the small peoples of the North. Perhaps the most important function of the kolkhozy is to serve as channels through which whatever funds are available can be poured and to integrate at least a portion of the population with the larger society.

Changes in traditional occupations—According to Marxist ideology, since economic activity is the basis of all human institutions, economic change precedes and predetermines all other types of change. The Soviet task in the North, as elsewhere, was that of placing the economy on a new footing—first materially, by means of improved technology, and then socially and intellectually, by means of changes in the organization of labor and of people's ideas. Actually in many parts of the Soviet Union, as a result of historical circumstances, the social changes came first and the new technology followed, sometimes after long delays. Nor were all branches of the economy equally amenable to technological change or mechanization, as the event proved. Hunting and reindeer herding proved particularly recalcitrant. Improved firearms and steel traps of modern design, of course, could be and were introduced; but even when this had been done, hunting still consumed large amounts of labor. There were several reasons for this, some of which lay in the nature of any hunting economy under any conditions—the very large areas to be covered, the uneven and irregular supply of game, and the variation in the price which the game finally brought. Other problems were generated or intensified by the weaknesses inherent in a centralized system for distribution and decision-making. New equipment did not always reach the point where it was needed. The supply of skilled hunters ran short because of biases in the educational policy (the same problem exists with regard to most traditional Northern occupations).[8]

Finally, there was the matter of the organization of the hunting economy as such. There are no hunting kolkhozy as such; there are only kolkhozy with hunters in them, and the hunting operation can be organized in one of two ways. Either the kolkhoz contracts with a purchasing agency of the state to sell the catch, in which case the kolkhoz sends out a brigade of hunters equipped from kolkhoz supplies; or the hunters contract individually with the purchasing agency, in which case they are responsible for their own equipment, the kolkhoz taking a percentage of the proceeds. In either case, the hunting economy becomes a poor relation in a kolkhoz that has many other things to do, and a potentially lucrative branch of the economy is neglected.[9]

The problems of reindeer herding are similar in broad outline to those of the hunting economy: lack of qualified personnel, lack of technology, general neglect. It is difficult at this distance to tell just what technology could be applied to the herding of reindeer, to what extent improved methods would help. Most of the ideas suggested by Soviet specialists (some of which have actually been tried out) relate not so much to the herding process itself as to various peripheral aspects of it: the transport of personnel to and from the job, means of communication between parties of herdsmen and the kolkhoz center, living conditions on the job. It has been suggested, for example, that tractors be used to pull portable accommodations over the tundra.[10] This would have the advantage of reducing or doing away with habitual (*bytovyi*) nomadism—the term used by Soviet specialists for that form of nomadic life in which entire families wander, following the herds, rather than merely males of working age who are assigned the task of reindeer herding within a diversified economy.[11] The proposal for portable tractor-hauled dwellings, however, encountered serious technical problems—fuel supply and spare parts for the tractors in the tundra, and the like—and required an investment not justified by the size of most reindeer herds. Transport of the herdsmen by helicopter or motor launch, making possible a fixed system of work shifts, has also been suggested. Something like this is in fact done for the reindeer herders of Murmansk Oblast in the European North, where the reindeer feeding-grounds are more accessible from settlements, railroads, and main highways than is the case over most of Siberia.

The processing of reindeer as such (veterinary service, butcher-ing, preparation of skins) is beset by severe problems of technology and supply. Because the necessary slaughtering points have not been constructed in the tundra, the animals must be driven back to the wintering area while they lose weight and their skins deterio-rate. Necessary items of harness are not commercially available and must be made by the people themselves according to traditional patterns. The reindeer are slaughtered and skinned with the most primitive equipment.[12] This is more or less true of all branches of the traditional economy, and the Soviet trade network has little in-centive to provide the necessary items.[13]

With the growing industrial development of Siberia and the in-creasing activity of prospectors for natural resources, a need has arisen for transport to inaccessible areas. This need is filled largely by the use of pack reindeer, from which many kolkhozy make a good part of their income. This branch of activity, although finan-cially profitable, has serious drawbacks both from a social point of view and from that of long-run economic development. Socially it removes many herdsmen from the kolkhoz and from their families for long periods of time and thus fosters, according to Vasil'ev, "a revival of what is termed occupational nomadism, and in its worst form, moreover, inasmuch as in the given instance this no-madism is not called for by the needs of production."[14] Econom-ically, the excessive use of reindeer for transport damages the food-producing operations of the kolkhoz, since the very high rates ob-tainable for pack reindeer—one ruble twenty kopaks per reindeer per day in 1960 plus replacement of any reindeer which die, at their book value of fifty rubles—induce the kolkhoz to use does as well for this purpose. As a result, the animals fail to bear and the herd deteriorates.

Fishing and marine hunting, unlike reindeer herding and dry-land hunting, were traditionally sedentary occupations or involved, at the most, periodic movements between fixed points. Economic development in some places, particularly in the Far East, led to the creation of large commercial fisheries of the industrial type. This was true even before the recent push in the development of Siberia. The establishment of commercial fisheries attracted large groups of people from other parts of the country for temporary or

permanent work. Thus, one might assume that the intensity of culture change, insofar as this depends on the amount of culture contact, would be greater among fishing populations. However, direct
data on this point are lacking. It could be assumed also that the
relatively sedentary nature of fishing as an occupation would permit more rapid culture change, better consumer services and the
like, than would be obtainable in a reindeer-herding economy.

Taksami's and Lar'kin's data, on the other hand, show a somewhat contradictory picture. Until 1960, the fishing kolkhoz where
most of the Orochi (this ethnic group numbers only about 780 in
all) are settled did not have its own equipment, but rented it from
the canning factory or the Motor Repair Station for twenty percent
of the maximum permissible purchase price of a tsentner of fish
caught.[15] After 1960, the kolkhoz spent 20,600 rubles for nets,
boats, and barges. Until the 1950s, fishing kolkhozy seem to have
been largely unmechanized. Furthermore, runs of fish vary widely,
which makes planning difficult and the population (except for the
basic membership of a particular kolkhoz) highly mobile. Much
depends on the availability of the equipment that makes offshore
fishing possible, and on the possession of a good central location
where if one run of fish fails others may still be exploited. Taksami
recommends that kolkhozy enter the field of fish processing; this
has in fact been done successfully in other areas, such as the Baltic.
He is also critical of the resettlement policy, as being disfunctional
in terms of fishing.[16]

One should not assume from this that Taksami or any other Soviet specialist on the Far North is opposed to collectivization *per
se*, or to the general policies and guidelines by which it has been
carried out. It is worth noting, however, that what is desirable
from the point of view of centralized investment policy—in terms
of utilities, consumer services, and the like—is not necessarily desirable from the point of view of local economics.

Sea-mammal hunting was traditionally engaged in by relatively
small groups of Eskimos (and Eskimoized Chukchi) on the Arctic
littoral of northeastern Siberia. Like fishing, this occupation permits a sedentary life if the locations are well chosen; archeological
data in fact show such a life going back thousands of years. The sea-
mammal hunting operation as now constituted suffers from lack of
mechanization and seems to suffer also from the persistent and

quixotic attempt to diversify the economy in ways that run counter to natural conditions. As of the time when Smoliak wrote,
motorized whaleboats, weapons, ammunition, fuel, and maintenance were provided by a Motor Hunting Station.[17] However, over
much of the year, hunting was confined to various species of seals,
and was carried on by entirely traditional methods, the greater part
of the catch being retained by the individual hunter.[18] Recent consolidation of the collectives, as a result of which they now contain
Eskimos, Chukchis, and Russians as well as families of mixed composition, has made it possible to diversify the economy of the collectives while drawing on traditional skills: in other words, each
people engages in specific occupations.[19]

New occupations—Over most of the area with which we are dealing, agriculture would seem to be *prima facie* impossible, or very
difficult, and in no case does it provide a stable livelihood. There
are certain partial exceptions: the Amur, the southerly or more
sheltered parts of Sakhalin, certain points on Kamchatka, and the
southern part of Yakutia.[20] Despite hostile natural conditions, the
regime has made repeated attempts to establish agriculture in many
parts of northern Siberia to the detriment of the traditional economy and of rational use of personnel. This course can be justified
only where the following conditions obtain: 1) the collective either
must be near an urban center or have adequate access to transportation in order that the products may be marketed directly, or 2)
the people must be able to consume the products themselves, thus
improving their diet; 3) the population must have the necessary
skills; 4) the collectives must have at their disposal plant varieties
adapted to Northern conditions, must have adequate technology,
and must enjoy a degree of autonomy that enables them to respond swiftly to changes in climate or other conditions. Although
in many areas none of these preconditions is completely met, the
regime has been compelled by demographic *force majeure* to develop agriculture on a wide scale, and has achieved a considerable
number of successes, although some of the victories may have been
won at too great a cost.[21]

From time to time, commercial fur farming (mink, sable, silver
fox) has been proposed as a potentially profitable sideline for Far
Northern collectives. There is no doubt that at some times and in
some places fur farming has worked well. More often, however, it

has given rise to severe technological and supply problems. The animals must be adequately fed and kept free of disease. This requires a relatively high level of skill on the part of those employed in this branch of the economy, a relatively small labor force, and a supply system that does not operate to the detriment of human beings. On many kolkhozy, a considerable proportion of slaughtered meat and fish catches, including prime-grade goods, goes to feed the caged animals, and the potential profits are thus literally eaten up. The ideal solution would of course be a synthetic food that could be distributed in large batches from a central point. This could be obtained as a by-product from milk-processing plants or fish canneries, which now do not fully utilize potentially useful materials. Activities in this direction have so far not been extensively pursued, apparently for reasons of priority and investment, and many kolkhozy have abandoned fur farming as unprofitable.

The development of industry, properly speaking, in the Far North shows a number of peculiarities. It is not evenly distributed over the area but is concentrated around a few focal points. The emphasis has been on the direct exploitation of natural resources (sources of electric power, oil, natural gas, mineral deposits, and timber), and the industry is thus primarily extractive in nature. It follows that such development as exists is not consumer-oriented, nor, in terms of consumer goods, can it begin to supply the needs of the people who service Northern industry. This aggravates the usual problems of priority and supply that flow from a centralized administrative system. More important than any of these considerations, however, is the fact that Northern industry, like any industry, requires large quantities of skilled manpower—and this requirement increases with mounting technological complexity and the consequent need of greater efficiency. In the nature of things, the skilled manpower required to man industry in the Far North must be brought from those parts of the Soviet Union that already have a pool of such skills—chiefly central and southern Russia and the Transcaucasus. The large-scale influx of people from these areas (now voluntary and encouraged by such devices as hardship pay and educational privileges) gives rise to serious problems in the fields of health, nutrition, and general living standards.[22] It has also created social problems that are perhaps equally severe in the long run, though less obvious.

By the same token, the high labor turnover prevalent in Siberian and Far Eastern industry is related not only to severe natural conditions but to the shortage of cultural facilities and opportunities for professional mobility. Furthermore, it is significant that, according to one report, both real and nominal income per capita in Irkutsk Oblast lags behind the rest of the R.S.F.S.R., and the same is true for the housing supply.[23] A statistical study of reasons for labor turnover in eastern Siberia shows that much of the turnover among young (and therefore relatively unskilled) workers is the result of "lack of prospects for growth" (meaning lack of opportunities for professional advancement) or of dissatisfaction with cultural and consumer-service facilities.[24] Taksami's data indicate that the Nivkhi working in the paper mills have an average of ten to fifteen years' seniority and received their training in the factory schools. This is apparently no longer a common method of training personnel. The ordinary schools that are expected to turn out people trained for jobs in industry are not set up to do this in the most efficient way. This gives rise to labor shortages in some places and surpluses in others. Though this phenomenon is not peculiar to Siberia, it is intensified there by factors relating to natural conditions and to the distribution of industry.[25]

It would have been possible to recruit large portions of the native population into industry only by making an all-out frontal attack on the native culture and social structure, a policy on which the regime has been unwilling or unable to embark. Such a program would have required an expansion of the market in foodstuffs in order to provide for the needs of those who were removed from food production. As a result of these factors, a situation was created where Far Northern industry, despite its importance in purely economic terms, has had less cultural impact on the native population as a whole than might have been expected.[26] Demographic and economic factors combine to make the question of attracting the small Northern peoples into industry an urgent one. Some specialists believe that the situation of these peoples is so substandard that absorbing them into the working class is the only solution.

Other specialists consider this impossible at present because of inadequate mobility of the small peoples.[27]

Social and Political Change

The problem faced by the Soviet government when it assumed control in Siberia (the date of effective assumption of control varied
from 1922 to 1925, depending on local military and political conditions) was one of establishing political institutions for a wide
variety of populations, many of which had never had such institutions as they are conceived of in the West. This work was carried
on with the aid of a complex set of concepts and instrumentalities
known collectively as the Soviet nationality policy. In essence, as
originally conceived by Lenin and as applied to the Soviet nationalities generally, the system consisted of a graded series of degrees of
autonomy, running from the autonomous raion (for the smallest
most scattered, and most primitive groups) to the union or constit-
uent republic, for those peoples which had already developed into
full-fledged nations at the time of the Revolution.[28] In accordance
with this conceptual scheme, a people could be "upgraded"—from
an autonomous oblast into an autonomous republic, or from an
autonomous to a union republic—when it was felt that its "national self-consciousness" had developed to the point where this was
appropriate or (looking at it another way) when such a course became politically expedient. Some autonomous units have also been
"downgraded" or abolished in response to particular situations.
These degrees of autonomy were expressed in various specific organs of power—local, district, and national (republican) soviets,
with their executive committees and officers. The political realities
behind this façade, as they relate to the Soviet Union as a whole,
need not concern us here. However, it is worth noting that the
categories in which the Soviet nationalistic policy was formulated,
artificial though they may be in many respects, determined what
was actually done by the organizers on the spot, in the Far North
as well as elsewhere.

In the spectrum of problems which the Soviet nationality policy
faced, the Far North and the Far East represented an extreme case
in terms of the small size of ethnic units, of their economic primi-
tiveness and lack of internal political structure, and of their widely

scattered settlement pattern. The usual concepts and methods of Soviet federalism soon proved unworkable. It was necessary to carry out considerable preparatory work before the Soviet political system could be applied to the small, primitive, and scattered groups of the area. The Soviet authorities at first found themselves compelled to make use of whatever rudiments of class and political structure existed among the small Northern peoples. Those who were elected to office in the "national councils" as late as 1927 were mostly shamans and "kulaks" (the heads of kin groups), who owned large herds of reindeer.[29] These were largely the same people whom the tsarist regime had used in its system of indirect rule. However, their continued privileged position was at marked variance with the stated goals of the Soviet government. In the Far East a rather special situation obtained, in that kin relations often crossed ethnic boundaries: the same clan might be found among several different peoples, and the members of this clan all considered themselves related. It was therefore considered preferable to organize the area on a territorial-economic, rather than on an ethnic, basis.[30]

The main role of the native organs (clan or local soviets, depending on the area under consideration) was to act as channels for the Soviet culture-change effort, expressed largely in terms of education. To a considerable extent this remains true to this day, although in many places apparently bona fide efforts have been made to give the local soviets a less passive role.

The Soviet educational and linguistic policy (the two must be considered in some respects as a unit) had two major aims: one economic, the other political and ideological. In the first place, the primitive Northern peoples had to be taught to use modern machinery (the fact that machinery is even now not widely available in the North is another matter) in order to make possible more rapid economic development; in the second place, they had to be taught to administer their own affairs within the limits permitted by the Soviet system, and to see themselves as working participants in this system.

At a very early stage the problem arose as to what medium or media should be used for education. Specifically, should the native languages be developed to the point where they would be capable of accommodating the content of European culture in its Russian form—science, technology, philosophy, political concepts, art, music, and all the rest? Or, on the other hand, should the native languages be used only to the extent necessary to teach the people Russian, and should their cultural development thereafter take place within a Russian context? It seems fair to say that the ultimate choice for the Far Northern and Far Eastern peoples was made in favor of the second alternative. However, the extent of "linguistic construction" which took place during the 1930s was considerable. This experience would make a fascinating study in itself.[31] The languages of fourteen Northern and Far Eastern peoples were reduced to writing, at first with an alphabet based on the Latin characters. In 1937, a Cyrillic-based alphabet was substituted.[32]

Strenuous efforts were made to liquidate illiteracy and to produce a population with at least a modicum of general education. Despite all the handicaps caused by bureaucratic interference and by the zigzags in linguistic policy, impressive results were achieved. However, it is now generally admitted that the use of native languages in written form was not in most cases an end in itself but a stage on the road to education in Russian.[33] There are sound practical reasons for such a policy; we should guard against assuming, as certain Western writers do, that it is part of a deep-laid Soviet plot to subvert the national self-consciousness of small and defenseless peoples. The primitive languages of the Far North are simply not equipped to absorb or handle the complex scientific, technical, and philosophical concepts necessary in dealing with the appurtenances of European civilization.

The present status of the languages of the Far North is a topic on which our sources are scanty and which, in any case, falls largely outside the purview of this discussion. However, it is safe to say that many of these languages now fall into the category of household vernaculars, since even elementary education is carried on in Russian, and Russian has become the lingua franca of social mobility and of communication on ethnically mixed kolkhozy and industrial projects. One might think that this situation would eventually bring about the death of the Northern languages, but many Soviet ethnographers appear to doubt that this is in prospect, at least within the near future. This becomes still more true when we consider that a large proportion of Far Northern reindeer herders remain to this day essentially nomadic, visiting the central settlements only at long intervals. Hence their grasp of Russian may be assumed to be elementary, an assumption confirmed by the fact that the children of reindeer herders or fishermen who are placed in boarding schools require preliminary instruction in so-called zero grades before taking up the regular curriculum. These zero grades have been prematurely eliminated in many cases, perhaps because of a certain overoptimism on the part of the authorities. The point is that even where kolkhozy are ethnically mixed and hence where Russian is supposedly the lingua franca, the individual brigades in which much of the life and work go on consist of members of one nationality, or even of one clan.

Small-scale social structure: kolkhoz, camp, family—In the interests of efficiency the kolkhozy have in many cases been expanded and centralized. However, where economic factors require wide dispersion of the population, as in reindeer herding, hunting, and fishing, for instance, this expansion of the kolkhozy does not necessarily affect the way the people actually live (see above, "Changes in traditional occupations"). The operative unit remains the brigade, which may be composed of members of one clan or of persons related by blood or marriage, although its specific make-up varies widely. It follows that the family, broadly interpreted, remains important as a social unit among the Far Northern peoples, as it does elsewhere in the Soviet Union, but for different reasons. Traditionally, children were fostered out within the larger kin group (to grandparents, uncles, or the like) or, among the Ekonda Evenki, outside it, and this continues to be done. The function of fosterage in most cases is to provide for those persons who lack physical support for their old age. Traditionally, large game (bear, seals, walrus, wild reindeer) was shared within the camp or the kin group, subject to ritual restrictions.[34] This practice still prevails, although the unit within which the game is shared is becoming increasingly territorial rather than being based on kinship. One of the reasons for the persistence of this custom is apparently the fact that in the absence of payment in meat for work on the kolkhoz many families were forced to buy meat for cash.

The family or kin group is important also because it is the child's first school, and traditionally (as among all primitive peoples before Western contact) his only one. The family teaches the child the skills needed by a competent reindeer herder, hunter, and fish-

erman, and, according to many Soviet ethnographers, it does this
more effectively than any state institution can. The placing of children in boarding schools in the central settlements of the kolkhozy
has produced a generation unadapted to the traditional life and unwilling to tolerate it, and has thereby created a problem of which
the more perceptive ethnographers, particularly Strakach, are becoming acutely aware.[35]

The kin group, which was the traditional locus of religious observance, retains this role to some extent, although the religious
system has been severely truncated. Most of the surviving ceremonies are connected with curing of the sick, with individual hunting magic, and with rites of passage, particularly the initiation of
hunters. The more elaborate manifestations of shamanism (where
they existed, as among the Evenki) have fallen into disuse; it is un-
likely that professional shamans of the traditional type still practice widely, although an Evenk who was a true shaman—i.e., one
who shamanized in full regalia, as opposed to a mere diviner or
curer—is mentioned by Tugolukov as recently as 1957. However, it
should be remembered that many ceremonies, both individual and
collective, and particularly those in the rite-of-passage category
(connected with birth, coming of age, marriage, and death, and in
general with transition from one status to another), were traditionally held with only minor participation of the shaman, or with
none at all. Some of these are still held. Funeral rites are especially
persistent and conservative. It was customary among most Siberian
peoples to equip the grave of the dead with objects for his use in
the next world. These were generally changed in some way in order to correspond symbolically with the changed condition of the
dead person. For example, spears or arrows were broken, dishes
had holes punched in them, etc. This custom is apparently still observed, except that the objects are not now the traditional ones.
"If an old Ul'chi woman brings to her son's grave not only food
products which, she thinks, he will need in his afterlife, but a ther-
mometer, aspirin tablets and a notebook and pencil, this means
that the new in her consciousness and way of life is interwoven
with the old religious concepts and customs."[36]

The Siberian peoples have a rich "cultural" heritage—folk music
and dance, arts and crafts, folklore—to which Soviet scholars have
paid considerable attention.[37] During the late 1920s and 1930s a

complex and voluminous argument was conducted as to whether there was such a thing as Soviet folklore and, if so, what it would be. The results were not particularly conclusive, and the items of folklore and folk art (in the form of new songs, ballads, craft articles, and the like) that were produced, particularly by Russians, for the most part continued older traditions. The point is that whereas among a more advanced people, such as the Russians, particular genres or items of folklore may be separated from the religious ideas and the archaic customs in which they originated and can live independently, the same is not possible to the same degree among primitive, originally hunting-and-gathering peoples like the small Siberian tribes. Recent Soviet writers make it quite clear that the traditional forms of Far Northern culture simply will not accommodate the content which is now being put into them.[38] Attempts are still being made to adapt popular festivals for Soviet use,[39] but how viable the results will be remains problematical.

Educational Change

Social mobility: the intelligentsia—One of the most striking changes produced by Soviet policy in the life of the peoples of northern Siberia has been the superimposition of a new mechanism of social mobility on the traditional social structure and way of life of these peoples. Beginning in the 1920s, it became possible for capable and lucky members of the Siberian nationalities to study at central and provincial institutions of higher learning and to prepare for such careers as physicians, teachers, and artists—a course of action that would have been unthinkable in pre-Revolutionary times. This process continues up to the present time, but the classifications of people who have been trained in these institutions show marked variations from people of similar background found elsewhere in the Soviet Union. For one thing, the Far Northern intelligentsia, while perhaps not smaller in proportion than that of the Soviet Union as a whole, includes relatively few engineers, industrial managers, physicians, and the like—those who are customarily included by both Soviet and Western sociologists in the category of "technical intelligentsia." Over the Soviet Union as a whole, this group is considerably larger than the cultural intelligentsia (teachers at all levels and academic personnel generally, practitioners of the arts, journalists, etc.), since the technical intelligentsia by some reckonings includes even mechanics and tractor-drivers. It is precisely the technicians—who in the North would include pilots and radio operators as well as the other categories—who are in short supply and who would transform the culture if they were available.

The category of what would be called in the West "civil servants" also falls within the technical intelligentsia. Under Soviet conditions, the classification includes elected members and staffs of local administrative bodies (the Soviets), who carry out the day-to-day work of governing the local areas, and also the officials of the Communist Party whose function is to oversee and regulate the activity of all administrative bodies and economic organs. Among these officials, whether elected or appointed, a considerable proportion belong to the native nationalities. Indeed, in some cases this proportion is higher than the percentage of natives in the population as a whole.[40] It remains to be seen whether, with the increasingly heavy responsibilities entrusted to local administrative bodies and the relatively low level of education of the members of these bodies, this situation will continue. We must remember, however, that this is a general problem faced all over the Soviet Union, and not merely— perhaps not even chiefly—in northern Siberia.

Considering the remoteness and continued technological backwardness of the area, it must be said that the Siberian peoples show as strong a tendency to migrate to cities as people anywhere in the Soviet Union.[41] This is particularly true of the intelligentsia and generally of people with any degree of education. In the process of getting an education, these people have gathered some inkling of what life has to offer, and they are naturally unwilling to remain in an isolated area that lacks amenities or cultural opportunities.

Siberian Russians and Nativized Groups

No discussion of the Russian impact on Siberia would be complete without at least cursory mention of the Russian population itself. This is a large and complex topic that, surely, deserves investigation by itself. However, in broad terms, the Russian population of Siberia is differentiated according to the time at which the people arrived, their reasons for coming, and the conditions under which they have lived. At most points, at least two categories are distinguishable: old settlers (Russian: *starozhily* or *Sibiriaki*; usually known also by various nicknames of historical or geographical origin) and new arrivals. The temporal dividing line between these two categories is somewhat vague and varies from place to place, but, generally speaking, anyone who arrived in Siberia (or whose ancestors did) later than about 1870 is considered a newcomer.

In terms of their reasons for coming to Siberia, the Russian old settlers fall into the following categories: 1) descendants of exiled religious dissenters (Old Believers and sectarians);[42] 2) descendants of political exiles, or ordinary convicts; 3) descendants of spontaneous voluntary migrants and runaway serfs (this category included also some groups of religious dissenters); 4) descendants of Cossacks and others in government service. By and large, only the first and fourth groups formed stable communities whose ethnic peculiarities are visible today. Those exiled for religious reasons maintained strict isolation and did not intermarry with other Russians, although in rare cases a man might take a native wife providing she converted. On the other hand, Cossacks and "service gentry" intermarried freely with the native population and formed biologically and culturally hybrid communities, as on Kamchatka,[43] although people of Russian descent are almost always sedentary and usually make some attempt to farm, no matter what the conditions.

It is quite natural that the Russian communities should have taken over much of the native material culture that is uniquely adapted to the climate and terrain. As for nonmaterial elements— religion, folklore, social structure, and customary law—the adoption of these seems to have depended on the remoteness of the point at which settlement was made and on the character of the original Russian population. Thus, the culture of the Russian old settlers of the Chuna Valley in what is now Krasnoiarsk Krai showed strong Tungus influence. The same was true of Russians in some parts of the present Buriat A.S.S.R. and Irkutsk Oblast.[44] Some Russian communities, besides borrowing cultural traits from the indigenous population, show a feature characteristic of transplanted groups in many parts of the world—the tendency to retain unaltered certain features of culture that have changed historically in the home country. It should be remembered that many Russian settler groups, particularly in the Baikal area and on the Angara River, were subject to a certain "leavening" influence by political exiles. However, since these people came as individuals and since their movements were dictated by chance or by individual factors, it is very difficult to offer any precise opinion as to what their effect may have been. The Russian old-settler communities in many areas remained practically undisturbed until the 1930s or in some cases until after World War II, when industrial development brought a large influx of Russian population. The previous isolation of the old settlers, which was often bolstered by religious separatism, is now breaking down and culture change is proceeding fairly rapidly, although some of the Sibiriaki remain among the most culturally conservative groups in the Soviet population.[45]

Cultural convergence (Russian: *sblizhenie*) is a topic on which Soviet specialists expend a great deal of effort without, in our view, having yet arrived at any very solid results. Certainly the most important data on this matter are not yet in. Isupov's data, which are based on the results of the 1959 census, show that while ethnically mixed marriages (one of the basic indices of cultural convergence) are proceeding at an accelerated rate, the number of such marriages among most Northern Siberian peoples is not such as to lead us to assume that a culture of definitely Russian type would emerge from these families. In the North generally, Russians intermarry only with sedentary groups, since the former are not used to nomadism and dislike it. The rather slim indications currently available are that the culture likely to result from the processes now taking place will not be identical with the present Russian culture, nor even a recognizable descendant of it (as the American is of the Western European). However, we are still in the process of working out these highly complex matters, and they must be left for the time being with only this somewhat cursory treatment.[46]

PROBLEMS AND UNANTICIPATED CONSEQUENCES

Human beings are recalcitrant creatures, and human society is the most complex organism known to science. The social planner, when he introduces measures to effect a given purpose, can never be sure that his measures will not also produce some entirely different result. The Soviet planners are no exceptions to this rule. We propose now to lay out some of the unintended results of Soviet policies and measures, in the form of a series of questions: Is the traditional way of life viable for the small Siberian peoples? If not, what should replace it? What are the elements militating against the creation of a new way of life?

The traditional way of life is not viable because in the process of collectivization and of educating the small peoples the traditional economy has been seriously distorted. The traditional economy needs a technological transformation that will take some time. Teachers will have to be trained in the new technology so that they in turn may teach their students. These students need to acquire not only such skills as how to pilot planes, how to drive mobile tractors, and how to operate radios, but also how to repair these machines. It goes without saying that they will need spare parts and equipment. We may well ask whether a reindeer herder who goes to his herd by helicopter, who lives in a mobile trailer, who cares for his animals according to the latest advances in veterinary science, and who returns to his settlement or even to a Far Eastern city after a tour of duty is really engaged in a traditional economy and whether, if that degree of mechanization is possible, another type of economy would not be more efficient. Most Soviet ethnographers maintain that in many areas the reindeer herds could be at least doubled if such a system as we have described were put into effect. Two simple facts of plant and animal biology need to be taken into account, however: a reindeer (no less than a human) needs a certain amount of vitamin-rich green fodder; and if a reindeer pasture becomes overgrazed because the herds are too large or too infrequently rotated the pasture takes years to grow again.

Reindeer, of course, are necessary in the North: they provide food, transportation, clothing, and even shelter for the nomadic populations (including geological expeditions). People must fish and hunt to feed and clothe themselves and, if possible, to feed and clothe the in-migrants. Therefore, the answer to the question of viability of the traditional economy is that for the immediate future it must be made viable, but probably will have to be replaced by something else.

That something else is utopian speculation, permissible only because millions of "Europeans" already live in the North. The process of urbanization in Siberia and the Far East will continue, but rather than being diffused it will be concentrated in relatively few large centers. These centers, in turn, will be supported not, as at present, by hundreds of fishing and reindeer-breeding sovkhozy and kolkhozy struggling to develop a Siberian agriculture but by highly specialized "food factories" using techniques that are now in the realm of science fiction.

The Soviet regime in the early period achieved remarkable results in the development of Siberia by what were essentially half-measures. In view of other demands on the national budget, the temptation is now strong to continue the policy of half-measures—to allow urbanization to proceed more or less spontaneously on the usual European model, to bring in personnel from outside and trust that they will be fed somehow, and to plan for the development of the area as though it were not geographically and environmentally unique. All the signs indicate, however, that the time is rapidly approaching, if not already here, when half-measures will no longer do. A number of conditions must obtain if Siberia is to be developed into a country that can take its place in the modern world. The fiscal demands of foreign policy and national defense must be held in line; a firm system of domestic priorities must be set up, and the people on the spot must be given a degree of autonomy sufficient to let them respond swiftly to changes in conditions. How probable it is that any of these conditions will be brought about in the near future no-one can tell without a crystal ball. In this presentation, we have merely endeavored to set forth some of the elements in the equation.

—9—

Russia and China:
the Structure of Contact

Mark Mancall

In a world characterized by ideological and political conflict on a vast scale, it is fashionable to link commerce and investment with the concepts of influence and impact. Depending on one's point of view and ideological commitments, foreign trade and investment may be perceived either as opening wedges for democratic liberalism or as a threat to national independence. Thus, the United States, for instance, tries to purchase influence and loyalty by increasing its client states' dependence on the American economy, which, in turn, is conceived as a conduit for the spread of liberalism and democratic ideas. The Soviet Union pursues the same course, with different ideological objectives in mind. The flag, it seems, is supposed to follow trade. But, historically, the study of Russia's impact on China leads to a startlingly different conclusion: her impact was not only tremendous; it was disproportionate in my view to the magnitude and structure of her actual political, commercial, military, and missionary presence inside China.[1] With the exception of Manchuria (and possibly also Outer Mongolia and Sinkiang), where her influence began to dominate the land from about 1890, Russia was far less in evidence on the Chinese (Han) scene than were other foreign powers. Some Russian firms operated in China Proper, to be sure, but they were small, few, and far between. While Harbin in Manchuria became a largely Russian city after the beginning of the twentieth century, foreigners and foreign settlements inside China were mostly Western European and North American. Even in cities such as Tientsin and Shanghai, where émigrés settled in significant numbers after the October Revolution in

1917, Russians remained picturesque and exotic: they dominated neither the foreign settlements nor the surrounding Chinese communities.

The comparative weakness of Russia's presence in China stands in sharp contrast to China's experience with the West. From the middle of the nineteenth century, Western European, especially Anglo-Saxon, missionaries and merchants flooded into China, establishing businesses, building churches, schools, and social services, introducing new political ideas, languages, sewing machines, and other consumer goods, including opium. Western liberalism was a pervasive influence in many segments of the Chinese population, but it was corrosive rather than constructive; liberalism prepared the seed bed for a more radical solution to China's ills, but Chinese and Westerners alike were unable to discover in it relevant solutions for the glaring problems of the Chinese polity. China received Christianity largely in its Roman or Protestant forms, while Orthodoxy, even in Manchuria, made relatively few converts. Chinese academic institutions were staffed often by personnel from, or trained in, North America and Western Europe; few Chinese before 1949 graduated from or even attended Russian institutions of higher education,[2] and such institutions as existed in Manchuria's Russian colony were intended primarily to educate Russians, not Chinese. Chinese who studied foreign languages were far more likely to learn English, French, or German, rather than Russian. Yet ultimately it was Russian culture, Russian concepts, or Russian filtrates of European ideas that were to flourish in the social and psychological atmosphere to which the West contributed so greatly.

The failure of the "Lao mao-tzu," the old hairy-ones from the north, to penetrate Chinese society and the Chinese economy to a greater degree than, or even to the same extent as, did the red-haired barbarians who came to China by sea from the West is explicable in several ways. Russia and China were in territorial contact from the middle of the seventeenth century, and by the beginning of the twentieth their common frontier ran for approximately 4,500 miles from the Pacific Ocean in the farthest east to the Pamir Mountains in Central Asia. Their common political frontier, however, did not represent cultural contiguity. It did not even create a zone—again with the exception of Manchuria after 1890—where a mixed population of Russians and Chinese could serve as a conduit for cultural influences.

The Sino-Russian frontier zone was divided into three major areas. Manchuria and the maritime provinces constituted the zone in the Far East. Here the Amur River system was the major line of division between the Manchu and the Romanov empires. Until after the middle of the nineteenth century, Manchuria was a sparsely inhabited forest region. From the very beginning of the Ch'ing, or Manchu, dynasty's reign in China, state ethnic policies inhibited Chinese emigration to Manchuria until late in the last century. The middle section of the frontier region comprised Mongolia, a land consisting largely of steppe and desert inhabited by a small population. In the west, Chinese Turkestan, or Sinkiang, supported a Turkish oasis culture.[3] Consequently, all along the frontier direct contact between Russian and Chinese populations took place only under very specialized circumstances, a situation that did not change significantly with the gradual growth of Russia's Siberian population. Russian caravans passed through the intermediate non-Chinese–non-Russian areas on their way to China, where they sojourned only briefly for commercial or diplomatic purposes. At such places as Kiakhta on the Russo-Mongolian frontier south of Urga, or Urumchi in Chinese Turkestan, Russian and Chinese merchants mingled in a common marketplace, but their concerns were primarily commercial and competitive, not intellectual or cultural.[4]

There were, of course, glaring departures from this pattern of Sino-Russian contact. The Russians maintained a religious mission at Peking continuously from the 1690s, but its major concern, when the good fathers were concerned at all, was to serve the souls of Russians in Peking or to study the Manchu empire rather than teach it. Russian and Chinese populations mixed in Northern Manchuria during and after the last decade of the nineteenth century, but they coexisted rather than interpenetrated. Aside from the adoption by the Chinese in Northern Manchuria of certain Russian customs and the use of a kind of pidgin Russian for communication between the two populations, it was the Russian revolutionary, not cultural, tradition that influenced local Chinese, and even this influence was little felt outside Manchuria. The Russians made almost no effort to reach out from the cities or the railway concession in Manchuria into other Chinese cities or into the Chinese country-side, as did Christian missionaries in China Proper. In Mongolia, particularly at Urga, it was Mongols rather than Chinese who felt the brunt of Russian influence. The Chinese had actually never been very numerous in the population of that settlement.

With the exception of outright military conquest or bandit raids, contact between China and other societies was carried on, until around the middle of the nineteenth century, within a traditional institutional structure and set of procedures intended to minimize the impact on China of commercial or political communications with external populations. Collectively known by Western scholars as the "tribute system" because of the central role played by for-eign envoys' presentation of tribute to the emperor, these institu-tions and procedures were in actuality an extension of accepted Chinese social relationships into the realm of intersocietal contact, particularly in the commercial and political fields.

In traditional Chinese Confucian political theory, the emperor of China (who was not necessarily Chinese) was not merely the su-preme cultural and political personage inside the empire; his posi-tion was unique in the universe, and he stood between man and Heaven, mediating between the two as the pivotal point in the uni-versal continuum. This concept was reenforced by, and in turn re-enforced, the image of China not as one empire among many but as civilization itself, surrounded by degrees of barbarism differenti-ated in terms of the barbarians' acceptance or rejection of, or in-difference to, the ways of civilization, that is, of China. Just as the various orders of Chinese society—the scholar-bureaucrat, the sol-dier, the peasant, the artisan, the merchant—surrounded the em-peror in a descending order of concentric circles, so the barbarians, or those who had not "turned toward civilization" by adopting Chi-nese ways, lay outside civilization in a similar, but lower, descend-ing order. Confucian officialdom, while denominating the barbar-ians both by ethnic and geographical terms, did not spatially place them in a larger geographical context around China but, rather, perceived them in cultural terms: those able to enter into contact with China on her own terms were conceptually closer to China than those who rejected intercourse with the Celestial Empire on any but their own conditions. Ignorance of, or opposition to, the ways of China involved spatial and physical exclusion of barbarians from the penumbra of the emperor's beneficence, which meant denial of access to China's markets. Entrance within the penumbra took place along a continuum of acceptance of China's ways. Viet Nam and Korea were at one end, both accepting Chinese forms of government, philosophy, and official language; the Mongols and other non-Sinitic barbarians were at the other end, willing to accept China's terms for intercourse while rejecting her culture. The rest of the world lived in a kind of Outer Limbo and, even when known to the Chinese, they were of little interest.

All official contacts with foreigners, therefore, were based on the principle of hierarchy, with Chinese officialdom taking the superior position. In this context, access to the emperor became a serious problem. Whereas in Europe rulers were considered equals, in China there was no concept of equality, and the emperor was uniquely superior to all. This superiority was represented in the requirement that all who entered the emperor's presence, be they Chinese or not, had to perform the ritual of the kowtow, or the three kneelings and nine prostrations. Access to the emperor's person could not be had without the performance of this ritual, and European diplomats were particularly loath to perform it, seeing it as a form of recognition of the emperor's superiority to their own masters. This problem was not resolved until 1873, when the emperor granted his first public audience to foreign diplomats who, indeed, had been residing in Peking only from 1861 on.

Commercial contacts between Chinese and foreigners were highly developed at an early period in China's history. The empire engaged in indirect trade with the Near East and Middle East at least as early as the Han dynasty, and during the Southern Sung dynasty a large foreign commercial settlement existed at Ch'uan-chou on the coast of Fukien Province. Traditionally, commercial contacts with foreigners took place in two forms. First, caravans from Central Asia visited Peking in the guise of, or in the train of, tribute missions. While in Peking, they were permitted to trade with the local inhabitants under specific regulations and within limited periods of time. The second, and more common, form of commercial contact was the frontier market place, located on both land and sea frontiers. Here again, under very controlled conditions, Chinese and foreign merchants engaged in commerce. These frontier markets were analogs of the "ports of trade" that characterized commerce along the West African coast and in Mezo-America, for instance.[5] By isolating foreign commerce in "ports of trade" and placing it under strict governmental supervision, China prevented foreign merchants from occupying a position from which they might penetrate the geographical or social space of China itself. The benefits of commercial activity were thus maximized, while the dangers of social disruption inherent in the presence of foreigners inside the empire were minimized.

Before 1860, the Ch'ing dynasty's foreign relations were managed by two offices in Peking. The "Board of Rites," charged with overseeing the correct performance of Confucian ritual, conducted relations with those barbarians who had accepted Confucian culture or whose societies were understood by the Chinese to most resemble their own, particularly the societies of maritime East Asia and continental Southeast Asia, or those whose merchants and representatives arrived in China by sea. The Li-fan yuan, or Barbarian Control Board, oversaw the conduct of relations with the societies of Central Asia and those who arrived in China by land from that direction, who were not presumed to have "turned toward civilization." More often than not, however, actual diplomatic and commercial negotiations took place along the frontiers themselves, and the conduct of diplomacy fell within the domain of provincial officials or bureaucrats dispatched from Peking for that purpose. The Tsung-li yamen, a prototypical foreign office in the Western sense of the term, was established in Peking only in 1861, and a centralized bureaucracy for the conduct of relations between China and foreign nations did not develop until later still. The first resident embassy abroad was established only in 1877.

Chinese traditional practice in the conduct of relations with foreign states therefore minimized the opportunities for the penetration of foreign influence into China; at the same time, it restricted the Chinese observation of foreign ways. Government policy, particularly after the first decades of the eighteenth century, inhibited Chinese travel abroad, a policy that grew out of China's deeply rooted suspicion of foreign or heterodox ideas. Chinese ethnocentricity, encouraged by her geographical separation from the other great centers of civilization in Europe and Western Asia, was reenforced by the heavy hand of Confucian orthodoxy. In a society where access to civil power rested primarily on the successful completion of a mighty battery of written examinations based on a carefully prescribed course of study and on an officially sanctioned philosophical and literary tradition, heterodox ideas were productive neither of power nor of normal happiness.

Chinese xenophobia and rejection of heterodoxy were nowhere more plainly exhibited than in the attitude toward foreign science. As early as the last years of the Ming dynasty, the imperial court and bureaucracy had looked not unfavorably on European mechanics and engineering. Clocks, maps, pictures, gadgets, and gewgaws were eagerly sought as curios by Chinese literati and court officials, indeed by the emperors themselves. Western astronomy and mathematics were given an honored position insofar as they contributed to the strengthening or reenforcement of bureaucratic orthodoxy. In the nineteenth century, however, when Chinese literati began to perceive, however dimly, that Western science, as distinct from engineering mechanics, carried with it the suggestion of a conceptual universe at variance with their own, that science fell under suspicion. The products of Western industry and ingenuity, in other words, were welcomed in China only so long as they did not threaten to upset the Chinese view of the universe. Philosophical and educational orthodoxy, supported by the powers of a state whose personnel were drawn from among the orthodox, combined with diplomatic and commercial practice to inhibit the penetration into China of foreigners as potential carriers of disruptive influences.

Russia's relations with China up to the middle of the nineteenth century developed within this structure, as did those of Western Europe. In the specifically Russian case, difficulties of geographical access to China provided a reenforcement of the pattern. The traditional structure could be challenged, after all, only when a power unwilling to operate within it accumulated sufficient strength along China's frontiers to challenge the structure itself to make it inoperative in terms of the satisfaction of the psychological, ideological, and material requirements of the parties working within it.

For two hundred years after the initiation of direct Sino-Russian relations—when Russian and Manchu forces clashed furtively in the forests of the Amur basin in the middle of the seventeenth century—Russia found it advantageous to work within the Chinese system. Indeed, the Manchus sought to entangle Russia in a complex net of carefully calibrated institutions and relationships that balanced Russian acquiescence to Chinese practice with satisfaction of Russian commercial requirements. From 1689, when the beginnings of a regulated frontier between the two empires were embodied in the Treaty of Nerchinsk and the first tentative efforts were made to create a rationalized system for the conduct of relations between the two powers, to 1727, when the Treaty of Kiakhta described the treaty system that, with only minor adjustments, was to govern Sino-Russian contacts down to 1860, various efforts and adjustments were made to develop the particular form of contact that would best serve the purposes of each empire. The Russians sought primarily access to the Chinese market, both for the sale of furs from Siberia and for the purchase of such goods as they required or desired: rhubarb, tea, and luxury items. The Chinese had two objectives in their Russian policy: first, Peking wished to neutralize Russia in the growing struggle with the Western Mongols, or Jungars, for supremacy in Central Asia and, concomitantly, to secure the Manchu northern homeland in Manchuria from Russian incursions. Second, the Manchus wished to raise barriers against Russian penetration of Chinese society, as they did against other foreigners as well.

To these ends, the Treaty of Kiakhta embodied institutions that were remarkably suited to permit intercourse between the two empires without challenging either party's ideological commitments. At the same time, these institutions were sufficiently flexible to allow the level of contact to rise or fall without endangering the structure itself. Commercially, the Kiakhta Treaty legitimized both frontier markets and caravan trade to Peking; culturally, it specified those acts that were considered criminal and prescribed punishments in terms of each party's traditional criminal practice. Politically, it sanctioned carefully defined forms of communications between officials designated for diplomatic negotiations, thus avoiding the issue of access to the imperial person, and at the same time provided for a system of passports and communications that recognized the future continuity of the relationship. Because the Russians viewed trade as their essential interest in the system, the Manchus, through the device of trade embargoes, were able to exert political pressure on the Russians within the context of the Kiakhta system itself, without the necessity of resorting to warfare. The ingeniousness of this system can be seen in the fact that it avoided all issues of culture conflict and permitted each side to continue to interpret the relationship in terms of its own tradition. The success of the system may easily be demonstrated by the fact that it remained essentially unchanged down to the middle of the nineteenth century, with only minor interruptions of commerce.

Nevertheless, the concept of a special Russian interest in China developed as early as 1731, long before Russia became entangled in a Far Eastern rivalry with the powers of Western Europe. In that year, Savva Vladislavich, the Russian diplomat primarily responsible for the negotiations that led to the creation of the Kiakhta system, drew on his observations in China and on his view of the significance of Sino-Russian frontier proximity, to submit a memorial to the tsar proposing the Russian conquest of China. A long period of peace in Europe, the accumulation of a sufficiently large treasury, and the development of a war machine, he suggested, would permit the consideration of a possible Russian military attack on the Manchu empire. Two factors, he believed, would make the conquest a relatively simple task. First, the Chinese, though prepared for war and outstandingly numerous and industrious, were not, in his opinion, a warlike people. Second, the Manchus were a small minority ruling a vast Chinese population that was prepared to rise against their Manchu overlords. A Russian invasion of the Ch'ing empire would encourage such an uprising, forcing the Manchus to divide their already very limited military resources. This would give the Russians their victory.[6]

It was a credit to the Kiakhta system that Vladislavich had helped to create that at no time were his proposals taken seriously. Indeed, neither Russia nor China was prepared for conquest. China was too strong to permit of easy conquest by any foreign power in the eighteenth century, and the myth of her strength was to be shattered only by the British victory in the First Opium War of 1839-42. For her part, Russia remained far too weak in her Siberian possessions to support any forward policy against China. Neither population nor the development of transportation and natural resources in Siberia would allow such aggression. Manchu policies were, therefore, successful; and Russia's European concerns, combined with her Asian weakness, prevented a rekindling of interest in the Far East for well over a century.

A confluence of circumstances in the middle of the nineteenth century led to a radical change in Russian policy toward China. Her interest in the Amur revived, and she began to think of a warm water port on the Pacific, on a coast claimed by the Ch'ing empire. In a sense, the Sino-Russian Treaty of Peking of 1860, which completely replaced the Kiakhta system, was the final act in the fulfillment of Russia's "manifest destiny" in the Far East. Russia's territorial aggrandizement at China's expense was influenced by Western politics. As a great European power, she was determined to counter the international maneuvers of her rivals wherever they might affect her; and her Siberian frontier lay exposed to the rising Anglo-French power in the Far East. Accordingly, St. Petersburg tried to oppose the growth of British power in China and to extend its own sphere of influence.

Count Nikolai Nikolaevich Muraviev was the chief architect of this change in Russia's Far Eastern policy. As governor general of Eastern Siberia, he was deeply impressed with the indeterminate nature of the occupation of those areas that lay between what was clearly Russian and what was clearly Manchu territory. A visionary, he foresaw a crucial role for Siberia in Russia's future. For both these reasons, Muraviev was acutely alert to the Anglo-French threat to Russian interests in East Asia, but because his dream of Asian empire ran counter to St. Petersburg's official policies, he was often forced to carry out his plans on his own responsibility. It is a curious note that precisely at this moment of transition from a passive to an active Far Eastern policy, Muraviev, Russia's Asian proconsul, fit perfectly the traditional Chinese pattern of a frontier official making foreign policy. Indeed, in 1853 the tsar granted Muraviev sovereign powers to carry on diplomatic negotiations in the Far East without reference to the Foreign Ministry in St. Petersburg.[7]

Muraviev used the threat of an Anglo-French attack on Siberia during the Crimean War to draw Russia's immediate attention to the Far East. He had already personally sponsored, and even actually participated in, the exploration and settlement of the basins of the Amur and Ussuri rivers and of the Pacific coast north from Korea. His recognition of the Manchu empire's weakness spurred him on. In 1852, for instance, he wrote the tsar that in view of the possible collapse of the Manchu dynasty in the face of the great Taiping Rebellion and its defeat in the Opium War of 1839-42, "assurance on our part might have the effect of inducing the Chinese emperor to seek our protection."[8] Although no offer of aid was actually made until 1858, rumors to the effect that some help might be forthcoming were already circulating along the China coast as early as 1853. This furnishes some indication of the increased awareness of Russia in the consciousness of both Chinese and Western officials in the Far East as a result of Muraviev's vigorous Siberian policies.

As a direct result of Russian military and diplomatic maneuvers along the Amur, Muraviev and the Manchu military governor of the Amur, I-shan, signed the Treaty of Aigun on 16 May 1858. This treaty recognized Russia's claim to the left bank of the Amur and established a condominium over the territories between the Ussuri River and the Pacific Ocean. At the same time, however, St. Petersburg, lest it lose a share of the spoils of the Anglo-French expedition of 1856-58, sent an ambassador, Count Putiatin, to Peking as a "disinterested observer." When the Allies entered Tientsin, Putiatin, not to be outdone, negotiated a separate Sino-Russian treaty which, not unnaturally, given the vagaries of diplomatic correspondence in the Far East at that time, was at variance with the Aigun settlement. Whereas the Aigun treaty tended toward an explicit delimitation of the boundary, the Tientsin treaty did no more than sanction the establishment of a boundary commission to consider the problem.

Muraviev, to secure his own more explicit and advantageous agreement with the Manchus, now resorted to an attempt at direct interference in China's internal affairs by offering Peking a Russian military assistance and advisory group that would aid in the training of Ch'ing forces, to be armed and supplied by Russia, for the suppression of the Taiping Rebellion. Incidentally, of course, a Russian-trained and -armed army would have given St. Petersburg a commanding position in Peking itself and a strong voice in the councils of the Ch'ing government. Although the Manchus refused Muraviev's offer, this first Russian attempt to interfere in Chinese affairs was by no means a failure. Muraviev now dispatched the commander of the proposed military mission, Colonel (later Major General) Nikolai Pavlovich Ignatiev, on a diplomatic mission to Peking to represent the governor general's interests.

Ignatiev's activities in Peking and along the China coast between June 1859 and November 1860 secured Russia's, and Muraviev's, objectives in the Far East without resort to arms. By a series of complex maneuvers in which Ignatiev sought to play the Anglo-French and Chinese negotiators off against each other, the Russian appeared to be using his good offices to bring about a settlement of Sino-Western differences. This placed him in the advantageous position of being able to demand in payment for his services a Sino-Russian treaty embodying Muraviev's objectives. Russia was thus converted from a passive, if willing, participant in the traditional East Asian international order into a member of the imperialist camp in the Far East at the very time when the traditional order itself was crumbling under the West's onslaught. This she achieved without the military force characteristic of the policy of the other European powers in China. But the Manchus did not mistake Russia for a friend of China. At least one important and influential Chinese specialist on foreign policy in the middle of the nineteenth century argued that Russia, not the other Western powers, represented the greatest threat to Ch'ing interests.[9]

Despite the success of Muraviev's China policy, it was not until 1880 and after that, fired by the Slavophile vision of Russia's "holy mission" and by the course of events in the Balkans after the Russo-Turkish War of 1877-78, a revival of Russian thought took place, supporting an aggressive policy toward China and, it might be added, the rest of Asia too. Fedor Dostoevskii wrote in 1881:

> In Europe, we were hangers-on and slaves, whereas we shall go to Asia as masters. In Europe we were Asiatics, whereas in Asia we, too, are Europeans. Our civilizing mission in Asia will bribe our spirit and drive us thither. It is only necessary that the movement should start. Build two railroads: begin with the one to Siberia, and then—to Central Asia,— and at once you will see the consequences.[10]

General M. N. Przhevalskii, the noted explorer in Central Asia, propagandized in favor of Russian espousal of the cause of non-Chinese Manchu subjects in Mongolia and Sinkiang. Professor F. F.

Martens, a leading specialist on international law, published works arguing that international law was not binding in relations between civilized and "semibarbarous" peoples. V. P. Vasil'ev, Russia's leading Sinologist, advocated in a public lecture in 1883, in terms curiously similar to later Soviet rationalizations of Russia's historical conquest of Siberia and Central Asia, an interpretation of Russian aggressiveness in Asia in terms of its instrumentality as a liberating force for peoples subjected to strife, oppression, and backwardness.[11]

In journalism, in government, and in business circles, the advocates of an aggressive policy in Asia, and particularly in the Far East, gained such influence and power that by the middle of the last decade of the nineteenth century Russia was embarked, not without European, particularly German, goading, on a forward Far Eastern policy that ultimately led to the disaster of the Russo-Japanese War of 1904-05.[12] In the event, however, the structure of Russian penetration of China inhibited, rather than encouraged, the growth of Russian influence inside China Proper. Russia's Far Eastern presence took the form of a colonial establishment directly linked to the Trans-Siberian and Chinese Eastern railways, just as Western colonial expansion was directly tied to its major form of external communication, the ocean. But whereas Western colonial or semicolonial expansion into China from the coast took place in that part of the empire that was from every point of view—economic, cultural, social, and political—the center of the nation's life, Russia's land-based colonialism infected a region itself of the colonial periphery of Chinese society.

The opening of the Suez Canal in 1869 contributed markedly to changing Russia's status from a participant in the traditional East Asian international order coexisting with China to a full member of the imperialist camp. Not only was sea transport between Russia's Black Sea port of Odessa and the China coast more convenient than the long trek through Siberia but it was also cheaper. Tea was the major Russian import from China in the nineteenth century. The cost of transporting a *pud* (36 lbs.) of tea to Kiakhta from the major tea-producing regions of southeast China in the second half of the century was approximately 10 rubles, while to regional ports the cost was only 1.32 rubles. Moreover, it sometimes took more than three months to supply tea from the point of production to the Kiakhta market, while it usually took only about twenty days to transport it to the coast. Consequently, once the major international shipping lanes from the Far East to Europe had moved closer to Odessa, it was both cheaper and more convenient for Russia to begin purchasing tea along the coast rather than through Kiakhta.[13]

Russian commercial shipping along the China coast was slow to develop, however, until 1880. The Kiakhta emporium was a going concern, and the Crimean War, together with the sale of Alaska and the Aleutian Islands to the United States in 1867, at first decreased Russian maritime interests in the Pacific. For instance, the last vessel of the Russian-American Company to visit the China coast did so in 1853. Regular shipping was established between Odessa and Vladivostok in 1880, however; and by the middle of the decade Russian vessels had begun calling regularly at Canton and Shanghai, primarily to purchase tea. This seaborne tea commerce grew rapidly thereafter: in 1885 Russian ships carried 246,193,000 *puds* of tea away from China to Odessa, while that figure increased in 1893 to 640,676,000. By the beginning of the 1890s, the value of maritime imports from China to Russia had reached some thirteen to fourteen million rubles a year, roughly equal to the value of Russian imports through Kiakhta at that same time.[14]

Even after the Manchu-Russian treaty of 1860 and the opening of the Suez Canal in 1869, Sino-Russian frontier commerce continued to develop, partly as a function of the growth of the Siberian population, which, far removed from sources of supply in European Russia, relied on China for certain necessities. In the two hundred years between 1697 and 1897, the Russian population of Siberia increased from 150,000 to 4.7 million, which constituted about 80 percent of the population of the entire country. This increase, which was particularly rapid in the second half of the nineteenth century, was reflected in trade figures. At Kiakhta, for instance, Russian imports from China, including tea, increased from 6,916,000 rubles in 1850 to 14,903,000 rubles in 1893, a growth of about 216 percent. As Russians moved into Central Asia, an even more remarkable increase took place along the Ch'ing-Russian frontier in Turkestan. Here, between 1850 and 1893, Russian imports from China increased from 530,500 rubles to 2,792,200 rubles, or by 526.3 percent. Alone in Central Asia along the entire extent of the Sino-Russian commercial frontier, Russian exports to China exceeded imports. In 1893 exports were valued at 3,036,400 rubles, as against 211,500 rubles in 1850, an increase of 1,435.4 percent.

Both the growth of trade and the singular balance of trade in favor of Russia, which was not characteristic of any other part of the commercial picture, may be explained by several factors. The Treaty of Kuldja of 1851 regularized Sino-Russian trade in Turkestan by extending the Kiakhta treaty system to that region. For instance, between 1850 and 1853, the total trade turnover in Turkestan increased by almost 200 percent. Furthermore, the Turkestan region was isolated from China Proper, where Russian trade competed, often unsuccessfully, with the commercial activities of other European powers.

It is important to note that the two areas of the Manchu empire in closest commercial contact with the Russian economy—Sinkiang and Mongolia—were both culturally non-Chinese and were isolated geographically from China Proper and the main routes of commercial communication. Thus, the pattern of Russian trade with China was not such as to encourage the development of Russian influence on Chinese commercial practices and organization, nor did it provide a base for the growth of Russian influence in the noncommercial sectors of the Chinese polity. The concentration and localization of Russian trade in non-Chinese areas continued up to and after World War I. In 1914, for instance, Russian imports from China by sea just barely exceeded the combined imports across the Sinkiang, Mongolian, and Amur frontiers. In sharp contrast, Russian exports to China by sea approximated only 5 percent of combined exports over the entire land frontier.

The pattern of Russian investments in the Ch'ing empire reflected the situation in trade. For instance, Russians established tea-processing factories in China Proper, at Hankow, as early as 1863, before any other foreigners, and by 1868 they owned factories over one hundred miles into the interior from that city. In the 1870s, they established tea factories in Foochow and Kiukiang, and by the 1890s these Russian firms employed about seven thousand Chinese.[15] But their investments were significantly less important than the Anglo-Americans'.

Russian capital investment in the Manchu empire by the end of

1904 was overwhelmingly concentrated in Manchuria, particularly in the Russian-owned Chinese Eastern Railway. Out of an investment of 563.5 million rubles at the end of 1904, 441 million rubles was invested in the construction of the railway, 17.6 million in the construction of a port at Dairen, 10.4 million in the city of Dairen itself, 12 million in Port Arthur, and another 11.9 million in the construction of railway-owned maritime and riverine shipping. Private investment in Manchuria amounted to some 15 million rubles, and in all of China Proper Russians invested only about 5 million rubles. This situation had not changed by the eve of the First World War. While Russian investments in all of the Ch'ing empire had risen to some 925.8 million rubles, of this sum only 9 million represented private capital investment in areas outside Manchuria.

Of all the foreign powers investing in the Ch'ing empire, Russia, with a capitalization equivalent to US$474.8 million, occupied second place only to Great Britain, with a total capital investment worth about US$607.6 million; but the Russian investments were overwhelmingly concentrated in one area, the Russian colony in Northern Manchuria, far removed from the major political, cultural, and economic centers of China Proper. Moreover, investment of the private sector of the Russian economy in all the rest of the empire, pegged at about 1 percent in 1904, remained at this level in 1914.[16]

A comparison with British and American investments in the Manchu empire by order of magnitude will indicate the degree of concentration of Russian capital in one area. Hou Chi-ming estimates that British investment amounted to 37.7 percent of total foreign investment in the Manchu empire in 1914, as opposed to 33.0 percent in 1902. Russian investments in 1902 amounted to 31.3 percent of total foreign investment, dropping to 16.7 percent in 1914. In both years, however, Russia was second only to Great Britain and was followed by Germany. The United States at 2.5 percent in 1902 and 3.1 percent in 1914 was far behind several other powers. However, according to Hou's estimates, Russian investments in Manchuria and Outer Mongolia in 1910 amounted to 98.8 percent of her total investments in the empire, and in 1914 to 97.7 percent. Furthermore, this heavy concentration of Russian investments outside the Chinese part of the Manchu empire or, after the Revolution of 1911, outside China Proper, was reenforced by the very structure of Russian investment itself. Foreign loans to the Manchu and, later, the Chinese governments were an important element in the structure of foreign investment in China and a vital mechanism for the wielding of political influence within government circles. In the case of Great Britain, loans to the government amounted to approximately 42 percent of her China investments in 1904 and 34 percent in 1914. In Russia's case, however, this same element amounted to only 11 and 12 percent, respectively.[17] Therefore, not only was the geographical concentration of Russian investments, but their very structure as well, not conducive to the growth of Russian influence inside the Chinese polity.[18]

Eventually, it was not Russia's impact as a commercial or as a colonial power that influenced China so profoundly. Instead, Russia's impact on China flowed from those elements in Russian experience that were of universal significance outside of (and perhaps in spite of) the particular form or content of the Russian-Chinese relationship itself. Neither Russia's commercial policies nor her colonial status in Manchuria were contributing factors.

It is perhaps in the field of literature that the strength and the quality of the Russian impact on China may best be indicated statistically. In the very first years of the twentieth century, out of 259 volumes of translations of foreign literature published by China's Commercial Press, the country's single most important publishing house, only ten were translations from Russian, all by Tolstoi. Some works by Pushkin, Lermontov, Chekhov, and Gor'kii were also available, mostly in Chinese versions of Japanese translations. In all China, probably only a few more than fifty literary works written by Russians or dealing with Russian themes, including some of Krylov's fables, were published. Of these, Russian revolutionary movements were the subject of at least twenty-nine. Curiously, these were mostly written by non-Russians, including Chinese, Japanese, English, and a Pole, a German, a Frenchman, and an American.[19]

Chinese publishing about Russia increased considerably after 1905 and, more particularly, after 1917, in both standard and revolutionary periodicals. The New Culture Movement, lasting approximately from 1915 to 1922, published a great deal of material in its journals about Russia and by Russians. After 1927, when Sino-Russian relations were broken, Chiang Kai'shek's government tried to ban Russian literature officially, and Chinese, especially students, were at times arrested merely for possessing copies of Tolsťoi's *War and Peace* or Dostoevskii's *The Brothers Karamazov.* However, interest in Russia and in Russian literature continued to grow rapidly. A list of the translations of foreign fiction into Chinese that were available on the Chinese market as of 31 March 1929 contains some 1,100 titles from twenty-one countries. The number of Russian works on this list exceeds those of any other single country. A year later, many more Russian works were available.

Olga Lang, discussing a study made in 1936-37 concerning reader interest among students in twenty-two colleges and eight high schools in China, indicates that interest in Russian literature had grown even further. English literature and the English language were taught in all the schools studied, while Russian was taught in only one. "Nevertheless, the students were familiar with almost all the Russian classics and outstanding contemporary authors." They named as their favorite foreign books English and American works 217 times; Russian books 162; and all other nationalities, including French, German, Italian, etc., a total of 186. Asked about their favorite authors, they named Russian writers 307 times, English and American authors 287 times, and all others 95. Moreover, the newspaper and periodical press constantly drew parallels between Russian and Chinese conditions.[20]

Lu Hsün, the greatest modern Chinese writer and critic, wrote in explanation of the great Chinese response to Russian literature at the turn of the century:

> Some of our youth had already felt the oppression. . .they were suffering, they looked for concrete advice or guidance. And at that time they found Russian literature. They understood that Russian literature is our teacher and friend. Russian literature opened to us the beautiful soul of the oppressed, their suffering, their struggle. Our souls were inflamed with hope when we read the writers of the 1840s. We suffered with the characters of the writers of the 1860s. Certainly we knew that the Russian empire was committing acts of aggression against China; nevertheless, its literature made us understand an essential truth: there are two classes in the world, the oppressors and the oppressed.[21]

Kuo Mo-jo, the great Chinese communist intellectual, declared in 1940 that Russian influence on Chinese literature was greater than that of any other country, and a French Catholic critic, writing in 1941, said that "in attraction for modern Chinese writers the Russian novels have no rivals. There is a great similarity between the souls of Russian and Chinese novelists."[22]

Literature by Russians or about Russia was one of the two major vehicles of Russian impact on China. The other, which lies outside the scope of this essay, was obviously communist political activity and its accompanying ideological writings. But it may be argued that it was Russian literature or literature about Russia that contributed substantially to the preparation of Chinese intellectuals and students for radical political thought and action.

In surveying and analyzing the influence of one society on another, we may begin simply by cataloguing points of contact and moments of imitation. This may appear to be a fairly simple task, requiring only basic linguistic proficiency and an eye for comparisons. However, such an approach must remain ultimately unsatisfying for two reasons. First, not all contacts involve influence. China's first formal treaties with a Western nation, the treaties of Nerchinsk and Kiakhta with Russia, are an example. The institutional system created by these treaties for the conduct of contacts between the Manchu and Russian empires consciously minimized the possibility of the development of either empire's influence within the other by creating an institutionally neutral form of intercourse. This was accomplished by the establishment of a set of institutions that in and of themselves were without cultural foundation in the traditions of either one or the other empire exclusively. Each party was left to interpret the course and the events of the relationship in terms of its own traditions.

Second, the cataloguing approach to the analysis of influence or impact encourages an essentially external view of the recipient society's history, and cannot provide explanations for the failure of certain factors in one culture to influence another. Why, for instance, did Orthodox Christianity have so little impact on China in comparison with Roman Catholicism or Protestantism? The failure of Russians to develop a concerted missionary effort inside China is certainly part of the explanation, but is it sufficient?

Nor can such an approach account for changes in the influencing elements in one culture once they cross the frontier into another. For instance, to say that Western liberalism failed in China is true, but it does not explain the failure. One may suggest that the political and social forces espousing Western liberalism in China were weak, but such a statement cannot serve as a basis for an explanation of the fact that ultimately the failure of liberalism in China was a Chinese, not a Western, phenomenon. It was not Western liberalism that failed in China but, rather, Chinese liberalism. Why, in a given culture, do some ideas gain credence while others do not? Why and how do ideas undergo transformation? The statement that Marxism is a Russian intrusion into China and that as Maoism it is adapted to Chinese conditions perpetuates the myth that Marxism is a foreign element intruded into the Chinese scene *unnaturally.* The very concept of "adaptation," or naturalization, contains within it the tacit implication that Marxism in China is condemned to remain forever foreign, forced, or in conflict with "traditional" Chinese values. The emphasis on "adaptation" leads to a simplistic reductionism, a view of the intruded foreign element, the "influence," as becoming nativized but never native. To carry this example farther, it may be pointed out that two opposing views of Marxism in China derive from it: either China under Marxist communism is radically different from its past because of foreign intrusions or domination by an "alien ideology," or it simply repeats the past in a different, more modern guise. Either "China always conquers her conquerors," or communism is the vehicle for the modernization of China. Both approaches are unsatisfactory because, first, neither explains how influence takes place and, second, they are conclusions rather than analytical tools. A different approach is required.

The structure, nature, and intensity of the Russian impact on China must be analyzed within the context of particular configurations in the total paradigmatic perceptual scheme through which the Chinese viewed themselves and reality. By paradigm, to paraphrase Thomas S. Kuhn, I mean to suggest the perceptual system—including institutions, laws, theories, conceptual schemes, on all levels of consciousness taken together—that exhibit throughout the total system regularities, discontinuities, oppositions, irregularities, lacunae, etc.[23] It is within this paradigmatic system that the Chinese felt the Russian impact or, for that matter, that any culture experiences the impact of another.

The traditional Chinese paradigm did not include concepts either of diachronic or of synchronic historical conflict and discontinuity. The universe, and all of history, were viewed as harmonious and endlessly repetitious. The iconographic representation of this perception was the famous *yin-yang* symbol; in philosophy and literature, it found expression in a statement such as "what is filled will become empty; what is empty will become filled." In logic, it was expressed in a chain system that declared, "if a, then b; if b, then c; if c, then d; if d, then x; if x, then d; if d, then c; if c, then b; if b, then a." One result of the impact of Western European, more particularly Anglo-Saxon, culture on China was the introduction of a perception of diachronic conflict and discontinuity, the past versus the present, the old versus the new. Russian influence in China resulted, among other things, in the introduction of the perception of synchronic conflict, the embodiment of diachronic conflicts in contemporaneous elements, such as class struggle, the struggle with the past in the present. This was not simply the product of Marxism; indeed, entering China through the vehicle of literature, it antedated the "intrusion" of Marxism into China.

These new perceptions were not just a matter of Russian or Anglo-Saxon influence on China. They became *facts* on the Chinese scene, functioning elements in the Chinese paradigmatic structure. For instance, the traditional Chinese viewed the world as a harmonious whole that included a four-part division, the parts existing in functional harmony with one another, and this constituted the natural social state of man. This concept was not disturbed by Western Anglo-Saxon influences on China, which, through Christianity and liberalism, introduced an antipathy between past and future. Rather, it was upset by Russian ideas (either as Russian ideas or as filtrates of European ideas through the medium of Russian literature) of a new dimension, the synchronic antithesis of class conflict. Synchronic conflict is a concept closely related to, but quite distinct from, diachronic conflict.

Once the new concepts of synchronic and diachronic conflict became part of the Chinese paradigmatic structure and therefore "facts" of the Chinese scene—while previously this kind of conflict may have existed, without an explicit concept of such conflict it would not have been perceived as such—the instrumentalities for dealing with these conflicts and discontinuities could also be introduced from the outside and become Chinese, not foreign, elements. Nihilism, anarchism, and socialism are examples, and they all became part of Chinese intellectual life. This is a very different process from what we call "adaptation," which ultimately means, or implies, deformation. The concept of synchronic conflict and discontinuity and its concomitant instrumentalities of anarchism, nihilism, or socialism came into China with tremendous force not because they filled places in the Chinese paradigm that had formerly been vacant but precisely because they added dimensions to it that had previously not existed. Conflict, to be sure, had existed in China, but no perceptual means existed for structuring it and, therefore, for analyzing it on a temporal or a social level.

In contrast, Anglo-Saxon liberalism failed in China because it tended to individualize the problem of conflict, to suggest perceptions of conflict on the microcosmic level of two human beings or, macrocosmically, on the almost purely temporal level of the past versus the present. Liberal individualism disturbed the Chinese scene because it introduced the concept of temporal conflict, but it was not profoundly disturbing because it harmonized with the Chinese view of the individual more than it conflicted with it. In China, as in the West, the individual was both the subject and the object of history as an individual, not as a member of a social class. Consequently, Western liberalism, revolutionary though it may have been in China, ultimately left a shallow imprint and led to a kind of pathetic pessimism born of the hopelessly vain effort to change a society by saving individual souls. This difference between the Russian and the Anglo-Saxon West outweighed the Russian on the Chinese scene.

The impact of Russia on China, particularly of Russian literature and sociopolitical ideas, both before and after 1917, was tremendous precisely because Russia provided a focus for thinking about problems inside China that had not been previously available to Chinese. In other words, Russia, as an arena of social conflict, itself became a Chinese symbol which made meaningful and conscious for Chinese what previously had been only latent or unconscious. Liberalism did no such thing. Science and democracy were introduced from the liberal Anglo-Saxon West and were even anthropomorphized on occasion as *Mr.* **Science** and *Mr.* **Democracy.**[24] This was well within the tradition of the Chinese political and intellectual style, which viewed politics in clique or personalistic rather than in social or structural terms.

Terrorism and assassination, which the Chinese learned chiefly through Russian novels or novels about Russia, were not part of the Chinese political style. In literature they were often presented in the personification of Sofia Perovskaia and Vera Figner, but Russian nihilists and anarchists did not just become foreign heroes and heroines to the Chinese; they became Chinese symbols where no such symbols had existed before, and in Chinese literature their characteristics were often attached to Chinese figures. Novelists wrote about Chinese Perovskaias and Figners, the ultimate in the integration of new symbols into the paradigmatic structure. Perovskaia and Figner became Chinese and acted as Chinese within the Chinese social structure and perceptual system. Young Chinese began patterning their lives and actions on these figures, perceiving them in no way as foreign, nor as adaptations. Russian individuals became Chinese concepts and as such influenced Chinese individuals. Western concepts such as science and democracy became, in a sense, individuals—Mr. Science and Mr. Democracy—who as foreigners interacted with individual Chinese; but they never *became* Chinese. They always remained external to the Chinese scene.

Social conflict had always existed in China, but social conflict as such was not an element in the Chinese paradigm and, consequently, was not recognized as such. Assassination as a social act was, therefore, not a recognized weapon in social conflict. The concepts of social conflict and of assassination as a weapon in that conflict both came to China from or through Russia (and France as well) with profound results. Had the Chinese paradigm previously contained formalized conceptions of either diachronic or synchronic conflict, social or individual, the impact of Russia or of the Anglo-Saxon West might have been different. The very absence of these concepts contributed to the weight of the Russian impact. On the other hand, the high degree of personalization of conflict already present in China ultimately lessened the impact of personifications of Anglo-Saxon concepts.

This argument is not meant to suggest that the paradigms characteristic of the Chinese world view did not change through time before the arrival in East Asia of Russia or the West. It is to suggest, rather, that in the Chinese paradigm certain symbols, ideas, or concepts simply did not exist, were not available, and therefore could not have changed. An example taken from the contemporary American view of China may serve for clarification. The American paradigmatic structure includes a category of contradictory good and evil, and this category cannot be left empty or vacant without causing extreme discomfort to be felt by all. The subcategory of bad or evil enemy is well-developed, and in recent years it has been filled successively by Germany and Japan, Russia, and now China, each filling the vacancy left by the departure of its predecessor. This is a very different matter from Russia's becoming a symbol of social redemption for Chinese. Russia did not just fill a vacancy; she added a new dimension to (or filled a lacuna in) the very structure of Chinese perception.

Historically, Russia's influence on China must be viewed as part of the larger impact of the West as a whole. From the point of view of the early Ch'ing dynasty, Moscow was nearer London and Amsterdam than it was to Peking, and today again the view from Peking is that Moscow is in the bourgeois, capitalist West. Russian institutions, concepts, and ideas were Western to China. Commercially and politically, especially after 1860, Russia took part in the general Western depredation of China. While on the one hand the impact of Russia on China was to a large extent determined by the configuration of Chinese perceptions, on the other it was determined by the structure of Western history.

In the late nineteenth and early twentieth centuries, Great Britain and the United States were societies without striking ideological conflicts. Americans and Englishmen themselves brought to China, or sent thither with their Chinese students, a view of the world that was primarily liberal. They did not introduce into China, because they could not, the ideological conflicts of the West that were not taking place within their own societies. But ideological conflict did develop in Moscow and, of course, in other places, such as Paris. London, England, and Peoria, Illinois, fought Moscow and Paris inside China, as it were. In the end, the victory went to Moscow and Paris. British- and American-educated Chinese who acted on the Chinese scene as liberals before 1949 tended to emigrate to Taiwan or to the United States in the face of the victorious communist revolution, while Russian- and French-educated Chinese tended to stay home to build a new society.

Consequently, the Russian impact on China can be understood in more than the purely parochial terms of a bilateral political or economic relationship. It is a simple fact that each culture exists in a context of other cultures: when changes occur in other cultures, any given culture is affected, minimally by a change in context, maximally by changes in the form and content of its own symbols. Lu Hsün's remarks concerning the impact of Russian literature on Chinese now take on a new meaning. Through Russian historical experience, as reported in the Chinese press or vicariously experienced by Chinese through Russian literature, Chinese perceived not Russian oppressed classes but the oppression of Chinese by other Chinese and foreigners. They viewed not Russian society with sympathy but Chinese society with anger. Russia itself, even with its legacy of imperialist relations with China, became a Chinese symbol as the Anglo-Saxon West never could or never did.

— 10 —

The Russian Impact on Japan

George Alexander Lensen

This essay was written as part of my research in the Soviet Union and Japan under the auspices of the Inter-University Committee on Travel Grants, the American Council of Learned Societies, the American Philosophical Society, and the National Endowment for the Humanities.

From the moment that Russians first set foot on Japanese soil in 1739, Japanese statesmen have been ever conscious of the proximity of Russia. "Guardians of Hakodate, beware! This is not the kind of age when only waves wash ashore," an eighteenth-century patriot warned his countrymen.[1]

Russia played a major role in drawing Japan out of the isolation in which she had sought shelter in the seventeenth century. In the present essay I propose to examine the relations between Russia and Japan in the diplomatic sphere, in the area of economics and trade, and in the field of cultural impact. In 1792-93 and in 1804-05 Russian envoys conferred with the Japanese. Though they did not establish commercial ties, they broke through the seclusion barrier without drawing fire and set the precedent for negotiation. The inept attempts of two young naval officers to frighten Japan into commercial relations by raiding her outlying possessions in 1806-07 and the tall tales told to the Japanese by a naval captain whom the Japanese seized and held captive in 1811-13 in retribution for the attacks aroused Japanese alarm. Increasingly the Japanese were forced to think about the heretofore unthinkable re-entry of Japan into world affairs.

Many Japanese looked upon Russia as a menace. They advocated strong defensive measures, including territorial expansion, to keep

338

the Russians at a distance. The colonization of Hokkaido was hastened as a matter of strengthening the northern frontier against Russian encroachment. Other Japanese saw in Russia strength and opportunity. They proposed that concessions be made to Russia in exchange for Russian protection against other countries. In the early 1850s, when the American Commodore Matthew C. Perry was negotiating with the Japanese, the Japanese told the Russian Vice-Admiral Putiatin, who was conferring with them in another part of Japan, that because Russia was a great country with boundaries adjacent to theirs, they considered her as a defense against other states.[2] Commodore Perry's refusal to join forces with the Russians, as Putiatin had proposed, enabled the Japanese to play the United States and Russia against each other, a policy to which they were to revert repeatedly.

DIPLOMATIC IMPACT

If we look at East Asian international relations as a whole, we can perceive a Russo-Japanese-American triangle. If we focus our attention on relations between Russia and Japan only, we get the impression of a pendulum swinging back and forth between the extremes of amity and enmity. But while the character of the relations changed from time to time, they remained constant in the sense that Russia was always a major factor in the considerations of Japanese policymakers.

Until 1875 the initiative in Russo-Japanese relations lay in Russian hands. Russian explorers pushed across the continent and across the ocean to Japan; Russian envoys entreated the Japanese to establish commercial relations and to define the territorial limits of their empires. The Treaty of Edo in 1858 authorized trade between the two states. The Treaty of Shimoda had begun the delineation of the frontier in 1855. The Kuril Islands had been divided, the northern ones being declared Russian, the southern ones Japanese; no agreement had been reached concerning Sakhalin, and the island had been left in joint possession. To lessen the friction that such an arrangement produced, the two countries came to a "final" agreement in 1875. By the Sakhalin-Kuril Islands Exchange Treaty the entire Kuril archipelago was recognized as Japanese and the entire island of Sakhalin as Russian. With Russia's main objectives—the establishment of trade and the delineation of the frontier—attained at last, an era of peaceful coexistence seemed at hand.[3]

The next two decades were peaceful. Although the seeds of future conflict were sown at this time as Russia and Japan both industrialized, the Russians did not yet appreciate the rising power of Japan nor pursue an active policy of their own in Korea or in Manchuria that might have threatened the Japanese. In fact, Russia supported Japanese action to make Korea independent of Manchu China, for she regarded China as the stronger and potentially more dangerous neighbor. There were some disputes about fishery between Russia and Japan, but on the whole Russian policy toward Japan was passive. Both economically and militarily Russia's position in the Far East was incredibly weak; her navy depended on Japanese harbors for year-round operation. Thus she conciliated the Japanese, hoping only to preserve as long as possible the general status quo in the Far East.

It was the smashing victory of Japan in the Sino-Japanese War of 1894-95 and the magnitude of Japanese demands and the ambitions they betrayed that startled the Russians out of their lethargy. They did not, however, assume an anti-Japanese stance at once but deliberated whether they could best protect their interests by working with Japan or against Japan, a question that was to arise repeatedly in later years. The Treaty of Shimonoseki, which ended the Sino-Japanese War, provided for the cession to Japan of the Liaotung Peninsula, including Port Arthur. This would have given the Japanese a beachhead for further expansion on the continent. Russia could accept the situation and demand from China an ice-free port for herself as "compensation"; or she could side with China and block the Japanese advance. Left to herself, Russia would probably have made common cause with Japan, but the offer of support from Germany and France swayed her to step athwart Japan's path of expansion. Her purpose was twofold: to keep Japanese forces at a distance while she strengthened her armaments and to bolster her own prestige and influence in China.

As the Russian fleet assembled in the Pacific Ocean and as Russian armies prepared for an invasion of Manchuria, the Japanese backed down before the demands of the three powers. But the tripartite intervention profoundly affected Japanese thinking. Not only was it brought home to Japanese statesmen that, all noble pronouncements notwithstanding, might was right everywhere but also that military success must be safeguarded by careful diplomatic preparations.

The active policy that Russia had assumed to contain the expansion of Japan continued of its own momentum. Realizing that she could no longer depend on Japanese ports as wintering places for her fleet, she turned to the acquisition of an ice-free naval base. In 1898 she occupied the very territory that she had denied Japan. Meanwhile she had taken advantage of her "championship" of China to conclude a defensive alliance with China against Japan (1896). By the terms of this agreement, all Chinese ports were opened to Russian warships in the event of operations against Japan, and construction of the Trans-Manchurian railway was authorized to expedite the movement of Russian troops. When the Boxer Uprising spilled into Manchuria in 1900 and Russian engineers and railroad workers and their families were attacked and Russian property destroyed, Russian armies hastened to the rescue.[4]

Meanwhile the Russians had begun to counteract Japanese intrigues in Korea. The flight of the Korean king, whose wife had been murdered by the Japanese, into the Russian legation in 1896 played into Russian hands. A series of agreements between Russia and Japan in 1896 and 1898 acknowledged Japan's special economic interests in the peninsula, but Russia refused to recognize Korea as a Japanese sphere of influence in exchange for Japanese recognition of Manchuria as a Russian sphere of influence.

The Russian drive into Manchuria and Korea was actually less determined than usually pictured. Russian resolution and vigilance faded at an early stage, and Russian objectives became entangled in a mass of red tape. There was divergence in Russian counsels and confusion of authority. But the very presence of Russians in Manchuria and Korea made a sufficient impact on Japanese policymakers to persuade a majority of them that war between the two countries sooner or later was inevitable.

In February 1904, believing that time was on the side of Russia, Japan struck suddenly. Her decision, however, had not been hasty. She had been preparing for the conflict since 1895 and had insured Russia's isolation by an alliance with Great Britain in 1902.[5]

Japan's victory shook the Russian Empire to its foundations. It did not, however, eliminate Russia as a major influence on Japanese policy. Though beaten and on the verge of revolution, Russia remained a great power. The Treaty of Portsmouth gave Japan important fishery rights and acknowledged Japanese domination of Korea and South Manchuria; it gave her no indemnity[6] and no Russian territory except for the southern half of Sakhalin, which had once been Japanese. The war demonstrated the futility of rivalry and bolstered the arguments of Russian and Japanese statesmen who favored Russo-Japanese collaboration. American efforts to share in the exploitation of Manchuria contributed to a Russo-Japanese rapprochement.

From 1907 to the outbreak of the Communist Revolution in November of 1917, Russia and Japan drew ever closer together. By 1916 their relationship had matured into a full-fledged alliance, Russia and Japan agreeing to cooperate in preventing any third power hostile to them from gaining domination over China; and if, in the process of taking such preventive action, either of them should become involved in war, the other would come to its partner's assistance upon request.[7] As Russia was cut off from her Western suppliers during the First World War, she became partly dependent on Japanese rifles, guns, and equipment. The magnitude of Russian needs boosted the Japanese economy as the Japanese government shipped to Russia all stocks of ammunition not needed for her own defense, and geared the entire output of several government arsenals and private factories to the needs of the Russian war machine.[8] By the time the revolution broke out, Japan had acquired a significant economic stake in the Russian Empire. She had purchased over a quarter of a billion yen worth of Russian government bonds. She had a prosperous trade with Vladivostok and Harbin, and there were branch offices of Japanese companies with Japanese nationals in major cities in Manchuria and Eastern Siberia. As one Russian contemporary complained, Japan had received "nothing else than the surrender of the vast Far Eastern region to full exploitation."[9]

When the communists denounced all secret treaties concluded by the imperial government, including those in which Russia and Japan had defined their respective interests, and refused to honor tsarist debts, they struck a heavy blow at legitimate Japanese interests in Russia as well as at Japan's less legitimate but determined desire to gain control over Manchuria and China. Japan's reaction was not immediate. She debated for a while whether it would be wiser, if the Bolsheviks stood to win, to conciliate them and renew a Russo-Japanese understanding, or whether she should take advantage of the Russian civil war to extend her influence over the region east of Lake Baikal.[10] The Japanese chose the latter course; and their intervention, like the intervention of the other Allied powers, was a fiasco. It cost the Japanese two-thirds as much as the Russo-Japanese War and netted them little. This defeat not only discredited the military temporarily at home, but in later years, when the military were in power again, the memory of it dulled their appetite for Siberia and contributed to the decision to expand southward.

The Soviet Union represented a much greater threat to the Japanese Empire than had tsarist Russia, for the Soviets sought to subvert the Japanese polity in the name of world revolution. Yet geographic relationships and economic needs were not altered by ideology. Japan required fishery grounds and oil, which the Soviets in 1925 were willing to share in exchange for Japanese recognition of their government and for the evacuation by Japan of northern Sakhalin. In the 1930s Japanese expansion into North China, North Manchuria, and Inner Mongolia precipitated a number of border clashes with Russian troops in which planes, tanks, and artillery were used by both sides, with casualties running high. In the summer of 1939 the clashes between the Japanese and the Russians erupted into an unofficial war, the troops from the Mongolian People's Republic fighting alongside Soviet troops. The strength and determination shown by the Russian forces at this time contributed to the deflection of Japanese efforts to Southeast Asia.[11]

When the tide of battle turned against Japan during the Pacific War, she made every effort to keep Russia out. By June of 1945 Japan was prepared to make territorial and economic concessions to the Soviet Union if she refrained from attacking Japan. But Russia had already made a deal with the Allies at Yalta, and true to her commitment entered the war against Japan. Brief as Russian participation was, it made a considerable impact on Japan. Prisoners whom she took were subject to thorough communist indoctrination before being repatriated. Russia regained South Sakhalin, which she had lost during the Russo-Japanese War, and the northern Kuril Islands, which she had traded for South Sakhalin in 1875. In addition to this, Russia received the southern Kuril Islands, which had never been Russian territory. This gave her a powerful bargaining position in years to come, when Japan actively reentered world affairs. Today the boundary issue commands headlines whenever Russian and Japanese officials meet.

The diplomatic impact of Russia on Japan, briefly sketched above, is relatively well known. The economic and cultural influences, on the other hand, have been studied little. Admittedly they are less dramatic and less extensive. Yet they constitute a vital part of the total picture of the Russian impact on Japan and deserve our attention.

ECONOMIC IMPACT

The Russian push toward Japan in the eighteenth and early nineteenth centuries had been motivated largely by economic considerations. The populous and fertile island empire had seemed ideally situated to supply needed commodities to the sparsely inhabited and underdeveloped regions of the Russian Far East and of Russian America. But the brisk trade that Russian and Japanese merchants had expected to follow the opening up of Japan had failed to materialize. This failure resulted partly from deliberate obstacles placed in the way of all trade by Japanese officials, who had been forced into foreign relations against their will. The prohibition in the commercial treaty of 1858 against the export of rice and wheat, which Russia desired most, hindered the development of Russo-Japanese trade, as did Russian lack of interest in Japanese silk and tea, Japan's major exports at that time. Russian inability to supply machinery and manufactured products from European Russia at competitive prices formed another hindrance. Hopes for increased Russo-Japanese commerce were aroused by the Kuril Islands-Sakhalin exchange of 1875, for the enormous fish resources of Sakhalin seemed to offer the major item of trade. But, as matters developed, the Russians were unable to compete with Japanese fishermen.[12]

In 1888 Russian exports received a boost with the sale of kerosene to Japan. Kerosene, the use of which was spreading rapidly in Japan, remained Russia's major export to that country until the

Russo-Japanese War, when it was displaced by American and British kerosene. This commodity exceeded in value the rice, flour, and wheat imports purchased from Japan. Yet even with the sale of kerosene, Russo-Japanese transactions remained insignificant both in terms of Japanese trade with other countries and in terms of the potentials of trade between Russia and Japan.

The potentials for expanded trade between the two countries were brought home by the fact that far more Russian and Japanese products were actually exchanged than the statistics indicated and that foreign middlemen dominated Russo-Japanese trade. The indirect purchase and transport of goods—in the name of foreign firms, often by way of Europe—went undocumented in the annals of Russo-Japanese commerce. But the strongest argument for an optimistic view of trade potential lay in the construction of the Chinese Eastern Railway. It was hoped that with the extension of the Trans-Siberian Railway at Vladivostok, Russia might become the natural intermediary of East-West commerce.

At the beginning of the twentieth century Russian trade with Japan still lagged far behind that of other countries. In 1902 Russia ranked eighth in exports to Japan and ninth in imports from Japan.[13] Russian trade with Japan differed not only in volume but also in place and in character with that of other powers. While most foreign merchants had moved from Hokkaido to the main island, Russians continued their dealings with Japan primarily through merchants based in Hokkaido. The merchants of industrially advanced states brought manufactured goods, which could be sold more readily in the populous and developed ports in the south. The fish from Russia's nearby Priamur region, on the other hand, could be marketed in Hokkaido, whose ocean treasures had been depleted by Japanese fishermen. In turn Russia obtained from Hakodate foodstuffs needed in her own underdeveloped regions, notably rice and fruit (particularly apples), and salt for salting fish.[14]

The balance of trade between Russia and Japan fluctuated. In the early years Russian imports from Japan had exceeded exports to Japan. By the beginning of the twentieth century, however, Russia had established a favorable balance of trade. The Russo-Japanese War of 1904-05 interrupted trade relations. Once relations were resumed, however, the balance shifted in favor of Japan.

This trend of mounting imports from Japan and declining exports to Japan continued for a decade and a half.

The steady rise in Japanese sales to Russia was due to the accelerated industrialization of Japan and to Japan's concerted effort to export, as well as to the various economic privileges obtained by Japan in the wake of her victory in the Russo-Japanese War. The free port arrangement in effect in the Priamur region furthered Japanese trade expansion. Russia, meanwhile, being preoccupied with internal problems and with the traditional European market, made no serious attempt to develop commercial relations with Japan. Russian merchants were unfamiliar with Japanese tastes and demands; they did not know the language; they had neither the desire nor the capital to expand their activities in this direction. The high cost of railway transport and the boycott of Russian goods by Japanese nationalists made their task even more difficult.

While Japanese foreign commerce in general expanded rapidly in the decade following the Russo-Japanese War, trade with Russia increased slowly. On the eve of World War I it amounted still to only one percent of Japan's total foreign trade. The major items exported by Russia at this time were oil cakes and beans from Manchuria as well as lumber; Japan sent primarily raw silk (for European Russia) and fruits and vegetables as well as charcoal (for Asiatic Russia). It was the First World War that gave an enormous boost to Russo-Japanese trade. The closing of the Black Sea and Baltic ports cut Russia off from her traditional markets and sources of supply. The interruption of internal communications and commerce left her with shortages in one area and surpluses in another. Thus she required chemical and apothecary products, rice, salt, and various metals and metal goods, while having extra raw materials that Japan needed. When Vladivostok was made a free port during the war, trade skyrocketed. Practically overnight Russia became Japan's number one customer.[15]

Throughout the civil war and the Japanese intervention in Siberia, Russo-Japanese trade continued on a large scale. Consumer goods were a major item of Russian import in the years from 1914 to 1924. But the situation was abnormal; with the end of hostilities and the consolidation of communist power in Asiatic Russia, the volume of commerce dropped sharply. Yet the feasibility of large-scale Russo-Japanese trade had been demonstrated. As "abnormal" conditions were to become increasingly normal and planned economies were to facilitate bilateral commercial exchanges on a vast scale, Japanese and Soviet economists and businessmen were to revert repeatedly to the subject of massive Russo-Japanese trade.

"Normal" trade relations were resumed between Russia and Japan in 1922, even though Japan did not yet recognize the Soviet regime. The amount of commerce was sharply reduced and the balance of trade was reversed. Soviet-Japanese trade differed in the nature as well as in the quantity of goods exchanged, as the U.S.S.R. tried to develop her Far Eastern regions industrially. The motivation was not merely economic, but political and ideological as well. The Soviet Union wanted to industrialize Asiatic Russia as a showplace of socialist building to impress and win over the neighboring colonial and "semicolonial" peoples. She continued to purchase some foodstuffs, notably tea and seafood, but thirty percent of her imports in 1926-27 consisted of spun materials such as nets and ropes for the fishing industry in the Okhotsk-Kamchatka region and the Amur estuary. She bought also ores, metals, metal products, lumber, and chemical products (mainly iodine and camphor). Russian exports consisted primarily of lumber and fish products as well as agricultural produce and oil cakes.[16]

While the volume of Russo-Japanese trade exceeded the prewar figures, the ratio of this trade to the total trade of Russia and Japan remained about the same—approximately one percent of the turnover of either country. Most Soviet economists, like their tsarist predecessors, favored the expansion of Russo-Japanese trade and demonstrated the feasibility of such a policy. The Soviet Union had grave foreign exchange problems; an increase in Soviet exports to Japan would enable her to obtain additional fishery equipment and needed products. She was already buying 15 to 20 percent of Japan's green tea exports, 60 percent of her iodine exports, and 80 percent of her fishing nets exports. Japanese economists also spoke highly of the possibilities of Russo-Japanese trade and pointed particularly to Russian resources in lumber and oil.[17]

With the growing industrialization of the U.S.S.R., a further change occurred in the character of trade. Shipments of fish, lumber, and agricultural produce from Russia declined while industrial exports rose. Oil, charcoal, manganese, asbestos, fertilizers, ferrous metal, and chemical and pharmaceutical goods that had once been

imported from Japan, now were sold to Japan. By 1930 industrial
exports accounted for almost 73 percent of Soviet sales to Japan,
and in 1932 for over 86 percent.

Soviet exports to Japan continued to exceed imports from Japan
until 1933. The total volume of trade between the two countries
continued to increase until 1930. Following the Japanese attack
on neighboring Manchuria, however, the renewed deterioration of
political relations between the two powers put a damper on economic dealings. But in 1935, partly in consequence of this friction,
the Soviet Union sold the Chinese Eastern Railway to the Japanese
puppet state of Manchukuo. The impact of this event on Russo-
Japanese trade was as dramatic as had been the impact of the First
World War. According to the terms of sale, only one-third of the
purchase price was to be paid in cash; two-thirds was to be paid in
Japanese and Manchurian goods. Consequently Russian imports
from Japan showed a remarkable increase, notably in 1936 and
1937, mostly in the form of machinery, apparatus, means of transportation, electrical equipment, building materials, and nonferrous
metals. As in the case of the First World War, the stimulus of the
sale of the railway was only temporary. In both instances serious
political differences and actual military clashes stunted the bur-
geoning trade.[18]

The Pacific War cut trade relations between the two countries.
The Japanese merchant fleet was sunk and Japan's economy was
crushed. The outbreak of the Cold War complicated the situation.
The United States, which occupied Japan until 1952 and maintained "security forces" there for a number of years afterward,
frowned upon Japanese trade with communist countries. The absence of a peace treaty between the Soviet Union and Japan—first
because the U.S.S.R. would not agree to the terms of the San
Francisco Conference, then because Japan wanted the return of
some of the islands taken by the Soviet Union—further delayed
the resumption of commercial relations. But the full economic recovery of Japan and the remarkable growth of her industry made
her increasingly interested in expanding her markets. In 1954 an
association for the promotion of Russo-Japanese trade was formed
in the Diet; in 1955 over thirty Japanese firms joined in an association of Japanese-Soviet trade to promote commerce between the
two countries. In 1956 Japan reestablished diplomatic relations

with the Soviet Union, even though the two countries could not agree on a peace treaty. In October of that year Japan concluded a commercial treaty with the Soviet Union that became effective upon the exchange of ratifications in May 1958—a century after the conclusion of the first commercial agreement between the two countries. This treaty provided for reciprocal most-favored-nation treatment in trade matters, duties, navigation, and protection of property and persons. Japan agreed to the establishment of a Soviet Trade Mission in Japan, foreign trade being a monopoly of the Soviet government. Both agreed to the arbitration of disputes that might arise in trade matters.[19]

The "normalization" of trade in 1956 did not result in large-scale transactions between the two powers, partly because Japan could not afford to alienate the United States, whose commercial patronage was essential. But a more important reason was the relative backwardness of the Russian economy and Soviet insistence that Japan buy from her as much as she sold, even though the U.S.S.R. lacked what Japan desired. While the Soviet Union wanted ships, heavy machinery, and steel piping she could still offer only such primary products as lumber, iron ore, and petroleum. Nevertheless, the prospects of a vast Russian market continued to excite the imagination of Japanese businessmen, particularly after Premier Nikita Khrushchev in 1962 publicly invited Japanese participation in the development of Siberia.[20]

A new commercial treaty, signed in 1963 to cover a period of three years, provided the Soviet Union with more Japanese tankers, dry-cargo ships, fishing vessels, machinery, and instruments in exchange for the usual crude oil, timber, coal, asbestos, pig iron, minerals, and chemicals. When the two countries signed another trade agreement in 1966 covering a period of five years, the Soviet Union expressed the hope that Soviet-Japanese trade would reach two-and-a-quarter billion dollars during this period.[21]

The hostility of China toward the Soviet Union and Japan, as well as Japan's determination not to be dependent on the United States or on any other power, encouraged a rapprochement between the Japanese and the Soviets. If there was no discernible Russian impact on the Japanese economy in terms of actual trade, except for the brief stimulus during the First World War and later in conjunction with the sale of the Chinese Eastern Railway, there was a definite impact on Japanese thinking in terms of the potentials of trade between the two countries. Considering the fact that foreign policy is often determined not by events but by expectations, the impact of the continued confidence in the prospects of Russia's trade is more significant than statistics would lead one to believe.

The decline of trade following the reestablishment of "normal" relations between the Soviet Union and Japan in 1925 did not mean a loss of interest in economic contacts on either side. What it did signify was a change in the character of economic relations, with concessions for the exploitation of oil and coal resources attracting most attention.

Japan was poor in raw materials and fuel; yet her industries and ships were steadily demanding them in greater and greater quantities. In 1928, for example, she consumed about a million tons of petroleum, while producing only about a quarter of a million tons. She thus had to import some 750,000 tons of petroleum, almost three-fourths of it from the United States, the rest mostly from the Dutch East Indies. While her demands for fuel increased, her sources of supply became less certain. As relations between the United States and Japan deteriorated, her dependence on American petroleum became as hazardous as the reliance of the Russian navy on Japanese harbors had been in the late nineteenth century. The Geneva Conference had failed to reduce armaments, and a naval race was on. Japan felt compelled to secure the necessary fuel in the event of war.

One nearby source of oil and coal was Sakhalin. Japan owned the southern half of the island, but the northern part was still in Russian hands. Ostracized by most of the world, the Soviet Union on her part desired diplomatic and economic relations with Japan. At the same time she was not yet in a position to exploit her distant resources. As Japan pressed for oil and coal concessions on Sakhalin, the Soviet Union agreed.[22]

In 1925, the U.S.S.R. granted to Japanese concerns recommended by the Japanese government the concession for the exploitation of 50 percent in area of each of the oil fields on North Sakhalin that had been exploited by the Japanese since their temporary occupation of the area during the Siberian intervention. Furthermore, the Soviet Union allowed Japanese concerns to prospect for new oil fields in a large coastal section of North Sakhalin and to exploit 50 percent in area of any oil fields discovered by them. In addition, the Soviet Union granted Japan coal-mining concessions on North Sakhalin. The oil and coal concessions were given for a period of forty-five years. Under the terms of the agreement the Soviet Union was to receive an annual royalty of 5 to 8 percent of the gross output of the coal fields and 5 to 15 percent of the gross output of the oil fields, a figure that could be raised to 45 percent of the gross output in the case of a gusher. A specific schedule was to be fixed in the contracts.[23]

In June 1926 the Japanese consolidated their oil exploitation of Sakhalin in a new joint-stock company, whose stockholders included the biggest oil-mining concerns of Japan. The results of Japanese operations exceeded all expectations. In 1926 the Japanese obtained under 30,000 tons of oil, the following year close to 70,000 tons. By 1928 they expected to get over 150,000 tons, or already 60 percent of the entire oil production of Japan proper. By 1930 they were close to 200,000 tons.

Japanese coal mining on North Sakhalin also dated back to the temporary occupation of this part of the island. While production increased from about 120,000 tons of coal in 1927 to about 186,000 tons in 1935-36, it was curtailed in 1937 to the current needs of the company. The Japanese justified a halt in some of their operations on the grounds that Soviet officialdom made it impossible for them to operate efficiently, but the Russians accused the Japanese of hurting the Soviet economic organizations that depended on the work and income of the Japanese concession.[24]

In addition to oil and coal the Japanese were allowed to exploit timber in the Russian Far East. In April of 1927 they received a concession for an area of over a million hectares along the north coast of the Maritime territory, bordering Sovetskaia Gavan'.

The general deterioration of Soviet-Japanese relations in the 1930s eventually extended to Sakhalin. Although the Soviet Union in 1936 extended for five years the eleven-year exclusive oil exploration rights she had given the Japanese as part of the general forty-five-year oil concession, she soon began to complain that Japanese companies were violating Soviet safety regulations, were employing a higher percentage of Japanese labor than stipulated,

were building oil pipe-lines without prior approval, and were forti-
fying South Sakhalin, although they had pledged not to do so. Japanese countercomplaints and demands were rejected by the Soviet
Union, and as Japan became increasingly eager to assure the neutrality of the Soviet Union in the approaching struggle with the United
States and Great Britain, the Russians pressed for the termination
of the concessions. But although Foreign Minister Matsuoka at the
time of the signing of the Soviet-Japanese Neutrality Pact in April
of 1941 promised in writing to solve the question in a matter of
months, Japan clung to the concession as long as possible. By 1944
the fortunes of war had forced Japan to placate the Soviet Union,
and in March of that year she surrendered the concessions twenty-
six years ahead of schedule.[25] While they had lasted, the concessions had strengthened the Japanese economy and had held out
promise of greater independence in international relations.

The products of the sea nourish Japan, and access to the fishing
grounds of Northeastern Asia has therefore been a vital Japanese
objective. When Japan surrendered her territorial claims to South
Sakhalin in 1875, she did not abdicate her economic interests in
the region.

The fisheries of Sakhalin and the coastal region of the mainland
were as vital—or at least potentially as vital—to the economy of
Russia as of Japan. On the world market, Russia was second only
to the United States in the volume of fish business. For the Russian Far East, fishery was more than a potential source of wealth.
The sparsely populated regions of the Russian Pacific coast already
lived on fish, and the development of the fish industry was basic
to the colonization of the Russian Far East. Fearful of the presence of an element "alien" to her interests, Russia thus sought to
"phase out" Japanese fishery on Sakhalin Island.[26]

The Japanese did not object in principle to Russian imposition
of fishery permits, but they took issue with the short term of the
leases that the Russians were prepared to grant and with the rate
of the duty they demanded. The regulations that were finally issued in 1885 and that governed Japanese fishing in Sakhalin waters
until 1894 provided for five-year licensing of fishing grounds, re-
newable for another five years. In 1894 licenses were reduced to a

period of three years, but the Russians threw open to Japanese fishing heretofore barred grounds along the northeastern coast and removed the surtax on fish meal.

During the negotiations between Russia and Japan in May 1895 concerning a treaty of commerce and navigation, and again in October of that year, Japan proposed the conclusion of a full-fledged fishery treaty. Russia declined because Russian fishery interests in the Maritime Region were still in their infancy and the Finance Ministry, which sought to develop the Russian fish industry, feared that the Japanese would gain a monopoly. Russian fears were not unfounded. By 1899 the Japanese employed 5,000 workers on 269 Sakhalin fishing grounds. They occupied practically all the fishing grounds on the southern and western coast or eight percent of all the fishing grounds of the island. This meant that Sakhalin would rapidly revert to Japanese domination. As a countermeasure the local Russian authorities cancelled the lease on some of the choicest Japanese fishing grounds and issued new fishing regulations which gave absolute preference to Russian applicants. Now it had become Japan's turn to worry about her legitimate fishing rights, and she renewed her demands for a fishery treaty.

In January 1902 the Japanese government sent a draft fishery treaty to the Russian government. It proposed to leave fishing regulations unchanged till the end of 1906; thereafter fishing grounds were to be awarded to the highest bidder without regard to nationality. Although Japan pressed for a speedy reply, Russia moved very slowly, extending the Marine Products Regulations for a year while she deliberated. Increasingly upset by mounting restrictions on their fishery on Sakhalin and in the Maritime Region, the Japanese had to accept annual extensions of the old regulations for 1903 and 1904.[27] The "reasonable and definite method" of deliberation on which the Russians insisted in this as in other matters of dispute between the two countries became entwined in a Gordian knot of procrastination, which the Japanese finally cut with the sword.

Japan's victory in the Russo-Japanese War gained her the southern half of Sakhalin Island with all its fisheries as well as fishery rights elsewhere. These gains were as important as the financial indemnity that Russia refused to pay, for they assured Japan of cheap food for her population and plentiful fertilizer for her crops.

The fishery convention of 1907, which grew out of the treaty of peace, gave the Japanese equal rights with Russian subjects in bidding for coastal fishery lots. Rivers and inlets were reserved for Russian exploitation. The granting to the Japanese of equal rights along the coast was tantamount to giving them a disguised concession, for there was no Russian capital that could exploit the fishing lots and no foreign enterprises could compete with the Japanese in waters adjacent to their own country. The Japanese received the additional advantage of being allowed to proceed to the fishing grounds directly from Japan, the necessary papers to be issued by Russian consuls abroad. Permitted to bring their own inexpensive supplies, equipment, and labor and to move about freely from one place to another, they were able to organize their fishery on a large scale.

By 1909 the Japanese had in Russian waters 221 fishing vessels with a displacement of over 40,000 tons, as compared with 6 Russian vessels with a tonnage of 4,600. The Japanese employed 6,000 crewmen and fishermen, the Russians 300. The Japanese caught over 70 million pounds of fish worth almost 3 million rubles. For this they paid to the Russian treasury a little over 100,000 rubles in lease money. It was the failure of their government to realize a greater gain from the leases that irked some Russians most and caused them to dub their fishery enterprises as "caterers" of the Japanese.[28]

The fishery convention of 1907 expired in 1919. By this time Russo-Japanese relations had run the full cycle from hostility to friendship and back to hostility. As the communist government refused to honor tsarist treaties and commitments and as Tokyo did not recognize the new regime, which was not yet in control of the eastern regions, the Japanese continued fishing without any agreement. At the time of the Siberian Intervention, when Japanese troops occupied the Russian Far East, Japan presented Seventeen Demands to the representatives of the Far Eastern Republic at the Dairen Conference (1921-22). Among these were suggestions for a new fishery convention, which would have given the Japanese broad rights of cabotage along the Russian shore, something they had desired for years.[29]

The Soviets, who emerged victorious in the civil war and annexed the Far Eastern Republic following the Japanese withdrawal, did not grant the right of cabotage; but the temporary regulations that they drew up in 1924 left the Japanese in a more advantageous position than ever. The regulations of 1924 did not take into consideration the basic changes that had occurred in the Russian economic structure. Foreign trade had become a state monopoly and the fishery industry had been brought into a complex network of planning and regulations subject to the tax policy of the Ministry of Finance and the wage policy of the Ministry of Commerce. Thus, while the Japanese, independent of a state monopoly on trade and unhampered by domestic taxes and licensing, furnished their fisheries with the necessary supplies at the lowest cost, their Russian counterparts were forced to bring a large part of their supplies from the Russian interior. Whatever this may have done for the economy as a whole, it made it impossible for the Russian fish industry to compete with the Japanese.

The Soviet-Japanese Convention embodying the Basic Principles of Interrelations between the Union of Soviet Socialist Republics and Japan, concluded at Peking in January 1925, recognized the Treaty of Portsmouth as remaining in full force. It provided for the "revision of the fishery treaty of 1907, taking into consideration those changes which might have taken place in the general conditions since the said fishing treaty was concluded." The new fishery convention, which was concluded in 1928, continued Japanese fishing rights in Russian waters and the lease of lots by public auction "without any discrimination being made between Japanese subjects and citizens of the Union of Soviet Socialist Republics." The Japanese also received permission to establish and operate canning factories. Yet there was no longer full freedom of competition. In an attempt to plan distribution the Soviets withheld (with Japanese consent) a number of lots from auction and excluded the Japanese from thirty-seven inlets. Furthermore, the Soviet Union reserved the right to set fishing norms to protect the multiplication of fish in Soviet waters.[30]

The convention of 1928 failed to resolve the fishery question. Squabbles and differences continued. The small, helpless Japanese fishery enterprises of pre-World War I days had been displaced by large capitalist firms that banded together in three major fishery associations. The Soviets resented the fact that the Japanese met their state monopoly with a united front, for small enterprises had not objected to Soviet restrictions. It was large concerns such as the Nichiro Gyogyo Company, whose fishery production was one and a half times larger than that of all Soviet enterprises combined (and twenty-four times larger in the production of canned goods) that clamored for unrestricted fishing rights, arguing that the Treaty of Portsmouth took precedence over the convention of 1928.

The convention of 1928 was to run until 1936. At Japanese request a revision was prepared, but was not signed by the Soviet Union when Japan joined the Anti-Comintern Pact with Germany (1936). The original convention of 1928 was extended at first to the end of 1936 and then annually with minor modifications through 1943.[31] When Japan agreed to the termination of her coal and petroleum concessions on North Sakhalin in March 1944, the Soviet Union extended the fishery convention of 1928 for another five years. She limited Japanese operations, however, by reducing the number of fishing lots, increasing the lease rental, and removing any restrictions on the activity of Soviet organizations. Most importantly, she forbade all fishery by the Japanese or any other foreigners in various sea regions, specified by the Soviet government in July 1941, for the duration of World War II.

With the entrance of the Soviet Union in the war against Japan, Russo-Japanese fishery came to a standstill. The return of South Sakhalin and the surrender to the Soviet Union of the entire Kuril archipelago by defeated Japan made the Japanese more dependent than ever on fishing in Soviet territorial waters. Without any agreement they resumed their fishery forays into waters near the shores of Kamchatka and the Kuril Islands. To protect her salmon fishery the Soviet Union in March 1956 proclaimed regulations limiting the amount of salmon that could be caught during the spawning period in the Bering Sea, in the Pacific Ocean adjoining the Kamchatka peninsula, and in the Sea of Okhotsk.

In May 1956 the Soviet Union and Japan concluded a new ten-year fishery convention that went into effect upon the official termination of the state of war between the two countries and the resumption of diplomatic relations in October of the same year. In July 1966 an agreement of fishery cooperation was initiated for a period of three years. This provided for cooperation between the two countries in increasing their fish catch in inland waters and in research on fishing resources as well as for technical cooperation. A joint communique issued at this time announced that the Fishery Agreement of 1956 would be renewed.[32]

Russian policy regarding the fishery question has been of vital importance to Japan. The impact of Russian actions in allowing or forbidding the Japanese to exploit Russian waters has been both economic and political. Soviet control of fishing areas vital to Japan remains a potential source of either friction or rapprochement.

CULTURAL IMPACT

Orthodox missionaries to Japan disseminated Russian concepts along with Christianity. The first Orthodox church in Japan, built in Hakodate in 1859, was to serve the Russian consulate and Russian community alone; but Father Nikolai (Kasatkin), who assumed the ministry of the Russian community in 1861, came with a missionary purpose. Although the propagation of Christianity was as yet forbidden, he converted a number of educated Hakodate residents and through them spread the Orthodox faith to other regions. The former Shinto priest and fencing master Sawabe Takuma, who became his faithful co-worker Pavel (Paul), was particularly effective in Sendai.

In 1870 a spiritual "mission" was formally established in Japan, with posts in Tokyo, Kyoto, and Nagasaki as well as in Hakodate. Nikolai, who headed the mission as archimandrite, moved to Tokyo (1872). Nikolai had spent the first seven years of his stay in Japan studying the Japanese language. During the half-century that he remained in the country he translated many Orthodox works into Japanese. Father Anatolii, who succeeded him in Hakodate, assisted in translating the liturgy into Japanese. One of Father Anatolii's contributions was the organization of a church choir. A psalmist and then a professional music teacher taught the Japanese how to sing in harmony. The lessons were not confined to sacred works, and Russian choral instruction in Hakodate and later in Tokyo influenced modern Japanese music.[33]

Japanese were drawn to the church by free instruction in the Russian language as well as in music. The fear of Japanese officials that the missionaries, the head of whose church was the Russian emperor, were subverting the political loyalties of the people contributed to anti-Christian persecutions in 1872. Although the Japanese government rescinded the centuries-old prohibition against Christianity in 1875, Japanese suspicion remained rife. Like Soviet historians in later years, Japanese nationalists regarded the priests as agents of the tsarist government. Nikolai, who became bishop in 1880, sought to allay Japanese mistrust by ordaining a native clergy and by keeping the number of Russian missionaries to a minimum. During the Russo-Japanese War of 1904-05 he specifically urged Japanese converts to remain loyal to their fatherland. But churchmen in Russia did express the expectation that the spread of the Orthodox faith in Japan would benefit Russian foreign policy.[34]

The major means of propagating the Orthodox faith were Russian schools in Japan. The catechist schools produced men who could disseminate the church teachings. But Russian-language instruction benefited converts and nonconverts alike. The first of these schools was established in Hakodate in 1871, the second in Tokyo the following year. The Tokyo school actually evolved into three schools: a catechist school, where catechists were trained to spread the Orthodox word among their countrymen; a translator school, to prepare translators of religious writings from Russian into Japanese; and a seminary, which at first was merely a school of Russian language and elementary studies for anyone who wanted to study Russian for any reason. It was the last-named that attracted most students. In 1875 a school for girls was added, patterned after one established in Hakodate.[35]

In 1880 a literary circle was formed by educated Japanese who knew the Russian language well. The group called itself the Aiai-sha or Love-love company, whose purpose was to publish the *Church Gazette.* Though the newspaper was dedicated to the dissemination of "scholarly and religious truths favorable to Christianity," it printed much general information about Russian life and culture. In 1892 the girls' school of the mission began publication of a new journal, *Oranishiki,* which contained many articles on Russian literature in general and Russian poetry in particular.

The Russian Cathedral of the Resurrection of Christ, which has become a well-known Tokyo landmark and is popularly known as "Nikolai-do," was begun by Nikolai in 1884 and completed seven years later, in 1891, at a cost of 300,000 rubles. Its library of

11,000 volumes contributed to Russian knowledge of Japan.[36] In 1908 Bishop Sergii (Tikhomirov) joined Archbishop Nikolai in the administration of the Orthodox Church in Japan, and became its head following the archbishop's demise in 1912. The Orthodox Church of Japan had by this time 266 congregations with a total of over 33,000 members.[37]

Although the Orthodox Church had been loyal to the tsar, it recognized the authority of the Provisional Government when the monarch abdicated in the spring of 1917. It would not, however, recognize the antireligious Bolshevik regime which overthrew the Provisional Government in the fall of the same year. The Orthodox Church sympathized with the Allied intervention and thus became in communist eyes "an obedient tool of the Japanese imperialists."[38]

With the victory of the communists in Russia, the Orthodox Church of Japan was deprived of public and private funds from Russia. At the same time, as fear of communism made everything Russian suspect, support for the church in Japan declined. The recognition by Sergii (by then archbishop) of the Moscow patriarchate contributed to this. Whereas there had been a steady increase in the number of converts before the Revolution, there was an equally pronounced decline thereafter. The White Russians who had sought refuge in Japan following the communist triumph had lost most of their possessions in Russia. In 1923 another disaster befell the mission. The great earthquake, which leveled much of Tokyo, severely damaged all the church buildings. Though Metropolitan Sergii with his meager funds succeeded in restoring the structures over a period of ten years, most of the mission's excellent library was lost forever. At the time of the Revolution the Orthodox Church of Japan had 174 houses of worship. By 1931 only 13 consecrated churches and 55 chapels were still in operation.[39]

In 1939 the Japanese government enacted new laws concerning the relations of the various religions with one another and with the state. While Christianity was treated on an equal basis with Shintoism and Buddhism, its foreign ties were limited. All sects had to work out their own bylaws for approval by the Japanese government. When Sergii failed to win consent for all the articles he had drafted and then refused to modify those that were rejected, he was forced to step down as metropolitan. He transferred the property of the Russian Orthodox Church to the Japanese national church and proposed three native candidates as possible successors.

The national Orthodox synod that met in the fall of 1940 was deeply divided. It cut the ties with the Moscow patriarchate but was unable to agree on a bishop. The government accepted a revised constitution in 1941 which provided that only native Japanese were allowed to hold a public position in the church. Ivan Ono, son-in-law of Pavel Sawabe, the first Japanese Orthodox priest and dean of the Tokyo congregation, became bishop. In honor of the founder of the Orthodox mission, Ivan Ono was named Bishop Nikolai. He was placed under the jurisdiction of the Metropolitan in Harbin in the puppet state of Manchukuo.[40]

During World War II the Japanese military did not think of the Orthodox priests as "tools of Japanese imperialism." On the contrary, they suspected them of loyalty to Russia. In May 1945 Sergii was hauled away by Japanese gendarmes. Accused of "economic espionage" on the grounds that he had told someone that Japanese money would soon be worthless, Sergii was imprisoned for thirty days. Upon his release he looked like a shadow of his former self. He died shortly afterward, just a few days before the end of the war.[41]

The general impoverishment of its erstwhile supporters by the war left the Japanese Orthodox Church prostrate. It could not have survived without "foreign" help. A special fund-raising committee that included Americans and Greeks as well as Russians was organized by Orthodox Christians. The American Metropolitan Council, the Federated Russian Orthodox Clubs of America, and various parishes and private individuals sent aid in the form of candles, incense, and regalia for the church and clothing and foodstuffs for the congregation. Yet in the long run American help was a mixed blessing, for it threatened to undermine Nikolai Kasatkin's efforts to make the Japanese church national, with leaders rising from its own ranks.

Following Japan's defeat Nikolai Ono renewed the ties with the Moscow patriarchate, a move that was opposed by part of the clergy. A new national synod was convened by the archpriest Samuil Uzawa, who was apparently elected metropolitan. When the quarrel was submitted to the Occupation authorities for solution, the matter was referred to Metropolitan Theophil Pashkovskii in New York, who appointed Bishop Veniamin Basaliga of Pittsburgh as head of the Japanese Church. Veniamin was succeeded by other bishops of the Russian Greek Orthodox Church of North America—Archbishops Irinei and Nikon, and in 1962 Bishop Vladimir. The Moscow faction meanwhile persisted in its opposition. During Irinei's tenure Nikolai Ono, backed by Soviet authorities, made a future attempt to obtain Irinei's position and the church property by a lawsuit. In December 1967 Father Sagayama visited Moscow.[42]

As we look back over the history of the Orthodox Church in Japan, we find that it exerted some influence in spreading Russian thought and culture. Even at the time of its greatest success, however, its impact on Japanese culture and on Japanese society was minimal. As in the case of economic relations, the religious impact of Russia on Japan remained a potential that never lived up to expectations.

With the victory of the Bolsheviks, state support of the Orthodox Church came to an end. But the communist regime, like its tsarist predecessor, financed the dissemination of Russian beliefs. If the Orthodox mission spread "Russianism," the Comintern did the same. Both the Orthodox Church and the Comintern were international in name more than in fact. Their mainspring was Russian. To be sure, communism was no more Russian in origin than Christianity. The development of Marxism in Japan antedated the Russian Revolution. But the establishment of the Communist Party in Japan was the result of communist success in Russia; and the type of communism that spread in Japan was essentially Russian in interpretation. The Comintern, which assisted and at times controlled the communist movement in Japan, was dominated by the Soviet government. It was on the specific instructions of the Comintern that the Communist Party was formally but secretly founded in Tokyo in the summer of 1922. It was under the guidance of the Comintern staff in Moscow that the program of the Japanese Communist Party was drafted. It was in Russia too, mainly at the Communist University for the Toilers of the East, that Japanese cadres were trained.[43]

While the Orthodox mission sought to change Japanese society gradually by persuasion, it was monarchist in outlook until the Revolution. The Comintern, on the other hand, advocated the overthrow of the Japanese government and tried to assist Soviet foreign policy by directives to its Japanese adherents. For example, recognition of the Soviet government by Japan was one of the planks of the Communist Party, determined in Moscow. Communist penetration of the labor movement increased the alarm of the Japanese authorities, and systematic suppression of the communist movement began shortly thereafter. When the Japanese leadership dissolved the Japanese Communist Party in 1924 in order to free its members from the stigma of belonging to an illegal party while they made more thorough preparations for a communist take-over, the Comintern expressed its indignation and ordered the reestablishment of the party.[44]

The revival of the party in 1925 did not change matters basically. The communists were hampered not only by government suppression, but by disagreement and disunity within the party and by the opposition of other left-wing groups. Above all, the communist propagandists, like the Orthodox missionaries, failed to overcome the traditional attitudes and loyalties firmly implanted in the minds of the populace by classroom teachers, Shinto priests, and drill sergeants. Only twenty years later, after the cataclysmic defeat of Japan in World War II had shaken old beliefs and values to their roots, were the communists able to make serious inroads in Japanese life. The Occupation authorities' democratic sufference of religious and political propaganda enabled the communists for the first time to participate in Japanese politics actively as an organization.

The attempt by the Japanese Communist Party to remain a "lovable party"—to expand its influence by peaceful means and to support those occupation reforms which it deemed desirable—was relatively successful in terms of the elections. In 1949 communists received almost ten percent of the vote, or a total of thirty-five seats in the Lower House. The "lovable party" approach was unsuccessful, however, in that it aroused the ire of the Cominform, which had succeeded the Comintern as Russia's channel of influence. When the Japanese Communist Party complied with Cominform demands for violent agitation, the Occupation authorities and the Japanese government instituted a purge of communists (1950-51), that seriously crippled the movement.

Japanese prosperity in the later 1950s and the 1960s undermined the appeal of communism. In 1967 there were only five communists in the Lower House and four in the Upper House out of a total of over 700 Diet members. The friction that had always existed between the Russian Communist Party and the Japanese Communist Party was heightened with the outbreak of the Sino-Soviet dispute, the Japanese Communist Party siding for a time with Peking. Not all Japanese communists agreed with this policy, however; and the party was split into pro-Russian and pro-Chinese wings. By 1967 the Japanese Communist Party claimed to be independent of both Moscow and Peking.[45]

Marxism had a greater impact on Japan than Christianity in that it molded the thinking of a larger number of professors and students and called for a basic transformation of Japanese society. The military, for all their anticommunism, assimilated some of its radicalism and anticapitalism in the 1930s. At the same time, communism had the "negative impact" of furnishing ultranationalists with a cause against which they could unite and a label which they could attach to any opponent. The Russian version of Marxism was more effective in gaining adherents than the Russian version of Christianity. Yet in a way its ideological impact was limited. Until the Sino-Soviet split, the Marxist doctrine was of potential importance as a tool of Russian foreign policy; after the split it lost some of its significance in this respect, too.

The schools operated by the Orthodox Church contributed, as we have seen, to the training of Russian linguists in Japan. Instruction in the Russian tongue served the dual purpose of conveying Russian thoughts and beliefs to the Japanese, and of attracting to the Orthodox faith Japanese who wanted to learn the language. It was the hope of Russian teachers and churchmen also that the literature of their country would dispose the Japanese favorably toward Russia. Japanese institutions such as the Ministry of Education's Tokyo Foreign Language School and Waseda University taught Russian language and literature too. Their purpose was equally patriotic: to make Japanese students understand the neighboring country, which loomed alternately as an ally or as an enemy of Japan. But the ideas of Russia's great writers could not be contained within the bounds of either objective. They awakened among Japanese readers thoughts that were looked upon with favor by neither the Russian nor the Japanese teachers.[46]

The impact of Russian literature on Japanese culture was more significant than the impact of Orthodox Christianity or Leninism in that it reached and influenced a larger number of intellectuals.

Japanese themselves played an active role in the translation and dissemination of Russian literature and literary criticism. They adopted Russian methods and attitudes to their own writings. For example, Futabatei ("The Hell with It") Shimei was at once the foremost translator of Russian works into Japanese in the late nineteenth century and the author of original novels that showed the
influence of Russian realism.

Futabatei Shimei was one of those Japanese who had begun the
study of Russian for patriotic reasons. He was dissatisfied with the
Sakhalin-Kuril Islands Exchange Agreement of 1875 and wanted
to become a Japanese diplomat—in fact, minister to Russia—to further Japan's national cause. But as he delved into Russian literature
his antagonism faded; and though he remained a loyal Japanese, he
spread Russian ideas in Japan rather than Japanese ideas in Russia.

Futabatei had an excellent command of the Russian language.
He studied for five years at the Tokyo Foreign Language School,
where he read Russian works in the original tongue. He visited Russia twice: in 1902 and in 1908-09. He taught Russian at an army
school and later at his alma mater, the Tokyo Foreign Language
School. He translated over thirty Russian works into Japanese,
among them the writings of Turgenev, Gogol, Goncharov, Lev
Tolstoi, Gor'kii, and Andreev. His own novels were influenced in
the process by the realism and style of Russian authors, notably
of Turgenev and Goncharov. Thus his novel *Ukigumo* (Floating
Clouds) showed the influence of Turgenev's *Fathers and Sons* and
Goncharov's *The Precipice*. His translation in 1888 of excerpts
from Turgenev's *Sportsman's Sketches* and *Three Encounters* had
been the first application of colloquial Japanese in modern literature.

The debate between Westerners and Slavophiles, in which most
Russian intellectuals participated to some extent, resembled the
conflict that rent Japanese souls with the onslaught of industrialization and modernization. Groping for a new way of life, Japanese
readers were attracted to Russian literature because it dealt with
similar problems and probed beneath the surface in search of truth
and justice. Authors learned how novels could be used as vehicles
for social ideas rather than merely as means of entertainment. They
gave Japanese literature a new dimension as they imitated Russian
novelists in examining the personality and psychology of literary

characters in depth. The philosophical and literary-esthetic writings of such men as Belinskii, Chernyshevskii, and Dobroliubov had a great impact on the views of Futabatei and through his works about literature on other Japanese authors.[47]

Another Japanese translator and literary critic of note who disseminated Russian writings and ideas was Nobori Shomu. He had studied Russian in the church school of the Orthodox mission in Tokyo. As his literary life-span encompassed the first half of the twentieth century, he translated both classics and Soviet works. Like Futabatei he appreciated realism, however, and preferred those modern novels that continued the old realistic style in new circumstances.[48]

The influence of Russia's greatest novelist, Lev Tolstoi, may serve to illustrate better than any other example the nature of the impact of Russian literature on Japan. All of Tolstoi's works were translated into Japanese from 1880 on, and have remained so popular to this day that not only individual books but voluminous sets of his complete works are brought out every two or three years. The interest in Tolstoi's writings has varied both in nature and in degree with conditions in Japan; at different times Japanese readers looked for different insights. In the late nineteenth century they admired the humanism expressed in Tolstoi's novels; in the first decade of the twentieth century they focused on his ethical and philosophical teachings. Tolstoi's famous essay against the Russo-Japanese War boosted his popularity in Japan. To be sure, his pacifism was as offensive to the Japanese government as to the tsarist government, and translations of his work were subjected to censorship. But the example of Tolstoi inspired Japanese intellectuals, and in 1918 agricultural-intellectual communes patterned after Tolstoi's colony in Russia sprang into existence.

Tolstoi entertained Japanese visitors in his home and corresponded with them and with other Japanese literati about Japanese culture as well as about his own thoughts. Among his Japanese guests were Konishi Matsutaro and Tokutomi Roka (Kenjiro). Konishi, who later became a well-known philosopher and publicist and a professor at universities in Kyoto and Tokyo, visited Tolstoi in 1892. Konishi was then studying for the Orthodox priesthood at the spiritual academy in Kiev and called himself Daniil Petrovich Konishi. Typically, Tolstoi tried to alienate Konishi from the church and succeeded in undermining his faith. Tokutomi Roka was already one of Japan's greatest realistic novelists when he visited Tolstoi in 1906. He had been influenced by Tolstoi's writings before this. His novel *Namiko*, published in 1899, embodied some of Tolstoi's ethical views and realistic principles of writing. On his return to Japan, Tokutomi retired to the land and lived frugally in the manner of Tolstoi. He eventually resumed a normal life, but did not abandon Tolstoi's teachings.[49]

The Russo-Japanese War had heightened Japanese interest in Russia. As Japanese readers devoured translations of the works of Tolstoi, Turgenev, Dostoevskii, Chekhov, Lermontov, Pushkin, Gogol, Merezhkovkskii, Korolenko, Garshin, Sologub, Kuprin, Andreev, Artsybashev, and Gor'kii, some patriots grumbled that Japan had defeated Russia in war but had been captured in literature.

The Communist Revolution, like the Russo-Japanese War, turned Japanese attention to Russia. In the intellectual flux of post-World War I and depression days the Japanese were once again eager for new ideas and looked with interest at Soviet writings. They found the fiction of Fadeev and Serafimovich as challenging in the twentieth century as they had the novels of Turgenev and Goncharov in the nineteenth. The literary theories of Plekhanov and Lenin influenced proletarian writers as Belinskii and Dobroliubov had influenced the preceding generation.[50] The works of Furmanov, Gladkov, Fedin, and Ehrenburg were translated. But the writer whose impact on modern Japanese literature compares most with that of Tolstoi was Maksim Gor'kii.

Like Tolstoi, Gor'kii had a personal interest in Japan. He was acquainted with intellectuals and exchanged letters with them. Like Tolstoi, Gor'kii used literature as a vehicle for social ideas. But the ideas that Tolstoi and Gor'kii advocated were very different. Tolstoi in his letters had argued not merely against Japanese adoption of Christianity (a sentiment that Gor'kii would have shared) but against Westernization in general. He believed that Japan and China could exert a major influence on world history only if they clung to their own culture; and by this he meant, if they returned to the "tao" or way of nature. In other words, Tolstoi advocated a retreat from action. An advocate of peace, he favored man's adjustment to the world about him. Gor'kii, on the other hand, became a spokesman for revolution. His literary characters became protesting heroes in contrast to the superfluous men of old.

As in the case of Tolstoi's works, the Japanese reacted different-ly to Gor'kii's writings at various times. In the first decade of the twentieth century Japanese romantics praised Gor'kii's works for the hope, for the strength and the beauty of man, and for the anti-capitalist and antibourgeois sentiments that they conveyed. With the growth of Japanese realism the realistic aspects of Gor'kii's writings were studied, and with the development of a proletarian literature his Socialist Realism became the model for a number of Japanese writers. In the 1920s Gor'kii's writings, including his lit-erary criticism as well as his fiction, were systematically translated. Japanese writers, particularly the female novelist Miyamoto Yuriko who visited him in Leningrad in 1928, were enthusiastic about Gor'kii's involvement in the political struggle of the masses.[51]

The impact of Russian literature extended also to the theater. In the second decade of the twentieth century the plays of Chekhov became exceedingly popular. *The Cherry Orchard* seemed almost as meaningful to intellectuals in Japan as to their counterparts in Russia. Gor'kii's dramas, notably *The Lower Depths*, made an even greater impact on the modern Japanese theater. *The Lower Depths* was performed regularly for decades following its first staging in 1910.[52]

The popularity of the classical Russian writers in Japan contin-ued until the early 1920s, when the Japanese Proletarian Literature Movement pushed them aside in favor of communist writers. The influence of the communist school was increased by the predomi-nance of Soviet literary criticism. As Japanese government authori-ties began to suppress the leftist movement, the prerevolutionary writers returned to popular favor. After the Second World War, Soviet literature was once more circulated freely, but now was read in addition to, rather than in place of, the classic authors.[53]

The impact of Russia on Japan has been remarkably slight in terms of direct effect on Japanese institutions. This may be accounted for by the fact that the Japanese have been very selective. They have adopted only the best or the most appropriate systems that they could find. They did not regard either tsarist Russia or the Soviet Union as ranking first in the world in its form of govern-ment, in economic development, in military organization, or in general cultural level. It was only in the area of the Russian novel that Japan's neighbor was supreme, and from this field the Japanese borrowed freely. The lack of general cultural influence and even the failure of commercial relations to develop according to expectations do not negate the impact of Russia on Japanese thinking, however. The proximity and the power of Russia do have a direct bearing on most major decisions made by Japanese statesmen and continue to affect, at least indirectly, both the foreign and domestic policies of Japan.

Notes

CHAPTER I

1. My, sam drug, nad step'iu v polnoch' stali:
Ne vernut'sia, ne vzglianut' nazad.
Za Nepriadvoi lebedi krichali,
I opiat', opiat' oni krichat. . .

Aleksandr Blok, "Na pole Kulikovom," *Stikhotvoreniia. Kniga Tret'ia (1907-1916)* (Berlin, 1922), p. 274.

2. V. P. Adrianova-Peretts, *Voinskie povesti drevnei Rusi* (Moscow and Leningrad, 1949), pp. 12-13. Historical research in general supports the impression of the contemporaries of the enormous scope of the massacre and the devastation caused in Russia by the Mongols. In addition to the already known works, see Michel Roublev, "Conséquences économiques de la domination mongole en Russie, 1233-1505," doctoral dissertation, Sorbonne, 1967.

3. For a brilliant outline of the organization of Muscovy as a "huge military camp," with the service gentry and therefore the serfs on their estates, created and located according to military need, see V. Kliuchevskii, *Istoriia soslovii v Rossii* (Petrograd, 1918), pp. 162-67.

4. See the treatment of the Mongol impact on Russia in A. Presniakov, *Obrazovanie velikorusskogo gosudarstva, ocherki po istorii XII-XV stoletii* (Petrograd, 1918).

5. For example, Platonov wrote: "And how could the Mongol influence on Russian life be considerable, when the Mongols lived far off, did not mix with the Russians, and came to Russia only to gather tribute or as an army, brought in for the most part by Russian princes for the princes' own purposes?. . . Therefore we can proceed to consider the internal life of Russian society in the thirteenth century without paying attention to the fact of the Mongol

yoke" (S. Platonov, *Lektsii po russkoi istorii*, St. Petersburg, 1904, pp. 92-93). Platonov went on to cite in support of his contention an earlier great Russian historian, S. Solov'ëv.

6. In contrast to old Russia, where the unity of the overwhelming experience of the struggle against the steppe and a certain unity of culture suggest that the attitude toward Asiatic nomads was shared by the people as a whole, the Russian view of Asia in modern times must refer, for lack of additional evidence, to the educated classes alone. As to the common people, some of them probably continued to hold to the old attitudes, especially on certain frontiers where these attitudes remained more relevant. As late as the 1870s there was genuine peasant enthusiasm to fight for the Balkan Christians against the infidel Turks. For most uneducated Russians the problem probably lost all importance. In any case they cannot be associated with the speculations of a Chaadaev or a Dostoevskii.

7. Raymond T. McNally, ed., *Chaadaev's Philosophical Letters Written to a Lady and his Apologia of a Madman*, in *Forschungen zur osteuropäischen Geschichte* (Berlin, 1966), 11: 114.

8. *Ibid.*, p. 112.

9. A. S. Khomiakov, *Polnoe sobranie sochinenii*, 8 vols. (Moscow, 1900-14), vols. 5-7. On the Slavophiles, see Nicholas V. Riasanovsky, *Russia and the West in the Teaching of the Slavophiles: A Study of Romantic Ideology* (Cambridge, Mass., 1952). Khomiakov's history is discussed on pp. 67-74. See also Nicholas V. Riasanovsky, "Khomiakov on *Sobornost'*," in *Continuity and Change in Russian and Soviet Thought*, Ernest J. Simmons, ed. (Cambridge, Mass., 1955), pp. 183-96. Khomiakov also wrote a play, *Ermak*, in which he opposed Russian civilization to Siberian, represented by a shaman. The play occupies pp. 303-418 of the fourth volume of Khomiakov's *Polnoe sobranie sochinenii*.

10. Khomiakov probably borrowed the principles from Friedrich Schlegel. See appendix, pp. 215-18, in my *Russia and the West*.

11. Khomiakov, himself an outstanding theologian, experienced constant tension between the traditional Christian approach and the newer romantic and racist trends. For instance, he wrote: "The dissemination of opinion or of faith is not limited by the natural division into tribes. . . Faith and enlightenment belong equally to every thinking being, whether his skin is as black as coal or as poetically white as snow, and whether his hair is the curly felt of the African or the chestnut ornament of an English head." And on the same page: "A certain nobility and purity from time immemorial distinguish the white tribe in Asia and in Europe." "In that tribe, and only in that tribe, were preserved the living tradition and the clear teaching of Iranian spirituality" (Khomiakov, *Polnoe sobranie sochinenii*, 4th ed., 5: 358-59).

12. On Official Nationality, see my *Nicholas I and Official Nationality in Russia, 1825-1855* (Berkeley and Los Angeles, 1959).

13. The phrase is taken from V. Botsianovskii, "Senkovskii (Osip-Iulian Ivanovich)," *Entsiklopedicheskii Slovar'* (Brockhaus-Efron), 29A: 531.

14. For a more detailed treatment of their views on Asia than the one given here, see my "Russia and Asia: Two Nineteenth-Century Russian Views," in *California Slavic Studies*, Berkeley and Los Angeles, 1 (1960): 170-81.

15. S. Uvarov, "Projet d'une académie asiatique," *Etudes de philologie et de critique*, Paris, 1845, pp. 1-48; quoted from pp. 3-4; italics in the original. Pages 49-66 contain an interesting letter written by De Maistre to Uvarov in 1810 in criticism of the project. For Goethe's very favorable comments, see G. Schmid, ed., *Goethe und Uwarow und ihr Briefwechsel* (St. Petersburg, 1888), pp. 9-13. The volume illustrates well Uvarov's interest in Asia.

16. Uvarov, "Projet d'une académie asiatique," p. 8.

17. *Ibid.*, p. 9.

18. *Ibid.* Italics in the original except for "Alexander," which in the original is in Roman capitals.

19. *Ibid.*, p. 24. Although the Asiatic Academy never became a reality, later, during his sixteen-year tenure of the office of minister of education, Uvarov was able to advance the knowledge of Asia in the universities, and even in certain high schools, of the Russian Empire. Oriental studies in Russia are discussed in Professor Richard Frye's contribution to this volume.

In addition to ideologists like Uvarov, many European writers were attracted to the exotic, colorful, and mysterious East. Russians in this group included such major figures as Pushkin, Lermontov, and Tolstoi, who found their Orient primarily in the Caucasus and the Crimea. Earlier, in the eighteenth century, Russians, such as Lomonosov, had participated in the enlightenment vogue of picturing certain mythical Orientals as truly wise, civilized beings. A full treatment of the subject would have to include also a discussion of Asiatic elements in Russian music, painting, and other arts.

20. N. Barsukov, *Zhizn' i trudy Pogodina*, 22 vols. (St. Petersburg, 1888-1910), quoted from 2: 17.

21. M. Pogodin, *Stat'i politicheskie i pol'skii vopros, 1856-1867* (Moscow, 1876), pp. 14-24, quoted from p. 16.

22. *Ibid.*, p. 21.

23. *Ibid.*, p. 92.

24. M. Pogodin, *Istoriko-politicheskie pis'ma i zapiski v prodolzhenii Krym-skoi Voiny, 1853-1856* (Moscow, 1874), p. 242. The article "About Russian Policy for the Future" ("O russkoi politike na budushchee vremia") occupies pp. 231-44.

25. *Ibid.*, p. 243. Pogodin idolized Peter the Great.

26. *Ibid.*

27. S. Uvarov, *Desiatiletie ministerstva narodnogo prosveshcheniia, 1833-1843* (St. Petersburg, 1864), p. 23.

28. McNally, ed., *Chaadaev's Philosophical Letters*, p. 114.

29. F. Dostoevskii, *Polnoe sobranie sochinenii* (St. Petersburg, 1896) 21: 514. The article, "Geok Tepe. Chto takoe dlia nas Asiia?" and its sequel, "Voprosy i otvety," occupy pp. 513-23.

30. *Ibid.*, p. 518. I am limiting myself on purpose to Dostoevskii's "Asiatic" articles which have given ground for misunderstanding. This is not the place to discuss the great writer's view of Christianity, or of Pan-Slavism, or of Russian Messiahship in Europe. Incidentally, following the words quoted above, Dostoevskii referred to his celebrated Pushkin anniversary speech which had formulated this Messiahship.

I am unable to cite a single Russian intellectual before the twentieth century who was consistently willing to identify himself or his country with Asia. References in this connection to M. L. Magnitskii are apparently mistaken. Magnitskii, a notorious reactionary, was an extreme and bitter critic of the West and a loud champion of Russian superiority, but he based this claim of superiority squarely on Orthodoxy and did not identify Russia with Asia. See M. L. Magnitskii, "Sud'ba Rossii," *Raduga* [Revel], vol. 1, 1833.

31. Quoted from Theodore H. Von Laue, *Sergei Witte and the Industrialization of Russia* (New York and London, 1963), pp. 87-88. Von Laue adds that "Witte's version of Russia's imperialist mission. . .was no more grandiloquent than the contemporary creeds of a Cecil Rhodes or a Lord Curzon."

32. In fact, this was a common point among imperialist writers. Pogodin, for instance, included the following lines in his discussion of the Sepoy Mutiny: "Wishing the English complete success in all the measures which they have undertaken, and the most rapid possible conclusion of the present internal war, we wish, together with that, moral, intellectual, and spiritual advance for those Eastern tribes which fate has brought under the rule of the English. We wish that the English should be able to place themselves in their position, and from their position, not from the English one, not in the English manner, devise for them a gradual progressive advance, with firm if slow steps. We condemn and curse, together with their own humane and impartial writers, authority that has as its sole purpose the desire to get rich at somebody else's expense, the

exploitation in every respect of miserable natives, which, according to their own admission, has been heretofore generally the rule where the English have been concerned, and also other Europeans. We by no means place the entire guilt upon the English. We do not exclude the Dutch, or the Spaniards, or the Italians, or even the Russians. What have these Europeans done for their subject tribes in Africa, in America, or for the northern Finnish tribes?" (Pogodin, *Stat'i politicheskie i pol'skii vopros, 1856-1867*, pp. 21-22).

33. *Iskhod k Vostoku. Predchustviia i sversheniia. Utverzhdenie evraziitsev. Stat'i: Petra Savitskogo, P. Suvchinskogo, kn. N. S. Trubetskogo i Georgiia Florovskogo* (Sofia, 1921). For the remainder of this essay, see Nicholas V. Riasanovsky, "The Emergence of Eurasianism," in *California Slavic Studies* (Berkeley and Los Angeles), 4 (1967): 39-72. Suvchinskii, a noted musicologist, is known best in the West as Pierre Souvtchinsky.

34. *Iskhod k Vostoku*, p. vii; italics in the original.

35. *Ibid.*, pp. 2-3.

36. *Ibid.*, p. 14.

37. *Ibid.*, p. 113.

38. *Ibid.*, p. 125.

39. *Ibid.*, pp. 96-97.

40. *Ibid.*, p. 100.

41. *Ibid.*, p. 101.

42. Kn. N. S. Trubetskoi, "O turanskom elemente v russkoi kul'ture," *Evraziiskii Vremennik, Nepereodicheskoe izdanie pod redaktsiei Petra Savitskogo, P. P. Suvchinskogo i kn. N. S. Trubetskogo. Kniga chetvërtaia* (Berlin, 1925), pp. 351-78. Also published, together with "The Upper and Lower Layers of Russian Culture" and two other studies by Trubetskoi, in Kn. N. S. Trubetskoi, *K probleme russkogo samopoznaniia. Sobranie statei* (Paris, 1927), pp. 34-53.

43. R. O. Jakobson, *K kharakteristike evraziiskogo iazykovogo soiuza* (Paris, 1931). Republished in Roman Jakobson, *Selected Writings. I: Phonological Studies* (The Hague, 1962), pp. 144-201. See also *Evarziia v svete iazykoznaniia* (Paris, 1931). (This booklet contains an "announcement of a discovery" by Savitskii and a report by Jakobson.)

44. As an example of the last approach, see an article in the eighth number of the *Eurasian Chronicle* asserting that because of the statistical distribution of blood types among the Russians "Russia is situated [in that respect, too] between the European and the Asiatic group; it virtually adjoins the Asiatic group, and it has very little in common with the European" (V. T., "Poniatie

Evrazii po antropologicheskomu priznaku," *Evraziiskaia Khronika*, Vypusk VIII [Paris, 1927], pp. 26-31, quoted from p. 26).

45. The best, although by no means exhaustive, bibliography of Eurasian literature is provided in the only book devoted to Eurasianism: Otto Boss, *Die Lehre der Eurasier. Ein Beitrag zur russischen Ideengeschichte des 20. Jahrhunderts* (Wiesbaden, 1961). The Eurasians' own annotated bibliography of Eurasian writings during the first decade of the existence of the movement may be found in Stepan Lubensky, "Bibliographie de l'Eurasisme," *Le Monde slave* (March 1931), pp. 388-422. The same bibliography was published in Russian as an appendix to the seventh Eurasian joint volume: S. Lubenskii, "Evraziiskaia bibliografiia 1921-1931," *Tridtsatye Gody. Utverzhdenie evraziitsev, Kniga VII* (Paris, 1931), pp. 185-317. "Stepan Lubenskii" was one of Savitskii's pseudonyms.

Professor G. V. Vernadsky's major Eurasian writings range in time from *Opyt istorii Evarzii s poloviny 6 veka do nastoiashchego vremeni* (Berlin, 1924) and *Nachertanie russkoi istorii* (Prague, 1927) to such post-World War II volumes as *The Mongols and Russia* (New Haven, 1953) and *The Origins of Russia* (Oxford, 1959). For bibliography, see Alan D. Ferguson, "Bibliography of the Works of George Vernadsky," in *Essays in Russian History. A Collection Dedicated to George Vernadsky*, Alan D. Ferguson and Alfred Levin, eds. (Hamden, Conn., 1964), pp. xi-xxv. Professor Vernadsky's latest relevant study is his article, "The Eurasian Nomads and Their Impact on Medieval Europe. A Reconsideration of the Problem," *Studi medievali*, Ser. 3, IV, 2 (Spoleto, 1963), pp. 1-34.

46. Kn. N. S. Trubetskoi, *Evropa i chelovechestvo* (Sofia, 1920). A revised German edition appeared soon afterward: *Europa und die Menschheit. Aus dem russischen Übersetzt von S. O. Jacobsohn [Yakobson] und F. Schlözer. Mit einem Vorwort von Otto Hoetzsch* (Munich, 1922). For a fuller discussion of this important book, see my "Prince N. S. Trubetskoy's 'Europe and Mankind'," *Jahrbücher für Geschichte Osteuropas*, July 1964, pp. 207-20.

47. Trubetskoi, *Europa i chelovechestvo*, p. iii.

48. See, e.g., Trubetskoi's article on "The Russian Problem" in the second Eurasian symposium, where the author argues that the utterly devastated Russia could never again be a great European power, that it would in fact fall into a colonial dependence on the West, but that this very development would give her the golden opportunity to lead other colonial countries, in particular her "Asiatic sisters," in a decisive struggle against the Romano-Germanic colonizers (Kn. N. S. Trubetskoi, "Russkaia problema," *Na Putiakh. Utverzhdenie evraziitsev. Kniga vtoraia. Stat'i Petra Savitskogo, A. V. Kartasheva, P. P. Suvchinskogo, kn. N. S. Trubetskogo, Georgiia V. Florovskogo, P. Bitsilli*, Moscow, Berlin, 1922, pp. 294-316).

49. The very term "Eurasia" was apparently introduced by an Austrian geologist, Eduard Suess. See Böss, *Die Lehr der Eurasier*, pp. 25-33, for a good discussion of Eurasian geopolitics and its antecedents.

50. V. Kliuchevskii, *Kurs russkoi istorii*, Part I, 4th ed. (Moscow, 1911), pp. 361-82. Trubetskoi, incidentally, started his ethnographic interest in the non-Russian peoples of the Russian Empire with the same Finnic tribes. See "Notes autobiographiques de N. S. Troubetskoy communiquées par R. Jakobson," in N. S. Troubetskoy, *Principes de phonologie* (Paris, 1949), pp. xv-xxix, esp. p. xv.

51. Velimir Khlebnikov, *Sobranie proizvedenii* (Leningrad, 1933) 5: 179. Khlebnikov's writings include such interesting "proto-Eurasian" pieces as "Khadzhi-Tarkhan," "Persian poems," and "Asia."

52. Belyi's earlier novel, *The Silver Dove* (1908-09), contained in a weaker form some "pro-Eurasian" elements. [Compare with the views of another writer in "Bely and the Mongols," *The Times* (London) *Literary Supplement*, 21 March 1968. Ed.] The two novels were meant to constitute the first two parts of a trilogy, *East and West*, the third part of which was never written.

53. A. Blok, *O. rodine* (Moscow, 1945), pp. 88-91. For the circumstances of the writing of the poem, see. e.g., K. Mochulskii, *Aleksandr Blok* (Paris, 1948), pp. 411-13.

54. Blok, *O rodine,* p. 88.

55. N. S. Trubetskoi's letter to R. O. Jakobson. I am very grateful to Professor Jakobson for letting me see and use Trubetskoi's unpublished correspondence. "Eurasian" elements may be found also in the writings of some other authors of approximately the same period, such as V. Bruisov, M. Tsvetaeva, B. Pil'niak, and M. G. Rozanov. See Gleb Struve, *Russkaia literatura v izgnanii. Opyt istoricheskogo obzora zarubezhnoi literatury* (New York, 1956), pp. 40-49. If Professor R. E. Steussy is to be believed, Pasternak's *Doktor Zhivago* constitutes the latest major Eurasian work, with the mysterious Evgraf as the prime representative of Eurasia in contrast to the main protagonist's Westernism. If so, the novel certainly continues the Eurasian literary "tradition" of love and hatred, violence and terror, revolution and epochal changes (R. E. Steussy, "The Myth behind 'Dr. Zhivago'," *Russian Review*, 18 (July 1959): 184-98). Pasternak did belong to the cultural renaissance, to the age of Belyi, Blok, etc.

CHAPTER II

1. The writer of this essay is a specialist on ancient Iran; and because Leningrad is the world center of Iranian studies, he has close acquaintance with the U.S.S.R. and with many Soviet Orientalists. He makes no pretense of being competent to discuss the cultural history of Russia, of which the development of Oriental studies is a very small part. He presents here a counterpart of the survey of Oriental studies in the U.S.A. that he gave in lectures in various cities of the U.S.S.R., a summary of which is published in the journal *Narody*

Azii i Afriki 4 (1966): 279-81, under the title "Razvitie Vostokovedenia v Soedinennykh Shtatakh Ameriki."

2. Some authors, however, argue that there is a close interconnection between politics, economics, and historiography (see W. Z. Laquer, "The Shifting Line in Soviet Orientology," *Problems of Communism*, No. 2 (March-April 1956), pp. 20-24)[Ed.].

3. Cf. G. Vernadsky, *Ancient Russia* (Yale Univ. Press, New Haven, 1943), p. 236.

4. Omeljan Pritsak is preparing an extensive study on the Varangians which reveals the existence in the tenth and eleventh centuries of Iranian colonies in South Russia.

5. Cf. F. Jakobson, "Slavic Mythology," in *Funk and Wagnalls Standard Dictionary of Mythology* (New York, 1950), pp. 1025-26.

6. Russian pilgrims from time to time went to Palestine and thus came in contact with Arabs and Turks, but their influence at home cannot be ascertained, since we do not have extensive travel reports from them.

7. Compare with Anatole G. Mazour, *Modern Russian Historiography* (Princeton, 1958), p. 1. Professor Mazour holds that this period is well covered: "There is hardly another country which possesses a richer stockpile of annalistic literature [or chronicles] than Russia." [Ed.] General literature, on the other hand, is very restricted and small in quantity [R.H.F.].

8. B. Nikitine, *apud* V. V. Bartol'd, *La découverte de l'Asie* (Paris, 1947), p. 205.

9. *Ibid.*, p. 226.

10. *Ibid.*, p. 230.

11. N. A. Smirnov, *Ocherki istorii izucheniia islama v SSSR* (Moscow, 1954), pp. 25-26.

12. *Ibid.*

13. *Ibid.*

14. E. Schuyler, *Peter the Great* (New York, 1884), p. 469.

15. I. Iu. Krachkovskii, *Ocherk po istorii russkoi arabistiki* (Moscow, 1950), p. 49.

16. *Ibid.,* pp. 47-48.

17. B. M. Dantsig, "Iz istorii izucheniia blizhnego vostoka v Rossii (vtoraia

polovina xviii v.)," *Ocherki po istorii russkogo vostokovedeniia*, 6 (Moscow, 1963): 135-36.

18. *Ibid.*, p. 137.

19. Bartol'd, *La découverte de l'Asie*, p. 256.

20. Smirnov, *Ocherki istorii izucheniia islama*, p. 29.

21. See, further, P. S. Savel'ev, "Predpolozhenie ob uchrezhdenii Vostochnoi Akademii v St. Petersburge," *Zhurnal Ministerstva narodnogo prosveshcheniia* (1855), no. 89, part 3.

22. N. I. Veselovskii, "Svedeniia ob offitsialnom prepodavanii vostochnykh iazykov v Rossii," *Travaux de la troisième session du congrès international des Orientalistes*, 1 (St. Petersburg, 1879): 111.

23. *Ibid.*, p. 114.

24. D. I. Tikhonov, "Iz istorii Aziatskogo muzeia," *Ocherki po istorii russkogo vostokovedeniia*, 2 (1956): 455.

25. Veselovskii, p. 117.

26. For what follows I have used mostly A. P. Baziiants, *Lazarevskii Institut vostochnykh iazykov* (Moscow, 1959), 55 pp.

27. *Ibid.*, p. 19.

28. *Ibid.*., p. 19.

29. *Ibid.*, p. 20.

30. *Ibid.,* p. 23.

31. Veselovskii, p. 137.

32. Krachkovskii, pp. 186, 204.

33. Veselovskii, pp. 155-56.

34. Krachkovskii, p. 188.

35. B. V. Lunin, *Sredniaia Aziia v dorevoliutsionnom i sovetskom vostokovedenii* (Tashkent, 1965), p. 58.

36. *Ibid.*, p. 56.

37. For an opposite view, see Olaf Caroe, *Soviet Empire* (London, 1953), pp. 148-49. See also Professor Bennigsen's discussion in this volume. Bennigsen

speaks of Soviet gerrymandering of the boundaries of the republics which did not truly correspond to population distribution patterns.

38. There is disagreement on the instability of religion in the Soviet Union. Harrison E. Salisbury, ed., *The Soviet Union: The Fifty Years* (New York, 1967), pp. 402-20, and others contend that religion in the Soviet Union is very strong. See, for example, Geoffrey Wheeler, *The Peoples of Soviet Central Asia* (Chester Springs, Pa., 1966), pp. 97-99; and Alexandre Bennigsen and Chantal Lemercier-Quelquejay, *Islam in the Soviet Union* (New York, 1967), pp. 178-83.

39. The exact location of Karakorum, the thirteenth-century Mongol capital, was discovered in 1889 by Russian archeologists N. M. Iadrintsev and A. M. Pozdneev.

CHAPTER III

1. One of the best and most up-to-date surveys of Soviet Oriental studies is N. A. Kuznetsova and L. M. Kulagina, *Iz istorii sovetskogo vostokovedeniia* [History of Soviet Oriental studies] (Moscow, 1970). See introductory pages for Oriental studies in Imperial Russia.

2. See G. Z. Sorkin, "S'ezd narodov Dal'nego Vostoka," *Problemy vostokovedeniia* (hereafter *PV*) [Congress of Peoples of the Far East], no. 5 (1960), pp. 76-86.

3. *Iz istorii*, pp. 11-12. The Central Asian State University published *Trudy Sredneaziatskogo gosudarstvennogo universiteta* [Works of the Central Asian University].

4. In 1922 transformed into the *Institut dlia vneshnykh snoshenii* [Institute for Foreign Relations], *ibid.*, p. 12.

5. In May 1919 the Eastern Department of the North-Eastern Archeological and Ethnographic Institute was founded in Kazan and published its own journal called *Izvestiia* [Reports].

6. In March 1919 Lazarev Institute was made an Armenian institute, later transformed into Near East Institute and in 1920 to Central Institute of Living Oriental Languages, which in 1921 became the Moscow Institute of Oriental Studies. See *Bol'shaia Sovetskaia Entsiklopediia* (hereafter *BSE*), 24 (1953): 226-27. In 1940 the Institute of Oriental Studies was made a higher educational institution, organized in 1953 into Far Eastern and Near Eastern Faculties. See *BSE*, 28 (1954): 416.

7. For the text of the directive (27 October 1920) founding the Central Institute of Living Oriental Languages, and its organization and functions, see *Iz istorii*, pp. 229-30.

8. For a full text of the directive founding the Institute of Oriental Studies in Moscow and its assigned functions, see *Iz istorii*, pp. 230-34. See also M. Blagoveshchenskii and P. Fesenko, "Dvatsat let moskovskogo Instituta vostokovedeniia" [Twenty years of the Moscow Institute of Oriental Studies], *Trudy Moskovskogo Instituta vostokovedeniia*, no. 2 (1940), pp. 9-11.

9. *Izvestiia Rossiiskoi Akademii nauk.* Seriia VI, nos. 1-18, vol. 15 (1926): 184. See also *Iz istorii*, pp. 13-16.

10. *Iz istorii*, pp. 13-14. *Spravochnye svedeniia po Leningradskom Institute zhivykh Vostochnykh iazykov za 1924-1925 uchebnyi god* [Information Bulletin on Leningrad Institute of Living Eastern Languages for the 1924-1925 School Year] (Leningrad, 1925), pp. 11-19. The bulletin contains names of professors, numbers of students, and other pertinent information.

11. The Asiatic Museum of the Academy had four departments (*otdelenii*). The first of these was in charge of books and periodicals in European languages, while the second, which was first called the Asiatic Archive and later the Archive of the Orientalists (*Arkhiv vostokovedov*), held the personal archives of prominent Orientalists. The third department was responsible for manuscripts and books in Oriental languages. The fourth department housed numismatic and epigraphic and archeological materials. On the Museum and its activities, its archival and book collections, and the names of staff members of the Asiatic Museum, see *Iz istorii*, pp. 45-49. See also *Aziatskii muzei Rossiiskoi Akademii nauk 1818-1918. Kratkaia pamiatka* [Asiatic Museum of the Russian Academy of Sciences, 1818-1918] (St. Petersburg, 1920); *Vostokovedenie v Petrograde 1918-1922 gg. Pamiatka Kollegii vostokovedov* [Oriental studies in Petrograd, 1918-1922. Memoir of the Collegium of Orientalists] (St. Petersburg, 1923); and S. A. Kozin, "Aziatskii arkhiv pri Institute vostokovedeniia v akademii nauk SSSR" [The Asiatic Museum in the Institute of Oriental Studies], *Bibliografiia Vostoka*, nos. 5-6 (1934), pp. 56-66. For the history of the Asiatic Museum see A. Baziiants *et al., Aziatskii muzei—Institut vostokovedeniia AN SSSR 1818-1968* [The Asiatic Museum—Institute of Oriental Studies of the Academy of Sciences of the U.S.S.R., 1818-1968] (Moscow, 1969).

12. For details on the College of Orientalists, see "Kollegiia Vostokovedov pri Aziatskom muzee Rossiiskoi Akademii nauk" [The College of Orientalists in the Asian Museum of the Russian Academy of Sciences], *Vostok*, 1 (1922): 107.

13. *Zapiski* were edited by V. V. Bartol'd. Research done by the members of the College of Arabists and the Asiatic Museum was published in *sborniks* (symposiums) issued by the Russian Academy of Sciences (*Aziatskii sbornik, Iran*, 2 vols. [1918-1919]), and by some other institutions (e.g., *Sbornik Muzeia antropologii i etnografii; Iafeticheskii sbornik* [Japhetic symposium], 1922 ff.); and in such series as *Pamiatniki indiiskoi filosofii* [Monuments of Indian Philosophy], 1922 ff.; *Monumenta hagiographica Georgica*, 1918 ff.; and in the *Bibliotheca Buddhica* and *Khristianskii Vostok*.

14. The Institute of Buddhist Culture, founded in 1926 under the directorship of F. I. Shcherbatskoi (1866-1942), published a series called *Bibliotheca Buddhica*. On the Buddhist studies in the Soviet Union, see N. L. Zhukovskaia, "Sovetskaia Buddologiia" [Soviet Buddhist Studies], *Narody Azii i Afriki* (hereafter NAiA), No. 6 (1970), pp. 148-156.

15. See *Sovetskoe iazykoznanie za 50 let* [Fifty years of Soviet linguistic studies] (Moscow, 1967), p. 8; and I. M. Tronskii, "Sravnitel'no-istoricheskie issledovaniia," *Teoreticheskie problemy sovetskogo iazykoznaniia* [Comparative historical investigations] (Moscow, 1968), pp. 7-8.

16. *Vestnik AN SSSR*, no. 8 (1950), p. 89; no. 11 (1950), p. 79.

17. *Iz istorii*, pp. 61-64. The Institute included an Asiatic Department consisting of a number of sectors and commissions for the study of specific regions and problems.

18. *Iz istorii*, p. 35.

19. *Ibid.*, p. 12.

20. *Novyi vostok*, no. 4 (1925), pp. 503-04.

21. Several years later (1926) a Committee for the Supervision of Teaching and Publication in Oriental Studies was established. The committee included representatives from VNAV, the Communist University of the Workers of the East, the Moscow Institute of Oriental Studies, the Leningrad Institute of Eastern Languages, the Institute of Marxism-Leninism, the Museum of Revolution, and the Central Asian University (*Izvestiia*, 6 February 1926). See *Iz istorii*, pp. 17-18.

22. KUTV had chairs and units set up along ethnic lines. Its functions were to train teachers and specialists; in addition it organized field expeditions. Compare with *Revoliutsionnyi vostok*, no. 8 (1930), p. 340. For text of decree founding the University of the Workers of the East, see *Iz istorii*, p. 234.

23. *Iz istorii*, pp. 31-32.

24. From the time of its founding in October 1918 until April 1919 this institution was called Socialistic Academy of Sciences. From 1919 to 1924 it was known as Socialistic Academy, and in April 1924 it was given the name Communist Academy. The Academy was the center of "Marxist-Leninist science." Its various branches investigated humanities (languages and literature) and social and natural sciences. Among its members were such prominent Orientalists as M. P. Pavlovich-Vel'tman. Within the Academy were a number of institutes, sections, commissions, and a library. Affiliated with the Academy were societies of Marxist agrarians, Marxist historians, Marxist Orientalists, and several others. It published several journals, including *Revoliutsiia i natsional'nost'* [Revolution and Nationality]. See *Sovetskaia istoricheskaia entsiklopediia* (hereafter *SIE*), 7 (Moscow, 1965): 589-90.

25. There were also the Society of Marxist Agrarians (*Agrarnikov-marksistov*) and Association of Marxist Orientalists (*Assotsiatsiia marksistov vostokovedov*).

26. *Problemy Kitaia*, no. 1 (1929), pp. 403, 419; *Iz istorii*, p. 33.

27. The proceedings were published. See *Trudy Pervoi Vsesoiuznoi konferentsii agrarnikov-marksistov* [Works of the First All-Union Conference of Agrarian-Marxists], 2 vols. (Moscow, 1930).

28. See "Deklaratsiia Vsesoiuznoi assotsiatsii marksistov-vostokovedov" [Declaration of the All-Union Association of Marxist Orientalists], *Novyi vostok*, no. 29 (1930), pp. xxi-xxiv.

29. For examples of the writings of communist Orientalists, see the pages of *Revoliutsionnyi vostok* [Revolutionary East]; *Mezhdunarodnaia zhizn* [International Life], published by the People's Commissariat for Foreign Affairs; *Torgovlia Rossii s vostokom* [Trade of Russia with the Orient], published by the All-Union Trade Chamber; the journals of the institutes of the Communist Academy: *Na agrarnom fronte* [On the Agrarian Front], *Istorik-Marksist* [Marxist Historian], *Problemy Kitaia* [The Problems of China], *Revoliutsiia i natsional'nost'* [Revolution and Nationality]; the publications of the Institute of Red Professorship (*Institut Krasnoi professury*), and those of the Sun Yatsen Communist University of the Workers of China. See also V. Gurkho-Kriazhin, "10 let vostokovednoi zhizni," *Novyi vostok*, no. 19 (1928), p. xlvi; and *Iz istorii*, p. 33.

30. RANION (*Assotsiatsiia nauchno-issledovatel'skikh institutov obshchestvennykh nauk*) was founded in Moscow in 1923 and existed until 1930. Fourteen institutes were members of the Association. For a list of these see *BSE*, 3 (1950): 271-72. Its functions were to organize scientific research, to investigate particular problems, to train specialists, and to popularize science. It was abolished in 1930 when the reorganization of scientific establishments took place.

31. Included in the list of societies, commissions, and associations were the following: Commission for the Investigation of the Ethnic Composition of the Population of Russia (in the Academy of Sciences); Eastern Commission of the Society of Archeology, History and Ethnography (in Kazan); the Scientific Palestinian Society (in the Academy of Sciences); the Ossetian Historical-Philological Society; the Turkestan (Central Asian) Committee for the Preservation of Monuments of Antiquity; the Azerbaijan Archeological Society; the Azerbaijan Committee for the Preservation of Monuments of Antiquity and Art; Society for the Study of the History, Economy, and Culture of the Countries of the Near East and the Middle East; Society for the Study of the Manchurian Region (at Harbin); Commission for the Study of the Revolutionary Movement in Turkestan; Scientific Eastern Commission (Tashkent); the Society for the Study of Tajikstan and Iranian Nationalities; Institute of Turkmen

Culture; Commission for the Study of National Minorities; and several others. See *Iz istorii*, pp. 29-30.

32. On VNAV see *Mezhvuzovskaia nauchnaia konferentsiia po voprosam istorii stran Azii i Afriki v sovetskoi istoriografii (20-22 dekabria, 1966 g.)* [Scientific Conference of Higher Institutions of Learning on the Problem of the History of the Countries of Asia and Africa in Soviet Historiography], *Tezisy dokladov* (Moscow, 1966), pp. 5-7. See also N. A. Kuznetsova, "U istokov marksistko-leninskogo vostokovedeniia v SSSR" [Sources of Marxist-Leninist Oriental Studies in the U.S.S.R.], *Narody Azii i Afriki* (hereafter *NAiA*), no. 3 (1969), pp. 55-66; and "Vostokovedenie" [Oriental Studies], *BSE*, 2nd ed., 9 (1951): 192-202. For the text of the decree founding VNAV, see *Iz istorii*, p. 235; and for the text of its constitution after it changed its name to *Vsesoiuznaia nauchnaia assotsiatsiia vostokovedeniia*, see *ibid.*, pp. 235-37.

33. After the abolition of NARKOMNATS (*Narodnyi komissariiat po delam natsional'nostei*), in April 1924, VNAV was attached to the Central Executive Committee of the U.S.S.R. See M. P. Pavlovich, *Piat' let sovetskogo vostokovedeniia* [Five Years of Soviet Oriental Studies] (Moscow, 1927), p. 3.

34. M. Pavlovich, "Zadachi i dostizheniia sovetskogo vostokovedeniia. K piatiletiiu Nauchnoi Assotsiatsii vostokovedeniia pri Ts K SSSR" [Goals and achievements of Soviet Oriental studies. Fifth anniversary of the Scientific Association of Oriental Studies attached to the Central Committee of the U.S.S.R.], *Novyi vostok*, nos. 16-17 (1927), pp. xii-xiii.

35. *Iz istorii*, p. 21.

36. I. Borozin, "M. P. Pavlovich i Vsesoiuznaia nauchnaia assotsiatsii vostokovedov" [M. P. Pavlovich and the All-Union Scientific Association of Orientalists], *Novyi vostok*, no. 28 (1927), p. xxxix.

37. *Iz istorii*, pp. 23, 28, 38. See also V. M. Zummer, *Moskovskie soveshchanie po izucheniiu kul'tury i iskusstva tiurskikh narodov* [Moscow consultations for study of the culture and art of Turkic peoples] (Baku, 1927).

38. *Iz istorii*, pp. 27, 28. VNAV had cells (*iacheiki*) in foreign countries, including one in Teheran.

39. VUNAV published its own journal called *Biulleten' Vseukrainskoi nauchnoi assotsiatsii vostokovedeniia*, published in Kharkov, as well as another called *Skhidnii svit*. On the history of VNAV in Kiev and of VUNAV, see I. M. Fal'kovich, "K istorii sovetskogo vostokovedeniia na Ukraine" [The history of Soviet Oriental studies in the Ukraine], *NAiA*, no. 4 (1966), pp. 270-78; and by the same author, "Vostokovedenie v Kieve" [Oriental studies in Kiev]; also *Iz istorii*, pp. 27-28, 38.

40. Among other journals and periodicals published were *Revoliutsionnyi vostok, Zhizn' natsional'nostei, Materialy po kolonial 'nym i natsional'nym*

problemami, and *Novyi Dal'nyi vostok.* Some of the more serious and scholarly periodicals published in the interwar period were *Zapiski kollegii vostokovedov pri Aziatskom Muzee Rossiiskoi Akademii nauk* (1925-30), 5 vols.; *Zapiski vostokovedeniia Akademii nauk SSSR* (1932-39), 7 vols.; *Izvestiia Rossiiskoi nauky (Novaia seriia), Iran* (1927-29), 3 vols.; *Rabochaia khronika Instituta vostokovedeniia za 1943 god.,* 2 vols. (Tashkent, 1944).

41. VNAV was divided into sections and commissions. There were commissions for the study of Eastern culture, Tatar culture, the culture of Turkic peoples, and for Finno-Ugrian nationalities; commissions for Eastern art, for natural resources of the East, for the Near East, and the Middle East; and commissions for Turkmenistan and for Japan. When the revolutionary activity in China became important, the Far Eastern Section was added.

42. Three of the better-known series were "The East in the struggle for independence," "Sketches on the revolutionary movement in the Middle East," and "The national movement in the Near East."

43. Pavlovich participated in the Bolshevik Revolution and was later on the staffs of the People's Commissariat on Nationality Affairs, the Eastern Trade Chamber (*Vostochnaia torgovaia palata*), and the Council of History and Propaganda (*Soviet istorii i propagandy*). He was assisted by V. Gurko-Kriazhin, L. N. Borozdin, and a number of other Marxist writers. See also N. A. Kuznetsova and L. M. Kulagina, "M. P. Pavlovich (Vel'tman) (1917-1927)," *NAiA*, no. 3 (1963), pp. 189-93.

44. Compare with S. Ol'denburg, "Pamiate M. P. Pavlovicha," *Novyi vostok,* no. 18 (1927), p. xxv. See also Pavlovich, "Zadachi i dostizheniia," nos. 16-17 (1927), pp. xii-xiii.

45. S. Dimanshtein, "Povorotnyi punkt v sovetskom vostokovedenii" [Turning-point in Soviet Oriental studies] , *Novyi vostok,* no. 28 (1930), p. xxi.

46. *Iz istorii,* pp. 24-25.

47. *Ibid.,* pp. 72-73. For the texts of the project for the reorganization of the Eastern Sector of the Academy of Sciences and the 1929 directive founding the Institute of Oriental Studies of the Academy of Sciences of the U.S.S.R. and on its duties and organization, see pp. 238-43. See also V. V. Struve *et al.,* "Institut vostokovedeniia AN SSSR," *Vestnik AN SSSR,* no. 3 (1932), p. 48; nos. 10-11 (1937), pp. 270-72. The Institute was divided into two sections and eleven cabinets (1937): Central Asia, the Caucasus, China, Japan-Korea, Mongolia and Buriat Mongolia, the Indo-Tibetan Cabinet, Turkey, Iran, the Arabic World, the Ancient East, and Modern India. It was directed in the thirties by four prominent Orientalists: S. F. Ol'denburg, A. N. Samoilovich, A. P. Barannikov, and V. V. Struve.

48. *Iz istorii,* p. 90.

49. For details, see *Iz istorii*, pp. 74-75.

50. *Vestnik AN SSSR*, nos. 4-5 (1936), pp. 34-35; and *Istorik-Marksist*, no. 1 (1937), p. 195.

51. The granting of the degrees of *aspirantura* and *doktorantura* was introduced in the Academy in 1927.

52. See *Vestnik AN SSSR*, no. 5 (1934), pp. 59-61; also *Iz istorii*, pp. 77-78.

53. *Vestnik AN SSSR*, nos. 2-3 (1938), pp. 132-33; nos. 7-8 (1938), p. 126.

54. S. F. Ol'denburg, "Edinaia vostokovednaia rabota" [Unified Oriental studies], *Vestnik AN SSSR*, no. 8 (1932), p. 72; and by the same author, "O deiatel'nostei Instituta vostokovedeniia Akademii nauk" [Activities of the Institute of Oriental Studies of the Academy of Sciences of the U.S.S.R.], *Revoliutsiia i natsional'nost'*, no. 6 (1932), p. 21.

55. In 1932 there were in the Institute of Oriental Studies 23 members of the Communist Party, 1 candidate, and 8 members of the Communist Youth. There is a discrepancy in the figures given for the staff during the 1930s. Compare *Iz istorii*, pp. 77, 100. See also V. V. Struve, Kh. I. Muratov, V. I. Kal'-ianov, *Institut vostokovedeniia*, p. 271; and *Vestnik AN SSSR*, no. 3 (1932), p. 48. On the text of the directive for the organization and work of the Institute of Oriental Studies, issued in 1936, see *Iz istorii*, pp. 243-44.

56. *Vestnik AN SSSR*, no. 7 (1933), pp. 1-8; and *Iz istorii*, pp. 75-76.

57. See A. Kovalevskii, "Rabota nad istochnikami po istorii vostochnoi Evropy i Kavkaza v Akademii nauk SSSR" [The work on sources for the history of Eastern Europe and the Caucasus in the Academy of Sciences of the U.S.S.R.], *Istorik-Marksist*, no. 1 (1937): 197-98. For titles of these collections, see *Iz istorii*, pp. 84-85.

58. *Iz istorii*, pp. 79-81. On the work of the Institute in the thirties, see also V. P. Volgin, "Akademiia nauk na novom etape" [The Academy of Sciences at a new stage], *Vestnik AN SSSR*, no. 4 (1935), p. 22.

59. See *Bibliografiia Vostoka* [Bibliography of the Orient], 10 vols. (Moscow, 1932-36).

60. For work done on folklore, see *Vestnik AN SSSR*, nos. 7-8 (1935), pp. 71-74.

61. See "Izuchenie drevnei istorii v Institute vostokovedeniia Akademii nauk SSSR" [Investigation of ancient history in the Institute of Oriental Studies of the Academy of Sciences of the U.S.S.R.], *Vestnik drevnei istorii* (hereafter *VDI*), no. 3(4) (1938), pp. 255-57.

62. See "Assotsiatsiia iapanovedeniia," *Zapiski Instituta vostokovedeniia Akademii nauk* (hereafter *Zapiski IVAN*), no. 3 (1935), p. 212.

63. *Zapiski IVAN*, no. 3 (1935), pp. 211-12.

64. *Ibid.*, no. 3 (1935), p. 211; no. 9 (1935), p. 64; nos. 4-5 (1937), p. 81.

65. A. E. Iskanderov, "Pervaia sessiia arabistov" [The First Session of the Arabicists], *Vestnik AN SSSR*, no. 9 (1935), p. 64.

66. *Trudy Vtoroi sessii Assotsiatsii arabistov 19-23 oktiabra 1937 g.* [Proceedings of the second session of the Association of Arabicists] (Moscow, 1941).

67. *Iz istorii*, p. 97.

68. *Ibid.*, p. 126. On the background of the Pacific Ocean Institute and its history, see "Institut tikhookeanskikh snoshenii SSSR [Relations of the U.S.S.R. with the Pacific Ocean Institute], *Tikhii Okean*, no. 1 (1934), pp. 217-18; and A. Klimov, "V Tikhookeanskom Institute AN SSSR" [The Pacific Ocean Institute of the Academy of Sciences of the U.S.S.R.], *Istoricheskii zhurnal*, nos. 3-4 (1943), p. 109. For text of the decision (28 July 1934) for the founding of the Pacific Ocean Institute, see *Iz istorii*, p. 244.

69. *Iz istorii*, p. 108.

70. I. Amusin, "Sektor drevnego i ranne-seradnevekovogo IVAN" [Sector on Ancient and Early Medieval History in the Institute of Oriental Studies of the Academy of Sciences], *VDI*, no. 2 (1948), pp. 164-67; also *ibid.*, no. 3 (1949), pp. 192-93.

71. G. A. Kniazev and A. V. Kol'tsov, *Kratkii ocherk istorii Akademii nauk SSSR* [Short sketch of the history of the Academy of Sciences of the U.S.S.R.] (Moscow-Leningrad, 1957), p. 122.

72. D. Tikhonov, "Institut vostokovedeniia AN SSSR" [The Institute of Oriental Studies of the Academy of Sciences of the U.S.S.R.], *Izvestia AN SSSR Otdeleniia literatury i iazyka*, no. 4 (1944), pp. 177-81. On the work and activities of the Institute of Oriental Studies in this period and the names of the Orientalists, see D. Tikhonov, "Institut vostokovedeniia Akademii nauk SSSR v 1946 g." [The Institute of Oriental Studies of the Academy of Sciences of the U.S.S.R. in 1946], *Izvestiia AN SSSR Otdeleniia literatury i iazyka*, no. 2 (1947): 167-70; and *Iz istorii*, pp. 107-110.

73. See "Otdelenie Vostoka istoricheskogo fakul'teta Moskovskogo universiteta" [Department of the East in the Historical Faculty of Moscow University], *Istoricheskii zhurnal*, nos. 1-2 (1945), p. 107. For the names of those who received degrees, see *Iz istorii*, p. 114.

74. On the Moscow Group, see D. Reder, "Moskovskaia grupa IVAN" [The Moscow Group of the Institute of Oriental Studies of the Academy of Sciences], *VDI*, no. 2 (1948), pp. 168-69; see also A. I. Falina, "V moskovskoi gruppe Instituta vostokovedeniia" [The Moscow Group of the Institute of Oriental Studies], *Vestnik AN SSSR*, no. 4 (1950), pp. 103-05; and *Iz istorii*, p. 115. For the text of the directive founding the MGIVAN, see *Iz istorii*, p. 245.

75. For the names of those who came from Moscow, see *Iz istorii*, p. 115.

76. *Iz istorii*, pp. 118-19. On the Moscow Group's work and activities, see *Izvestia AN SSSR Otdeleniia literatury i iazyka*, no. 1 (1947), pp. 85-88.

77. In recent years the Soviet Union has actively promoted interest in the Oriental world and in Oriental causes both at home and abroad. The Soviet Committee for the Solidarity of the Countries of Asia and Africa (*Sovetskii komitet solidarnosti stran Azii i Afriki*) was established in 1956. This body organizes programs and ceremonies, arranges visits, and provides stipends to Asian students. There is the Society for Friendship and Cultural Ties with the Countries of the Arab East (*Obshchestvo druzhby i kul'turnoi sviazi so stranami Arabskogo vostoka*), and comparable societies promoting Soviet cultural relations with most other Oriental countries (e.g., the Society of Soviet-Chinese Friendship, the Soviet-Iranian Society and the Society for Soviet-Indian Cultural Ties). All these societies, numbering almost fifty, were in 1958 centralized into the organization called the Union of Soviet Societies of Friendship and Cultural Ties with Foreign Countries (*Soiuz sovetskikh obshchestv druzhby i kul'turnoi sviazi s zarubezhnymi stranami*). The societies meet occasionally to choose the Union Council, the Revision Commission, the Presidium, and the President. In Moscow there is a Home of Friendship with the Peoples of Foreign Countries and in Leningrad a Home of Peace and Friendship with Peoples of Foreign Countries. See *NAiA*, no. 3 (1968), pp. 222-23; no. 3 (1970), p. 206; no. 5 (1970), p. 245.

78. The *Islamic Review*, September 1955, p. 3.

79. *Vestnik AN SSSR*, no. 9 (1950), pp. 80-87; and *Iz istorii*, pp. 134-35.

80. "Perspektivnyi plan raboty Instituta vostokovedeniia AN SSSR v blizhaishee piatiletie" [Outline of projected work of the Institute of Oriental Studies of the Academy of Sciences of the U.S.S.R. in the approaching Five-Year Plan], *Kratkie soobshcheniia Instituta vostokovedeniia AN SSSR* (hereafter *KSIV*), no. 1 (1951), pp. 3-16.

81. *Iz istorii*, pp. 136-37.

82. *Vestnik AN SSSR*, no. 9 (1950), pp. 80-87.

83. See "Otchet o rabote Instituta vostokovedeniia AN SSSR za 1950 g."

[An account of the work of the Institute of Oriental Studies of the Academy of Sciences of the U.S.S.R. for 1950], cited in *Iz istorii*, p. 138.

84. *Vestnik AN SSSR*, no. 6 (1951), pp. 89-90. On the status of the cadre, see *ibid.*, no. 4 (1953), pp. 76-77. See also P. P. Bushev's comment in *Voprosy istorii*, no. 9 (1954), pp. 170-72, and *Sovetskoe vostokovedenie*, no. 2 (1955), pp. 158-64.

85. For a good discussion of the controversy centering on Shamil and Muridism, see Lowell Tillett, *The Great Friendship* (Chapel Hill, N. C., 1969), pp. 194-224.

86. *Izvestiia AN SSSR*, no. 9 (1952), pp. 80-87.

87. A. A. Guber spoke on the influence of the Russian Revolution on Asian peoples in general; A. M. Reisner on the impact of the Russian Revolution on India; M. S. Ivanov on its impact on Iran; and A. F. Miller on its impact on Turkey. See *Voprosy istorii*, no. 1 (1956), pp. 205-08.

88. *Voprosy istorii*, no. 9 (1954), pp. 170-72.

89. *Vestnik AN SSSR*, no. 4 (1953), pp. 76-77.

90. The Council for the Coordination has itself been criticized on one occasion for doing little more than facilitating the exchange of information and for not doing enough on the planning of historical research. See *Voprosy istorii*, no. 9 (1954), pp. 170-72. On coordination of scholarly work of the academies of sciences, see *Izvestiia AN SSSR*, no. 9 (1952), pp. 99-104; *Voprosy istorii*, no. 5 (1953), pp. 130-32. The Council on Coordination of Scientific Work of the Union of the Republic's Academies of Sciences is attached to the Presidium of the Academy of Sciences of the Soviet Union.

91. *Voprosy istorii*, no. 9 (1954), pp. 170-72; and no. 3 (1957), pp. 196-201.

92. *Iz istorii*, pp. 141-42.

93. *Vestnik AN SSSR*, no. 4 (1953), pp. 76-77.

94. The fundamental problems were listed as the origin of languages, the ethnogenesis of the Turkish-speaking peoples of the Middle Volga region, the interpretation of the past of various peoples in the light of Stalin's ideas, the formation of the bourgeois nations, the historical significance of the "union" between Russia and the non-Russian peoples and the concept of the "lesser evil," the formation of the Soviet socialist nations, and the unmasking of American imperialism.

95. *Bol'shevik*, no. 13 (1952), pp. 60-70.

96. *Voprosy istorii*, no. 11 (1952), p. 153.

97. *Ibid.*, no. 10 (1952), pp. 4-32; and no. 12 (1952), pp. 3-10.

98. On this occasion Tolstov was replaced as director of the Institute by V. I. Avdiev, who in turn was replaced in 1955 by A. A. Guber. On details and names of sectional heads, see *Iz istorii,* pp. 142-43.

99. *Iz istorii,* p. 152.

100. *Iz istorii,* p. 142.

101. These cabinets were 1) history and economy of China, 2) language and literature of the peoples of China, 3) history and economics of Mongolia and China, 4) language and literature of the peoples of Korea, Mongolia, and Japan, 5) history and economy of Japan, 6) history and economy of India and Southeast Asia, 7) language and literatures of the peoples of India and Southeast Asia, 8) history and literatures of the countries of the Middle East and the Near East, 9) languages of the peoples of the Middle East, 10) history and culture of the peoples of Soviet Asia, 11) the Ancient East, and 12) Oriental manuscripts in Leningrad (*Iz istorii,* pp. 143-44).

102. Thus, the Historical Section had five groups: medieval history, history of Russian Oriental studies, the problem of the formation of nations, historiography, and study of the liberation movement. The Philological Section had two groups: the problem of lexicography and the problem of transcription.

103. *Iz istorii,* pp. 144-45.

104. *Vestnik AN SSSR,* no. 12 (1954), p. 65; *Iz istorii,* pp. 145-46.

105. The first issue of "Brief Reports" was dedicated to "International Relations in the Far East, 1870-1945."

106. *Iz istorii,* p. 146.

107. *Ibid.,* p. 147.

108. For a listing, see *Iz istorii,* pp. 145-48. See, for example, Z. N. Petrunicheva, "Izuchenie iazykov i literatur narodov Indii" [Study of the languages and literatures of the peoples of India], *Vestnik AN SSSR,* no. 3 (1945), pp. 100-101.

109. There were conferences on the Soviet liberation of Korea, on the founding of the Viet Nam Democratic Republic, on the fifty years of the First Russian Revolution, on the thirty years of the Mongol People's Republic, on the anniversary of the Bandung Conference, on the literature and languages of the peoples of India and Southeast Asia, on the Egyptian struggle against imperialistic oppression, on the founding of Russian Sinology, on the centenary of Bichurin's death (see *Vestnik AN SSSR,* no. 7 [1953], pp. 98-102), on socialist realism in the literature of the peoples of Asia (see *KSIV,* no. 17 [1955],

pp. 3-9), on the economies of colonial and dependent countries in the period of imperialism, on periodization of the recent history of Oriental countries, on the influence of the first Russian Revolution on the Oriental peoples, on the hundredth anniversary of Dorzhi Banzarov (the Buriat thinker), on the ancient Indian writer Kalidasy, and on Sun Yat-sen. There were a number of sessions on prominent Russian and Soviet Orientalists, on national traditions among peoples of the Soviet Union, on the character of peoples' democracies of the East, and on the economies of Eastern countries. For details, see *Iz istorii*, p. 151, and no. 30, p. 199. On conferences dealing with China, see *Vestnik AN SSSR*, no. 12 (1953), pp. 106-10; no. 11 (1954), pp. 49-50; no. 3 (1955), pp. 97-99; no. 11 (1955), pp. 112-13; no. 4 (1960), p. 141.

110. *Iz istorii*, p. 200.

111. For a full text of the directive by the Presidium of the Academy of Sciences of the Soviet Union, issued on 7 September 1956, see *Iz istorii*, pp. 245-48.

112. *Ibid.*, pp. 152-53.

113. *Iz istorii*, no. 97, p. 203.

114. *Vestnik AN SSSR*, no. 3 (1951), pp. 101-10.

115. *Iz istorii*, pp. 245-48.

116. For full details and the text of the directive by the Presidium, see *Iz istorii*, pp. 246-48.

117. The Institute of World Economy and International Relations (*Institut mirovoi ekonomiki i mezhdunarodnykh otnoshenii*), whose purpose was to investigate economic problems in Oriental and other countries, was founded in 1956 (*Vestnik AN SSSR*, no. 6 [1956], pp. 117-18).

118. The six sections and sectors were 1) the Far East and Southeast Asia (sectors: Japan, Korea, Mongolia, Philippines, Indonesia, Indo-China); 2) China (replaced by the Institute of Chinese Studies, founded on 26 October 1956); 3) India (sectors: history of philosophy, economy, language, and literature); 4) the Near East and the Middle East (sectors: Iran, Turkey, Pakistan); 5) the Arab East (sectors: Arab countries of the Near East, Arabs of North Africa); and 6) Africa (on 2 October 1959, the Institute of African Studies was founded in the Academy of Sciences). See *Iz istorii*, pp. 248-49.

119. These sections were 1) ancient history (in 1958 merged with the Leningrad Branch to become the Section of Ancient History); 2) current developments; 3) publication of Eastern documents and monuments; and 4) the contemporary East. See *Iz istorii*, p. 154.

120. *Voprosy istorii*, no. 3 (1957), pp. 19-24.

121. The three sectors were South China and Southeast Asian languages; Turco-Mongolian and Far Eastern languages; and Iranian and Semitic languages (*Iz istorii*, pp. 154-55).

122. *Iz istorii*, pp. 134, 158; and B. G. Gafurov, "Aktual'nye zadachi sovetskogo vostokovedeniia" [Current objectives of Soviet Oriental studies], *Vestnik AN SSSR*, no. 9 (1957), pp. 19-21.

123. A. Litman, "Piatiletni plan Instituta vostokovedeniia Akademii nauk SSSR" [The Five-Year Plan of the Institute of Oriental Studies of the Academy of Sciences of the U.S.S.R.], *Sovremennyi vostok*, no. 5 (1957), pp. 39-40; and P. A. Brovtsinov, "Plan nauchno-issledovatel'skikh rabot Instituta vostokovedeniia AN SSSR na 1959-1965 gg." [Plan for scientific investigation work of the Institute of Oriental Studies of the Academy of Sciences of the U.S.S.R. for 1959-1965], *Voprosy istorii*, no. 11 (1959), pp. 179-81. See also *PV*, no. 1 (1960), pp. 234-37; and *Iz istorii*, pp. 153-54.

124. *Iz istorii*, pp. 201-02.

125. On the Institute's publication record, see *Iz istorii*, pp. 158-59.

126. *Institut vostokovedeniia* (Moscow). *Gosudarstvennyi plan nauchno-issledovatel'skikh rabot Instituta vostokovedeniia AN SSSR na 1959-1965 gg.* [State plan for scientific investigation work of the Institute of Oriental Studies of the Academy of Sciences of the U.S.S.R.] (Moscow, 1959), 63 pp.

127. On the duties and organization of the Institute of the Peoples of Asia, see directive of the Presidium of the Academy of Sciences, 16 December 1960 (*Vestnik AN SSSR*, no. 2 [1961], p. 100); and *Iz istorii*, pp. 160-61.

128. The topics to be investigated included the national liberation movements, the crisis in and the collapse of the colonial system, imperialism, the economic and political developments in Eastern countries, economic ties between the Asian countries and the capitalist and socialist countries, international relations in Asia, workers' and peasants' movements, development of cultural and social thought, the languages and literatures of the peoples of Asia, socialist and state construction, the development of socialist culture, and the history of socialist countries. See *Iz istorii*, pp. 160-61.

129. The sections and sectors are 1) the Near East and the Middle East (sectors: economy and contemporary problems; history); 2) the Arabic countries of Asia and Africa; 3) India, Pakistan, Ceylon, and Nepal (sectors: economy and contemporary problems; history). (In 1964 the Sector of the history and economy of Pakistan was added and the existing sectors were renamed the Sector of the economy of India, Ceylon, and Nepal, and the Sector of the history of India, Ceylon, and Nepal [see *Iz istorii*, no. 82, p. 202]); 4) Southeast Asia and Oceania (sectors: economy and contemporary problems; history); 5) China (sectors: social and state construction; contemporary problems; his-

tory); 6) Korea, Mongolia, Viet Nam (sectors: socialist and state construction; history); 7) Japan (since 1965 has sectors for economy, history, and contemporary problems).

130. The cabinets were Arabic, Near Eastern, Iranian, Kurdish, Caucasian, Indian, Turco-Mongolian, Chinese, and Ancient Indian.

131. These were groups for Eastern philology (in the Cabinet for the Ancient East); description and publication of manuscripts and xylographs; Japan; and Korea. Under the Leningrad Branch of the Institute were also Archives of the Orientalists and the Section of Manuscripts (*Iz istorii*, p. 163). The author gives the names of the heads of the cabinets and groups.

132. *Iz istorii*, pp. 164-66.

133. On the Plan, see *PV*, no. 1 (1960), pp. 234-37. See also P. A. Brovtsinov, "Plan nauchno-issledovatel'skikh rabot Instituta vostokovedeniia AN SSSR na 1959-1965 gg." [Plan of scientific research work for 1959-65 of the Institute of Oriental Studies of the Academy of Sciences of the U.S.S.R.], *Voprosy istorii*, no. 11 (1959), pp. 179-81.

134. *Iz istorii*, pp. 167-68.

135. *Ibid.*, pp. 167-70. On the latest Soviet interpretations of the national liberation movement and the role of the national bourgeoisie, the communists, the working class, and peasants in that movement, see A. A. Iskenderov, *Natsional'no-osvoboditel'noe dvizhenie* [The national liberation movement] (Moscow, 1970), 392 pp.; and V. L. Tiagunenko, *Problemy sovremennykh natsional'no-osvoboditel'nykh revoliutsii* [Problems of contemporary national liberation revolutions] (Moscow, 1969), 352 pp.

136. Publishes *Sovetskaia ethnografiia.* For an excellent list of Russian bibliographies of ethnographic materials, see Z. D. Titova, *Etnografiia* (Moscow, 1970), 142 pp.

137. Publishes *Sovetskaia arkheologiia, Kratkie soobshcheniia o dokladakh i polevykh issledovaniiakh*, and *Materialy i issledovaniia po arkheologii.* The Leningrad Branch of the Institute publishes *Epigrafiki vostoka.*

138. Publishes *Vestnik drevnei istorii* [Journal of ancient history]. Of some importance on the medieval history of the Near East is *Vizantiiskii vremennik* [Byzantine chronicle].

139. This department consists of the Institute of State and Law, Institute of Philosophy, Chair of Philosophy, Leningrad Chair of Philosophy, Scientific Council on Development of the State, Administration and Law, Scientific Council on Joint Research in Atheism and Religious Criticism, Soviet Association of International Law, Soviet Association of Political Sciences, and Soviet Sociological Association.

140. Consists of Institute of Africa, World Economics and International Relations, Economics, Economics of International Socialism, the Far East, International Working Class Movement, and various other groups, such as Scientific Council on Transitional Economics from Socialism to Communism, Department of Economic Studies, Scientific Council on "Economic Competition of Two Systems and Underdeveloped Countries," and Association of Soviet Economic Scientific Institutions.

141. Consists of A. M. Gor'kii Institute of World Literature, Institute of Linguistic Studies, Kazan Institute of Language-Literature-History, Petrozavodsky Institute of Language-Literature-History, Scientific Councils for the Development of National Languages in Developing Socialist Nations, Lexicology and Lexicography, Folklore, Dialectology, History of Language, and a Commission on History of Philological Science.

142. The Siberian Department has under its jurisdiction the Institute of Geography of Siberia and the Far East (located at Irkutsk), the Institute of History-Philology and Philosophy (located at Novosibirsk), Joint Scientific Council on Economic Sciences, Joint Scientific Council on Historical-Philological and Philosophical Sciences, Bureau of Siberian and Far Eastern Branches and Department of the U.S.S.R. Geographic Society, Siberian Section on the Commission of International Relations, and Scientific Council on the History of Siberia. The Siberian Department also has several branches: the East Siberian Department (at Irkutsk), the V. L. Komarov Far Eastern Branch (at Vladivostok), the Department of History, the Institute of Linguistics-Literature and History, the Department of Economics, the Buriat Branch (at Ulan-Ude), the Irkutsk Branch (at Irkutsk), and the Buriat Institute of Social Sciences. There are also research centers of the Branch in Krasnoiarsk, Khabarovsk, Magadan, Petropavlovsk on Kamchatka, and in Sakhalin. Compare with M. A. Lavrent'ev, "10-letie sibirskogo otdeleniia Akademii nauk SSSR," [A ten-year record of the Siberian Branch of the Academy of Sciences of the U.S.S.R.], *Vestnik AN SSSR*, no. 5 (1967), pp. 5-13.

143. On Oriental studies in Armenia, see G. Indzhikian, "Vostokovedenie v sovetskoi Armenii' [Oriental studies in Soviet Armenia], *NAiA*, no. 3 (1969), pp. 227-30; also A. Baziiants, *Lazarevskii institut* (Moscow, 1960).

144. The Sector for Oriental Studies (*Sektor vostokovedeniia*) has sections on the history, economics, and literature of Turkey; the history, economics, and culture of Iran; the history and economy of the Arabic countries; Kurdish studies; and a group for editing and publication of manuscripts and scientific information.

145. The Sector for Oriental Studies has published among other things three symposiums. See *Vostokovedcheskii sbornik* [Orientological symposium], 3 vols. (Erevan, 1960-67).

146. See *NAiA*, no. 3 (1969), pp. 217-20.

147. On the activities of the Institute of Oriental Studies of the Azerbaijan Academy of Sciences, see *NAiA*, no. 2 (1967), pp. 227-29. See also "O rabote vostokovednykh uchrezhdenii v soiuznykh respublikakh" [The work of the Orientological institutions in the Federal Republics], *PV*, no. 6 (1961), pp. 220-23.

148. On Oriental studies in Azerbaijan, see A. S. Sumbat-zade, ed., *Vostokov edenie v sovetskom Azerbaidzhane* [Oriental studies in Soviet Azerbaijan] (Baku, 1964), 47 pp. See also B. Guseinov, "Nad chem rabotaiut literaturovedy Azerbaidzhana" [Literary studies in progress by Azerbaijan scholars], *NAiA*, no. 3 (1968), pp. 217-19.

149. On Oriental studies in Georgia, see N. V. Komakhidze, "Vostokovedenie v Gruzii za piat'desiat let" [Oriental studies in Georgia during the past fifty years], *NAiA*, no. 1 (1968), pp. 235-37. See also *NAiA*, no. 2 (1962), pp. 256-58; and "O rabote vostokovednykh uchrezhdenii," *PV*, no. 6 (1961), pp. 220-23.

150. On the Institute of Oriental Studies in Georgia, see "O rabote vostokovednykh uchrezhdenii," *PV*, no. 6 (1961), pp. 220-23; also *NAiA*, no. 1 (1968), pp. 235-37; and no. 2 (1968), pp. 247-50.

151. The sectors of the Department of Oriental Studies are contemporary East, history of literature, Oriental manuscripts, and textology and publication. On Oriental studies in Tajikistan, see D. S. Komissarova, ed., *Braginskii, Iosif Samuilovich* (Dushanbe, 1966), 95 pp. This includes a bibliography of published works.

152. *NAiA*, no. 3 (1965), p. 249.

153. See L. Maksudov, "Razvitie vostokovedeniia v Tashkentskom universitete" [Development of Oriental studies in Tashkent University], *PV*, no. 4 (1961), pp. 247-48.

154. *NAiA*, no. 3 (1964), pp. 211-12.

155. On the Institute of Oriental Studies of the Academy of Sciences of the Uzbek S.S.R. (full name, Abu Reikhani Biruni Institute of Oriental Studies), see *PV*, no. 6 (1961), pp. 220-23; also *NAiA*, no. 3 (1964), pp. 210-11.

156. On Arabistics in the Institute of Oriental Studies of the Uzbek Academy of Sciences, see A. Irisov, *Arabistika v Tashkente* (Tashkent, 1964), 72 pp. On the development of the Institute of Oriental Studies and its activities, see L. Maksudov, "Razvitie vostokovedeniia v Tashkentskom universitete" [Development of Oriental studies in Tashkent University], *PV*, no. 4 (1961), pp. 247-48.

157. See *Mezhvuzovskaia nauchnaia konferentsiia. . .(20-22 dekabria 1966 g.)*, pp. 9-11. See also A. Kh. Babakhodzhaev *et al.*, eds., *Materialy po Vostoke*

[Materials on the Orient] (Tashkent, 1966), 127 pp. A collection of articles on the history, economy, and culture of countries bordering on Central Asia.

158. See, for example, A. Ia. Sokolov, "Prisoedinenie Srednei Azii k Rossii i razvitie russko-afganskikh torgovykh otnoshenii" [Union of Central Asia with Russia and the development of Russian-Afghan commercial relations], *Nauchnye trudy*, no. 223 (Tashkent, 1964), pp. 191-214.

159. The Buriat Institute succeeded the earlier Institute of Culture of the Buriats and the Group of the Eastern Siberian Branch of the Academy of Sciences of the U.S.S.R. It specializes on the Mongols, the Buriats, China, Buddhism, and regional archeology and history. See *NAiA*, no. 6 (1963), pp. 259-261. On the Buriat studies and research, see D. D. Lubsanov, R. E. Pubaev, "Vostokovednye issledovaniia v Buriatii" [Oriental Investigations in Buriatia], *NAiA*, no. 5 (1970), pp. 237-241.

160. *NAiA*, no. 6 (1962), pp. 215-16.

161. Interest in Oriental studies in Central Asia predates the Bolshevik Revolution. Such studies were promoted particularly by the Turkestan Branch of the Russian Geographical Society and the Turkestan Circle of the Lovers of Geography.

162. On the linguistic, literary, and historical work by the staff of the Tashkent State University, see *Nauchnye trudy*, no. 229 (Tashkent, 1964), 219 pp.

163. *Azerbaidzhanskii gosudarstvennyi universitet. Pervoe desiatiletie, 1919-1929* [Azerbaijan State University; the first ten years, 1919-1929] (Baku, 1930), pp. 10-89.

164. *Irkutskii gosudarstvennyi universitet, 1918-1921* [Irkutsk State University, 1918-1921] (Irkutsk, 1921), p. 30. See also *Iz istorii*, p. 12. In 1921 the Faculty was reorganized into the Faculty of Social Sciences, and the Eastern Department became the Eastern Department of Foreign Relations.

165. G. Petrosian, *Erevanskii gosudarstvennyi universitet* [Erevan State University] (Erevan, 1941), pp. 3-8.

166. *Novyi vostok*, no. 3 (1922), pp. 580-81.

167. The list includes S. M. Kirov State University (Azerbaijan, in Baku), Bashkir State University (Ufa), Cheboksary State University (Chuvash), Daghestan State University (Makhachkala), Erevan State University (Erevan, Armenia), Far Eastern State University (Vladivostok), Irkutsk A. A. Zhdanov State University (Irkutsk), Kabardo-Balkar State University (Nal'chik), Kazakh S. M. Kirov State University (Alma-Ata), Kazan V. I. Lenin State University (Kazan), Kharkov A. M. Gor'kii State University (Kharkov), Kirghiz State University (Frunze), Novosibirsk State University (Novosibirsk), Ordzhonikidze State University (Ordzhonikidze, North Ossetian A.S.S.R.), Samarkand

Alisher Navai State University (Samarkand), Tadjik V. I. Lenin State University (Dushanbe), Tashkent V. I. Lenin State University (Tashkent), Tbilisi State University, Turkomen A. M. Gor'kii State University (Ashkhabad), Urals A. M. Gor'kii State University (Sverdlovsk), and Iakutsk State University (Iakutsk).

168. See I. M. Fal'kovich, "K istorii vostokovedeniia na Ukraine," [History of Oriental studies in the Ukraine], *NAiA*, no. 4 (1966), pp. 270-79. See also *NAiA*, no. 1 (1970), p. 244.

169. On the history of Moscow University, see I. G. Petrovskii *et al.*, eds., *Moskovskii universitet za piat'desiat let Sovetskoi vlasti* [Moscow University during the fifty years of Soviet rule] (Moscow, 1967), 758 pp. (See section "Vostokovedenie," pp. 595-613.)

170. Since 1967 the Institute of Oriental Languages has chairs in Arabic, Turkish, Iranian, and Chinese philologies; Far Eastern and Southeast Asian languages and literatures; Near East and Middle East, Indian, Chinese, Far Eastern and Southeast Asian histories; African studies; economics and economic geography of the countries of Asia and Africa; and Western European languages (V. I. Tropin, ed., *Spravochnik dlia postupaiushchikh v Moskovskii universitet* [Guide for those entering Moscow University] (Moscow, 1969), pp. 85-87.

171. Instruction in major Oriental languages is not offered every year. Thus, for the school year 1969-70 Moscow State University admitted only students wishing to study Arabic, Afghan (Pushtu), African (Swahili), Viet Namese, Indian (Hindi), Chinese, Khmer, Persian, Turkish, and Japanese (Tropin, p. 85).

172. S. A. Tokarev, *Etnografiia narodov SSSR* [Ethnography of the peoples of the Soviet Union] (Moscow, 1958).

173. K. S. Kozlov, *Etnografiia narodov Povol'ozhia* [Ethnography of the peoples of the Volga region] (Moscow, 1963).

174. On the history of Oriental studies in Leningrad University, see V. V. Mavrodin *et al.*, eds., *Istoriia Leningradskogo universiteta 1819-1969* [History of Leningrad University, 1819-1969] (Leningrad, 1969), 663 pp.

175. I. M. Petrushevskii, *Ocherki po istorii feodal'nykh otnoshenii v Azerbaidzhane i Armenii v XVI-nachale XIX veka* [Sketches of history of feudal relations in Azerbaijan and Armenia from the sixteenth to the beginning of the nineteenth century] (Leningrad, 1949).

176. A. N. Kononov is currently working on a history of the Oriental Faculty of Leningrad University in which it is planned to give full details on the accomplishments of this great institution since its founding in the early nineteenth century.

177. On the organization of the translation work, see *NAiA*, no. 2 (1967), pp. 234-36.

178. See *Mezhvuzovskaia nauchnaia konferentsiia po istoriografii i istochnikovedenii istorii stran Azii i Afriki. Tezisy dokladov* [Inter-Academic Scientific Conference on historiography and source study of the history of countries of Asia and Africa] (Leningrad, 1963), 68 pp. See particularly G. V. Efimov, ed., *Istoriografiia i istochnikovedenie istorii stran Azii. Materialy mezhvuzovskoi nauchnoi konferentsii 25-27 ianvaria, 1963* [Historiography and study of sources on the history of countries of Asia. Materials relating to Inter-Academic Scientific Conference 25-27 January 1963], 2 vols. (Leningrad, 1965, 1968).

179. See *Reshenie Mezhvuzovskoi nauchnoi konferentsii po voprosam istorii stran Azii i Afriki v sovetskoi istoriografii* [Decision of the Scientific Conference of Higher Institutions of Learning on the Questions Concerning the History of the Countries of Asia and Africa in Soviet Historiography] (Moscow, 1967), 6 pp.

180. V. I. Avdiev, *Istoriia drevnego vostoka* [History of the Ancient East] (Moscow, 1948).

181. For details, see *Pravda*, 19 April 1952, p. 2.

182. For topics and questions that Soviet historians should consider when writing ancient history, see review of Vol. 1 in *VDI*, no. 4 (1951), pp. 130-36.

183. *VDI*, no. 1 (1951), pp. 9-14.

184. *Ibid.*, no. 2 (1953), pp. 80-102. On the criticism of the texts in ancient history, see *ibid.*, no. 4 (1953), pp. 136 ff. For a critical assessment of V. D. D'iakov and N. M. Nikol'skii, *Istoriia drevnego mira dlia uchitel'skikh institutov* [History of the ancient world for teaching institutes] (Moscow, 1952), see *ibid.*, no. 2 (1953), pp. 80-102.

185. Discussed in bimonthly journal *Prepodavanie istorii v shkole* [Teaching of History in Schools], published by the Ministry of Education of the R.S.F. S.R. See review of this journal in *Voprosy istorii*, no. 9 (1957), pp. 152-58.

186. From 1964 on, *Vysshaia shkola* and *Prosveshchenie*, the principal journals on pedagogical questions, often discussed this and related questions.

187. L. S. Klimovskii *et al.*, eds., "Problemy prepodavaniia istorii stran Azii i Afriki v universitetakh i pedagogicheskikh institutakh" [Problems of teaching the history of the countries of Asia and Africa in the universities and pedagogical institutes], *NAiA*, no. 4 (1965), p. 91.

188. On the errors in ethnography, see *Sovetskaia etnografiia*, no. 1 (1954), pp. 171-77.

189. See, for example, *NAiA*, no. 4 (1966), pp. 130-38. Klimovskii, "Problemi prepodavaniia istorii," pp. 90-92. On "practicum" see A. V. Raikov, "K

voprosu o praktikume po istorii stran Azii" [On the question of practicum in the history of the countries of Asia], *NAiA*, no. 4 (1965), pp. 97-99; and N. A. Akimkin and M. A. Liuksemburg, *Praktikum po istorii stran zarubezhnogo Vostoka (India, Iran, Turtsiia). Uchebnoe posobie dlia vysshykh uchebnykh zavedenii SSSR* [Practicum for the history of the countries of the foreign East (India, Iran, Turkey). A teaching guide for higher educational institutions of the U.S.S.R.] (Moscow, 1963). On this highly regarded work, see *NAiA*, no. 1 (1967), pp. 245-46. See also N. A. Koroleva, "Kurs istorii stran Azii i Afriki v pedegogicheskom institute" [A course of history of the countries of Asia and Africa in pedagogical institutes], *NAiA*, no. 4 (1965), pp. 95-96.

190. N. G. Kukanova, "Sptezseminar po novoi istorii stran Azii i Afriki" [Special seminar on modern history of the countries of Asia and Africa], *NAiA*, no. 4 (1965), pp. 93-94.

191. *NAiA*, no. 5 (1967), pp. 237-60.

192. *Ibid.*, no. 1 (1965), pp. 253-55. See also Akademiia Nauk S.S.S.R. Institut narodov Azii, *Konferentsiia aspirantov i molodykh nauchnykh sotrudnikov Aprel' 1967. Tezisy dokladov* [Conference of aspirants and young scientific collaborators in April 1967] (Moscow, 1967), 74 pp.

193. A. A. Freiman, V. A. Levshits, M. N. Bogoliubova *et al.*, eds., *Sogdiiskie dokumenty s gory Mug* [Sogdian documents from the mountain Mug], 3 vols. (Moscow, 1962-63).

194. See A. S. Tvertinova, *Vostokovednye fondy krupneishikh bibliotek Sovetskogo Soiuza. Stat'i i soobshcheniia* [Oriental collections of the major libraries of the Soviet Union. Articles and reports] (Moscow, 1963), 240 pp. The symposium is composed of articles by librarians who contribute short histories of the origins and development of the collections. See review in *NAiA*, no. 1 (1964), pp. 202-06.

195. *NAiA*, no. 3 (1965), pp. 243-46.

196. For a list and description of the Eastern manuscripts of the Institute of Oriental Studies, see D. I. Tikhonov, "Vostochnye rukopisi Instituta vostokovedeniia Akademii Nauk SSSR" [Eastern manuscripts of the Institute of Oriental Studies of the Academy of Sciences of the U.S.S.R.], *Uchenye zapiski Instituta vostokovedeniia* (hereafter *UZIV*), no. 6 (1955), pp. 3-35. See also N. P. Zhuraviev and A. M. Muginov, "Kratkii obzor arkhivnykh materialov khraniashchikhsia v sektore vostochnykh rukopisei Instituta vostokovedeniia AN SSSR" [Short review of archival materials in the sector for Oriental manuscripts of the Institute of Oriental Studies of the A.S. U.S.S.R.], *UZIV*, no. 6 (1953), pp. 34-53. The author describes manuscripts on the Middle East, the Caucasus, Central Asia, and the Far East.

197. On the origin and character of the Arabic collection, see V. I. Beliaev,

"Arabskie rukopisi v sobranii Instituta vostokovedeniia AN SSSR" [Arabic manuscripts in the collections of the Institute of Oriental Studies of the Academy of Sciences of the U.S.S.R.], *UZIV*, no. 6 (1953), pp. 54-103. The article includes a number of facsimili. See also A. A. Kartsev, "Arkhivnye istochniki po istorii russko-arabskikh sviazi v XIX-nachale XX v." [Archival sources on the history of Russo-Arab relations from the nineteenth to the beginning of the twentieth century], *Kratkie soobshcheniia Instituta narodov Azii* (hereafter *KSINA*), no. 58 (1962), pp. 16-23; and A. L. Khalidov and A. I. Mikhailova, *Katalog arabskikh rukopisei Instituta narodov Azii. Akademiia nauk SSSR* [Catalogue of Arabic manuscripts of the Institute of the Peoples of Asia, Academy of Sciences U.S.S.R.], 3 vols. (Moscow, 1960-65).

198. L. V. Dimitrieva, "Kratkii obzor dokumentov i fragmentov na tiurskikh iazykakh iz sobraniia Instituta vostokovedeniia Akademii nauk SSSR" [Short review of documents and fragments in Turkic languages in the collection of the Institute of Oriental Studies of the Academy of Sciences of the U.S.S.R.], *UZIV*, no. 9 (1954), pp. 214-45; A. N. Kononov, *Opisanie tiurskikh rukopisei Instituta narodov Azii* [A description of Turkish manuscripts of the Institute of the Peoples of Asia] (Moscow, 1965), 257 pp., A. Kh. Rafikov, *Istoricheskaia literatura na turetskom iazyke, khraniashchaiasia v bibliotekakh Leningrada* [Historical literature in the Turkish language in the libraries of Leningrad] (Leningrad, 1968); and by the same author, "Sobranie russkikh izdanii XVIII v. o Turtsii v Biblioteke Akademii nauk SSSR" [Collection in the Library of the Academy of Sciences of the U.S.S.R. of Russian editions of the eighteenth century about Turkey], *Sbornik statei i materialov Biblioteki AN SSSR* (Leningrad, 1965), pp. 282-320. The Institute of Oriental Studies has an important collection of ancient Turkic runic texts—the oldest written monuments of Turkic-speaking peoples of Central and Inner Asia—probably dating from the seventh to the tenth centuries. They are written in old Sogdian script of the fifth to the sixth centuries.

199. N. D. Miklukho-Maklai, *Opisanie tadzhikskikh i persidskikh rukopisei Instituta vostokovedeniia* [A description of Tajik and Persian manuscripts of the Institute of Oriental Studies] (Moscow, 1955), 106 pp.; and N.D. Miklukho-Maklai and S. I. Baevskii, *Opisanie persidskikh i tadzhikskikh rukopisei Instituta narodov Azii* [A description of Persian and Tajik manuscripts of the Institute of Oriental Studies] (Moscow, 1955), 106 pp.; and N. D. Miklukho-Maklai and collaborators have also edited a two-volume catalogue, which appeared in 1964, of Persian and Tajik documents.

200. The Syrian collection, consisting of several medieval manuscripts, is small but unique. For a description see N. V. Pigulevskaia, "Pamiatniki siriiskoi pis'mennosti" [Monuments of Syrian writing], *Vestnik AN SSSR*, no. 1 (1968), pp. 67-72.

201. L. S. Puchkovskii, *Mongol'skie, buriat-mongol'skie i oiratskie rukopisi i khsilografy Instituta vostokovedeniia* [Mongol, Buriat-Mongol and Oirat man-

uscripts and xylographs of the Institute of Oriental Studies] (Moscow, 1957), 277 pp.; and by the same author, "Sobranie mongol'skikh rukopisei i khsilografov Instituta vostokovedeniia Akademii nauk SSSR" [A collection of Mongol manuscripts and xylographs of the Institute of Oriental Studies of the Academy of Sciences of the U.S.S.R.], *UZIV*, no. 9 (1954), pp. 90-127. See also I. I. Iorish, *Materialy o mongolakh, kalmykakh i buriatakh v arkhivakh Leningrada* [Materials about Mongols, Kalmyks, and Buriats in the Archives of Leningrad] (Moscow, 1966), 206 pp.

202. M. I. Vorob'eva-Desiatkovskaia *et al.*, eds., *Opisanie kitaiskikh rukopisei Dun'khuanskogo fonda Instituta narodov Azii* [Description of Chinese manuscripts in the Tun-huang Collection of the Institute of the Peoples of Asia], 2 vols. (Moscow, 1963). See also L. N. Men'shikov, "Izuchenie drevnokitaiskikh pis'mennykh pamiatnikov" [An investigation of ancient Chinese written monuments], *Vestnik AN SSSR*, no. 5 (1967), pp. 59-62 (a description of Tunhuang documents).

203. Z. I. Gorbacheva and E. I. Kychanov, *Tangutskie rukopisei i ksilografi* [Tangut manuscripts and xylographs] (Moscow, 1963), 171 pp. Tangut manuscripts in the Leningrad Branch of the Institute of Oriental Studies are useful for an understanding of socioeconomic conditions in the twelfth and thirteenth centuries. They were first discovered at Karakhoto in 1908 by a Russian traveler, P. K. Kozlov. Subsequent finds of Tangut documents have augmented the collection. For a description see G. F. Efimov, "Tangutskie pis'mennye pamiatniki iz Khara-Khoto kak istoricheskii istochnik," *Istoriografiia i istochnikovedenie*, I: 44-49. See also N. A. Nevskii, *Tangutskiia Filologiia* [Tangut philology], 2 vols. (Moscow, 1960). The author discussed the Tangut written monuments as a historical source. See also Tvertinova, *Vostokovednye fondy*, pp. 55-109.

204. M. P. Volkova, *Opisanie man'zhurskikh rukopisei instituta narodov Azii* [A description of the Manchurian manuscripts of the Institute of the Peoples of Asia] (Moscow, 1965), 139 pp.

205. B. D. Dandaron, *Opisanie tibetskikh rukopisei i ksilografov Buriatskogo kompleksnogo nauchno-issledovatel'skogo instituta* [Description of Tibetan Manuscripts and Xylographs in the Buriat Complex Scientific-Research Institute], 2 vols. (Moscow, 1960, 1965).

206. G. A. Zograf, *Opisanie rukopisei khindi i pandzhabi Instituta vostokovedeniia Akademii nauk SSSR* [A description of Hindi and Punjabi manuscripts in the Institute of Oriental Studies of the Academy of Sciences U.S.S.R.] (Moscow, 1960), 100 pp.

207. A. M. Muginov, *Opisanie uigurskikh rukopisei Instituta narodov Azii* [A description of Uighur manuscripts of the Institute of the Peoples of Asia] (Moscow, 1962), 207 pp. Uighur documents are valuable for an understanding of social conditions in China and Central Asia. The first documents were dis-

covered in the nineteenth century, but recent archeological excavations uncovered more of them. See D. I. Tikhonov, "Drevnie uigurskie dokumenty—
vazhneishie istochniki dlia izucheniia obshchestvennogo stroia Tsentral'noi
Azii" [Ancient Uighur Documents—most important sources for study of the
social order in Central Asia], in G. V. Efimov, *Istoriografiia i istochnikovedenie*, I: 31-43.

208. M. B. Rudenko, *Opisanie kurdskikh rukopisei leningradskikh sobranii*
[A description of Kurdish manuscripts in Leningrad collections] (Moscow,
1961), 125 pp.

209. O. P. Petrova, *Opisanie pis'mennykh pamiatnikov koreiskikh kul'tury*
[A description of written monuments of Korean culture] (Moscow, 1963),
152 pp. (Description of Korean manuscripts, xylographs, and old books in
the Leningrad Branch of the Institute of Oriental Studies).

210. O. P. Petrova, *Opisanie iaponskikh rukopisei, ksilografov i staropechat-
nikh knig* [A description of Japanese manuscripts, xylographs, and old printed
books], 3 vols. (Moscow, 1963-66).

211. R. R. Orbeli, "Sobranie armianskikh rukopisei instituta vostokovedenii
AN SSSR" [A collection of Armenian Manuscripts of the Institute of Oriental Studies of the A.S. U.S.S.R.], *UZIV*, no. 6 (1953), pp. 104-30.

212. R. R. Orbeli, "Sobranie gruzinskikh rukopisei Instituta vostokovedeniia
AN SSSR" [A collection of Georgian manuscripts of the Institute of Oriental
Studies of the Academy of Sciences U.S.S.R.], *UZIV*, no. 9 (1954), pp. 30-
66. Some Georgian manuscripts are in Persian and Turkish. They span the
time from 1038 to midnineteenth century and shed light on travels, history,
archeology, philosophy, law, art, literature, linguistics, church history, science, and military matters. See also R. R. Orbeli, *Gruzinskie rukopisi instituta
vostokovedeniia* [Georgian manuscripts of the Institute of Oriental Studies]
(Moscow, 1956), 185 pp.; and S. S. Kakabadze, *Gruzinskie dokumenty Instituta narodov Azii* [Georgian documents of the Institute of the Peoples of
Asia] (Moscow, 1967), 511 pp.; and *NAiA*, no. 5 (1970), pp. 236-37.

213. Puchkovskii, *Mongol'skie, buriat-mongol'skie i oiratskie rukopisi.*

214. *Ibid.*

215. *UZIV*, no. 11 (1954), pp. 67-145.

216. Tvertinova, *Vostokovednye fondy*, pp. 110-26. Compare with *Iz istorii*,
p. 217.

217. A. A. Semenov, ed., *Sobranie vostochnykh rukopisei Akademii nauk
Uzbekskoi SSR* [Collection of Oriental manuscripts in the Academy of Sciences of the Uzbek S.S.R.], 2 vols. (Tashkent, 1952, 1954). A catalogue of
manuscript collections in the Uzbek Academy of Sciences.

218. In recent years a number of works have been published, including books by Abu Raihani (*History of India*), Abu al-Faiz Raihaki (*Tarikh-i Mas'udi*), Sidi 'Ali Rais (*Mir'at al-Mamalik*), 'Abd al-Razzaq Samarqandi (*Travels to India*), Gulbadan Begum (*Humayun-nama*); and a new edition of Zahir al-Din Muhammad Babur's *Babur-nama* has been brought out.

219. See *Katalog vostochnykh rukopisei fonda AN Tadzhikskoi SSR* [Catalogue of Oriental manuscripts in the collection of the Academy of Sciences of the Tajik S.S.R.] , 2 vols. (Stalinabad, 1960-62).

220. *PV*, no. 6 (1959), pp. 222-23; *NAiA*, no. 3 (1962), pp. 238-39; no. 4 (1962), pp. 236-37; and no. 3 (1964), p. 212. On the activities of the Department of Oriental Studies of the Tajik Academy of Sciences, see *NAiA*, no. 3 (1963), pp. 184-85.

221. Tvertinova, *Vostokovednye fondy*, pp. 127-41.

222. *Persidskie, arabskie i tiurskie ofitsial'nye dokumenti Matenadarana XIV-XIX vekov i ikh znachenie dlia izucheniia sotsial'no-ekonomicheskoi zhizn stran Blizhnego vostoka* [Persian, Arabic and Turkish official documents in the Matenadaran from the 14th to the 19th centuries and their significance for the study of the socioeconomic life of the countries of the Near East] (Moscow, 1960).

223. A. D. Papazian, *Ukazy persidskikh shakov* [The decrees of the Persian Shahs] (Erevan, 1956); and *Persidskie dokumenty Matenadarana* [Persian documents in the Matenadaran] (Erevan, 1959).

224. A. D. Papazian, "Istorigraficheskaia tsennost' persidskikh rukopisei gosudarstvennogo Matenadarana" [Historiographic value of Persian manuscripts of the State Matenadaran] , *Materialy Pervoi vsesoiuznoi nauchnoi konferentsii vostokovedov v Tashkente 4-11 iiunia 1957 g.*

225. V. S. Puturidze, *Persidskie istoricheskie dokumenti v knigokhranilishchakh Gruzii* [Persian historical documents in Georgian libraries] (Tbilisi, 1962).

226. V. S. Puturidze, "Persidskie istoricheskie dokumenty v drevne khranilishchakh Gruzinskoi SSR," *Materialy Pervoi vsesoiuznoi nauchnoi konferentsii vostokovedov v Tashkente 4-11 iiunia 1957 g.* (Tashkent, 1958), pp. 900-05.

227. Tvertinova, *Vostokovednye fondy*, pp. 142-45.

228. *Ibid.*, pp. 156-71. *Gosudarstvennaia publichnaia biblioteka im. M. E. Saltykova-Shchedrina*, the library's full name. One might mention also the Eastern Section of the Scientific Library of Gor'kii in Moscow (*Vostochnyi otdel nauchnoi biblioteki im. A. M. Gor'kogo*). See Tvertinova, *Vostokovednye fondy*, pp. 218-27.

229. Tvertinova, *Vostokovednye fondy*, pp. 146-55. The official name of the library is *Gosudarstvennaia biblioteka SSSR im. V. I. Lenina.*

230. Tvertinova, *Vostokovednye fondy*, pp. 146-55.

231. *Ibid.*, pp. 192-201.

232. *Ibid.*, pp. 202-17.

233. *NAiA*, no. 3 (1968), pp. 221-22.

234. For details on collections of Sinological, Tun huang, and Tangut collections, see *Sinology*, U.S.S.R. Academy of Sciences, Institute of the Peoples of Asia (Moscow, 1968), pp. 26-29.

235. In 1955 the Central Organization of the Geographical Society (*Tsentral'-naia organizatsiia geograficheskogo obshchestva SSSR*) organized the Eastern Commission (*Vostochnaia Kommissiia*) for the coordination of geographic work on the Oriental world.

236. *NAiA*, no. 6 (1968), pp. 219-22.

237. N. N. Nikolaeva *et al.*, eds., *Muzei vostochnykh kul'tur* [Museum of Oriental Cultures] (Moscow, 1957), 167 pp.

238. *NAiA*, no. 1 (1965), p. 248.

239. The name of the journal is *Uchenye zapiski kafedri istorii stran vostoka* [Scientific notes of the Chair of History of the Eastern Countries] . The Institute of Marxism-Leninism has branches throughout the Soviet Union.

240. The Academy has several chairs (*kafedras*): political economy, economics and politics of foreign countries, theory of state and law, international law, general history, international relations, history of the Soviet Communist Party, theory and history of literature, theory and history of art, dialectical and historical materialism, history of Russian and Western European philosophy, and a chair of logic and psychology. On the Academy of Social Sciences, see *BSE*, 1 (1949): 582.

241. O. E. Livotov and V. B. Portugal', *Vostokovedenie v izdaniikah Akademii nauk, 1726-1917 gg. Bibliografiia* [Oriental studies in editions of the Academy of Sciences, 1726-1917. A bibliography] (Moscow, 1966), 144 pp.; and Ia. Ia. Bychkov, *Knigi glavnoi redaktsii vostochnoi literatury izdatel'stva "Nauka" 1957-1966* [Books of the main editorial office of Eastern literature of the publishing house "Nauka" 1957-1966] (Moscow, 1968). A catalogue.

242. I. M. Aksel'rod and E. P. Bochkarev, *Khudozhestvennaia literatura zarubezhnogo Vostoka* [Artistic literature of the Foreign East] (Moscow, 1963), 132 pp. A bibliography of translations into languages of the peoples of the Soviet Union from 1918 to 1960; includes also children's stories, fables, literature for the blind, etc.

Footnotes

403

243. *Bibliografiia vostoka* [Bibliography of the Orient], 10 vols. (Moscow, 1932-37).

244. *Ezhegodnik knig SSSR* [Yearbook of books of the U.S.S.R.] (Moscow, 1935 ff.); published by *Vsesoiuznaia knizhnaia palata* [All-Union Book House].

245. *Bibliografiia Sovetskoi bibliografii 1965* [Bibliography of Soviet bibliography 1965] (Moscow, 1966), 388 pp., publ. by *Vsesoiuznaia knizhnaia palata*; M. L. Borukhin *et al.*, eds., *Istoriia SSSR. Annotirovannyi perechen russkikh bibliografii izdanykh do 1965 g.* [History of the U.S.S.R.: an annotated listing of Russian bibliographies published up to 1965] (Moscow, 1966), 427 pp. See also *Istoriia zarubezhnykh stran. Bibliografiia russkikh bibliografii opublikovannykh s 1857 do 1965* [History of foreign countries. Bibliography of Russian bibliographies published from 1857 to 1965] (Moscow, 1966).

246. See, for example, *Letopis' pechati Tadzhikskoi SSR* [Chronicle of the publications of the Tajik S.S.R.] (Stalinabad, 1939 ff.); and *Letopis' pechati Turkmenskoi SSR* [Chronicle of the publications of the Turkmen S.S.R.] (Ashkhabad, 1930 ff.).

247. T. I. Kukhtin, *Bibliografiia Afganistana. Literatura na russkom iazyke* [Bibliography of Afghanistan. Literature in the Russian language] (Moscow, 1962), 272 pp. The work lists books and periodical and newspaper articles with brief comments.

248. D. A. Birman and G. G. Kotovskii, *Bibliografiia Indii. Dorevoliutsionnaia i sovetskaia literatura na russkom iazyke i iazykakh narodov SSSR, original'naia i perevodnaia* [Bibliography of India. Pre-Revolution and Soviet literature in the Russian language and languages of the peoples of the U.S.S.R., originals and translations] (Moscow, 1965), 608 pp. The work includes dissertation titles and book reviews. Soviet reviewers consider this the best in the series of bibliographies. In 1959 a comparable but much shorter "Bibliography of India" was published.

249. A. K. Sverchevskaia, ed., *Bibliografiia Irana* [Bibliography of Iran] (Moscow, 1967). Includes 9,000 entries. Also N. A. Kuznetsova, ed., *Bibliografiia Irana. Literatura na Russkom iazyke* [Bibliography of Iran. Literature in the Russian language] (Moscow, 1967), 390 pp.

250. V. S. Grivin *et al.*, eds., *Bibliografiia Iaponii. Literatura, izdannaia v Rossii s 1734 po 1917* [Bibliography of Japan. Literature published in Russia from 1734 to 1917] (Moscow, 1965), 389 pp. Lists books, documents, articles, and notes. See also V. A. Vlesov *et al.*, eds., *Bibliografiia iaponii. Literatura, izdannaia v Sovetskom Soiuze na russkom iazyke s 1917 do 1958 g* [Bibliography of Japan. Literature published in the Soviet Union in the Russian language from 1917 to 1958] (Moscow, 1960), 328 pp. Lists books as well as articles.

251. R. L. Baldaev and N. N. Vasil'ev, *Bibliografiia Mongol'skoi Narodnoi*

Respubliki [Bibliography of the Mongol People's Republic] (Moscow, 1963), 119 pp. Lists books and articles published in the U.S.S.R. from 1951 to 1961.

252. A. K. Sverchevskaia and T. P. Cherman, *Bibliografiia Turtsii (1713–1917)* [Bibliography of Turkey, 1713-1917] (Moscow, 1961), 267 pp. Lists books, articles, and popular items; annotated. By the same author, *Bibliografiia Turtsii (1917-1958)* [Bibliography of Turkey, 1917-1958] (Moscow, 1959), 190 pp. Lists originals and translations, books and articles, in Russian.

253. A. M. Grishin, *Bibliografiia Iugo-Vostochnoi Azii. Dorevoliutsionnaia i sovetskaia literatura na russkom iazyke original'naia i perevodnaia* [Bibliography of Southeast Asia. Pre-Revolution and Soviet literature in the Russian language, originals and translations] (Moscow, 1960), 256 pp.

254. P. E. Skachkov, *Bibliografiia Kitaia* [Bibliography of China] (Moscow, 1960), 691 pp. Lists books and articles published in Russian between 1730 and 1957.

255. See, for example, O. E. Livotov, "Bibliografiia izdaniia aziatskogo Muzeia i Instituta vostokovedeniia Akademii nauk SSSR (1917-1958)" [Bibliography of the publications of the Asiatic Museum and the Institute of Oriental Studies of the Academy of Sciences of the U.S.S.R.], *Ocherki po istorii russkogo vostokovedeniia*, 3 (Moscow, 1960): 196-297. See also, by the same author, "Osnovnaia literatura ob aziatskom Muzee—Institute vostokovedeniia Akademii nauk SSSR (1776-1954)" [Basic literature about the Asiatic Museum—Institute of Oriental Studies of the Academy of Sciences, U.S.S.R.], *Ocherki po istorii russkogo vostokovedeniia*, 2 (1956): 469-511.

256. Z. L. Amitin-Shapiro, *Annotirovannyi ukazatel' literatury po istorii, arkheologii i etnografii Kirgizii (1750-1917)* [Annotated guide to literature on the history, archeology, and ethnography of Kirghizia, 1750-1917] (Frunze, 1968); *Bibliografiia trudov Instituta etnografii im. N. N. Miklukho-Maklaia 1900-1962* [Bibliography of works published by the Miklukho-Maklai Institute of Ethnography from 1900 to 1962] (Leningrad, 1967); and *Bibliografiia Kirgizii*, 4 vols. (Frunze, 1965).

257. *Bibliografiia Kirgizii.*

258. N. A. Burov, *Dorevoliutsionnaia pechat' Turkestana* [Pre-Revolution Press of Turkestan], vol. 1 (1868-79) (Tashkent, 1964).

259. E. A. Bekmakhanov, ed., *Bibliografiia po istorii Kazakhstana. Dorevoliutsionnyi period* [Bibliography of the history of Kazakhstan. Pre-Revolutionary period], vol. 1 (Alma-Ata, 1964), 410 pp.

260. B. G. Bek-Nazarova, *Istoriia Uzbekistana. Bibliografskii ukazatel'* [History of Uzbekistan. Bibliographical index] (Tashkent, 1960), 119 pp.

261. *Bibliografiia Tuvinskoi Avtonomnoi Oblasti (1774-1958)* [Bibliography of the Tuva Autonomous Region, 1774-1958] (Moscow, 1959), 167 pp.

262. N. M. Alekseev, *Bibliografiia Iakutskoi ASSR (1931-1955)* [Bibliography of the Yakut A.S.S.R., 1931-1955], vol. 1 (Moscow, 1958), 167 pp.

263. V. P. Martynenko, *Kratkii ukazatel' literatury po istorii i geografii Kamchatki* [A short guide to literature on the history and geography of Kamchatka] (Petropavlovsk Kamchatskii, 1965), 20 pp.

264. Zh. S. Musaelian, *Bibliografiia po Kurdovedeniiu* (Moscow, 1963), 184 pp.

265. R. L. Baldnev, *Ukazatel' bibliografii po mongolovedeniiu na russkom iazyke 1824-1860* [Guide to bibliography on Mongol studies in the Russian language, 1824-1860] (Leningrad, 1962), 89 pp.

266. For a critical review, see *PV*, no. 2 (1960), pp. 212-15.

267. For a review of some of the volumes, see *PV*, no. 2 (1960), pp. 174-80; and *NAiA*, no. 2 (1962), pp. 154-57. See criticism of vol. 10, which appeared in 1965, in *NAiA*, no. 5 (1965), pp. 188-90.

268. *Vestnik Akademii nauk SSSR*, no. 2 (1954), pp. 84-85.

269. *VDI*, no. 1 (1952), pp. 3-16; no. 3 (1952), pp. 165-68; no. 4 (1952), p. 164; and *Voprosy istorii*, no. 5 (1954), pp. 175-78. On the criticism of interpretations and contents of the sections on ancient history in "Universal History," see *VDI*, no. 1 (1953), pp. 214-32; no. 2 (1953), pp. 216-37. See also *Voprosy istorii*, no. 5 (1954), pp. 175-78. The article gives additional data on "Universal History," On the topics treated in the first volume, see *Voprosy istorii*, no. 12 (1954), pp. 167-71.

270. It is charged furthermore that Western historians distort history. A Soviet critic asks how one can say that Ibn Sina (c. 980-1037) is Asia's Leonardo da Vinci, when it should be said that Leonardo da Vinci (1452-1519) is Europe's Ibn Sina. After all, Ibn Sina lived and wrote long before Leonardo was born.

271. Iu. P. Furtseva *et al.*, eds., *Vsemirnaia istoriia* [Universal History], vol. 1 (Moscow, 1955), 747 pp. Contains many maps, illustrations, and an index. Preface presents a statement on the objectives of the ten-volume "Universal History" and lists the errors of the "bourgeois historians."

272. *Vestnik AN SSSR*, no. 3 (1967), p. 151.

273. *Ibid.*, no. 1 (1966), pp. 9-12.

274. *Ibid.*

275. In this series were published diaries of V. M. Alekseev on his travels to China in 1907, diaries and notes of a number of Russians who visited Korea in the nineteenth century, Fedot Kotov's travel to Persia in 1623-24, and others. Reprints and original studies in history, archeology, and ethnography of the Far East are being published in the series "Dal'nevostochnaia istoricheskaia biblioteka." Five books have already appeared. See *Voprosy istorii*, no. 5 (1971), pp. 156-58.

276. For instance, stories, novels, sayings, legends, aphorisms of India; Afghan, Persian, Dargintsy, Viet Namese, and other stories; Mongol-Oirot stories; Japanese kёgen; Korean and Chinese poetry; Turkish satire; Malay popular songs; ancient Tamil legends, etc.

277. *Kratkie soobshcheniia Instituta narodov Azii* (hereafter *KSINA*), vols. 44 (1961), 53 (1963), 80 (1965), and 84 (1965).

278. V. Nikitina *et al.*, eds., *Literatury drevnego vostoka* [Literatures of the Ancient East] (Moscow, 1962). Includes treatment of the literatures of Mesopotamia, Egypt, Palestine, Phoenicia, Iran, India, and China.

279. N. I. Konrad, *Zapad i vostok* [West and East] (Moscow, 1966). See also I. S. Braginskii, ed., *Vzaimosviazi literatur Vostoka i Zapada* [Interrelations between the literatures of East and West] (Moscow, 1961).

280. I. S. Braginskii *et al.*, eds., *Problemy stanovleniia realizma v literaturakh Vostoka. Materialy diskussi* [The question of realism in the literatures of the Orient] (Moscow, 1964), 357 pp.

281. B. B. Parnikel', "Ob osnovakh literaturnoi periodizatsii" [The basis of literary periodization], *NAiA*, no. 6 (1965), pp. 136-40.

282. I. S. Braginskii *et al.*, eds., *Problemy teorii literatury i estetiki v stranakh Vostoka* [Problems of literary and esthetic theory in the countries of the East] (Moscow, 1964), 340 pp. Theoretical problems concerning the literatures of Asian peoples were discussed at Leningrad conference, February 2-6, 1970. See *NAiA*, no. 5 (1970), pp. 231-234.

283. A. T. Grigor'ian, ed., *Iz istorii nauki i tekhniki v stranakh Vostoka* [The history of science and technology in Eastern countries], 3 vols. (Moscow, 1960-63).

284. A. T. Grigor'ian, *Fiziko-matematicheskie nauki v stranakh Vostoka*, [Physical-mathematical sciences in Eastern countries], vol. 1 (Moscow, 1966), 358 pp.

285. A number of issues of *KSINA*, vols. 40, 57 (1961); 57, 67, 72 (1963); 62, 68, 86 (1964); 65, 69, 86 (1965), have been dedicated to Oriental languages.

286. M. N. Tikhomirov, M. V. Nechkina, *et al.*, eds., *Ocherki po istorii istoricheskoi nauki v SSSR* [Sketches on the history of historiography in the

U.S.S.R.], 6 vols. (Moscow, 1955-63). For a list of works on Russian and Soviet Oriental studies see vol. III, p. 796; for a list of historiographies of individual Asian countries, see vol. III, pp. 799-805. For a list of works on the Russian and Soviet Oriental studies, see vol. III, p. 796 and a list of historiographies of individual Asian countries, see vol. III, pp. 799-805.

287. V. I. Avdiev, N. P. Shastina, and V. A. Zhukovskii, *Ocherki po istorii russkogo vostokovedeniia* [Sketches on the history of Russian Oriental studies], 5 vols. (Moscow, 1953-60); also Vasilii V. Bartol'd, *Istoriia izucheniia Vostoka v Evrope i Rossii* [History of the study of the East in Europe and Russia] (Leningrad, 1925), 318 pp.

288. See, for example, "Vostokovedenie" [Oriental studies], *BSE*, 9 (1951): 193-202. G. F. Kim (et al), *Obshchʿe i osobennoe v istoricheskom razvitti stran vostoka* [Common and Special in Historical Development of Eastern Countries] (Moscow, 1966), 248 pp.

289. A. N. Kononov, ed., *Vostokovedenie v leningradskom universitete Sbornik statei* [Oriental studies in Leningrad University. A collection of articles] (Leningrad, 1960).

290. L. Maksudov, "Razvitie vostokovedeniia v Tashkentskom universitete" [Development of Oriental studies in Tashkent University], *Problemy vostokovedeniia*, no. 4 (1961), pp. 247-48. See also *NAiA*, no. 6 (1970), pp. 211-13.

291. S. Z. Zakhirov, "Izdaniia na vostochnykh iazykakh v Kazani v pervoi polovine XIX v." [Publications in Oriental languages in Kazan in the first half of the nineteenth century], *PV*, no. 6 (1961), pp. 109-11.

292. Boris V. Lunin, *Srednaia Aziia v dorevoliutsionnom i sovetskom vostokovedeniiu* [Central Asia in Pre-Revolution and Soviet Oriental studies] (Tashkent, 1965), 408 pp.

293. S. A. Azimdzhanova, "Raboty uzbekskikh vostokovedov" [The work of Uzbek Orientalists], *Vestnik AN SSSR*, no. 1 (1968), pp. 73-75.

294. *Josif Samuilovich Braginskii* (Dushanbe, 1966), 93 pp. A biography of the leading Tajik and Soviet Orientalist. Lists Braginskii's contributions to the advancement of Tajik and other Oriental studies.

295. B. V. Lunin, *Iz istorii russkogo vostokovedeniia i arkheologii v Turkestane* [The history of Russian Oriental studies and archeology in Turkestan] (Tashkent, 1958).

296. V. P. Sherstobitov and B. F. Vinnik, "Razvitie istoricheskoi nauki v Sovetskoi Kirgizii (1917-1964)" [The development of historical science in Soviet Kirghizia, 1917-1964], *Voprosy istorii*, no. 2 (1965), pp. 3-26.

297. Grigorii F. Dakhshleiger, *Istoriografiia sovetskogo Kazakhstana* [Historiography of Soviet Kazakhstan] (Alma-Ata, 1969); and by the same author,

"Osnovnye etapy razvitiia istoricheskoi nauki v Sovetskom Kazakhstane" [Basic stages in the development of historical science in Soviet Kazakhstan], *Voprosy istorii*, no. 10 (1964), pp. 3-35.

298. G. P. Basharin, *Obozrenie istoriografii dorevoliutsionnoi Iakuti* [A review of the historiography of pre-Revolution Yakutia] (Yakutsk, 1965).

299. G. Indzhikian, "Vostokovedenie v sovetskoi Armenii" [Oriental studies in Soviet Armenia], *NAiA*, no. 3 (1969), pp. 217-20; Sh. R. Arutiunian, "Armianskaia sovetskaia istoriografiia za sorok let" [Forty years of Armenian Soviet historiography], *Voprosy istorii*, no. 7 (1960), pp. 101-20; G. Kh. Sarkisian, "Izuchenie istorii drevnei Armenii v Armianskoi sovetskoi istoriografii" [A study of the history of Ancient Armenia in Armenian Soviet historiography], *VDI*, no. 2 (1967), pp. 201-2.

300. A. S. Sumbat-zade, "Razvitie istoricheskoi nauki v Azerbaidzhanskoi SSR za gody Sovetskoi vlasti" [The development of historical science in Azerbaijan during the years of Soviet rule], *Voprosy istorii*, no. 11 (1957), pp. 206-18; by the same author, "Istoricheskaia nauka Azerbaidzhana mezhdu XX i XXI s'ezdami KPSS i perspektivy ee razvitiia" [Historical science in Azerbaijan between the Twentieth and Twenty-First Congress of the CPSU and perspectives on its development], *Voprosy istorii*, no. 10 (1959), pp. 121-36; and by the same author, *Istoriografiia Sibiri. Domarksistskii period* [Historiography of Siberia. Pre-Marxist Period] (Moscow, 1970).

301. Komakhidze, "Vostokovedenie v Gruzii."

302. V. G. Mirzoev, *Istoriografiia Sibiri. Pervaia polovina XIX veka* [Historiography of Siberia. First half of the nineteenth century] (Kemerovo, 1965). See also A. I. Andreev, *Ocherki po istochnikovedeniiu Sibiri* [Sketches on the study of Siberian sources] (Moscow-Leningrad, 1960). By the same, *Istoriografiia Sibiri. Domarksistskii period* [Historiography of Sibiria. Pre-Marxist Period] (Moscow, 1970).

303. G. D. Sanzhev *et al.*, eds., *Filologiia i istoriia mongol'skikh narodov* [The philology and history of the Mongol Peoples] (Moscow, 1958), 346 pp. A symposium dedicated to Boris Iakovlevich Vladimirtsov (1884-1931). See esp. the first three chapters; also n. 425.

304. *Mezhvuzovaia nauchnaia konferentsiia, 20-22 dekabria 1966*, pp. 23-24.

305. A. K. Boravkov, ed., *Turkologicheskie issledovaniia* [Turkological investigations] (Moscow-Leningrad, 1962), 298 pp.; L. N. Gumilev, *Drevnie tiurki* [The ancient Turks] (Moscow, 1967); and *Mongolovedenie i tiurkologiia* [Mongolian studies and Turcology] (Moscow, 1964).

306. K. K. Kurdoev comments in *Zapiski Instituta vostokovedeniia*, 25 (1960): 55-67, and also in "Trudy P. I. Lerkha po Kurdovedeniiu (k voprosam

ob izucheniiu istorii Kurdov v Rossii)" [Works of P. I. Lerkh on Kurdish studies: Investigation of the history of the Kurds in Russia], *Ocherki po istorii russkogo vostokovedeniia*, 4 (1959): 39-51.

307. I. Iu. Krachkovskii, *Ocherki po istorii russkoi arabistiki* [Sketches on the history of Russian Arabic studies] (Moscow-Leningrad, 1950).

308. *Istoriia i filologiia Blizhnego Vostoka; Semitologiia* [History and philology of the Near East: Semitology] (Moscow, 1965), 223 pp. A symposium dedicated to the late N. V. Pigulevskaia.

309. E. V. Skazin, *Dagestan v sovetskoi istoricheskoi literature* [Daghestan in Soviet historical literature] (Makhachkale, 1963), 196 pp.

310. A. E. Kuprava, "Kratkii obzor izucheniia istorii Abkhazii za 40 let" [A brief review of forty years of investigation of the history of Abkhazia], *Trudy Abkhazskogo instituta iazyka, literatury i istorii*, 32 (1962): 67-76.

311. N. A. Smirnov, *Ocherki istorii izucheniia Islama v SSSR* [Sketches on the history of the investigation of Islam in the U.S.S.R.] (Moscow, 1954), 275 pp.

312. V. I. Avdiev, *Sovetskaia nauka o drevnem Vostoke za 40 let* [Forty years of Soviet science on the Ancient East] (Moscow, 1958), 103 pp.

313. A. A. Azat'ian, M. I. Belov, *et al.*, eds., *Istoriia otkrytiia i issledovaniia sovetskoi Azii* [History of the discovery and investigation of Soviet Asia] (Moscow, 1969), 534 pp.

314. See, for example, "O rabote vostokovednykh uchrezhdenii v soiuznykh respublikakh" [The work of Oriental institutions in the federal republics], *PV*, no. 6 (1961), pp. 220-23.

315. Soviet writers distinguish between Soviet Asia and Asia beyond the Soviet frontiers (*zarubezhnaia Aziia*). Among other terms employed by Soviet writers are *Dal'nyi vostok* (the Far East), *Iuzhno-vostochnaia Aziia* (Southeast Asia), *Tsentral'naia Aziia* (inner Asia: Mongolia, Manchuria, and the adjacent region), *Srednaia Aziia* (central Asia: The Soviet republics of Uzbekistan, Kirghizstan, Turkmenistan, Tajikstan, and Kazakhstan [the last-named, however, is often treated as a separate geographic region]), *Peredniaia Aziia* (forward Asia: the Near East and the Middle East, as understood in the West), *Blizhnyi vostok* (the Near East: coincides more or less with the Middle East, as understood in the West); *Srednyi vostok* (the Middle East: Iran and Afghanistan), and *Primorie* (the Soviet maritime region: Siberia, Transcaucasia, and the Caucasus).

316. See, for example, *Trudy Tadzhikskoi arkheologicheskoi ekspeditsii Instituta istorii material'noi kul'tury AN SSSR, Instituta istorii, arkheologii i*

etnografii AN Tadzhikskoi SSR i Gosudarstvennogo Ermitazha [Works of the Tajik Archeological Expedition of the Institute of Material Culture of the Academy of Sciences of the U.S.S.R., Institute of History, Archeology and Ethnography of the Academy of Sciences of the Tajik S.S.R. and State Hermitage], 5 vols. (Moscow, 1950-58).

317. See, for example, S. A. Kozlov, *Etnografiia narodov SSSR* (Moscow, 1958); and S. I. Rudenko, *Kul'tura naseleniia Tsentral'nogo Altaia v skifskoe vremia* [Culture of the Central Altain population in the Scythian Era] (Moscow, 1960).

318. On the Gorno-Badakhshan Autonomous Region Expedition to search for documents, see *NAiA*, no. 3 (1964), p. 212.

319. See, for example, I. A. Guseinov *et al., Istoriia Azerbaidzhana* [History of Azerbaijan], 3 vols. (Baku, 1958-63); A. P. Okladnikov *et al., Istoriia buriat-mongol'skoi ASSR* [History of the Buriat Mongolian A.S.S.R.] (Ulan-Ude, 1951); S. A. Tokarev *et al., Istoriia iakutskoi ASSR* [History of the Yakutian A.S.S.R.], 2 vols. (Moscow, 1957); A. P. Okladnikov, *Iakutiia do prisoedineniia k Russkomu gosudarstvu* [Yakutia up to the union with the Russian state] (Moscow, 1955); N. A. Smirnov *et al., Istoriia Kabardy s drevneishikh vremen do nashikh dnei* [History of Kabarda from the earliest times to our day] (Moscow, 1957), 394 pp.; M. O. Auezov *et al., Istoriia Kazakhskoi SSR* [History of the Kazakh S.S.R.], 2 vols. (Alma-Ata, 1957-59); K. K. Karakev *et al., Istoriia Kirgizskoi SSR* [History of the Kirghiz S.S.R.], 3rd ed., 2 vols. (Frunze, 1957-68); S. K. Bushuev *et al., Istoriia Severo-Osetinskoi ASSR* [History of the North Ossetian A.S.S.R.] (Moscow, 1959), 335 pp.; B. G. Gafurov *et al., Istoriia Tadzhikskogo naroda* [History of the Tajik people], 4 vols. (Tashkent, 1963-64); A. Karryev *et al., Istoriia Turkmenskoi SSR* [History of the Turkmen S.S.R.], 2 vols. (Ashkhabad, 1957); R. Kh. Aminov *et al., Istoriia Uzbekskoi SSR*, 4 vols. (Tashkent, 1967-68); and L. P. Potapov, *Istoriia Tuvy* (Moscow, 1964).

A long list of shorter historical surveys has been published. See, for example, G. A. Dzidzariia *et al., Ocherk istorii abkhazskoi ASSR* [Sketch of the history of the Abkhazian A.S.S.R.] (Sukhumi, 1960); S. K. Bushuev *et al., Ocherki istorii Adygei* [Sketches of the history of Adygei] (Maikop, 1957); L. P. Potapov, *Ocherki po istorii Altaitsev* [Sketches of the history of the Altaians] (Moscow, 1953); T. Kh. Kumykov *et al., Ocherki istorii balkarskogo naroda* [Sketches of the history of the Balkar people] (Nal'chik, 1961); M. O. Kosven *et al., Ocherki istorii Dagestana* [Sketches of the history of Daghestan) (Makhachkala, 1957); S. P. Tolstov *et al., Ocherki istorii Karakalpakskoi ASSR* [Sketches of the history of the Karakalpak A.S.S.R.], 2 vols. (Tashkent, 1964).

320. See B. N. Arakelian and A. R. Ioannisian, *Istoriia armianskogo naroda* [History of the Armenian people], vol. 1 (Erevan, 1951); also I. M. D'iakonov,

Predistoriia armianskogo naroda [Prehistory of the Armenian people] (Erevan, 1969); N. A. Berdzenishvili *et al., Istoriia Gruzii* [History of Georgia], vol. 1 (Tbilisi, 1962), 510 pp. The last-named work covers the period from ancient times to the nineteenth century.

321. See, for example, M. S. Totoev, *Iz istorii druzhby osetinskogo naroda s velikim russkim narodom* [History of the friendship of the Ossetian people with the Great Russian people], 2nd ed. (Ordzhonikidze, 1954); S. K. Bushuev, *Iz istorii russko-kabardinskikh otnoshenii* [History of Russo-Kabardin relations] (Nal'chik, 1956); N. A. Khalfin, *Prisoedinenie Serednei Azii k Rossii* [Union of Central Asia with Russia] (Moscow, 1965); Sh. A. Meskhia and Ia. Z. Tsinadze, *Iz istorii russko-gruzinskikh vzaimootnoshenii X-XVIII veka* [History of Russo-Georgian relations between the tenth and the eighteenth centuries] (Tbilisi, 1958); E. P. Alekseeva *et al., Dobrovol'noe prisoedinenie Cherkesii k Rossii (k 400-letnemu iubileiu)* [The voluntary union of Cherkesia with Russia] (Cherkessk, 1957); B. Dzhamgerchinov, *Prisoedinenie Kirgizii k Rossii* [The union of Kirghizia with Russia] (Moscow, 1959); A. N. Usmanov, *Prisoedinenie Bashkirii k moskovskomu gosudarstvu* [The union of Bashkiria with the state of Moscow] (Ufa, 1949); V. P. Nevskaia, *Prisoedinenie Cherkesii k Rossii i ego sotsial'no-ekonomicheskie posledstviia* [The union of Cherkesie to Russia and the socioeconomic consequences] (Cherkessk, 1956).

The whole question of the annexation of non-Russian Asian peoples is still very much alive in Soviet historiography, and widely differing views are being expressed on the subject. Some historians, for example, argue that Russia conquered Cherkesia by force in 1899, while others contend that Cherkesia had voluntarily submitted to Russia in 1557. For a discussion of these and other conflicting views, see M. M. Bliev, "O vremeni prisoedineniia narodov Severnogo Kavkaza k Rossii" [When did the peoples of the North Caucasus unite with Russia?], *Voprosy istorii*, no. 7 (1970), pp. 43-56.

On the Russian impact on Asiatic peoples see, for example, K. Beisembiev, *Mirovozzrenie Abaia Kunanbaeva* [The world outlook of Abai Kunanbaev] (Alma-Ata, 1956); and G. G. Gadzhiev, *Rol' Rossii v istorii Dagestana* [The role of Russia in the history of Daghestan] (Moscow, 1965).

322. For a good coverage of the discussion on the meaning and the importance of the annexation of Asian peoples by Russia, see Lowell Tillett, *The Great Friendship* (Chapel Hill, N. C., 1969), pp. 358-81. For examples of the studies of Russian annexation, see n. 325.

323. M. Abdykalykov and A. Pankratova, *Istoriia Kazakhskoi S.S.R.* [History of the Kazakh S.S.R.] (Alma-Ata, 1943). Histories of other Asian peoples followed a similar line. See, for example, K. G. Kafadarian and M. T. Nersisian, *Istoriia armianskogo naroda* [History of the Armenian people], I (Erevan, 1944); B. Gafurov and N. Prokhorov, *Tadzhikhskii narod v bor'be za svobodu i nezavisimost'* [The Tajik people in their struggle for freedom and independence] (Stalinabad, 1944); E. B. Bekmakhanov, *Kazakhstan v 20-40 gody XIX*

veka [Kazakhstan in the twenties to the forties of the nineteenth century] (Alma-Ata, 1947). Bakmakhanov argued that the Kenesary movement had a popular character and was progressive. After being condemned by official spokesmen he revised his views and accepted the line that the Kenesary movement was reactionary. See E. B. Bekmakhanov, "Feodal'no-monarkhisticheskie dvizheniia v Kazakhstane" [The feudal-monarchistic movements in Kazakhstan], *Uchenye zapiski Kazakhskogo gosudarstvennogo universitetata*, 20 (1965): 66-85.

324. *Geseriade* and *Alpamysh* (depicting the popular struggles of the Uzbeks, the Kazakhs, and the Karakalpaks against nomadic invaders); *Manas* (dealing with the struggle of the Kirghiz people against Oirot, Kalmyk, and other invaders); *Kër-Ogly* (an Azerbaijani epic depicting the popular struggle against the Turkish and Iranian conquerors).

325. One author contends that Jadidism—"a bourgeois nationalist movement"—included honest enlighteners. See M. G. Vakhanov, "O sotsial'noi prirode seredne-aziatskogo dzhadidizma" [The social nature of Central Asian Jadidism], *Istoriia SSSR*, no. 2 (1963), pp. 35-36.

326. Tillett, *The Great Friendship*, pp. 171-93. See Kh. T. Tursunov, *Vosstanie 1916 goda v Srednei Azii i Kazakhstane* [Uprising of 1916 in Central Asia and Kazakhstan] (Tashkent, 1962); and K. U. Usenbaev, *Vosstanie 1916 goda v Kirgizii* [Uprising of 1916 in Kirghizia] (Frunze, 1967). The latter work has been received in the Soviet Union as a definitive study of Kirghiz people against their two enemies—the *baimanapstvo* and tsarism.

327. *Ibid.*, p. 251.

328. See, for example, I. P. Tsamerian *et al.*, *Stroitel'stvo komunizma i preodolenie religioznykh perezhitkov* [The building of communism and the overcoming of religious survivals] (Moscow, 1966), 253 pp.

329. Some of these topics were discussed at a conference held in Dushanbe on 15-17 May 1968. See *Vestnik AN SSSR*, no. 9 (1968), pp. 136-38.

330. See Krachkovskii, *Ocherki po istorii russkoi arabistiki.* On Arabic studies in Russia and the Soviet Union, see the following studies by B. M. Dantsig: *Izuchenie Blizhnego Vostoka v Rossii (XIX nachale XX v)* [Investigations of the Near East in Russia in the nineteenth and early twentieth centuries] (Moscow, 1968); "Iz istorii izucheniia Blizhnego Vostoka v Rossii v vtoroi polovine XVIII v." [History of the investigation of the Near East in Russia in the second half of the eighteenth century], *Sessiia po voprosam istorii i ekonomiki Afganistana, Irana i Turtsii* (Tezisy dokladov) (Moscow, 1962), pp. 91-93; "Iz istorii izucheniia Blizhnego Vostoka" [History of the investigation of the Near East], *Ocherki po istorii russkogo vostokovedeniia*, 2 (1956): 381-414; "Iz istorii russkikh puteshestvii i izucheniia Blizhnego Vostoka v dopetrovskoi Rossii" [History of Russian travels in and studies on the Near East in pre-

Petrine Russia], *ibid*., pp. 185-231; and "Iz istorii izucheniia Blizhnego Vostoka v Rossii (vtoraia chetvrt' XVIII v.)" [History of the investigation of the Near East in Russia during the second quarter of the eighteenth century], *ibid*., 4 (1959): 3-38; and A. G. Karimullin, "Vozniknovenie Rossiiskogo knigopechataniia arabskim shriftom" [Origin of Russian bookprinting in Arabic script], *NAiA*, no. 3 (1969), pp. 95-103.

331. S. S. Korneev, *Nauchnye sviazi Akademii nauk SSSR so stranami Azii i Afriki* [Scientific relations of the Academy of Sciences of the U.S.S.R. with countries of Asia and Africa] (Moscow, 1969), 313 pp.

332. Space does not permit an examination of Soviet work on ancient Egypt, Phoenicia, Assyria, Sumeria, the Hittites, Urartu, and other ancient civilizations. A large quantity of material has been published on early archeology, history, and culture. The Soviet Union produced no historians in this area of the stature of B. A. Turaev (1868-1920), specialist on Egypt, Assyria, and Ethiopia. Turaev was a man of enormous erudition—historian, archeologist, philologist, and historian of art. His "History of the Ancient East" went through a number of editions, and he is considered the founder of the Russian school of ancient Oriental history.

333. Il'ia Pavlovich Petrushevskii, *Islam v Irane v VII-XV vekakh* [Islam in Iran from the seventh to the fifteenth centuries] (Leningrad, 1966).

334. E. A. Beliaev, *Araby, islam i arabskii khalifat v ranee srednevekov'e* [Arabs, Islam, and the Arabic caliphate in the early medieval period] (Moscow, 1965), 280 pp.; also by the same author, *Arabskii khalifat* [The Arab caliphate] (Moscow, 1951).

335. V. B. Lutskii, *Novaia istoriia arabskikh stran* [Modern history of Arab countries] (Moscow, 1965); by the same author, *Modern history of the Arab countries* (Moscow, 1969), a translation.

336. D. R. Voblikov *et al.*, *Noveishaia istoriia arabskikh stran* [Recent history of Arab countries] (Moscow, 1968).

337. I. Iù. Krachkovskii, *Izbrannye sochineniia* [Selected works], 6 vols. (Moscow-Leningrad, 1955-60).

338. N. A. Smirnov, *Ocherki istorii izucheniia Islama*. Under the imprimatur "Ateist" was published in 1931 a symposium *Islam*, which contained a number of essays on various aspects of Islam as well as a bibliography of works on Islam in the Russian language.

339. L. I. Klimovich, *Islam* (Moscow, 1962).

340. S. Bushuev, *Bor'ba gortsev za nezavisimost' pod rukovodstvom Shamilia* [Struggle of the mountaineers for independence under the leadership of Shamil] (Moscow, 1939); and by the same author, *O dvizhenii Shamila* [The movement of Shamil] (Makhach-Kale, 1949).

341. T. Izimbetov, *Kritika ideologii sovremennogo Islama* [A critique of the ideology of contemporary Islam] (Moscow, 1962); and by the same author, *Islam i sovremennost'* [Islam and contemporaneity] (Nukus, 1963), 161 pp. See also S. M. Gadziev, *Osnovnye cherty sovremennogo Islama* [Basic features of contemporary Islam] (Makhach-Kale, 1962).

342. N. A. Smirnov, *Sovremennyi Islam* [Contemporary Islam] (Moscow, 1959).

343. E. A. Beliaev, *Klassovaia sushchnost Islama* [Class essence of Islam] (Moscow, 1934).

344. E. A. Beliaev, *Musul'manskoe sektantstvo* [Muslim sectarianism] (Moscow, 1957).

345. E. A. Beliaev, *Proiskhozhdenie Islama. Khrestomatiia* [Origin of Islam. A chrestomathy] (Moscow, 1931).

346. D. A. Petrushev, *Islam i ego reaktsionnaia sushchnost'* [Islam and its reactionary essence] (Moscow, 1960).

347. I. P. Tsamerian *et al.*, eds., *Stroitel'stvo kommunizma i preodolenie religioznykh perezhitkov* [The building of communism and the overcoming of religious survivals] (Moscow, 1966); O. A. Sukharev, *Islam v Uzbekistane* [Islam in Uzbekistan] (Tashkent, 1960); G. S. Snesarev, "O nekotorykh prichinakh sokhraneniia religiozno-bytovykh perezhitkov u Uzbekov Khorezma" [Some reasons for the preservation of religious survivals among the Uzbeks of Khoresm], *Sovetskaia etnografiia*, no. 2 (1957), p. 68.

348. A. E. Bertel's, *Nasir-i-Khosrov i ismailism* [Nasir-i Khosrov and Ismailism] (Moscow, 1959); and L. V. Stroeva, "Ismaility Irana i Sirii v Zarubezhnoi i sovetskoi istoriografii" [Ismailis of Iran and Syria in foreign and Soviet historiography], in G. V. Eftimov, *Istoriografiia i istochnikovedenie*, 1: 138-48.

349. E. A. Beliaev, *Puritane Islama?* (Moscow, 1967), 262 pp.

350. I. Iu. Krachkovskii, *Koran* (Moscow, 1962), 714 pp.

351. The entire issue of the *Vizantiiskii vremennik*, no. 7 (1953), is dedicated to the Ottoman conquest of Constantinople; Soviet writers reject Western and Turkish interpretation of the conquest.

352. A. Davidovich Novichev, *Istoriia Turtsii* [History of Turkey], 2 vols. (Leningrad, 1963-68). The first volume covers the period from the eleventh to the eighteenth centuries and the second from the eighteenth century on.

353. A. L. Narochnitskii *et al.*, eds., *Vneshnaia politika Rossii XIX i nachala XX veka* (Moscow, 1960-). The six volumes of the first series have appeared;

the series has been suspended, perhaps for ideological and political considerations.

354. Korneev, *Nauchnye sviazi Akademii nauk*, p. 183.

355. On Iranian studies in the Soviet Union, see I. P. Petrushevskii, *History of Iranian studies* (Moscow, 1967), 29 pp.; N. A. Kuznetsova and L. M. Kulagina, "Izuchenie v SSSR istorii, ekonomiki i kul'tury Irana v novoe i noveishee vremia" [Investigations in the U.S.S.R. on the history, economics, and culture of Iran during modern and recent times], *KSINA*, 73 (Moscow, 1963): 213-18; and by the same author, "Osnovnye problemi noveishei istorii Irana v osveshchenii sovetskikh istorikov" [Basic problems of the recent history of Iran in the works of Soviet historians], in D. S. Komissarova and N. A. Kuznetsova, eds., *Iran. Sbornik statei* (Moscow, 1963), pp. 253-67.

356. M. M. D'iakonov, *Ocherk istorii drevnego Irana* [A sketch on the history of Ancient Iran] (Moscow, 1961); and M. A. Dandamaev, *Iran pri pervykh Akhemenidakh* [Iran during the time of the first Achaemenides] (Moscow, 1963).

357. N. V. Pigulevskaia, *Vizantiia i Iran na rubezhe VI i VII vekov* [Byzantium and Iran at the end of the sixth century] (Moscow, 1946).

358. I. P. Petrushevskii, *Zemledelie i agrarnye otnosheniia v Irane XIII-XIV vekakh* [Agriculture and agrarian relations in Iran in the thirteenth and fourteenth centuries] (Leningrad, 1960).

359. N. V. Pigulevskaia, *Goroda Irana v rannem srednevekovie* [Towns of Iran in the early medieval period] (Moscow, 1956), 366 pp.

360. I. P. Petrushevskii, *Islam v Irane v VII-XV vekakh* [Islam in Iran in the seventh to fifteenth centuries] (Leningrad, 1966).

361. N. V. Pigulevskaia *et al., Istoriia Irana s drevneishikh vremen do kontsa XVIII veka* [History of Iran from the earliest times to the end of the eighteenth century] (Leningrad, 1958), 390 pp.

362. Korneev, *Nauchnye sviazi*, pp. 185-94.

363. See *Vestnik AN SSSR*, no. 6 (1966), pp. 64-68, a report on Soviet archeological work in Afghanistan. On Soviet-Afghan scientific relations and cooperation, see Korneev, *Nauchnye sviazi*, pp. 196-203.

364. M. S. Ivanov, *Razvitie feodalizma i obrazovanie gosudarstva u Afgantsev* [The development of feudalism and the formation of the Afghan state] (Moscow, 1956), 416 pp.

365. R. T. Akhramovich, *Afganistan posle vtoroi mirovoi voiny* [Afghanistan after the Second World War] (Moscow, 1961).

366. F. S. Nukhovich, *Vneshnaia politika Afganistana* [Foreign policy of Afghanistan] (Moscow, 1962).

367. L. B. Teplinskii, *Sovetsko-afganskie otnosheniia, 1919-1960. Kratkii ocherk* [Soviet-Afghan relations, 1919-60. A short sketch] (Moscow, 1961).

368. V. M. Masson and V. A. Romodin, *Istoriia Afganistana* [History of Afghanistan], 2 vols. (Moscow, 1957-64).

369. On Indian studies in the Soviet Union, see L. B. Alaev, "Izuchenie istorii Indii v SSSR v 1917-1934 godakh" [Investigation of the history of India in the U.S.S.R., 1917-34], *NAiA*, no. 2 (1963), pp. 160-72; and by the same author, *Indology* (Moscow, 1967), 45 pp.; also Aleksandr A. Guber, *Izuchenie Indii v Sovetskom Soiuze* [The study of India in the Soviet Union] (Moscow, 1954), 30 pp. On Indian studies in Russia before the Revolution, see L. S. Gamaiunov, "Iz istorii izucheniia Indii v Rossii" [History of the study of India in Russia], *Ocherki po istorii russkogo vostokovedeniia*, 2 (1956): 74-117; and G. G. Kotovskii, ed., *Ivan Pavlovich Minaev* (Moscow, 1967).

370. For a discussion of the Indian socioeconomic order during ancient and medieval times, see L. S. Gamaiunov, "O marksovoi kontseptsii sotsial'no-ekonomicheskogo stroia Indii" [Marx's conception of the socioeconomic order in India], *NAiA*, no. 3 (1968), pp. 57-67; also M. K. Kudriavtsev, "Kontseptsiia Indiiskogo feodalizma v sovetskoi istoriografii" [Conception of Indian feudalism in Soviet historiography], *NAiA*, no. 1 (1970), pp. 72-84; also E. M. Medvedev, "Feodal'nye otnosheniia v derevnei i srednevekovoi Indii" [Feudal relations in ancient and medieval India], *NAiA*, no. 3 (1970), pp. 71-79.

371. A. M. D'iakov, *India vo vremia i posle vtoroi mirovoi voiny* [India during and after the Second World War] (Moscow, 1952), 262 pp.

372. G. M. Bongard-Levin and G. F. Il'in, *Drevnaia Indiia* [Ancient India] (Moscow, 1969), 735 pp.; *Srednevekovaia istoriia Indii* [Medieval history of India] (Moscow, 1968), a collective work; K. Antonov *et al.*, *Novaia istoriia Indii* [Modern history of India] (Moscow, 1961), 833 pp.; and V. V. Balabushevich and A. M. D'iakov, *Noveishaia istoriia Indii* [Recent history of India] (Moscow, 1959), 758 pp.

373. Iu. V. Gankovskii, *Narody Pakistana. Osnovnye etapi etnicheskoi istorii* [Peoples of Pakistan. Basic stages in their ethnic history] (Moscow, 1964).

374. Iu. V. Gankovskii, *Natsional'nyi vopros i natsional'noe dvizhenie v Pakistane* [The national question and the national movement in Pakistan] (Moscow, 1967).

375. Iu. V. Gankovskii and L. R. Gordon-Polonskaia, *Istoriia Pakistana* (Moscow, 1961).

376. On Soviet studies of Southeast Asia, see A. B. Belen'kii, "Sovetskie

nauchnye trudy po Indonezii" [Soviet scientific works on Indonesia], *NAiA*, no. 4 (1961), pp. 207-11; no. 1 (1969), pp. 182-90; and A. Guber *et al.*, "Kolonial'naia politika zapadnykh derzhav v iugo-vostochnoi Azii v svete russkikh arkhyvnykh istochnikov" [Colonial policy of Western states in Southeast Asia in the light of Russian archival sources], *Trudy XXV Mezhdunarodnogo kongressa vostokovedov*, 4 (Moscow, 1963), pp. 301-11; N. N. Miklukho-Maklai, *Puteshestviia* [Travels], 2 vols. (Moscow-Leningrad, 1940-41); and by the same author, *Sobranie sochinenii* [Collected works], 4 vols. (Moscow-Leningrad, 1950-53).

377. A. A. Guber *et al.*, *Politika evropeiskikh derzhav v Iugovostochnoi Azii (60-e gody XVIII–60-e gody XIX v)*. *Dokumenty i materialy* [Policy of European states in Southeast Asia from the sixties of the eighteenth century to the sixties of the nineteenth century. Documents and materials] (Moscow, 1962), 655 pp.

378. A. B. Belen'kii, *Natsional'noe probuzhdenie Indonezii* [National awakening of Indonesia] (Moscow, 1965), 346 pp. Since the appearance of this book others have written extensively about the Indonesian national liberation movement and contemporary political situation. See symposium *Natsional'no-osvoboditel'noe dvizhenie v Indonezii (1942-1965)* [National-liberation movement in Indonesia (1942-1965)] (Moscow, 1970), 295 pp.; V. A. Tsyganov, *Natsional'no-revoliutsionnye partii Indonezii* [National revolutionary parties of Indonesia] (Moscow, 1969); A. Iu. Drugov and A. B. Reznikov, *Indoneziia v period napravliaemoi demokratii* [Indonesia in the period of Guided Democracy] (Moscow, 1969).

379. E. Alioshin, *Sovetskoe-Indoneziiskoe otnoshenie v mae 1945-1962 godakh* [Soviet-Indonesian relations from May 1945 to 1962] (Moscow, 1963).

380. Korneev, *Nauchnye sviazi.*

381. *Problemy Kitaia* (1929-35), published by *Institut mirovogo khoziaistva i mirovoi politiki*, organ of the Communist Academy; *Novyi Dal'nyi vostok*, organ of the VNAV; *Novyi vostok*; and *Revoliutsionnyi vostok.*

382. On Chinese studies in Russia and the Soviet Union, see *Sinology*, Academy of Sciences of the U.S.S.R. Institute of the Peoples of Asia (Moscow, 1967), 15 pp.; Tikhomirov *et al.*, *Ocherki istoricheskoi nauki v SSSR*; and Iu. V. Chudodeev, ed., *Velikii Oktiabr' i razvitie sovetskogo Kitaevedeniia* [Great October and the development of Soviet Oriental studies] (Moscow, 1968), 171 pp. There are several items on Sinological studies in Russia in the previously cited five-volume *Ocherki po istorii russkogo Vostokovedeniia*. See also V. N. Nikiforov, ed., *Materialy k khronike Sovetskogo vostokovedeniia. Istoriia Mongolii i Kitaia* [Materials relating to the chronicle of Soviet Oriental studies. The history of Mongolia and China] (Moscow, 1965), 227 pp.; G. V. Eftimov, "Problemy novoi i noveishei istorii Kitaia v sovetskoi istoriografii (1964-1966 gg)" [The problems of the new and the recent history of China in

Soviet historiography (1964-1966 gg)], *Vestnik Leningradskogo universiteta*, no. 2 (1967), pp. 13-20; and A. N. Khokhlov *et al.*, *Voprosy istorii i istoriografii Kitaia* [Problems of history and historiography of China] (Moscow, 1968), 278 pp.

383. For a very recent work, see M. V. Kriukov, *Formy sotsial'noi organizatsii drevnikh Kitaitsev* [Forms of social organization of ancient Chinese] (Moscow, 1967). On Soviet interpretations of Chinese history and institutions, see also B. N. Zanegin, ed., *Istoriografiia i istochnikovedenie stran zarubezhnogo vostoka* [Historiography and study of sources of the countries of Foreign East] (Moscow, 1967), 197 pp.; and G. V. Eftimov, ed., *Istoriografiia i istochnikovedenie istorii stran Azii i Afriki* [Historiography and study of sources of the history of the countries of Asia and Africa] (Moscow, 1967), 197 pp.

383a. For the latest Soviet position on the "Asiatic mode of production" see essays by N. B. Ter-Akopian and V. N. Nikiforov in *Obshchee i osobennoe v istoricheskom razvitii stran Vostoka* [Common and Special in Historical Development of Eastern Countries] (Moscow, 1966).

384. L. S. Vasil'ev, "Izuchenie problemy genezisa kitaiskoi tsivilizatsii" [Investigation of the problem of the genesis of Chinese civilization], in G. V. Eftimov, ed., *Istoriografiia i istochnikovedenie istorii stran Azii*, 1 (Leningrad, 1965): 8-11. See also N.N. Cheboksarov, "K voprosu proizkhodstva Kitaetsev" [The question of the origin of the Chinese], *Sovetskaia etnografiia*, no. 1 (1947), p. 53.

385. On the antifeudal movements in China, from the tenth to the thirteenth centuries, and the interpretation of these movements, with accompanying bibliography, see G. Ia. Smolin, "Antifeodal'nye narodnye vosstaniia v Kitae kontsa X-XIII vekov v sovetskoi i kitaiskoi istoriografii" [The antifeudal peoples' uprisings in China from the end of the tenth to the thirteenth centuries in Soviet and Chinese historiography], in Eftimov, *Istoriografiia i istochnikovedenie istorii stran Azii*, 1: 12-21.

386. See, for example, N. A. Vinogradova, *Iskusstvo srednevekovogo Kitaia* [The art of medieval China] (Moscow, 1962).

387. N. F. Demidova and V. S. Miasnikov, *Pervye russkie diplomaty v Kitae* [The first Russian diplomats in China] (Moscow, 1966), 157 pp.; also P. I. Iakovleva, *Pervyi russko-kitaiskii dogovor 1689 g.* [The first Russo-Chinese Agreement, 1689], (Moscow, 1958), 235 pp.

388. See particularly V. P. Iliushechkin and O. G. Soloviev, eds., *Taipinskoe vosstanie 1850-1865* [The Taipei Uprising, 1850-1864] (Moscow, 1966); and V. P. Iliushechkin, *Krest'ianskaia voina taipinov* [The Taipei Peasant Uprising] (Moscow, 1967).

389. I. Irmashev, *Sun Yat-sen* (Moscow, 1964), 318 pp. Many studies have

been published on Sun Yat-sen, "a staunch supporter of friendship between the Soviet and Chinese peoples." On 10-11 November 1966, the one-hundredth anniversary of his birth was the occasion for a professional meeting. See *Vestnik AN SSSR*, no. 12 (1966), pp. 92-93.

390. On the character of people's democracies in Eastern countries, see E. M. Zhukov, "Ob kharaktere i osobennostiakh narodnoi demokratii v stranakh Vostoka" [The specifics of people's democracies in Eastern countries], *Izvestiia AN SSSR*, Seriia istorii i filologii, no. 1 (1952), pp. 99-104.

391. G. V. Eftimov, *Ocherki po novoi i noveishei istorii Kitaia* [Sketches of modern and recent history of China], 1st ed. (Moscow, 1949), 2nd ed.(Moscow, 1951).

392. L. V. Simonskaia *et al.*, eds., *Ocherki istorii Kitaia* [Sketches of the history of China] (Moscow, 1956); also N. P. Vinogradov *et al.*, eds., *Ocherki istorii Kitaia v noveishee vremia* [History of China in most recent times] (Moscow, 1959). Though other surveys of modern Chinese history have appeared since then, the quality has not improved.

393. R. F. Etes and G. I. Smolin, *Ocherki istorii Kitaia s drevneishikh vremen do serediny XVII v* [Sketches of the history of China from the earliest times to the midseventeenth century] (Moscow, 1961). Since the sixties Soviet Chinese studies have suffered as a result of strained relations between Peking and Moscow. In 1960 the Institute of Chinese Studies was converted into the Section for Chinese Studies in the Institute of the Peoples of Asia. Some of the Sinologists were transferred to such organizations as the Institute of Economy of the World Socialist System, the Institute of Philosophy, the Institute of Law (a part of Moscow State University), and the Institute of International Workers Movements. See *Iz istorii*, p. 192.

394. V. A. Bogoslovskii, *Ocherki istorii tibetskogo naroda* [Sketches of the history of the Tibetan people] (Moscow, 1962).

395. A. I. Vostrikov, *Tibetskaia istoricheskaia literatura* [Tibetan historical literature] (Moscow, 1962), 427 pp.

396. A. P. Okladnikov, *Daleko proshloe Primor'ia* [The distant past of the maritime region] (Vladivostok, 1959); *Ocherki istorii sovetskogo Primor'ia* [Sketches of the history of the Soviet maritime region] (Vladivostok, 1963); and *Istoriia Sibiri* (Ulan-Ude, 1964). See also the symposiums *Narody Azii* [Peoples of Asia] (Moscow-Leningrad, 1965), and *Narody vostochnoi Azii* [Peoples of East Asia] (Moscow-Leningrad, 1966).

397. On Russian investigation of Mongol history, see A. Iu. Iakubovskii, "Iz istorii izucheniia Mongolov perioda XI-XIII vv." [History of the investigation of the Mongols from the eleventh to the thirteenth centuries], *Ocherki po istorii russkogo vostokovedeniia* (Moscow, 1953), pp. 31-95; also R. L. Baldaev

and N. N. Vasil'ev, *Ukazatel' bibliografii po Mongolovedeniiu na russkom iazyke* [Guide to the bibliography of Mongol studies in the Russian language] (Leningrad, 1962).

398. B. D. Grekov and A. Iu. Iakubovskii, *Zolotaia orda i ee padenie* [The Golden Horde and its fall] (Moscow, 1950), 428 pp.

399. Nina Pavlovna Shastin, *Izuchenie mongol'skikh letopisei v SSSR* [Investigation of Mongol chronicles in the U.S.S.R.] (Moscow, 1963), a pamphlet; also Sh. Bira, *Mongol'skaia tibetoiazychnaia istoricheskaia literatura (XVII-XIX vv)* [Mongol historical literature in the Tibetan language] (Ulan Bator, 1960), 82 pp.; and A. G. Galstian, ed., *Armianskie istochniki o Mongolakh* [Armenian sources on the Mongols] (Moscow, 1962).

400. N. Ts. Munkuev, *Kitaiskii istochnik o pervykh mongol'skikh khanakh* [A Chinese source on the first Mongol khans] (Moscow, 1965).

401. See, for example, *NAiA*, no. 6 (1969), pp. 10-22, an article on the Mongolian People's Republic's realization of the "Leninist Cooperative Plan." Several short books have appeared on the founding and the history of the Mongolian People's Republic.

402. See, for example, I. Ia. Ziatkin, *Ocherki novoi i noveishei istorii Mongolii* [Sketches of modern and recent history of Mongolia] (Moscow, 1957).

403. See, for example, *NAiA*, no. 1 (1969), pp. 28-43.

404. See a short note on Japanese cultural ties with Europe in *NAiA*, no. 3 (1969), pp. 88-94.

405. A. L. Galperin, *Ocherki sotsial'no-politicheskoi istorii Iaponii v period pozdnego feodalizma* [Sketches on the sociopolitical history of Japan during the late feudalism period] (Moscow, 1963).

406. E. I. Fainberg, *Russko-Iaponskie otnosheniia v 1697-1875 gg* [Russo-Japanese relations from 1697 to 1875] (Moscow, 1960).

407. L. N. Kutakov, *Portsmutskii mirnyi dogovor 1905-1945* [The Portsmouth Peace Treaty, 1905-1945] (Moscow, 1961); and by the same author, *Istoriia sovetsko-iaponskikh diplomaticheskikh otnoshenii* [History of Soviet-Japanese diplomatic relations] (Moscow, 1962).

408. B. A. Romanov, *Ocherki diplomaticheskoi istorii russko-iaponskoi voiny 1895-1907* [Sketches on the diplomatic history of the Russo-Japanese War, 1895-1907] (Moscow, 1947), 496 pp.; 2nd ed. (Moscow, 1955), 696 pp.

409. D. Petrov, *Rabochee i demokraticheskoe dvizhenie v Iaponii* [Workers and the democratic movement in Japan] (Moscow, 1961).

410. V. A. Popov, *Krest'ianskoe dvizhenie i Iaponiia posle vtoroi mirovoi voiny* [The peasant movement and Japan after the Second World War] (Mos-

cow, 1961); and G. I. Podpalova, *Krest'ianskoe petitsionnoe dvizhenie v Iaponii vo vtoroi polovine XVII-XVIII vekov* [The peasant petition movement in Japan in the second half of the seventeenth and the eighteenth centuries] (Moscow, 1960). There is also a study of a medieval town in Japan by A. A. Iskanderov.

411. A. L. Galperin, ed., *Ocherki novoi istorii Iaponii* [Sketches of the modern history of Japan] (Moscow, 1958).

412. On Russian investigations of Korea, see G. D. Tiagai, "Trudy russkikh issledovatelei kak istochnik po novoi istorii Korei" [Works of Russian investigators as a source of modern history of Korea], *Ocherki po istorii russkogo Vostokovedeniia*, pp. 122-47.

413. Iu. V. Vanin, *Feodal'naia Koreia v XIII-XIV vekakh* [Feudal Korea in the thirteenth and fourteenth centuries] (Moscow, 1962).

414. M. V. Vorobiev, *Drevnaia Koreia* [Ancient Korea] (Moscow, 1961).

415. G. D. Tiagai, *Krest'ianskoe vostanie v Koree 1893-1895* (Moscow, 1961).

416. G. D. Tiagai, *Ocherk istorii Korei vo vtoroi polovine XIX v* [A sketch of the history of Korea in the second half of the nineteenth century] (Moscow, 1961).

417. G. D. Tiagai, *Narodnoe dvizhenie v Koree v vtoroi polovine XIX veka* [The nationalist movement in Korea in the second half of the nineteenth century] (Moscow, 1958), 78 pp.

418. I. Shipaev, *Koreiskaia burzhuaziia v natsional'no-osvoboditel'nom dvizhenii* [The Korean bourgeoisie in the national liberation movement] (Moscow, 1966).

419. I. S. Kazakevich, *Agrarnyi stroi v Iuzhnoi Koree* [The agrarian order in southern Korea] (Moscow, 1954).

420. F. I. Shabshin, *Sotsialisticheskaia Korea* [Socialistic Korea] (Moscow, 1963).

421. V. Griaznov, *Sotsialisticheskaia industrializatsiia v KNDR* [Socialistic industrialization in the Korean People's Democratic Republic] (Moscow, 1966). There is also a book on the general economic situation in southern Korea; see B. V. Sinitsyn, *Ocherki ekonomiki Iuzhnoi Korei* (Moscow, 1967).

422. Tiagai, *Ocherk istorii Korei.*

CHAPTER IV

1. A theocratical state established in Daghestan by Sheik Shamil, third Imam of the Nakshbandi Sufi order in the early thirties of the nineteenth century.

This state, based on the strict application of the koranic law (*shari'at*), lasted up to the definitive Russian conquest of Daghestan in 1859.

2. Sporadic contacts between the Russians and Muslims have existed since the ninth century, and probably there were even earlier contacts.

3. Cf. A. Bennigsen and Ch. Quelquejay, *Les mouvements nationaux chez les Musulmans de Russie: Vol. 1, Le "Sultangaliévisme" au Tatarstan* (Paris–La Haye, 1960), pp. 21-26; also N. N. Firsov, *Proshloe Tatarii* [The past of Tataria] (Kazan, 1926), p. 25 *passim*.

4. *Istoriia Tatarskoi A.S.S.R.* [History of the Tatar A.S.S.R.] (Kazan, 1955) 1: 188 *passim*.

5. G. Gubaidullin, "Iz proshlogo Tatar" [The past of the Tatars], in *Materialy po izucheniiu Tatarstana* [Materials for the study of Tatarstan] (Kazan, 1925), pt. II, p. 83; also N. A. Firsov, *Inorodcheskoe naselenie Kazanskogo tsarstva i novoi Rossii do 1762 i kolonizatsiia Zakamskikh zemel'* [The autochthonous population of the Kingdom of Kazan and of the New Russia before 1762 and the colonization of the Transkama territories] (Kazan, 1869), one of the best works on early Russian colonization of Middle Volga.

6. On this problem, see *Istoriia Tatarskoi ASSR*, p. 208; and A. N. Grigor'ev, "Khristianizatsiia nerusskikh narodnosteii kak odin iz metodov natsional'noi politiki tsarizma" [The Christianization of non-Russian peoples as one of the methods of national policy of tsarism], in *Materialy po istorii Tatarii*, 1 (Kazan, 1948): 234 ff. The tsarist attitude is reflected in two excellent works: A. O. Malov, *O Novokreshchenskoi Kontore* [Concerning the Novokreshchenskaya Kontora] (Kazan, 1878); and A. F. Mozharovskii, *Izlozhenie khoda missionerskogo dela po prosveshcheniiu kazanskikh inorodtsev s 1552 po 1867 gody* [Description of missionary activity among the non-Russian natives of Kazan from 1552 to 1867] (Moscow, 1880).

7. G. Gubaidullin, "K istorii razlozheniia feodal'nogo klassa u privolkhskikh Tatar" [The decline of feudal class among Volga Tatars], *Vostokovedenie*, 1 (Baku, 1926): 49-74.

8. *Ukaz* of 1713 in *Polnoe sobranie zakonov Rossiiskoi Imperii*, VI, art. 27-34, pp. 66-67. Cf. Gubaidullin, "Iz proshlogo Tatar," p. 91.

9. On this subject, see the works by Grigor'ev, Malov, and Mozharovskii; also S. L. Ursynovich, "Novokreshchenskaia Kontora–k voprosu o roli pravoslavnogo missionerstva v kolonizatsionnoi i natsionnal'noi politiki samoderzhaviia" [The Novokreshchenskaia Kontora and the role of the Orthodox missionaries in the colonial and national policy of the autocracy], *Ateist*, Moscow, no. 54 (1930), pp. 22-56.

10. G. Gubaidullin, "Pugachevshchina i Tatary" [Tatars and the revolt of Pugachev], *Izvestiia Obshchestva obsledovaniia i izucheniia Azerbaidzhana*

(Baku, 1927), no. 4, pp. 74-103; and by the same author, "Uchastie Tatar v Pugachevchine" [The participation of Tatars in the revolt of Pugachev], *Novyi vostok* (Moscow, 1924), no. 1, pp. 262-68.

11. *Ukaz* of 17 April 1773, *Polnoe sobranie zakonov Rossiiskoi Imperii*, vol. 19, no. 13996, pp. 795-96.

12. *Ukaz* of 22 September 1782, *ibid.*, vol. 22, no. 16710, pp. 1107-08.

13. Grigor'ev, "Khristianizatsiia nerusskikh," p. 257.

14. Cf. G. Gubaidullin, "Iz istorii torgovogo klassa u privolzhskikh Tatar" [The history of the merchant class among Volga Tatars], *Vostokovedenie* (Baku, 1926), 1: 59-61; also K. Fuks, *Kazanskie Tatary v statisticheskom i etnograficheskom otnoshenii* [Kazan Tatars from the statistical and ethnographical point of view] (Kazan, 1844). This book remains one of the best works on Tatar society.

15. On this little-known problem, see D. Koblov, *O tatarizatsii inorodtsev privolzhskogo kraia* [The Tatarization of the Volga natives] (Kazan, 1910); also S. A. Tokarev, *Etnografiia narodov S.S.S.R.* [Ethnography of the peoples of the U.S.S.R.] (Moscow, 1958), p. 171.

16. Completed with the annexation of the khanate of Kokand in 1876 and the construction of the Transcaspian and Orenburg-Tashkent railways in 1899 and 1906.

17. This policy was inaugurated by Nikolai Ivanovich Il'minskii, professor of the Theological Academy of Kazan and first director of the Central School for Christian Tatars in Kazan. On this subject, cf. *Kazanskaia Tsentral'naia Kreshcheno-tatarskaia Shkola* [The Central School for Christian Tatars in Kazan] (Kazan, 1887). For the Soviet point of view, see M. Gorokhov, *Reaktsionnaia shkol'naia politika tsarizma v otnoshenii tatar Povolzh'ia* [Reactionary education policy of tsarism among Volga Tatars] (Kazan, 1941); and I. Levin, "Materialy k politike tsarizma v oblasti pis'mennosti inorodtsev" [Contribution to the study of tsarist literary policy among natives], *Kul'tura i pis'mennost' Vostoka*, 6 (Baku, 1930).

18. N. V. Nikol'skii, *Naibolee vazhnye statisticheskie svedeniia ob inorodtsakh Vostochnoi Rossii i Zapadnoi Sibiri podverzhennykh vliianiiu Islama* [The most important statistical information concerning natives of Eastern Russia and Western Siberia subjected to the influence of Islam] (Kazan, 1912); and by the same author, *Kreshchenie Tatary—Statisticheskie svedeniia za 1911 god* [Christian Tatars—statistical information for 1911] (Kazan, 1914).

19. Cf. the excellent work by Jemaleddin Validov, a former Muslim Tatar reformist who joined the Soviet regime in 1920, *Ocherki istorii obrazovannosti*

i literatury Tatar do revoliutsii 1917 goda [Outline of Tatar education and literature before the 1917 Revolution] (Moscow, 1933).

20. The best work on prerevolutionary Tatar society is Galimjan Ibragimov, *Tatary v Revoliutsii 1905 goda* [The Tatars in the 1905 Revolution] (Kazan, 1926).

21. The Tatar historian Fatyh Sayfi wrote in his "Tatary do fevral'skoi Revoliutsii" [The Tatars before the February Revolution], in *Ocherki po izucheniiu mestnogo kraia* (Kazan, 1930), pp. 192-93, "[at this moment] the Tatar society possessed all the elements of a capitalist society."

22. Cf. *1906 sene 12-16 Augustda iftima etmish Rusiya Müsülmanlarinin nedvesi* [Congress of the Muslims of Russia, August 1906] (Kazan, 1906), in Tatar; and *Bütün Rusiya Müsülmanlarinin 1917-nchi yilda 1-2 Mayda Meskvede bulgan umumi isyezdinin protokollari* [Proceedings of the Pan-Russian Muslim Congress in Moscow, on 1-2 May, 1917], in Turkish; also Musa Jarulla Bigi (Bigiyev), *Eslahat Esaslari* [The basis of the reform] (Petrograd, 1915-17), in Tatar.

23. Our best source on this problem are two books by Soviet authors, A. Arsharuni and K. H. Gabidullin, *Ocherki panislamizma i panturkizma v Rossii* [Outline of Pan-Islamism and Pan-Turkism in Russia] (Moscow, 1931); and Galimjan Ibramigov, *Tatary v Revoliutsii 1905 goda.* In Western languages, see Richard Pipes, *The Formation of the Soviet Union*, 2nd ed. (Cambridge, Mass., 1964); and Gerhard von Mende, *Der Nationale Kampf der Russland Tuerken* (Berlin, 1936).

24. Among many others, the Tatar Yusuk Ahchura, publisher in Istanbul of the famous *Türk Yurdu*; the Azeri, Ali Husein Zade, member of the Central Committee of the "Ittihad ve Tarakki" party; and Ahmed Aga oglu, in 1924 deputy of Kars Province in the Turkish Parliament.

25. On this subject, see the exhaustive work of Edige Kirimal, a Crimean Tatar émigré in Germany, *Der Nationale Kampf der Krim Tuerken* (Emsdetten, 1952); and a good article by a Soviet author, V. Elagin, "Natsionalisticheskie illiuzii Krymskikh Tatar v revoliutsionnye gody" [The nationalist delusions of the Crimean Tatars during the Revolution], *Novyi vostok* (Moscow, 1924), no. 5, pp. 190-216; and no. 6, pp. 205-25.

26. Cf. A. I. Markevich, "Pereselenie krimskikh Tatar v Turtsiiu" [The emigration of Crimean Tatars into Turkey], in *Biulleten' Akademii Nauk*, 7th series (1928), pp. 375-405; and 1929, pp. 1-16; and A. K. Bochagov, *Milli Firka—Natsional'naia kontrevoliutsiia v Kryma* [Milli Firka—the national counterrevolution in the Crimea] (Simferopol, 1930).

27. On this little-known subject the basic work is A. A. Takho-Godi, *Revoliutsiia i kontrrevoliutsiia v Dagestane* [Revolution and counterrevolution in Daghestan] (Moscow, 1927).

28. There are few really good works devoted to the intellectual and political life of the Muslim community in prerevolutionary Russian Azerbaijan. One of the best is the work of an émigré Azeri, M. Z. Mirza Balla, *Milli Azerbaycan Hareketi* [The National Movement in Azerbaijan] (Berlin, 1938), in Turkish.

29. The so-called Lithuanian and Kasymov Tatars, numbering fewer than 20,000 and cut off from their coreligionists in the fifteenth and sixteenth centuries.

30. English text in Richard Pipes, *The Formation of the Soviet Union*, 2nd ed. (Cambridge, Harvard Univ. Press, 1964), p. 155.

31. Cf. Bennigsen and Quelquejay, *Islam in the Soviet Union* (London, 1967), p. 82.

32. For more details, cf. Bennigsen and Quelquejay, "The Evolution of the Muslim Nationalities of the U.S.S.R. and their Linguistic Problems," *Central Asian Research Centre*, London, 1961.

33. The leader of Muslim "national communism" in the U.S.S.R., the Tatar Sultan Galiev, was arrested and officially condemned in early 1928. Cf. Bennigsen and Quelquejay, *Les mouvements nationaux chez les Musulmans de Russie*, p. 180 *passim*.

34. The French translation in Bennigsen and Quelquejay, *Les mouvements nationaux*, pp. 226-39.

35. First of all, by Stalin himself, at the 4th conference of the Central Committee of the Russian Communist Party (RCP) with the workers of the republics and national regions, Moscow, 9-12 June 1923 (text in Stalin's *Works*, in Russian [Moscow, 1952], 5: 301-2; French translation in *Les mouvements nationaux*, pp. 239-45). The text of the resolution of the conference condemning Muslim "national deviations" was published some ten years later in *Revoliutsiia i natsional'nosti*, no. 11 (1933), pp. 107-8; French text in *Les mouvements nationaux*, pp. 246-48.

36. The *waqfs* were liquidated in 1925, the religious courts closed in 1927 (Decree of the Central Executive Committee of the U.S.S.R., 21 September 1927), and the closing of mosques began in 1927. Their number was reduced from more than 26,000 in 1912 (excluding Bukhara and Khiva) to fewer than 2,000 in 1939.

37. With the antireligious campaign in Muslim Transcaucasia we are very familiar, thanks to the excellent work of Djeyhun Hadjibeyli, *Antiislamistskaia propaganda i ee metody v Azerbaidzhane* [Anti-Islamic propaganda in Azerbaijan and its methods] (Munich, Institute for the Study of the U.S.S.R., 1959).

38. On this subject, cf., for the Volga Region (Tatarstan and Bashkiria), *Les mouvements nationaux*, pp. 188-93; for the Crimea, Bochagov, *Milli-Firka*,

and Elagin, "Natsionalisticheskie illiuzii"; for Azerbaijan, Hadjibeyli, *Antiis-lamistskaia propaganda*; and Mehmed Emin Rasul-Zade, *L'Azerbayjan en lutte pour l'independance* (Paris, 1930).

39. The most typical "nationalist" crisis that shook Azerbaijan in 1950-56 opposed Russians to Muslims on the problem of interpretation of the Russian conquest of North Caucasus and of the Muridism. Cf. Bennigsen and Quelque-jay, *Islam in the Soviet Union*, pp. 218-22.

40. For instance, S. Dorjehov, "Musul'manin li ia?" [Am I a Muslim?], *Nauka i Religiia*, 4 (1967): 50-52.

41. Cf. my article, "La littérature antireligieuse dans les Républiques Soviét-iques musulmanes," *Revue des Etudes Islamiques* (Paris, 1958), pp. 73-85.

42. Statistics according to the latest Soviet census (1959); see table 2 (general statistics of Muslim National Languages), *Islam in the Soviet Union*, p. 233.

43. For instance, in 1963 there were 7,209 Azeri and 6,251 Tatar research workers [*Nauchnye rabotniki*] as against 5,990 Uzbeks, 3,793 Kazakhs, 1,211 Tajiks, 1,011 Turkmens, and 834 Kirghiz (cf. *Islam in the Soviet Union*, table 7, p. 235).

44. In this brief account we have had to neglect discussion of many impor-tant aspects concerning Russian-Muslim relations. Problems such as the rural collectivization and its effects are more strongly felt in Central Asia and Kazakhstan, where the Russian rural colonization is still active, than in the Caucasus or in the Mid-Volga. In these two regions, rural collectivization did not bring the Russians and the Muslims closer because collective farms (*kol-khozes*) seldom have a mixed population.

CHAPTER V

1. On the ravages and impact on Armenia of the Mongol invasions of the eleventh to the fourteenth centuries, see Hakob Manandian, *Knnakan tesutiun hai zhogovurdi patmutian* [A critical exposition of the history of the Arme-nian people] (Erevan, 1952), vol. 3, chaps. X-XI, XIII, XVI, XVIII; L. H. Babayan, *Hayastani Sotsial-tntesakan ev kaghakakan patmutiune XIII-XIV darerum* [The social-economic and political history of Armenia in the 13th to 14th centuries] (Erevan, 1964), pp. 525-67; also for Turkic invasions. On Ot-toman-Persian wars and their consequences for Armenia, see H. Kh. Nadjarian, *Turk-Iranakan haraberutiunnere XVI darum ou XVII dari aradjin kesin ev Haystane* [Armenia and Turco-Iranian relations during the 16th century and the first half of the 17th century] (Erevan, 1961), pp. 104-13, 152-58, 199-229; and Leo (pseud. for Arakel Babakhanian), *Hayots patmutiun* [History of the Armenians] (Erevan, 1946), 3: 171 ff.

2. For the text of the 1639 agreement, see Nadjarian, pp. 282-86; A. Kh. Safrastian (compiler), *Turkakan aghbiurnere Hayastani, Hayeri ev Andrkovkasi mius zhogovurdneri masin* [The Turkish sources pertaining to Armenia, the Armenians, and the other peoples of Transcaucasia] (Erevan, 1961); 1: 210-12. See also J. Hammer, *Geschichte der osmanischen Reiches* (Budapest, 1834), 3: 44-45; and J. C. Hurewitz, ed., *Diplomacy in the Near and Middle East: A Documentary Record, 1535-1914* (Princeton, 1956), 1: 21-23.

3. On the administrative divisions of the Ottoman and Persian Armenias, see T. Kh. Hakobian, *Urvagdser Hayastani Patmakan ashkharagrutian* [Outlines of the historical geography of Armenia] (Erevan, 1960), pp. 347-68; and Leo, 3: 51-53, 59-66. For the organization, rights, and prerogatives of the five Armenian principalities, see Leo, 3: 499-512.

4. For instance, in 1578 during the Ottoman-Persian wars, the Ottomans took some sixty thousand Armenians captive from the region of Erevan and transferred them to the western regions of their empire. In 1603-04, under the orders of the Safawid ruler Shah Abbas, an estimated 350,000 Armenians were forced out of Eastern Armenia for resettlement in Persia. In 1618-23 the Khan of Erevan in his raids on Western Armenia forced Armenian populations out of there to resettle them in various districts of his domain. See Hakobian, *Urvagdser*, pp. 383-84, 345-47; Leo, pp. 239-69; and Nadjarian, p. 153.

5. A. G. Abrahamian, *Hamarot urvagids hai gaghtavaireri patmutian* [A concise outline of the history of the Armenian colonial settlements] (Erevan, 1964), on the colonies of Georgia, pp. 91-111; on Kiev and Volga regions, pp. 112-25; on Poland, pp. 197-233; on Bulgaria, pp. 305-27; on Rumania, pp. 328-61; on Russia, pp. 362-402; on the Crimea, pp. 157-96. On the last-named colony see also the monographic study of V. A. Mikaelian, *Ghrimi haikakan gaghuti patmutiun* [History of the Armenian colony of Crimea] (Erevan, 1964). For a historiographic survey of that colony, see *ibid.*, pp. 5-22. For a general survey of the Armenian colonies of the period, see Arshak Alpoyajian, *Patmutiun hai gaghtakanutian; hayeru tsrvume ashkari zanazan masere* [A history of the Armenian emigration: Dispersion of the Armenians in various parts of the world] (Cairo, 1955, 1961), vols. 2 and 3.

6. For a survey of these early relations, see Ashot Hovhannisian, "Hayeri Rusakan koghmnvoroshman nakhapatmutiunits" [On the background of the Russian orientation of the Armenians], in *Patma-Banasirakan Handes* [Historical-philological journal] (henceforth *PBH*) (Erevan, 1958), no. 1, pp. 65-70.

7. The two works were "The Life of Grigor Partev" and "The Life and Acts of Hripsimiantz Virgins." The Russian work was "The Life and Acts of Boris (Roman) and Gleb (David)." See V. Parsamian, "Hai-Rusakan haraberutiunneri patmutiunits" [Of the history of Russian-Armenian relations], in *Teghekagir* [*Izvestiia*] of the Social Sciences of the Armenian S.S.R. Academy of Sciences, Erevan (henceforth *Teghekagir*), no. 7 (1952), pp. 60, 61.

8. Academician B. D. Grekov, *Kievaskaia Rus* (Moscow, 1949), p. 429; David Talbot Rice, *Byzantine Art* (Oxford, 1935), p. 213; O. M. Dalton, *East Christian Art* (Oxford, 1925), p. 25; G. H. Hamilton, in *The Art and Architecture of Russia* (Baltimore, 1954), pp. 35-36, says: "the character of the carved ornament on the Vladimir-Suzdal churches. . .[has] such close analogies with the tenth- and eleventh-century churches of the Caucasus and Armenia that one must accept the possibility that Andrei's architects, or the artisans collaborating in their structures, were familiar with the plan and distribution of relief sculpture on the Armenian cathedrals"; see also pp. 37 and 38. One of the frescoes of the Cathedral of Novgorod represented Armenian saints Gregory the Illuminator and Hripsimé. In the thirteenth century one of the churches of Ani was decorated by a Russian painter (see Parsamian, p. 61).

9. Mikaelian, pp. 41-82, 157-94; Hovhannisian, p. 74.

10. L. Melikset-Bek, *Drevniaia Rus' i Armenia* (in "Scientific Studies," publ. by the Linguistic Institute of the Academy of Sciences of the Armenian S.S.R., Erevan, 1946), p. 118; Abrahamian, pp. 118-19.

11. L. Khachikian, "Haikakan gaghtavayrer Ukraniaium XVI-XVII DD" [Armenian colonial settlements in the Ukraine in the 16th-17th centuries], *Teghekagir*, no. 4 (1954), p. 50.

12. Abrahamian, p. 118; Khachikian, pp. 48-49, 52, 54; Parsamian, p. 62; A. Hovhannisian, p. 73.

13. I. A. Linichenko, *Lehastani ev arevmtian-haravain Rusiayi Hayere* [The Armenians of Poland and Southwest Russia], trans. from the Polish (Moscow, 1894); Simeon Lehatsi, *Ughegrutiun* [Travelogue], Father Nerses Akinian, ed. (Vienna, 1935). For the prerogatives and privileges of the Polish Armenians, see M. L. Hovhannisian, "Lehahayeri iravakan vitjake 16-17 rd darerum" [The legal status of the Polish Armenians in the 16th-17th centuries], *Teghekagir*, no. 9 (1965), pp. 35-48; Abrahamian, pp. 211-17; Khachikian, p. 51; Ashot Hovhannisian, pp. 39, 42.

14. H. E. Galstian, "Hai dprotsakan tatrone arevmtian Ukraniaium" [The Armenian school-theatre in the Western Ukraine], *Teghekagir*, no. 6 (1959), pp. 51-64. On the cultural and literary contributions of Ukrainian-Polish Armenian communities, see Khachikian, pp. 67-80; and Abrahamian, pp. 227-33.

15. Abrahamian, pp. 210-11; A. Hovhannisian, p. 42. A great deal has been written by Ukrainian historians on the position and the role of the Armenian colonies in the Ukraine. For a historiographic survey, see I. R. Dashkevich, "Ukrainakan patmagrutian nerdrume Hai-Ukrainakan pokharaberutiunneri usumnasirutian gordsum" [The contributions of Ukrainian historiography in the task of the study of Armenian-Ukrainian relations], *Teghekagir*, no. 6 (1964), pp. 27-40.

16. M. I. Tikhomirov, *Srednevekovaia Moskva v XIX-XV vekakh* (Moscow, 1957), pp. 215-16; and his *Drevniaia Moskva* (Moscow, 1947), p. 142; Parsamian, pp. 63-64.

17. A. Hovhannisian, p. 73.

18. V. O. Kliuchevskii, *Skazaniia inostrantsev o moskovskom gosudarstve* (Petrograd, 1918), p. 252.

19. For the interesting background and origins of this concession and its future political and economic implications for Russia and for Armenian capital in Persia, see V. Voskanian's article based on archival materials, "Hai-Rusakan haraberutiunnere XVII darum" [Armenian-Russian relations in the 17th century], *Teghekagir*, no. 1 (1948), pp. 59-62; Parsamian, pp. 67-77. See also Samuel H. Baron, ed. and trans., *The Travels of Olearius in 17th Century Russia* (Stanford, 1967), Introduction, p. ii. For the text and correspondence relating to the concession of the tsar, see V. A. Parsamian *et al.*, eds., *Armiano-russkie otnosheniia v XVII v: Sbornik dokumentov*, 1: 34 ff., 139. For the position of the Armenian merchants in Persia and India, see Abrahamian, pp. 234-64, 435-85.

20. Parsamian, *Armiano-russkie otnosheniia*, 1: 224, 237 ff.; also his "Hai-Rusakan," pp. 78-79.

21. Baron, p. 328. N. Kostomarov attests to the great commercial importance of Astrakhan as an emporium for merchants of the Caucasus-Caspian region and the East. See his *Ocherki torgovli moskovskogo gosudarstva v XVI-XVII stoletiakh* (St. Petersburg, 1862), pp. 43, 47, 107-12. See also Kliuchevskii, p. 297.

22. A. Iukht, "Vostochnaia torgovlia Rossii v 30-40 godakh XVIII i pole v nei armianskikh kuptsov," *Izvestiia Akademii Nauk Armianskoi S.S.R.*, no. 8 (1956), pp. 57, 60-61; also in the same publication, his "Astrakhani Haikakan Gaghuti Bnakchutian sotsialakan kazme 18-rd dari aradjin kesum" [The social structure of the Astrakhan Armenian colony during the first half of the 18th century], no. 7 (1957), pp. 48-53.

23. E. I. Zaozerskaia, *Rabochaia sila i klassovaia bor'ba na tekstil'nykh manufakturakh Rossii v 20-26kh gg XVIII v.* (Moscow, 1960), p. 298; P. I. Mikhailov, "O vozniknovenii kapaliticheskoi manufaktury v Rossii," *Voprosy istorii*, no. 2 (1957), p. 81; also V. A. Khachatrian, "Naselenie armianskoi kolonii v Astrakhane vo vtoroi polovine XVIII veka," *Izvestiia (Teghekagir)*, Erevan, no. 7 (1965), pp. 77-87.

24. A. P. Gritskevich, "Armianskaia manufaktura v Belorussii v kontse XVIII v," in *Lraber Hasarakakan Gitutiunneri* (Vestnik Obshchestvennykh Nauk, Akademiia Nauk Armianskoi S.S.R.), Erevan, no. 4 (1967), pp. 44-53.

25. Abrahamian, pp. 379-80.

26. E. I. Zaozerskaia, *Razvitie legkoi promyshlennosti v Moskve v pervoi chetverti XVIII v* (Moscow, 1953), p. 308.

27. P. G. Liubomirov, *Ocherki po istorii Russkoi promyshlennosti* (Moscow, 1947), p. 578.

28. A. Semënov, *Izuchenie istoricheskikh svedenii o Russkoi vneshnei torgovle i promyshlennosti* (St. Petersburg, 1859), 1: 173.

29. For the Armenian community of St. Petersburg, see Abrahamian, pp. 377-81; and V. A. Diloyan, "Edjer Rusastani hai vadjarakan kapitali patmutiunits" [Pages from the history of the Armenian mercantilistic capital in Russia], *PBH*, no. 2 (1962), pp. 73-74.

30. Diloyan, pp. 75, 81.

31. M. G. Nersisian, *Iz istorii russko-armianskikh otnoshenii* (Erevan, 1956), 1: 99-100; also his "A. V. Souvorov ev Rus-Haikakan haraberutiunnere 1770-1790" [A. V. Suvorov and Russian-Armenian relations: 1770-1790], *Teghekagir*, no. 2 (1943), pp. 28-34. On other details of the emigration of Armenians of the Crimea, see Mikaelian, pp. 337-83.

32. Kh. Porksheian, "Nor Nakhidjevani gaghuti patmutiunits" [On the history of New Nakhichevan colony], *Teghekagir*, no. 10 (1957), pp. 54-55.

33. Abrahamian, pp. 376-78.

34. *Ibid.*, pp. 378-92. For the correspondence of Suvorov regarding the matter, see Nersisian, "Souvorove," pp. 43-45.

35. V. B. Barkhudarian, "Nor Nakhichevani inknavarutiune" [The self-rule of New Nakhichevan], *PBH*, no. 2 (1965), pp. 176-86; and Abrahamian, p. 388.

36. Diloyan, p. 80; Abrahamian, pp. 401-02; Porksheian, p. 59.

37. Porksheian, p. 59.

38. A. A. Adamian, "Vaveragrer 1812T. Hairenakan Paterazmi masin" [Documents pertaining to the War of the Fatherland in 1812], *Teghekagir*, no. 8 (1964), pp. 77-83.

39. For these diplomatic moves, see respectively Ghevond Alishan, *Hai-Venet* [Armenia-Venice] (Venice, 1898), pp. 325-30; H. Kurdian, "Hai azatagrakan pordz me XVI darum" [An attempt at Armenian liberation in the 16th century], *Anahit* (Paris, 1937), nos. 5-6; Leo, 3: 188-97; Archbishop Malachia Ormanian, *Azgapatum* [Story of the Nation] (vol. 1, Constantinople, 1913; vol. 2, Jerusalem, 1927), 2: 2252-81. For a detailed analysis of these missions, see Ashot Hovhannisian, *Drvagner Hai azatagrakan mtki patmutian* [Episodes in the history of Armenian liberation thought] (Erevan, 1959), 2: 26-50.

40. *Ibid.*, pp. 163-222; Leo, 2: 343-48.

41. For the text of the letter, see Parsamian, *Armiano-russkie otnosheniia,* pp. 257-58. For an analysis of the letter, see A. Hovhannisian, *Drvagner,* 2: 214-17.

42. For the text of the letter, see Parsamian, *Armiano-russkie otnosheniia,* pp. 91-92.

43. *Ibid.*, pp. 40, 71, 78, 84. For details of Lusikov's activities, see Voskanian, pp. 63-68. For a survey of prehistory of Armenian orientation toward Russia, see A. Hovhannisian, *Drvagner,* 2: 419, 494.

44. For the life and activities of Israyel Ori, see A. Hovhannisian, *Drvagner,* 2: 227-415; and Leo, 3: 513-89. For his Russian project see A. Hovhannisian, *Drvagner,* 2: 494-521. For a thesis arguing against Israyel Ori's intended national-liberation mission, see H. Kurdian, "Israyel Orii Kiankin Aradjin Shrdjane" [The first period of Israyel Ori's life], *Hairenik* (Boston), 34 (Jan. 1956): 70-78; "Israyel Orin Moskvayi Medj" [Israyel Ori in Moscow], *ibid.* (Feb. and March 1956).

45. For the developments of the period, see S. P. Poghossian, *Hai zhoghovurdi patmutiun* [History of the Armenian people] (Erevan, 1965), 2: 278-300; P. Arutiunian, "Poslanie Mkhitar-Beka Russkomu pravitelstvu," *Teghekagir,* no. 3 (1952), pp. 83-99; A. Mirzoian, "Mkhitar Begi koghmits Russakan karava rutian ughvats ugherdzi hartsi shurdj" [Regarding the problem of the Mkhitar Beg's message to the Russian government], *Teghekagir,* no. 8 (1952), pp. 87-98. For the documents pertaining to Peter the Great's policies vis-à-vis Armenians, see G. A. Ezov, ed., *Snosheniia Petra Velikogo s Armianskim narodom* (St. Petersburg, 1898).

46. Leo, 3: 769.

47. Poghossian, pp. 303-13; Leo, 3: 773-803. For the life of Emin, see his autobiography: Joseph Emin, *Life and Adventures of Emin Joseph Emin 1726-1809* (1st ed., London, 1792; 2nd ed., Calcutta, 1918), 2 vols. For a detailed critical study of his activities, see A. R. Ioannisian, *Iosef Emin* (Erevan, 1945); and his *Rossiia i armianskoe osvoboditel'noe dvizhenie v 80kh godakh XVIII stoletiia* (Erevan, 1947).

48. Ioannisian, *Iosif Emin,* pp. 266-78; Poghossian, pp. 318-20.

49. Leo, 2: 900-24; Poghossian, 2: 303-25. To further their aims they entered into correspondence with General Suvorov; see Nersisian, "Souvorov," pp. 40-45. For the socioeconomic character of the move, see T. Avdalbegian, "Hai azatagrakan sharjman erku hosank XVIII dari verdjum" [Two currents in the Armenian liberation movement at the end of the 18th century], *Nork,* Erevan, 1922.

50. G. H. Grigorian, *Hai Aradjavor Hasarakakan Kaghakakan Mtki Patmutiun*

[The history of Armenian progressive social-political thought] (Erevan, 1959), pp. 341-43; Leo, 2: 1024-44; Avdalbegian, *ibid.*

51. John F. Baddeley, *The Russian Conquest of the Caucasus* (London, 1908), pp. 65-82; V. Parsamian, *Haiastane XIX dari arajin kesin* (Erevan, 1960). For the Treaty of Gulistan, see Hurewitz, 2: 84-86.

52. For Turkmenchai, see Hurewitz, 2: 91-102; Ali Akbar Bina, *La question iranienne au début du XIX siècle* (Paris, 1939), chap. IV and pp. 236-47; also Firuz Kazemzadeh, "Russia and the Middle East," in Ivo J. Lederer, ed., *Russian Foreign Policy* (New Haven, 1962), p. 491. For a detailed account of the military operations of 1826-27 based on archival materials, see D. Muradian and V. Martirosian, "Arevelian Haiastane Rusastanin mianalu taregrutiunits" [A chronological account of the union of Eastern Armenia with Russia], *Teghekagir*, no. 12 (1957), pp. 18-30.

53. For a detailed account of this assistance and cooperation, see V. Parsamian, *Haiastane*, pp. 33, 54; and Z. T. Grigorian, *Rus ev. Hai zhoghovurdneri razmakan hamagortsaktsutiune XIX dari skzbin* [The mutual military assistance of the Russian and Armenian peoples at the beginning of the 19th century] (Erevan, 1957); also his "Hayeri masnaksutiune arevelian Haiastani azatagrman gordzin" [The participation of Armenians in the liberation of Eastern Armenia], *Teghekagir*, no. 11 (1951), pp. 13-39. For another account see "Vaveragrer Hai ev Rus zhoghovrdneri kaperits 1827-1833TT" [Documents pertaining to the relations of Armenian and Russian peoples, 1827-1833], *Banber Haiastani Arkhivneri* (Erevan, 1961), no. 1, pp. 99-122. For the attempts of Decembrist Mikhail Ivanovich to organize an Armenian volunteer army during 1827-28, see *Teghekagir*, no. 4 (1952), pp. 103-10.

54. G. Lazian, *Haiastan ev Hai Dat* [Armenia and the Armenian question] (Cairo, 1946), p. 24; Mikael Varandian, *Haikakan sharjman nakhapatmutiun* [Prehistory of the Armenian movement] (Geneva, 1912), 1: 212.

55. Lazian, p. 25.

56. A. Hovhannisian, *Nalbandiane ev nra amanake* [Nalbandian and his times] (Erevan, 1955), 1: 42-43; Al. Yeritsian, *Amenayn hayots katoghikosutiune ev Kovkasi haik XIX darum* [The Catholicosate of All Armenians and the Armenians of the Caucasus in the 19th Century] (Tbilisi, 1894), Part I, pp. 276, 375; Varandian, 1: 225.

57. N. B. Sarukhanian, "Arevelian Haiastani miatsume Rusastanin jamanaki hai gordzitchneri gnahatumov" [The union of East Armenia with Russia as evaluated by the Armenian political activists of the time], *Lraber*, no. 7 (1967), pp. 52-62.

58. Parsamian, *Haiastane XIX dari kesin*, p. 93.

59. Hakobian, *Urvagdser*, pp. 391-94.

60. V. Parsamian, *Tsarizmi gaghutain kaghakakanutiune Haiastanum* [The colonial policy of tsarism in Armenia] (Erevan, 1940); and his *A. S. Griboedove ev Hai-Rusakan haraberutiunnere* [A. S. Griboedov and Armeno-Russian relations] (Erevan, 1947), as well as his *Haiastane XIX dari kesin*, pp. 123-26.

61. For the administrative changes, see Hakobian, pp. 391-99; E. Esadze, *Istoricheskaia zapiska ob upravlenii kavkazom* (Tbilisi, 1907), 2: 45. V. N. Ivanenko, *Grazhdanskoe upravlenie Zakavkazia* (Tbilisi, 1901), p. 376.

62. B. Parsamian, "Hai zhoghovurdi patmutiun (1830-1850)" [The history of the Armenian people, 1830-1850], *Teghekagir*, no. 1 (1956), p. 70.

63. For the unfavorable socioeconomic position of the Armenian peasantry on the eve of the annexation of Eastern Armenia to the Russian Empire, see V. H. Rshtuni, "Feodalakan haraberutiunnere arevelian Haiastanum" [Feudal relations in Eastern Armenia], *PBH*, no. 2 (1958), pp. 13-37; and S. S. Markosian, "Rusastani mianalu nakhoriakin arevelian Haiastani hoghatirutian ev tjortatirutian hartsi shurj" [On the problem of land-ownership and serfdom in Eastern Armenia on the eve of its union with Russia], *PBH*, nos. 3-4 (1961), pp. 245-72. For a monographic study of the history of the Armenian peasantry, see V. H. Rshtuni, *Urvagdser Haiastani gughatsiutian patmutian: 1828-1917* [Outlines of the history of the Armenian peasantry] (Erevan, 1960), Part I, 1828-1878, pp. 7-72, 256, 261.

64. David Ananun, *Rusahayeri hasarakakan zargatsume: 1870-1900* [The social development of Russian Armenians] (Echmiadzin, 1922), 2: 25; also G. Guzalian, "Hai heghapokhutunits aradj" [Before the Armenian Revolution], in *Hushapatum H. H. Dashnaktsutian 1890-1950* [On the memories of the Armenian Revolutionary Federation, 1890-1950] (Boston, 1950). p. 29.

65. For statistical data, see I. Shopen, *Istoricheskii pamiatnik sostoianiia Armianskoi oblasti v epokhu ee prisoedineniia k Rossiiskoi imperii* (St. Petersburg, 1852), pp. 1219-22, as quoted by Rshtuni, *Urvagdser*, pp. 110-16.

66. Parsamian, *Tsarizmi gaghutain kaghkakanutiune*, pp. 109-25. For modern assessments, see Rshtuni, *Urvagdser*, pp. 119-26, and his *Krest'ianskaia reforma v Armenii v 1870g* (Erevan, 1947), p. 88; and M. A. Adontz, *Ekonomicheskoe razvitie vostochnoi Armenii v XIX v.* (Erevan, 1957), pp. 231 ff., 241.

67. Parsamian, "Hai zhoghovurdi patmutiun, 1830-1850," p. 72; Rshtuni, *Urvagdser*, pp. 122-24.

68. Rshtuni, *Krest'ianskaia reforma*, pp. 86-87.

69. Rshtuni, "Haiastani XIX dari giughatsiakan sharjumneri masin" [Concerning peasant movements in 14th-century Armenia], *Teghekagir*, no. 6 (1945), pp. 40-42, 46-50; also his *Urvagdser*, chap. III.

70. Ananun, 2: 33-34.

71. *Ibid.*, p. 35.

72. Rshtuni, *Urvagdser*, pp. 247-49.

73. Ananun, 2: 35-36.

74. Rshtuni, *Krest'ianskaia reforma*, pp. 166-68.

75. Rshtuni, *Urvagdser*, p. 250. Such a policy had already been in effect in the Northern Caucasus since the 1830s. See N. A. Smirnov, *Miuridizm na Kavkaze* (Moscow, 1963), pp. 222-23.

76. For statistical sources and analyses, see Ananun, 2: 36-37.

77. Rshtuni, *Krest'ianskaia reforma*, pp. 168-70.

78. Ananun, 2:37.

79. *Ibid.*, 2: 40-44.

80. Rshtuni, *Krest'ianskaia reforma*, pp. 170-71.

81. For a unique statistical breakdown of these villages and their population make-up, see Ananun, 2: 7-13.

82. Ananun, 2: 11.

83. Rshtuni, "Haiastani XIX dari giughatsiakan sharjumnere," pp. 62-63; D. A. Muradian, *Haiastane Rusakan Aradjin revoliutsiai tarinerin: 1905-1907* [Armenia during the years of the first Russian Revolution 1905-1907] (Erevan, 1964), p. 16.

84. A. M. Esayan, *Mulkdarskoe pravo v Armenii; Ocherki po istorii krupnogo chastnogo zemlevladeniia v dorevoliutsionnoi Armenii v XVIII-XX vv.* (Erevan, 1948), pp. 141-49; M. Nersisian, "Hai zhoghovurdi patmutiun 1901-1917 TT" [History of the Armenian people, 1901-1917], *Teghekagir*, no. 5 (1955), p. 39.

85. O. E. Tumanian, *Razvitie ekonomiki Armenii nachala XIX veka do ustanovleniia Sovetskoi vlasti* (Erevan, 1947), p. 267; Ananun, 2: 44-45. On the economic plight of the Armenian peasants and their exodus from the villages, see also M. Nersisian, "Haiastani tntesakan ev kaghakakan drutiune 1860-1880 TT" [The economic and political situation of Armenia in the years 1860-1880], *Teghekagir*, no. 10 (1946), pp. 37-38.

86. F. Makharadze, *Ocherki revoliutsionnogo dvizheniia v Zakavkazii* (Tbilisi, 1927), p. 43; Adontz, p. 519; Z. Korkotian, *Khorhrdain Haiastani bnakchutiune verjin hariuramiakum, 1831-1931* [The population of Soviet Armenia during the past one hundred years] (Erevan, 1935), pp. 164-67.

87. *Kratkii ocherk ekonomicheskogo polozheniia Kavkaza* (Tbilisi, 1888), p. 12, as quoted by Nersisian, "Haiastani tntesakan ev kaghakakan," p. 39. For other statistical data, see Ananun, 2: 48-49.

88. Ananun, 2: 47-48.

89. Nersisian, "Haiastani tntesakan," p. 40.

90. Ananun, 2: 53.

91. *Ibid.*, pp. 53-54, 56-57; Nersisian, "Haiastani tntesakan," p. 40; also A. M. Yeghiazarian, "Andrkovkasi hai bnakchutian sotsialakan kazmi masin," [On the social make-up of the Armenian population of Transcaucasia], *Teghekagir*, no. 9 (1961), p. 64.

92. Yeghiazarian, p. 64.

93. *Ibid.*, p. 64; Ananun, 2: 58, 65.

94. Ananun, pp. 62-64.

95. *Ibid.*, pp. 65-66.

96. I. Nikoladze, *Armiano-Gruzinskiie otnosheniia v 1893-1898 gg* (Tbilisi, 1920); Ananun, 2:111-15.

97. Ananun, 2: 111-12. In Baku during 1906-09, among citizens with the right to vote in municipal elections, out of a total of 2,807 there were 944 Armenian electors; 1,399 Tatar-Turk electors; and of the 464 remaining, some were Russian, others mixed (Ananun, 3: 423).

98. Yeghiazarian, pp. 62, 63.

99. For an excellent article based on first-hand statistical accounts and an analysis of the Armenian population of Transcaucasia, see Nersisian, "Haiastani Tntesakan Ev Kaghakakan Drutiune 1860-1880TT," pp. 34, 35.

100. *Ibid.*, p. 37.

101. H. Tumanian, "Haiastanum kapitalizmi zargatsman mi kani arandznahatkutiunneri masin," [Concerning a few peculiar characteristics of the development of capitalism in Armenia], *Teghekagir*, no. 3 (1947), p. 26.

102. Muradian, p. 18.

103. Nersisian, "Haiastani Tntesakan," pp. 38-39; H. Tumanian, "Haiastanum Kapitalizmi," p. 29.

104. For instance, in 1891 some 379,864 *puds* of goods from Persia passed through Armenia, in 1892 some 482,395, and in 1893 639,910 *puds* (see Muradian, pp. 31-32).

105. Tumanian, *Razvitie ekonomiki Armenii s nachala XIX veka do ustanov-leniia Sovetskoi vlasti*, p. 67.

106. Adontz, pp. 187-88. On the early exploitation of the mineral resources of the Alaverdi mines in the Lori district, see V. A. Melkonian, *Metallurgia medi v Armenii* (Moscow, 1955), pp. 5 ff.

107. Shopen, p. 754; S. Gulishambarov, *Obzor fabrik i zavodov Zakavkazskogo kraia* (Tbilisi, 1894), p. 379.

108. *Kavkazskii kalendar'* (Tbilisi, 1902), p. 56; 1909, p. 507; Muradian, pp. 22-23.

109. *Kavkazskii kalendar'* (Tbilisi, 1909), pp. 507 ff., 561-62; and Nersisian, "Haiastani tntesakan ev kaghakakan drutiune," p. 39. See also O. E. Tumanian, *Ekonomichekoe razvitie Armenii* (Erevan, 1954), 1: 208-11; Adontz, p. 415.

110. A. S. Hambarian, "Gordzaranian artadrutian zargatsume nakhasovetakan Haiastanum" [The development of factory production in pre-Soviet Armenia], *Teghekagir*, no. 10 (1959), pp. 17, 18.

111. *Ibid.*, p. 19; Muradian, p. 25; and Tumanian, "Haiastanum," pp. 32-33. The number of small wineries increased rapidly from 1892 on. Thus, whereas at that time there were only some 274 in Erevan Province, by 1900 the number had reached 517 (see A. Hambarian, "Manufakturayi zargatsume Haiastani ardunaberutian medj" [The development of manufactures in Armenian industry], *Teghekagir*, no. 12 (1958), p. 32.

112. Hambarian, *Manufakturayi*, p. 29; Muradian, pp. 27-28.

113. Hambarian, "Gordzaranain," pp. 20-21, 24-25.

114. Muradian, p. 28.

115. Hambarian, "Gordzaranain," pp. 22-23; Tumanian, *Razvitie ekonomiki*, p. 67.

116. V. A. Parsamian, *Hai zhoghovurdi patmutiun, 1801-1917* [History of the Armenian people] (Erevan, 1967), p. 373; and Tumanian, *Razvitie ekonomiki Armenii*, p. 268.

117. Parsamian, *Hai zhoghovurdi patmutiun*, p. 373.

118. Ananun, 2: 123. See also V. S. Yerkanian, "Edjer Andrkovkasi haikakan dprotsi patmutiunits" [Pages from the history of the Armenian school in Transcaucasus], *Lraber*, no. 1 (1967), p. 21.

119. F. Makharadze, *Gruziia v XIX veke* (Tbilisi, 1933).

120. M. Ormanian, *The Church of Armenia* (London, 1912), p. 152; and H. F. B. Lynch, *Armenia* (London, 1901), 1: 234-35.

121. Ananun, 2: 106-9.

122. Ananun, 2: 128-64. See also V. S. Yerkanian, "Hayeri krtakan gordzi zargatsman endhanur bnutagzere" [The general characteristics of the development of educational work of the Armenian], *Lraber*, no. 6 (1967), pp. 35-37.

123. Ananun, 3: 494-45; see also pp. 27-66.

124. A. Astvadzatrian, "Rusahai mshakutayin hastatutiunnere" [Cultural establishments of Russian Armenians], *Hairenik Amsagir*, May 1939, p. 150.

125. Lynch, 1: 220-21.

126. Yerkanian, "Hayeri krtakan gordze," p. 37; M. G. Gamaghelian, "Aradjdimakan gaghaparneri tapantsume Gevorkian Djemaran" [On the advent of progressive ideas in Gevorkian Djemaran], *Teghekagir*, Oct. 1964, pp. 45-50.

127. In 1919 it became Armenian Institute, in 1920 Central Institute of Living Oriental Languages, and in 1921 Moscow Institute of Oriental Studies.

128. V. A. Diloyan, "Lazarian Djemarane" [Lazarian Academy], *Teghekagir*, Dec. 1965, pp. 43 f.

129. Armenian Academy of Sciences, *Hai nor grakanutian patmutiun* [History of New Armenian Literature] (Erevan, 1962), vol. 1, chap. 7; and Henry Gabrielian, *Hai pilisopayakan mtki patmutiun* [History of Armenian philosophical thought] (Erevan, 1959), vol. 3, chap. 3.

130. See S. Sarinian, "Hiusisapaili realistakan ardzake" [The realist prose of Hiusisapail], *Teghekagir*, no. 12 (1953), pp. 41-59; Armenian Academy of Sciences, *Hai nor grakanutian patmutiun*, vol. 1, chap. 1; and Henry Gabrielian, chap. 3.

131. See Armenian Academy of Sciences, *Hai nor grakanutian patmutiun*, 1: 38-40; G. Hovnan, "Pushkini yerkerits katarvats hayeren aradjin targmanutiune" [The first Armenian translation from the works of Pushkin], *Teghekagir*, no. 4 (1950), pp. 56-59; Gh. Ayvazian, "A. S. Pushkine yev hai grakanutiune" [A. S. Pushkin and Armenian literature], *ibid.*, no. 5 (1949), pp. 3-8.

132. G. Harutiunian and V. Vartanian, "Tiflisi hayeren grkeri hratarakchakan enkerutian ev hai groghneri pokhharaberutiunnere" [The mutual relationship of Armenian writers and the Armenian publishing company of Tbilisi], *Banber Haiastani Arkhivneri*, no. 1 (1960), pp. 178-211; Ayvazian, pp. 3, 6-20. See also A. Injikian, "Lermontove ev hai vatsunakannere" [Lermontov and the Armenians in the sixties], *Teghekagir*, no. 8 (1946), pp. 61-69.

133. Using this as a base, during the last phase of the Stalinist period the Soviet-Marxist theoreticians and linguists stressed the desirability of using standard Russian words that dealt with Marxist-Leninist ideology; i.e.: a) dialektika, materializm, utopiia, proletariat, diktatura, konstitutsiia, teoriia, revoliutsiia, evolutsiia; b) those that dealt with the revolutionary movement: agitator, demokrat, interventsiia, minimum, maksimum, tsentrist, opozitsiia, oportunist, funksiia, conspiratsiia; c) technical words such as agregat, avto, kino, radio, traktor, tekhnika, gaz, fond, faktura; d) technical words in the sports: alpinist, rekord, shakhmaty, gol, chempion, sport, tennis. See G. Ghazarian, "Rusereni azdetsutian mi kani drsevorumner ardi hayerenum" [A few manifestations of the influence of Russian in present-day Armenian], *Teghekagir*, no. 8 (1946), pp. 43-57.

134. V. Terzibashian, *Hai dramaturgiai patmutiun*, 1668-1868 (Erevan, 1959), vol. 1, chap. 6. See also A. Babaian, "Mi edj hai tatroni patmutiunits" [A page from the history of the Armenian theater], *Teghekagir*, no. 3 (1958), pp. 61-67.

135. Armenian Academy of Sciences, *Hai nor Grakanutiun*, 3: 66-67.

136. V. Terzibashian, *Hai dramaturgiai patmutiun* (Erevan, 1964), vol. 2, chaps. 3-6. See also R. Zarian, "Paikare hai tatronum Maxim Gorku dramaturgiaii hamar" [The struggle in the Armenian theater for the dramaturgy of Maksim Gor'kii], *Teghekagir*, no. 10 (1954), pp. 25-48.

137. M. Muradian, "Hai-Ukraniakan yerazhshtakan kaperi patmutiunits," *Teghekagir*, no. 10 (1954), pp. 49-58; Alexander Shahverdian, *Hai yerazhshtutian patmutian aknarkner* [Glimpses of the history of Armenian music] (Erevan, 1959), pp. 148-92.

138. Armenian Academy of Sciences, *Hai nor grakanutian patmutiun*, 3: 55-58; and 1: 47-48. See also Izabella Ginzburg, "Armianskie khudozhniki pervoi polovine XIX v," *Patmabanasirakan Handes*, no. 3 (1958), pp. 106-35. The author traces the development of Armenian painting in Russia from the 1820s to the 1860s; and the careers of such Armenian painters as M. Melikian, H. Katanian, S. Nersisian, H. Hovnatanian, and others who studied in the Academy of Fine Arts at St. Petersburg.

139. A. G. Hovhannisian, "Tasnevinnerord dari 50-60-akan tvakanneri arevelahai hasarakakan-kaghakakan hosanknere" [East Armenian social-political movements in the 50s and 60s of the 19th century], *Patmabanasirakan handes*, no. 4 (1965), p. 75.

140. M. G. Nersisian, *Hai zhoghovrdi azatagrakan paykare tiurkakan brnapetutian dem 1850-1870* [The Armenian peoples' liberation struggle against Turkish despotism, 1850-1870] (Erevan, 1955), p. 361.

141. Ananun, 2: 174-75.

142. V. Rshtuni, "Haikakan liberalizmi patmutiunits" [On the history of Armenian liberalism] , *Teghekagir*, no. 9 (1946), pp. 28-53.

143. Ananun, 2: 184-85. See also V. H. Kalashian, "Grigor Ardzrunin ev Haikakan Hartse" [Grigor Ardzruni and the Armenian Question] , *Teghekagir*, no. 3 (1949), pp. 65-73; and A. G. Babakhanian, "Grigor Ardzrunin hasarakakan zargatsman masin" [Grigor Ardzruni on social development] , *ibid.*, no. 1 (1961), pp. 61-78.

144. S. Spandarian in *Mshak*, no. 57 (1877), as quoted by Ananun, 2: 179-80.

145. For the similarities and the relationship of the writings of Nalbandian and such Russian intellectuals, see S. Sh. Zurabian, *Hai tntesagitakan mtki zargatsman urvagtser* [Outlines of the history of Armenian economic thought] (Erevan, 1959), chap. 7; A. Ohanian, "Arevelahai tntesagitakan mtki putmutiunits" [On the history of Armenian economic thought] (Erevan, 1955), vol. 1; and H. Mamikonian, "N. G. Chernishevskin ev antsial dari 50-60-akan tvakanneri hai revoliutsion demokratian" [N. G. Chernyshevskii and the Armenian revolutionary democrats of the 50s and 60s of the last century] , *Teghekagir*, no. 7 (1953).

146. The first national-liberation organization to emerge in Russian Armenia, the secret "Barenpatak Enkerutiun" (Goodwill, or Good Purpose, Society), which had some 43 members, mostly teachers, high-school seniors, artisans, and merchants, was influenced by the writings of Nalbandian, as well as of other Armenian nationalists. The society and its founder, Arsen Kritian, aimed at spreading patriotic and nationalist sentiments and promoting education and culture. Its ultimate aim was to free Armenia from foreign rule. It carried on local propaganda activities and collected money to buy arms. The organization was dissolved in 1875 when its members were arrested by tsarist authorities. See Nersisian, *Hai zhoghovrdi azatagrakan paikare*, pp. 142-48; Parsamian, *Hai zhoghovrdi patmutiun*, 3: 311-14; and *Hai azatagrakan sharjumneri patmutiunits* [On the history of Armenian national-liberation movements] (Erevan, 1958).

147. H. Mamikonian, pp. 33-36; and Gurgen Hovnan, "N. G. Chernishevsku kapere haikakan shrjanneri het, 19-rd dari 80-akan tvakannerin" [N. G. Chernyshevskii's ties with Armenian circles in the 80s of the 19th century] , *Teghekagir*, no. 7 (1953), pp. 37-40, 46-47; and A. Karinian, "Chernishevskin ev parberakan mamuli patmutian mi kani hartser" [Chernyshevskii and a few problems of the history of the periodical press] , *Teghekagir*, no. 7 (1953), pp. 58-59.

148. Leo, *Turkahai heghapokhutian gaghaparabautiune* [The ideology of the Ottoman Armenian revolutionary movement] (Paris, 1934), 1: 27.

149. M. Nersisian, *Narodnikakan khmbaknern Andrkovkasum* [Populist cells in Transcaucasia] (Erevan, 1940).

440   Footnotes

150. Nersisian, *Hai zhoghovrdi azatatagrakan paikare*, p. 278.

151. Kristapor Mikaelian, "Bekorner im husherits" [Fragments from my memoirs], *Hairenik Amsagir*, Aug. 1924, p. 56.

152. Ohanian, *Arevelahai tntesagitakan mtki patmutiunits*, pp. 127-48; and V. Rshtuni's *Hai narodnik Hovsep Ter Movsisian* [Armenian Narodnik Hovsep Ter Movsisian] (Erevan, 1946); *Hai hasarakakan hosanknere ev 1861-1864-1870 tvakanneri giughatsiakan reforme* [Armenian social movements and the 1861-1864-1870 peasant reforms] (Erevan, 1940); *Hai narodnikakan gagha-parakhosutian patmutiunits* [Of the history of Armenian Narodnik ideology] (Erevan, 1944).

153. Mikael Varandian, *H. H. Dashnaktsutian Patmutiun* [History of the Armenian Revolutionary Federation] (Paris, 1932), 1: 45-51; S. Vratzian, ed., *Hushapatum H. H. Dashnaktsutian 1890-1950* [Historical recollections of the Armenian Revolutionary Federation, 1890-1950] (Boston, 1950), pp. 73-76; Parsamian, *Hai zhoghovrdi patmutiun*, pp. 318-20; and Louise Nalbandian, *The Armenian Revolutionary Movement* (Berkeley, 1963), pp. 141-43.

154. Aram Ohanian, pp. 148-53; S. Zurabian, pp. 413-65. See also Leo, *Turkahai heghapokhutian gaghaparabanutiune*, 1: 148-52.

155. For the history and ideology of the Hnchakian party, see Ananun, 2: 206-13; Ruben Khan-Azat, "Hai heghapokakani husherits" [From the memoirs of an Armenian Revolutionary], *Hairenik Amsagir*, June 1927-May 1929; and Nalbandian, pp. 104-31.

156. Vratzian, *Hushapatum*, pp. 87-140. See also Varandian, *H. H. Dashnaktsutian*, 1: 88-106.

157. See Ananun, vols. 2 and 3; S. Vratzian, *Hushapatum; H. H. Dashnaktsutian Vatsunamiak (1890-1950)* [Sixtieth Anniversary of the A. R. F.] (Boston, 1950); Varandian, *H. H. Dashnaktsutian Patmutiun*, vols. 1 and 2; and Nalbandian.

158. Among those present were Chernov, Miliukov, Struve, Prince Dolgorukov, Iodko-Vronsky, Gabiunashvili, Dekanoze, Tsiliakus, Dmowski, and Varandian.

159. Varandian, *H. H. Dashnaktsutian*, vol. 1, chap. XIX.

160. For a list, see Vratzian, *Hushapatum*, pp. 580-84.

161. S. Tigranian, *Dashnaktsakan patgamavornere yerkrord petakan dumayum* [The representative of Dashnaktsutiun in the Second Duma] (Tbilisi, 1907), pp. 80-90.

162. Ananun, 3: 67-106.

163. Gabrielian, *Hai pilisopaiakan mtki patmutiun*, vol. 4; Kh. G. Gulanian, *Marxistakan tntesagitakan mtki taratsume hai irakanutian medj 1890-1961*; and A. Voskerchian, *Hai marxistakan knnadatutian himnadirnere* [The founders of Armenian Marxist critique] (Erevan, 1967).

CHAPTER VI

1. Svetlana Alliluyeva, *Twenty Letters to a Friend.* Trans. from the Russian by Priscilla Johnson (London, 1967), p. 83.

2. V. Shaduri, *Russkie pisateli o Gruzii* (Tbilisi, 1948), 1: 124-60, 288-96.

3. D. M. Lang, *The Georgians* (New York, 1966), pp. 64-69.

4. D. M. Lang, *Lives and Legends of the Georgian Saints* (New York, 1956), pp. 13-39.

5. D. M. Lang, *The Last Years of the Georgian Monarchy* (New York, 1957), pp. 183-85.

6. D. M. Lang, *A Modern History of Soviet Georgia* (New York, 1962), p. 78.

7. A. S. Griboedov, *Sochineniia*, ed. V. Orlov (Leningrad, 1945), p. 565.

8. G. K. Bakradze, *Vozniknovenie i razvitie kapitalisticheskoi promyshlennosti v Gruzii v XIX veke* (Tbilisi, 1938), pp. 25-26.

9. F. I. Makharadze and G. V. Khachapuridze, *Ocherki po istorii rabochego i krest'ianskogo dvizheniia v Gruzii* (Moscow, 1932), p. 164.

10. Quoted by Lang in *Modern History of Soviet Georgia*, p. 156.

11. F. Kazemzadeh, *The Struggle for Transcaucasia, 1917-1921* (New York, 1951), p. 34.

12. Sir Harry Luke, *Cities and Men* (London, 1953), 2: 88.

13. *Ibid.*, p. 156.

14. Stalin's excesses, it should be noted, were fiercely resented even by the local Bolsheviks. The entire Central Committee of the Georgian Communist Party resigned in protest.

15. The affair is treated fully in the late Isaac Deutscher's *Stalin*; also in Richard Pipes, *The Formation of the Soviet Union*, 2nd ed. (Cambridge, Mass., 1964), pp. 266-93. The most recent account is by Moshé Lewin, "Les derniers mois de la vie de Lénine," in *Cahiers du Monde Russe et Soviétique*, vol. 8, no. 2 (1967): 270-79 ("Staline, Trotski et les Géorgiens").

16. Due to a misprint, this figure is given as 17,000 in Lang, *Modern History of Soviet Georgia*, p. 251.

17. Joshua Rothenberg, "The Special Case of the Georgian Jews," in *Jewish Frontier* (June, 1967), p. 17. I owe this reference to my good friend Jay D. Frierman of the University of California at Los Angeles.

18. Yet he was, in his own twisted way, a patron of Georgia during this period. Robert Conquest, in his article "The Real Man from Smersh," *New York Times Magazine*, 5 November 1967, writes: "In Georgia. . .he enjoyed genuine popularity, under the rule of his nominees, the republic was an oasis of comparative prosperity through the dreadful postwar shortages and famines."

19. Alec Nove and J. A. Newth, *The Soviet Middle East: A Model for Development?* (London, 1967), pp. 86-90, 106-07.

20. *Ibid.*, p. 97.

21. There are disagreements on this point. See, for example, Walter Kolarz, *Russia and Her Colonies* (Hamden, Conn., 1967), pp. 231-33.

CHAPTER VII

1. F. Steinmann and E. Hurwicz, *Konstantin Petrovitsch Pobjedonoszew, der Staatsmann der Reaktion unter Alexander III* (Königsberg, 1933), pp. 77-78.

2. A. S. Khomiakov, *Polnoe sobranie sochinenii* (Moscow, 1911), 7: 77.

3. K. Leont'ev, *Sobranie sochinenii* (Moscow, 1912), 5: 351, 386.

4. A. Gertsen, *Sobranie sochinenii* (Moscow, 1919), 5: 549; 8: 47; *Kolokol* (1 April 1860), pp. 557.

5. E. Sarkisyanz, *Russland und der Messianismus des Orients. Sendungsbewusstsein und Chiliasmus des Ostens* (Tübingen, 1955), pp. 154 ff.

6. P. P. Ivanov, *Ocherki po istorii Srednei Azii* (Moscow, 1958), pp. 36-40.

7. This summary of Kazakh history is based mainly on M. Abdykalykov and A. Pankratova, *Istoriia Kazakhskoi S.S.R.* (Alma-Ata, 1943).

8. A. Lobanov-Rostovsky, *Russia and Asia* (New York, 1933), pp. 147, 152-61.

9. E. Sarkisyanz, *Geschichte der orientalischen Völker Russlands bis 1917* (Munich, 1961), p. 329.

10. K. Kereeva-Kanafieva, *Dorevoliutsionnaia russkaia pechat' o Kazakhstane;*

iz istorii russko-kazakhskikh literaturnykh sviazei (Alma-Ata, 1963), pp. 241-43, on Potanin.

11. On Semënov-Tian-Shanskii see L. S. Berg, *Geschichte der russischen geographischen Entdeckungen* (Leipzig, 1954), pp. 193-97.

12. Akademiia Nauk Kazakhskoi S.S.R.: Chokan Valikhanov, *Izbrannye proizvedeniia* (Alma-Ata, 1953), pp. 16 ff., 23 ff., 32 ff., 45, 49, 51, 59-71, 77 ff.

13. M. S. Silchenko, *Tvorcheskaia biografiia Abaia* (Alma-Ata, 1957), pp. 51, 54 ff., 67, 69.

14. Examples of undidactic lyrical poetry of Abai Kunanbaev in Russian translations may be found in *Pesni Kazakhskikh stepei* (Moscow and Leningrad, 1951), pp. 21-28.

15. K. Beisembiev, *Ideino-politicheskie techeniia v Kazakhstane kontsa XIX-nachala XX veka* (Alma-Ata, 1961), pp. 87 ff., 90-96.

16. *Ibid.*, pp. 101-07.

17. G. N. Potanin, "V iurte poslednego kirgizskogo tsarevicha," in *Russkoe Bogatstvo*, no. 8 (1896), pp. 60-88.

18. K. Beisembiev, *Progressivno-demokraticheskaia i marksistskaia mysl' v Kazakhstane nachala XX veka* (Alma-Ata, 1965), pp. 23, 41.

19. On N. I. Il'minskii: P. Josef Glazik, *Die Islammission der russisch-orthodoxen Kirche* (Münster, 1959: *Missionswissenschaftliche Abhandlungen und Texte*, 23), pp. 133-36.

20. Beisembiev, *Progressivno-demokraticheskaia i marksistskaia mysl' v Kazakhstane*, pp. 24-37, 46-49.

21. *Ibid.*, pp. 37-40; Beisembiev, *Ideino-politicheskie techeniia v Kazakhstane*, pp. 250-68, 272-76.

22. Saken Seifullin, "Asau Tulpar" (Orenburg, 1922), p. 98, quoted in *Zhizn' Natsional'nostei*, no. 2 (1923), p. 167.

23. The livestock had increased by forty percent since 1916, but had not until recently reached pre-1914 level; cf. Lawrence Krader, *Peoples of Central Asia* (Bloomington, Indiana University, 1963), p. 260.

24. Ian Murray Matley, "Agricultural Development" in *Central Asia: A Century of Russian Rule*, Edward Allworth, ed. (New York, 1967), pp. 305 ff.; and in the same volume, Ian Murray Matley, "Industrialization," pp. 337-42.

25. The other propagandistic extreme is represented by such literature as Marcel Egretaud, *L'Orient soviétique* (Paris, 1959).

26. K. I. Petrov, *K istorii dvizheniia kirgizov na Tian'-shan'* (Frunze, 1961), pp. 87-208.

27. The above summary of Kirghiz history is based mainly on Akademiia Nauk Kirgizskoi S.S.R., Institut Istorii, *Istoriia Kirgizii*, I (Frunze, 1963): 182-326.

28. B. Dzhamgerchinov, *Ocherk politicheskoi istorii Kirgizii XIX veka* (Frunze, 1966), pp. 79-187.

29. Kushbek Usenbaev, *Prisoedinenie iuzhnoi Kirgizii k Rossii* (Frunze, 1960), pp. 63-126.

30. Baymirza Hayit, *Turkestan im zwanzigsten Jahrhundert* (Darmstadt, 1956), p. 20.

31. A. Abyshkaev, *Karateginskie Kirgizy v kontse XIX-nachale XX veka* (Frunze, 1965), pp. 29, 42.

32. R. Pierce, *Russian Central Asia, 1867-1917*: a study in colonial rule (Berkeley, 1960), pp. 87-89.

33. Soviet poetry of Toktogul may be found in L. I. Klimovich, *Khrestomatiia po literature narodov SSSR* (Moscow, 1959), pp. 840-55.

34. Akademiia Nauk Kirgizskoi, *Istoriia Kirgizii*, I: 567.

35. D. Shmelev, *Kirgizskaia SSR* (Moscow, 1957), pp. 50-53.

36. W. Kolarz, *Russia and Her Colonies* (New York, 1952), p. 272.

37. On other Kirghiz folklore: Kirgizgosizdat, *Skazanie ob okhotnike Kodzodzhashe. Kirgizskii epos* (Frunze, 1958); K. Eshmambetov and D. Brudnoi (trans.), *Kirgizskie narodnye skazski* (Frunze, 1965).

38. On the *Weltanschauung* of Kirgiz epics, see B. Amanaliev, *Iz istorii filosofskoi mysli kirgizskogo naroda* (Frunze, 1963), pp. 41-46.

39. M. I. Bogdanova, "Kirgizskaia literatura," in *Istoriia literatur narodov Srednei Azii* (Moscow, 1960), pp. 466-77.

40. *Ibid.*, p. 457.

41. B. A. Akhmedov, *Gosudarstvo kochevykh Uzbekov* (Moscow, 1965), pp. 32-68.

42. M. K. Rozhkova, *Ekonomicheskie sviazi Rossii so Srednei Aziei* (Moscow, 1963), pp. 48-60.

43. S. B. Bakhrushin, *Istoriia narodov Uzbekistana* (Tashkent, 1947), Vol. II.

44. Arminius Vambery, *Travels in Central Asia. . .across the Turkoman Desert. . .to Khiva, Bokhara and Samarcand* (London, 1864), pp. 66 ff., 74.

45. See V. Nalivkin, *Histoire du Chanat de Khokand* (trans. A. Dozon; Paris, 1889), on pre-Russian history of the area.

46. Cf. Sh. Iusupov, *Ocherki istorii Kuliabskogo Bekstva v kontse XIX i nachale XX veka* (Dushanbe, 1964), pp. 31 ff.

47. On Bukharan law enforcement, cf. N. A. Kisliakov, *Patriarkhal'no feodal' nye otnosheniia. . .Bukharskogo khanstva v kontse XIXgo-XX veka* (Moscow, 1962) Akademiia Nauk S.S.S.R., Trudy Instituta Etnografii, Novaia seriia, LXXIV, pp. 47-50.

48. Akhmad Donish, *Puteshestvie iz Bukhary v Peterburg. Izbrannie* (Dushanbe?, 1960), pp. 74-121.

49. Sadriddin Aini, "Bukhara (Vospominaniia)": *Sobranie sochinenii*, 3 (Moscow, 1960): 472-74.

50. Cf. O. A. Sukhareva, *Bukhara XIX-nachala XX veka* (Moscow, 1966), pp. 26-30.

51. Hélène Carrère d'Encausse, *Réforme et révolution chez les Musulmans de l'Empire Russe. Bukhara 1867-1924* (Paris, 1966), pp. 168-81.

52. On administrators and divisions of Russian Turkestan, see E. Hamburger, *Geschichte der Behördenorganisation Russlands. . .bis 1917* (Leiden, 1966), pp. 409-11.

53. V. Bartol'd, *Istoriia kul'turnoi zhizni Turkestana* (Leningrad, 1927), p. 127.

54. On Jadids of Russian Turkestan, see S. A. Zenkovsky, *Pan-Turkism and Islam in Russia* (Cambridge, Mass., 1960), pp. 82-84.

55. Edward Allworth, "The Changing Intellectual and Literary Community," in Allworth, ed., *Central Asia*, p. 359.

56. Edward Allworth, *Uzbek Literary Politics* (The Hague, 1964).

57. R. Pierce, *Russian Central Asia, 1867-1917: A study in colonial rule* (Berkeley, 1960).

58. A. Park, *Bolshevism in Turkestan, 1917-1927* (New York, Columbia Univ. Press, 1957), p. 14.

59. J. Castagne, *Le bolchévisme et l'Islam*, Vol. II (Paris, 1922).

60. Akademiia Nauk Uzbekskoi S.S.S.R., Karakalpakskii Filial, *Ocherk istorii Karakalpakskoi ASSR*, 2 (Tashkent, 1964): 134.

61. On the previous situation of the peasantry of Khiva, see M. Iuldashev, *K istorii krestian Khivy XIX veka* (Tashkent, 1966), pp. 35-59.

62. Hayit, *Turkestan im zwanzigsten Jahrhundert*, pp. 156 ff.

63. Allworth, *Uzbek literary politics*.

64. Said Alim Khan, *La voix de la Boukharie opprimée* (Paris, 1929), pp. 34-48.

65. J. Castagne, *Les basmatchis* (Paris, 1925), pp. 71 ff.

66. On social revolutionary movements in the name of Islam, see Sarkisyanz, *Russland und der Messianismus des Orients,* pp. 223-80.

67. On Muslim-Marxist syncretism which historical developments had produced among the Tatars, see A. Bennigsen and Ch. Quelquejay, *Les mouvements nationaux chez les Musulmans de Russie. Le "Sultangaliévisme" au Tatarstan* (Paris, 1960), pp. 52 ff., 70 ff., 77, 82 ff., 90-99, 105-10.

68. Park, *Bolshevism in Turkestan*, p. 237.

69. R. Pipes, *The formation of the Soviet Union. communism and nationalism* (Cambridge, Mass., 1954).

70. Park, *Bolshevism in Turkestan*, pp. 286, 343-46.

71. Allworth, *Uzbek literary politics*.

72. O. A. Sukhareva, *Islam v Uzbekistane* (Tashkent, 1960), pp. 69-78, exemplifies the slogan about Islam's being an instrument of exploitation.

73. Hayit, *Turkestan im zwanzigsten Jahrhundert*, pp. 334-40.

74. Allworth, "Changing Intellectual and Literary Community," pp. 388, 383.

75. See T. E. Markov, *Ocherk istorii formirovaniia severnykh Turkmen* (Moscow, 1961), pp. 43-45.

76. See Iu. E. Bregel', *Khorezmskie Turkmeny v XIX veke* (Moscow, 1961), pp. 176-220.

77. L. Karryev and A. Rosliakov, *Kratkii ocherk istorii Turkmenistana 1868-1917* (Ashkhabad, 1956), pp. 12-43.

78. G. Nepeson, *Iz istorii khorezmskoi revoliutsii, 1920-1924* (Tashkent, 1962), pp. 67, 97-100.

79. E. L. Shteinberg, *Ocherki istorii Turkmenii* (Moscow, 1934). A basic work is Akademiia Nauk Turkmenskoi S.S.R., *Istoriia Turkmenskoi SSR* (1957).

80. Sarkisyanz, *Geschichte der orientalischen Völker Russlands*, pp. 181 ff., 184.

81. Kolarz, *Russia and Her Colonies*, pp. 259 ff.

82. Cf. Baymirza Hayit, *Sowjetrussische Orientpolitik am Beispiel Turkestans* (Cologne-Berlin, 1962), pp. 208 ff.

83. Akademiia Nauk S.S.S.R., *Ocherki po istorii filosofskoi i obshchestvenno-politicheskoi mysli narodov SSSR* (Moscow, 1955), pp. 91-92, 84.

CHAPTER VIII

1. An exception must be made in this respect, as in many others, for the Yakuts, a part of whom were horse and cattle pastoralists, and some of whom may have had primitive forms of agriculture even before the Russians came. On these points see A. P. Okladnikov, *Istoriia Iakutskoi ASSR*, vol. 1 (Moscow, 1955), English translation forthcoming. Soviet scholars usually handle the Yakuts separately from the other Siberian and Far Eastern peoples because of their cultural and linguistic distinctiveness. In view of the relative scarcity of data in the Soviet literature on the modern Yakuts (as distinct from the vast mass of archeological and historical material handled by Okladnikov), we will not be dealing with the Yakuts in detail in this report, even though certain Yakut-speaking groups will fall within our purview.

2. On these groups, see V. A. Tugolukov, "The Vitim-Olekma Evenki," *Soviet Anthropology and Archeology*, vol. 2, no. 2 (1963), pp. 15-40; and V. A. Tugolukov, "Izmeneniia v khoziaistve i byte evenkov Irkutskoi oblasti za poltora veka," *Sovetskaia etnografiia*, no. 3 (1965), pp. 12-26.

3. The Evenki in the vicinity of Lake Orel', Lower Amur region, considered themselves zealous Christians and held themselves apart from the neighboring peoples on this account. To judge by the rare occurrence of intermarriage between Evenki of this group and other peoples such as the Negidals and the Nivkhi, this situation appears to persist even today (A. V. Smoliak, "O sovremennom etnicheskom razvitii narodov Nizhnego Amura i Sakhalina," *Sovetskaia etnografiia*, no. 3 [1967], p. 101).

4. Kolkhozy in the current sense were preceded by a variety of "simpler" forms of collectivization which did not involve socialization of the means of production (reindeer herds and major fishing and hunting equipment) or were organized on a short-term basis for specific purposes—to exploit a particular run of fish or the like. On the history of collectivization in northern Siberia and the Far East, see V. A. Tugolukov, "Khantaiskie Evenki," *Sibirskii etnograficheskii sbornik V*, TIE, 84 (Moscow, 1963), pp. 10 ff.; A. V. Smoliak,

"Zametki po etnografii nivkhov Amurskogo Limana," *Sovremennoe khozia-istvo, kul'tura i byt malykh narodov Severa,* TIE, 56 (Moscow, 1960), pp. 98-101; I. S. Vdovin, *Ocherki istorii i etnografii chukchei* (Moscow-Leningrad, 1965), pp. 345-60; and V. I. Vasil'ev, Iu. B. Simchenko, and Z. P. Sokolova, "Problems of the reconstruction of daily life among the small peoples of the Far North," *Soviet Anthropology and Archeology*, vol. 5, no. 2 (1966), p. 11.

5. Ch. M. Taksami, *Nivkhi* (Leningrad, 1967), pp. 36-66.

6. Vdovin (*Ocherki istorii*, p. 356, 359-60) notes that before the final collectivization drive in the 1950s, a kolkhoz member on Chukotka might have as many as fifty head of reindeer and that in 1854 only 81.9 percent of the reindeer herd was collectivized. The number of reindeer privately held obviously varied from place to place. Iu. B. Strakach writes that "in the 1930s the permissible norm for one household in the tundra zone was 250-300 reindeer, not counting the young (and in the taiga fewer); later this figure was repeatedly lowered, but without sufficient foundation" (Iu. B. Strakach, "Nekotorye voprosy izucheniia khoziaistvenno-kul'turnogo stroitel'stva u malykh narodov Sibiri," *Izvestiia Sibirskogo otdeleniia Akademii Nauk SSSR, Seriia obshchest-vennykh nauk*, no. 1, vyp. 1 [1965], p. 76). It should be noted that taiga reindeer herding is a quite different operation from that carried on in the tundra, and the total number of animals has always been smaller.

7. Taksami (*Nivkhi*, p. 160) notes that the old Nivkhi in some cases refused to move into the central settlements and so were left where they were, in settlements that had been inhabited for generations precisely because they made good bases of operation. Taksami considers that some aspects of collectivization—particularly the resettlement policy—have been mistakes, an opinion shared in greater or lesser degree by most of the Northern specialists.

8. Iu. B. Strakach has documented in some detail the place of education within the family group for preparing future hunters, fishermen, and reindeer breeders. His implied conclusion is that the Soviet educational policy as presently constituted is inferior in this respect to the traditional education, (Strakach, *Narodnye traditsii i podgotovka sovremennykh promyslovo-sel'sko-khoziaistvennykh kadrov: Taezhnye i tundrovye raiony Sibiri*, Novosibirsk, 1966).

9. See Stephen P. Dunn and Ethel Dunn, "The transformation of economy and culture in the Soviet North," *Arctic Anthropology*, vol. 1, no. 2 (1963), pp. 7-10; V. A. Tugolukov, "Ekondskie Evenki," in *Sovremennoe khoziaistvo, kul'tura i byt malykh narodov Severa* (Moscow, 1960), pp. 148-77; K. G. Kuzakov, "Khoziaistvo, kul'tura i byt kolkhoznikov Aianka," *ibid.*, pp. 199-213.

10. I. S. Gurvich, "Directions to be taken in the further reorganization of the economy and culture of the peoples of the North," *Soviet Anthropology and Archeology*, vol. 1, no. 2 (1962), p. 28.

11. Vasil'ev, Simchenko, and Sokolova, "Problems of Reconstruction of Daily Life," p. 12; p. 21, n. 5. In most places, under present conditions, this distinction is largely specious, since material facilities for settling down the population do not yet exist.

12. *Izvestiia*, 26 Oct. 1965, p. 3, describing the Yamalo-Nen National Okrug. More or less the same points are made by all the sources cited in the present study and those in our previous one (Dunn and Dunn, "Transformation of economy and culture").

13. The chairman of Bolshevik kolkhoz, Ust'-Yenisei raion Taimyr (Dolgan-Nen) National Okrug, wrote a bitter letter to *Izvestiia* (2 Feb. 1966, p. 3) in which he charged that although the Semenov Gas Exploration Administration is the nominal "sponsor" of the kolkhoz, no one actually looks after its needs. In order to fulfill the plan for sale of goods, trading organizations bring lots of vodka. Salt, soap, nails, and eau de cologne are not always available. The chairman concluded his letter by saying that the towns of Dudinka, Ust'-Port, and Karaul are serviced by the same organizations and that they get good clothes and shoes. Providing the same to the kolkhoz should be the responsibility of some central organization if no local one will do an adequate job. We should note that under tsarism, vodka was the most widely sold commodity because it had a high value relative to its bulk. Soviet claims of a radical change in the trade pattern in Siberia and the Far East are not always borne out, as may be deduced from data presented by I. S. Gurvich and K. G. Kuzakov (*Koriakskii Natsional'nyi Okrug* [Moscow, 1960], pp. 159-65). Here the major export is fish, and nearly all industrial goods and most foodstuffs are imported; the food imports, of course, satisfy the demands of a population accustomed to a Western diet. When Gurvich and Kuzakov wrote, consumer-oriented industries were virtually nonexistent, except for boot-making and the tailoring of essential winter clothing in the native style.

14. V. A. Vasil'ev, "The Forest Entsy (An Essay on Their History, Economy and Culture)," *Soviet Anthropology and Archeology*, vol. 4, no. 3 (1965-66), p. 22. The herder's pay in 1960 was 100 rubles a month, probably more than he got on the kolkhoz.

15. V. G. Lar'kin, *Orochi* (Moscow, 1964), p. 148. The Motor Repair Station is the equivalent of a Machine Tractor Station in agriculture—a state-owned facility that supplied equipment and services to the individual collectives. Lar'kin does not give the interval to which this rental applied, but presumably it was only for the duration of a fish run.

16. Taksami, *Nivkhi*, p. 88.

17. A. V. Smoliak, "Materialy k kharakteristike sotsialisticheskoi kul'turi i byta korennogo naseleniia Chukotskogo raiona," in *Sibirskii etnograficheskii sbornik II*, TIE, 35 (Moscow-Leningrad, 1957), pp. 3-37.

18. Vdovin (*Ocherki istorii*) indicates that until the end of the 1950s the collectives of the Chukchi National Okrug were exempt from compulsory sales to the state.

19. I. S. Gurvich and L. A. Fineberg (Fainberg) comment on C. C. Hughes' "Under four flags: Recent culture change among the Eskimos," *Current Anthropology*, vol. 6, no. 1 (1965), p. 60; see also the comment by Stephen P. Dunn and Ethel Dunn, *ibid.*, p. 59. Gurvich and Kuzakov (*Koriakskii Natsional'nyi Okrug*, pp. 240-46) provide further data which would seem to indicate that sea-mammal hunting could be more highly developed.

20. In many other parts of Siberia, agriculture is traditional and is now carried on to good effect, but even here, those who farm are usually Russians, or in some cases strongly Russified native groups such as the "horse Tungus" mentioned by Tugolukov (see fn. 2). These Russians and Russified populations present in most respects a separate ethnographic problem.

21. The nonnative population of Siberia has tripled, the major influx occurring since 1939. These in-migrants must be fed; eating Northern style almost by definition means going out and hunting for one's food personally. Indications are, however, that the majority of the nonnative population either demands or requires a Western-style diet. See Ethel Dunn, "Educating the small peoples of the Soviet North: The limits of culture change," *Arctic Anthropology*, vol. 5, no. 1 (1968), pp. 1-31.

22. See Ethel Dunn, "Educating the small peoples," pp. 17-29; and also Ethel Dunn, "Education and the native intelligentsia in the Soviet North: Further thoughts on the limits of culture change," *Arctic Anthropology*, vol. 6, no. 2 (1970), pp. 112-22.

23. *Izvestiia* (30 March 1967, p. 5). The reporter, L. Shinkarev, states that on the basis of a calculation showing that the number of sunny days in Eastern Siberia was about equal to that in the Crimea, it was decided to apply standards for the building of child-care facilities and the like similar to those in the Crimea. Shinkarev cites a little-known speech by the early Soviet official G. M. Krzhizhanovskii before the Presidium of the State Planning Commission (4 February 1930) in which Krzhizhanovskii said that the wealth of Siberia was such that its development had to be planned on a world scale. Shinkarev obviously considers Krzhizhanovskii's statement even more relevant today than when it was made, and he is not alone in this.

24. N. Tokarskaia, "Zakreplenie kadrov v promyshlennosti Vostochnoi Sibiri," *Ekonomicheskie nauki*, no. 4 (1967); see especially table 3 on p. 47 and text following. The author suggests that the "lack of prospects for growth" is only apparent and not real, and that turnover attributed to this cause is actually due to poor indoctrination and explanatory work.

25. Taksami, *Nivkhi*, p. 144; V. N. Shubkin, "Youth starts out in life," *Soviet Sociology*, vol. 4, no. 3 (1965-66), pp. 3-15. Shubkin attributes many of these

problems to the absence, since early in the Stalin era, of any government agency bearing direct responsibility for the distribution of the labor supply.

26. Data on industrial recruitment of the native nationalities are hard to obtain, and tend to be fragmentary and anecdotal. We are indebted to Terence Armstrong, Scott Polar Research Institute, Cambridge, England, for the following data taken from T. T. Egorov ("O natsional'nykh kadrakh v promyshlennosti Yakutii," in V. G. Mel'nikov, ed., *Voprosy ekonomiki promyshlennosti Yakutii* [Yakutsk, 1962], pp. 45-51). In the early years of Northern industrialization the number of members of the native nationalities employed in industry was small, partly because natives were not eligible for hardship pay for Northern service. This provision was abolished in 1960. The percentage of Yakuts in various types of mining (gold, diamonds, tin, mica, and coal) and in the timber industry in the Yakut A.S.S.R. amounted to 2.6 percent in 1957 and 4.0 percent in 1958. The only category showing wide departures from these percentages was diamond mining, where the figures were 14.7 percent in 1957 and 26.1 percent in 1958. Egorov, according to Armstrong, points out the social and economic necessity of increasing the number of natives in industry. It is worth noting that Egorov's percentage data apparently pertain only to the Yakuts, one of the more numerous and highly developed of the Siberian peoples. Armstrong himself has written (Terence Armstrong, "The Administration of Northern Peoples: the USSR," in *The Arctic Frontier*, R. St. J. Macdonald, ed. [Toronto, 1966], p. 74): "in 1935, 2.3 percent of the industrial labour force in the North were classified as members of the Northern peoples." He believes that the proportion of industrial workers among the Yakuts and the Komi (a Finnic-speaking people of the European North) was probably somewhat higher, because these peoples were more highly developed culturally and were partially literate. A very interesting exception to this generalization is provided by the Shors, an Altaic-speaking people inhabiting Kemerovo Oblast in Western Siberia and numbering in 1959 14,900, of whom 41.6 percent were urban (Strakach, *Narodnye traditsii*, pp. 6-7). They were studied in 1949 by L. P. Potapov, who found that as of 1 July 1949 28.0 percent were miners and 20.4 percent were classified as "employees and others"—i.e., nonmanual workers. At this time, only 2.5 percent were engaged in hunting, which had been the major occupation of the Shors before the Revolution (L. P. Potapov, "The Shors," in *The Peoples of Siberia*, M. G. Levin and L. P. Potapov, eds. [Chicago, 1964], pp. 466-67).

27. Z. P. Sokolova and B. F. Shapalin, "Naselenie i trudovye resursy zony Severa (Soveshchanie v Magadane)," *Sovetskaia etnografiia*, no. 3 (1966), pp. 152-57; Strakach, "Nekotorye voprosy," p. 75. Strakach connects this phenomenon with collectivization, which, by purportedly establishing the northern Siberian groups in centralized establishments, has considerably reduced their mobility.

28. A "nation," according to Marxist-Leninist theory, is a social formation characteristic of a specific historical era—that of capitalism. Therefore, only

those peoples could be classified as true nations which, like the Russians, Ukrainians, Georgians, and Armenians, had already experienced some degree of
capitalist development.

29. Vdovin, *Ocherki istorii*, p. 293.

30. Taksami, *Nivkhi*, p. 47: "the native raions were formed within general
administrative regions, to which they were subordinate in their concrete activity."

31. L. M. Zak and M. I. Isaev, "Problemy pis'mennosti narodov SSSR v
kul'turnoi revoliutsii," *Voprosy istorii*, no. 1 (1966): 3-20; V. A. Avrorin,
"Leninskaia natsional'naia politika i razvitie literaturnykh iazykov narodov
SSSR," *Voprosy iazykoznaniia*, no. 4 (1960), pp. 3-19; V. A. Avrorin, "Iazyki
narodov Sibiri v period razvernutogo stroitel'stva kommunizma," *Izvestiia Sibirskogo otdeleniia Akademii Nauk SSSR, seriia obshchestvennykh nauk*, no.
1, vyp. 1 (1963), pp. 101-12.

32. Certain peoples did not receive written languages because of their small
numbers or because the use of Russian was widespread among them; these included the Sel'kups, Kets, and Aleuts (a hybrid Russian-Eskimo population
inhabiting the Komandorsky Islands and the western Aleutians). See Zak and
Isaev, "Problemi pis'mennosti narodov SSSR," p. 13 n. The Udegei and
Nivkhi, according to Zak and Isaev, were omitted from the list because there
were no specialists at the time who knew their language. It is curious that this
statement is in direct contradiction to the testimony of Taksami, himself a
Nivkhi, who speaks of classes for the liquidation of illiteracy (*likbezy*) held
among the Nivkhi in the early 1930s (Taksami, *Nivkhi*, p. 241). Apparently
the language at this point was written in Latin characters, since Taksami men-
tions the work done by the Committee for the New Alphabet, an organization
identified with Latinization. It is possible that at the time of the switchover
from Latin to Cyrillic script, the Nivkhi language was merely permitted to return to preliterate status. However, in this case the question arises why there
should have been a lack of qualified specialists after 1937 when there was no
lack before.

The switchover from Latin to Cyrillic characters was prompted by a complex tangle of both ideological and practical considerations. Interestingly
enough, Zak and Isaev ("Problemi pis'mennosti narodov SSSR," p. 11) point
out that the Latin alphabet was defended by many authors at the time, on
what now sound like Trotskyist ideological grounds. "I. Khansuvarov [*Latini-
zatsiia−orudie Leninskoi natsional'noi politiki*, Moscow, 1932, p. 21], for example, held that an internationalist can defend only the Latin alphabet which
allegedly will be basic for all peoples 'with the coming victory of the world
revolution.' Any attempt to consider the Russian alphabet as the basis for the
written languages of non-Russian peoples was branded as a counterrevolutionary action, which 'pours water in the mill of the medieval bourgeoisie.' " In
its enthusiasm for the Latin alphabet, the Committee for the New Alphabet

had transferred into Latin characters a number of languages (Udmurt, Mordvin, Komi, Oirot [Mongol], and others) that had previously been written in Cyrillic. This whole matter is a fascinating illustration of the tension between resurgent nationalism and the doctrine of world revolution in which this nationalism was for a time clothed.

33. "Writing and education in the languages of the peoples of the Far North as a *transitional stage* in acclimatizing these people to a higher culture played a very positive role *in its time* [emphasis added]" (V. K. Gardanov, B. O. Dolgikh, and T. A. Zhdanko, "Major trends in ethnic processes among the peoples of the USSR," *Soviet Anthropology and Archeology*, vol. 1, no. 1 (1962), p. 14.

34. For obligatory sharing of game, see B. O. Dolgikh and L. A. Fainberg, "Taimyrskie Nganasany," in *Sovremennoe khoziaistvo, kul'tura i byt malykh narodov Severa* (Moscow, 1960), p. 45; and V. A. Tugolukov, "Ekondskie Evenki," p. 176. For the bear festival and the restrictions applying to the consumption of the bear, see Taksami, *Nivkhi*, pp. 185-86, 217-21. The bear in particular is traditionally a sacred animal among many Siberian peoples, and to this day bears must be killed "courteously," and among some peoples, the hunters must disclaim responsibility for their acts.

35. Strakach, *Narodnye traditsii*, pp. 106-08. Taksami (*Nivkhi*, pp. 144-45) says that Nivkhi young people going away to study tend to go to those schools that are attended by their fellow villagers; and when they go away to work in industry, they generally enter those branches and those enterprises in which relatives are already working. Rarely does an enterprise contain only one Nivkhi family, a situation that makes the hiring of Nivkhi comparatively difficult. This of course is a phenomenon common to all societies undergoing industrialization. Strong family or ethnic feeling is not the only factor, however; plant managers still prefer contract labor, even though it is inefficient.

36. I. A. Kryvelev, "Overcoming the vestiges of religion in the lives of the peoples of the USSR," *Soviet Anthropology and Archeology*, vol. 1, no. 2 (1962), p. 20. For an account of a very colorful initiation ceremony performed recently by the Avam Nganasans, see Iu. B. Simchenko, "Prazdnik An'go Dialy u avamskikh Nganasan," *Sibirskii etnograficheskii sbornik V* (1963), pp. 168-79. An excellent description of traditional Evenki shamanism, originally written in the 1930s, is A. F. Anisimov, "The Shaman's Tent of the Evenks and the Origin of the Shamanistic Rite," in *Studies in Siberian Shamanism*, H. N. Michael, ed. (Toronto, 1963), pp. 84-124. Taksami (*Nivkhi*, p. 177) points out that the Nivkhi are generally buried in traditional costume, even when they did not wear the costume during life. This fact has many parallels in other parts of the Soviet Union. Finally, we should note a complicating factor in the religious situation among some Siberian peoples, particularly though not solely in Irkutsk Oblast, where the population is now ethnically quite diverse and where native populations (once nominally Christians) mix

both Christian and shamanistic elements in their ritual (see Tugolukov, "Khantaiskie Evenki," pp. 29-32). Furthermore, even Russians have been known to consult shamans on various matters which it is assumed that science is ill-equipped to handle; this is not solely a post-Revolutionary phenomenon but it is certainly intensified by the lack of adequate church controls among all the faiths in the Soviet Union (see *Stroitel'stvo kohmunizma i preodolenie religioznykh perezhitkov*, I. P. Tsamerian *et al.*, eds., Moscow, 1966).

37. See Levin and Potapov, eds., *The Peoples of Siberia*. The illustrations in the American edition are poorly reproduced but may be compared with the original. The bibliographies on individual peoples carry full references on folklore and folk art.

38. See Vdovin (*Ocherki istorii*, p. 393). Several members of the Far Northern intelligentsia have translated Pushkin into their native languages—a formidable exercise for any writer. For the problems that can arise for a non-Western translator, compare Z. Gasanov, "Some problems in the translation of Pushkin's *Eugene Onegin* into Turkic languages (from the Example of translation of the novel into Azerbaijani)," *Soviet Anthropology and Archeology*, vol. 4, no. 4 (1966), pp. 46-54. Problems of translation into Northern languages would be, if anything, more severe than those discussed by Gasanov, since these languages have no equivalents whatever for the complex and subtle social distinctions on which much of classical Russian literature depends.

39. Strakach (*Narodnye traditsii*, pp. 143-46) describes a festival which he helped to organize in 1962-63 in the Taimyr and Nen National Okrugs.

40. See Armstrong, "Administration of Northern Peoples," p. 82.

41. Let us cite some comparative data. According to Strakach (*Narodnye traditsii*, pp. 6-7), the Orochi population by the 1959 census was 32 percent urban. Lar'kin (*Orochi*, p. 147) notes that 35 Orochi families left the "Oroch" kolkhoz between 1956 and 1960; since the average-sized family is one to four persons and the entire people numbers 780, this represents a substantial population loss. These figures are reported in Ethel Dunn, "Educating the small peoples." For comparative purposes, see the results of a survey conducted in Smolensk Oblast, western Russia, in 1964, reported in Stephen P. Dunn and Ethel Dunn, *The Peasants of Central Russia* (New York, 1967), pp. 87-88.

42. In Russian usage, the term "sectarians" applies to adherents of non-Orthodox Christian denominations, and according to some reckonings includes Old Believers.

43. See I. S. Gurvich, "Russian Old Settlers along the Kamchatka River Valley (A contribution to the question of the history and ultimate destiny of isolated groups of the Russian people in Siberia)," *Soviet Anthropology and Archeology*, vol. 2, no. 3 (1963-64), pp. 39-48.

44. See N. I. Vorob'ev, "Materialy po bytu russkogo starozhilcheskogo naseleniia Vostochnoi Sibiri (naseleniia Prichunskogo kraia Eniseiskoi gubernii)," *Izvestiia obshchestva arkheologii, istorii i etnografii pri Kazanskom gosudarstvennom universitete*, vol. 33, nos. 2-3 (1926), pp. 59-112; G. Vinogradov, "Smert' i zagrobnaia zhizn' v vozzreniiakh russkogo starozhilogo naseleniia Sibiri," *Sbornik trudov professorov i prepodavatelei gosudarstvennogo Irkutskogo universiteta* (Irkutsk, 1923), pp. 261-345. It would be a very difficult matter to determine which of the omens and "superstitions" described by Vinogradov were brought by the settlers from European Russia, and which were picked up on the spot. However, both Vinogradov and Vorob'ev mention the presence among the Russians of forms of shamanism that are certainly of local origin.

45. See L. P. Potapov *et al.*, "Historical-Ethnographic Survey of the Russian Population of Siberia in the Prerevolutionary Period," in *The Peoples of Siberia*, pp. 105-99. In recent years expeditions have been at work in the Angara and Baikal region studying the material culture and social structure of the Russian Old Believer populations in the area; see G. S. Maslova and L. M. Saburova, "An ethnographic study of the Russian collective-farm peasantry of Eastern Siberia in 1957-59," *Soviet Anthropology and Archeology*, vol. 1, no. 1 (1962), pp. 19-26; L. M. Saburova, "Nekotorye cherty obshchestvennogo i semeinogo byta russkogo naseleniia Priangar'ia v pervye gody Sovetskoi vlasti (1919-1929 gg.)," *Sovetskaia etnografiia*, no. 2 (1965): 28-39; G. F. Okhrimenko, "Russian decorative house painting of the Transbaikal," *Soviet Anthropology and Archeology*, vol. 6, no. 2 (1967), pp. 38-51; G. I. Il'ina, "Ob izuchenii sovremennogo byta 'semeiskikh' [Old Believers]," *Etnograficheskii sbornik*, issue 1 (Ulan-Ude, 1960), pp. 108-22; I. S. Gurvich, "Etnograficheskaia ekspeditsiia v bassein r. Indigirke," *Kratkie soobshcheniia Instituta etnografii AN SSSR*, no. 19 (1953): 28-43.

46. A. A. Isupov, *Natsional'nyi sostav naseleniia SSSR* (Moscow, 1964), p. 41; see also Smoliak ("O sovremennom etnicheskom razvitii") and Taksami (*Nivkhi*).

CHAPTER IX

1. The terminology referring to China from 1644 to 1912 presents certain difficulties. China Proper, inhabited by the Chinese-speaking Han people, became a part of the Manchu empire through conquest in 1644. The Manchu empire, sometimes called the Ch'ing empire, included, in addition to China Proper, Manchuria, Mongolia, Sinkiang (Chinese Turkestan), and Tibet. Ch'ing was the Chinese dynastic name by which the Manchu dynasty denominated itself. This essay does not concern the entire range of relations between Russia and the Ch'ing dynasty; it concentrates on the institutionalization of contact

with the Ch'ing empire before 1860, the patterns of Russian trade and investment with the empire, particularly in Manchuria, and with the Russian impact on China, that is, on the most important component of the Ch'ing empire, China Proper. After the Chinese Revolution of 1911, Manchuria remained a part of China, the successor state to the Manchu dynasty; Mongolia, Sinkiang, and Tibet remained under Chinese suzerainty, though in each case the exact nature of the relationship to China differed.

2. Chiang Kai-shek and his son, Chiang Ching-kuo, are among the very few prominent Chinese who had direct experience of Russian (Soviet) educational institutions.

3. W. A. Douglas Jackson, *Russo-Chinese Borderlands* (New York, 1962).

4. On Kiakhta as a Sino-Russian emporium, see E. P. Silin, *Kiakhta v XVIII veke: iz istorii russko-kitaiskoi torgovli* (Irkutsk, 1947).

5. Karl Polanyi, Conrad M. Aresberg, and Harry W. Pearson, eds., *Trade and Market in the Early Empires* (Glencoe, Ill., 1957), pp. 38-63, 114-53, 154-76.

6. N. Bantysh-Kamenskii, *Diplomaticheskoe sobranie del mezdhu rossiiskim i kitaiskim gosudarstvami s 1619 po 1792 god: sostavlennoe po dokumentam, khraniashchimsia v Moskovskom Arkhive Gosudarstvennoi Kollegii Inostrannykh del, v 1792-1803 godu* (Kazan, 1882), pp. 373-75.

7. On the activities of Muraviev and Ignatiev in China, see Mark Mancall, "Major-General Ignatiev's Mission to Peking, 1859-1860," *Papers on China*, 10: 55-96 (Cambridge, Mass., October 1956).

8. Quoted in *ibid.*, p. 58.

9. Shao I-shan, *Ch'ing-tai t'ung-shih* (Taipei, 1963), 2: 993.

10. Fedor M. Dostoevskii, *The Diary of a Writer*, trans. by Boris Brasol (New York, 1954), p. 1048.

11. Andrew Malozemoff, *Russian Far Eastern Policy 1881-1904: with Special Emphasis on the Causes of the Russo-Japanese War* (Berkeley, 1958), pp. 41-50, as reprinted in George Alexander Lensen, ed., *Russia's Eastward Expansion* (Englewood Cliffs, N. J., 1964), pp. 90-96.

12. On the Russian occupation of Manchuria after the Boxer Rebellion, see Chester C. Tan, *The Boxer Catastrophe* (New York, 1955), esp. pp. 157 ff. On the Russo-Japanese war, see Malozemoff.

13. Unless otherwise specifically stated, the data on Sino-Russian trade are taken from M. I. Sladkovskii, *Ocherki ekonomicheskikh otnoshenii SSSR s Kitaem* (Moscow, 1957).

14. The balance of trade both at Kiakhta and in the maritime provinces were in China's favor. This further decreased Russia's desire to participate in the market in China Proper. Local commerce along the Far Eastern frontier also developed slowly. See Sladkovskii, esp. p. 120.

15. Hou Chi-ming, *Foreign Investment and Economic Development in China* (Cambridge, Mass., 1965), pp. 83-85.

16. The value of the property of the Russian religious mission in China in 1914 is estimated at 1.5 million rubles, or U.S.$8,000,000 (Sladkovskii, p. 158). While figures for the value of Roman Catholic and Protestant mission-ary properties are unavailable, the number of missionaries and converts sug-gests that value of their properties was considerably higher, indicating the vastly greater Western European and North American interest in missionary activities in China. See, for instance, John K. Fairbank, Edwin O. Reischauer, and Albert M. Craig, *East Asia: the Modern Transformation* (Boston, 1965).

17. Hou, pp. 17, 20.

18. For Russian activities in Mongolia and Sinkiang, see Robert Rupen, *Mon-gols of the Twentieth Century* (Bloomington, Ill., 1964); Owen Lattimore, *Pivot of Asia* (Boston, 1950); and Allen S. Whiting and General Sheng Shih-ts'ai, *Sinkiang: Pawn or Pivot?* (East Lansing, Mich., 1958).

19. On the influence of Russian literature in China, see Olga Lang, *Pa Chin and His Writings: Chinese Youth between the Two Revolutions* (Cambridge, Mass., 1967), esp. pp. 220-24 and 232 ff.

20. *Ibid.*, p. 222.

21. Quoted in *ibid.*, pp. 223-24.

22. *Ibid.*, p. 224.

23. Thomas S. Kuhn, *The Structure of Scientific Revolutions* (Chicago, 1962).

24. Chow Tse-tsung, *The May Fourth Movement: Intellectual Revolution in Modern China* (Cambridge, Mass., 1960), esp. chaps. 12, 13.

CHAPTER X

1. George Alexander Lensen, *The Russian Push Toward Japan: Russo-Japan-ese Relations, 1697-1875* (Princeton Univ. Press, 1959), p. 181.

2. G. A. Lensen, *Russia's Japan Expedition of 1852 to 1855* (Gainesville, Univ. of Florida Press, 1955), p. 63.

3. For a detailed account of Russo-Japanese relations up to this point, see Lensen, *Russian Push Toward Japan*; and E. Ia. Fainberg, *Russko-iaponskie otnosheniia v 1697-1875 gg.* [Russo-Japanese relations, 1697-1875] (Moscow, 1960).

4. For the story of the conflict, see Lensen, *The Russo-Chinese War* (Tallahassee, Fla., The Diplomatic Press, 1967).

5. The most recent studies of events leading up to the outbreak of the Russo-Japanese War are John Albert White, *The Diplomacy of the Russo-Japanese War* (Princeton Univ. Press, 1964); Ian H. Nish, *The Anglo-Japanese Alliance: The Diplomacy of Two Island Empires 1894-1907* (London, 1966); Shinobu Seizaburo and Nakayama Jiichi, comp., *Nichi-Ro senso-shi no kenkyu* [Study of the history of the Russo-Japanese War] (Tokyo, 1959); Lensen, ed., *Korea and Manchuria between Russia and Japan 1895-1904: The Observations of Sir Ernest Satow, British Minister Plenipotentiary to Japan (1895-1900) and China (1900-1906)* (Tallahassee, Fla., The Diplomatic Press, 1966); and Lensen, ed., *The d'Anethan Dispatches from Japan, 1894-1910* (Tokyo, Sophia University in cooperation with The Diplomatic Press, Tallahassee, 1967). A readable compilation of eyewitness accounts of the war itself is J. N. Westwood, *Witnesses of Tsushima* (Tokyo, Sophia University in cooperation with The Diplomatic Press, Tallahassee, 1970).

6. Ernest Batson Price speaks of a "camouflaged indemnity." See his *The Russo-Japanese Treaties of 1907-1916 Concerning Manchuria and Mongolia* (Baltimore, Johns Hopkins Press, 1933), p. 26.

7. Peter Alexander Berton, *The Secret Russo-Japanese Alliance of 1916* (Ann Arbor, Mich., University Microfilms, Inc., 1956), pp. 340-42.

8. Kikujiro Ishii, *Diplomatic Commentaries* (Baltimore, 1936), p. 106.

9. Vasilii Ivanovich Nemirovich-Danchenko, *Elliny velikago okeana* [Hellenes of the Pacific Ocean] (St. Petersburg, 1916), p. 260. For a recent Japanese study of Russo-Japanese relations from 1905 to 1917, see Yoshimura Michio, *Nihon to Roshia* [Japan and Russia] (Tokyo, 1968).

10. See James William Morley, *The Japanese Thrust into Siberia, 1918* (New York, Columbia Univ. Press, 1957); Hosoya Chihiro, *Shiberia shuppei no shiteki kenkyu* [Historical study of the Siberian intervention] (Tokyo, 1955).

11. For a detailed study of Soviet-Japanese relations from 1921 to 1930, see Lensen, *Japanese Recognition of the U.S.S.R.* (Tokyo, Sophia University in cooperation with The Diplomatic Press, Tallahassee, 1970). The conflict in 1939 is discussed in Larry W. Moses, "Soviet-Japanese Confrontation in Outer Mongolia: The Battle of Nomonhan-Khalkin Gol," *Journal of Asian History* (Wiesbaden, 1967), vol. 1, pt. 1, pp. 64-85; Katsu H. Young, "The Nomonhan Incident: Imperial Japan and the Soviet Union," *Monumenta Nipponica* (Tokyo, 1967), vol. 22, nos. 1-2, pp. 82-102; and Alvin D. Coox, "High Com-

mand and Field Army: The Kwantung Army and the Nomonhan Incident, 1939," *Military Affairs* (Manhattan, Kansas, 1969), vol. 33, no. 2, p. 312. Japanese policy toward Russia before and during the Pacific War is examined in Carl Gilbert, Jr., *The Hirota Ministries: An Appraisal. Japan's Relations with China and the U.S.S.R., 1933-1938* (Ann Arbor, Mich., University Microfilms, Inc., 1967); Hubertus Lupke, *Japans Russlandpolitik von 1939 bis 1941* [Japan's Russia policy from 1939 until 1941] (Frankfurt am Main, 1962); Robert J. C. Butow, *Tojo and the Coming of the War* (Princeton Univ. Press, 1961); and Nobutake Ike, ed., *Japan's Decision for War: Records of the 1941 Policy Conferences* (Stanford Univ. Press, 1967). The Soviet-Japanese conflict in 1945 is related in Raymond L. Garthoff, "The Soviet Manchurian Campaign, August 1945," *Military Affairs* (1969), pp. 312-36. *Contest over Japan* by Herbert Feis (New York, 1968) deals with the period from 1945 to 1952; and Donald C. Hellmann, *Japanese Domestic Politics and Foreign Policy: The Peace Agreement with the Soviet Union* (Berkeley, Univ. of Calif. Press, 1969), with the period from 1954 to 1956. For the Soviet point of view, see L. N. Kutakov, *Istoriia sovetsko-iaponskikh diplomaticheskikh otnoshenii* [History of Soviet-Japanese diplomatic relations] (Moscow, 1962); G. N. Sevost'ianov, *Podgotovka voiny na Tikhom okeane 1939-1941* [The making of the war in the Pacific 1939-1941] (Moscow, 1962); G. N. Sevost'ianov, *Diplomaticheskaia istoriia voiny na Tikhom okeane* [Diplomatic history of the war in the Pacific Ocean] (Moscow, 1969); D. I. Gol'dberg, *Vneshniaia politika Iaponii v 1941-1945 gg.* [The foreign policy of Japan in 1941-1945] (Moscow, 1962); L. N. Vnotchenko, *Pobeda na Dal'nem Vostoke* [Victory in the Far East] (Moscow, 1966); R. Ia. Malinovskii, ed., *Final* [The finale] (Moscow, 1966); Kh. T. Eidus, *SSSR i Iaponiia. Vneshnepoliticheskie otnosheniia posle vtoroi mirovoi voiny* [The U.S.S.R. and Japan: foreign relations after the Second World War] (Moscow, 1964).

12. Lensen, *Russian Push Toward Japan*, pp. 417-24, 502-03; A. L. Narochnitskii, *Kolonial'naia politika kapitalisticheskikh derzhav na Dal'nem Vostoke 1860-1895* [The colonial policy of the capitalist powers in the Far East 1860-1895] (Moscow, 1956), pp. 269, 550.

13. *Entsiklopedicheskii Slovar'* ([Brockhaus-Efron] Encyclopedia), Vol. XLI-A (St. Petersburg, 1904), p. 727; Narochnitskii, p. 551; "O torgovle Iaponii s Rossieiu" [Concerning Japan's trade with Russia], compiled by the Office of the Committee of Ministers and printed as a supplement to No. 8 of *Priamurskiia Vedomosti* for 1894, pp. 4-7.

14. A. Kobelev, "Obzor goroda Khakodate i ego torgovo-promyshlennoi deiatel'nosti v 1901 godu. Po iaponskim istochnikam" [Survey of the city of Hakodate and its commercial-industrial activity in 1901. On the basis of Japanese sources], *Izvestiia vostochnago instituta*, vol. 12, no. 1 (1904), pp. 52-56.

15. K. Kurteev, "Russko-iaponskii tovaroobmen i ekonomicheskoe sblizhenie" [Russo-Japanese trade and economic rapprochement], *Zapiski Priamurskogo*

Obshchestva vostokovedeniia, no. 3 (1915), pp. 111-13; *Entsiklopedicheskii Slovar',* p. 727; A. Dobrotin, "Torgovyia snosheniia mezhdu Iaponiei i Rossiei" [Commercial relations between Japan and Russia], *Vestnik finansov promyshlennosti i torgovli* [Financial, industrial, and commercial gazette], no. 5 (1907), pp. 187-88; K. Popov, *Iaponiia. Ocherki geografii i ekonomiki* [Japan, Sketches of geography and economy] (Moscow, 1931), pp. 380-81; Nomura, "O russko-iaponskikh torgovykh snosheniiakh" [Concerning Russo-Japanese commercial relations], *Zapiski Priamurskogo otdela imperatorskogo obshchestva vostokovedeniia,* no. 3 (1916), pp. 122-26; Vl. Braude, "Sovetsko-iaponskie ekonomicheskie vzaimootnosheniia" [Soviet-Japanese economic relations], *Novyi vostok,* no. 22 (1928), p. 148; "K voprosu ob ekonomicheskom sblizhenii Rossii s Iaponiei" [Concerning the question about the economic rapprochement of Russia with Japan], *Zapiski Priamurskogo otdela imperatorskogo obshchestva vostokovedeniia,* 1915, pp. 260-61.

16. Popov, *Iaponiia,* pp. 381-82; Braude, p. 149; A. Gal'perin, *Dal'nevostochnyi krai i tikhookeanskii rynok* [The Far Eastern region and the Pacific market], *Voprosy torgovli,* no. 10 (1930), pp. 22-33.

17. A. Bonch-Osmolovskii, "Bol'she vnimamie torgovle s Iaponiei" [More attention to trade with Japan], *Sovetskaia torgovlia,* no. 22 (1930), pp. 9-10; "Vtorostepennyi eksport iz SSSR v Iaponiiu" [Secondary export from the U.S.S.R. to Japan], *Ekonomicheskoe obozrenie,* no. 2 (1938), p. 22.

18. Iu. Davydov, "Ekonomicheskie otnosheniia Iaponii i SSSR" [Economic relations of Japan and the U.S.S.R.], *Mirovoe khoziaistvo i mirovaia politika,* no. 9 (1938), pp. 52-53; Ministry of Foreign Trade of the U.S.S.R., *Vneshniaia torgovlia SSSR za 1918-1940 qq.* [Foreign trade of the U.S.S.R. for 1918-1940] (Moscow, 1960), pp. 1032, 1036.

19. Boris M. Pichugin, *Iaponiia: Ekonomika i vneshniaia torgovlia* [Japan: Economy and foreign trade] (Moscow, 1957), p. 201; "Torgovyi dogovor mezhdu Soiuzom Sovetskikh Sotsialisticheskikh Respublik i Iaponiei" [Commercial treaty between the U.S.S.R. and Japan], *Vneshniaia torgovlia,* no. 7 (1958), pp. 46-49.

20. "Expanding Japanese business with Russia," *The Economist,* 208 (13 July 1963): 170.

21. *Keesing's Contemporary Archives,* 13-20 August 1966, p. 21565.

22. Braude, pp. 132-51.

23. Great Britain, Foreign Office, *British and Foreign State Papers,* 1925, part II, pp. 898-905.

24. Davydov, p. 61; Braude, pp. 138-41; A. Il'in, "K likvidatsii iaponskikh kontsessii na Severnom Sakhaline i prolongatsii na piat' let rybolovnoi konventsii" [Concerning the liquidation of the Japanese concessions on North

Sakhalin and the extension of the fishery convention for five years], *Bol'* *shevik*, no. 9 (1944), p. 70; William C. Amidon, "The issue of Sakhalin in Russo-Japanese relations," in Robert E. Ward, ed., *Five Studies in Japanese Politics*, Center for Japanese Studies (Univ. of Michigan), Occasional Papers, no. 7 (1957), p. 78.

25. "Sovetsko-iaponskie soglasheniia o likvidatsii iaponskikh kontsessii na Severnom Sakhaline i o prolongatsii rybolovnoi konventsii mezhdu SSSR i Iaponiei s vnesennymi v konventsiiu izmeneniiami" [Soviet-Japanese agreements regarding the liquidation of the Japanese concessions on North Sakhalin and the extension of the fishery convention between the U.S.S.R. and Japan with the changes made in the convention], *Mirovoe khoziaistvo i mirovaia politika*, nos. 3-4 (1944), p. 79; Il'in, pp. 69-71.

26. Tanaka Bunichiro, *Nichi-Ro kosho-shi* [History of Russo-Japanese relations] (Tokyo, 1944), p. 213; Narochnitskii, p. 516; D. Bogdanov, *Sovremennoe polozhenie nashei rybopromyshlennosti na Dal'nem Vostoke* [Current state of our fishery in the Far East] (Vladivostok, 1911), pp. 2, 70; N. Sliunin, *Promyslovye bogatstva Kamchatki, Sakhalina i Komandorskikh ostrovov* [The fishery and hunting riches of Kamchatka, Sakhalin and the Komandorskie Islands] (St. Petersburg, 1895), p. 88; Ma. A. Kozakov, "Kratkii ocherk rybolovstva na Dal'nem Vostoke" [Brief sketch of fishery in the Far East], *Ezhegodnik Departamenta Zemledeliia*, 1911, pp. 562-63; B. Geineman, "Rybnyi promysel' v nizov'iakh reki Amura v 1907 i 1908 godakh" [Fishery in the lower reaches of the Amur in 1907 and 1908], *Vestnik rybopromyshlennosti* [Fishery gazette], no. 6 (1909), p. 339; A. P. Chekhov, *Ostrov Sakhalin* [Sakhalin Island], in *Polnoe sobranie sochinenii i pisem*, 10 (Moscow, 1948): 147, 251.

27. Tanaka, pp. 213-24; Narochnitskii, pp. 516-17; Russia, Ministry of Foreign Affairs, *Sbornik dogovorov i diplomaticheskikh dokumentov po delam Dal'niago Vostoka 1895-1905* [Collection of treaties and diplomatic documents concerning the affairs of the Far East 1895-1905] (St. Petersburg, 1906), pp. 49-52.

28. Bogdanov, pp. 19-20, 49-50, 59, 71, 74; V. V. Trautshol'd, *Okhotsko-Kamchatskii rybolovnyi sezon 1906 goda i uchastie v nem iapontsev* [The Okhotsk-Kamchatka fishing season of 1906 and Japanese participation in it] (St. Petersburg, 1907), p. 73; Popov, p. 383; Kozakov, pp. 574, 575, 582; "K voprosu o nashikh vzaimootnosheniiakh s Iaponiei v oblasti rybnoi promyshlennosti na Dal'nem Vostoke" [Regarding the question of our relations with Japan in the area of fishery in the Far East], *Biulleten' rybnogo khoziaistva*, no. 6 (1925), p. 13.

29. B. Sokolov, "Rybolovnyi vopros v kontsessionykh vodakh SSSR" [The fishery question in the concession waters of the U.S.S.R.], *Tikhii Okean*, no. 2 (1936), p. 90; Kozakov, p. 589.

30. Victor A. Yakhontoff, *Russia and the Soviet Union in the Far East* (London, 1932), pp. 404-05; "K voprosu o nashikh vzaimootnosheniiakh," pp. 13-14; "Fishery Convention Between Japan and the Soviet Socialist Republics," Russo-Japanese Treaties collection of the Japanese Archives, microfilmed by the Library of Congress, 32-1; Homer E. Gregory and Kathleen Barnes, *North Pacific Fisheries, with special reference to Alaska salmon* (New York, 1939), pp. 289-90.

31. Popov, pp. 384-85; Sokolov, pp. 91-92; "K podpisaniiu sovetsko-iaponskogo protokola o prolongatsii rybolovnoi konventsii na 1943 g." [Regarding the signing of the Soviet-Japanese protocol about the extension of the fishery convention for 1943], *Vneshniaia torgovlia*, nos. 3-4 (1943), pp. 7-8; "Sovetsko-iaponskoe soglashenie ot 31 dekabria 1939 g." [The Soviet-Japanese agreement of 31 December 1939], *Mirovoe khoziaistvo i mirovaia politika*, no. 1 (1940), p. 142.

32. S. Nevskii, "Sovetsko-iaponskie otnosheniia" [Soviet-Japanese relations], *Mezhdunarodnaia zhizn'*, no. 4 (1956), pp. 33-34; *Keesing's Contemporary Archives*, 1956, p. 15195A.

33. "Tserkov' Voskreseniia Khristova pri russkom konsul'stve v Khakodate (v Iaponii)" [The Church of the Resurrection of Christ at the Russian consulate in Hakodate (in Japan)], *Missioner*, no. 31 (1874), pp. 279-81; P. Prokoshev, "Russkaia pravoslavnaia missiia v Iaponii" [The Russian-Orthodox mission in Japan], *Strannik*, February 1896, pp. 270-71; "O rasprostranenii v Iaponii Provoslavnoi Khristianskoi very russkimi veropropovednikami" [Regarding the propagation of the Orthodox Christian faith in Japan by Russian missionaries], *Vladimirskiia eparkhial'nyia vedomosti*, no. 3 (1875), pp. 135-40; "Dokladnaia zapiska ieromonakha Nikolaia direktoru Aziatskago Departamenta P.N. Stremoukhovu" [Report of the regular priest Nikolai to the Director of the Asiatic Department P.N. Stremoukhov], dated 12 (24) July 1869, *Russkii Arhiv*, vol. 45, part 1 (1907), p. 570. "Polozhenie dlia rossiiskoi dukhovnoi missii v Iaponii" [Statutes of the Russian ecclesiastical mission in Japan], *Pribavleniia k Irkutskim eparkhial'nym vedomostiam*, no. 47 (1871), pp. 810-15; no. 48 pp. 821-30; Anatolii, "Pis'mo Khakodatskago (v Iaponii) missionera i iaponskikh khristian k preosviashchenneishemu Veniaminu episkopu Irkutskomu i Nerchinskomu" [Letter of the Hakodate (in Japan) missionary and Japanese Christians to the Most Reverend Veniamin Bishop of Irkutsk and Nerchinsk], *Pribavleniia k Irkutskim eparkhial'nym vedomostiam*, no. 8 (1875), pp. 79-81; "Vesti iz Iaponii. Pis'mo iaponskago missionerstva ieromonakha Anatoliia iz Khakodate ot 16 aprelia sego 1875 goda" [News from Japan. Letter of the Japanese missionary the regular priest father Anatolii from Hakodate of 16 (28) April of this year 1875], *Tserkovaia letopis'*, no. 33 (1875), p. 108.

34. "Pravoslavnaia russkaia missiia v Iaponii" [The Orthodox Russian mission in Japan], *Domashniaia beseda*, 1873, pp. 505-35; "Pravoslavnaia

russkaia missia v Iaponii" [The Orthodox Russian mission in Japan], *Russkii vestnik*, no. 5 (1873): 429-30; Prokoshev, pp. 437, 630; B. Kandidov, "Iaponskaia pravoslavnaia tserkov' na sluzhbe russkogo imperializma" [The Japanese Orthodox Church in the service of Russian imperialism], *Antireligioznik*, nos. 11-12 (1932), pp. 6-7; "O rasprostranenii v Iaponii," p. 150; "Poezdka preosviashchennago Veniamina episkopa Kamchatskago v Iaponiiu" [Voyage of the Most Reverend Veniamin, Bishop of Kamchatka, to Japan], *Izvestiia po Kazanskoi eparkhii*, no. 5 (1873), p. 152; "Posledniia izvestiia o pravoslavnoi iaponskoi missii: pis'mo arkhimandrita Nikolaia, nachal'nika iaponskoi dukhovnoi missii, k ego preosviashchenstvu, preosviashchenneishemu Veniaminu, episkopu Irkutskomu i Nerchinskomu" [Latest news about the Orthodox Japanese mission, to his eminence, the Most Reverend Veniamin, Bishop of Irkutsk and Nerchinsk], *Pribavleniia k Irkutskim eparkhial'nym vedomostiam*, no. 43 (1873), pp. 673-74; Prokoshev, pp. 440-44.

35. Prokoshev, pp. 445-50; "Zapiski russkoi pravoslavnoi missionerki v Iaponii Marii Aleksandrovny Cherkasovoi" [Notes of the Russian Orthodox woman missionary in Japan Mariia Aleksandrovna Cherkasova], *Missioner*, no. 43 (1897), pp. 366-70.

36. "Tserkov' v Iaponii. (Novyi episkop i novyi ieromonakh v iaponskoi tserkvi)" [The Church in Japan. (A new bishop and a new regular priest in the Japanese Church)], *Tserkovnyi vestnik*, no. 10 (1881), p. 8; I.G., "Iz deiatel'nosti 'Apostola' Iaponii" [Regarding the activity of the "Apostle" of Japan], *Istoricheskii vestnik*, 33 (1912): 1017-24; "Dokladnaia zapiska," pp. 570-615.

37. "Konchina arkhiepiskopa Nikolaia" [The demise of Archbishop Nikolai], *Zapiski Priamurskogo otdela imperatorskogo obshchestva vostokovedeniia*, no. 1 (1912), pp. 259-62; I.E. Ivanov, *Na praktike v Iaponii v 1908 g.* [Practicing in Japan in 1908] (St. Petersburg, 1909), pp. 58-61; Pravoslavnyi, "Pravoslavie v Iaponii" [The Orthodox faith in Japan], *Pribavleniia k tserkovym vedomostiam*, no. 2 (1912), p. 55; D. Pozdneev, "Izdoneseniia nachal'nika rossiiskoi dukhovnoi missii o sostoianii pravoslavnoi tserkvi v Iaponii za 1911 god" [From the report of the head of the Russian mission about the state of the Orthodox church in Japan in 1911], *Pribavleniia k tserkovnym vedomostiam*, nos. 12-13 (1911), pp. 500-11.

38. Kandidov, p. 6.

39. Josef Glazik, *Die Russisch-Orthodoxe Heidenmission seit Peter dem Grossen* [The Russian Orthodox mission to the heathens since Peter the Great] (Münster, 1954), pp. 178-95; Lensen, "The Orthodox Church in Occupied Japan," *Florida State University Studies*, no. 8 (1952), pp. 93-94.

40. Glazik, pp. 194-95.

41. Lensen, ed., "White Russians in Wartime Japan: Leaves from the Diary of Dmitri Abrikossow," *The Russian Review*, vol. 25, no. 3 (1966), pp. 270-72.

42. Glazik, pp. 178-79; Lensen, "The Orthodox Church," pp. 94-95.

43. Rodger Swearingen and Paul Langer, *Red Flag in Japan: International Communism in Action 1919-1951* (Cambridge, Mass., Harvard Univ. Press, 1951), pp. 14-17, 24.

44. *Ibid.*, p. 19; Robert A. Scalapino, *Democracy and the Party Movement in Prewar Japan: The Failure of the First Attempt* (Berkeley, Univ. of Calif. Press, 1953), pp. 328-29.

45. W. G. Beasley, *The Modern History of Japan* (New York, 1963), p. 235; Hans H. Baerwald, "The Japanese Communist Party," in Robert A. Scalapino, ed., *The Communist Revolution in Asia: Tactics, Goals, and Achievements* (Englewood Cliffs, N. J., 1965), pp. 198-99, 213-17; *Keesing's Contemporary Archives*, 1967, pp. 21897A, 21966.

46. For a description of Russian studies in Japan, see Peter Berton, Paul Langer, and Rodger Swearingen, *Japanese Training and Research in the Russian Field* (Los Angeles, Univ. of Southern Calif. Press, 1956), pp. 92-111.

47. Bruno Lewin, *Futabatei Shimei in seinen Beziehungen zur russischen Literatur* [Futabatei Shimei in his relations to Russian literature] (Hamburg, 1955); Lensen, *Report from Hokkaido: The Remains of Russian Culture in Northern Japan* (Hakodate, 1954), pp. 165-66; R. Karlina, "Belinskii i iaponskaia literatura" [Belinskii and Japanese literature], *Literaturnoe nasledstvo*, 56 (1950): 501; Okazaki Yoshie, *Japanese Literature in the Meiji Era*, translated and adapted by V. H. Viglielmo (Tokyo, 1955), pp. 79, 199-203, 613-15; N. I. Konrad, *Zapad i vostok* [West and East] (Moscow, 1966), pp. 338, 340-41; Yoshiyuki Nakai, "Futabatei Shimei (1864-1909)," *Papers on Japan*, 4 (Cambridge, East Asian Research Center, Harvard University, September 1967): 1-63. For an example of the Japanization of Russian manners of speech and behavior in Futabatei's translations, see E. M. Pinus, "M. Gor'kii i iaponskaia literature" [M. Gor'kii and Japanese literature], *Vestnik Leningradskogo Universiteta*, no. 8 (1950), p. 143.

48. Konrad, *Zapad i vostok*, pp. 412-14.

49. N. I. Konrad, "Tolstoi v Iaponii" [Tolstoi in Japan], *Literaturnoe nasledstvo*, vol. 75 (1965), bk. 2, pp. 347-59; A. Shifman, *Lev Tolstoi i vostok* [Lev Tolstoi and the East] (Moscow, 1960), pp. 285-86, 345, 366-69; "Iaponskii palomnik. Vospominaniia Tokutomi Roka" [A Japanese pilgrim. The recollections of Tokutomi Roka], pub. by A. I. Shifman, trans. V. A. Kostereva, *Literaturnoe nasledstvo*, vol. 75 (1965), bk. 2, 166. For a German doctoral dissertation, see Claus M. Fischer, *Lev N. Tolstoj in Japan (Meiji-und Taisho-Zeit)* [Lev Tolstoi in Japan during the Meiji and Taisho periods] (Weisbaden, 1969).

50. Konrad, *Zapad i vostok*, pp. 412-14.

51. K. Rekho, *M. Gor'kii i iaponskaia literatura* [M. Gor'kii and Japanese literature] (Moscow, 1965), pp. 11-116; Pinus, "M. Gorkii i iaponskaia literatura," pp. 139-56. For a brief account of the impressions of Soviet writers, notably Boris Pilniak, of Japan, see Konstantin Popov, *Japan: Essays on National Culture and Scientific Thought* (Moscow, 1969), pp. 482-87.

52. A popular beer parlor in the Shinjuku section of Tokyo, where Soviet songs are sung in Japanese, is called Traktir Nadne (Lower Depths Tavern). For Russian influence on the Japanese dance and the performing arts in general, see Osei Keishi, *Nichi-Ro bunko-soden* [Essays on Japanese-Russian culture] (Tokyo, 1941); and "Gastroli v Iaponii. Beseda s narodnym artistom SSSR D. F. Oistrakhom" [Guest performances in Japan. An interview with the People's Artist of the U.S.S.R. D. F. Oistrakh], *Novoe vremia*, no. 14 (1955), pp. 28-31.

53. Rekho, pp. 124-28; Konrad, *Zapad i vostok*, p. 419; Lensen, *Report from Hokkaido*, p. 169.

According to a Soviet scholar, "Japanese-American censorship" blocked the publication of translations of some Soviet works during the occupation. He asserts that the study of Russian and Soviet literature consequently became "one of the forms in the struggle of the vanguard of the Japanese intelligentsia for the real rebirth of Japan, for the establishment of a free and democratic Japan." (Pinus, "M. Gorkii i iaponskaia literatura," p. 156; Pinus, "Gogol' i Russkaia klassicheskaia literatura v Iaponii" [Gogol and Russian classical literature in Japan], in *Gogol'. Stat'i i materialy* [Gogol. Articles and materials] (Leningrad, Leningrad State University, 1954), pp. 352-55; Pinus, "M. Sholokhov v Iaponii" [M. Sholokhov in Japan], in *Mikhail Sholokhov, Sbornik statei* [Mikhail Sholokhov. Collection of articles] (Leningrad, Leningrad State University, 1956), pp. 234-36.

Index

467

74

75
76
77
79
81

83
88